PRINCIPLES
of MORAL
PHILOSOPHY

Classic and Contemporary
Approaches

EDITED BY

STEVEN M. CAHN *and*
ANDREW T. FORCEHIMES

New York   Oxford
OXFORD UNIVERSITY PRESS

Oxford University Press is a department of the University of Oxford.
It furthers the University's objective of excellence in research,
scholarship, and education by publishing worldwide.

Oxford   New York
Auckland   Cape Town   Dar es Salaam   Hong Kong   Karachi
Kuala Lumpur   Madrid   Melbourne   Mexico City   Nairobi
New Delhi   Shanghai   Taipei   Toronto

With offices in
Argentina   Austria   Brazil   Chile   Czech Republic   France   Greece
Guatemala   Hungary   Italy   Japan   Poland   Portugal   Singapore
South Korea   Switzerland   Thailand   Turkey   Ukraine   Vietnam

For titles covered by Section 112 of the US Higher Education
Opportunity Act, please visit www.oup.com/us/he for the
latest information about pricing and alternate formats.

Published by Oxford University Press
198 Madison Avenue, New York, New York 10016
http://www.oup.com

Oxford is a registered trademark of Oxford University Press

Library of Congress Cataloging-in-Publication Data

Names: Cahn, Steven M. editor. | Forcehimes, Andrew, 1987- editor.
Title: Principles of moral philosophy : classic and contemporary readings in
    normative ethics / [edited] by Steven M. Cahn and Andrew T. Forcehimes.
Description: New York : Oxford University Press, 2017. | Includes index.
Identifiers: LCCN 2015041248 | ISBN 9780190491000
Subjects: LCSH: Normativity (Ethics)
Classification: LCC BJ1458.3 .P75 2017 | DDC 171--dc23 LC record available
    at http://lccn.loc.gov/2015041248

Printing number: 9 8 7 6 5 4 3 2 1

Printed in the United States of America
on acid-free paper

Contents

PART X VIRTUE ETHICS

PART XI THE ETHICS OF CARE

PART XII PARTICULARISM

PART XIII APPLIED ETHICS

PART XIV METAETHICS

Preface

Normative ethics explores competing explanations of why certain actions are judged to be right and others wrong. Most anthologies in ethics combine readings in normative ethics with extensive studies of the nature of moral judgments, an inquiry known as "metaethics," as well as consideration of numerous practical moral problems, such as abortion or world hunger. Such anthologies, however, do not contain sufficient available space to consider in depth the numerous variations on reasons that may be offered to justify any particular moral judgment. While we have included short sections on moral problems and metaethics for those instructors and students who wish to touch on these subjects, the focus of this book is normative ethics.

While some of the readings are reprinted in their entirety, most are shortened to sharpen their focus and increase their accessibility. The major historical works presented unabridged are Kant's *Groundwork for the Metaphysics of Morals* and Mill's *Utilitarianism*. Extended contemporary essays by Marilyn Friedman and Barbara Herman are also reprinted uncut. In addition, extensive material is presented from the work of Aristotle, Thomas Aquinas, Henry Sidgwick, Julia Annas, Shelly Kagan, Christine Korsgaard, and T. M. Scanlon. Approximately one-third of the contemporary articles are authored by women.

Co-editor Andrew Forcehimes has provided a glossary as well as an extensive introduction that offers a detailed guide to the field of normative ethics. Headnotes and study questions for each selection are also included.

Acknowledgments

We are grateful to our editor, Robert Miller, for his support and guidance. We also wish to thank assistant editor Kaitlin Coats and assistant editor Alyssa Palazzo, who have helped in numerous ways. Our thanks also to production editor Marianne Paul for her conscientiousness and to the staff of Oxford University Press for thoughtful assistance throughout production.

We have been guided in part by suggestions from reviewers chosen by the Press. We would like to thank them individually:

Dennis Arjo, Johnson County Community College
Larry A. Herzberg, University of Wisconsin Oshkosh
Joshua Johnston, Auburn University
Ari Krupnick, Berkeley City College
Judith Lichtenberg, Georgetown University
Greg Lynch, North Central College
Ellen M. Maccarone, Gonzaga University
Elizabeth A. Oljar, University of Detroit Mercy
Paul Pistone, American InterContinental University
Nancy Nyquist Potter, University of Louisville
Kenneth Shockley, University at Buffalo–SUNY
Fernando Zapata, Hunter College of the City University of New York

Resources for Students and Instructors

Co-editor Andrew Forcehimes has prepared a comprehensive set of resources to assist teachers and students.

The Oxford University Press Ancillary Resource Center (ARC) at www.oup-arc.com/cahn-principles-of-philosophy houses a wealth of Instructor Resources to accompany *Principles of Moral Philosophy*, including the following:

- A Computerized Test Bank with
  - 5–15 multiple-choice questions per reading
  - 5–10 true/false questions per reading
- An Instructor's Manual with
  - A traditional "pencil-and-paper" version of the Computerized Test Bank
  - 5–7 essay/discussions questions per reading
  - A summary of each reading
  - Suggested web links and media resources for each part
  - A glossary of key terms and definitions from the text
- A PowerPoint Lecture Outline for each reading

Student Resources are available on the Companion Website at www.oup.com/us/cahn, including the following:

- Practice quizzes with
  - 5–8 multiple-choice questions per reading, selected from the Test Bank
  - 3–5 true/false questions per reading, selected from the Test Bank
  - 3–4 essay/discussion questions per reading, selected from the Instructor's Manual
- Suggested web links and media resources for each part
- Flashcards of key terms and definitions from the text

Instructor and Student Resources are also available as course cartridges for virtually any learning management system. For more information, please contact your Oxford University Press representative or call 1-800-280-0280.

NOTE

Some of the materials throughout the book were written when the custom was to use the noun "man" and the pronoun "he" to refer to all persons, regardless of gender, and we have retained the authors' original wording. With this proviso, let us now embark on the study of normative ethics.

Part I

INTRODUCTION

The Anatomy of Normative Ethics

Andrew T. Forcehimes

§0. INTRODUCTION

I went to a small high school. When something happened, word got around. Midway through my sophomore year my friend's parent had an affair. The affair gave rise to a fascinating phenomenon. Most people I spoke with seemed to think my friend's parent had done something wrong, but nearly all supplied different rationales. These, if memory serves, were some of the proposed explanations for why it was wrong: It was wrong because my friend's parent broke a vow, because it was disrespectful, because the Bible says one should not commit adultery, because that is just not what people do around here, because it harms family and friends, because it will make them both unhappy.

This divergence in rationales was unsettling. Though there was largely consensus on the verdict, the agreement appeared to be merely a haphazard convergence. And, perhaps more disturbing, the conflict was not only *inter*personal: it was *intra*personal. For example, a few days later, I overheard the person who explained the wrongness of the action in terms of disrespect tell another student that it was wrong to be rude, because being rude makes the world an unhappier place. Why not, I thought, turn to disrespect to explain the wrongness of rudeness too?

Consider the issues surrounding this case. There were claims made about the normative status of the action, which most people agreed on. There were the various reasons—the rationales—for why the action was thought to be wrong. Here people diverged. In addition, there was the apparent intrapersonal conflict. In short, on the surface things seemed to be a mess.

But perhaps things weren't so bad. Maybe the disagreement wasn't deep. If, for instance, what makes disrespect problematic is traceable to the unhappiness it produces, the intrapersonal disagreement dissolves. And the same might hold for the interpersonal disagreement as well. If there were one core rationale from which all the others were derived, the disagreement would be merely apparent. That's a reassuring thought.

We can now be a bit more precise. It was the lack of a unified, ultimate rationale that I found disturbing. I didn't know then, but what I was after was a coherent *ethical theory*—an account of what we are required to do and who we are required to be. This collection brings together the most promising attempts to provide such a theory, or, in some cases, explain why we shouldn't be after such a theory in the first place.

My aim in this introduction is to provide the tools that should make the task of understanding and assessing these theories easier. To this end, I'll present the formal elements of normative ethics. These elements—the deontic verdicts, evaluative claims, determining grounds, and core normative principles—offer only a skeleton. Yet, once understood, they provide a clear way to categorize the various ethical theories. Having a firm grasp of the elements of normative ethics, how they fit together, and how they can be filled out, will prove invaluable as you read this volume.

There are, I should note, no knockout arguments in ethics. Success is instead best measured by showing that other theories fare worse. Accordingly, though the anatomy of normative ethics might seem initially unexciting, gauging a theory's defensibility depends on understanding the alternatives. Without such an understanding, we operate in the dark.

§1. DEONTIC VERDICTS

Let's begin by identifying the central elements of normative ethics. Take again the case of my friend's adulterous parent. Here, most people held that the committing of adultery was impermissible. This is a *deontic verdict*—a claim about the normative status of an action. Different theories arrive at different deontic verdicts. Indeed, some of the people I talked with said my friend's parent acted permissibly. Or, more intriguing, they said they would have to wait and see—maybe they'd get happily divorced.

So here we have two deontic verdicts, 'impermissible' and 'permissible'. Put precisely,

An action is *impermissible* if and only if refraining from the action is required.

An action is *permissible* if and only if it is an action that is not impermissible.

But these are not the only verdicts. After all, we cashed out the definition of 'impermissible' in terms of an act's being 'required'. So we'll need a definition for that deontic verdict too:

An action is *required* if and only if it is an action that is not optional—it is the uniquely permissible action available.

Of course, now we need a definition of 'optional'. So let us say,

An action is *optional* if and only if it is permissible to perform or not perform the action.

With these definitions in hand, we now have four ways of classifying my friend's parent's action:

The committing of adultery was

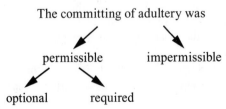

permissible   impermissible

optional   required

An astute reader will notice that the definitions for our four deontic verdicts have been partly defined in terms of one another. That's unsatisfying. Definitional circles are uninformative. Yet, how these definitions relate, and which we should take as primary, is a controversial matter.

Nevertheless, we can make some headway toward more satisfying definitions if we introduce the concept of a *reason*—a consideration that counts in favor of, or justifies, our acting in certain ways. As, for instance, when we say, the fact that you are on fire gives you a reason to stop-drop-and-roll. The fact—that you are on fire—counts in favor of your stopping, dropping, and rolling, such that you are justified in so acting. By deploying the concept of a reason, we could break out of our definitional circle by analyzing 'required' in the following, more informative way:

> An action is *required* if and only if there is decisive (or conclusive) reason to perform the action.

Defining 'required', and thereby our other deontic verdicts, in terms of reasons sits well with what we intuitively think normative theories are in the business of doing: namely, locating the considerations that count in favor of our actions. Normativity is, at base, justificatory. We could say, for example, the fact that committing adultery is disrespectful, gives my friend's parent decisive reason to refrain from committing it. Here we are not trying to explain how the world is; rather we're trying to justify how it should be. It should be a world where my friend's parent does not commit adultery.

§2. DETERMINING GROUNDS

Notice, however, that in supplying the reason that gets us the deontic verdict that refraining from adultery was required we've made a subtle shift. We've started supplying specific justifications—e.g., citing disrespect—for *why* we should give certain deontic verdicts as opposed to others. We've moved, in other words, in the direction of supplying grounds for our deontic verdicts. This—the *determining grounds*—is our second central element of normative ethics.

The grounds of a theory determine the facts that are relevant for our deontic verdicts. In other words, a theory's determining grounds tell us which facts are genuinely reason-providing. Now, many facts seem to be reason-providing. One might think, for instance, that many of the explanations I cited in the opening paragraph for the impermissibility of the adultery seem plausible. This could well be the case. But remember the reassuring thought above: our surface disagreement might vanish if we agree on some ultimate rationale. So before opting for a long list of reason-providing facts, we need to introduce an important distinction between *instrumental*, *derivative*, and *non-derivative* reasons.

Suppose you and a close friend are enjoying supper at your favorite restaurant. But then, in walks a gang of powerful jerks. They credibly tell you that, unless you dance, they are going to cause you great suffering. You then have a reason to dance, provided by the gang's threat. This reason is *derivative*: the force of the gang's threat is parasitic on the nature of suffering. This reason is also *instrumental*: dancing is merely a means to avoiding the threatened suffering. Your reason to dance supplied by the gang's threat thus owes its force to the connection it has to suffering. Absent the threatened suffering, the gang's threat fails to provide you with a reason to dance. Facts about suffering provide the ultimate ground for the reasons you have. Hence only suffering, in this case, provides *non-derivative* reasons. Once we see that only the reasons provided by suffering have this special status—being non-derivative—we see that only suffering has normative significance for our deontic verdict.

To be clear, facts about suffering seem like a good candidate for providing non-derivative reasons. But at this point we are only trying to distinguish the facts that are relevant to the deontic verdicts from those that are not. And perhaps, in the end, suffering is not one such fact. No matter. The lesson here is general: the reasons grounding our deontic verdicts should be non-derivative. Thus, though there might be many plausible explanations for why my friend's parent's adultery was wrong, only the non-derivative reasons are relevant to the status of the action. When it comes to reaching the correct deontic verdicts, we can ignore the others. The driving question behind a theory's determining grounds is accordingly this: what things provide agents with non-derivative reasons?

§3. EVALUATIVE-FIRST THEORIES

One tempting answer to this question brings us to the next element of normative ethics, *evaluative claims*. Evaluative claims are claims about what is good or valuable. The tempting answer, what we might call an *evaluative-first* theory, treats deontic verdicts as a function of evaluative claims. The evaluative-first approach, in other words, treats goodness facts as the only facts that supply non-derivative reasons. For example, your reason to dance is provided by the fact that suffering is bad, and hence to be avoided.

A prominent version of the evaluative-first approach has an intimidating name: a *teleological theory*. 'Telos' is Greek for end or goal. Accordingly, a teleological theory tells us to promote a certain outcome or state of affairs. But which outcome or state of affairs should we aim to bring about? Coupling teleology with the evaluative-first approach provides one answer. We are, according to this approach, given the end or goal of promoting the good. The reasons relevant to our deontic verdicts are provided by facts about the good, and the response demanded by these reasons is always the same: promotion—i.e., aim at the good's greater overall realization. This is a compelling idea. Take whatever seems non-derivatively good or bad, say, suffering. Then, conjure a choice situation with two options, one with more suffering and the other with less. In such a situation, a teleological theory tells us to choose the option with less suffering. Less abstractly, suppose you had to undergo an agonizing surgery. The doctor tells you that she can either perform the surgery with or without anesthesia. Which should you choose? All other things equal, the answer is obvious. Why endure unnecessary badness? For an evaluative-first teleological theory, this thought globalizes for the rest of the normative domain: it is always permissible to bring about the best outcome.

To better understand the evaluative-first teleological approach, we need to better understand evaluative claims. When it comes to evaluative claims we often speak loosely, as I did when talking about your suffering being bad. We could say that your suffering is *bad-for-you*—personally bad. Or, we could say that your suffering is *bad-simpliciter*—impersonally bad. Since, to supply the ground for our deontic verdicts, we are only after non-derivative reasons, we could ignore either good-for or good-*simpliciter*, if one were reducible to the other. Unfortunately, this is a thorny issue. For now, let's turn to how each, taken separately, might be combined with an evaluative-first teleological theory.

§3.1 UNIVERSAL EGOISM

We've reached an exciting juncture. We are now in a position to sketch an ethical theory. Suppose we take a teleological approach to our deontic verdicts. And we also think that the only facts of intrinsic normative significance are facts about what is good-for-you. That is, facts about what is good-for-you ground all deontic verdicts. We could then formulate a *core normative principle*, which is our next element of normative ethics, as follows:

> For all persons, each person, for example, Becky, is permitted to do (of the available actions open to her) only what will bring about the most good-for-Becky.

This theory is known as *universal egoism* (see Part 3). It tells each agent to do whatever will best promote her own good.

If we combine the core principle of universal egoism with non-normative facts about the world, we can generate a host of deontic verdicts. My friend's parent was, for example, *required* to commit adultery, if committing adultery would uniquely promote the most overall good for my friend's parent. Committing adultery was *impermissible* if doing so would not have produced the most overall good for my friend's parent. And committing adultery was *optional* if doing so would have produced the most overall good for my friend's parent, but there was some other available action that tied with committing adultery in the amount of overall good it could produce for my friend's parent.

§3.2 ACT-CONSEQUENTIALISM

After hearing these deontic verdicts, universal egoism might not look very promising. Is the impermissibility of committing adultery really located in the narcissistic fact that it wouldn't be best for *me*? Can't the good of others bear, non-derivatively, on deontic verdicts? The thought driving these questions seems to be this: universal egoism makes evaluative claims overly and implausibly focused on a specific person—me. An ethical theory should be more impersonal. This brings us to our next evaluative-first teleological theory. This time, however, only facts concerning what is good-*simpliciter* supply us with non-derivative reasons. The theory we then get is:

> For all persons, each person is permitted to do (of the available actions) only what will bring about the most good-*simpliciter*.

This principle captures the core of *act-consequentialism* (see Part 7). It tells each agent to do whatever will best promote the good overall, impartially assessed.

Again, once combined with non-normative facts, the core principle of act-consequentialism immediately generates deontic verdicts. My friend's parent was *required* to commit adultery, if committing adultery would uniquely promote the most overall good. Committing adultery was *impermissible* if doing so would not have produced the most overall good. Put otherwise, there was another action available to my friend's parent that would have produced more good-*simpliciter*. And committing adultery was *optional* if doing so would have produced the most overall good, but there was some other available action that tied with committing adultery in that it would also produce the most overall good.

Unlike universal egoism, the deontic verdicts supplied by act-consequentialism might initially seem plausible. But a moment's reflection on what act-consequentialism demands invites reassessment. Act-consequentialism's impartiality leaves little room for people to live their own lives. One is required, for every available action, to act in the way that produces the greatest amount of good, period. For example, I plan to spend the bulk of my day writing this introduction. Maybe it will do some good. It will help some people better understand normative ethics. But that, act-consequentialism says, is not enough. My writing this introduction is not permissible unless, of the available alternatives, this is the action that produces the *most* good. That is a daunting demand. Recall the deontic verdict concerning what it would take for committing adultery to be optional—it would have to produce the most good and also be tied with some other available action that produced an equal amount of good. Here's a gross understatement: act-consequentialism doesn't hand out a lot of optional deontic verdicts. This dearth of options appears to be a damning problem. And, unfortunately for act-consequentialism, the problems do not end here.

Recall that, if it uniquely produces the most good-*simpliciter*, act-consequentialism tells us that committing adultery is required. Intuitively, that seems like a mistake. One might have thought that adultery is impermissible. So it's bad enough that act-consequentialism does not rule out adultery in principle; even worse, it could require it. To put the point more generally, any action can be made permissible, indeed required, by being the action the produces the most good. This might not seem worrisome if the margins were large enough—for example, if committing adultery was the only way to save many people's lives. Yet one outcome can be better than another by only the smallest degree. So pick an act that is as abhorrent as you can imagine. Next, rig two outcomes such that one outcome, the one where *you* are performing the abhorrent action, is infinitesimally better overall than the outcome where you do not perform the action. Act-consequentialism always comes back with the same verdict. It's not just permissible for you to perform the abhorrent action, it's required.

These two problems—the lack of options and lack of limits—are not new. Act-consequentialists have compelling ways of responding to both. The best strategy, as suggested above, is to show the implausibility of alternative theories. So we shouldn't write off act-consequentialism quite yet. Its rivals might be worse. We'll have to wait and see.

In any case, the seemingly troubling implications of universal egoism and act-consequentialism provide a helpful way to orient our discussion. Egoism requires too little of us; act-consequentialism requires too much. The remaining normative theories can thus be seen as attempts to forge a middle path. They try to resist the pull of consequentialism's impartiality without being driven all the way to egoism. How might this be accomplished?

§3.3 NATURAL LAW THEORY

Let's pause to remember what seems to be the force driving egoism and act-consequentialism to their extremes. Surprisingly, the source of these problems seems to be what was initially so compelling about teleological theories in the first place. Specifically, that it is always permissible, and perhaps required, to act so as to promote the good. Once pointed in a certain direction, with nothing holding them back, the deontic verdicts of teleological theories have no bounds. So, if we hope to stick with the evaluative-first approach, we might try to avoid these problems by jettisoning the demand to bring about the best outcome.

A *non-teleological approach* gains some plausibility once we notice that there is more than one way we can respond to the things we find good or valuable. Consider friendship. If friendship facts provide us with non-derivative reasons, the teleological approach tells us to promote friendship. That sounds off. We fail to properly understand the nature of friendship if we respond by trying to maximize the number of friendships overall. Instead, the appropriate response seems to be to *respect* or *honor* friendship in our own person. Suppose this is on the right track. We would then need a defensible list of the good things that provide us with non-derivative reasons. But once we had such a list, we could combine it with a non-teleological theory. This evaluative-first non-teleological theory would then supply us with the following principle:

> For all persons, each person, for example, Becky, is required to respect or honor those things that are non-derivatively good in her own person.

This captures the core of the *natural law theory* (see Part 5). It tells us to honor or respect those things that are non-derivatively good, where what is 'natural' determines what is good and what is 'unnatural' determines what is bad.

Unfortunately, properly making the natural/unnatural distinction raises significant complications. So, to see the kinds of deontic verdicts natural law generates, let's simply assume that marriage is a non-derivative good. Then, according to the natural law theory, my friend's parent was *required* to refrain from committing adultery, since committing adultery fails to respect the institution of marriage. Committing adultery was, accordingly, *impermissible*. Adultery, the natural law theorist might say, is unnatural.

Natural law allows us to escape the problems of act-consequentialism without collapsing into egoism. Still, difficulties loom. Suppose that there are many non-derivative goods. To get natural law theory to generate contradictory deontic verdicts, all we need to do is pit two goods against one another. For example, suppose that if you tell your friend the truth—that his parent committed adultery—it would destroy your friendship. If both friendship and honesty are to be honored, then the core principle of natural law theory tells us to lie to honor friendship and not lie to honor honesty. In response to such conflicts, the natural law theorist might try to provide a ranking of the importance of the non-derivative goods. But this would do little to help. Indeed, we could grant that the list of non-derivative goods consists of only one item, and still generate conflicting deontic verdicts. Assume, for instance, that only human life is non-derivatively good. Now imagine a situation where you must choose between your life and the life of another. Natural law theory would then tell you to honor your life and act to preserve it. But it would also tell you to honor the other person's life and act to preserve it. In this case, however, we've stipulated that you cannot do both.

Theories that generate conflicting deontic verdicts are hard to defend. Yet, like act-consequentialism, natural law theorists have ways of responding to these problems. Nevertheless, at this point we might start to wonder if the evaluative-first approach led us down the wrong path. We might do better if we simply ensure certain deontic verdicts. That is, perhaps we should turn to a *deontic-first* approach.

§4. DEONTIC-FIRST THEORIES

On a deontic-first approach, in providing the grounds of our deontic verdicts, we eschew talk about goodness facts, and opt for a set of constraints. Constraints, as their name implies, are a kind of normative barrier. They tell us that we are required to refrain from performing certain actions, even if so refraining comes at the cost of the overall good. For example, suppose that there is a constraint on performing adultery. We could then say that my friend's parent acted impermissibly, even if committing adultery ultimately led to the best outcome overall.

This last claim might strike you as puzzling. If I do what is normatively *required*, how could things turn out worse? The evaluative-first teleological approach's compelling idea has reemerged. Remember, however, that we found act-consequentialism worrisome because, under the right circumstances, it requires that we perform certain intuitively abhorrent acts. The deontic-first approach gives credence to this worry by erecting constraints to block the performance of such acts. Nonetheless, there does seem to be something perplexing about the deontic-first account. Relying on goodness facts seems to provide a straightforward, intuitive grounding of our deontic verdicts. Without relying on these evaluative claims, where do these constraints come from? This is the *explanatory burden* incurred by deontic-first theories.

To fully grasp this burden, we need to have a better grip on the nature of constraints. To begin, think back on our discussion of the evaluative-first approach. There we always spoke of specific actions. The explanation for this should be obvious. If evaluative-first theories treat deontic verdicts as a function of evaluative claims, then we need to assess each available action to identify which should be performed. But part of the worry we had about act-consequentialism stems from the thought that some acts are simply abhorrent. And here we've arrived at an important distinction, the distinction between act-types and act-tokens. To help see this distinction, consider the question: how many letters are in the word 'fool'? This question is instructively imprecise. We might plausibly answer: four—counting each specific letter. Or, we might plausibly answer: three—counting each type of letter, and so counting 'o'only once. If we answer four, we took the question to be a question concerning letter-tokens. If we answer three, we took the question to be about letter-types. The same distinction applies to acts. On an evaluative-first approach, we are only concerned with *act-tokens*. But, once we take up the deontic-first approach, we're inclined to start thinking in terms of *act-types*. Constraints are formulated as barriers, blocking the performance of certain act-types—for example, performing adultery is impermissible. If you then perform the act-token—you commit adultery—you've violated the constraint, and thereby done something impermissible.

Even once we've noticed this important point concerning the nature of constraints—that they are typically formulated in terms of act-types—a teleological thought still haunts us. If constraints give us the goal of not performing certain act-types, why not think that we should promote the outcome with the fewest performances of such acts? Consider a schematic case. Suppose that my friend's parent is in the following position: if my friend's parent committed adultery, this would prevent two other people from each committing adultery. The teleological thought here is that if violations of constraints are to be avoided, then we should have the goal of minimizing violations. If constraints are so important, then it might seem that my friend's parent should commit adultery to prevent two additional adulterous actions. Generalizing, why not combine a deontic-first approach with a teleological theory—what we might call *constraints-teleology*? The answer, which is what drove us to the deontic-first theory to begin with, is that we want to avoid having to be the one performing the abhorrent act. To avoid constraints-teleology, the deontic-first approach thus needs to make a slight retreat toward egoism. We need to formulate constraints in a way that makes essential reference to *me*—the person to whom the constraint applies.

This leads us to the next feature of constraints. Deploying some fancy terminology, we could say that constraints need to provide *agent-relative*, as opposed to *agent-neutral*, reasons. To help see the distinction between agent-relative and agent-neutral reasons, suppose you are on a road trip with your family. Your parents tell you and your two siblings to make sure there is as little fighting as possible. Not long after, your two siblings get in a fight. Suppose you know that unless you intervene the fight will continue for the rest of the trip. Your parents' command thus provides you with a reason to fight, because your intervention would bring about less fighting. The reason provided by your parents' constraint against fighting is thus agent-neutral; it gives all the children the same aim—minimize fighting. Now imagine the same scenario, but this time your parents tell you and your siblings, each individually: no fighting! Again not long after, your two siblings get in a fight, which unless you intervene will last the rest of the trip. Yet, this time you cannot fight to reduce the fighting, for if you did, you would disobey your parents' command. In this second case, the reason provided by your parents' constraint against fighting is agent-relative; it makes essential reference to you, telling *you* not to fight. To avoid consequentialism, the deontic-first approach needs to mimic your parents' in this latter case. Constraints need to be formulated in such a way that it gives *you* a weighty, perhaps decisive, reason to avoid violation of the constraint, even if your violation would prevent additional future violations of that very constraint. If the constraint doesn't make this essential reference to the agent to whom it applies, if the reason attached to the constraint is, in other words, agent-neutral, then the deontic-first approach seems unable to resist constraints-teleology. It would give everyone the same aim: minimize constraint violations. A deontic-first theory, in short, needs to be articulated in agent-relative terms, meaning that such a theory could potentially give different persons different aims.

We are now in a position to feel the full weight of the deontic-first approach's explanatory burden. Not only do agent-relative constraints wall us off from the good, they wall us off from other deontic verdicts. The viability of the deontic-first approach thus hinges on locating a plausible source of agent-relative constraints. Three promising sources might here spring to mind: something above us (God), something around us (culture), or something within us (rational nature). Let's take these in turn.

§4.1 DIVINE COMMAND THEORY

Most religious views take God to supply a number of agent-relative constraints. Drawing on this theological tradition, we could then formulate a deontic-first non-teleological theory as:

> For all persons, each person, for example, Becky, is required to do whatever God commands her to do.

This is the core principle of *divine command theory* (see Part 4). On its face, divine command theory has some plausibility, and it seems to provide a powerful explanation of the source of our agent-relative constraints. Yet a serious difficulty lurks.

Divine command theory faces an old problem, a dilemma that directly calls into question its ability to discharge the explanatory burden. Either what is normatively required is required because God commands it, or it isn't. If performing an action is required because God commands it, then the demands of normativity are arbitrary. God could have commanded that we do the most abhorrent acts; and in so commanding, these acts would then be required. That looks worse than act-consequentialism. At least with act-consequentialism, we got some good out of performing abhorrent acts. But if we go for the other horn of the dilemma, maintaining that God commands certain acts because they are required, then the explanatory burden returns in full force. God is superfluous to the normative story. At best, God identifies the constraints we already had.

§4.2 CULTURAL RELATIVISM

There's nonetheless something attractive about looking for the source of the constraints in God. That there is something outside of us handing down the constraints seems to imbue them with the special authority they seem to have. So even if God may not undergird agent-relative constraints, perhaps something outside of us still can. For example, as was the case with my friend's adulterous parent, we often hear people saying that there are certain things we just don't do around here. The thought seems to be this: certain constraints apply to people simply in virtue of being a member of a social group with certain norms and customs. Being part of a particular culture, then, provides another possible way of meeting the explanatory burden. We can formulate the core principle of such a theory as follows:

> For all persons, each person, for example, Becky, is required to do whatever the norms of her culture tell her to do.

This theory is known as *cultural relativism* (see Part 2). It holds that deontic verdicts are indexed to cultural norms.

Cultural relativism, for example, tells us that my friend's parent acted *impermissibly* because the norms of our culture include an agent-relative constraint against committing adultery. But what would have made committing adultery permissible? Interestingly, cultural relativism gives us two answers. Committing adultery would have been *permissible* had our culture not had norms that include a constraint against committing adultery. Or, even if the norms of our culture contain a constraint against committing adultery, the adulterous action of my friend's parent would be *permissible* from the perspective of other cultures whose norms lack such a constraint.

Having these two ways of arriving at permissibility is a puzzling feature. But that's the relativism. The correctness of a deontic verdict concerning an act, whatever it is, depends entirely on the norms of the culture from which the verdict is issued. Cultural relativism thus asserts a bold thesis. It does not merely make the uncontroversial claim that deontic verdicts are context sensitive; rather it denies the existence of moral truths that cut across all cultures. Maybe that's not wildly unintuitive for acts like adultery. But if we turn to other acts, things look different. Could the norms of a culture really determine the correct deontic verdict concerning torturing for fun? If that seems mistaken, then we're led to accept an important desideratum on normative theories: their deontic verdicts must be *universal*. They must not be relative to a particular culture, but apply to all persons in relevantly similar circumstances.

We now have an even better handle on what a non-teleological deontic-first theory is after: discharging the explanatory burden while retaining universality. So perhaps the source of agent-relative constraints can be derived from something about all of us. After all, we are the entities to whom they apply. We are agents—beings capable of recognizing and responding to reasons.

§4.3 KANTIANISM

The recognition that we are agents is a thought worth exploring. Right now I am writing this essay. Outside my window there is a red maple. In a minute, I am going to leave my desk for coffee. In about thirty minutes, the sun is going to rise, and the red maple will bend slightly east. In an hour, let's suppose my rather nosy neighbor who's been watching all of this comes in and asks: "Why did you get the coffee?" I might respond, "Because I'm writing this introduction, and wanted to be sharp." I cite a reason. If my neighbor, for example, asks me why I chose coffee and not tea, I could deploy this reason to justify my choice: coffee has more caffeine. Next suppose the conversation shifts to the red maple, and my neighbor asks: "Why did that tree bend to the east?" I might respond, hoping to shut him up: "Because of positive phototropism." Though this answer sounds similar to my previous one, it is not. It is an explanatory reason, not a justificatory one. The red maple, unlike me, does not have a rational nature. I, not the maple, am sensitive to reasons. External forces, like the sun, do not drive me. Hence, there is a kind of freedom that I have, which the maple lacks. And it is only in virtue of this freedom that normative questions become salient. The maple does not ask: What ought I to do? Or, who should I be? Only persons, beings with rational natures, confront such questions.

That I have a rational nature, of course, does not mean that I always act rationally. Depressingly, I act irrationally all too often. But now we've arrived at an intriguing idea. Perhaps agent-relative constraints fall directly out of our own rational nature, such that violating the constraint can only be done on pain of our own rationality. That would be a neat result. But how could we establish this tight connection between rationality and agent-relative constraints?

To answer this question, return to universality—the thought that our deontic verdicts need to apply to all persons in relevantly similar circumstances. Previously, we concluded that universalizability seemed like a plausible desideratum on normative theories. Given our discussion of rationality, we can now defend this desideratum. The connection between rationality and universality is easiest to see in the theoretical domain. Insofar as we are rational, we cite reasons for our beliefs. I don't simply believe, for example, that the gas in my car is low. Rather, if I am to rationally form a belief concerning how much fuel my car has, I look for reasons. For instance, I see that my car's reliable gas light is on, and this justifies my belief that the gas is low. Notice an interesting feature concerning the evidence that my gas light provides: it is not person specific. If it's rational for me to believe that the gas is low because of the gas light, then, based on this same reason, were you in my situation, it would also be rational for you to believe the gas is low. I don't have a monopoly on gas light reasons. Universalizability thus appears to be a constitutive principle of rationality. But there is no reason to think this principle is restricted to the theoretical domain. Presumably, universalizability is also a constitutive principle of practical rationality. To act rationally is to act on reasons I can coherently see others, in relevantly similar circumstances, acting on as well.

The link between universalizability and rationality leads us to a *universalizability test*. If a purported reason for acting can't apply to all rational beings in relevantly similar circumstances, the reason is merely apparent. With this test in place, we are in a position to discharge the explanatory burden. We apply the universalizability test broadly, identifying acts whose features are such that any purported reason in their favor fails the test. If permission-granting reasons for such acts systematically fail, we can conclude that there is an agent-relative constraint against performing them.

To see how this works, return to my friend's adulterous parent. To make things manageable, let's focus on the breaking of the vows. To apply the universalizability test, start by provisionally granting that all persons, in similar circumstances, could act as my friend's parent did. Let's stipulate that my friend's parent broke the vow because of the pleasure adultery would afford. Consider a world where everyone adhered to, or even just believed in, the permissibility of vow-breaking for pleasure-based reasons. What would vows or promises look like in this world? Imagine you went to a wedding and heard the bride say to the groom: "I promise to always be faithful. But remember, we both know it is perfectly permissible for me to be unfaithful to you when it pleases me." This vow is funny, because a vow that is permissible to break whenever pleasurable is no vow at all. This tells us something about a world where everyone acts like my friend's parent. In such a world, the very institution of vow-making would cease. It would be pointless to make vows, since no one would believe them. Accordingly, if not everyone could rationally act on such reasons, no one could rationally act on them. Failing universalizability is the hallmark of irrationality. No one gets a monopoly on pleasure-based reasons to break vows. Thus my friend's adulterous parent failed the universalizability test, and hence acted irrationally. But perhaps we can say more. Perhaps no reasons in favor of vow-breaking can pass the universalizability test. If so, there would be an agent-relative constraint against vow-breaking—vow-breaking, as such, would be impermissible. That would be a substantial result; it would show the possibility of discharging the explanatory burden through rationality alone.

The non-teleological deontic-first theory we've been exploring brings us close to the theory espoused by Immanuel Kant. Kant's theory is complex. But one of Kant's central ideas is that the reasons that serve as the determining grounds of our deontic verdicts need to be sharable by all rational beings. In his words, "Act only in accordance with that maxim [i.e., the statement describing what you are going to do, and why you are going to do it] through which you at the same time can will that it become a universal law." We can thus state the core principle of Kant's theory as:

> For all persons, each person, for example, Becky, is required to refrain from acting according to a maxim she couldn't rationally will as a universal law.

Despite its complexity, *Kantian ethics* (see Part 6) provides an elegant solution to the deontic-first approach's explanatory problem. Rationality is what makes normativity possible; we must have agents to have reasons. But rationality, fully appreciated, is also the source of our agent-relative constraints. Moreover, there is an intuitive thought—how would you feel if everyone did that?—which Kantianism nicely captures.

Yet there are problems for Kant too. The universalizability test seems to generate false negatives. The day I graduated college—May 10, 2010—I pulled all of my money out of the bank. About two years ago, because I wanted to focus on my work, I decided never to have children. And the other day, I took the last chair in a packed auditorium. Not everyone could have acted on the maxim that I acted on when I did these things. The universalizability test thus tells us that I acted impermissibly. That looks like the wrong verdict. These actions were obviously permissible. And the problems for Kantians might not end here. The universalizability test seems to generate false positives too. For example, were I to fight in a duel, I would aim to miss. But not everyone could act on this maxim. For then, like vows that are permissible to break, the very institution of dueling would be laughable. According to the universalizability test, then, it would be impermissible for me to aim to miss. Again, that seems like the wrong verdict. The universalizability test thus either needs to be refined or abandoned.

My disclaimer should by now be familiar: Kantians have plausible rejoinders to these criticisms. Nevertheless, we might now be suspicious that discharging the explanatory burden is possible. The deontic-first approach leaves too many normative mysteries. Act-consequentialism might, at this point, appear rather alluring. However, before we succumb to consequentialism's pull, we should explore a final approach.

§5. CHARACTER-FIRST THEORIES

Perhaps our focus on acts and actions—on conduct—pointed us in the wrong direction. Think about the last funeral you attended. If you're like me, you've probably noticed are markable pattern. When people give a eulogy they don't start listing the actions the deceased performed. Instead, they start talking about the kind of person the deceased was. In other words, they talk about the deceased's character. And this talk is not limited to funeral homes. Often, in everyday discourse, character is primary to conduct. When my parents wanted me to act in a certain way, they would tell me to be more like my sister. And when I was a kid, a ubiquitous Gatorade commercial demanded that young basketball players "Be like Mike." Perhaps we should follow this linguistic evidence, and treat our deontic verdicts as a function of our character. On this *character-first* approach, it is only by first figuring out who we ought to be that we can figure out how we are required to act. Character facts, in other words, serve as the determining grounds of our deontic verdicts.

To understand this approach, we first need to understand what it is to have a certain character. Consider Gatorade's claim that young basketball players should be like Michael Jordan. The idea seems to be that Jordan has traits or dispositions to respond in certain ways that make him a good basketball player. (None of which, it's worth mentioning, include the disposition to drink Gatorade.) So, the thought continues, if you want to be a good basketball player too, then you should also try to cultivate Jordan-like dispositions. Of course, dispositions can also be bad. My dispositions, when it comes to basketball, are dispositions young basketball players should not cultivate. We might distinguish the good from the bad dispositions by calling the good dispositions *virtues*, and the bad ones *vices*.

At this point it should be clear that the character-first approach is a species of the evaluative-first approach. But we need to be careful. Notice the difference between evaluative claims like "suffering is bad" and "Michael Jordan is a good basketball player." In the former, we use 'bad' as a predicate. In the latter, we use 'good' as a predicate modifier. To differentiate the latter type of evaluative claim from good-*simpliciter* and good-for, let's call this a claim of *attributive goodness*. Attributive uses of good pick out those things that are good-of-a-kind. For example, a sharp pair of scissors is better than a dull pair. Accordingly, we call a pair of scissors that has certain traits that make it better than other scissors, within a certain comparison class, a good pair of scissors. This thought is easy to apply to Michael Jordan. He is better than most, if not all, basketball players.

Once we see the character-first approach's appeal to attributive goodness, it is not hard to predict how the rest of the story unfolds. We generalize the point we've been making about Michael Jordan to human beings. The answer to the question—who should we be?—is then determined by identifying those dispositions that good humans have. Once we've identified the goodness-making traits for humans—for example, honesty, beneficence, courageousness—we're told by the character-first approach to promote them in our lives. The character-first approach is, accordingly, a teleological theory. But the goal is not the promotion of the good overall; rather, we are given the goal of becoming good persons.

How might this goal be accomplished? Well, consider how one cultivates certain dispositions. If one wants to be a good basketball player, one does not practice like me; instead, one practices like Michael Jordan. Similarly, if one wants to be a good person one emulates what good people do. Virtuous persons serve as exemplars. They inform us how we ought to act. Looking to them tells us what to do. And here we've arrived at a core normative principle:

> For all persons, each person, for example, Becky, is required to do whatever a fully virtuous person (acting in character) would do in her circumstances.

This principle lies at the heart of the theory known as *virtue ethics* (see Part 10).

Like other evaluative-first theories, once combined with non-normative facts, the core principle of virtue ethics generates deontic verdicts. My friend's parent, for example, was *required* to commit adultery if committing adultery is what the fully virtuous person would have done in the circumstances. Committing adultery was *impermissible* if doing so is what the fully virtuous person would not have done. And committing adultery was *optional* if doing so is what the fully virtuous person might have done.

That we should act only as the fully virtuous act is an attractive idea. However, a closer inspection of virtue ethics' core principle raises concerns. The principle analyzes actions in terms of a counterfactual—were the fully virtuous person in my situation, she would do such-and-such. But this seems to rule out the requirement to do certain actions that would make us more like the virtuous. Let's return to scissors. When I was in elementary school, I was shown a cartoon where pairs of scissors, with finger-hole eyes and blade legs, interacted with each other. It was terrifying, and I'm still not sure what the point was. In any case, let's suppose these scissors were virtue ethicists, holding that each pair is required to do whatever the fully good pair of scissors would do in the circumstances. Now, obviously, the fully good pair of scissors would be extremely sharp. If a class—Sharpening Your Blades 101—were offered, she wouldn't attend. But we can imagine that other scissors would, on their path to becoming virtuous scissors, need to take this class. The example is silly, but the point here is serious. If we're required to do only what the *fully* virtuous person would do, then it looks like we're never required to become *more* virtuous. And that looks like a devastating problem for a view whose main focus is character development.

Virtue ethicists, of course, have rejoinders to this objection, which I will not address. Instead, let's now take stock. Here is the normative landscape we've been traversing.

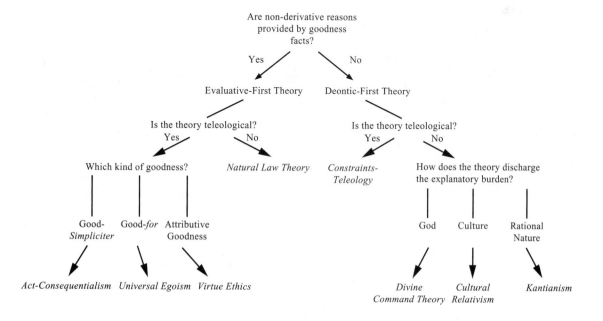

§6. OMISSIONS

The accompanying chart should help you navigate the views presented in this anthology. I should note that some of the included theories—*rule-consequentialism* (see Part 7), *social contract theory* (see Part 9), *care ethics* (see Part 11), *pluralism* (see Part 8), and *particularism* (see Part 12)—have not been addressed. This should not be taken as evidence of their unimportance. They were difficult to fit in the narrative I've been telling. My aim here was to introduce the elements of normative ethics and describe how they might be filled out. The views discussed in detail earlier fill out the elements of normative ethics in a natural way. They are, we might say, standard package views. Once one feature is in place, it is easy to see how we get the rest of the package. In contrast, rule-consequentialism, social contract theory, care ethics, pluralism, and particularism are revisionary views. By filling out the elements of normative ethics in non-standard ways, they hope to avoid the problems that confront standard approaches. Again, these are formidable positions, worth taking seriously. Yet we should flag a worry that revisionary views invite: they often turn out to be unstable. That is, when pressed, they tend to collapse into one of the standard package views. Of course proponents of revisionary theories think this worry can be assuaged. Fair enough. But we'll need to see the details.

I've also not discussed *metaethical theories* (see Part 14). Theories in metaethics attempt to answer second-order questions concerning the nature of ethics. For example, are ethical claims apt for truth, or merely expressions of our attitudes? If there are such truths, are they part of the natural, spatiotemporal world? If they are not part of the natural world, how can we come to know them? Why, when we think we know ethical truths, do we feel compelled to act in accordance with them? These second-order questions about ethics are deeply important. We often clarify and improve our ethical thinking by pursuing both normative and metaethical questions together. Only space prevents me from doing so here.

§7. CONCLUSION

Throughout this introduction I've pressed objections to all the views we've confronted. This helps make the anatomy of normative ethics vivid. Yet we should not be discouraged; this was not an autopsy. All views have objections. And, as I stressed, the proponents of these views have powerful responses. It's our goal, as we peel through the layers of the debate, to see which view comes out on top.

After reading this collection, I expect you'll be left with the sense that normative ethics makes progress. Of course we do not know what the next stage in the development of ethics will bring. But we have strong reasons to be optimistic. I, for one, am.

Part II

RELATIVISM

Moral Relativism: A Defense

Ruth Benedict

Ruth Benedict (1887–1948) was Professor of Anthropology at Columbia University. Drawing on her research, she defends cultural relativism: the view that the right depends on the norms of one's social group. Benedict argues that because different cultures have different moral norms, no universal moral truths exist. Rather, because morality differs in every society, many moralities exist. Hence what is good or bad, right or wrong, is culturally dependent.

Modern social anthropology has become more and more a study of the varieties and common elements of cultural environment and the consequences of these in human behavior. For such a study of diverse social orders primitive peoples fortunately provide a laboratory not yet entirely vitiated by the spread of a standardized worldwide civilization. Dyaks and Hopis, Fijians and Yakuts are significant for psychological and sociological study because only among these simpler peoples has there been sufficient isolation to give opportunity for the development of localized social forms. In the higher cultures the standardization of custom and belief over a couple of continents has given a false sense of the inevitability of the particular forms that have gained currency, and we need to turn to a wider survey in order to check the conclusions we hastily base upon this near-universality of familiar customs. Most of the simpler cultures did not gain the wide currency of the one which, out of our experience, we identify with human nature, but this was for various historical reasons, and certainly not for any that gives us as

its carriers a monopoly of social good or of social sanity. Modern civilization, from this point of view, becomes not a necessary pinnacle of human achievement but one entry in a long series of possible adjustments.

These adjustments, whether they are in mannerisms like the ways of showing anger, or joy, or grief in any society, or in major human drives like those of sex, prove to be far more variable than experience in any one culture would suggest. In certain fields, such as that of religion or of formal marriage arrangements, these wide limits of variability are well known and can be fairly described. In others it is not yet possible to give a generalized account, but that does not absolve us of the task of indicating the significance of the work that has been done and of the problems that have arisen.

One of these problems relates to the customary modern normal-abnormal categories and our conclusions regarding them. In how far are such categories culturally determined, or in how far can we with assurance regard them as absolute? In how far can

From Ruth Fulton Benedict, "Anthropology and the Abnormal," *Journal of General Psychology*, vol. 10, no. 1, 1934. Reprinted by permission of the Helen Dwight Reid Educational Foundation.

we regard inability to function socially as diagnostic of abnormality, or in how far is it necessary to regard this as a function of the culture? . . .

The most spectacular illustrations of the extent to which normality may be culturally defined are those cultures where an abnormality of our culture is the cornerstone of their social structure. It is not possible to do justice to these possibilities in a short discussion. A recent study of an island of northwest Melanesia by Fortune describes a society built upon traits which we regard as beyond the border of paranoia. In this tribe the exogamic groups look upon each other as prime manipulators of black magic, so that one marries always into an enemy group which remains for life one's deadly and unappeasable foes. They look upon a good garden crop as a confession of theft, for everyone is engaged in making magic to induce into his garden the productiveness of his neighbors'; therefore no secrecy in the island is so rigidly insisted upon as the secrecy of a man's harvesting of his yams. Their polite phrase at the acceptance of a gift is, "And if you now poison me, how shall I repay you this present?" Their preoccupation with poisoning is constant; no woman ever leaves her cooking pot for a moment untended. Even the great affinal economic exchanges that are characteristic of this Melanesian culture area are quite altered in Dobu since they are incompatible with this fear and distrust that pervades the culture. They go farther and people the whole world outside their own quarters with such malignant spirits that all-night feasts and ceremonials simply do not occur here. They have even rigorous religiously enforced customs that forbid the sharing of seed even in one family group. Anyone else's food is deadly poison to you, so that communality of stores is out of the question. For some months before harvest the whole society is on the verge of starvation, but if one falls to the temptation and eats up one's seed yams, one is an outcast and a beachcomber for life. There is no coming back. It involves, as a matter of course, divorce and the breaking of all social ties.

Now in this society where no one may work with another and no one may share with another, Fortune describes the individual who was regarded by all his fellows as crazy. He was not one of those who periodically ran amok and, beside himself and frothing at the mouth, fell with a knife upon anyone he could reach. Such behavior they did not regard as putting anyone outside the pale. They did not even put the individuals who were known to be liable to these attacks under any kind of control. They merely fled when they saw the attack coming on and kept out of the way. "He would be all right tomorrow." But there was one man of sunny, kindly disposition who liked work and liked to be helpful. The compulsion was too strong for him to repress it in favor of the opposite tendencies of his culture. Men and women never spoke of him without laughing; he was silly and simple and definitely crazy. Nevertheless, to the ethnologist used to a culture that has, in Christianity, made his type the model of all virtue, he seemed a pleasant fellow. . . .

. . . Among the Kwakiutl it did not matter whether a relative had died in bed of disease, or by the hand of an enemy, in either case death was an affront to be wiped out by the death of another person. The fact that one had been caused to mourn was proof that one had been put upon. A chief's sister and her daughter had gone up to Victoria, and either because they drank bad whiskey or because their boat capsized they never came back. The chief called together his warriors, "Now I ask you, tribes, who shall wail? Shall I do it or shall another?" The spokesman answered, of course, "Not you, Chief. Let some other of the tribes." Immediately they set up the war pole to announce their intention of wiping out the injury, and gathered a war party. They set out, and found seven men and two children asleep and killed them. "Then they felt good when they arrived at Sebaa in the evening."

The point which is of interest to us is that in our society those who on that occasion would feel good when they arrived at Sebaa that evening would be the definitely abnormal. There would be some, even in our society, but it is not a recognized and approved mood under the circumstances. On the Northwest Coast those are favored and fortunate to whom that mood under those circumstances is congenial, and those to whom it is repugnant are unlucky. This latter minority can register in their own culture only by doing violence to their congenial responses and acquiring others that are difficult for them. The person, for instance, who, like a Plains Indian whose wife has been taken from him, is too proud to fight, can deal with the Northwest Coast civilization only by ignoring its strongest bents. If he cannot achieve it, he is the deviant in that culture, their instance of abnormality.

This head-hunting that takes place on the Northwest Coast after a death is no matter of blood revenge or of organized vengeance. There is no effort to tie up the subsequent killing with any responsibility on the part of the victim for the death of the person who is being mourned. A chief whose son has died goes visiting wherever his fancy dictates, and he says to his host, "My prince has died today, and you go with him." Then he kills him. In this, according to their interpretation, he acts nobly because he has not been downed. He has thrust back in return. The whole procedure is meaningless without the fundamental paranoid reading of bereavement. Death, like all the other untoward accidents of existence, confounds man's pride and can only be handled in the category of insults. . . .

These illustrations, which it has been possible to indicate only in the briefest manner, force upon us the fact that normality is culturally defined. An adult shaped to the drives and standards of either of these cultures, if he were transported into our civilization, would fall into our categories of abnormality. He would be faced with the psychic dilemmas of the socially unavailable. In his own culture, however, he is the pillar of society, the end result of socially inculcated mores, and the problem of personal instability in his case simply does not arise.

No one civilization can possibly utilize in its mores the whole potential range of human behavior. Just as there are great numbers of possible phonetic articulations, and the possibility of language depends on a selection and standardization of a few of these in order that speech communication may be possible at all, so the possibility of organized behavior of every sort, from the fashions of local dress and houses to the dicta of a people's ethics and religion, depends upon a similar selection among the possible behavior traits. In the field of recognized economic obligations or sex tabus this

selection is as nonrational and subconscious a process as it is in the field of phonetics. It is a process which goes on in the group for long periods of time and is historically conditioned by innumerable accidents of isolation or of contact of peoples. In any comprehensive study of psychology, the selection that different cultures have made in the course of history within the great circumference of potential behavior is of great significance.

Every society, beginning with some slight inclination in one direction or another, carries its preference farther and farther, integrating itself more and more completely upon its chosen basis, and discarding those types of behavior that are uncongenial. Most of those organizations of personality that seem to us most incontrovertibly abnormal have been used by different civilizations in the very foundations of their institutional life. Conversely the most valued traits of our normal individuals have been looked on in differently organized cultures as aberrant. Normality, in short, within a very wide range, is culturally defined. It is primarily a term for the socially elaborated segment of human behavior in any culture; and abnormality, a term for the segment that that particular civilization does not use. The very eyes with which we see the problem are conditioned by the long traditional habits of our own society.

It is a point that has been made more often in relation to ethics than in relation to psychiatry. We do not any longer make the mistake of deriving the morality of our locality and decade directly from the inevitable constitution of human nature. We do not elevate it to the dignity of a first principle. We recognize that morality differs in every society, and is a convenient term for socially approved habits. Mankind has always preferred to say, "It is morally good," rather than "It is habitual," and the fact of this preference is matter enough for a critical science of ethics. But historically the two phrases are synonymous.

The concept of the normal is properly a variant of the concept of the good. It is that which society has approved. A normal action is one which falls well within the limits of expected behavior for a particular society. Its variability among different peoples is essentially a function of the variability of the behavior patterns that different societies have created for themselves, and can never be wholly divorced from a consideration of culturally institutionalized types of behavior.

Each culture is a more or less elaborate working-out of the potentialities of the segment it has chosen. In so far as a civilization is well integrated and consistent within itself, it will tend to carry farther and farther, according to its nature, its initial impulse toward a particular type of action, and from the point of view of any other culture those elaborations will include more and more extreme and aberrant traits.

Each of these traits, in proportion as it reinforces the chosen behavior patterns of that culture, is for that culture normal. Those individuals to whom it is congenial either congenitally, or as the result of childhood sets, are accorded prestige in that culture, and are not visited with the social contempt or disapproval which their traits would call down upon them in a society that was differently organized. On the other hand, those individuals whose characteristics are not congenial to the selected type of human behavior in that community are the deviants, no matter how valued their personality traits may be in a contrasted civilization. . . .

The problem of understanding abnormal human behavior in any absolute sense independent of cultural factors is still far in the future. The categories of borderline behavior which we derive from the study of the neuroses and psychoses of our civilization are categories of prevailing local types of instability. They give much information about the stresses and strains of Western civilization, but no final picture of inevitable human behavior. Any conclusions about such behavior must await the collection by trained observers of psychiatric data from other cultures. Since no adequate work of the kind has been done at the present time, it is impossible to say what core of definition of abnormality may be found valid from the comparative material. It is as it is in ethics: all our local conventions of moral behavior and of immoral are without absolute validity, and yet it is quite possible that a modicum of what is considered right and what wrong could be disentangled that is shared by the whole human race. When data are available in psychiatry, this minimum definition of abnormal human tendencies will be probably quite unlike our culturally conditioned, highly elaborated psychoses such as those that are described, for instance, under the terms of schizophrenia and manic-depressive.

STUDY QUESTIONS

1. Is the distinction between the normal and abnormal equivalent to the distinction between the moral and immoral?
2. In any disagreement, does the disputed issue always result from a different point of view?
3. If cultural relativism is true, can people from different cultures have moral disagreements?
4. Is the claim that killing innocent people is wrong best described as normative or descriptive?

Moral Isolationism

Mary Midgley

Some claim that the search for universal answers to moral questions is futile because morality differs from one culture to another. This view, sometimes referred to as "cultural relativism," maintains that while we can seek understanding of a particular culture's moral system, we have no basis for judging it, for morality is only a matter of custom. Mary Midgley, who was Senior Lecturer in Philosophy at Newcastle University in England, argues against cultural relativism, maintaining that moral reasoning requires the possibility of judging the practices of other cultures.

All of us are, more or less, in trouble today about trying to understand cultures strange to us. We hear constantly of alien customs. We see changes in our lifetime which would have astonished our parents. I want to discuss here one very short way of dealing with this difficulty, a drastic way which many people now theoretically favour. It consists in simply denying that we can ever understand any culture except our own well enough to make judgements about it. Those who recommend this hold that the world is sharply divided into separate societies, sealed units, each with its own system of thought. They feel that the respect and tolerance due from one system to another forbids us ever to take up a critical position to any other culture. Moral judgement, they suggest, is a kind of coinage valid only in its country of origin.

I shall call this position "moral isolationism." I shall suggest that it is certainly not forced upon us, and indeed that it makes no sense at all. People usually take it up because they think it is a respectful attitude to other cultures. In fact, however, it is not respectful. Nobody can respect what is entirely unintelligible to them. To respect someone, we have to know enough about him to make a *favourable* judgement, however general and tentative. And we do understand people in other cultures to this extent. Otherwise a great mass of our most valuable thinking would be paralysed.

To show this, I shall take a remote example, because we shall probably find it easier to think calmly about it than we should with a contemporary one, such as female circumcision in Africa or the Chinese Cultural Revolution. The principles involved will still be the same. My example is this. There is, it seems, a verb in classical Japanese which means "to try out one's new sword on a chance wayfarer." (The word is *tsujigiri,* literally "crossroads-cut.") A samurai sword had to be tried out because, if it was to work properly, it had to slice through someone at a single blow, from the shoulder to the opposite flank. Otherwise, the warrior bungled his stroke. This could injure his honour, offend his ancestors, and even let down his

From Mary Midgley, *Heart and Mind: The Varieties of Moral Experience,* Routledge, 2003. Reprinted by permission of Taylor & Francis.

emperor. So tests were needed, and wayfarers had to be expended. Any wayfarer would do—provided, of course, that he was not another Samurai. Scientists will recognize a familiar problem about the rights of experimental subjects.

Now when we hear of a custom like this, we may well reflect that we simply do not understand it; and therefore are not qualified to criticize it at all, because we are not members of that culture. But we are not members of any other culture either, except our own. So we extend the principle to cover all extraneous cultures, and we seem therefore to be moral isolationists. But this is, as we shall see, an impossible position. Let us ask what it would involve.

We must ask first: Does the isolating barrier work both ways? Are people in other cultures equally unable to criticize *us?* This question struck me sharply when I read a remark in *The Guardian* by an anthropologist about a South American Indian who had been taken into a Brazilian town for an operation, which saved his life. When he came back to his village, he made several highly critical remarks about the white Brazilians' way of life. They may very well have been justified. But the interesting point was that the anthropologist called these remarks "a damning indictment of Western civilization." Now the Indian had been in that town about two weeks. Was he in a position to deliver a damning indictment? Would we ourselves be qualified to deliver such an indictment on the Samurai, provided we could spend two weeks in ancient Japan? What do we really think about this?

My own impression is that we believe that outsiders can, in principle, deliver perfectly good indictments—only, it usually takes more than two weeks to make them damning. Understanding has degrees. It is not a slapdash yes-or-no matter. Intelligent outsiders can progress in it, and in some ways will be at an advantage over the locals. But if this is so, it must clearly apply to ourselves as much as anybody else.

Our next question is this: Does the isolating barrier between cultures block praise as well as blame? If I want to say that the Samurai culture has many virtues, or to praise the South American Indians, am I prevented from doing *that* by my outside status? Now, we certainly do need to praise other societies in this way. But it is hardly possible that we could praise them effectively if we could not, in principle, criticize them. Our praise would be worthless if it rested on no definite grounds, if it did not flow from some understanding. Certainly we may need to praise things which we do not *fully* understand. We say "there's something very good here, but I can't quite make out what it is yet." This happens when we want to learn from strangers. And we can learn from strangers. But to do this we have to distinguish between those strangers who are worth learning from and those who are not. Can we then judge which is which?

This brings us to our third question: What is involved in judging? Now plainly there is no question here of sitting on a bench in a red robe and sentencing people. Judging simply means forming an opinion, and expressing it if it is called for. Is there anything wrong about this? Naturally, we ought to avoid forming—and expressing—*crude* opinions, like that of a simple-minded missionary, who might dismiss the whole Samurai culture as entirely bad, because non-Christian. But this is a different objection. The trouble with crude opinions is that they are crude, whoever forms them, not that they are formed by the wrong people. Anthropologists, after all, are outsiders quite as much as missionaries. Moral isolationism forbids us to form *any* opinions on these matters. Its ground for doing so is that we don't understand them. But there is much that we don't understand in our own culture too. This brings us to our last question: If we can't judge other cultures, can we really judge our own? Our efforts to do so will be much damaged if we are really deprived of our opinions about other societies, because these provide the range of comparison, the spectrum of alternatives against which we set what we want to understand. We would have to stop using the mirror which anthropology so helpfully holds up to us.

In short, moral isolationism would lay down a general ban on moral reasoning. Essentially, this is the programme of immoralism, and it carries a distressing logical difficulty. Immoralists like Nietzsche are actually just a rather specialized sect of moralists. They can no more afford to put moralizing out of business than smugglers can afford to abolish customs regulations. The power of moral judgement is, in fact, not a luxury, not a perverse indulgence of the self-righteous. It is a necessity. When we judge something to be bad or good, better or worse than something else, we are taking it as an example to aim at or avoid. Without opinions of this sort, we would have no framework of comparison for our own policy, no chance of profiting by other people's insights or mistakes. In this vacuum, we could form no judgements on our own actions.

Now it would be odd if *Homo sapiens* had really got himself into a position as bad as this—a position where his main evolutionary asset, his brain, was so little use to him. None of us is going to accept this sceptical diagnosis. We cannot do so, because our involvement in moral isolationism does not flow from apathy, but from a rather acute concern about human hypocrisy and other forms of wickedness. But we polarize that concern around a few selected moral truths. We are rightly angry with those who despise, oppress or steamroll other cultures. We think that doing these things is actually *wrong*. But this is itself a moral judgement. We could not condemn oppression and insolence if we thought that all our condemnation were just a trivial local quirk of our own culture. We could still less do it if we tried to stop judging altogether.

Real moral scepticism, in fact, could lead only to inaction, to our losing all interest in moral questions, most of all in those which concern other societies. When we discuss these things, it becomes instantly clear how far we are from doing this. Suppose, for instance, that I criticize the bisecting Samurai, that I say his behaviour is brutal. What will usually happen next is that someone will protest, will say that I have no right to make criticisms like that of another culture. But it is most unlikely that he will use this move to end the discussion of the subject. Instead, he will justify the Samurai. He will try to fill in the background, to make me understand the custom, by explaining the exalted ideals of discipline and devotion which produced it. He will probably talk of the lower value which the ancient Japanese placed on individual life generally. He may well suggest that this is a healthier attitude than our own

obsession with security. He may add, too, that the wayfarers did not seriously mind being bisected, that in principle they accepted the whole arrangement.

Now an objector who talks like this is implying that it *is* possible to understand alien customs. That is just what he is trying to make me do. And he implies, too, that if I do succeed in understanding them, I shall do something better than giving up judging them. He expects me to change my present judgement to a truer one—namely, one that is favourable. And the standards I must use to do this cannot just be Samurai standards. They have to be ones current in my own culture. Ideals like discipline and devotion will not move anybody unless he himself accepts them. As it happens, neither discipline nor devotion is very popular in the West at present. Anyone who appeals to them may well have to do some more arguing to make *them* acceptable, before he can use them to explain the Samurai. But if he does succeed here, he will have persuaded us, not just that there was something to be said for them in ancient Japan, but that there would be here as well.

Isolating barriers simply cannot arise here. If we accept something as a serious moral truth about one culture, we can't refuse to apply it—in however different an outward form—to other cultures as well, wherever circumstances admit it. If we refuse to do this, we just are not taking the other culture seriously. This becomes clear if we look at the last argument used by my objector—that of justification by consent of the victim. It is suggested that sudden bisection is quite in order, *provided* that it takes place between consenting adults. I cannot now discuss how conclusive this justification is. What I am pointing out is simply that it can only work if we believe that *consent* can make such a transaction respectable—and this is a thoroughly modern and Western idea. It would probably never occur to a Samurai; if it did, it would surprise him very much. It is *our* standard. In applying it, too, we are likely to make another typically Western demand. We shall ask for good factual evidence that the wayfarers actually do have this rather surprising taste—that they are really willing to be bisected. In applying Western standards in this way, we are not being confused or irrelevant. We are asking the questions which arise *from where we stand,* questions which we can see the sense of. We do this because asking questions which you can't see the sense of is humbug. Certainly we can extend our questioning by imaginative effort. We can come to understand other societies better. By doing so, we may make their questions our own, or we may see that they are really forms of the questions which we are asking already. This is not impossible. It is just very hard work. The obstacles which often prevent it are simply those of ordinary ignorance, laziness and prejudice.

If there were really an isolating barrier, of course, our own culture could never have been formed. It is no sealed box, but a fertile jungle of different influences—Greek, Jewish, Roman, Norse, Celtic and so forth, into which further influences are still pouring—American, Indian, Japanese, Jamaican, you name it. The moral isolationist's picture of separate unmixable cultures is quite unreal. People who talk about British history usually stress the value of this fertilizing mix, no doubt rightly. But this is not just an odd fact about Britain. Except for the very smallest and most remote, all cultures are formed out of many streams. All have the problem of digesting and assimilating things which, at the start, they do not understand. All have the choice of learning something from this challenge, or, alternatively, of refusing to learn, and fighting it mindlessly instead.

This universal predicament has been obscured by the fact that anthropologists used to concentrate largely on very small and remote cultures, which did not seem to have this problem. These tiny societies, which had often forgotten their own history, made neat, self-contained subjects for study. No doubt it was valuable to emphasize their remoteness, their extreme strangeness, their independence of our cultural tradition. This emphasis was, I think, the root of moral isolationism. But, as the tribal studies themselves showed, even there the anthropologists were able to interpret what they saw and make judgements—often favourable—about the tribesmen. And the tribesmen, too, were quite equal to making judgements about the anthropologists—and about the tourists and Coca-Cola salesmen who followed them. Both sets of judgements, no doubt, were somewhat hasty, both have been refined in the light of further experience. A similar transaction between us and the Samurai might take even longer. But that is no reason at all for deeming it impossible. Morally as well as physically, there is only one world, and we all have to live in it.

STUDY QUESTIONS

1. What does Midgley mean by "moral isolationism"?
2. Are those opposed to our judging other cultures equally opposed to other cultures judging ours?
3. Do those who live in a culture necessarily understand it better than those who don't live in that culture?
4. If criticisms of other cultures are always inappropriate, can praise of other cultures ever be appropriate?

Part III

EGOISM

The Republic

Plato

Plato (c. 428–347 B.C.E.), the famed Athenian philosopher, wrote a series of dialogues, most of which featured his teacher Socrates (469–399 B.C.E.). In this excerpt from *The Republic*, Plato's greatest work, Socrates is challenged by Plato's brothers, Glaucon and Adeimantus, to defend the Socratic belief that a life of injustice leads to unhappiness, whereas living justly results in happiness. To motivate this challenge, Glaucon draws a distinction between different kinds of goods: *intrinsic goods,* goods for their own sake, and *instrumental goods,* goods for their consequences. Glaucon asks Socrates to consider cases where none of the usual benefits accompany being moral. Suppose, for example, that those who are just appear to others as if they were unjust, while those who are unjust enjoy a reputation for being just. Under these conditions, why be just? Why not merely appear to be just?

BOOK II

357 Glaucon, with that eminent courage which he displays on all occasions, . . . began thus: Socrates, do you wish really to convince us that it is on every account better to be just than to be unjust, or only to
b seem to have convinced us?

If it were up to me, I replied, I should prefer convincing you really.

Then, he proceeded, you are not doing what you wish. Let me ask you, Is there, in your opinion, a class of good things of such a kind that we are glad to possess them, not because we desire their consequences, but simply welcoming them for their own sake? Take, for example, the feelings of enjoyment and all those pleasures that are harmless, and that

are followed by no consequences, beyond simple enjoyment in their possession.

Yes, I certainly think there is a class of this description.

Well, is there another class, do you think, of those which we value, both for their own sake and c for their results? Such as intelligence, and sight, and health—all of which we surely welcome on both accounts.

Yes.

And do you further recognize a third class of good things, which would include gymnastics training, and submission to medical treatment in illness, as well as the practice of medicine, and all other means of making money? Things like these we should describe as irksome, and yet beneficial to us;

From *The Republic,* translated by John Llewelyn Davies and David James Vaughan, revised by Andrea Tschemplik, Rowman & Littlefield Publishers, 2005. Used by permission of the publisher. The notes are provided by Andrea Tschemplik.

and while we should reject them viewed simply in themselves, we accept them for the sake of the rewards, and of the other consequences which result

d from them.

Yes, undoubtedly there is such a third class also; but what then?

In which of these classes do you place justice?

358 I should say in the highest—that is, among the good things which will be valued by one who is in the pursuit of true happiness, alike for their own sake and for their consequences.

Then your opinion is not that of the many, by whom justice is ranked in the irksome class, as a thing which in itself, and for its own sake, is disagreeable and repulsive, but which it is well to practice for the advantages to be had from it, with an eye to rewards and to a good name.

I know it is so . . .

b Listen to my proposal then, and tell me whether you agree to it. . . . I am not satisfied as yet with the exposition that has been given of justice and injustice; for

c I long to be told what they respectively are, and what force they exert, taken simply by themselves, when residing in the soul, dismissing the consideration of their rewards and other consequences. This shall be my plan then, if you do not object. I will . . . first state the common view respecting what kind of thing justice is and how it came to be; in the second place, I will maintain that all who practice it do so against their will, because it is indispensable, not because it is a good thing; and thirdly, that they act reasonably in so doing, because the life of the unjust man is, as men say, far better than that of the just. Not that I think so myself, Socrates;

d only my ears are ringing so with what I hear . . . that I am puzzled. Now I have never heard the argument for the superiority of justice over injustice maintained to my satisfaction; for I should like to hear it praised, considered simply in itself; and from you if from anyone, I should expect such a treatment of the subject. Therefore I will speak as forcibly as I can in praise of an unjust life, and I shall thus display the manner in which I wish to hear you afterwards blame injustice and praise justice. See whether you approve of my plan.

Indeed I do, for on what other subject could a sensible man like better to talk and to hear others talk, again and again?

Most beautifully spoken! So now listen to me e while I speak on my first theme, what kind of thing justice is and how it came to be.

To commit injustice is, they say, in its nature, a good thing, and to suffer it a bad thing; but the bad of suffering injustice exceeds the good of doing injustice; and so, after the two-fold experience of both 359 doing and suffering injustice, those who cannot avoid the latter and choose the former find it expedient to make a contract of neither doing nor suffering injustice. Hence arose legislation and contracts between man and man, and hence it became the custom to call that which the law enjoined just, as well as lawful. Such, they tell us, is justice, and so it came into being; and it stands midway between that which is best, to commit injustice with impunity, and that which is worst, to suffer injustice without any power of retaliating. And being a mean between these two extremes, the just is cared for, not as good in itself, but is honored because of the inability to commit in- b justice; for they say that one who had it in his power to be unjust, and who deserved the name of a man, would never be so weak as to contract with anyone neither to commit injustice nor to suffer it. Such is the current account, Socrates, of the nature of justice, and of the circumstances in which it originated.

Even those men who practice justice do so unwillingly, because they lack the power to violate it, will be most readily perceived, if we use the following reasoning. Let us give full liberty to the just man and to the unjust alike, to do whatever they please, c and then let us follow them, and see whither the inclination of each will lead him. In that case we shall surprise the just man in the act of traveling in the same direction as the unjust, owing to that desire to gain more, the gratification of which every creature naturally pursues as a good, only that it is forced out of its path by law, and constrained to respect the principle of equality. That full liberty of action would, perhaps, be most effectively realized if they were invested with a power which they say was in old times possessed by the ancestor of Gyges the Lydian. He was a shepherd, so the story runs, in the d service of the reigning sovereign of Lydia, when one day a violent storm of rain fell, the ground was rent asunder by an earthquake, and a yawning gulf appeared on the spot where he was feeding his flocks. Seeing what had happened, and wondering at it, he went down into the gulf, and among other marvelous objects he saw, as the legend relates, a hollow bronze horse, with windows in its sides, through which he looked, and beheld in the interior a corpse, apparently of superhuman size; from which he took the only thing remaining, a golden ring on the hand,

e and therewith made his way out. Now when the usual meeting of the shepherds occurred, for the purpose of sending to the king their monthly report of the state of his flocks, this shepherd came with the rest, wearing the ring. And, as he was seated with the company, he happened to turn the hoop of the

360 ring round towards himself, until it came to the inside of his hand. Whereupon he became invisible to his neighbors, who were talking about him as if he were gone away. While he was marveling at this, he again began playing with the ring, and turned the hoop to the outside, upon which he became once more visible. Having noticed this effect, he made experiments with the ring, to see whether it possessed this power. And so it was, that when he turned the hoop inwards he became invisible, and when he turned it outwards he was again visible. After this discovery, he immediately contrived to be appointed one of the messengers to carry the report to the king; and upon his arrival he seduced the queen, and conspiring

b with her, slew the king, and took possession of the throne.

If then there were two such rings in existence, and if the just and the unjust man were each to put on one, it is to be thought that no one would be so steeled against temptation as to abide in the practice of justice, and resolutely to abstain from touching the property of his neighbors, when he had it in his power to help himself without fear to anything he pleased in the market, or to go into private houses

c and have intercourse with whom he would, or to kill and release from prison according to his own pleasure, and in everything else to act among men with the power of a god. And in thus following out his desires the just man will be doing precisely what the unjust man would do; and so they would both be pursuing the same path. Surely this will be allowed to be strong evidence that none are just willingly, but

only by compulsion, because to be just is not a good to the individual; for all violate justice whenever they imagine that there is nothing to hinder them. And they do so because everyone thinks that, in the individual case, injustice is much more profitable than justice; and they are right in so thinking, as d the speaker of this speech will maintain. For if anyone having this license within his grasp were to refuse to do any injustice, or to touch the property of others, all who were aware of it would think him a most pitiful and irrational creature, though they would praise him before each other's faces, deceiving one another, through their fear of suffering injustice. And so much for this topic.

But in actually deciding between the lives of e the two persons in question, we shall be enabled to arrive at a correct conclusion, by contrasting together the thoroughly just and the thoroughly unjust man, and only by so doing. Well then, how are we to contrast them? In this way. Let us take nothing away from the injustice of the unjust or from the justice of the just, but let us suppose each to be perfect in his own line of conduct. First of all then, the unjust man must act as clever craftsmen do. For a first-rate pilot or physician perceives the difference between what is possible and what is impossible in his art; and while he attempts the former, he leaves the latter 361 alone; and moreover, should he happen to make a false step, he is able to recover himself. In the same way, if we are to form a conception of a consummately unjust man, we must suppose that he makes no mistake in the prosecution of his unjust enterprises, and that he escapes detection. But if he be found out, we must look upon him as a bungler, for it is the perfection of injustice to seem just without really being so. We must therefore grant to the perfectly unjust man, without taking anything away, the most perfect injustice; and we must concede to him, that while committing the grossest acts of injustice b he has won himself the highest reputation for justice; and that should he make a false step, he is able to recover himself, partly by a talent for speaking with effect in case he be called in question for any of his misdeeds, and partly because his courage and strength, and his command of friends and money, enable him to employ force with success, whenever

force is required. Such being our unjust man, let us, in speech, place the just man by his side, a man of true simplicity and nobleness, resolved, as Aeschylus says, not to seem, but to be, good. We must certainly take away the seeming, for if he be thought to be a just man, he will have honors and
c gifts on the strength of this reputation, so that it will be uncertain whether it is for justice's sake, or for the sake of the gifts and honors, that he is what he is. Yes, we must strip him bare of everything but justice, and make his whole case the reverse of the former. Without being guilty of one unjust act, let him have the worst reputation for injustice, so that his justice may be thoroughly tested, and shown to be proof against infamy and all its consequences; and let him go on until the day of his death, steadfast in his justice, but with a lifelong reputation for injus-
d tice, in order that, having brought both the men to the utmost limits of justice and of injustice respectively, we may then give judgment as to which of the two is the happier.

Good heavens! my dear Glaucon, said I, how vigorously you work, scouring the two characters clean for our judgment, like a pair of statues.

I do it as well as I can, he said. And after describing the men as we have done, there will be no further difficulty, I imagine, in proceeding to sketch
e the kind of life which awaits them respectively. Let me therefore describe it. And if the description be somewhat coarse, do not regard it as mine, Socrates, but as coming from those who commend injus-
362 tice above justice. They will say that in such a situation the just man will be scourged, racked, fettered, will have his eyes burnt out, and at last, after suffering every kind of torture, will be crucified; and thus learn that it is best to resolve, not to be, but to seem, just. Indeed those words of Aeschylus are far more applicable to the unjust man than to the just. For it is in fact the unjust man, they will maintain, inasmuch as he devotes himself to a course which is allied to reality, and does not live with an eye to appearances, who "is resolved not to seem, but to be," unjust,

Reaping a harvest of wise purposes,
b Sown in the fruitful furrows of his mind.[1]

First of all he rules in the city through his reputation for justice, and in the next place he chooses a wife wherever he will, and marries his children into whatever family he pleases. He enters into contracts and joins in partnership with anyone he likes, and besides all this, he enriches himself by large profits, because he is not too nice to commit a fraud. Therefore, whenever he engages in a contest, whether public or private, he defeats and over-reaches his enemies, and by so doing grows rich, and is enabled to benefit his friends and injure his enemies, and to offer sacrifices and dedicate gifts to the gods in magnificent abundance. And thus having greatly the advantage over the just man to do service to the gods, c as well as to such men as he chooses, he is also more likely than the just man to be dearer to the gods. And therefore they affirm, Socrates, that a better provision is made both by gods and men for the life of the unjust, than for the life of the just.

When Glaucon had said this, before I could make the reply I had in mind, his brother Adeimantus ex- d claimed, You surely do not suppose, Socrates, that the argument has been satisfactorily expounded.

Why not? said I.

The very point which was most needed has been omitted.

Well then, according to the proverb, "May a brother be present to help one," it is for you to supply his deficiencies, if there are any, by your assistance. But indeed, for my part, what Glaucon has said is enough to bring me to my knees, and puts it beyond my power to come to the rescue of justice.

You are not in earnest, he said. Listen to the following argument also; for we must now go e through those representations which, reversing the declarations of Glaucon, commend justice and disparage injustice, in order to bring out more clearly what I take to be his meaning. Now, surely, fathers tell their sons, as do all those who have someone in their care, that one must be just. But when they impress this upon their children, they do not praise justice in itself, but only the respectability which it 363 gives—their object being that a reputation for justice may be gained, and that this reputation may bring the offices, marriages, and the other good things which, as Glaucon has just told us, are secured to the just man by his high character. And these persons carry the advantages of a good name still further; for, by introducing the good opinion of the gods, they are enabled to describe innumerable blessings which the gods, they say, grant to the pious, as the excellent Hesiod tells us, and Homer too—the former saying, that the gods cause the oak-trees of the just

b
> On their tops to bear acorns, and swarms of
> bees in the middle; Also their wool-laden sheep
> sink under the weight of their fleeces.[2]

with many other good things of the same sort; while the latter, in a similar passage, speaks of one,

c
> Like to a blameless king, who, godlike in virtue
> and wisdom, Justice ever maintains; whose rich
> land fruitfully yields him Harvests of barley
> and wheat, and his orchards are heavy with
> fruit; Strong are the young of his flocks; and the
> sea gives him fish in abundance.[3]

But the blessings which Musaeus[4] and his son represent the gods as bestowing upon the just, are still more delectable than these; for they bring them
d to the abode of Hades, and describe them as reclining on couches at a banquet of the pious, and with garlands on their heads spending all time in wine-bibbing, the fairest reward of virtue being, in their estimation, an ever-lasting drunken party. Others, again, do not stop even here in their enumeration of the rewards bestowed by the gods; for they tell us that the man who is pious and true to his oath leaves children's children and a posterity to follow him. Such, among others, are the commendations which they lavish upon justice. The ungodly, on the other hand, and the unjust, they plunge into a swamp in Hades, and condemn them
e to carry water in a sieve; and while they are still alive, they bring them into ill repute, and inflict upon the unjust precisely those punishments, which Glaucon enumerated as the lot of the just who are reputed to be unjust; more they cannot say. Such is their method of praising the one character and condemning the other.

Once more, Socrates, take into consideration another and a different mode of speaking with regard to justice and injustice, which we meet with both in common life and in the poets. All as with one mouth   364 proclaim, that to be moderate and just is an admirable thing certainly, but at the same time a hard and an irksome one; while moderation and injustice are pleasant things and of easy acquisition, and only rendered shameful by law and public opinion. But they say that justice is in general less profitable than injustice, and they do not hesitate to call wicked men happy, and to honor them both in public and in private, when they are rich or possess other sources of power, and on the other hand to treat with dishonor   b and disdain those who are in any way feeble or poor, even while they admit that the latter are better men than the former. But of all their statements the most wonderful are those which relate to the gods and to virtue; according to which even the gods allot to many good men a calamitous and bad life, and to men of the opposite character an opposite portion. And there are quacks and soothsayers who flock to the rich man's doors, and try to persuade him that they have a power procured from the gods, which enables them, by sacrifices and incantations performed amid feasting and indulgence, to make amends for   c any crime committed either by the individual himself or by his ancestors; and that, should he desire to do a mischief to anyone, it may be done at a trifling expense, whether the object of his hostility be a just or an unjust man. They profess that by certain invocations and spells they can prevail upon the gods to do their bidding. And in support of all these assertions they produce the evidence of poets—some, to exhibit the facilities of vice, quoting the words

> Whoever seeks wickedness, may even in abun-   d
> dance obtain it Easily. Smooth is the way, and
> short, for near is her dwelling. Virtue, Heav'n
> has ordained, shall be reached by the sweat of
> the forehead,
>   and by a long and up-hill road,[5]

while others, to prove that the gods may be turned from their purpose by men, adduce the testimony of Homer, who has said:

e   Yea, even the gods do yield to entreaty; Therefore to them men offer both victims and meek
supplications, Incense and melting fat, and turn
them from anger to mercy; Sending up sorrowful
prayers, when trespass and error is committed[6]

And they produce a host of books written by
Musaeus and Orpheus, children, as they say, of
Selene and of the Muses, which form their ritual, per-
suading not individuals merely, but whole cities also,

365 that men may be absolved and purified from crimes,
both while they are still alive and even after their
death, by means of certain sacrifices and pleasurable
amusements which they call initiations—which deliver us from the torments of the other world, while
the neglect of them is punished by an awful doom.

    When views like these, he continued, my dear
Socrates, are proclaimed and repeated with so much
variety, concerning the honors in which virtue and
vice are respectively held by gods and men, what can
we suppose is the effect produced on the minds of all
those good-natured young men, who are able, after
skimming like birds, as it were, over all that they
hear, to draw conclusions from it as to what sort of
man one must be, and the path in which he must

b walk, in order to live the best possible life? In all
probability a young man would say to himself in the
words of Pindar, "Shall I by justice or by crooked
wiles climb to a loftier stronghold, and, having thus
fenced myself in, live my life?" For common opinion
declares that to be just without being also thought
just, is no advantage to me, but only entails manifest
trouble and loss; whereas if I am unjust and get
myself a name for justice, an unspeakably marvelous
life is promised me. Very well then, since the appear-

c ance, as the wise inform me, overpowers the truth,
and is the sovereign dispenser of happiness, to this I
must of course wholly devote myself; I must draw
round about me a picture of virtue to serve as an ex-
terior front, but behind me I must keep the fox with
its cunning and shiftiness—of which that most clever
Archilochus tells us.[7] Yes but, it will be objected, it is
not an easy matter always to conceal one's wicked-

d ness. No, we shall reply, nor yet is anything else easy
that is great; nevertheless, if happiness is to be our
goal, this must be our path, as the steps of the

argument indicate. To assist in keeping up the deception, we will form secret societies and clubs. There
are, moreover, teachers of persuasion, who impart
skill in popular and court oratory; and so by persuasion or by force, we shall gain our ends, and carry on
our dishonest proceedings with impunity. But, it is
urged, neither evasion nor violence can succeed with
the gods. Well, but if they either do not exist, or do
not concern themselves with the affairs of men, why
need *we* concern ourselves to evade their observation? But if they do exist, and do pay attention to us, e
we know nothing and have heard nothing of them
from any other quarter than the current traditions
and the genealogies of poets; and these very authori-
ties state that the gods are beings who may be persuaded and diverted from their purpose by sacrifices
and meek supplications and votive offerings. Therefore we must believe them in both statements or in
neither. If we are to believe them, we will act unjustly, and offer sacrifices from the proceeds of our 366
crimes. For if we are just, we shall, it is true, escape
punishment at the hands of the gods, but we renounce
the profits which accrue from injustice; but if we are
unjust, we shall not only make these gains, but also
by putting up prayers when we overstep and make
mistakes, we shall prevail upon the gods to let us go
unscathed. But then, it is again objected, in Hades we
shall pay the just penalty for the crimes committed
here, either in our own persons or in those of our
children's children. But my friend, the champion of
the argument will continue, the mystic rites, again, b
are very powerful, and the absolving gods, as we are
told by the mightiest cities, and by the sons of the
gods who have appeared as poets and inspired prophets, who inform us that these things are so.

    What consideration, therefore, remains which
should induce us to prefer justice to the greatest injustice? Since if we combine injustice with a spurious decorum, we shall fare to our liking with the
gods and with men, in this life and the next, according to the most numerous and the highest authori-
ties. Considering all that has been said, by what c
device, Socrates, can a man who has any advantages, either of high talent, or wealth, or personal
appearance, or birth, bring himself to honor justice,
instead of smiling when he hears it praised? Indeed,

if there is anyone who is able to show the falsity of what we have said, and who is fully convinced that justice is best, far from being angry with the unjust, he doubtless makes great allowance for them, knowing that, with the exception of those who may possibly refrain from injustice through the disgust of a godlike nature or from the acquisition of knowledge, there is certainly no one else who is willingly just; but it is from cowardice, or age, or some other infirmity, that men condemn injustice, simply because they lack the power to commit it. And the truth of this is proved by the fact, that the first of these people who comes to power is the first to commit injustice, to the extent of his ability. And the cause of all this is simply that fact, which my brother and I both stated at the very beginning of this whole argument, Socrates, saying: With all due respect, to you who profess to be admirers of justice—beginning with the heroes of old, of whom accounts have descended to the present generation—have every one of you, without exception, made the praise of justice and condemnation of injustice turn solely upon the reputation and honor and gifts resulting from them; but what each is in itself, by its own peculiar force as it resides in the soul of its possessor, unseen either by gods or men, has never, in poetry or in prose, been adequately discussed, so as to show that injustice is the greatest curse that a soul can receive into itself, and justice the greatest blessing. Had this been the language used by all of you from the start, and had you tried to persuade us of this from our childhood, we should not be on the watch to check one another in the commission of injustice, because everyone would be his own watchman, fearful lest by committing injustice he might attach to himself the greatest of evils.

All this, Socrates, and perhaps still more than this, would be put forward respecting justice and injustice, . . . thus vulgarly, in my opinion, turning around the power of each. For my own part, I confess— for I do not want to hide anything from you—that I have a great desire to hear you defend the opposite view, and therefore I have exerted myself to speak as forcefully as I can. So do not limit your argument to the proposition that justice is stronger than injustice, but show us what is that influence exerted by each of them on its possessor, whereby the one is in itself a blessing, and the other a curse; and take away the estimation in which the two are held, as Glaucon urged you to do. For if you omit to withdraw from each quality its true reputation and to add the false, we shall declare that you are praising, not the reality, but the appearance of justice, and blaming, not the reality, but the semblance of injustice; that your advice, in fact, is to be unjust without being found out, and that you hold . . . that justice is another man's good, being for the advantage of the stronger; injustice a man's own interest and advantage, but against the interest of the weaker. Since then you have allowed that justice is one of the greatest goods, the possession of which is valuable, both for the sake of their results, and also in a higher degree for their own sake, such as sight, hearing, understanding, health, and everything else which is genuinely good in its own nature and not merely reputed to be good. Select for commendation this particular feature of justice, I mean the benefit which in itself it confers on its possessor, in contrast with the harm which injustice inflicts. The rewards and reputations leave to others to praise; because in others I can tolerate this mode of praising justice and condemning injustice, which consists in eulogizing or reviling the reputations and the rewards which are connected with them; but in you I cannot, unless you require it, because you have spent your whole life in investigating such questions, and such only. Therefore do not content yourself with proving to us that justice is better than injustice; but show us what is that influence exerted by each on its possessor, by which, whether gods and men see it or not, the one is in itself a good, and the other a detriment.

NOTES

1. Aeschylus, *Seven Against Thebes* 1.592–94.
2. Hesiod, *Works and Days* 232–33.
3. Homer, *Odyssey* 19.109.
4. Musaeus was a singer and poet of myth and legend.
5. Hesiod, *Works and Days* 287–89.
6. Homer, *Iliad* 9.497–501.
7. Archilochus (675?–635? B.C.E.) was a poet from Paros.

STUDY QUESTIONS

1. Might the same goods be intrinsic in one situation and instrumental in another?
2. What points are illustrated by the story of the Ring of Gyges?
3. Can someone appear to be just while being unjust?
4. Can you offer a scenario in which being unjust has better consequences for you than being just?

In Defense of Egoism

Jesse Kalin

Morality is usually thought to be an essentially social enterprise. Ethical egoism, however, holds that the right act is the act that best promotes the agent's overall self-interest. Accordingly, the egoist is, at base, anti-social. Ethical egoism is thus often charged with failing to qualify as a moral theory at all. Jesse Kalin, Professor Emeritus of Philosophy and Film at Vassar College, responds to this charge. He argues that we can reject the claim that morality is essentially social. To qualify as moral, Kalin maintains, a theory needs to answer the question: what ought I to do? Because ethical egoism provides a coherent answer to this question, the theory should be taken seriously as a viable contender.

I

Ethical egoism is the view that it is morally right—that is, morally permissible, indeed, morally obligatory—for a person to act in his own self-interest, even when his self-interest conflicts or is irreconcilable with the self-interest of another. The point people normally have in mind in accepting and advocating this ethical principle is that of justifying or excusing their own self-interested actions by giving them a moral sanction.

This position is sometimes construed as saying that selfishness is moral, but such an interpretation is not quite correct. "Self-interest" is a general term usually used as a synonym for "personal happiness" and "personal welfare," and what would pass as selfish behavior frequently would not pass as self-interested behavior in this sense. Indeed, we have the suspicion that selfish people are characteristically, if not always, unhappy. Thus, in cases where selfishness tends to a person's unhappiness it is not in his self-interest, and as an egoist he ought not to be selfish. As a consequence, ethical egoism does not preclude other-interested, nonselfish, or altruistic behavior, as long as such behavior also leads to the individual's own welfare.

That the egoist may reasonably find himself taking an interest in others and promoting their welfare perhaps sounds nonegoistic, but it is not. Ethical egoism's justification of such behavior differs from other accounts in the following way: The ethical egoist acknowledges no general obligation to help people in need. Benevolence is never justified unconditionally or "categorically." The egoist has an obligation to promote the welfare only of those whom he likes, loves, needs, or can use. The source of this obligation is his interest in them. No interest, no obligation. And when his interest conflicts or is irreconcilable with theirs, he will reasonably pursue his own well-being at their expense, even when this other person is his wife, child, mother, or friend, as well as when it is a stranger or enemy.

From Jesse Kalin, "In Defense of Egoism," in *Morality and Rational Self-Interest*, ed. D. P. Gauthier, Prentice-Hall, 1970. Reprinted by permission of the publisher.

Such a pursuit of one's own self-interest is considered *enlightened*. . . . On this view, a person is to harmonize his natural interests, perhaps cultivate some new interests, and optimize their satisfaction. Usually among these interests will be such things as friendships and families. . . . And, of course, it is a part of such enlightenment to consider the "long run" rather than just the present and immediate future. . . .

Taking the long run fully into account, the egoist must hold his position silently if he is to remain prudent. This restriction is more serious than might be suspected, for it means the egoist must refrain not only from advocating his doctrine, but also from a wide range of behavior typical of any morality. For instance, he will not be able to enter into moral discussions, at least not sincerely or as an egoist. . . . This will not be to his interest for at least the reason that others will become suspicious of him and cease to trust him. They will learn he is an egoist and treat him accordingly. It would be even worse if he should win the debate and convince them.

Nor will he be able to give or receive moral advice. If it is objected that he can advise others as long as interests do not conflict, it will do to note that it is not to his interest to have his egoistic views known. Giving of advice involves giving reasons for certain actions; inquiries about the moral principle upon which that advice is based are therefore appropriate. Of course, the egoist can lie. When Harry comes to Tom about his affair with Dick's wife, Tom can approve, professing enlightened views about marriage, noting that there are no children, that both are adults, and so forth, although he knows Harry's behavior will soon lead to a scandal ruining Harry's career—all to Tom's advantage. Tom has advised Harry, but not sincerely; he has not told Harry *what he thinks Harry really ought to do*—what would be most in Harry's overall self-interest. And Tom ought not. . . . This all goes to make the point; the egoist is not sincerely advising Harry, but rather pretending to sincerely advise him while really deceiving and manipulating him.

This use of advice—to manipulate others—is limited, and perhaps bought at a price too great for the egoist to pay. Since advising is a public activity, urging others to be benevolent (in order to benefit

from their actions) gives them grounds to require one to be benevolent toward them, and thus to create sanctions restricting the scope of his self-interested behavior.

Worst of all, it will do the egoist himself no good to *ask* for moral advice for he is bound not to get what he wants. If he asks nonegoists, he will be told to do things which might be in his self-interest, but usually won't be. What sort of help could he get from a Kantian or a utilitarian? Their advice will follow from the wrong moral principle. If he asks another egoist, he is no better off, since he cannot be trusted. Knowing that he is an egoist, he knows that he is . . . acting in his own self-interest, and lying if he can benefit from it. The egoist is truly isolated from any moral community, and must always decide and act alone, without the help of others.

It will not be to the egoist's self-interest to support his moral principle with sanctions. He will be unable to praise those who do what they ought, unable to blame those who flagrantly shirk their moral tasks. Nor will he be able to establish institutions of rewards and punishments founded on his principle. The egoist cannot sincerely engage in any of these activities. He will punish or blame people for doing what they ought not to do (for doing what is not in their self-interests) only by coincidence. . . . To punish people for not being egoists is to encourage them to be egoists, and this is not to his interest. Similarly, the egoist, if he engages in such an activity at all, will praise people for doing what they ought to do only by chance, and always under a different, nonegoistic label.

A corollary to this is the egoist's inability to teach . . . his children. . . . It is imprudent to raise egoistic children, since among other things, the probability of being abandoned in old age is greatly increased. Therefore, the egoist can give his children no sincere moral instruction, and most likely will be advised to teach them to disapprove of his actions and his character, should they become aware of their true nature.

Finally, one of the points of appealing to a moral principle is to justify one's behavior *to others*—to convince them that their (sometimes forcible) opposition to this behavior is unwarranted and ought to be withdrawn. When we do convince someone of the rightness of our actions, he normally comes onto our side, even if reluctantly. Thus, the teenage daughter tries to convince her father that it is right and proper for sixteen year old girls to stay out until 12:30 (rather than 11:00) because if she is successful and he agrees with her, he then has *no excuse* (other things being equal) for still withholding his permission. For an ethical egoist, this point is doomed to frustration for two reasons: first, because justifying one's behavior . . . gives an opponent no reason to cease his opposition if maintaining it would be in his own interest; and second, because it will not be to the egoist's interest to publicly justify his behavior to others on egoistic grounds, thereby running the risk of converting them to egoism. Therefore, the egoist is unable to engage in *interpersonal reasoning* with his moral principle as its basis—he can neither justify nor excuse his egoistic actions as such in the interpersonal sense of "justify" and "excuse."

Adherence to the egoistic principle makes it impossible, because imprudent, for one to sincerely engage in any of these moral activities. There are also typical moral attitudes and emotions which, while perhaps not impossible for an egoist to sincerely have, it is impossible for him to sincerely express. I have in mind remorse, regret, resentment, repentance, forgiveness, revenge, outrage and indignation, and the form of sympathy known as moral support. Let us take forgiveness. When can the egoist forgive another, and for what? One forgives the other's wrongs, wrongs which are normally done against oneself. First, it is hard to see how someone could wrong someone else given ethical egoism, for [it] . . . gives one no obligations to others, and hence no way of shirking those obligations. At least, one has no such obligations directly. Second, what is the nature of the wrong action which is to be forgiven? It must be a failure to properly pursue self-interest. Suppose Harry makes this lapse. Can Tom forgive him? In so far as such forgiveness involves nonexpressed beliefs and attitudes, yes. But Tom would be unwise to express this attitude or to forgive Harry in the fuller, public sense. Partly because if their interests conflict, Tom's good will involve Harry's harm; Tom does not want Harry to do what he ought, and Tom

ought not to encourage him to do so, which would be involved in overtly forgiving him. And partly because of the general imprudence of making it known that one is an egoist, which would be involved in expressing forgiveness of nonegoistic behavior. If the egoist is to forgive people where this involves the expression of forgiveness, his doing so must be basically insincere.

Similar considerations hold for the expression of the other emotions and attitudes mentioned. As for those which are not so clearly dependent upon some manner of public expression, such as resentment and remorse, it is perhaps not impossible for the egoist to have them (or to be capable of having them), but it is clear that their objects and occasion will be quite different from what they are in the standard morality. Resentment as a moral attitude involves taking offense at someone's failure to do what they ought. But why should the egoist be offended if other people don't look after their interests, at least when their interests are not connected with his own? And when their interests are connected, the offense does not arise from the fact that the other did something wrong—failed to properly pursue his own interests—but because of the further and undesirable consequences of this failure, but consequences for which that person was not liable. Resentment here is very strange, all the more so because of the formal rather than material commitment of the egoist to the obligation to pursue one's own self-interest. Since he doesn't value others' doing what they ought, any resentment he feels must be slight and rather abstract, amounting to little more than the belief that they ought not to behave that way.

Granting that it would not be in his overall self-interest for others to be egoists too, the ethical egoist has compelling reasons not to engage sincerely in any of the activities mentioned above, as well as not to give expression to various typical moral attitudes and emotions. This is strange not because the egoist is in some sense required to promulgate his doctrine while at the same time faithfully follow it, for we saw above that he can coherently reject this demand, but strange because his position seems to have lost most of the features characterizing a morality. When put into practice, ethical egoism discards the moral activities of advocacy, moral discussion, giving and asking of advice, using sanctions to reward and punish, praising and blaming, moral instruction and training, and interpersonal excusing and justification, as well as the expressing of many moral attitudes and emotions. With these features gone, what remains that constitutes a morality? The egoist may, indeed, have a coherent practical system, but since it lacks certain major structural features of a morality, it is not a *moral theory.* Consider a legal theory which, when put into practice, turns out to have neither trials, nor judges, nor juries, nor sentencing, nor penal institutions, nor legislating bodies. Could it still be a legal theory and lack all of these? Isn't the case similar with ethical egoism? . . .

I personally think that it makes sense to speak of egoism as a morality, since I think it makes sense to speak of a "private morality" and of its being superior to "public moralities." The egoist's basic question is "What ought I to do; what is most reasonable for me to do?" This question seems to me a moral question through and through, and any coherent answer to it thereby deserves to be regarded as a moral theory. What is central here is the rational justification of a certain course of behavior. Such behavior will be justified in the sense that its reasonableness follows from a coherent and plausible set of premises. This kind of justification and moral reasoning can be carried out on the desert island and is not necessarily interpersonal—it does not have as one of its goals the minimal cooperation of some second party. Whether one *calls* the result a "morality" or not is of no matter, for its opponents must show it to be a poor competitor to the other alternatives. . . .

If one insists that egoism is without the pall of morality, the obvious question one must face is: "Why be moral?" It is not at all easy to convincingly show that the egoist should (that it would be most reasonable for him to) abandon his position for one which could require him to sacrifice his self-interest, even to the point of death. What must be shown is not simply that it is to the egoist's interests to *be in* a society structured by various social, moral, and legal institutions, all of which limit categorically certain expressions of self-interest (as do the penalty rules in football), . . . but that the egoist also has compelling reasons (always) to abide by its rules. . . .

The egoist can acknowledge that it is in his long range self-interest to be in a moral system and thus that there should be categorical public rules restricting his egoistic behavior. Publicly, these rules will be superior to self-interest, and will be enforced as such. But according to his private morality, they will not be superior. Rather, they will be interpreted as hypotheticals setting prices (sometimes very dear) upon certain forms of conduct. Thus, the egoist will believe that, while it is always reasonable to be in a moral system, it is not always reasonable to act morally while within that system (just as it is not always reasonable to obey the rules of football). The opponent of egoism, in order to soundly discredit it, must show that moral behavior is always reasonable. . . . I do not see how such attempts could be successful.

STUDY QUESTIONS

1. What is a selfish action?
2. Do morality and self-interest ever conflict?
3. If you were the sole person on a desert island, could you have moral obligations?
4. Is moral behavior always reasonable?

Egoism and Moral Scepticism

James Rachels

Whereas ethical egoism asserts that we ought never act against our own interest, psychological egoism affirms that we always act in this way. James Rachels (1941–2003), who was Professor of Philosophy at the University of Alabama in Birmingham, finds both doctrines untenable. He argues, contrary to the claim made by psychological egoists, that selfishness should not be conflated with self-interest, and that feeling good after doing an action should not be confused with doing the action because it feels good. Against ethical egoism, Rachels maintains that concern for one's own welfare is compatible with concern for the welfare of others. He agrees that ethical egoism is a coherent position but concludes that it should not be accepted because it yields intuitively implausible moral verdicts.

1. Our ordinary thinking about morality is full of assumptions that we almost never question. We assume, for example, that we have an obligation to consider the welfare of other people when we decide what actions to perform or what rules to obey; we think that we must refrain from acting in ways harmful to others, and that we must respect their rights and interests as well as our own. We also assume that people are in fact capable of being motivated by such considerations, that is, that people are not wholly selfish and that they do sometimes act in the interests of others.

Both of these assumptions have come under attack by moral sceptics, as long ago as by Glaucon in Book II of Plato's *Republic*. Glaucon recalls the legend of Gyges, a shepherd who was said to have found a magic ring in a fissure opened by an earthquake. The ring would make its wearer invisible and thus would enable him to go anywhere and do anything undetected. Gyges used the power of the ring to gain entry to the Royal Palace, where he seduced the Queen, murdered the King, and subsequently seized the throne. Now Glaucon asks us to imagine that there are two such rings, one given to a man of virtue and one given to a rogue. The rogue, of course, will use his ring unscrupulously and do anything necessary to increase his own wealth and power. He will recognize no moral constraints on his conduct, and, since the cloak of invisibility will protect him from discovery, he can do anything he pleases without fear of reprisal. So, there will be no end to the mischief he will do. But how will the so-called virtuous man behave? Glaucon suggests that he will behave no better than the rogue: "No one, it is commonly believed, would have such iron strength of mind as to stand fast in doing right or keep his hands off other men's goods, when he could go to the market-place and fearlessly help himself to anything he wanted, enter houses and sleep with any woman he chose, set prisoners free and kill men at his pleasure, and in a word go about among men with the powers of a god. He would behave no better than the other; both would take the same course."[1] Moreover, why shouldn't he? Once he is freed from the fear of reprisal, why shouldn't a man simply do what he pleases, or what he thinks is best for himself? What reason is there for him to continue being "moral" when it is clearly not to his own advantage to do so?

These sceptical views suggested by Glaucon have come to be known as *psychological egoism* and *ethical egoism,* respectively. Psychological egoism is the view that all men are selfish in everything that they do, that is, that the only motive from which anyone ever acts is self-interest. On this view, even when men are acting in ways apparently calculated to benefit others, they are actually motivated by the belief that acting in this way is to their own advantage, and if they did not believe this, they would not be doing that action. Ethical egoism is, by contrast, a normative view about how men *ought* to act. It is the view that, regardless of how men do in fact behave, they have no obligation to do anything except what is in their own interests. According to ethical egoists, a person is always justified in doing whatever is in his own interests, regardless of the effect on others.

Clearly, if either of these views is correct, then "the moral institution of life" (to use Butler's well-turned phrase) is very different than what we normally think. The majority of mankind is grossly deceived about what is, or ought to be, the case, where morals are concerned.

2. Psychological egoism seems to fly in the face of the facts. We are tempted to say, "Of course people act unselfishly all the time. For example, Smith gives up a trip to the country, which he would have enjoyed very much, in order to stay behind and help a friend with his studies, which is a miserable way to pass the time. This is a perfectly clear case of unselfish behavior, and if the psychological egoist thinks that such cases do not occur, then he is just mistaken." Given such obvious instances of "unselfish behavior," what reply can the egoist make? There are two general arguments by which he might try to

show that all actions, including those such as the one just outlined, are in fact motivated by self-interest. Let us examine these in turn:

a. The first argument goes as follows: If we describe one person's action as selfish, and another person's action as unselfish, we are overlooking the crucial fact that in both cases, assuming that the action is done voluntarily, *the agent is merely doing what he most wants to do.* If Smith stays behind to help his friend, that only shows that he wanted to help his friend more than he wanted to go to the country. And why should he be praised for his "unselfishness" when he is only doing what he most wants to do? So, since Smith is only doing what he wants to do, he cannot be said to be acting unselfishly.

This argument is so bad that it would not deserve to be taken seriously except for the fact that so many otherwise intelligent people have been taken in by it. First, the argument rests on the premise that people never voluntarily do anything except what they want to do. But this is patently false; there are at least two classes of actions that are exceptions to this generalization. One is the set of actions which we may not want to do, but which we do anyway as a means to an end which we want to achieve, for example, going to the dentist in order to stop a toothache, or going to work every day in order to be able to draw our pay at the end of the month. These cases may be regarded as consistent with the spirit of the egoist argument, however, since the ends mentioned are wanted by the agent. But the other set of actions are those which we do, not because we want to, nor even because there is an end which we want to achieve, but because we feel ourselves *under an obligation* to do them. For example, someone may do something because he has promised to do it, and thus feels obligated, even though he does not want to do it. It is sometimes suggested that in such cases we do the action because, after all, we want to keep our promises; so, even here, we are doing what we want. However, this dodge will not work: if I have promised to do something, and if I do not want to do it, then it is simply false to say that I want to keep my promise. In such cases we feel a conflict precisely because we do *not* want to do what we feel obligated to do. It is reasonable to think that Smith's action falls roughly into this second category: he might stay behind, not because he wants to, but because he feels that this friend needs help.

But suppose we were to concede, for the sake of the argument, that all voluntary action is motivated by the agent's wants, or at least that Smith is so motivated. Even if this were granted, it would not follow that Smith is acting selfishly or from self-interest. For if Smith wants to do something that will help his friend, even when it means forgoing his own enjoyments, that is precisely what makes him *un*selfish. What else could unselfishness be, if not wanting to help others? Another way to put the same point is to say that it is the *object* of a want that determines whether it is selfish or not. The mere fact that I am acting on *my* wants does not mean that I am acting selfishly; that depends on *what it is* that I want. If I want only my own good, and care nothing for others, then I am selfish; but if I also want other people to be well-off and happy, and if I act on *that* desire, then my action is not selfish. So much for this argument.

b. The second argument for psychological egoism is this: Since so-called unselfish actions always produce a sense of self-satisfaction in the agent,[2] and since this sense of satisfaction is a pleasant state of consciousness, it follows that the point of the action is really to achieve a pleasant state of consciousness, rather than to bring about any good for others. Therefore, the action is "unselfish" only at a superficial level of analysis. Smith will feel much better with himself for having stayed to help his friend—if he had gone to the country, he would have felt terrible about it—and that is the real point of the action. According to a well-known story, this argument was once expressed by Abraham Lincoln:

> Mr. Lincoln once remarked to a fellow-passenger on an old-time mud-coach that all men were prompted by selfishness in doing good. His fellow-passenger was antagonizing this position when they were passing over a corduroy bridge that spanned a slough. As they crossed this bridge they espied an old razor-backed sow on the bank making a terrible noise because her pigs had got into the slough and were in danger

of drowning. As the old coach began to climb the hill, Mr. Lincoln called out, "Driver, can't you stop just a moment?" Then Mr. Lincoln jumped out, ran back, and lifted the little pigs out of the mud and water and placed them on the bank. When he returned, his companion remarked: "Now, Abe, where does selfishness come in on this little episode?" "Why, bless your soul, Ed, that was the very essence of selfishness. I should have had no peace of mind all day had I gone on and left that suffering old sow worrying over those pigs. I did it to get peace of mind, don't you see?"[3]

This argument suffers from defects similar to the previous one. Why should we think that merely because someone derives satisfaction from helping others this makes him selfish? Isn't the unselfish man precisely the one who *does* derive satisfaction from helping others, while the selfish man does not? If Lincoln "got peace of mind" from rescuing the piglets, does this show him to be selfish, or, on the contrary, doesn't it show him to be compassionate and good-hearted? (If a man were truly selfish, why should it bother his conscience that *others* suffer—much less pigs?) Similarly, it is nothing more than shabby sophistry to say, because Smith takes satisfaction in helping his friend, that he is behaving selfishly. If we say this rapidly, while thinking about something else, perhaps it will sound all right; but if we speak slowly, and pay attention to what we are saying, it sounds plain silly.

Moreover, suppose we ask *why* Smith derives satisfaction from helping his friend. The answer will be, it is because Smith cares for him and wants him to succeed. If Smith did not have these concerns, then he would take no pleasure in assisting him; and these concerns, as we have already seen, are the marks of unselfishness, not selfishness. To put the point more generally: if we have a positive attitude toward the attainment of some goal, then we may derive satisfaction from attaining that goal. But the *object* of our attitude is *the attainment of that goal*; and we must want to attain the goal *before* we can find any satisfaction in it. We do not, in other words, desire some sort of "pleasurable consciousness" and then try to figure out how to achieve it; rather, we desire all sorts of different things—money, a new fishing boat, to be a better chess player, to get a promotion in our work, etc.—and because we desire these things, we derive satisfaction from attaining them. And so, if someone desires the welfare and happiness of another person, he will derive satisfaction from that; but this does not mean that this satisfaction is the object of his desire, or that he is in any way selfish on account of it.

It is a measure of the weakness of psychological egoism that these insupportable arguments are the ones most often advanced in its favor. Why, then, should anyone ever have thought it a true view? Perhaps because of a desire for theoretical simplicity: In thinking about human conduct, it would be nice if there were some simple formula that would unite the diverse phenomena of human behavior under a single explanatory principle, just as simple formulae in physics bring together a great many apparently different phenomena. And since it is obvious that self-regard is an overwhelmingly important factor in motivation, it is only natural to wonder whether all motivation might not be explained in these terms. But the answer is clearly No; while a great many human actions are motivated entirely or in part by self-interest, only by a deliberate distortion of the facts can we say that all conduct is so motivated. This will be clear, I think, if we correct three confusions which are commonplace. The exposure of these confusions will remove the last traces of plausibility from the psychological egoist thesis.

The first is the confusion of selfishness with self-interest. The two are clearly not the same. If I see a physician when I am feeling poorly, I am acting in my own interest but no one would think of calling me "selfish" on account of it. Similarly, brushing my teeth, working hard at my job, and obeying the law are all in my self-interest but none of these are examples of selfish conduct. This is because selfish behavior is behavior that ignores the interests of others, in circumstances in which their interests ought not to be ignored. This concept has a definite evaluative flavor; to call someone "selfish" is not just to describe his action but to condemn it. Thus, you would not call me selfish for eating a normal meal in normal

circumstances (although it may surely be in my self-interest); but you would call me selfish for hoarding food while others about are starving.

The second confusion is the assumption that every action is done *either* from self-interest or from other-regarding motives. Thus, the egoist concludes that if there is no such thing as genuine altruism then all actions must be done from self-interest. But this is certainly a false dichotomy. The man who continues to smoke cigarettes, even after learning about the connection between smoking and cancer, is surely not acting from self-interest, not even by his own standards—self-interest would dictate that he quit smoking at once—and he is not acting altruistically either. He *is,* no doubt, smoking for the pleasure of it, but all that this shows is that undisciplined pleasure-seeking and acting from self-interest are very different. This is what led Butler to remark that "the thing to be lamented is, not that men have so great regard to their own good or interest in the present world, for they have not enough."[4]

The last two paragraphs show (*a*) that it is false that all actions are selfish, and (*b*) that it is false that all actions are done out of self-interest. And it should be noted that these two points can be made, and were, without any appeal to putative examples of altruism.

The third confusion is the common but false assumption that a concern for one's own welfare is incompatible with any genuine concern for the welfare of others. Thus, since it is obvious that everyone (or very nearly everyone) does desire his own well-being, it might be thought that no one can really be concerned with others. But again, this is false. There is no inconsistency in desiring that everyone, including oneself *and* others, be well-off and happy. To be sure, it may happen on occasion that our own interests conflict with the interests of others, and in these cases we will have to make hard choices. But even in these cases we might sometimes opt for the interests of others, especially when the others involved are our family or friends. But more importantly, not all cases are like this: sometimes we are able to promote the welfare of others when our own interests are not involved at all. In these cases not even the strongest self-regard need prevent us from acting considerately toward others.

Once these confusions are cleared away, it seems to me obvious enough that there is no reason whatever to accept psychological egoism. On the contrary, if we simply observe people's behavior with an open mind, we may find that a great deal of it is motivated by self-regard, but by no means all of it; and that there is no reason to deny that "the moral institution of life" can include a place for the virtue of beneficence.[5]

3. The ethical egoist would say at this point, "Of course it is possible for people to act altruistically, and perhaps many people do act that way— but there is no reason why they *should* do so. A person is under no obligation to do anything except what is in his own interests."[6] This is really quite a radical doctrine. Suppose I have an urge to set fire to some public building (say, a department store) just for the fascination of watching the spectacular blaze: according to this view, the fact that several people might be burned to death provides no reason whatever why I should not do it. After all, this only concerns *their* welfare, not my own, and according to the ethical egoist the only person I need think of is myself.

Some might deny that ethical egoism has any such monstrous consequences. They would point out that it is really to my own advantage not to set the fire—for, if I do that I may be caught and put into prison (unlike Gyges, I have no magic ring for protection). Moreover, even if I could avoid being caught it is still to my advantage to respect the rights and interests of others, for it is to my advantage to live in a society in which people's rights and interests are respected. Only in such a society can I live a happy and secure life; so, in acting kindly toward others, I would merely be doing my part to create and maintain the sort of society which it is to my advantage to have.[7] Therefore, it is said, the egoist would not be such a bad man; he would be as kindly and considerate as anyone else, because he would see that it is to his own advantage to be kindly and considerate.

This is a seductive line of thought, but it seems to me mistaken. Certainly it is to everyone's advantage (including the egoist's) to preserve a stable society where people's interests are generally protected.

But there is no reason for the egoist to think that merely because *he* will not honor the rules of the social game, decent society will collapse. For the vast majority of people are not egoists, and there is no reason to think that they will be converted by his example—especially if he is discreet and does not unduly flaunt his style of life. What this line of reasoning shows is not that the egoist himself must act benevolently, but that he must encourage *others* to do so. He must take care to conceal from public view his own self-centered method of decision making, and urge others to act on precepts very different from those on which he is willing to act.

The rational egoist, then, cannot advocate that egoism be universally adopted by everyone. For he wants a world in which his own interests are maximized; and if other people adopted the egoistic policy of pursuing their own interests to the exclusion of his interests, as he pursues his interests to the exclusion of theirs, then such a world would be impossible. So he himself will be an egoist, but he will want others to be altruists.

This brings us to what is perhaps the most popular "refutation" of ethical egoism current among philosophical writers—the argument that ethical egoism is at bottom inconsistent because it cannot be universalized.[8] The argument goes like this:

To say that any action or policy of action is *right* (or that it *ought* to be adopted) entails that it is right for *anyone* in the same sort of circumstances. I cannot, for example, say that it is right for me to lie to you, and yet object when you lie to me (provided, of course, that the circumstances are the same). I cannot hold that it is all right for me to drink your beer and then complain when you drink mine. This is just the requirement that we be consistent in our evaluations; it is a requirement of logic. Now it is said that ethical egoism cannot meet this requirement because, as we have already seen, the egoist would not want others to act in the same way that he acts. Moreover, suppose he *did* advocate the universal adoption of egoistic policies: he would be saying to Peter, "You ought to pursue your own interests even if it means destroying Paul"; and he would be saying to Paul, "You ought to pursue your own interests even if it means destroying Peter." The attitudes expressed in these two recommendations seem clearly inconsistent—he is urging the advancement of Peter's interest at one moment, and countenancing their defeat at the next. Therefore, the argument goes, there is no way to maintain the doctrine of ethical egoism as a consistent view about how we ought to act. We will fall into inconsistency whenever we try.

What are we to make of this argument? Are we to conclude that ethical egoism has been refuted? Such a conclusion, I think, would be unwarranted; for I think that we can show, contrary to this argument, how ethical egoism can be maintained consistently. We need only to interpret the egoist's position in a sympathetic way: we should say that he has in mind a certain kind of world which he would prefer over all others; it would be a world in which his own interests were maximized, regardless of the effects on the other people. The egoist's primary policy of action, then, would be to act in such a way as to bring about, as nearly as possible, this sort of world. Regardless of however morally reprehensible we might find it, there is nothing *inconsistent* in someone's adopting this as his ideal and acting in a way calculated to bring it about. And if someone did adopt this as his ideal, then he would not advocate universal egoism; as we have already seen, he would want other people to be altruists. So, if he advocates any principles of conduct for the general public, they will be altruistic principles. This could not be inconsistent; on the contrary, it would be perfectly consistent with his goal of creating a world in which his own interests are maximized. To be sure, he would have to be deceitful; in order to secure the good will of others, and a favorable hearing for his exhortations to altruism, he would have to pretend that he was himself prepared to accept altruistic principles. But again, that would be all right; from the egoist's point of view, this would merely be a matter of adopting the necessary means to the achievement of his goal—and while we might not approve of this, there is nothing inconsistent about it. Again, it might be said, "He advocates one thing, but does another. Surely *that's* inconsistent." But it is not; for what he advocates and what he does are both calculated as means to an end (the *same* end, we might note); and as such, he is doing what is rationally required in

each case. Therefore, contrary to the previous argument, there is nothing inconsistent in the ethical egoist's view. He cannot be refuted by the claim that he contradicts himself.

Is there, then, no way to refute the ethical egoist? If by "refute" we mean show that he has made some *logical* error, the answer is that there is not. However, there is something more that can be said. The egoist challenge to our ordinary moral convictions amounts to a demand for an explanation of why we should adopt certain policies of action, namely, policies in which the good of others is given importance. We can give an answer to this demand, albeit an indirect one. The reason one ought not to do actions that would hurt other people is other people would be hurt. The reason one ought to do actions that would benefit other people is other people would be benefited. This may at first seem like a piece of philosophical sleight-of-hand, but it is not. The point is that the welfare of human beings is something that most of us value *for its own sake,* and not merely for the sake of something else. Therefore, when *further* reasons are demanded for valuing the welfare of human beings, we cannot point to anything further to satisfy this demand. It is not that we have no reason for pursuing these policies, but that our reason *is* that these policies are for the good of human beings.

So if we are asked, "Why shouldn't I set fire to this department store?" one answer would be, "Because if you do, people may be burned to death." This is a complete, sufficient reason which does not require qualification or supplementation of any sort. If someone seriously wants to know why this action shouldn't be done, that's the reason. If we are pressed further and asked the sceptical question, "But why shouldn't I do actions that will harm others?" we may not know what to say—but this is because the questioner has included in his question the very answer we would like to give: "Why shouldn't you do actions that will harm others? Because, doing those actions would harm others."

The egoist, no doubt, will not be happy with this. He will protest that *we* may accept this as a reason, but *he* does not. And here the argument stops: there are limits to what can be accomplished by argument, and if the egoist really doesn't care about other people—if he honestly doesn't care whether they are helped or hurt by his actions—then we have reached those limits. If we want to persuade him to act decently toward his fellow humans, we will have to make our appeal to such other attitudes as he does possess, by threats, bribes, or other cajolery. That is all that we can do.

Though some may find this situation distressing (we would like to be able to show that the egoist is just *wrong*), it holds no embarrassment for common morality. What we have come up against is simply a fundamental requirement of rational action, namely, that the existence of reasons for action always depends on the prior existence of certain attitudes in the agent. For example, the fact that a certain course of action would make the agent a lot of money is a reason for doing it only if the agent wants to make money; the fact that practicing at chess makes one a better player is a reason for practicing only if one wants to be a better player; and so on. Similarly, the fact that a certain action would help the agent is a reason for doing the action only if the agent cares about his own welfare, and the fact that an action would help others is a reason for doing it only if the agent cares about others. In this respect ethical egoism and what we might call ethical altruism are in exactly the same fix: both require that the agent *care* about himself, or about other people, before they can get started.

So a nonegoist will accept "It would harm another person" as a reason not to do an action simply because he cares about what happens to that other person. When the egoist says that he does *not* accept that as a reason, he is saying something quite extraordinary. He is saying that he has no affection for friends or family, that he never feels pity or compassion, that he is the sort of person who can look on scenes of human misery with complete indifference, so long as he is not the one suffering. Genuine egoists, people who really don't care at all about anyone other than themselves, are rare. It is important to keep this in mind when thinking about ethical egoism; it is easy to forget just how fundamental to human psychological makeup the feeling of sympathy is. Indeed, a man without any sympathy at all

would scarcely be recognizable as a man; and that is what makes ethical egoism such a disturbing doctrine in the first place.

4. There are, of course, many different ways in which the sceptic might challenge the assumptions underlying our moral practice. In this essay I have discussed only two of them, the two put forward by Glaucon in the passage that I cited from Plato's *Republic*. It is important that the assumptions underlying our moral practice should not be confused with particular judgments made within that practice. To defend one is not to defend the other. We may assume—quite properly, if my analysis has been correct—that the virtue of beneficence does, and indeed should, occupy an important place in "the moral institution of life"; and yet we may make constant and miserable errors when it comes to judging when and in what ways this virtue is to be exercised. Even worse, we may often be able to make accurate moral judgments, and know what we ought to do, but not do it. For these ills, philosophy alone is not the cure.

NOTES

1. *The Republic of Plato,* translated by F. M. Cornford (Oxford, 1941), p. 45.
2. Or, as it is sometimes said, "It gives him a clear conscience," or "He couldn't sleep at night if he had done otherwise," or "He would have been ashamed of himself for not doing it," and so on.
3. Frank C. Sharp, *Ethics* (New York, 1928), pp. 74–75. Quoted from the Springfield (IL) *Monitor* in the *Outlook,* vol. 56, p. 1059.
4. *The Works of Joseph Butler,* edited by W. E. Gladstone (Oxford, 1896), vol. II, p. 26. It should be noted that most of the points I am making against psychological egoism were first made by Joseph Butler. Butler made all the important points; all that is left for us is to remember them.
5. The capacity for altruistic behavior is not unique to human beings. Some interesting experiments with rhesus monkeys have shown that these animals will refrain from operating a device for securing food if this cause other animals to suffer pain. See Jules H. Masserman, Stanley Wechkin, and William Terris, "'Altruistic' Behavior in Rhesus Monkeys," *American Journal of Psychiatry,* vol. 121 (1964), pp. 584–85.

6. I take this to be the view of Ayn Rand, insofar as I understand her confused doctrine.

7. Cf. Thomas Hobbes, *Leviathan* (London, 1651), chap. 17.

8. See, for example, Brian Medlin, "Ultimate Principles and Ethical Egoism," *Australasian Journal of Philosophy,* vol. 35 (1957), pp. 111–18; and D. H. Monro, *Empiricism and Ethics* (Cambridge, 1967), chap. 16.

STUDY QUESTIONS

1. What is the distinction between psychological egoism and ethical egoism?
2. If you do what you want to do, are you being selfish?
3. Is a concern for yourself incompatible with a concern for others?
4. Is it self-defeating for the ethical egoist to urge everyone to act egoistically?

Part IV

DIVINE COMMAND THEORY

God and Morality

Steven M. Cahn

According to divine command theory, an act is right if and only if God wills that it is right. Steven M. Cahn, coeditor of this book, argues instead that whether God exists has no implications for morality. An act is not rendered right because God commands it; rather, if God commands it, God does so because the action is in accord with an independent moral standard. In that case, you could act in accord with the standard regardless of whether you believe in God.

According to many religions, although not all, the world was created by God, an all-powerful, all-knowing, all-good being. Although God's existence has been doubted, let us for the moment assume its truth. What implications of this supposition would be relevant to our lives?

Some people would feel more secure in the knowledge that the world had been planned by an all-good being. Others would feel insecure, realizing the extent to which their existence depended on a decision of this being. In any case, most people, out of either fear or respect, would wish to act in accord with God's will.

Belief in God by itself, however, provides no hint whatsoever which actions God wishes us to perform or what we ought to do to please or obey God. We may affirm that God is all-good, yet have no way of knowing the highest moral standards. All we may presume is that, whatever these standards, God always acts in accordance with them. We might expect God to have implanted the correct moral standards in our minds, but this supposition is doubtful in view of the conflicts among people's intuitions. Furthermore, even if consensus prevailed, it might be only a means by which God tests us to see whether we have the courage to dissent from popular opinion.

Some would argue that if God exists, then murder is immoral, because it destroys what God with infinite wisdom created. This argument, however, fails on several grounds. First, God also created germs, viruses, and disease-carrying rats. Because God created these things, ought they not be eliminated? Second, if God arranged for us to live, God also arranged for us to die. By killing, are we assisting the work of God? Third, God provided us with the mental and physical potential to commit murder. Does God wish us to fulfill this potential?

Thus God's existence alone does not imply any particular moral precepts. We may hope our actions are in accord with God's standards, but no test is available to check whether what we do is best in God's eyes. Some seemingly good people suffer great ills, whereas some seemingly evil people achieve happiness. Perhaps in a future life these outcomes will be reversed, but we have no way of ascertaining who, if anyone, is ultimately punished and who ultimately rewarded.

Over the course of history, those who believed in God's existence typically were eager to learn

God's will and tended to rely on those individuals who claimed to possess such insight. Diviners, seers, and priests were given positions of great influence. Competition among them was severe, however, for no one could be sure which oracle to believe.

In any case prophets died, and their supposedly revelatory powers disappeared with them. For practical purposes what was needed was a permanent record of God's will. This requirement was met by the writing of holy books in which God's will was revealed to all.

But even though many such books were supposed to embody the will of God, they conflicted with one another. Which was to be accepted? Belief in the existence of God by itself yields no answer.

Let us suppose, however, that an individual becomes persuaded that a reliable guide to God's will is contained in the Ten Commandments. This person, therefore, believes to murder, steal, or commit adultery is wrong.

But why is it wrong? Is it wrong because God says so, or does God say so because it *is* wrong?

This crucial issue was raised more than two thousand years ago in Plato's remarkable dialogue, the *Euthyphro.* Plato's teacher, Socrates, who in most of Plato's works is given the leading role, asks the overconfident Euthyphro whether actions are right because God says they are right, or whether God says actions are right because they are right.

In other words, Socrates is inquiring whether actions are right because of God's fiat or whether God is subject to moral standards. If actions are right because of God's command, then anything God commands would be right. Had God commanded adultery, stealing, and murder, then adultery, stealing, and murder would be right—surely an unsettling and to many an unacceptable conclusion.

Granted, some may be willing to adopt this discomforting view, but then they face another difficulty. If the good is whatever God commands, to say that God's commands are good amounts to saying that God's commands are God's commands, a mere tautology or repetition of words. In that case, the possibility of meaningfully praising the goodness of God would be lost.

The lesson here is that might does not make right, even if the might is the infinite might of God. To act morally is not to act out of fear of punishment; it is not to act as one is commanded to act. Rather, it is to act as one ought to act, and how one ought to act is not dependent on anyone's power, even if the power be divine.

Thus actions are not right because God commands them; on the contrary, God commands them because they are right. What is right is independent of what God commands, for to be right, what God commands must conform to an independent standard.

We could act intentionally in accord with this standard without believing in the existence of God; therefore morality does not rest on that belief. Consequently those who do not believe in God can be highly moral (as well as immoral) people, and those who do believe in the existence of God can be highly immoral (as well as moral) people. This conclusion should come as no surprise to anyone who has contrasted the benevolent life of the inspiring teacher, the Buddha, an atheist, with the malevolent life of the monk Torquemada, who devised and enforced the boundless cruelties of the Spanish Inquisition.

In short, believing in the existence of God does not by itself imply any specific moral principles, and knowing God's will does not provide any justification for morality. Thus regardless of our religious commitments, the moral dimension of our lives remains to be explored.

STUDY QUESTIONS

1. If God exists, is murder immoral?
2. Is murder wrong because God prohibits it, or does God prohibit it because it is wrong?
3. Can those who do not believe in God be moral?
4. Can adherents of different religions resolve moral disagreements?

A Modified Divine Command Theory

Robert M. Adams

Robert M. Adams, Recurring Research Professor of Philosophy at Rutgers University, considers the possibility that God might command us to act immorally. Should we obey such a command? If so, we act immorally. If not, we act against the will of God, whose commands are not then supreme. Adams seeks a way out of this impasse by defining a moral act as one in accord with the commands of a loving God. Whether taking this step avoids the problem is the crucial issue.

It will be helpful to begin with the statement of a simple, *unmodified* divine command theory of ethical wrongness. This is the theory that ethical wrongness *consists in* being contrary to God's commands, or that the word 'wrong' in ethical contexts *means* 'contrary to God's commands'. It implies that the following two statement forms are logically equivalent.

(1) It is wrong (for A) to do X.
(2) It is contrary to God's commands (for A) to do X.

Of course that is not all that the theory implies. It also implies that (2) is conceptually prior to (1), so that the meaning of (1) is to be explained in terms of (2), and not the other way around. It might prove fairly difficult to state or explain in what that conceptual priority consists, but I shall not go into that here. I do not wish ultimately to defend the theory in its unmodified form, and I think I have stated it fully enough for my present purposes. . . .

The following seems to me to be the gravest objection to the divine command theory of ethical wrongness, in the form in which I have stated it. Suppose God should command me to make it my chief end in life to inflict suffering on other human beings, for no other reason than that he commanded it. (For convenience I shall abbreviate this hypothesis to 'Suppose God should command cruelty for its own sake'.) Will it seriously be claimed that in that case it would be wrong for me not to practice cruelty for its own sake? I see three possible answers to this question.

(1) It might be claimed that it is logically impossible for God to command cruelty for its own sake. In that case, of course, we need not worry about whether it would be wrong to disobey if he did command it. It is senseless to agonize about what one should do in a logically impossible situation. This solution to the problem seems unlikely to be available to the divine command theorist, however. For why would he hold that it is logically impossible for God to command cruelty for its own sake? Some theologians (for instance, Thomas Aquinas) have believed (a) that what is right and wrong is independent

of God's will, *and* (b) that God always does right by the necessity of his nature. Such theologians, if they believe that it would be wrong for God to command cruelty for its own sake, have reason to believe that it is logically impossible for him to do so. But the divine command theorist, who does not agree that what is right and wrong is independent of God's will, does not seem to have such a reason to deny that it is logically possible for God to command cruelty for its own sake.

(2) Let us assume that it is logically possible for God to command cruelty for its own sake. In that case the divine command theory seems to imply that it would be wrong not to practice cruelty for its own sake. There have been at least a few adherents of divine command ethics who have been prepared to accept this consequence. William Ockham held that those acts which we call "theft," "adultery," and "hatred of God" would be meritorious if God had commanded them.[1] He would surely have said the same about what I have been calling the practice of "cruelty for its own sake."

This position is one which I suspect most of us are likely to find somewhat shocking, even repulsive. We should therefore be particularly careful not to misunderstand it. We need not imagine that Ockham disciplined himself to be ready to practice cruelty for its own sake if God should command it. It was doubtless an article of faith for him that God is unalterably opposed to any such practice. The mere logical possibility that theft, adultery, and cruelty might have been commanded by God (and therefore meritorious) doubtless did not represent in Ockham's view any real possibility.

(3) Nonetheless, the view that if God commanded cruelty for its own sake it would be wrong not to practice it seems unacceptable to me; and I think many, perhaps most, other Jewish and Christian believers would find it unacceptable too. I must make clear the sense in which I find it unsatisfactory. It is not that I find an internal inconsistency in it. And I would not deny that it may reflect, accurately enough, the way in which some believers use the word 'wrong'. I might as well frankly avow that I am looking for a divine command theory which at least might possibly be a correct account of how *I* use the word 'wrong'. I do not use the word 'wrong' in such a way that I would say that it would be wrong not to practice cruelty if God commanded it, and I am sure that many other believers agree with me on this point.

But now have I not rejected the divine command theory? I have assumed that it would be logically possible for God to command cruelty for its own sake. And I have rejected the view that if God commanded cruelty for its own sake, it would be wrong not to obey. It seems to follow that I am committed to the view that in certain logically possible circumstances it would not be wrong to disobey God. This position seems to be inconsistent with the theory that 'wrong' means 'contrary to God's commands'.

I want to argue, however, that it is still open to me to accept a modified form of the divine command theory of ethical wrongness. According to the modified divine command theory, when I say, 'It is wrong to do X', (at least part of) what I *mean* is that it is contrary to God's commands to do X. 'It is wrong to do X' *implies* 'It is contrary to God's commands to do X'. But 'It is contrary to God's commands to do X' implies 'It is wrong to do X' only if certain conditions are assumed—namely, only if it is assumed that God has the character which I believe him to have, of loving his human creatures. If God were really to command us to make cruelty our goal, then he would not have that character of loving us, and I would not say it would be wrong to disobey him.

But do I say that it would be wrong to obey him in such a case? This is the point at which I am in danger of abandoning the divine command theory completely. I do abandon it completely if I say both of the following things.

(A) It would be wrong to obey God if he commanded cruelty for its own sake.
(B) In (A), 'wrong' is used in what is for me its normal ethical sense.

If I assert both (A) and (B), it is clear that I cannot consistently maintain that 'wrong' in its normal ethical sense for me means or implies 'contrary to God's commands'.

But from the fact that I deny that it would be wrong to disobey God if He commanded cruelty for its own sake, it does not follow that I must accept (A) and (B). Of course someone might claim that obedience and disobedience would both be ethically permitted in such a case; but that is not the view that I am suggesting. If I adopt the modified divine command theory as an analysis of my present concept of ethical wrongness (and if I adopt a similar analysis of my concept of ethical permittedness), I will not hold either that it would be wrong to disobey, or that it would be ethically permitted to disobey, or that it would be wrong to obey, or that it would be ethically permitted to obey, if God commanded cruelty for its own sake. For I will say that my concept of ethical wrongness (and my concept of ethical permittedness) would "break down" if I really believed that God commanded cruelty for its own sake. Or to put the matter somewhat more prosaically, I will say that my concepts of ethical wrongness and permittedness could not serve the functions they now serve, because using those concepts I could not call any action ethically wrong or ethically permitted, if I believed that God's will was so unloving.

NOTE

1. Guillelmus de Occam, *Super 4 libros sententiarum,* bk. II, qu. 19, O, in vol. IV of his *Opera plurima* (Lyon, 1494–6; réimpression en fac-similé, Farnborough, Hants., England: Gregg Press, 1962). I am not claiming that Ockham held a divine command theory of exactly the same sort that I have been discussing.

STUDY QUESTIONS

1. What does Adams mean by "an unmodified divine command theory of ethical wrongness"?
2. What does he consider the gravest objection to that theory?
3. What does he mean by "a modified divine command theory of ethical wrongness"?
4. Does the modified theory avoid the objection he saw to the unmodified theory?

Part V

NATURAL LAW

Summa Contra Gentiles

Thomas Aquinas

Thomas Aquinas (1225–1274) was a Dominican monk who taught at the University of Paris. His work synthesizes Aristotelian thought and Christian doctrine. Aquinas argues that each thing's proper operation determines its final end, and in the case of human beings that final end is happiness (or beatitude). It is achieved by the fulfillment of our capacity for contemplating that which is most perfect, namely, God. Aquinas defends this conclusion against rival contenders for happiness, such as pleasure, power, or the arts.

BOOK THREE

Providence

Chapter II

That Every Agent Acts for an End

Accordingly we must first show that every agent, by its action, intends an end.

For in those things which clearly act for an end, we declare the end to be that towards which the movement of the agent tends; for when this is reached, the end is said to be reached, and to fail in this is to fail in the end intended. This may be seen in the physician who aims at health, and in a man who runs towards an appointed goal. Nor does it matter, as to this, whether that which tends to an end be endowed with knowledge or not; for just as the target is the end of the archer, so is it the end of the arrow's flight. Now the movement of every agent tends to something determinate, since it is not from any force that any action proceeds, but heating proceeds from heat, and cooling from cold; and

therefore actions are differentiated by their active principles. Action sometimes terminates in something made, as for instance building terminates in a house, and healing in health; while sometimes it does not so terminate, as for instance, in the case of understanding and sensation. And if action terminates in something made, the movement of the agent tends by that action towards the thing made; while if it does not terminate in something made, the movement of the agent tends to the action itself. It follows therefore that every agent intends an end while acting, which end is sometimes the action itself, sometimes a thing made by the action.

Again. In all things that act for an end, that is said to be the last end beyond which the agent seeks nothing further; and thus the physician's action goes as far as health, and when this is attained, his efforts cease. But in the action of every agent, a point can be reached beyond which the agent does not desire to go; or else actions would tend to infinity, which is impossible, for since *it is not possible to pass through an infinite medium*,[1] the agent would never begin to act, because nothing moves towards what it cannot reach. Therefore every agent acts for an end.

Moreover. If the actions of an agent proceed to infinity, these actions must needs result either in something made, or not. If the result is something made, the being of that thing made will follow after an infinity of actions. But that which presupposes an infinity of things cannot possibly be, since *an infinite medium cannot be passed through*. Now impossibility of being argues impossibility of becoming, and that which cannot become, it is impossible to make. Therefore it is impossible for an agent to begin to make a thing for the making of which an infinity of actions is presupposed.—If, however, the result of such actions be not something made, the order of these actions must be either according to the order of active powers (for instance, if a man feels that he may imagine, and imagines that he may understand, and understands that he may will), or according to the order of objects (for instance, I consider the body that I may consider the soul, which I consider in order to consider a separate substance, which again I consider so that I may consider God). Now it is not possible to proceed to infinity, either in active powers (as neither is this possible in the forms of things, as is proved in *Metaph.* ii,[2] since the form is the principle of activity), or in objects (as neither is this possible in beings, since there is one first being, as we have proved above).[3] Therefore it is not possible for agents to proceed to infinity, and consequently there must be something, upon whose attainment the efforts of the agent cease. Therefore every agent acts for an end.

Further. In things that act for an end, whatsoever comes between the first agent and the last end, is an end in respect to what precedes, and an active principle in respect of what follows. Hence if the effort of the agent does not tend to something determinate, and if its action, as stated, proceeds to infinity, the active principles must needs proceed to infinity; which is impossible, as we have shown above. Therefore the effort of the agent must of necessity tend to something determinate.

Again. Every agent acts either by nature or by intellect. Now there can be no doubt that those which act by intellect act for an end, since they act *with* an intellectual preconception of what they attain by their action, and they act *through* such a preconception; for this is to act by intellect. Now just as in the preconceiving intellect there exists the entire likeness of the effect that is attained by the action of the intellectual being, so in the natural agent there pre-exists the likeness of the natural effect, by virtue of which the action is determined to the appointed effect; for fire begets fire, and an olive produces an olive. Therefore, even as that which acts by intellect tends by its action to a definite end, so also does that which acts by nature. Therefore every agent acts for an end.

Moreover. Fault is not found save in those things which are for an end, for we do not find fault with one who fails in that to which he is not appointed; and thus we find fault with a physician if he fail to heal, but not with a builder or a grammarian. But we find fault in things done according to art, as when a grammarian fails to speak correctly, and in things that are ruled by nature, as in the case of monstrosities. Therefore every agent, whether according to nature, or according to art, or acting of set purpose, acts for an end.

Again. Were an agent not to act for a definite effect, all effects would be indifferent to it. Now that which is indifferent to many effects does not produce one rather than another. Therefore, from that which is indifferent to either of two effects, no effect results, unless it be determined by something to one of them. Hence it would be impossible for it to act. Therefore every agent tends to some definite effect, which is called its end.

There are, however, certain actions which would seem not to be for an end, such as playful and contemplative actions, and those which are done without attention, such as scratching one's beard, and the like. Whence some might be led to think that there is an agent that acts not for an end.—But we must observe that contemplative actions are not for another end, but are themselves an end. Playful actions are sometimes an end, when one plays for the mere pleasure of play; and sometimes they are for an end, as when we play that afterwards we may study better. Actions done without attention do not proceed from the intellect, but from some sudden act of the imagination, or some natural principle; and thus a disordered humor produces an itching sensation and is the cause of a man scratching his beard, which he does without his intellect attending to it. Such actions do tend to an end, although outside the order of the intellect. Hereby is excluded the error of certain natural philosophers of old, who maintained that all things happen by the necessity of matter, thus utterly banishing the final cause from things.[4]

Chapter III

That Every Agent Acts for a Good

Hence we must go on to prove that every agent acts for a good.

For that every agent acts for an end clearly follows from the fact that every agent tends to something definite. Now that to which an agent tends definitely must needs be befitting to that agent, since the agent would not tend to it save because of some fittingness thereto. But that which is befitting to a thing is good for it. Therefore every agent acts for a good.

Further. The end is that wherein the appetite of the agent or mover comes to rest, as also the appetite of that which is moved. Now it is the very notion of good to be the term of appetite, since *good is the object of every appetite.*[5] Therefore all action and movement is for a good.

Again. All action and movement would seem to be directed in some way to being, either for the preservation of being in the species or in the individual, or for the acquisition of being. Now this itself, namely, being, is a good; and for this reason all things desire being. Therefore all action and movement is for a good.

Furthermore. All action and movement is for some perfection. For if the action itself be the end, it is clearly a second perfection of the agent. And if the action consist in the transformation of external matter, clearly the mover intends to induce some perfection into the thing moved, towards which perfection the movable also tends, if the movement be natural. Now we say that this is to be good, namely, to be perfect. Therefore every action and movement is for a good.

Also. Every agent acts according as it is actual. Now by acting it tends to something similar to itself. Therefore it tends to an act. But an act has the nature of good, since evil is not found save in a potentiality lacking act. Therefore every action is for a good.

Moreover. The intellectual agent acts for an end, as determining for itself its end; whereas the natural agent, though it acts for an end, as was proved above,[6] does not determine its end for itself, since it knows not the nature of end, but is moved to the end determined for it by another. Now an intellectual agent does not determine the end for itself except under the aspect of good; for the intelligible object does not move except it be considered as a good, which is the object of the will. Therefore the natural agent also is not moved, nor does it act for an end, except in so far as this end is a good, since the end is determined for the natural agent by some appetite. Therefore every agent acts for a good.

Again. To shun evil and to seek good are of the same nature, even as movement from below and upward are of the same nature. Now we observe that all things shun evil, for intellectual agents shun a thing for the reason that they apprehend it as evil, and all natural agents, in proportion to their strength, resist corruption which is the evil of everything. Therefore all things act for a good.

Again. That which results from the agent's action outside his intention, is said to happen by chance or luck. Now we observe in the works of nature that either always or more often that happens which is best: thus in plants the leaves are so placed as to protect the fruit; and the parts of an animal are so disposed as to conduce to the animal's safety. Therefore, if this happens outside the intention of the natural agent, it will be the result of chance or luck. But that is impossible, because things that happen always, or frequently, are not by chance or fortuitous, but those which occur seldom.[7] Therefore the natural agent tends to that which is best; and much more evidently is this so with the intellectual agent. Therefore every agent intends a good in acting.

Moreover. Whatever is moved is brought to the term of movement by the mover and agent. Therefore mover and moved tend to the same term. Now that which is moved, since it is in potentiality, tends to an act, and consequently to perfection and goodness; for by its movement it passes from potentiality to act. Therefore mover and agent by moving and acting always intend a good.

Hence the philosophers in defining the good said: *The good is the object of every appetite*; and Dionysius says that *all things desire the good and the best.*[8]

Chapter XXV

That to Know God Is The End of Every Intellectual Substance

Now, seeing that all creatures, even those that are devoid of reason, are directed to God as their last end, and that all reach this end in so far as they have some share of a likeness to Him, the intellectual creature attains to Him in a special way, namely, through its proper operation, by understanding Him. Consequently this must be the end of the intellectual creature, namely, to understand God.

For, as we have shown above,[9] God is the end of each thing, and hence, as far as it is possible to it, each thing intends to be united to God as its last end. Now a thing is more closely united to God by reaching in a way to the very substance of God; which happens when it knows something of the divine substance, rather than when it reaches to a divine likeness. Therefore the intellectual substance tends to the knowledge of God as its last end.

Again. The operation proper to a thing is its end, for it is its second perfection; so that when a thing is well conditioned for its proper operation it is said to be fit and good. Now understanding is the proper operation of the intellectual substance, and consequently is its end. Therefore, whatever is most perfect in this operation is its last end; and especially in those operations which are not directed to some product, such as understanding and sensation. And since operations of this kind take their species from their objects, by which also they are known, it follows that the more perfect the object of any such operation, the more perfect is the operation. Consequently to understand the most perfect intelligible, namely God, is the most perfect in the genus of the operation which consists in understanding. Therefore to know God by an act of understanding is the last end of every intellectual substance.

Someone, however, might say that the last end of an intellectual substance consists indeed in understanding the best intelligible object, but that what is the best intelligible for this or that intellectual substance is not absolutely the best intelligible; and that the higher the intellectual substance, the higher is its best intelligible. So that possibly the supreme intellectual substance has for its best intelligible object that which is best absolutely, and its happiness will consist in understanding God; whereas the happiness of any lower intellectual substance will consist in understanding some lower intelligible object, which however will be the highest thing understood by that substance. Especially would it seem not to be in the power of the human intellect to understand that which is absolutely the best intelligible, because of its weakness; for it is as much adapted for knowing the supreme intelligible *as the owl's eye for seeing the sun.*[10]

Nevertheless it is evident that the end of any intellectual substance, even the lowest, is to understand God. For it has been shown above that God is the last end towards which all things tend.[11] And the human intellect, although the lowest in the order of intelligent substances, is superior to all that are devoid of understanding. Since then a more noble substance has not a less noble end, God will be the end also of the human intellect. Now every intelligent being attains to its last end by understanding it, as we have proved. Therefore the human intellect attains to God as its end, by understanding Him.

Again. Just as things devoid of intellect tend to God as their end by way of assimilation, so do intellectual substances by way of knowledge, as clearly appears from what has been said. Now, although things devoid of reason tend towards a likeness to their proximate causes, the intention of nature does not rest there, but has for its end a likeness to the highest good, as we have proved,[12] although they are able to attain to this likeness in a most imperfect manner. Therefore, however little be the knowledge of God to which the intellect is able to attain, this will be the intellect's last end, rather than a perfect knowledge of lower intelligibles.

Moreover. Everything desires most of all its last end. Now the human intellect desires, loves and enjoys the knowledge of divine things, although it can grasp but little about them, more than the perfect knowledge which it has of the lowest things. Therefore man's last end is to understand God in some way.

Further. Everything tends to a divine likeness as its own end. Therefore a thing's last end is that whereby it is most of all like God. Now the intellectual creature is especially likened to God in that it is intellectual, since this likeness belongs to it above other creatures, and includes all other likenesses. And in this particular kind of likeness it is more like God in understanding actually than in understanding habitually or potentially, because God is always actually understanding, as we proved in the First Book.[13] Furthermore, in understanding actually, the intellectual creature is especially like God in understanding God; for by understanding Himself God understands all other things, as we proved in the First Book.[14] Therefore the last end of every intellectual substance is to understand God.

Again. That which is lovable only because of another is for the sake of that which is lovable for its own sake alone; because we cannot go on indefinitely in the appetite of nature, since then nature's desire would be in vain, for it is impossible to pass through an infinite number of things. Now all practical sciences, arts and powers are lovable only for the sake of something else, since their end is not knowledge, but work. But speculative sciences are lovable for their own sake, for their end is knowledge itself. Nor can we find any action in human life that is not directed to some other end, with the exception of speculative consideration. For even playful actions, which seem to be done without any purpose, have some end due to them, namely that the mind may be relaxed, and that thereby we may afterwards become more fit for studious occupations; or otherwise we should always have to be playing, if play were desirable for its own sake, and this is unreasonable. Accordingly, the practical arts are directed to the speculative arts, and again every human operation, to intellectual speculation, as its end. Now, in all sciences and arts that are mutually ordered, the last end seems to belong to the one from which others take their rules and principles. Thus the art of

sailing, to which belongs the ship's purpose, namely its use, provides rules and principles to the art of ship-building. And such is the relation of first philosophy to other speculative sciences, for all others depend thereon, since they derive their principles from it, and are directed by it in defending those principles; and moreover first philosophy is wholly directed to the knowledge of God as its last end, and is consequently called the *divine science*.[15] Therefore the knowledge of God is the last end of all human knowledge and activity.

Furthermore. In all mutually ordered agents and movers, the end of the first agent and mover must be the end of all, even as the end of the commander-in-chief is the end of all who are soldiering under him. Now of all the parts of man, the intellect is the highest mover, for it moves the appetite, by proposing its object to it; and the intellective appetite, or will, moves the sensitive appetites, namely the irascible and concupiscible. Hence it is that we do not obey the concupiscence, unless the will command; while the sensitive appetite, when the will has given its consent, moves the body. Therefore the end of the intellect is the end of all human actions. *Now the intellect's end and good are the true,*[16] and its last end is the first truth. Therefore the last end of the whole man, and of all his deeds and desires, is to know the first truth, namely, God.

Moreover. Man has a natural desire to know the causes of whatever he sees; and so through wondering at what they saw, and not knowing its cause, men first began to philosophize, and when they had discovered the cause they were at rest. Nor do they cease inquiring until they come to the first cause; and *then do we deem ourselves to know perfectly when we know the first cause.*[17] Therefore man naturally desires, as his last end, to know the first cause. But God is the first cause of all things. Therefore man's last end is to know God.

Besides. Man naturally desires to know the cause of any known effect. But the human intellect knows universal being. Therefore it naturally desires to know its cause, which is God alone, as we proved in the Second Book.[18] Now one has not attained to one's last end until the natural desire is at rest. Therefore the knowledge of any intelligible object is not enough for man's happiness, which is his last end, unless he know God also, which knowledge terminates his natural desire as his last end. Therefore this very knowledge of God is man's last end.

Further. A body that tends by its natural appetite to its place is moved all the more vehemently and rapidly the nearer it approaches its end. Hence Aristotle proves that a natural straight movement cannot be towards an indefinite point, because it would not be more moved afterwards than before.[19] Hence that which tends more vehemently to a thing afterwards than before is not moved towards an indefinite point but towards something fixed. Now this we find in the desire of knowledge, for the more one knows, the greater one's desire to know. Consequently, man's natural desire in knowledge tends to a definite end. This can be none other than the highest thing knowable, which is God. Therefore the knowledge of God is man's last end.

Now the last end of man and of any intelligent substance is called *happiness* or *beatitude,* for it is this that every intellectual substance desires as its last end, and for its own sake alone. Therefore the last beatitude or happiness of any intellectual substance is to know God.

Hence it is said (*Matt.* v. 8): *Blessed are the clean of heart, for they shall see God; and (Jo. xvii. 3): This is eternal life, that they may know thee, the only true God.* Aristotle himself agrees with this judgment when he says that man's ultimate happiness is *speculative, and this with regard to the highest object of speculation.*[20]

Chapter XXVI

Does Happiness Consist in an Act of the Will?

Since the intellectual substance attains to God by its operation, not only by an act of understanding but also by an act of the will, through desiring and loving Him, and through delighting in Him, someone might think that man's last end and ultimate happiness consists, not in knowing God, but in loving Him, or in some other act of the will towards Him; [1] especially since the object of the will is the good, which has the nature of an end, whereas the

true, which is the object of the intellect, has not the nature of an end except in so far as it also is a good. Therefore, seemingly, man does not attain to his last end by an act of his intellect, but rather by an act of his will.

[2] Further. The ultimate perfection of operation is delight, *which perfects operation as beauty perfects youth,* as the Philosopher says,[21] Hence, if the last end be a perfect operation, it would seem that it must consist in an act of the will rather than of the intellect.

[3] Again. Delight apparently is desired for its own sake, so that it is never desired for the sake of something else; for it is silly to ask of anyone why he seeks to be delighted. Now this is a condition of the ultimate end, namely, that it be sought for its own sake. Therefore, seemingly, the last end consists in an act of the will rather than of the intellect.

[4] Moreover. All agree in their desire of the last end, for it is a natural desire. But more people seek delight than knowledge. Therefore delight would seem to be the last end rather than knowledge.

[5] Furthermore. The will is seemingly a higher power than the intellect, for the will moves the intellect to its act; since when a person wills, his intellect considers by an act what he holds by a habit. Therefore, seemingly, the action of the will is more noble than the action of the intellect. Therefore, it would seem that the last end, which is beatitude, consists in an act of the will rather than of the intellect.

But this can be clearly shown to be impossible.

For since happiness is the proper good of the intellectual nature, it must needs become the intellectual nature according to that which is proper thereto. Now appetite is not proper to the intellectual nature, but is in all things, although it is found diversely in diverse things. This diversity, however, arises from the fact that things are diversely related to knowledge. For things wholly devoid of knowledge have only a natural appetite; those that have a sensitive knowledge have also a sensitive appetite, under which the irascible and concupiscible appetites are comprised; and those which have intellectual knowledge have also an appetite proportionate to that knowledge, namely, the will. The will, therefore, in so far as it is an appetite, is not proper to the intellectual nature, but only in so far as it is dependent on the intellect. On the other hand, the intellect is in itself proper to the intellectual nature. Therefore, beatitude or happiness consists principally and essentially in an act of the intellect, rather than in an act of the will.

Again. In all powers that are moved by their objects, the object is naturally prior to the acts of those powers, even as the mover is naturally prior to the movable being moved. Now the will is such a power, for the appetible object moves the appetite. Therefore the will's object is naturally prior to its act, and consequently its first object precedes its every act. Therefore an act of the will cannot be the first thing willed. But this is the last end, which is beatitude. Therefore beatitude or happiness cannot be the very act of the will.

Besides. In all those powers which are able to reflect on their acts, their act must first bear on some other object, and afterwards the power is brought to bear on its own act. For if the intellect understands that it understands, we must suppose first that it understands some particular thing, and that afterwards it understands that it understands; for this very act of understanding, which the intellect understands, must have an object. Hence either we must go on forever, or if we come to some first thing understood, this will not be an act of understanding, but some intelligible thing. In the same way, the first thing willed cannot be the very act of willing, but must be some other good. Now the first thing willed by an intellectual nature is beatitude or happiness; because it is for its sake that we will whatever we will. Therefore happiness cannot consist in an act of the will.

Further. The truth of a thing's nature is derived from those things which constitute its substance; for a true man differs from a man in a picture by the things which constitute man's substance. Now false happiness does not differ from true in an act of the will; because, whatever be proposed to the will as the supreme good, whether truly or falsely, it makes no difference to the will in its desiring, loving, or enjoying that good: the difference is on the part of the intellect, as to whether the good proposed as supreme be truly so or not. Therefore

beatitude or happiness consists essentially in an act of the intellect rather than of the will.

Again. If an act of the will were happiness itself, this act would be an act either of desire, or love, or delight. But desire cannot possibly be the last end. For desire implies that the will is tending to what it has not yet; and this is contrary to the very notion of the last end.—Nor can love be the last end. For a good is loved not only while it is in our possession, but even when it is not, because it is through love that we seek by desire what we have not; and if the love of a thing we possess is more perfect, this arises from the fact that we possess the good we love. It is one thing, therefore, to possess the good which is our end, and another to love it; for love was imperfect before we possessed the end, and perfect after we obtained possession.—Nor again is delight the last end. For it is possession of the good that causes delight, whether we are conscious of possessing it actually, or call to mind our previous possession, or hope to possess it in the future. Therefore delight is not the last end.—Therefore no act of the will can be happiness itself essentially.

Furthermore. If delight were the last end, it would be desirable for its own sake. But this is not true. For the desirability of a delight depends on what gives rise to the delight, since that which arises from good and desirable operations is itself good and desirable, but that which arises from evil operations is itself evil and to be avoided. Therefore its goodness and desirability are from something else, and consequently it is not itself the last end or happiness.

Moreover. The right order of things agrees with the order of nature, for in the natural order things are ordered to their end without any error. Now, in the natural order delight is for the sake of operation, and not conversely. For it is to be observed that nature has joined delight with those animal operations which are clearly ordered to necessary ends: for instance, to the use of food that is ordered to the preservation of the individual, and to sexual matters, that are appointed for the preservation of the species; since were there no pleasure, animals would abstain from the use of these necessary things. Therefore delight cannot be the last end.

Again. Delight, seemingly, is nothing else than the quiescence of the will in some becoming good, just as desire is the inclining of the will towards the attaining of some good. Now just as by his will a man is inclined towards an end, and rests in it, so too natural bodies have a natural inclination to their respective ends, and are at rest when they have once attained their end. Now it is absurd to say that the end of the movement of a heavy body is not to be in its proper place, but that it is the quiescence of the inclination towards that place. For if it were nature's chief intent that this inclination should be quiescent, it would not give such an inclination; but it gives the inclination so that the body may tend towards its proper place, and when it has arrived there, as though it were its end, quiescence of the inclination follows. Hence this quiescence is not the end, but accompanies the end. Neither therefore is delight the ultimate end, but accompanies it. Much less therefore is happiness any act of the will.

Besides. If a thing have something extrinsic for its end, the operation whereby it first obtains that thing will be called its last end. Thus, for those whose end is money possession is said to be their end, but not love or desire. Now the last end of the intellectual substance is God. Hence that operation of man whereby he first obtains God is essentially his happiness or beatitude. And this is understanding, since we cannot will what we do not understand. Therefore man's ultimate happiness is essentially to know God by the intellect; it is not an act of the will.

From what has been said we can now solve the arguments that were objected in the contrary sense. For it does not necessarily follow that happiness is essentially the very act of the will, from the fact that it is the object of the will, through being the highest good, as the *first argument* reasoned. On the contrary, the fact that it is the first object of the will shows that it is not an act of the will, as appears from what we have said.

Nor does it follow that whatever perfects a thing in any way whatever must be the end of that thing, as the *second objection* argued. For a thing perfects another in two ways: first, it perfects a thing that has its species; secondly, it perfects a thing that it may have its species. Thus the perfection of a house, considered as already having its species, is that to which the species "house" is directed, namely to be a dwelling; for one would not build a house but for that purpose, and consequently we must include this in the definition of a house, if the definition is to be perfect. On the other hand, the perfection that conduces to the species of a house is both that which is directed to the completion of the species, for instance, its substantial principles; and also that which conduces to the preservation of the species, for instance, the buttresses which are made to support the building; as well as those things which make the house more fit for use, for instance, the beauty of the house. Accordingly, that which is the perfection of a thing, considered as already having its species, is its end; as the end of a house is to be a dwelling. Likewise, the operation proper to a thing, its use, as it were, is its end. On the other hand, whatever perfects a thing by conducing to its species is not the end of that thing; in fact, the thing itself is its end, for matter and form are for the sake of the species. For although the form is the end of generation, it is not the end of the thing already generated and having its species, but is required in order that the species be complete. Again, whatever preserves the thing in its species, such as health and the nutritive power, although it perfects the animal, is not the animal's end, but vice versa. And again, whatever adapts a thing for the perfection of its proper specific operations, and for the easier attainment of its proper end, is not the end of that thing, but vice versa; for instance, a man's comeliness and bodily strength, and the like, of which the Philosopher says that they *conduce to happiness instrumentally.*[22]—Now delight is a perfection of operation, not as though operation were directed thereto in respect of its species, for thus it is directed to other ends (thus, eating, in respect of its species, is directed to the preservation of the individual); but it is like a perfection that is conducive to a thing's species, since for the sake of the delight we perform more attentively and becomingly an operation we delight in. Hence the Philosopher says that *delight perfects operation as beauty perfects youth,*[23] for beauty is for the sake of the one who has youth and not *vice versa.*

Nor is the fact that men seek delight not for the sake of something else but for its own sake a sufficient indication that delight is the last end, as the *third objection* argued. Because delight, though it is not the last end, nevertheless accompanies the last end, since delight arises from the attainment of the end.

Nor do more people seek the pleasure that comes from knowledge than knowledge itself. But more there are who seek sensible delights than intellectual knowledge and the delight consequent thereto; because those things that are outside us are better known to the majority, in that human knowledge takes its beginning from sensible objects.

The suggestion put forward by the *fifth argument,* that the will is a higher power than the intellect, as being the latter's motive power, is clearly untrue. Because the intellect moves the will first and *per se,* for the will, as such, is moved by its object, which is the apprehended good; whereas the will moves the intellect accidentally as it were, in so far, namely, as the act of understanding is itself apprehended as a good, and on that account is desired by the will, with the result that the intellect understands actually. Even in this, the intellect precedes the will, for the will would never desire understanding, did not the intellect first apprehend its understanding as a good.—And again, the will moves the intellect to actual operation in the same way as an agent is said to move; whereas the intellect moves the will in the same way as the end moves, for the good understood is the end of the will. Now the agent in moving presupposes the end, for the agent does not move except for the sake of the end. It is therefore clear that the intellect is higher than the will absolutely, while the will is higher than the intellect accidentally and in a restricted sense.

Chapter XXVII

That Human Happiness Does Not Consist in Carnal Pleasures

From what has been said it is clearly impossible that human happiness consists in pleasures of the body, the chief of which are pleasures of the table and of sex.

It has been shown that according to nature's order pleasure is for the sake of operation, and not conversely.[24] Therefore, if an operation be not the ultimate end, the consequent pleasure can neither be the ultimate end, nor accompany the ultimate end. Now it is manifest that the operations which are followed by the pleasures mentioned above are not the last end; for they are directed to certain manifest ends: eating, for instance, to the preservation of the body, and carnal intercourse to the begetting of children. Therefore the aforesaid pleasures are not the last end, nor do they accompany the last end. Therefore happiness does not consist in them.

Again. The will is higher than the sensitive appetite, for it moves the sensitive appetite, as was stated above.[25] But happiness does not consist in an act of the will, as we have already proved.[26] Much less therefore does it consist in the aforesaid pleasures which are seated in the sensitive appetite.

Moreover. Happiness is a good proper to man, for it is an abuse of terms to speak of brute animals as being happy. Now these pleasures are common to man and brute. Therefore we must not assign happiness to them.

The last end is the most noble of things belonging to a reality, for it has the nature of that which is best. But the aforementioned pleasures do not befit man according to what is most noble in him, namely, the intellect, but according to the sense. Therefore happiness is not to be located in such pleasures.

Besides. The highest perfection of man cannot consist in his being united to things lower than himself, but consists in his being united to something above him; for the end is better than that which tends to the end. Now the above pleasures consist in man's being united through his senses to things beneath him, namely, certain sensible things. Therefore we must not assign happiness to such pleasures.

Further. That which is not good unless it be moderate is not good in itself, but receives its goodness from its moderator. Now the use of the aforesaid pleasures is not good for man unless it be moderate; for otherwise they would frustrate one another. Therefore these pleasures are not in themselves man's good. But the highest good is good of itself, because that which is good of itself is better than what is good through another. Therefore such pleasures are not man's highest good, which is happiness.

Again. In all *per se* predications, if A be predicated of B absolutely, an increase in A will be predicated of an increase in B. Thus if a hot thing heats, a hotter thing heats more, and the hottest thing will heat most. Accordingly, if the pleasures in question were good in themselves, it would follow that to use them very much would be very good. But this is clearly false, because it is considered sinful to use them too much; besides, it is hurtful to the body, and hinders pleasures of the same kind. Therefore they are not per se man's good, and human happiness does not consist in them.

Again. Acts of virtue are praiseworthy through being ordered to happiness.[27] If therefore human happiness consisted in the aforesaid pleasures, an act of virtue would be more praiseworthy in acceding to them than in abstaining from them. But this is clearly untrue, for the act of temperance is especially praised in abstinence from pleasures; whence that act takes its name. Therefore man's happiness is not in these pleasures.

Furthermore. The last end of everything is God, as was proved above.[28] We must therefore posit as man's last end that by which especially man approaches to God. Now man is hindered by the aforesaid pleasures from his chief approach to God, which is effected by contemplation, to which these same pleasures are a very great hindrance, since more than anything they plunge man into the midst of sensible things, and consequently withdraw him from intelligible things. Therefore human happiness is not to be placed in bodily pleasures.

Hereby is refuted the error of the Epicureans who ascribed man's happiness to pleasures of this kind. In their person Solomon says (*Eccles.* v. 17): *This therefore hath seemed good to me, that a man should eat and drink, and enjoy the fruit of his labor . . . and this is his portion*; and (*Wis.* ii. 9): *Let us everywhere leave tokens of joy, for this is our portion, and this is our lot.*

The error of the Cerinthians is also refuted. For they *pretended that,* in the state of final happiness, *after the resurrection Christ will reign for a thousand years, and men will indulge in the carnal pleasures of the table. Hence they are called "Chiliastae,"*[29] or believers in the Millennium.

The fables of the Jews and Mohammedans are also refuted, who pretend that the reward of the righteous consists in such pleasures. For happiness is the reward of virtue.

Chapter XXVIII

That Happiness Does Not Consist in Honors

From the foregoing it is also clear that neither does man's highest good, or happiness, consist in honors.

For man's ultimate end and happiness is his most perfect operation, as we have shown above.[30] But man's honor does not consist in something done by him, but in something done to him by another who shows him respect.[31] Therefore man's happiness must not be placed in honors.

Again. That which is for the sake of another good and desirable thing is not the last end. Now such is honor, for a man is not rightly honored, except because of some other good in him. For this reason men seek to be honored, as though wishing to have a voucher for some good that is in them; so that they rejoice more in being honored by the great and the wise. Therefore we must not assign man's happiness to honors.

Besides. Happiness is obtained through virtue. Now virtuous deeds are voluntary, or else they would not be praiseworthy. Therefore happiness must be a good obtainable by man through his will. But it is not in a man's power to secure honor, rather is it in the power of the man who pays honor. Therefore happiness is not to be assigned to honors.

Moreover. Only the good can be worthy of honor, and yet it is possible even for the wicked to be honored. Therefore it is better to become worthy of honor, than to be honored. Therefore honor is not man's supreme good.

Furthermore. The highest good is the perfect good. Now the perfect good is incompatible with any evil. But that which has no evil in it cannot possibly be evil. Therefore that which is in possession of the highest good cannot be evil. Yet it is possible for an evil person to receive honor. Therefore honor is not man's supreme good.

Chapter XXIX

That Man's Happiness Does Not Consist in Glory

Therefore it is evident also that man's supreme good does not consist in glory, which is the recognition of one's good name.

For glory, according to Cicero, is *the general recognition and praise of a person's good name,*[32] and, in the words of Ambrose, consists in *being well known and praised.*[33] Now men seek praise and distinction through being famous, so that they may be honored by those whom their fame reaches. Therefore glory is sought for the sake of honor, and consequently if honor be not the highest good, much less is glory.

Again. Those goods are worthy of praise, whereby a man shows himself to be ordered to his end. Now he who is directed to his end has not yet reached his last end. Therefore praise is not bestowed on one who has reached his last end; rather does he receive honor, as the Philosopher says.[34] Therefore glory cannot be the highest good, since it consists chiefly in praise.

Besides. It is better to know than to be known, because only the higher realities know, whereas the lowest are known. Therefore man's highest good cannot be glory, which consists in a man's being known.

Further. A man does not seek to be known except in good things; in evil things he seeks to be hidden. Therefore, to be known is good and desirable, because of the good things that are known in a man. Therefore these good things are better still. Consequently glory, which consists in a man's being known, is not his highest good.

Moreover. The highest good must needs be perfect, for it satisfies the appetite. But the knowledge of one's good name, wherein glory consists, is imperfect, for it is beset with much uncertainty and error. Therefore glory of this kind cannot be the supreme good.

Furthermore. Man's highest good must be supremely stable in human things, for it is natural to desire unfailing endurance in one's goods. Now glory, which consists in fame, is most unstable, since nothing is more changeable than human opinion and praise. Therefore such glory is not man's highest good.

Chapter XXX

That Man's Happiness Does Not Consist in Wealth

Hence it is evident that neither is wealth man's highest good. For wealth is not sought except for the sake of something else, because of itself it brings us no good, but only when we use it, whether for the support of the body or for some similar purpose. Now the highest good is sought for its own, and not for another's sake. Therefore wealth is not man's highest good.

Again. Man's highest good cannot consist in the possession or preservation of things whose chief advantage for man consists in their being spent. Now the chief advantage of wealth is in its being spent, for this is its use. Therefore the possession of wealth cannot be man's highest good.

Moreover. Acts of virtue deserve praise according as they lead to happiness. Now acts of liberality and magnificence, which are concerned with money, are deserving of praise because of money being spent rather than because of its being kept; and it is from this that these virtues derive their names. Therefore man's happiness does not consist in the possession of wealth.

Besides. Man's highest good must consist in obtaining something better than man. But man is better than wealth, since wealth is something directed to man's use. Therefore man's supreme good does not consist in wealth.

Further. Man's highest good is not subject to fortune.[35] For things that are fortuitous escape the forethought of reason, whereas man has to attain his own end by means of his reason. But fortune occupies the greatest place in the attaining of wealth. Therefore human happiness does not consist in wealth.

Moreover. This is evident from the fact that wealth is lost unwillingly; also because wealth can come into the possession of evil persons, who, of necessity, must lack the highest good. Again because wealth is unstable. Other similar reasons can be gathered from the arguments given above.[36]

Chapter XXXI

That Happiness Does Not Consist in Worldly Power

In like manner, neither can worldly power be man's highest happiness, since in the achievement thereof chance can effect much. Again, it is unstable, and not subject to man's will; and it is often obtained by evil men. These are incompatible with the highest good, as was already stated.[37]

Again. Man is said to be good especially according as he approaches the highest good. But in respect to his having power, he is not said to be either good or evil, since not everyone who can do good deeds is good, nor is a person evil because he can do evil deeds. Therefore the highest good does not consist in being powerful.

Besides. Every power implies reference to something else. But the highest good is not referred to anything further. Therefore power is not man's highest good.

Moreover. Man's highest good cannot be a thing that one can use both well and ill; for the better things are those that we cannot abuse. But one can use one's power both well and ill, for *rational powers can be directed to contrary objects*.[38] Therefore human power is not man's good.

Further. If any power be man's highest good, it must be most perfect. Now human power is most imperfect, for it is based on human will and opinion, which are full of inconstancies. Also, the greater a power is reputed to be, the greater number of people does it depend on; which again conduces to its weakness, since what depends on many is in many ways destructible. Therefore man's highest good does not consist in worldly power.

Consequently man's happiness does not consist in any external good, for all external goods, which are known as *fortuitous goods,* are contained under those we have mentioned.[39]

Chapter XXXII

That Happiness Does Not Consist in Goods of the Body

Like arguments avail to prove that man's highest good does not consist in goods of the body, such as health, beauty and strength. For they are common to good and evil, they are unstable, and they are not subject to the will.

Besides. The soul is better than the body, which neither lives nor possesses these goods without the soul. Therefore, the soul's good, such as understanding and the like, is better than the body's good. Therefore the body's good is not man's highest good.

Again. These goods are common to man and other animals, whereas happiness is a good proper to man.

Therefore man's happiness does not consist in the things mentioned.

Moreover. Many animals surpass man in goods of the body, for some are fleeter than he, some more sturdy, and so on. Accordingly, if man's highest good consisted in these things, man would not excel all animals; which is clearly untrue. Therefore human happiness does not consist in goods of the body.

Chapter XXXIII

That Human Happiness Is Not Seated in the Senses

By the same arguments it is evident that neither does man's highest good consist in goods of his sensitive nature. For these goods, again, are common to man and other animals.

Again. Intellect is superior to sense. Therefore the intellect's good is better than that of the sense. Consequently man's supreme good is not seated in the senses.

Besides. The greatest sensual pleasures are those of the table and of sex, wherein the supreme good must needs be, if seated in the senses. But it does not consist in them. Therefore man's highest good is not in the senses.

Moreover. The senses are appreciated for their utility and for knowledge. Now the entire utility of the senses is referred to the goods of the body. Again, sensitive knowledge is ordered to intellectual knowledge, and hence animals devoid of intellect take no pleasure in sensation except in reference to some bodily utility, in so far as by sensitive knowledge they obtain food or sexual intercourse. Therefore, man's highest good which is happiness is not seated in the sensitive part of man.

Chapter XXXIV

That Man's Ultimate Happiness Does Not Consist in Acts of the Moral Virtues

It is clear that man's ultimate happiness does not consist in moral activities.

For human happiness, if ultimate, cannot be directed to a further end. But all moral activities can be directed to something else. This is clear from a consideration of the principal among them.

Because deeds of fortitude in time of war are directed to victory and peace; for it were foolish to go to war merely for its own sake.[40] Again, deeds of justice are directed to keeping peace among men, for each man possesses with contentment what is his own. The same applies to all the other virtues. Therefore man's ultimate happiness is not in moral deeds.

Again. The purpose of the moral virtues is that through them we may observe the mean in the passions within us, and in things outside us. Now it is impossible that the moderation of passions or of external things be the ultimate end of man's life, since both passions and external things can be directed to something less. Therefore it is not possible that the practice of moral virtue be man's final happiness.

Further. Since man is man through the possession of reason, his proper good, which is happiness, must needs be in accordance with that which is proper to reason. Now that which reason has in itself is more proper to reason than what it effects in something else. Seeing, then, that the good of moral virtue is a good established by reason in something other than itself, it cannot be the greatest good of man which happiness is; rather this good must be a good that is in reason itself.

Moreover. We have already proved that the last end of all things is to become like God.[41] Therefore that in which man chiefly becomes like God will be his happiness. Now this is not in terms of moral actions, since such actions cannot be ascribed to God, except metaphorically; for it is not befitting to God to have passions, or the like, with which moral virtue is concerned. Therefore man's ultimate happiness, which is his last end, does not consist in moral actions.

Furthermore. Happiness is man's proper good. Therefore that good, which of all goods is most proper to man in comparison with other animals, is the one in which we must seek his ultimate happiness. Now this is not the practice of moral virtue, for animals share somewhat either in liberality or in fortitude, whereas no animal has a share in intellectual activity. Therefore man's ultimate happiness does not consist in moral acts.

Chapter XXXV

That Ultimate Happiness Does Not Consist in the Act of Prudence

It is also evident from the foregoing that neither does man's happiness consist in the act of prudence.

For acts of prudence are solely about matters of moral virtue. But human happiness does not consist in the practice of moral virtue.[42] Neither therefore does it consist in the practice of prudence.

Again. Man's ultimate happiness consists in man's most excellent operation. Now man's most excellent operation, in terms of what is proper to man, is in relation to most perfect objects. But the act of prudence is not concerned with the most perfect objects of intellect or reason; for it is not about necessary things, but about contingent practical matters.[43] Therefore its act is not man's ultimate happiness.

Besides. That which is ordered to another as to its end is not man's ultimate happiness. Now the act of prudence is ordered to another as to its end, both because all practical knowledge, under which prudence is comprised, is ordered to operation, and because prudence disposes a man well in choosing means to an end, as may be gathered from Aristotle.[44] Therefore man's ultimate happiness is not in the practice of prudence.

Furthermore. Irrational animals have no share of happiness, as Aristotle proves.[45] Yet some of them have a certain share of prudence, as may be gathered from the same author.[46] Therefore happiness does not consist in an act of prudence.

Chapter XXXVI

That Happiness Does Not Consist in the Practice of Art

It is also evident that it cannot consist in the practice of art.

For even the knowledge of art is practical, and so is directed to an end, and is not the ultimate end.

Besides. The end of the practice of art is the thing produced by art, and such a thing cannot be the ultimate end of human life, since it is rather we who are the end of those products, for they are all made for man's use. Therefore final happiness cannot consist in the practice of art.

Chapter XXXVII

That Man's Ultimate Happiness Consists in Contemplating God

Accordingly, if man's ultimate happiness does not consist in external things, which are called goods of fortune; nor in goods of the body; nor in goods of the soul, as regards the sensitive part; nor as regards the intellectual part, in terms of the life of moral virtue; nor in terms of the intellectual virtues which are concerned with action, namely, art and prudence:—it remains for us to conclude that man's ultimate happiness consists in the contemplation of truth.

For this operation alone is proper to man, and it is in it that none of the other animals communicates.

Again. This is not directed to anything further as to its end, since the contemplation of the truth is sought for its own sake.

Again. By this operation man is united to beings above him, by becoming like them; because of all human actions this alone is both in God and in the separate substances. Also, by this operation man comes into contact with those higher beings, through knowing them in any way whatever.

Besides, man is more self-sufficing for this operation, seeing that he stands in little need of the help of external things in order to perform it.

Further. All other human operations seem to be ordered to this as to their end. For perfect contemplation requires that the body should be disencumbered, and to this effect are directed all the products of art that are necessary for life. Moreover, it requires freedom from the disturbance caused by the passions, which is achieved by means of the moral virtues and of prudence; and freedom from external disturbance, to which the whole governance of the civil life is directed. So that, if we consider the matter rightly, we shall see that all human occupations appear to serve those who contemplate the truth.

Now, it is not possible that man's ultimate happiness consists in contemplation based on the understanding of first principles; for this is most imperfect, as being most universal, containing potentially the knowledge of things. Moreover, it is the beginning and not the end of human inquiry, and comes to us from nature, and not through the pursuit of the truth.

Nor does it consist in contemplation based on the sciences that have the lowest things for their object, since happiness must consist in an operation of the intellect in relation to the most noble intelligible objects. It follows then that man's ultimate happiness consists in wisdom, based on the consideration of divine things.

It is therefore evident also by way of induction that man's ultimate happiness consists solely in the contemplation of God, which conclusion was proved above by arguments.[47]

NOTES

1. Aristotle, *Post. Anal.,* I, 22 (82b 38).
2. Aristotle, *Metaph.,* I a, 2 (994, 6).
3. *C. G.* I, 42.
4. Cf. Aristotle, *Phys.,* II, 8 (198b 12).
5. Aristotle, *Eth.,* I, 1 (1094a 1).
6. Ch. 2.
7. Cf. Aristotle, *Phys.,* II, 5 (196b 11).
8. *De Div. Nom.,* IV, 4 (PG 3, 699).
9. Ch. 17.
10. Aristotle, *Metaph.,* I a, 1 (993b 9).
11. Ch. 17.
12. Ch. 19.
13. *C. G.,* I, 56.
14. *C. G.,* I, 49.
15. Aristotle, *Metaph.,* I, 2 (983a 6).
16. Aristotle, *Eth.,* VI, 2 (1139a 27).
17. Aristotle, *Metaph.,* I, 3 (983a 25).
18. *C. G.,* II, 15.
19. *De Caelo,* I, 8 (277a 18).
20. *Eth.,* X, 7 (1177a 18).
21. *Eth.,* X, 4 (1174b 31).
22. *Eth.,* I, 8 (1099b 2); 9 (1099b 28).
23. *Op. cit.,* X, 4 (1174b 31).
24. Ch. 26.
25. *Ibid.*
26. *Ibid.*
27. Cf. Aristotle, *Eth.,* I, 12 (1101b 14).
28. Ch. 17.
29. St. Augustine, *De Haeres.,* 8 (PL 42, 27).
30. Ch. 25.
31. Cf. Aristotle, *Eth.,* I, 5 (1095b 25).
32. *De Inventione,* II, 55 (p. 150^b).
33. Cf. St. Augustine, *Contra Maximin.,* II, 13 (PL 42, 770).
34. *Eth.,* I. 12 (1101b 24).

35. *Eth.,* I, 9 (1099b 24).
36. Ch. 28ff.
37. Ch. 28ff.
38. Aristotle, *Metaph.,* IX, 2 (1046b 25).
39. Ch. 28ff.
40. Cf. Aristotle, *Eth.,* X, 7 (1177b 9).
41. Ch. 19.

42. Ch. 34.
43. Cf. Aristotle, *Eth.,* VI, 5 (1104a 35).
44. *Op. cit.,* VI, 13 (1145a 6).
45. *Op cit.,* I, 9 (1099b 33).
46. Aristotle, *Metaph.,* I, 1 (980a 30).
47. Ch. 25.

STUDY QUESTIONS

1. Can you act to achieve an end that you believe is bad?
2. Can the human intellect understand God?
3. Can animals be happy?
4. Does luck play any role in achieving happiness?

Natural Law

John Finnis

John Finnis is Professor Emeritus of Law at the University of Oxford. He provides an overview of the core tenets of natural law theory, arguing that the theory provides a firm foundation for making correct moral decisions. Finnis maintains that acting in accord with natural law leads us to respect the basic human goods, such as knowledge, life, health, and friendship, thus leading all human beings to flourish.

I. WHY CALLED 'NATURAL'? WHY CALLED 'LAW'?

In the discourse of ethics, political theory, or *philosophie de droit* (philosophy of law), the claim that there is a natural law is an offer to explain and defend the substance of certain assertions often made in different terms in pre-theoretical discourse (moral argument, politics, and/or law). Pretheoretically (so to speak), choices, actions, and/or dispositions may be said to be 'inhuman', 'unnaturally cruel', 'perverse', or 'morally unreasonable'; proposals, policies, or conduct may be described as violations of 'human rights'; actions of states, groups, or individuals may be described as 'crimes against humanity' and citizens may claim immunity from legal liability or obligations by appealing to a 'higher law'. A natural law theory offers to explain why such assertions can be rationally warranted and true. It offers to do so by locating these assertions in the context of a general theory of good and evil in human life so far as human life is shaped by deliberation and choice.

Such a theory of good and evil can also be called a general theory of right and wrong in human choices and actions. It will contain both (i) normative propositions identifying types of choice, action, or disposition as right or wrong, permissible, obligatory, etc., and (ii) non-normative propositions about the objectivity and epistemological warrant of the normative propositions.

Theorists who describe their account of good and evil, right and wrong, as a 'natural law theory' are not committed to asserting that the normative propositions they defend are 'derived from Nature' or 'read off' or 'inspected in' 'the nature of things'. Indeed, it is rare for a natural law theory to make such assertions, for their sense is deeply obscure; it is difficult, if not impossible, to understand what epistemic or rational processes would be involved in such 'derivation' or 'reading off' or 'inspection in'.

Still less are natural law theorists committed to claiming that the normative propositions they defend stand in some definite relationship to, or are warranted by, the 'laws of nature' in the sense of the

From John Finnis, *Reasons in Action: Collected Essays*, Oxford University Press, 2011. Reprinted by permission of the publisher.

regularities observed, and explanatory factors adduced, by the 'natural sciences' (physics, biology, 'experimental psychology', ecology, etc.). Thomas Aquinas, a leading natural law theorist, sharply differentiates the propositions of moral and political philosophy (in which the principles and norms of natural law are identified and elaborated) from (1) the propositions which constitute the natural sciences, (2) the principles and norms of logic, and what others have called the 'laws of thought', and (3) the principles and norms of any and every human technique of manipulating matter which is subject to our will.[1]

Nor is the typical natural law theory (classical, mediaeval, or contemporary) concerned with any alleged 'state of nature', in the sense of some golden age or state of affairs prior to human wrongdoing or to the formation of human societies or of states or political communities.

As for the term 'law', as understood in the phrase 'natural law', it does not connote that the relevant principles and norms have their directive force precisely as the commands, imperatives, or dictates of a superior will. Even those natural law theorists who argue (as most do) that the most ultimate explanation of those principles and norms (as of all other realities) is a transcendent, creative, divine source of existence, meaning, and value, will also argue that the principles and norms are inherently fitting and obligatory (not fitting or obligatory because commanded), or that the source of their obligation is rather divine wisdom than divine will.

Instead, the term 'law' in the phrase 'natural law' refers to standards of right choosing, standards which are normative (that is, rationally directive and 'obligatory') because they are true and choosing otherwise than in accordance with them is unreasonable.

And the term 'natural' (and related uses of 'by nature', 'in accordance with nature', and 'of nature') in this context signifies any one or more of the following: (a) that the relevant standards (principles and norms) are not 'positive', that is, are directive prior to any positing by individual decision or group choice or convention; (b) that the relevant standards are 'higher' than positive laws, conventions, and practices, that is, provide the premises for critical evaluation and endorsement or justified rejection of or disobedience to such laws, conventions, or practices; (c) that the relevant standards conform to the most demanding requirements of critical reason and are objective, in the sense that a person who fails to accept them as standards for judgment is in error; (d) that adherence to the relevant standards tends systematically to promote human flourishing, the fulfilment of human individuals and communities.

II. CRITIQUE OF SCEPTICISM AND DOGMATISM

Historically, natural law theories have been articulated as part or product of a philosophical critique of ethical scepticisms (whether nihilism, relativism, subjectivism, or hedonism). Since the sceptical views thus criticized and rejected by theorists of natural law (e.g. Plato) or natural right/justice (e.g. Aristotle) were themselves articulated in reaction to uncritically accepted conventions or religiously promoted norms, the philosophical critique of scepticism included a differentiation of the rationally grounded norms of natural law (or natural right) from moral dogmatism or conventionalism.

In contemporary thought, scepticism about natural law (and about other moral theories claiming to be objective or true) is very often based upon a logically illicit and rationally unwarranted inference from certain propositions about what 'is' the case to certain propositions about what is good or obligatory. . . .

Examples of the invalid reasoning commonly encountered today include the following:

> — X is not universally regarded as good/obligatory; therefore X is not good/obligatory.
> — In modern thought ('modernity') X is widely regarded as not good/obligatory; therefore X is not good/obligatory.
> — In contemporary society X is widely regarded as good/obligatory; therefore X is good/obligatory.
> — I have a sentiment of approval of X; therefore X is good (or worthwhile . . . or obligatory . . .), at least for me.

— I have opted for or decided upon or am committed to the practical principle that X ought to be done; therefore X ought to be done, at least by me.

As this list of *non sequiturs* suggests, there is a link between ethical scepticism (at least in its popular forms) and ethical conventionalism. There are many natural law theories, on the other hand, which are not guilty of these or other fallacies, fallacies which consist in concluding to a normative judgment from premises which include no normative proposition. . . .

III. COGNITIVISM AND NATURAL LAW

Not every non-sceptical ethics is appropriately called a natural law theory. Natural law theories are distinguished from the broader set of cognitivist or objectivist ethical theories in four main ways.

First, they are differentiated . . . by their willingness to identify certain basic human goods, such as knowledge, life and health, and friendship, as the core of substantive first principles of practical reasoning. Taken together, these basic human goods give shape and content to a conception of human flourishing and thus, too, to a conception of human nature. For: an axiom of Aristotle's method . . . deployed more generally by Aquinas, shows that while nature is metaphysically (ontologically) fundamental, knowledge of a thing's nature is epistemically derivative: an animate thing's nature is understood by understanding its capacities, its capacities by understanding its activities, and its activities by understanding the objects of those activities. In the case of the human being the 'objects' which must be understood before one can understand and know human nature are the basic goods which are the objects of one's will, i.e. are one's basic reasons for acting and give reason for everything which one can intelligently take an interest in choosing.

Secondly, natural law theories are distinguished from any theory which asserts that moral truths are known essentially by discrete 'intuitions'. Rather, natural law theories contend that specific moral judgments concerning obligation or right are applications or specifications of higher principles. The first principles of the 'system' are known by insight. . . . But the insights whose content is the self-evident principles of practical knowledge are not intuitions—'insights' without data. Rather they are insights whose data are, in the first place, natural and sensory appetites and emotional responses. These data are subsequently enriched by theoretical knowledge or true opinion about possibilities (e.g. about what threatens and enhances health, or about what knowledge is available), and by experience of disharmony (frustrated intentions). . . . The first principles of natural law are not inclinations, but fundamental human goods understood as reasons for action.

Thirdly, natural law theories are distinguished from any fundamentally aggregative conception of the right and the just. For: viable natural law theories postulate no one end to which all human actions might be effective means, no one value in terms of which one might commensurate alternative options as simply better or worse, and no one principle which, without further specification in other principles and norms, should guide deliberation and choice. Rather they claim to identify a number of basic human goods, none of which is simply a means to or simply a part of any other such basic good; they further identify also a number of principles to guide ('morally') the choices necessitated by (i) the variety of basic goods and reasons for action and (ii) the multiple ways of instantiating these goods and acting on these reasons for action by intelligent and creative choice (or indeed by misguided choices whose primary motivation is not reasons but emotion).

Fourthly, natural law theories typically differ from other ethical theories by offering to clarify not only the normative disciplines and bodies of discourse, but also the methods of the descriptive and explanatory social theories (political theory or political science, economics, legal theory . . .). How best can human societies and their formative concepts be understood, without illusions, but in a general way . . . ? Could such projects be 'value-free'? Or must even descriptive-explanatory theorists, in selecting their concepts, rely upon some definite conceptions of what is important in human existence? Must they not use such conceptions as criteria for selecting topics for study and concepts for describing those topics? Must they not also employ such criteria in judging some types and instantiations of human institutions or practices to be the 'central cases' of such institutions or practices, and also in judging some uses of terms such as 'law' or 'constitution' or 'authority' to be, for critical descriptive theory, the 'focal' uses and senses of those terms? And must not such conceptions and criteria of importance be the subject, not of selection by 'demonic' personal preference . . . or silent conformism to academic fashion or political *parti pris,* but rather of an open, public, critical justification? Natural law theories of the classical type, as Aristotle and Aquinas, claim to offer such a justification.[2]

IV. CONCLUSION

. . . [T]heoretical reflection has yielded a more systematic and unifying 'master principle of morality'. This principle is reached by way of the consideration that, so far as it is in one's power, one should allow nothing but the principles corresponding to the basic human goods to shape one's practical thinking.

Aquinas's first principle, 'Good is to be done and pursued and evil avoided', taken as it stands, is not yet moral; it requires only that one not act pointlessly, that is, without reason; it requires only that one take at least one of the principles corresponding to a basic human good and follow through to the point at which one somehow instantiates that good through action. The first *moral* principle makes the stronger demand, not merely that one be reasonable enough to avoid pointlessness, but that one be entirely reasonable in one's practical thinking, choice, and action. It can be formulated: in voluntarily acting for human goods and avoiding what is opposed to them, one ought to choose and otherwise will those and only those possibilities whose willing is compatible with a will toward integral human fulfilment (i.e. the fulfilment of all human persons and communities).

NOTES

1. Aquinas, *Sententia Libri Ethicorum*, prol.
2. On this issue see John Finnis, *Natural Law and Natural Rights* (2nd edn, OUP, 2011), 3–22.

STUDY QUESTIONS

1. What does Finnis mean by "natural law"?
2. Can basic goods, such as knowledge and friendship, ever come into conflict?
3. If human beings were different, would morality be different?
4. Do facts alone ever imply values?

Natural Law

Russ Shafer-Landau

Natural law theory, as its name suggests, relies on nature to dictate the basic human goods. But why suppose that nature and morality converge? Russ Shafer-Landau, Professor of Philosophy at the University of North Carolina at Chapel Hill, argues that they don't. To begin with, what is meant by "natural"? Does the word refer to what is innate in human beings, what they have in common, or what they are designed to do? Furthermore, even if we grant that one of these answers is correct, why should we suppose that what is natural is moral, and what is moral is natural? For example, if violence is natural, is it moral? Or if kindness is moral, is it natural?

THE THEORY AND ITS ATTRACTIONS

You are an animal.

I'm not trying to insult you. Just stating a fact. I am an animal, too. And so is everyone else we know. The basic needs of animals—food, water, security, companionship, freedom from pain—are the basic needs of human beings. All humans, like every other animal, share the same fundamental plight: certain one day to die, and vulnerable to harm in the meantime. Perhaps the key to morality lies in understanding our place in the natural order of things. Many have thought so.

In trying to discover what makes for a good human life, we might take a cue from the rest of the animal kingdom and ask about why their lives go well, when they do. It seems that there is a common answer. Animals live good lives when their nature is fulfilled, and bad lives when it isn't. A race horse, by

nature, is built for speed. English pointers are meant to aid in the hunt. Chameleons naturally blend in with their background. When fillies break a leg, or chameleons cannot camouflage themselves, their lives go poorly. A good pointer will be able to track and give chase; a bad one will sit lazily and ignore nearby prey.

We can extend this sort of thinking even beyond animals. Impurities in a diamond render it flawed. A lake choked with algae is a poor lake. A torn aorta is a bad aorta. And so on.

In each of these cases, nature is dictating the terms of appraisal. The things *in* nature *have* a nature. Such things are bad when they are unnatural, and good to the extent that they fulfill their nature. Perhaps we can say the same thing about human beings.

That is the guiding thought of the natural law theory. By its lights, good human beings are those who fulfill their true nature; bad human beings are those who don't. The moral law is the natural law— the law that requires us to act in accordance with our

From Russ Shafer-Landau, *The Fundamentals of Ethics*, Oxford University Press, 2010. Reprinted by permission of the publisher.

nature. (As we'll see, this is a different kind of natural law from the one that physicists use to describe the workings of molecules or galaxies.) At its most basic, natural law theory tells us that *actions are right just because they are natural, and wrong just because they are unnatural. And people are good to the extent that they fulfill their true nature, bad insofar as they flout it*. . . .

TWO CONCEPTIONS OF HUMAN NATURE

We often voice our approval of actions by declaring them to be perfectly natural, or excuse someone's harmful conduct by saying that it was the natural thing to do under the circumstances. We also condemn certain actions as unnatural, or say of an especially awful act that it was a crime against nature. This all makes excellent sense, on the assumption that natural law theory is true.

The central claim of the theory is that the moral is the natural: The ideal for human beings is to fulfill their nature. Much depends, then, on what our nature really is.

In general terms, human nature is what makes us humans. It is the set of features that is essential to being human, so that if we were to lose these features, we would also lose our humanity. Natural law theorists are committed to the idea that there is a human essence, a set of traits that define us as human beings, and that mark us off as distinct from anything else in the world.

What is the nature of human nature? Here are two familiar—and problematic—answers.

Human Nature Is What Is Innately Human

Innate traits are ones we have from birth. They are natural in the sense of being inborn, natural as opposed to being learned, or acquired from parents and society. In this line of thinking, our true nature is the one we are born with; traits we acquire through socialization are artificial, and stain the purity of our earliest days. . . .

The view that the natural is what is innate is widely held. This is what explains why so many people think that studies of animal behavior, or those focused on human infants, will unlock the key to human nature. The thought is that society is bound to change our natural state, and so we gain the deepest insight into human nature by discovering what we are like before society exerts its influences.

Yet if natural law theory is correct, and if the natural is the very same thing as the innate, then we need to solve the nature/nurture debate before we can know what is right and wrong. And that seems mistaken. We are *very* confident that morality is not a counsel of selfishness, mistrust, and competition, even if we are uncertain about whether such traits are innate. We can be very sure that killing people because of their skin color is immoral, even if we aren't sure whether we have an innate tendency to harm people who don't look like us.

This raises a general point: *The ultimate origins of our impulses are irrelevant to the morality of our actions.* Rape and robbery are immoral, no matter whether the impulse to commit these crimes is innate or acquired. Cheerfully comforting the sick is a good thing, even if we weren't born with a desire to offer such help. Since the morality of our actions and character traits does not depend on whether they are innate or acquired, natural law theorists must look elsewhere for an understanding of human nature.

Human Nature Is What All Humans Have in Common

Many people think that our nature is fixed by those things that we all have in common. These universal human traits would make up the essence of humanity. Such a view lets us scientifically determine our human nature. The data wouldn't always be easy to come by. But with a lot of effort, we could reveal the essence of human nature just by observing the features that every person shares.

There are two problems with such a view. First, there may be no universal human traits. And second, even if there are, they may not provide good moral guidance.

It may seem silly to deny that there are any universal human traits. Doesn't everyone want to have enough food and water to remain alive? Don't all adults have a sex drive? Aren't we all capable, to one degree or another, of complex thinking about our future? Yet some people want to die, not to live; others are indifferent to the attractions of sex; still others are so mentally impaired as to be unable to think at all about their future. For just about any trait (perhaps every trait) that is said to be part of human nature, we can find exceptions that undermine the rule.

Natural law theorists have a reply to this, which is best appreciated by considering an example. Return to the case of nonhuman animals, and think about their nature. For instance, it is part of a buck's nature to be alert to predators, to have four legs, to grow antlers, and to be fawn-colored. Still, there are bucks with only three legs. A few fail to grow antlers; others are deaf to predators; still others are albinos. We might say of such specimens that they aren't really bucks, not fully bucks, or not all that bucks should be.

If that sounds right, then we might adopt the following strategy. Perhaps human nature, like that of nonhuman animals, is determined not by what *every* member of the species shares, but only by what *most* members share. Bucks can have a nature, even if some bucks fail to perfectly live up to it. The same goes for human beings.

But this strategy won't work. There is the difficult problem of setting a threshold. Just how many humans need to have a trait before it qualifies as part of human nature? But leave that aside. The real problem is this: the fact that most humans have a certain trait is morally irrelevant.

Suppose, for instance, that most of us are selfish and vindictive. In this line of thinking, being selfish and vindictive would then be part of human nature. That would make such behavior morally right, on the natural law view. But no natural lawyer accepts that. And they are right to reject such thinking.

Even if everyone, or most of us, were cruel and malicious, that would not make cruelty and malice morally good. Even if people were ordinarily, usually, or typically vindictive and petty, these traits would still be vices, not virtues. The fact that many, most, or all people behave a certain way, or have certain character traits, is not enough to show that such behaviors and traits are morally good. . . .

NATURAL PURPOSES

If human nature is not a matter of the (innate) traits that all or most of us have, then what is it? The answer given by most natural law theorists is this: Human nature is what we are designed to be and to do. It is some function of ours, some purpose that we are meant to serve, some end that we were designed for. . . .

For instance, nature designed our brains to enable us to think, our liver to detoxify our blood, and our pancreas to regulate glucose levels. We can say what mitochondria are for, what the heart and kidneys are meant to do. In each case, there is a purpose that these organs serve, even if no one assigned them this purpose. But that sort of talk doesn't easily translate to human lives. What is a human being *for*? Does the question even make sense?

To answer this question, we need to understand the idea of a natural purpose. Two basic secular accounts might offer some insight. Call the first account the *Efficiency Model,* and the second, the *Fitness Model.*

Consider the Efficiency Model. Sticking with the example of a heart, we can say that pumping blood is its natural purpose, because nothing pumps blood as well as a heart. Hearts have a certain structure that enables them to pump blood more efficiently than anything else in the body. That is why the purpose of a heart is to pump blood.

Human beings can have a function or a purpose, then, if we are more efficient than anything else when it comes to certain tasks. Well, we are. But there are so many of them. We are, for instance, better than anything else at designing puzzles and writing essays. But on this model, natural law theory cannot be correct, given its claim that unnatural action is immoral. For that would mean that we act immorally whenever we are inept at puzzle design or essay writing. We are also far better at building weapons than any other animal, and far more talented at using instruments of torture. But if acting naturally is always morally acceptable, then these actions, if they really are among our natural purposes, are beyond reproach. Something has gone wrong.

If the Efficiency Model is correct—if human nature is given by our natural purposes, and these purposes are whatever we are best able to accomplish—then natural law theory must fail. There are too many such purposes, and many have nothing moral about them. Perhaps the Fitness Model will do better.

On this account, our organs have the purposes they do because it is extremely *adaptive* for them to serve these roles. The natural purpose of the heart, brain, liver and lungs is to do what enhances fitness: roughly, our success at survival and reproduction. We are able to survive, and pass on our genes to our offspring, only because these organs function as well as they do. Nature has designed hearts and kidneys and brains (etc.) to improve our chances of survival. This is their natural purpose; it is ours, too. We are meant to survive, and to transmit our genes to the next generation. That is what a human life is *for*. . . .

Since our natural purposes are survival and procreation, we can see why so many natural law theorists have thought suicide immoral, and have condemned birth control and homosexual activity. We also have a ready explanation of why courage, endurance, and fortitude are true virtues—those who possess them are (in the relevant sense) fitter than those who don't.

Suppose that the natural law theory is true. And suppose that we fulfill our human nature just when we fulfill our natural purposes. Two things follow:

(1) Acting naturally—fulfilling our natural purpose—is always moral.
(2) Acting unnaturally—frustrating our natural purposes—is always immoral.

But if the Fitness Model is correct, then both claims are false.

Claim 1 is false. To see this, recall that natural actions are those in which we use our mind and body to satisfy the purposes they were designed for. In the Fitness Model, these purposes are survival and

reproduction. So natural actions are those that increase the chances of our survival and reproduction. But . . . [s]ometimes those best schooled in treachery, intimidation, and violence are the ones likeliest to live another day. If we understand natural purposes as the Fitness Model advises, then claim 1 is false.

Claim 2 is also false. Not every act that frustrates a natural purpose is immoral. Nature has engineered our ears to be capable of hearing—the better to detect predators, to listen to the advice of our allies, to hear the threats posed by our attackers. But there is nothing immoral about wearing a set of headphones that block out noise. We have eyes so that we can see. But there is nothing wrong with crossing your eyes to make a joke, or closing them to shut out an unwanted sight.

It is worth noting that these examples can be successful even if it is God, and not nature alone, that has endowed us with these various purposes. Suppose that God made eyes to see, ears to hear. Still, isn't it morally acceptable to put on blindfolds, or wear headphones? Despite being "unnatural," these actions are perfectly acceptable.

What this shows is that the Fitness Model is as vulnerable as the Efficiency Model. Neither gives us a solid understanding of what human nature is. Until we are given a better method for determining our nature, the natural law theory is in trouble.

The weakness of the various understandings of human nature allows us to see why a classic moral argument fails. That argument—call it the *Natural Law Argument*—goes like this:

(1) If an act is unnatural, then it is immoral.
(2) Suicide, contraception, and homosexual activity are unnatural.
(3) Therefore suicide, contraception, and homosexual activity are immoral.

The first premise is false on all of the interpretations we have so far considered. Whether unnatural actions spring from acquired traits, rather than innate ones; whether they are rare or unusual, rather than typical or even universal; whether they frustrate nature's purposes rather than conform to them; still, such actions can be morally acceptable.

This does not prove that suicide, contraception, or homosexual activity are morally okay. What it shows, however, is that this popular argument designed to reveal their immorality is highly suspect, and will certainly fail unless we have a better understanding of human nature to rely on. . . .

CONCLUSION

The deep appeal of the natural law theory is its promise to base morality on something clear and unmysterious: nature and its workings. Moral laws, on this account, are just natural laws, though ones that regulate human beings, rather than planets, molecules, or gravitational forces. But as we have seen, it is terribly difficult to try to read off recommendations for how we ought to act from descriptions of how nature actually operates.

And that shouldn't be too surprising. Natural laws describe and predict how things will behave. They summarize the actual behavior of things, and, unless they are statistical laws (of the sort that assign a probability to outcomes, rather than a certainty), they cannot be broken.

Moral laws are different in every respect. They can be broken, and often are. They are not meant to describe how we actually behave, but rather to serve as ideals that we ought to aim for. Nor are they designed to predict our actions, since we so often fall short of meeting the standards they set.

Nature can define the limit of our possibilities. Our nature does not allow us to leap tall buildings in a single bound, or to hold our breath for hours at a time. On the assumption that morality does not demand the impossible of us, nature can, in this way, set the outer bounds of what morality can require. But it can do no more. It cannot, in particular, tell us what we *are* required to do. Nor can it tell us what we are forbidden from trying to achieve. Nature has, at best, only a limited role to play in moral theory.

STUDY QUESTIONS

1. How do moral laws differ from scientific laws?
2. Does the function of your eyes imply what you should be viewing?
3. Do we possess traits that are both innate and immoral?
4. If all human beings share a characteristic, is it necessarily good?

Part VI

KANTIAN ETHICS

Groundwork for the Metaphysics of Morals

Immanuel Kant

Immanuel Kant (1724–1804) was a dominant figure in the history of modern philosophy, making groundbreaking contributions in virtually every area of the subject. He argues that the moral worth of an action is to be judged not by its consequences but by the nature of the maxim or principle that motivated the action. Thus right actions are not necessarily those with favorable consequences but those performed in accord with correct maxims. But which maxims are correct? According to Kant, the only correct ones are those that can serve as universal laws because they are applicable without exception to every person at any time. In other words, you should act only on a maxim that can be universalized without contradiction. Kant refers to his supreme moral principle as the "categorical imperative," categorical because it does not depend on anyone's particular desires, and imperative because it is a command of reason. Kant also claims that the categorical imperative can be reformulated as follows: so act that you treat humanity, whether in your own person or in any other person, always as an end, never merely as a means. In short, treat others as rational beings worthy of respect. To act otherwise, according to Kant, is immoral and irrational.

PREFACE

387 Ancient Greek philosophy was divided into three sciences: *physics, ethics,* and *logic.* This division fits the nature of the subject perfectly and needs no improvement except perhaps to add the principle on which that division rests. By doing this we may be able to guarantee its completeness as well as to determine its necessary subdivisions correctly.

All rational knowledge is either *material* and considers some object or other or *formal,* concerned just with the form of the understanding and the form of reason itself, and with the universal rules of thinking as such, whatever its objects might be. Formal philosophy is called *logic.* Material philosophy, which is concerned with specific objects and their laws, consists of two parts; for those laws are either laws of *nature* or laws of *freedom.* The science of the first is called *physics,* that of the second *ethics.* The former science is also called natural philosophy, the latter moral philosophy.

Logic can have no empirical part, that is, it can have no part in which the universal and necessary laws of thinking are based on facts taken from experience. Otherwise it would not be logic—that is, it would not be an authoritative set of rules for the

From Immanuel Kant, *Groundwork for the Metaphysics of Morals*, translated by Thomas E. Hill Jr. and Arnulf Zweig. Copyright © 2002. Reprinted by permission of Oxford University Press. Minor adjustments to the translation by the editors.

understanding or for reason, rules that are valid, and must be shown to be valid, for all thinking. On the other hand, both natural philosophy and moral philosophy can have an empirical part. The reason is that natural philosophy has to formulate nature's laws in so far as nature is an object of experience, while moral philosophy has to define the laws of the human will, to the extent that the will is affected by nature. Laws of nature are laws according to which everything happens; laws of freedom are laws according to which everything ought to happen, although these laws also weigh the conditions under which what ought to happen very often does not happen.

388

We can call any philosophy that is based on experience *empirical.* We can call it *pure* philosophy if it sets forth its teachings entirely on the basis of a priori principles. When pure philosophy is merely formal, it is called *logic;* but if it is limited to specific objects of the understanding, pure philosophy is then called *metaphysics.*

In this way there arises the idea of a two-fold metaphysics—*a metaphysics of nature* and *a metaphysics of morals.* Thus physics will have an empirical part, but also a rational part; and similarly ethics, although here the empirical part might be given the special title *practical anthropology,* the term *moral philosophy* being properly used to refer just to the rational part.

All professions, handicrafts, and arts have made progress by the division of labour. That is to say, one person can accomplish something most perfectly and easily if he confines himself to a particular job that differs significantly from other jobs in the treatment it requires. Where various tasks are not thus distinguished and divided, where everyone is a jack-of-all-trades, industry remains at a primitive level. It might be worth considering whether pure philosophy, in all its divisions, does not require its own specialist. Perhaps the learned profession as a whole would be better off if a warning were issued—a warning to those who call themselves 'independent thinkers' but who belittle as 'hair-splitters' those who work on the purely rational part of philosophy: For these people are used to marketing a mixture of the empirical and the rational (in various proportions unknown even to themselves, as they pander to the public's taste), but they should be warned against engaging at one and the same time in rational and empirical disciplines, two so different enterprises, involving such different techniques. For each job perhaps requires a special talent and the attempt to combine both in one person produces mere bunglers. Here, however, I ask only whether the nature of science does not require that the empirical part should always be scrupulously separated from the rational one, and that (empirical) physics proper should be prefaced by a metaphysic of nature, while practical anthropology should be prefaced by a metaphysic of morals. Each of these prior sciences must be scrupulously cleansed of everything empirical if we are to know how much pure reason can accomplish in each case and from what sources it can by itself create its own teaching a priori. I leave it an open question whether the latter business is to be conducted by all moralists (whose name is legion) or only by those who feel a calling for the subject.

389

Since my aim here is directed strictly to moral philosophy, I confine the proposed question to this single point. Is it not a matter of utmost importance to forge for once a pure moral philosophy, completely cleansed of everything that may be only empirical and that really belongs to anthropology? That there must be such a philosophy is already evident if one looks at the common idea of duty and of moral laws. For everyone must admit that a law has to carry with it absolute necessity if it is to be morally valid—valid, that is, as a basis of obligation; and everyone must grant that the commandment, 'Thou shalt not lie' could not hold merely for human beings, as if other rational beings had no obligation to abide by it. So it is with all other genuine moral laws. Consequently, the ground of obligation must here be sought, not in the nature of human beings or in facts about the way the world is, but solely a priori in concepts of pure reason. Every other precept, based on principles of mere experience—even a precept that might in a certain sense be considered universal—can indeed be called a practical rule, but never a moral law, so far as it rests even slightly (perhaps only in its motive) on empirical grounds.

Thus moral laws and their principles are essentially different from all the rest of practical knowledge, in which there is some empirical element. Furthermore, the whole of moral philosophy is based entirely on the part of it that is non-empirical, i.e., pure. When applied to man, it does not borrow in the slightest from our knowledge of human beings (i.e., from anthropology). Rather, it prescribes to man, as a rational being, laws a priori. These laws certainly require in addition a power of judgement sharpened by experience, partly in order to distinguish the cases to which they apply, partly to obtain for these laws access to the human will and impetus to their practice. For man, affected by so many inclinations, is indeed capable of grasping the idea of a pure practical reason, but it is not so easy for him to render this idea concretely effective in his conduct of life.

A metaphysic of morals is thus indispensably necessary not merely because one wants to investigate and understand the source of practical principles which are present a priori in our reason, but because morality itself remains subjected to all sorts of corruption as long as this guiding thread, this ultimate norm for correct moral judgement, is lacking. For if any action is to be morally good, it is not enough that it should *conform* to the moral law—it must also be done *for the sake of that law.* Where this is not the case, the conformity is just very coincidental and precarious, since the non-moral ground will now and then produce actions that accord with the law, but it will often produce actions that transgress it. But the moral law in its purity and authenticity (and in the field of action it is precisely this that matters most) can be found nowhere else than in a pure philosophy. Pure philosophy (metaphysics) must therefore come first, and without it there can be no moral philosophy at all. A philosophy that mixes these pure principles with empirical ones does not even deserve to be called philosophy (since philosophy is distinguished from common rational knowledge precisely because it treats in separate sciences what the latter apprehends only in a disordered way). Still less does it deserve to be called moral philosophy, since by this confusion of a priori and empirical principles it spoils the purity of morality itself and works against its own purpose.

It would be a mistake to think that what is here demanded has already been done by the celebrated Wolff in the preparatory study to his moral philosophy—that is, in what he entitles 'Universal Practical Philosophy'—and consequently to think that we do not need to break entirely new ground. Precisely because Wolff's work was supposed to be a universal practical philosophy, it did not take into consideration a special kind of will—a will motivated completely by a priori principles apart from any empirical motives, a pure will, as we might call it. Rather, Wolff's concern was with willing in general, together with all the actions and conditions that belong to volition in this general sense. Because of this it differs from a metaphysic of morals in the same way that general logic differs from transcendental philosophy. General logic sets forth the activities and rules of thinking *in general,* while transcendental philosophy speaks of the special activities and rules of *pure* thinking—that is, of thinking whereby objects are cognized completely a priori. For the metaphysics of morals has to examine the idea and the principles of a possible *pure* will, and not the acts and conditions of human volition generally, which are drawn largely from psychology. The fact that this 'universal practical philosophy' does talk (though quite unjustifiably) of moral laws and duty is no objection to what I am claiming. For the authors of that science remain true to their idea of it in this respect as well: they do not distinguish motives which, as such, are prescribed completely a priori by reason alone and are genuinely moral, from empirical motives which the understanding promotes to general concepts merely by comparison of experiences. On the contrary, without taking into account the difference in their origin they consider motives only as regards to their relative strength or weakness (looking upon all of them as of the same kind) and construct on this basis their concept of *obligation.* This concept is anything but moral; but a concept of that sort is all we can expect from a philosophy which ignores the question of *origin* and fails to decide whether all possible practical concepts are a priori or only a posteriori.

As a prelude to a metaphysics of morals, which I intend to publish someday, I present this *Groundwork.* Strictly speaking, there is no other foundation for a metaphysics of morals than the critique of *pure practical reason,* just as there is no other foundation for metaphysics than the critique of pure speculative reason, which I have already published. But, in the first place, the former critique is not as indispensable as the latter, since even the most ordinary human intelligence can easily be brought to a high degree of correctness and completeness in moral matters, while reason's theoretical but pure employment is, by contrast, totally dialectical. Secondly, I hold that a critique of practical reason, if it is to be complete, must demonstrate the unity of practical and theoretical reason under a single comprehensive principle, since ultimately there can only be one reason which has to be differentiated solely in its application. However, I found that I could not as yet achieve this completeness without bringing up considerations of quite another sort and confusing the reader. This is why I have used the title *Groundwork for the Metaphysics of Morals* rather than *Critique of Pure Practical Reason.*

392 But, in the third place, since a metaphysics of morals, in spite of its frightening title, is capable of a high degree of popularity and appeal to ordinary minds, I think it useful to publish this preliminary work on its foundation separately, so as to avoid having to insert the subtleties unavoidable here into the later, more easily understood work.

The present groundwork, however, aims only to seek out and establish *the supreme principle of morality.* This aim constitutes a complete project all by itself and must be kept separate from every other moral investigation. It is true that my claims about this central question, a question so important and yet until now so inadequately debated, would be greatly clarified by seeing the application of that supreme principle to the whole system, and they would be strongly confirmed by the adequacy the principle would manifest throughout. All the same, I had to forgo this advantage, which in any case would be more flattering to myself than helpful to others. For the convenience of a principle in use and its apparent adequacy do not constitute a secure proof of its correctness. They rather awaken a certain bias against examining and weighing it rigorously and independently of its consequences.

The method I have adopted in this book is, I believe, one which will work best if we proceed analytically from common knowledge to the formulation of its supreme principle and then back again synthetically from an examination of this principle and its origins to the common knowledge in which we find its application. Hence the division turns out to be as follows:

(1) Chapter One: Passage from the common rational knowledge of morality to the philosophical.
(2) Chapter Two: Transition from popular moral philosophy to a metaphysic of morals.
(3) Chapter Three: Final step from a metaphysic of morals to critique of pure practical reason.

CHAPTER ONE

393

Passage from the Common Rational Knowledge of Morality to the Philosophical

It is impossible to imagine anything at all in the world, or even beyond it, that can be called good without qualification—except a *good will.* Intelligence, wit, judgement, and the other mental talents, whatever we may call them, or courage, decisiveness, and perseverance, are, as qualities of *temperament,* certainly good and desirable in many respects; but they can also be extremely bad and harmful when the will which makes use of these *gifts of nature* and whose specific quality we refer to as *character,* is not good. It is exactly the same with *gifts of fortune.* Power, wealth, honour, even health and that total well-being and contentment with one's condition which we call '*happiness,*' can make a person bold but consequently often reckless as well, unless a good will is present to correct their influence on the mind, thus adjusting the whole principle of one's action to render it conformable to universal ends. It goes without saying that the sight of a creature enjoying uninterrupted prosperity, but never feeling the slightest pull of a pure and good will, cannot excite approval in a rational and impartial spectator. Consequently, a good will seems to constitute the indispensable condition even of our worthiness to be happy.

Some qualities, even though they are helpful to this good will and can make its task very much easier, nevertheless have no intrinsic unconditional worth. Rather, they presuppose a good will which puts limits on the esteem in which they are rightly held and forbids us to regard them as absolutely good. Moderation in emotions and passions, self-control, and sober reflection are not only good in many respects: they may even seem to constitute part of the inner worth of a person. Yet they are far from being properly described as good without qualification (however unconditionally they were prized by the ancients). For without the principles of a good will those qualities may become exceedingly bad; the passionless composure of a villain makes him not merely more dangerous but also directly more detestable in our eyes than we would have taken him to be without it.

A good will is not good because of its effects or accomplishments, and not because of its adequacy to achieve any proposed end: it is good only by virtue of its willing—that is, it is good in itself. Considered in itself it is to be treasured as incomparably higher than anything it could ever bring about merely in order to satisfy some inclination or, if you like, the sum total of all inclinations. Even if it were to happen that, because of some particularly unfortunate face or the miserly bequest of a step-motherly nature, this will were completely powerless to carry out its aims: if with even its utmost effort it still accomplished nothing, so that only good will itself remained (not, of course, as a mere wish, but as the summoning of every means in our power), even then it would still, like a jewel, glisten in its own right, as something that has its full worth in itself. Its utility or ineffectuality can neither add to nor subtract from this worth. Utility would be merely, as it were, its setting, enabling us to handle it better in our ordinary dealings or to attract to it the attention of those who are not yet experts, but not why we recommend it to experts and determine its worth.

Yet there is something so strange in this idea of the absolute worth of a mere will, all utility being left out of account, that, in spite of all the agreement this idea receives even from common reason, the suspicion must arise that perhaps its hidden basis is merely some high-flown fantasy, and that we may have misunderstood the purpose of nature in appointing reason as ruler of our will. Let us therefore examine this idea from this perspective.

In the natural constitution of an organized being—that is, a being properly equipped for life—we take it as a principle that no instrument for any purpose will be found in that being unless it is also the most appropriate and best adapted for that purpose. Now if nature's real purpose for a being possessed of reason and a will were its *preservation*, its *welfare*, or in a word its *happiness*, then nature would have hit on a very bad arrangement if it assigned the creature's reason the job of carrying out this purpose. For all the actions this creature has to perform with this end in view, and the whole rule of its conduct, would have been disclosed to it far more precisely by instinct; and the end in question could have been attained far more surely by instinct than it ever could be by reason. If, in that case, reason had been given to this favoured creature additionally, its service would have been only to contemplate the fortunate constitution of the creature's nature, to admire it, enjoy it, and be grateful to its beneficent Cause. But reason would not have been given in order that this creature would subject its faculty of desire to such feeble and defective guidance or to meddle incompetently with nature's purpose. In a word, nature would have prevented reason from striking out into a practical use and from presuming, with its feeble insights, to think out for itself a plan for happiness and for the means of attaining it. Nature would herself have taken over not only the choice of ends but also that of means, and would with wise foresight have entrusted both to instinct alone.

And in fact we do find that the more one devotes one's cultivated reason to the enjoyment of life and happiness, the further away does one get from true contentment. This is why a certain degree of *misology,* i.e., hatred of reason, arises in many people, including those who have been most tempted by this use of reason, if only they are candid enough to admit it. For, according to their calculation of all the benefits they draw—I will not say from the invention of all the arts of common luxury but even from the sciences (which in the final analysis seem to them to be only luxury of the understanding)—they find that

396 instead of gaining in happiness they have in fact only brought more trouble on their heads. They therefore come to envy, rather than despise, more ordinary people, who are closer to being guided by mere natural instinct and who do not let their reason have much influence on conduct. To this extent we must admit that the judgement of those who seek to moderate—and even to reduce below zero—the boasting glorification of benefits that reason is supposed to provide in the way of happiness and contentment with life, is by no means morose or ungrateful for the kindness of the world's ruler. That judgement rather is based on the idea that our existence has another and much worthier purpose, for which, and not for happiness, our reason is properly intended, an end which, therefore, is the supreme condition to which our private ends must for the most part be subordinated.

For since reason is not sufficiently competent to guide the will safely with regard to its objects and the satisfaction of all our needs (which it in part even multiplies)—a goal to which an implanted natural instinct would have led us much more certainly—and since reason is nevertheless given to us as a practical faculty—that is, as one which is supposed to influence the will; since, finally, reason was absolutely necessary for this purpose, as nature has everywhere distributed her abilities so as to fit the functions they are to perform; reason's true vocation must therefore be to produce a *will* which is *good in itself,* not just *good as a means* to some further end. Such a will must not be the sole and complete good, but it must be the highest good and the condition of all the rest, even of all our longing for happiness. In that case it is entirely compatible with the wisdom of nature that the cultivation of reason, which is required for the former unconditional purpose, may in many ways, at least in this life, restrict the attainment of the second, conditional purpose—happiness—and indeed that it can even reduce it to less than nothing. Nor does nature here violate its own purpose, for reason, which recognizes as its highest practical vocation the establishment of a good will, is capable only of its own peculiar kind of satisfaction—satisfaction from fulfilling a purpose which reason alone determines, even if this fulfilment damages the ends of inclination.

We must thus develop the concept of a will estimable in itself and good apart from any further aim. This concept is already present in the natural, healthy mind, which requires not so much instruction as merely clarification. It is this concept that always holds the highest place in estimating the total worth of our actions and it constitutes the condition of all the rest. Let us then take up the concept of *duty,* which includes that of a good will, the latter however being here under certain subjective limitations and obstacles. These, so far from hiding a good will or disguising it, rather bring it out by contrast and make it shine forth more brightly. 397

I will here omit all actions already recognized as opposed to duty, even if they may be useful from this or that perspective; for about these it makes no sense even to ask the question whether they might have been done *out of duty* since they are directly opposed to it. I will also set aside actions that in fact accord with duty, yet for one has no *direct inclination,* but which one performs because impelled to do so by some other inclination. For in such a case it is easy to decide whether the action [which accords with duty] was done *out of duty* or for some self-interested goal. This distinction is far more difficult to perceive when the action accords with duty but the agent has in addition a *direct* inclination to do it. For example, it is certainly in accord with duty that a shopkeeper should not overcharge an inexperienced customer; and, where there is much business, a prudent merchant refrains from doing this and maintains a fixed general price for everybody, so that a child can buy from him just as well as anyone else. People thus get *honest* treatment. But this is not nearly enough to justify our believing that the shopkeeper acted in this way out of duty or from principles of honesty; his interests required him to act as he did. We cannot assume him to have in addition a direct inclination towards his customers, leading him, as it were out of love, to give no one preferential treatment over another person in the matter of price. Thus the action was done neither out of duty nor from immediate inclination, but solely out of self-interest.

On the other hand, it is a duty to preserve one's life, and every one also has a direct inclination to do it.

But for that reason the often-fearful care that most people take for their lives has no intrinsic worth, and the maxim of their action has no moral merit. They do protect their lives *in conformity with duty,* but not *out of duty.* If, by contrast, disappointments and hopeless misery have entirely taken away someone's taste for life; if that wretched person, strong in soul and more angered at fate than fainthearted or cast down, longs for death and still preserves life without loving it—not out of inclination or fear but out of duty—then indeed that person's maxim has moral worth.

It is a duty to help others where one can, and besides this many souls are so compassionately disposed that, without any further motive of vanity or self-interest, they find an inner pleasure in spreading joy around them, taking delight in the contentment of others, so far as they have brought it about. Yet I maintain that, however dutiful and kind an action of this sort may be, it still has no genuinely moral worth. It is on a level with other inclinations—for example, the inclination to pursue honour, which if fortunate enough to aim at something generally useful and consistent with duty, something consequently honourable, deserves praise and encouragement but not esteem. For its maxim lacks the moral merit of such actions done not out of inclination but out of *duty.* Suppose then that the mind of this humanitarian were overclouded by sorrows of his own which extinguished all compassion for the fate of others, but that he still had the power to assist others in distress; suppose though that their adversity no longer stirred him, because he is preoccupied with his own; and now imagine that, though no longer moved by any inclination, he nevertheless tears himself out of this deadly apathy and does the action without any inclination, solely out of duty. Then for the first time his action has its genuine moral worth. Furthermore, if nature had put little sympathy into this or that person's heart; if he, though an honest man, were cold in temperament and indifferent to the sufferings of others—perhaps because he has the special gifts of patience and fortitude in his own sufferings and he assumes or even demands the same of others; if such a man (who would in truth not be the worst product of nature) were not exactly fashioned by nature to be a humanitarian, would he not still find in himself a source from which he might give himself a worth far higher than that of a good-natured temperament? Assuredly he would. It is precisely in this that the worth of character begins to show—a moral worth, and incomparably the highest—namely, that he does good, not out of inclination, but out of duty.

To secure one's own happiness is a duty (at least indirectly); for discontent with one's condition when pressed by many cares and amidst unsatisfied needs might easily become a *great temptation to transgress one's duties.* But even apart from duty, all human beings already have by their own nature the strongest and deepest inclination towards happiness, because it is precisely in this idea that all the inclinations come together. The prescription for happiness is, however, often so constituted that it greatly interferes with some inclinations, and yet we cannot form a precise conception of the satisfaction of all inclinations as a sum, the conception to which we give the name "happiness". Hence it is not surprising that a single inclination, well defined as to what it promises and as to the time at which it can be satisfied, may outweigh a fluctuating idea; so, for example, a man who suffers from gout, may choose to enjoy whatever he likes and put up with what he must—because according to his calculations he has at least not sacrificed the enjoyment of the present moment to some possibly groundless expectations of happiness allegedly attached to health. But even in this case, if the universal inclination to happiness has failed to determine his will, and if good health, at least for him, did not enter into his calculations, what would remain, as in other cases, is a law—the law that he ought to promote his happiness, not out of inclination, but out of duty. And only from this law would his conduct begin to have real moral worth.

It is doubtless in this sense that we should understand too the passages from Scripture in which we are commanded to love our neighbour and even our enemy. For love as inclination cannot be commanded; but kindness done out of duty—although no inclination impels us, and even although natural and unconquerable aversion stands in our way—is *practical love,* not *pathological love.* It resides in the will and not in the partiality of feeling, in principles

398

399

of action and not in melting compassion; and it is this practical love alone that can be commanded.

The second proposition[1] is this: The moral worth of an action done out of duty has its moral worth, not *in the objective* to be reached by that action, but in the maxim in accordance with which the action is decided upon; it depends, therefore, not on actualizing the object of the action, but solely on the *principle of volition* in accordance with which the action was done, without any regard for objects of the faculty of desire. It is clear from our previous discussion that the objectives we may have in acting, and also our actions' effects considered as ends and as what motivates our volition, can give to actions no unconditional or moral worth. Where then can this worth be found if not in the willing of the action's hoped for effect? It can be found nowhere but *in the principle of the will,* irrespective of the ends that can be brought about by such action. For the will stands, so to speak, at the crossroads between its a priori principle, which is formal, and its a posteriori motivation, which is material; and since it must be determined by something, it will have to be determined by the formal principle of volition, since every material principle is ruled out when an action is done out of duty.

The third proposition, which follows from the two preceding, I would express in this way: *Duty is the necessity of an act done out of respect for the law.* While I can certainly have an *inclination* for an object that results from my proposed action, I can never *respect* it, precisely because it is nothing but an effect of a will and not its activity. Similarly I cannot respect any inclination whatsoever, whether it be my own inclination or that of another. At most I can approve of that towards which I feel an inclination, and occasionally I can like the object of somebody else's inclination myself—that is, see it as conducive to my own advantage. But the only thing that could be an object of respect (and thus a commandment) for me is something that is conjoined with my will purely as a ground and never as a consequence, something that does not serve my inclination but overpowers it or at least excludes it entirely from my decision-making— consequently, nothing but the law itself. Now if an action done out of duty is supposed to exclude totally

the influence of inclination, and, along with inclination, every object of volition, then nothing remains that could determine the will except objectively *the law* and subjectively *pure respect* for this practical law. What is left therefore is the maxim,[2] to obey this sort of law even when doing so is prejudicial to all my inclinations.

Thus the moral worth of an action depends neither on the result expected from that action nor on any principle of action that has to borrow its motive from this expected result. For all these results (such as one's own pleasurable condition or even the promotion of the happiness of others) could have been brought about by other causes as well. It would not require the will of a rational being to produce them, but it is only in such a will that the highest and unconditional good can be found. That pre-eminent good which we call "moral" consists therefore in nothing but *the idea of the law* in itself, which certainly *is present only in a rational being*—so far as that idea, and not an expected result, is the determining ground of the will. And this pre-eminent good is already present in the person who acts in accordance with this idea; we need not await the result of the action in order to find it.[3]

But what kind of law can it be, the idea of which must determine the will, even without considering the expected result, if that will is to be called good absolutely and without qualification? Since I have robbed the will of every inducement that might arise for it from its obeying any particular law, the only thing remaining that could serve the will as a principle is the universal conformity of actions to law as such. That is, I ought never to act in such a way *that I could not also will that my maxim should become a universal law.* Here it is the mere conformity to law as such (without presupposing any law prescribing particular actions) that serves the will as its principle, and must so serve it if duty is not to be a totally empty delusion and a chimerical concept. Common human reason, when engaged in making practical judgements, also agrees with this completely and has that principle constantly in view.

Suppose, for example, the question is this: May I, when in distress, make a promise with the intention not to keep it? Here I easily distinguish the different

400

401

402

meanings this question can have, whether it is prudent to make a false promise, or whether it is in accord with duty. The first no doubt can often be the case. Of course I see that [even for prudence] it is not enough just to extricate myself from my present predicament by means of this deception; I need to consider whether this lie might give rise to even greater troubles than those from which I am escaping, since, for all my supposed *cunning,* it is not so easy to foresee all the consequences, e.g., the loss of trust may cost me more than all the misfortune I am now trying to avoid. I must consider therefore whether it might be *more* prudent for me to act on a general maxim and make it a habit to issue a promise only when I intend to keep it. But it is soon clear to me that such a maxim is always based solely on fear of consequences. To tell the truth out of duty is something entirely different from telling the truth out of fear of troublesome consequences; for in the first case the concept of the action itself already contains a law for me, while in the second case I must first look around to see how I am likely to be affected by the action. For deviating from the principle of duty is quite certainly bad; but deserting my prudential maxim can often be greatly to my advantage, though it is admittedly safer to stick to it. If, on the other hand, I want to find out most quickly but unerringly the answer to a different question—whether a deceitful promise accords with duty—I must ask myself 'Would I really be content if my maxim (the maxim of getting out of a difficulty by making a false promise) were to hold as a universal law (one valid both for myself and for others)?' And could I really say to myself, 'Let everyone be allowed to make a false promise if they find themselves in difficulties from which there is otherwise no escape'? I immediately see that I can indeed will the lie, but I cannot will a universal law to lie. For with such a law, there would actually be no promising at all, since it would be futile for me to allege my intentions with regard to some future actions to others who would not believe me, or who, if they did so over-hastily, would pay me back in the same coin. Consequently my maxim, as soon as it became a universal law, would necessarily subvert itself.

Thus I need no far-reaching acuteness to know what I have to do in order that my volition can be morally good. Inexperienced in the ways of the world and incapable of anticipating all its actual events, I ask myself only, 'Can you will that your maxim become a universal law?' If not, that maxim must be repudiated, and not because of any impending disadvantage to you or even to others, but because it cannot fit as a principle into a possible universal legislation, and reason forces me to offer my immediate respect to such legislation. As yet I have no *insight* into the grounds of that respect (something the philosopher may investigate), but I do at least understand this much: it is the appreciation of something whose worth far exceeds all the worth of anything favoured by inclination. I understand too that the necessity that I act out of *pure* respect for the practical law is what constitutes duty. To duty every other motive must give way, because it is the condition of a will good *in itself,* whose worth transcends all else.

Considering the moral knowledge of common human reason we have thus arrived at its principle, a principle it admittedly does not think about abstractly in such a universal formulation; but which it really does always have in view and employs as the standard in its judging. It would be easy to show here how common human reason, with this compass in hand, knows very well how to distinguish what is good or evil, consistent or inconsistent with duty, in all cases that present themselves. Without attempting to teach it anything new, one merely has to make reason attend, as Socrates did, to its own principle. Therefore neither science nor philosophy is needed in order for us to know what one has to do to be honest and good, and even to be wise and virtuous. This is something that we could have suspected from the start: that knowledge of what it is incumbent upon everyone to do, and so also to know, would be attainable by everyone, even the most ordinary human being. Here we cannot help but be impressed when we notice the great advantage that the power of practical judgement has over theoretical judgement, in the minds of ordinary people. In theoretical judgements, if common reason dares to go beyond the laws of experience and the perceptions of the senses, it falls into sheer inconceivabilities and self-contradictions, or at least into a chaos of uncertainty, obscurity, and vacillation. On the practical side, however, the power of judgement first begins to look its best when the ordinary mind excludes all sensuous motives from its practical laws. The ordinary mind then becomes even subtle—perhaps vexing itself with its conscience or with other claims regarding what is to be called "right", or trying to determine honestly for its own instruction the worth of various actions. But what is most important, the common understanding has, in the latter case, as good a chance of hitting the mark as any philosopher has. Indeed its chances are almost better than a philosopher's, since the latter's judgement has no principle different from that of ordinary intelligence, and a philosopher's judgement may easily be confused by a mass of strange and irrelevant considerations and caused to turn from the right path. Would it not be wise therefore to accept the judgement of common reason in moral matters, or to bring in philosophy at most to make the system of morals more complete and comprehensible and to present its rules in formulations more convenient to use (especially in disputation)—but not to lead the common human understanding away from its happy simplicity in matters of action and set it on a new path of inquiry and instruction?

405   A wonderful thing about innocence—but also something very bad—is that it cannot defend itself very well and is easily led astray. For this reason even wisdom—which otherwise is more a matter of acting than knowing—also needs science, not in order to learn from it, but in order to gain access and durability for what it prescribes. Human beings feel within themselves a powerful counterweight opposed to all the commandments of duty, which reason portrays as so worthy of esteem: the counterweight of needs and inclinations, whose total satisfaction people sum up under the name 'happiness'. But reason, without promising anything to inclination, dictates its prescriptions relentlessly, thus treating with neglect and contempt those blustering and seemingly legitimate claims (which refuse to be suppressed by any commandment). From this there arises a *natural dialectic*—that is, a tendency to quibble with these strict laws of duty, to cast doubt on their validity or at least on their purity and strictness, and, if possible, to make them conform better to our wishes and inclinations. This means

corrupting their very foundations and destroying their dignity—a result that even common practical reason cannot ultimately endorse.

In this way *common human reason* is driven, not by any cognitive need (which never touches it so long as it is content to be mere sound reason), but on practical grounds, driven to leave its own sphere and take a step into the field of *practical philosophy*. There it seeks instruction and precise direction as to the source of its own principle and about the correct function of this principle in contrast with maxims based on need and inclination. It ventures into philosophy so as to escape from the perplexity caused by conflicting claims and so as to avoid the risk of losing all genuine moral principles through the obscurity into which it easily falls. Thus, just as happens in its theoretical use, a *dialectic* arises unnoticed when practical common reason is cultivated, and it is forced to seek help in philosophy. As with the theoretical use of reason, the conflict will be resolved only by a thorough critical examination of our reason.

CHAPTER TWO

406

Transition from Popular Moral Philosophy to a Metaphysics of Morals

Although we have drawn our previous concept of duty from the common use of our practical reason, this by no means implies that we have treated it as a concept derived from experience. On the contrary, if we pay attention to our experience of what human beings do and fail to do, we encounter frequent and, I must admit, justified complaints that one cannot in fact point to any sure examples of the disposition to act out of pure duty. Thus we hear the charge that, although many things may be done that are in accord with what duty commands, it still remains doubtful whether those actions are really done out of duty, and doubtful therefore whether they have moral worth. That is why there have always been philosophers who absolutely denied the reality of this disposition in human conduct and ascribed everything we do to more or less refined self-love. But those philosophers have not denied the correctness of the concept of morality. Rather, they have spoken with sincere regret of the frailty and corruption of human nature, noble enough to fake as its rule an Idea so worthy of respect, but at the same time too weak to follow it, so that reason, which should serve as the law-giver to human nature, is used only to serve the interests of our inclinations, either singly or, at most, to maximize their compatibility. It is in fact absolutely impossible to identify by experience, with complete certainty, a single case in which the maxim of an action—an action that accords with duty—was based exclusively on moral reasons and the thought of one's duty. There are cases when the most searching self-examination comes up with nothing but duty as the moral reason that could have been strong enough to move us to this or that good action or to some great sacrifice. But we cannot conclude from this with certainty that the real determining cause of our will was not some secret impulse of self-love, disguising itself as that Idea of duty. So we like to flatter ourselves with the false claim to a nobler motive but in fact we can never, even with the most rigorous self-examination, completely uncover our hidden motivations. For when moral worth is the issue, what counts is not the actions which one sees, but their inner principles, which one does not see.

Furthermore, there is no better way to serve the interests of those who mock all morality as a mere phantom of the brain, an illusion with which, out of vanity, the human imagination puffs itself up, than to concede that concepts of duty must be drawn solely from experience (as people find it only too easy to believe about all other concepts). For by conceding this we prepare an assured victory for those scoffers. Out of charity I am willing to grant that most of our actions are in accord with duty; but if we look more closely at the devising and striving that lies behind them, then everywhere we run into the dear self which is always there; and it is this and not the strict command of duty (which would often require self-denial) that underlies our intentions. One need not be an enemy of virtue but only a dispassionate observer who does not immediately confuse even the liveliest wish for goodness with its reality, to become doubtful at certain moments whether any genuine virtue can really be found in the world. (Such doubts occur particularly as one grows older and experience renders one's power of judgement and observation shrewder and more discerning.) And at that point only one thing can protect us against a complete abandonment of our Ideas of duty, or can preserve in us a well-founded respect for its law: the clear conviction that even if there never were any actions springing from such pure sources, the question at issue here is not whether this or that actually occurs. The question is rather whether reason, by itself and independently of all appearances, commands what ought to be done, actions of which the world has perhaps never until now provided an example—actions whose feasibility might well be doubted by those who rest everything on experience—which are nevertheless commanded inexorably by reason. For example, the duty to be totally sincere in one's friendships can be demanded of everyone even if up to now there may never have existed a totally sincere friend. For this duty, as duty in general, lies prior to all experience in the Idea of a power of reason which determines the will by a priori grounds.

Unless we wish to deny to the concept of morality all truth and all application to a possible object, we must grant that its law is so broad in meaning that it must be valid not merely for human beings, but for all rational beings as such, and valid not merely under contingent conditions and subject to exceptions, but with absolute necessity. It is therefore clear that no experience could warrant even the possibility of such absolutely certain and necessary laws. For by what right can we make something that is perhaps valid only under the contingent human conditions into an object of unlimited respect and view it as universally prescribed for every rational creature? And how could laws for determining our will be taken as laws for determining the will of rational beings in general—and only on that account laws for determining our will—if these laws were merely empirical and did not have their source completely a priori in pure, but practical, reason?

Nor could one give morality worse advice than by trying to derive it from examples. For every example of morality presented to me must itself first be assessed with moral principles to see whether it deserves to be used as an original example, i.e., as a model. By no means can it have the authority to give us the concept of morality. Even the Holy One of the Gospels must first be compared with our ideal of moral perfection before we can acknowledge Him to be such. Even He says of Himself: 'Why do you call Me (whom you see) good? There is none good (the archetype of the good) but the one God alone (whom you do not see).' But where do we get the concept of 409 God as the highest good? Only from the *Idea* of moral perfection which reason designs a priori and connects inseparably with the concept of a free will. Imitation has no place in moral matters, and examples serve us only for encouragement—that is, they set beyond doubt the feasibility of doing what the law commands and they make perceptible what the law prescribing conduct expresses in more general terms; but examples can never justify our guiding our selves by examples and setting aside their true origin which resides in reason.

If, then, there is no genuine supreme principle of morality that is not grounded on pure reason alone, independently of all experience, I think it should be unnecessary even to ask whether it is desirable to exhibit these concepts in general (abstractly)—these concepts which, together with their corresponding principles, hold a priori, in so far as knowledge which establishes this is to be distinguished from common knowledge and described as philosophical. But nowadays it may well be necessary to raise this question. For if we took a vote on which is to be preferred, pure rational knowledge detached from everything empirical—that is to say, a metaphysic of morals—or popular practical philosophy, we can easily guess on which side the majority would stand.

It is certainly most commendable to descend to the level of folk concept once the ascent to the principles of pure reason has been satisfactorily completed. This ascent could be described as first *grounding* moral philosophy on metaphysics and subsequently, when moral philosophy has been established, winning *acceptance* for it by giving it a popular character. But it is utterly absurd to aim at popularity in our first investigation, on which the whole correctness of our principles depends. Not only can such a procedure never lay claim to the extremely rare merit of *truly philosophical popularity.* since it takes no skill to be generally

understandable once one renounces all thorough probing: what that popularizing produces is a disgusting mishmash of second-hand observations and half-reasoned principles. Empty-headed people regale themselves with this, because it is something useful in everyday chitchat. More insightful people, on the other hand, are confused by it and avert their eyes, dissatisfied but not knowing how to help themselves. They turn away, but philosophers who see through this deception gel little hearing if they urge those moralists to postpone this so-called popularizing for a while until the 410 achievement of some definite insight earns them the right to be popular.

We need only look at essays on morality written in this fashionable style. What we run into is a marvellous medley—now the talk is of the particular vocation of human nature (but along with this also the Idea of a rational nature as such), now they talk of perfection, now of happiness, here moral feeling and there the fear of God; a little of this and a little of that. But it never occurs to anyone to ask whether the principles of morality are to be sought at all in our knowledge of human nature (which we can get only from experience); nor does it occur to them that if this is not so—if these principles are to be found completely a priori and free from empirical elements in concepts of pure reason and absolutely nowhere else, even to the slightest extent—they had better pursue the latter investigation altogether separately, as pure practical philosophy, or (if one may use a word so much vilified) as a metaphysics[4] of morals. They do not see that this investigation must be completed entirely by itself and that the public, which demands popularity, should be put off until the outcome of this undertaking is at hand.

Nevertheless, such a completely isolated metaphysics of morals, mixed with no anthropology, no theology, no physics or hyperphysics, still less with occult qualities (which one might call 'hypophysical'), is not only an indispensable underlying support for all theoretical and precisely defined knowledge of duties; it is also something to be desired and of the utmost importance for the actual fulfilment of moral precepts. For the pure thought of duty and of the moral law generally, unmixed with any additional empirical

411 inducements, has an influence on the human heart much more powerful than all other motivations[5] that may arise from the field of experience, so much so that reason, conscious of its own dignity, despises these and is able gradually to become their master. The thought of duty and the moral law has this influence through reason alone (and reason first learns from this that by itself it is able to be practical [as well as theoretical]). A mixed moral theory, on the other hand, compounded of motives derived from feeling or inclination and also of rational concepts, must make the mind vacillate between [different] sources of motivation that cannot be brought under any single principle and that can guide us only by sheer accident to the good, and often to the evil.

From what has been said, it is clear that all moral concepts have their seat and origin in reason completely a priori, and this is just as true of the most ordinary human intellect as of the most highly theoretical. Moral principles cannot be abstracted from any empirical, and therefore merely contingent, cognition. Their worthiness to serve as supreme practical principles lies precisely in this purity of their origin. Everything empirical added to them subtracts just that much from their genuine influence and from the unqualified worth of the corresponding actions. It is of the utmost necessity—and not only from a cognitive point of view, where our concern is exclusively with theory, but it is also of the utmost importance for action, that we derive these concepts and laws from pure reason, enunciating them pure and unmixed, and indeed determine the scope of this whole practical but pure sphere of rational cognition—that is, of this whole faculty of pure practical reason. But in doing this, we must not 412 make its principles depend on the particular nature of human reason—as speculative philosophy allows and even at times requires. Since moral laws must hold for every rational being as such, our principles must instead be derived from the universal concept of a rational being as such. In this way the whole of ethics, which does require anthropology for its *application* to human beings, should at first be expounded independently of this and fully, as pure philosophy, that is, as metaphysics (which is quite possible to do in a totally separate branch of knowledge

such as this). We are well aware that without possessing such a metaphysics it is not only futile to try to determine precisely, for purposes of speculative judgement, the moral element of duty in all actions which accord with duty; it is impossible to establish morality on genuine principles even for merely ordinary practical purposes and particularly for moral instruction, if we lack such a metaphysics. Only in this way can we produce pure moral dispositions and engraft them onto the minds of human beings for the sake of the world's highest good.

In this study we must not go merely from common moral judgement (which is here worthy of great respect) to philosophical judgement, as has already been done, but advance by natural steps from a popular philosophy which goes no further than it can grope by means of examples, to metaphysics (which is not restricted by anything empirical, and—since it must survey the totality of this kind of rational knowledge—extends itself even to Ideas, where examples themselves forsake us). We must pursue and portray in detail the faculty of practical reason, from its general ordinances right up to the point where the concept of duty arises from it.

Everything in nature works in accordance with laws. Only a rational being has the power to act in accordance with the idea of laws—that is, in accordance with principles—and thus has a will. Since reason is required if we are to derive actions from laws, the will is nothing else than practical reason. If reason were inevitably to determine the will, then, in a being of this kind, actions which are recognized as objectively necessary would also be subjectively necessary—that is to say, the will would be a power to choose only that which reason independently of inclination recognizes to be practically necessary, that is, sees to be good. But if reason by itself alone is not sufficient to determine the will; if the will is exposed also to subjective conditions (certain incentives) which do not always harmonize with the objective ones; if, in a word, (as is actually the case with human beings) the will is not of itself com- 413 pletely in accord with reason; then actions which are recognized to be objectively necessary are subjectively contingent, and the determining of such a will in accordance with objective laws is constraint: that is, the relation between objective laws and an in-completely good will can be represented as the de-termining of a rational being's will by principles that are indeed principles of reason, but principles to which this will by its own nature is not necessarily obedient.

The idea of an objective principle, in so far as it constrains a will, is called a commandment (of reason), and the formulation of this commandment is called an Imperative.

All imperatives are expressed by a 'must'. Thereby they mark a constraint, that is to say, the relation of an objective law of reason to a will that in its subjective constitution is not necessarily deter-mined by this law. Imperatives say that something would be good to do or to leave undone; but they say this to a will that does not always do something simply because it has been informed that it is a good thing to do. Practical good however is something that determines the will by means of what reason presents to it, and therefore not by means of subjec-tive causes but objectively—that is, by reasons that are valid for every rational being as such. The prac-tical good is distinguished from the pleasant, which influences the will solely through the medium of sensation as a result of purely subjective causes, ef-fective only for the senses of this person or that, not as a principle of reason valid for everyone.[6]

414 A perfectly good will would thus be just as much subject to objective laws (laws of the Good), but it could not for that reason be thought to be constrained to act lawfully, since by its own subjective constitu-tion, it can be moved only by the concept of the Good. Hence no imperatives hold for the divine will or, more generally, for a holy will. The "must" is here out of place, because the "willing" is already of itself necessarily in agreement with the law. For this reason imperatives are only formulas for expressing the re-lation of objective laws of willing in general to the subjective imperfection of the will of this or that ra-tional being—for example, the human will.

All imperatives command either hypotheti-cally or categorically. Hypothetical imperatives de-clare a possible action to be practically necessary as a means to the attainment of something else that one wants (or that one may want). A categorical

imperative would be one that represented an action as itself objectively necessary, without regard to any further end.

Since every practical law presents a possible action as good and therefore as necessary for a sub-ject whose actions are determined by reason, all im-peratives are therefore formulae for determining an action which is necessary according to the principle of a will in some way good. If the action would be good only as a means to something else, the imper-ative is hypothetical; if the action is thought of as good in itself and therefore as necessary for a will which of itself conforms to reason as its principle, then the imperative is categorical.

An imperative therefore states which of my possible actions would be good. The imperative for-mulates a practical rule for a will that does not per-form an action immediately just because that action is good, partly because the subject does not always know that a good action is good, partly because, even if he did know this, his maxims might still be contrary to the objective principles of practical reason.

A hypothetical imperative thus says only that an action is good for some purpose or other, either possible or actual. In the first case it is a problematic practical principle; in the second case an assertoric practical principle. A categorical imperative, which declares an action to be objectively necessary of itself without reference to any purpose—that is, even without any further end—ranks as an apodic-tic practical principle.   415

What is possible only through the powers of some rational being can also be thought of as a possible purpose of some will. Consequently, if we think of principles of action as stating what is necessary in order to achieve some possible pur-pose, there are in fact infinitely many principles of action. All sciences have a practical part consisting of projects, which suppose that some end is possible for us, and imperatives, which tell us how that end is to be reached. These imperatives can in general be called imperatives of *skill*. Here there is no ques-tion at all as to whether the end is reasonable and good, but only about what one would have to do to attain it. The prescriptions required by a doctor in order to cure a patient and those that a poisoner needs in order to bring about certain death are of equal value so far as each will accomplish its purpose perfectly. Since young people do not know what ends may occur to them in the course of life, parents try to make their children learn *many kinds* of things. They try carefully to teach *skill* in the use of means to *various* desired ends, not knowing with certainty which possible end may in the future become an actual goal adopted by their pupil. Their anxiety in this matter is so great that they commonly neglect to form and correct their children's judgements about the worth of things that they might possibly adopt as ends.

There is, however, *one* end that we may presuppose as actual in all rational beings (so far as they are dependent beings to whom imperatives apply); and thus there is one aim which they not only *might* have, but which we can assume with certainty that they all *do* have by a necessity of nature and that aim is *perfect happiness*. The hypothetical imperative which affirms the practical necessity of an action as a means to the promotion of perfect happiness is an assertoric imperative. We must not characterize it as necessary merely for some uncertain, merely possible purpose, but as necessary for a purpose that we can presuppose a priori and with certainty to be present in everyone because it belongs to the essence of human beings. Now we can call skill in the choice of the means to one's own greatest well-being "prudence"[7] in the narrowest sense of the word. So the imperative concerning the choice of means to one's own happiness—that is, the precept of prudence—still remains hypothetical; the action is commanded not absolutely but only as a means to a further end.

Finally, there is one imperative which commands a certain line of conduct directly, without assuming or being conditional on any further goal to be reached by that conduct. This imperative is categorical. It is concerned not with the material of the action and its anticipated result, but with its form and with the principle from which the action itself results. And what is essentially good in the action consists in the [agent's] disposition, whatever the result may be. This imperative may be called the imperative of morality.

Volition in accordance with these three kinds of principles is also sharply distinguished by the dissimilarity in how they constrain the will. To make this dissimilarity obvious, I think we would name them most appropriately if we called them rules of skill, counsels of prudence, or commandments (laws) of morality, respectively. For only law carries with it the concept of necessity, an unconditional and objective and therefore universally valid necessity; and commandments are laws that must be obeyed, even against inclination. Counsels do indeed involve necessity, but a necessity valid only under a subjective and contingent condition—namely, depending on whether this or that human being counts this or that as essential to his happiness. As against this, a categorical imperative is limited by no condition and can actually be called a commandment in the strict sense, being absolutely, although practically necessary. We could also call imperatives of the first kind technical (concerned with art), imperatives of the second kind pragmatic[8] (concerned with well-being), and imperatives of the third kind moral (concerned with free conduct as such—that is, with morals).

The question now arises 'How are all these imperatives possible?' This question does not ask how an action commanded by the imperative can be performed, but merely how we can understand the constraining of the will, which imperatives express in setting us a task. How an imperative of skill is possible requires no special discussion. Whoever wills the end also wills (so far as reason has decisive influence on his actions) the means which are indispensably necessary and in his power. This proposition is analytic as far as willing is concerned. For when I will an object as an effect of my action I already conceive of my causality as an acting cause—that is, the use of means is included in the concept of the end; and the imperative merely extracts the concept of actions necessary to this end from the concept of willing an end. (Of course synthetic propositions are required in determining the means to a proposed end, but these propositions are concerned, not with the ground, the act of will, but with how to actualize the object.) Mathematics teaches, and certainly by synthetic propositions alone, that in order to bisect a line according to a reliable principle I must make two intersecting arcs from each of its extremities. But if I know that the aforesaid effect can be produced only by such an action, then the proposition 'If I fully will the effect, I must also will the action required to produce it' is analytic. For it is one and the same thing to think of something as an effect that is in a certain way possible through me and to think of myself as acting in this same way.

If it were only that easy to provide a definite concept of perfect happiness the imperatives of prudence would coincide entirely with those of skill and would be equally analytic. For then it could be said in this case as in the former case, 'Whoever wills the end, also (necessarily, according to reason) wills the sole means which are in his power.' Unfortunately, however, the concept of perfect happiness is such a vague concept that although everyone wants it, they can never say definitely and self-consistently what it really is that they wish and will. The reason for this is that all the elements that belong to the concept of happiness are empirical—that is, they must be borrowed from experience; but the Idea of perfect happiness requires an absolute whole, a maximum, of well-being in my present and in every future state. Now it is impossible for even the most insightful and most capable but finite being to form here a definite concept of what he really wants. Is it riches that he wants? How much anxiety, envy, and intrigue might he not bring on his own head in this way! Is it knowledge and insight? This might just give him an eye even sharper in seeing evils at present hidden from him and yet unavoidable, making those evils all the more frightful, or it might add a load of still further needs to the desires which already give him trouble enough. Is it long life? Who will guarantee that it would not be a life of long misery? Is it at least health? How often has not physical infirmity kept someone from excesses into which perfect health would have let him fall!—and so on. In short, he has no principle by which he is able to decide with complete certainty what would make him truly happy, since for this he would require omniscience. Thus we cannot act on definite principles in order to be happy, but only on empirical counsels, for example, of diet, frugality, politeness, reserve, and so on— things which experience shows contribute most to

well-being on the average. Hence the imperatives of prudence, strictly speaking, do not command at all—that is, they cannot exhibit actions objectively as practically necessary. They should be taken as pieces of advice (*consilia*), rather than as commandments (*praecepta*), of reason. The problem of determining certainly and universally what action will promote the perfect happiness of a rational being is completely insoluble; and consequently in regard to this there is no imperative possible which in the strictest sense could command us to do what will make us happy, since perfect happiness is an ideal, not of reason, but of imagination—an ideal resting merely on empirical grounds, of which it is vain to expect that they should determine an action by which we could attain the totality of a series of consequences which is in fact infinite. Nevertheless, if we were to assume that the means to happiness could be discovered with certainty, this imperative of prudence would be an analytic practical proposition; for it differs from the imperative of skill only in this— that in the latter the end is merely possible, while in the former the end is given. In spite of this difference, since both command solely the means to something assumed to be willed as an end, the imperative that commands him who wills the end to will the means is in both cases analytic. Thus, the possibility of an imperative of prudence also poses no difficulty.

By contrast, 'How is the imperative of morality possible?' is beyond all doubt the one question in need of solution. For the moral imperative is in no way hypothetical, and consequently the objective necessity, which it affirms, cannot be supported by any presupposition, as was the case with hypothetical imperatives. But we must never forget that it is impossible to settle by any example, i.e., empirically, whether there is any imperative of this kind at all; we should rather worry that all imperatives that seem to be categorical may yet be hypothetical in some hidden way. For example, when it is said, 'You must abstain from making deceitful promises,' one assumes that the necessity for this abstention is not mere advice so as to avoid some further evil—as though the meaning of what was said was, You ought not to make a deceitful promise lest, when it comes to light, you destroy your credit. On the contrary, an action of this kind would have to be considered as bad in itself, and the imperative of the prohibition would be therefore categorical. Even so, no example can show with certainty that the will would be determined here solely by the law without any further motivation, although it may appear to be so; for it is always possible that fear of disgrace, perhaps also hidden dread of other risks, may unconsciously influence the will. Who can prove by experience the non-existence of a cause? For experience shows only that we do not perceive it. In such a case, however, the so-called moral imperative, which as such appears to be categorical and unconditional, would in fact be only a pragmatic prescription calling attention to our own advantage and merely instructing us to take this into account.

420   We shall thus have to investigate entirely a priori the possibility of a categorical imperative, since here we do not enjoy the advantage of having its reality given in experience so that the discussion of its possibility would be needed merely to explain, and not to establish it. However, we can see the following at least provisionally: that the categorical imperative alone purports to be a practical law, while all the rest may be called principles of the will but not laws; for an action that is necessary merely to achieve some arbitrary purpose can be considered as in itself contingent, and we can always escape from the prescription if we abandon the purpose; whereas an unconditional commandment does not leave it open to the will to do the opposite at its discretion and therefore alone carries with it that necessity which we demand from a law.

In the second place, with this categorical imperative or law of morality the reason for our difficulty (in comprehending its possibility) is a very serious one. We have here a synthetic a priori practical proposition;[9] and since in theoretical knowledge there is so much difficulty in comprehending the possibility of propositions of this kind, we may well assume that the difficulty will be no less in the practical sphere.

The first part of our task is to see whether perhaps the mere concept of a categorical imperative might also give us the formula containing the only proposition that can be a categorical imperative. Showing how such an absolute commandment is possible will still require special and difficult effort,

even when we know what the commandment asserts. But we postpone this to the last section.

If I think of a *hypothetical* imperative as such, I do not know beforehand what it will contain—not until I am given its condition. But if I think of a *categorical imperative,* I know right away what it contains. For since this imperative contains,[10] besides the law, only the necessity that the maxim[10] conform to this law, while the law, as we have seen, contains no condition limiting it, there is nothing left over to which the maxim of action should conform except the universality of a law as such; and it is only this conformity that the imperative asserts to be necessary.   421

There is therefore only one categorical imperative and it is this: 'Act only on that maxim by which you can at the same time will that it should become a universal law.'

Now if all imperatives of duty can be derived from this one imperative as their principle, then even though we leave it unsettled whether what we call duty is or is not an empty concept, we shall still be able to indicate at least what we understand by it and what the concept means.

Because the universality of law according to which effects occur constitutes what is properly called nature in its most general sense (nature as regards its form)—that is, the existence of things so far as this is determined by universal laws—the universal imperative of duty could also be formulated as follows: 'Act as though the maxim of your action were to become by your will a universal law of nature.'

We shall now enumerate some duties, dividing them in the usual way into duties towards ourselves and duties towards others and into perfect and imperfect duties.[11]

1. A man feels sick of life as the result of a mounting series of misfortunes that has reduced him to hopelessness, but he still possesses enough of his   422 reason to ask himself whether it would not be contrary to his duty to himself to take his own life. Now he tests whether the maxim of his action could really become a universal law of nature. His maxim, however, is: 'I make it my principle out of self-love to shorten my life if its continuance threatens more evil than it promises advantage.' The only further question

is whether this principle of self-love can become a universal law of nature. But one sees at once that a nature whose law was that the very same feeling meant to promote life should actually destroy life would contradict itself, and hence would not endure as nature. The maxim therefore could not possibly be a general law of nature and thus it wholly contradicts the supreme principle of all duty.

2. Another finds himself driven by need to borrow money. He knows very well that he will not be able to pay it back, but he sees too that nobody will lend him anything unless he firmly promises to pay it back within a fixed time. He wants to make such a promise, but he still has enough conscience to ask himself, 'Isn't it impermissible and contrary to duty to get out of one's difficulties this way?' Suppose, however, that he did decide to do it. The maxim of his action would run thus: 'When I believe myself short of money, I will borrow money and promise to pay it back, even though I know that this will never be done.' Now this principle of self-love or personal advantage is perhaps quite compatible with my own entire future welfare; only there remains the question 'Is it right?' I therefore transform the unfair demand of self-love into a universal law and frame my question thus: 'How would things stand if my maxim became a universal law?' I then see immediately that this maxim can never qualify as a self-consistent universal law of nature, but must necessarily contradict itself. For the universality of a law that permits anyone who believes himself to be in need to make any promise he pleases with the intention of not keeping it would make, promising, and the very purpose one has in promising, itself impossible. For no one would believe he was being promised anything, but would laugh at any such utterance as hollow pretence.

3. A third finds in himself a talent that, with a certain amount of cultivation, could make him a useful man for all sorts of purposes. But he sees himself in comfortable circumstances, and he prefers to give himself up to pleasure rather than to bother about increasing and improving his fortunate natural aptitudes. Yet he asks himself further 'Does my maxim of neglecting my natural gifts, besides agreeing with my taste for amusement, agree also

with what is called duty?' He then sees that a nature could indeed endure under such a universal law, even if (like the South Sea Islanders) every man should let his talents rust and should be bent on devoting his life solely to idleness, amusement, procreation—in a word, to enjoyment. Only he cannot possibly *will* that this should become a universal law of nature or should be implanted in us as such a law by a natural instinct. For as a rational being he necessarily wills that all his powers should be developed, since they are after all useful to him and given to him for all sorts of possible purposes.

4. A fourth man, who is himself flourishing but sees others who have to struggle with great hardships (and whom he could easily help) thinks to himself: 'What do I care? Let every one be as happy as Heaven intends or as he can make himself; I won't deprive him of anything; I won't even envy him; but I don't feel like contributing anything to his well-being or to helping him in his distress!' Now admittedly if such an attitude were a universal law of nature, the human race could survive perfectly well and doubtless even better than when everybody chatters about sympathy and good will, and even makes an effort, now and then, to practise them, but, when one can get away with it, swindles, traffics in human rights, or violates them in other ways. But although it is possible that a universal law of nature in accord with this maxim could exist, it is impossible to *will* that such a principle should hold everywhere as a law of nature. For a will that intended this would be in conflict with itself, since many situations might arise in which the man needs love and sympathy from others, and in which, by such a law of nature generated by his own will, he would rob himself of all hope of the help he wants.

These are some of the many actual duties—or at least of what we take to be actual—whose derivation from the single principle cited above is perspicuous. We must be able to will that a maxim of our action should become a universal law—this is the authoritative model for moral judging of action generally. Some actions are so constituted that we cannot even *conceive* without contradiction that their maxim be a universal law of nature, let alone that we could *will*

423

424

that it *ought* to become one. In the case of other actions, we do not find this inner impossibility, but it is still impossible to *will* that their maxim should be raised to the universality of a law of nature, because such a will would contradict itself. We see readily that the first kind of action is opposed to strict or narrow duty, the second opposed only to wide (meritorious) duty; Thus all duties—so far as the type of obligation (not the object of its action) is concerned—are fully set out in these examples as dependent on our single principle.

If we now look at ourselves whenever we transgress a duty, we find that we in fact do not intend that our maxim should become a universal law. For this is impossible for us. What we really intend is rather that its opposite should remain a law generally; we only take the liberty of making an *exception* to it, for ourselves or (of course just this once) to satisfy our inclination. Consequently if we weighed it all up from one and the same perspective—that of reason—we should find a contradiction in our own will, the contradiction that a certain principle should be objectively necessary as a universal law and yet subjectively should not hold universally but should admit of exceptions. But there is actually no contradiction here, since we are first considering our action from the perspective of a will wholly in accord with reason, and then considering exactly the same action from the point of view of a will affected by inclination. What we have is rather an opposition (antagonism) of inclination to the precept of reason whereby the universality of the principle (*universalitas*) is transformed into a mere generality (*generalitas*) in order that the practical principle of reason can meet the maxim halfway. This procedure, though unjustifiable in our own impartial judgement, proves nevertheless that we in fact recognize the validity of the categorical imperative and (with all respect to it) merely allow ourselves a few exceptions that are, as we pretend, unimportant and apparently forced upon us.

425 We have thus at least shown this much—that if duty is a concept that is to have meaning and actual legislative authority for our actions, it can be expressed only in categorical imperatives and not at all in hypothetical ones. At the same time—and this is already a great deal—we have set forth clearly, and

defined for every use, the content of the categorical imperative, which must contain the principle of all duty (if there is to be such a thing at all). But we are still not so far advanced as to prove a priori that there actually is an imperative of this kind—that there is a practical law which by itself commands absolutely and without any further motivation, and that it is our duty to follow this law.

If we really intend to arrive at this proof it is extremely important to remember that we should not let ourselves think for a moment that the reality of this principle can be derived from *the particular characteristics of human nature.* For duty has to be a practical, unconditional necessity of action; it must therefore hold for all rational beings (to whom alone an imperative can apply at all), and *only for that reason* a law that holds also for all human wills. Whatever, on the other hand, is derived from the special predisposition of humanity, from certain feelings and propensities, and even, if this were possible, from some special bent peculiar to human reason and not holding necessarily for the will of every rational being—all this can indeed supply a personal maxim, but not a law: it can give us a subjective principle—one on which we have a natural disposition and inclination to act—but not an objective principle on which we should be directed to act even though our every propensity, inclination, and natural bent were opposed to it. This is so much the case that the sublimity and inner dignity of the commandment is even more manifest in a duty, the fewer subjective causes there are for obeying it and the more there are against it, but without this weakening in the slightest the constraint exercised by the law or diminishing its validity.

Here we see philosophy placed in what is actually a precarious position, a position that is supposed to be firm though it is neither suspended from heaven nor supported by the earth. Here she must show her purity as the sustainer of her own laws—not as the herald of laws that some implanted sense or who knows what guardian-like nature has whispered to her. Such laws, though perhaps always better than nothing, can never furnish us with fundamental 426 principles dictated by reason, principles whose origin must be completely a priori and, because of this, have commanding authority. Such fundamental principles expect nothing from human inclinations but everything from the supremacy of the law and the respect owed it. Without this they condemn human beings to self-contempt and inner disgust.

Everything empirical is thus not only wholly unfit to contribute to the principle of morality; it is highly damaging to the purity of moral practices themselves. For, in morality, the proper worth of an absolutely good will, a worth exalted above all price, lies precisely in the freedom of its principle of action from any influence by contingent reasons that only experience can provide. We cannot warn too strongly or too often against the slack, or indeed vulgar, attitude which searches among empirical motives and laws for the principle; for human reason in its weariness is glad to rest on this cushion, and in a dream of sweet illusions (which allow it to embrace a cloud instead of Juno) to substitute for morality a bastard patched up from limbs of very diverse parentage, looking like anything one wishes to see in it, only not resembling virtue to anyone who has once beheld her in her true form.[12]

Our question then is this: 'Is it a necessary law *for all rational beings* to judge their actions always in accordance with those maxims which they can themselves will that they should serve as universal laws?' If it is a necessary law, it must already be connected (entirely a priori) with the concept of the will of a rational being as such. But in order to discover this connection we must, however reluctantly, venture into metaphysics, although into a region of metaphysics different from that of speculative philosophy, 427 namely, the metaphysics of morals. In a practical philosophy we are not concerned with assuming reasons for what happens, but with acknowledging laws for what ought to happen, even if it may never happen— that is, objective practical laws. And here we have no need to investigate the reasons why anything pleases or displeases, how the pleasure of mere sensation differs from taste, and whether the latter is distinct from general satisfaction of reason. We need not inquire on what the feelings of pleasure and displeasure are based, or how from these feelings there arise desires and inclinations; and how from these, with the cooperation of reason, there arise maxims. For all this

belongs to empirical psychology, which would constitute the second part of the study of nature, if we regard the latter as the *philosophy of nature* to the extent to which it rests on *empirical laws*. Here, however, we are discussing objective practical laws, and consequently the relation of a will to itself insofar as it determines itself solely by reason. Everything related to the empirical then falls away of itself; for if *reason all by itself* determines conduct (and the possibility of this is what we now wish to investigate), it must necessarily do so a priori.

We think of the will as a power of determining oneself to act *in conformity with the idea of certain laws*. And such a power can be found only in rational beings. Now, what serves the will as the objective ground of its self-determining is an *end;* and this end, if it is given by reason alone, must be equally valid for all rational beings. On the other hand, something that contains merely the ground of the possibility of an action, where the result of that action is the end, is called a *means*. The subjective ground of desiring is a *driving-spring;* the objective ground of willing is *a motivating reason*. Hence the difference between subjective ends, which depend on driving-springs, and objective ends, which depend on motivating reasons that are valid for every rational being. Practical principles are 428 *formal* if they abstract from all subjective ends; they are *material,* on the other hand, if they are based on subjective ends and consequently on certain driving-springs. Those ends that a rational being at his own discretion sets for himself as *what he intends to accomplish* through his action (material ends) are in every case only relative; for what gives them worth is only their relation to some subject's particularly constituted faculty of desire. Such worth can therefore provide no universal principles, no principles valid and necessary for all rational beings and for every act of will—that is, it can provide no practical laws. Consequently all these relative ends are only the ground of hypothetical imperatives.

Suppose, however, there were something *whose existence in itself* had an absolute worth, something that, as an end *in itself,* could be a ground of definite laws. Then in it and in it alone, would the ground of a possible categorical imperative, that is, of a practical law, reside.

Now, I say, a human being, and in general every rational being, *does exist* as an end in himself, *not merely as a means* to be used by this or that will as it pleases. In all his actions, whether they are directed to himself or to other rational beings, a human being must always be viewed *at the same time as an end.* All the objects of inclination have only a conditional worth; for if these inclinations and the needs based on them did not exist, their object would be worthless. But inclinations themselves, as sources of needs, are so far from having absolute value to make them desirable for their own sake that it must rather be the universal wish of every rational being to be wholly free of them. Thus the value of any object *that is to be acquired* by our action is always conditional. Beings whose existence depends not on our will but on nature still have only a relative value as means and are therefore called *things,* if they lack reason. Rational beings, on the other hand, are called *persons* because, their nature already marks them out as ends in themselves—that is, as something which ought not to be used *merely* as a means—and consequently imposes restrictions on all choice making (and is an object of respect). Persons, therefore, are not merely subjective ends whose existence as an effect of our actions has a value *for us.* They are *objective ends—* that is, things whose existence is in itself an end, and indeed an end such that no other end can be substituted for it, no end to which they should serve *merely* as a means. For if this were not so, there would be nothing at all having *absolute value* anywhere. But if all value were conditional, and thus contingent, then no supreme principle could be found for reason at all.

If then there is to be a supreme practical principle and a categorical imperative for the human will, it must be such that it forms an objective principle of the will from the idea of something which is necessarily an end for everyone because *it is an end in itself,* a principle that can therefore serve as a universal prac-

429 tical law. The ground of this principle is: *Rational nature exists as an end in itself.* This is the way in which a human being necessarily conceives his own existence, and it is therefore a *subjective* principle of human actions. But it is also the way in which every other rational being conceives his existence, on the same rational ground which holds also for me;[13] hence

it is at the same time an *objective* principle from which, since it is a supreme practical ground, it must be possible to derive all laws of the will. The practical imperative will therefore be the following: *Act in such a way that you treat humanity, whether in your own person or in any other person, always at the same time as an end, never merely as a means.* We will now see whether this can be carried out in practice.

Let us keep to our previous examples.

First, as regards the concept of necessary duty to oneself, the man who contemplates suicide will ask himself whether his action could be compatible with the Idea of humanity as *an end in itself.* If he damages himself in order to escape from a painful situation, he is making use of a person *merely as a means* to maintain a tolerable state of affairs till the end of his life. But a human being is not a thing—not something to be used *merely* as a means: he must always in all his actions be regarded as an end in himself. Hence I cannot dispose of a human being in my own person, by maiming, corrupting, or killing him. (I must here forego a more precise definition of this principle that would forestall any misunderstanding—for example, as to having limbs amputated to save myself or exposing my life to danger in order to preserve it, and so on—this discussion belongs to ethics proper.)

Secondly, as regards necessary or strict duty owed to others, the man who has in mind making a false promise to others will see at once that he is intending to make use of another person *merely as a means* to an end which that person does not share. For the person whom I seek to use for my own purposes by such a promise cannot possibly agree with my way of treating him, and so cannot himself share the end of the action. This incompatibility with the principle of duty to others can be seen more distinctly when we bring in examples of attacks on the freedom and property of others. For then it is manifest that a violator of the rights of human beings intends to use the person of others merely as a means without taking into consideration that, as rational beings, they must always at the same time be valued as ends—that is, treated only as beings who must themselves be able to share in the end of the very same action.[14]

Thirdly, as regards contingent (meritorious) duty to oneself, it is not enough that an action not

430

conflict with humanity in our own person as an end in itself: it must also *harmonize with this end.* Now there are in humanity capacities for greater perfection that form part of nature's purpose for humanity in our own person. To neglect these can perhaps be compatible with the *survival* of humanity as an end in itself, but not with the *promotion* of that end.

Fourthly, as regards meritorious duties to others, the natural end that all human beings seek is their own perfect happiness. Now the human race might indeed exist if everybody contributed nothing to the happiness of others but at the same time refrained from deliberately impairing it. This harmonizing with humanity *as an end in itself* would, however, be merely negative and not positive, unless everyone also endeavours, as far as he can, to further the ends of others. For the ends of any person who is an end in himself must, if this idea is to have its full effect in me, be also, as far as possible, *my* ends.

This principle of humanity, and in general of every rational agent, *as an end in itself* (a principle which is the supreme limiting condition on every person's freedom of action) is not borrowed from experience: first, because it is universal, applying to all rational beings generally, and no experience is sufficient to determine anything about all such beings; secondly, because in this principle we conceive of humanity not as an end that one happens to have (a subjective end)—that is, as an object which people, as a matter of fact, happen to make their end. We conceive of it rather as an objective end—one that, as a law, should constitute the supreme limiting condition on all subjective ends, whatever those ends may be. This principle must therefore spring from pure reason.

That is to say, the ground of all practical legislation *objectively in the rule* and in the form of universality that (according to our first principle) makes the rule fit to be a law (and possibly a law of nature); *subjectively,* however, the ground of practical legislating lies in the *end.* But, according to our second principle, the *subject* of all ends is every rational being as an end in itself. From this there follows our third practical principle of the will: the supreme condition of the will's harmony with universal practical reason is the Idea of *the will of every rational being as a will that legislates universal law.*

By this principle all maxims are rejected which are inconsistent with the will's own universal lawgiving. The will is therefore not merely subject to the law, but subject in such a way that it must be considered as also *giving the law to itself* and only for this reason as first of all subject to the law (of which it can regard itself as the author).

Imperatives as formulated above excluded from their legislative authority every admixture of interest as a motivation. They either commanded a conformity of actions to universal law, a conformity analogous to a *natural order,* or they asserted the prerogative of rational beings to be regarded universally as *supreme ends* in themselves. (This followed from the mere fact that these imperatives were conceived as categorical.) But the imperatives were only *assumed* to be categorical because we had to make this assumption if we wished to explain the concept of duty. That there were practical propositions that command categorically could not itself be proved, any more than it can be proved here in this chapter. But one thing might have been done—namely, to show that in willing something just out of duty the renunciation of all interest is the specific mark distinguishing a categorical from a hypothetical imperative. This is what we are doing in the present third formulation of the principle—namely, in the Idea of the will of every rational being as *a will that legislates universal law.*

For once we think of a will of this kind, it becomes clear that while a will *that is subject to laws* may be bound to this law by some interest, a will that is itself a supreme lawgiver cannot possibly depend on any interest; for such a dependent will would itself require yet another law in order to restrict the interest of self-love by the condition that this interest must be valid as a universal law.

Thus the *principle* that every human will is *a will that enacts universal laws in all its maxims*[15] *would be well adapted* to be a categorical imperative, provided only that this principle is correct in other ways. Because of the Idea of giving universal law, it is *based on no interest,* and consequently, of all possible imperatives it alone can be *unconditional.* Or better still, let us take the converse of this proposition: if there is a categorical imperative (a law that applies to the will of every rational being), it can command us only to act always on the maxim of its will as one which could at the same time look upon itself as giving universal laws. For only then is the practical principle, and the imperative that the will obeys, unconditional, because the imperative cannot be based on any interest.

If we look back on all the previous efforts to discover the principle of morality, it is no wonder that they have all had to fail. One saw that human beings are bound to laws by their duty, but it never occurred to anyone that they are subject only to *laws which they themselves have given* but which are nevertheless *universal,* and that people are bound only to act in conformity with a will that is their own but that is, according to nature's purpose, a will that gives universal law. For when one thought of human beings merely as subject to a law (whatever it might be), the law had to carry with it some interest, as stimulus or compulsion to obedience, because it did not spring as law from their *own* will: in order to conform to the law, their will had to be compelled by *something else* to act in a certain way. But this strictly necessary consequence meant that all the labour spent in trying to find a supreme foundation for duty was irrevocably lost. For what one discovered was never duty, but only the necessity of acting from a certain interest. This interest might be one's own or another's. But the resulting imperative was bound to be always a conditional one and could not at all serve as a moral commandment. I therefore want to call my principle the principle of the *Autonomy* of the will in contrast with all others, which I therefore count as *Heteronomy.*

The concept of every rational being as a being who must regard itself as making universal law by all the maxims of its will, and must seek to judge itself and its actions from this standpoint, leads to a closely connected and very fruitful concept—namely, that of *a kingdom of ends.*

I understand by a 'kingdom' the systematic union of different rational beings under common laws. Now since laws determine ends as regards their universal validity, we can—if we abstract from the personal differences between rational beings, and also from the content of their private ends—conceive

433

a whole of all ends systematically united (a whole composed of rational beings as ends in themselves and also of the personal ends which each may set for himself); that is, we can conceive of a kingdom of ends which is possible in accordance with the aforesaid principles.

For rational beings all stand under the *law* that each of them should treat himself and all others *never merely as a means* but always *at the same time as an end in himself.* But from this there arises a systematic union of rational beings through shared objective laws—that is, a kingdom. Since these laws aim precisely at the relation of such beings to one another as ends and means, this kingdom may be called a kingdom of ends (admittedly only an ideal).

A rational being, however, belongs to the kingdom of ends as a *member,* if, while legislating its universal laws, he is also subject to these laws. He belongs to the kingdom as its *head,* if, as legislating, he is not subject to the will of any other being.

434

A rational being must always regard himself as lawgiving in a kingdom of ends made possible through freedom of the will—whether as member or as head. But he cannot maintain the position of head merely through the maxim of his will, but only if he is a completely independent being, without needs and with an unlimited power adequate to his will.

Thus morality consists in the relation of all action to just that lawgiving through which a kingdom of ends is made possible. But this lawgiving must be found in every rational being itself and must be capable of arising from the will of that being. The principle of its will is therefore this: never to perform any action except one whose maxim could also be a universal law, and thus to act only on a maxim *through which the will could regard itself at the same time as enacting universal law.* If maxims are not already by their very nature in harmony with this objective principle of rational beings as legislating universal law, the necessity of acting on this principle is called a constraint on the choice of actions, i.e., *duty.* Duty does not apply to the head in a kingdom of ends, but it does apply to every member and to all of them in equal measure.

The practical necessity of acting on this principle—that is, duty—is not based at all on feelings, impulses, and inclinations, but only on the relation of a rational beings to one another, a relation in which the will of a rational being must always be regarded as *lawgiving,* because otherwise it could not be thought of as *an end in itself.* Reason thus relates every maxim of a universally legislating will to every other will and also to every action towards oneself: it does so, not because of any further motive or future advantage, but from the Idea of the *dignity* of a rational being who obeys no law other than one which he himself also enacts.

In the kingdom of ends everything has either a *price or a dignity.* Whatever has a price can be replaced by something else as *equivalent.* Whatever by contrast is exalted above all price and so admits of no equivalent has a dignity.

Whatever is relative to universal human inclinations and needs has a *market price.* Whatever, even without presupposing a need, accords with a certain taste—that is, with satisfaction in the mere random play of our mental powers—has an *attachment price.* But that which constitutes the sole condition under which anything can be an end in itself has not mere relative worth, that is, a price, but an inner worth— i.e., *dignity.*

Now morality is the only condition under which a rational being can be an end in itself; for only through this is it possible to be a lawgiving member in the kingdom of ends. Therefore morality, and humanity so far as it is capable of morality, is the only thing that has dignity. Skill and diligence in work have a market price; wit, lively imagination, and humour have an attachment price but fidelity to promises and benevolence out of basic principles (not out of instinct) have an inner worth. Nature and art alike offer nothing that could replace their lack; for their worth consists not in the effects which result from them, not in the advantage or profit they produce, but in the intentions—that is, in the maxims of the will—which are ready in this way to reveal themselves in action even if they are not favoured by success. Such actions too need no recommendation from any subjective disposition or taste in order to be regarded with immediate favour and approval; they need no direct predilection or feeling for them. They exhibit as an object of immediate respect the will that performs them; since nothing but reason is

435

required in order to *impose* them on the will. Nor is the will to be *coaxed* into them, which would anyhow be a contradiction in the case of duties. This assessment lets us recognize the value of such a mental attitude as dignity and puts it infinitely above all price, with which it cannot be brought into comparison or computation without, as it were, violating its holiness.

And what is it then that justifies a morally good disposition, or virtue, in making such lofty claims? It is nothing less than the *sharing* which it allows to a rational being in *giving universal laws,* which therefore renders him fit to be a member in a possible kingdom of ends. His own nature as an end in himself already marked out this fitness and therefore his status as lawgiver in a kingdom of ends and as free from all laws of nature, obedient only to those laws which he himself prescribes, laws according to which his maxims can participate in the making of universal law (to which he at the same time subjects himself). For nothing can have worth other than that determined for it by the law. But the lawgiving that determines all worth must therefore have a dignity, i.e., an unconditional and incomparable worth. The word *'respect'* is the only suitable expression for the esteem that a rational being must necessarily feel for such lawgiving. *Autonomy* is thus the basis of the dignity of human nature and of every rational nature.

436

Our three ways of presenting the principle of morality are basically only so many formulations of precisely the same law, each one of them by itself uniting the other two within it. There is nevertheless a difference among them, which, however, is more subjectively than objectively practical: that is to say, the different formulations aim to bring an Idea of reason closer to intuition (by means of a certain analogy) and thus nearer to feeling. All maxims have:

1. A *form,* which consists in universality: and in this respect the formula of the moral imperative is expressed thus: 'Maxims must be chosen as if they were to hold as universal laws of nature.'

2. A *matter*—that is, an end; and in this respect the formula says: 'A rational being, as by its very nature an end and thus an end in itself, must serve

every maxim as the limiting condition restricting the pursuit of all merely relative and arbitrary ends.'

3. A *complete determination* of all maxims by means of the following formula: 'All maxims which stem from autonomous lawgiving are to harmonize with a possible kingdom of ends and with a kingdom of nature.'[16] Progression that takes place here as elsewhere is through the categories of unity, plurality, and totality: *unity* of the form of the will (its universality); *plurality* of its matter (its objects—that is, its ends); and the totality or *all-comprehensiveness* of its system of ends. It is, however, better if in moral *judgement* one proceeds always in accordance with the strict method and takes as one's basic principle the universal formula of the categorical imperative: *'Act on that maxim that can at the same time make itself into a universal law.'* If, however, we wish also to *gain a hearing* for the moral law, it is very useful to bring one and the same action under the three stated formulae and thereby, as far as possible, bring the moral law closer to intuition.

We can now end at the point from which we began—namely, with the concept of an unconditionally good will. *A will* is *absolutely good if* it cannot be evil—that is, if its maxim, when made into a universal law, can never be in conflict with itself. This principle is therefore also its supreme law: 'Act always on that maxim whose universality as a law you can at the same time will.' This is the one principle on which a will can never be in conflict with itself, and such an imperative is categorical. Since the validity of the will, as a universal law for possible actions, is analogous to the universal connection of the existence of things under universal laws, which is the formal aspect of nature in general, we can also express the categorical imperative as follows: *'Act on maxims which can at the same time have as their object [making] themselves into universal laws of nature.'* This then gives us the formula for an absolutely good will.

A rational nature distinguishes itself from others by the fact that it sets itself an end. That end would be the matter for every good will. But in the idea of an absolutely good will, good without any limiting condition (the attaining of this or that end),

we must abstract completely from every end that has to be *brought about* (for such an end would make any will only relatively good). Hence the proposed end must here be conceived, not as an end to be produced, *but as a self-sufficient* end. It must therefore be conceived only negatively—that is, as an end which we should never act against, and consequently one which in all our willing we must never value merely as a means, but always at the same time as an end. Now this end can be nothing other than the subject of all possible ends itself, because this subject is also the subject of a will that may be absolutely good; for such a will cannot without contradiction be subordinated to any other object. The principle 'So act in relation to every rational being (both yourself and others) that this being may at the same time count in your maxim as an end in itself' is thus basically the same as the principle 'Act on a maxim which at the same time embodies in itself its own universal validity for every rational being.' For to say that, in using means to any end, I ought to restrict my maxim by the condition that it should also be universally valid as a law for every subject, is just the same as to say this: a subject of ends, i.e., a rational being itself, must be made the foundation of all maxims of action, and must thus be treated never merely as a means, but as the supreme condition restricting the use of all means—that is, always at the same time as an end.

Now from this it unquestionably follows that every rational being, as an end in itself, must be able to regard himself as also the maker of universal law in respect of any law whatever to which he may be subject; for it is precisely the fitness of his maxims to make universal law that marks him out as an end in himself. It follows equally that this dignity (or prerogative) he possesses above all merely natural beings carries with it the necessity of always choosing his maxims from the point of view of himself, but also of every other rational being (which is why they are called persons) as lawgiving beings. It is in this way that a world of rational beings (*mundus intelligibilis*) [intelligible world] is possible as a kingdom of ends— possible, that is, through the giving of their own laws by all persons as its members. Accordingly every rational being must act as if he were always by his maxims a lawgiving member in the universal kingdom of ends. The formal principle of such maxims is 'Act as if your maxims had to serve at the same time as a universal law (for all rational beings).' A kingdom of ends is thus possible only by analogy with a kingdom of nature. A kingdom of ends is possible only through maxims—that is, self-imposed rules—while nature is possible only through laws of efficient causes externally necessitated. In spite of this difference, we give to nature as a whole, even though it is regarded as a machine, the name of a 'kingdom of nature' so far as and because rational beings are its ends. Now a kingdom of ends would actually come into existence through maxims whose rule the categorical imperative prescribes for all rational beings, *if these maxims were universally followed.* Yet even if a rational being were himself to follow such a maxim strictly, he cannot count on everybody else therefore being faithful to the same maxim, nor can he count on the kingdom of nature and its purposive order harmonizing with him, as a fitting member, towards a kingdom of ends made possible through himself, i.e., that the kingdom of nature will favour his expectations of perfect happiness. Nevertheless the law 'Act on the maxims of a universally lawgiving member of a merely possible kingdom of ends' remains in full force, because it commands categorically. And precisely here we encounter the paradox that, without any further end or advantage to be attained by it, the mere dignity of humanity as rational nature—and consequently respect for a mere Idea—should serve as an inflexible precept for the will; and that it is just this independence from any motivations based on his expectations of perfect happiness that constitutes the sublimity of a maxim and the worthiness of every rational subject to be a lawgiving member in the kingdom of ends; for otherwise he would have to be regarded as subject only to the natural law of his own needs. Even if both the kingdom of nature and the kingdom of ends were imagined to be united under one head and thus the kingdom of ends ceased to be a mere Idea and achieved genuine reality, the Idea would indeed gain additional motivating power by this, but no increase in its inner worth. For, even if this were so, this unique and absolute lawgiver would have to be conceived as judging the worth of rational

439

beings solely by the disinterested behaviour they prescribed to themselves from this Idea alone. The essence of things is not changed by their external relations; and, leaving aside such relations, whatever constitutes by itself the absolute worth of human beings is that by which they must be judged—by everyone whatsoever, even by the Supreme Being. *Morality* is thus the relation of actions to the autonomy of the will—that is, to a possible universal lawgiving by means of its maxims. An action that is compatible with the autonomy of the will is *permitted*; one that does not harmonize with it is *forbidden*. A will whose maxims necessarily agree with the laws of autonomy is a *holy,* absolutely good will. The dependence of a will not absolutely good on the principle of autonomy (that is, moral necessitation) is *obligation*. Obligation can thus not apply to a holy being. The objective necessity of an action out of obligation is called *duty*.

From what has just been said we can now easily explain how it happens that, although the concept of duty includes the idea of a person's subjection to the law, we nevertheless attribute a certain sublimity and *dignity* to the person who fulfils all his duties. For although there is nothing sublime about him just in so far as he is *subject* to the law, there is sublimity to him in his being at the same time its *author* and being subordinated only for this reason to this very same law. We have also shown above how neither fear nor inclination, but only respect for the law, is the motivation that can give an action moral worth. Our own will, provided it would act only under the condition of being able to give universal law by means of its maxims—this ideal will, which is possible for us, is the proper object of respect. The dignity of humanity consists precisely in this power of giving universal law, though only on condition of also being subject to this same lawgiving.

440

Autonomy of the Will
As the Supreme Principle of Morality

Autonomy of the will is the property the will has of being a law to itself (independently of any property of the objects of volition). Hence the principle of autonomy is 'Never choose except in such a way that the maxims of your choice are also comprehended as universal law in the same act of will.' That this practical rule is an imperative, that is, that the will of every rational being is necessarily bound to the rule as a condition, cannot be proved by a mere analysis of the concepts contained in it, since it is a synthetic proposition. To prove it we would have to go beyond knowledge of objects and to a critique of the subject—that is, to a critique of pure practical reason—since this synthetic proposition, which commands apodictically, must be capable of being known entirely a priori. This task does not belong to the present chapter. However, by mere analysis of the concepts of morality we can quite well show that the above principle of autonomy is the sole principle of ethics. For analysis discloses that the principle of morality must be a categorical imperative, and that the imperative in turn commands nothing neither more nor less than precisely this autonomy of the will.

Heteronomy of the Will

As the Source of All Spurious Principles of Morality

If the will seeks the law that is to determine it *anywhere else* than in the fitness of its maxims for its own giving of universal law, and if therefore it goes outside itself and seeks this law in a property of any of its objects—the result is always *heteronomy.* In that case the will does not give itself the law; rather, the object gives the law to it, in virtue of its relation to the will. This relation, whether based on inclination or on rational ideas, can give rise only to hypothetical imperatives: 'I ought to do something *because I want something else'.* As against this, the moral, and therefore categorical imperative, says. 'I ought to act thus or thus, even though I did not want anything else'. For example, the first says 'I ought not to lie if I want to maintain my reputation' while the second says 'I ought not to lie even if it would not bring me the slightest disgrace'. The second imperative must therefore leave out of consideration all objects to this extent; that they have no *influence* at all on the will, so that practical reason (the will) may not merely administer some alien interest but may simply manifest its own sovereign authority as the supreme legislation. Thus, for example, the reason why I ought to promote the happiness of others is not

because the realization of their happiness concerns me (whether because of direct inclination or on account of some satisfaction gained indirectly through reason), but simply because a maxim that excludes this cannot be included as a universal law in one and the same act of will.

Classification af all Possible Principles of Morality Based on Heteronomy as Their Assumed Foundation

Here, as everywhere else in the pure use of reason—so long as a critique of it is lacking—human reason tries every possible wrong way before it succeeds in finding the only true way.

All the principles that can be adopted from this point of view are either *empirical* or *rational*. Principles of the *first* kind, drawn from the principle of *perfect happiness,* are built on either physical or moral feeling. Principles of the *second* kind, drawn from the principle of *perfection,* are built either on the rational concept of perfection as a possible effect of our will or on the concept of an independently existing perfection (God's will) as a determining cause of our will.

Empirical principles are never fit to serve as a foundation for moral laws. For the universality with which these laws must hold for all rational beings without exception—the unconditioned practical necessity that they thus impose—is lost if their basis is taken from the *particular constitution of human nature* or from the accidental circumstances in which it is placed. The principle of *one's own perfect happiness* is, however, the most objectionable, not just because it is false and because its claim that well-being always adjusts itself to well-doing is contradicted by experience; nor merely because it contributes nothing whatever towards establishing morality, since making people happy is quite different from making them good, and making them prudent or clever in seeking their own advantage is quite different from making them virtuous. It is most objectionable because by basing morality on sensuous motives which undermine it and totally destroy its sublimity, since it puts the motives of virtue in the same class as those of vice and teaches us only to become better at calculation, the specific difference between virtue and vice is completely obliterated. On the other hand, moral feeling, this alleged special sense[17] (however shallow be the appeal to it, when people who are unable to *think* hope to help themselves out by *feeling,* even when the question is solely one of universal law, and however little feelings, differing as they naturally do from one another by an infinity of degrees, can supply a uniform measure of good and evil—let alone the fact that one person by his feeling can make no valid judgements at all for others)—moral feeling still remains closer to morality and to its dignity in this respect: it does virtue the honour of ascribing to her *directly* the approval and esteem in which she is held, and does not, as it were, tell her to her face that we are attached to her, not for her beauty, but only for our own advantage.

Among the *rational* or reason-based foundations of morality, the ontological concept of *perfection* is better than the theological concept that derives morality from a divine and supremely perfect will. It is of course empty, indefinite, and consequently useless for discovering in the boundless field of possible reality, the greatest sum which is appropriate to us; and, in trying to distinguish specifically between the reality here in question from every other reality, it inevitably tends to move in a circle and cannot avoid tacitly presupposing the morality it is meant to explain. Still, it is better than the theological concept, which derives morality from an all-perfect, divine will, not merely because we cannot directly apprehend God's perfection and can only derive it from our own concepts, among which that of morality is pre-eminent; but because, if we do not do this (and to do it would be to give a grossly circular explanation), the concept of God's will that remains for us is made up of such attributes as lust for glory and dominion, bound up with frightful ideas of power and vengefulness—inevitably the foundation for a moral system that would be directly opposed to morality.

Yet if I had to choose between the concept of moral sense and that of perfection in general (both of which at least do not undermine morality, though they are totally unfit to support it as its foundation), I should decide for the latter. For this, since it at least withdraws the decision of this question from sensibility and brings it before the court of pure reason, even though it there decides nothing, does still preserve undistorted the indeterminate Idea (of a will good in itself) for more precise definition.

For the rest I believe I may be excused from a lengthy refutation of all these systems. This is so easy and is presumably so well understood even by those whose office requires them to declare themselves for one or other of these theories (since their audience will not lightly put up with a suspension of judgement) that to spend time on it would be merely superfluous labour. But what is of more interest to us here is to know that these principles never lay down anything but heteronomy as the first basis of morality and must in consequence necessarily fail in their objective.

Whenever an object of the will has to be assumed as prescribing the rule that is to determine the will, the rule is nothing but heteronomy. The imperative is then conditional: '*If* or *because* one wants this object, one ought to act thus or thus'. Consequently this imperative can never command morally, that is, categorically. In whatever way the object determines the will—whether by means of inclination, as in the principle of one's own perfect happiness, or by means of reason directed to objects of our possible volitions generally, as in the principle of perfection—the will in these cases never determines itself *directly* by the thought of an action, but only by the motivation which the anticipated effect of the action exercises on the will: '*I ought to do something because I want something else'.* And the basis for this imperative must be the assumption of yet another law in my person, whereby I necessarily will this 'something else'—and this law in turn requires an imperative to limit this maxim. Because the idea of an object commensurate to our own powers stimulates in the will of the subject an impulse in accordance with our natural constitution, this impulse belongs to the nature of the subject, whether to sensibility, (i.e., inclinations and taste) or to understanding and reason, whose operation on an object is accompanied by delight due to the particular constitution of their nature. Strictly speaking, therefore, it is nature that would prescribe the law. This law, as a law of nature, not only must be known and proved by experience and therefore is in itself contingent and consequently unfitted to serve as an apodictic rule of action such as a moral rule must be, but it is *always merely heteronomy of the will*: The will would not prescribe the law to itself, but an alien stimulus would do so through the medium of the subject's own nature which is attuned to receive it.

An absolutely good will, whose principle must be a categorical imperative, will therefore be undetermined with respect to all objects and will contain only the *form* of *willing* in general and that form is autonomy. In other words, the fitness of the maxim of every good will to make itself a universal law is itself the sole law that the will of every rational being spontaneously imposes on itself without requiring any incentive or interest for support.

445   *How such a synthetic practical proposition is possible a priori* and why it is necessary—that is a problem whose solution does not lie within the boundaries of the metaphysics of morals; nor have we claimed it to be true or, still less, pretended to have a proof of it in our power. We have merely shown by developing the generally accepted concept of morality that autonomy of the will is unavoidably bound up with it or rather is its very foundation. Whoever therefore takes morality to be something real and not merely an illusory idea that lacks truth, must at the same time admit its principle, which we have presented here. This chapter, consequently, like the first, has been merely analytical. To prove that morality is not a mere phantom of the brain—a conclusion that follows if the categorical imperative, and with it the autonomy of the will is true and is absolutely necessary as an a priori principle—requires a *possible synthetic use of pure practical reason.* But we cannot venture on this synthetic use of reason without prefacing it by a *critique* of this faculty of reason itself. In our final chapter we outline, sufficiently for our purpose, the main features of such a critique.

446   # CHAPTER THREE

Final Step from a Metaphysics of Morals to a Critique of Pure Practical Reason

The Concept of Freedom Is the Key to Explain Autonomy of the Will

The will is a kind of causality that living beings have so far as they are rational. *Freedom* would then be that property whereby this causality can be active,

independently of alien causes *determining* it; just as *natural necessity* is a property characterizing the causality of all non-rational beings—the property of being determined to activity by the influence of alien causes.

The above definition of freedom is *negative* and therefore sterile when it comes to grasping freedom's essence; but a *positive* concept springs from it, which is richer and more fruitful. Since the concept of causality carries with it that of *laws,* implying that because of something we call a cause, something else—namely, its effect—must be posited, so freedom, although it is not a property the will has by virtue of natural laws, is not for that reason totally lawless. Freedom must rather be a causality that accords with immutable laws, though laws of a special kind; for otherwise a free will would be a fiction. Natural necessity, as we have seen, is a heteronomy of efficient causes; for we saw that every effect was only possible according to the law that something else gets the efficient cause to act as a cause. What   447 else then can freedom of will be but autonomy—that is, the property that a will has of being a law to itself? However, the proposition 'Will is in all its actions a law to itself' expresses only the principle of acting on no other maxim than one that can also have being itself a universal law for its object. But this is precisely the formula of the Categorical Imperative and the principle of morality. Thus a free will and a will under moral laws are one and the same.

Consequently if freedom of the will is presupposed, then morality, together with its principle, follows from this presupposition by mere analysis of its concept. Nevertheless the principle of morality is still a synthetic proposition, namely: An absolutely good will is one whose maxim can always include itself considered as a universal law; for this characteristic of its maxim cannot be discovered by analysis of the concept of an absolutely good will. Such synthetic propositions are however possible only if two cognitions are bound together by their connection with a third in which both of them are to be found. The *positive* concept of freedom supplies this third cognition, which cannot, as is the case with physical causes, be the nature of the sensible world (in the concept of which the concepts of something as a cause in relation to *something else* as effect come together). What this third cognition is, to which freedom directs us and of which we have an Idea a priori, cannot yet be shown here; nor can we as yet make comprehensible the deduction of the concept of freedom from pure practical reason and so the possibility of a categorical imperative. Some further preparation is needed.

1. Freedom Must be Presupposed as a Property of the Will of All Rational Beings

It is not enough to ascribe freedom to our will, on whatever basis, unless we have sufficient reason to attribute the same freedom to all rational beings. For since morality serves as a law for us only insofar as we are *rational beings,* it must be equally valid for all rational beings; and since it must be derived solely from the property of freedom, we need to prove that freedom too is a property of the will of all rational beings. And it is not enough to demonstrate freedom by appeal to certain alleged experiences of human nature (though to demonstrate freedom in this way is in any case absolutely impossible—it can be demonstrated only a priori). Rather, we must prove that freedom belongs universally to the activity of rational beings endowed with a will. Now I say that every being who cannot act except *under the Idea of freedom* is just for that reason really free—from the standpoint of practice. That is to say, all laws inseparably bound up with freedom are valid for such a being just as if his will could be proved to be free in itself and by means of proofs taken from theoretical philosophy.[18] I maintain too that we must necessarily grant the idea of freedom to every rational being who has a will, since only under that idea can such a being act. For we think of such a being as having a power of reason that is practical, i.e., that has causality in regard to its aims. But it is impossible to conceive of a power of reason that consciously regards its own judgements as directed from outside; for in that case the subject would attribute the determination of his power of judgement to some impulse, not to his reason. Reason must regard itself as the author of its own principles independently of alien influences. It follows that reason, as practical reason, or as the will of a rational being, must regard

itself as free. That is to say, the will of a rational being can be a will of its own only under the idea of freedom, and it must therefore—for purposes of action—be attributed to all rational beings.

2. Of the Interest Attached to the Ideas of Morality

We have at last traced the distinct concept of morality back to the Idea of freedom, but we could not demonstrate freedom as something real in human nature nor even in ourselves. We saw only that we must presuppose it if we want to conceive a being as rational and as endowed with consciousness of his causality in regard to actions—that is, as endowed with a will. Thus we find that on precisely the same grounds we must attribute to every being endowed with reason and a will this property of determining himself to action under the Idea of his freedom.

From the presupposition of this Idea there sprang also, as we saw, the consciousness of a law governing action, the law that subjective principles of action—that is, maxims—must always be so chosen that they can also hold as objective principles—that is, universally—and can therefore serve for our own enactment of universal law. But why should I subject myself to this principle simply as a rational being and in so doing also subject to it every other being endowed with reason? I am willing to admit that no interest *drives* me to do so, since that would not produce a categorical imperative. Yet I must necessarily *take* an interest in it and understand how this happens; for this 'I ought to' is actually an 'I intend to' that would hold necessarily for every rational being—if reason in him were practical without hindrance. For beings like us, who are affected also by the senses—that is, by motives of a different kind—and who do not always act as reason by itself would act, this necessity of action is only an 'ought' and the subjective necessity is distinguished from the objective.

It thus looks as though we have in fact merely presupposed the moral law in our Idea of freedom—that is, presupposed the principle of the autonomy of the will itself—without being able to give an independent proof of its reality and objective necessity. But in that case we would still have gained

448

449

something quite considerable, since we would at least have formulated the genuine principle more precisely than has been done before. However, we would have made no progress at all with proving the principle's validity and the practical necessity of subjecting ourselves to it. For if someone asks us: Why must the universal validity of our maxim as a law be the condition that restricts our action, and what is the basis of the worth we ascribe to this way of acting—a worth supposedly so great that there cannot be any interest higher than it—and asks how it happens that human beings believe this alone to be the source of their personal worth, in contrast to which the worth of a pleasant or painful condition counts as nothing? To these questions we could give no sufficient answer.

We do indeed find that we can take an interest in a personal characteristic that involves no interest in any condition, but only if that characteristic makes us fit to share in the latter condition in case reason were to determine its distribution. That is to say, the mere fact of deserving to be happy, even without the motive of sharing in this happiness, can by itself interest us. But such a judgement is in fact merely the result of the importance we have already assumed moral laws to have (when by means of the Idea of freedom we detach ourselves from every empirical interest). But we cannot as yet see why we ought to detach ourselves from such interest—that is, why we ought to regard ourselves as free in our actions and yet bound by certain laws, in order to find solely in our own person a worth that can compensate us for the loss of everything that makes our condition valuable. We do not see how this is possible nor consequently *on what grounds the moral law can be binding.*

We must frankly admit that a kind of circle shows up here, from which there seems to be no escape. We suppose ourselves to be free in the order of efficient causes in order that we may conceive ourselves to be under moral laws in the order of ends; and then we proceed to think of ourselves as subject to moral laws on the ground that we have ascribed freedom of will to ourselves. For freedom and the will's lawgiving of its own laws are both autonomy, and therefore reciprocal concepts. But just

for this reason one of them cannot be used to explain the other or to furnish its ground. It can at most be used for the logical purpose of reducing seemingly different ideas of the same object to a single concept (as different fractions of the same value can be reduced to the lowest common terms).

One route, however, still remains open to us. We can inquire whether we do not take one standpoint when, through freedom, we think of ourselves as causes acting a priori, and another standpoint when we contemplate ourselves in the light of our actions as effects that we see before our eyes.

A remark that does not require any subtle reflection and that we may assume even the most ordinary intelligence can make—no doubt in its own way, by some obscure distinction in the power of judgement that it calls 'feeling', is this: all ideas that come to us involuntarily (as do those of the senses) allow us to know objects only as they affect us: what those objects may be in themselves remains unknown. Consequently, ideas of this kind, no matter how strenuously the understanding attempts to exert focus and clarity on them, serve only to give us knowledge of *appearances,* never of *things in themselves.* Once this distinction is drawn (it may be merely by noting the difference between ideas given to us from without, where we ourselves are passive, and ideas which we produce entirely from ourselves, ideas that therefore manifest our own activity), it follows directly that behind appearances we must admit and assume something else which is not appearance—namely, things in themselves. Since we can never be acquainted with these, but only with the way in which they affect us, we must however resign ourselves to the fact that we can never get any nearer to them and can never know what they are in themselves. This thought must yield a distinction, however rough, between a *sensible world* and the *intelligible world,* the first of which can vary a great deal because of differences in sensibility among different observers, while the second, which is its foundation, always remains the same. Even as regards himself—so far as a human being is acquainted with himself by inner sensation—he has no right to claim to know what he is in himself. For since he does not as it were create himself and since he acquires his concept of himself not a priori but empirically, it is natural that he can get information even about himself only through inner sense and so only through the way his nature appears and the way his consciousness is affected. Beyond this constitution of himself as a subject, compounded of nothing but appearances, he must assume that there is something else that is its foundation—namely, his ego, however it may be constituted in itself. Thus, as far as mere perception and the capacity for receiving sensations are concerned, he must count himself as belonging to the *world of sense,* but as regards whatever pure activity there may be in him (whatever reaches consciousness directly and not by affecting the senses), *he* must count himself as belonging to the *intellectual world.* Of that world, however, he knows nothing more.

A reflective human being must reach a conclusion of this kind about all things that may present themselves to him. Such a conclusion is presumably to be found even in the most common understanding, which, as is well known, is always inclined to look behind the objects of the senses for something further that is invisible and is spontaneously active. But such an understanding goes on to spoil this invisible something by immediately trying to make it into something sensible—that is to say, it wants to make it an object of intuition, so by this procedure the common understanding does not become the least bit wiser.

Now, a human being actually finds in himself a power by which he distinguishes himself from all other things—and even from himself so far as he is affected by objects. That power is *reason.* As pure spontaneity, reason is elevated even above the *understanding* in the following respect: although the latter too is spontaneous activity and is not, like sense, confined to ideas that arise only when we are affected by things (and therefore are passive), it can produce by its own activity only concepts whose sole purpose is *to bring sensuous representations under rules* and so to unite them in one consciousness. Without using sensibility, the understanding would think nothing at all. Reason, on the other hand—in what are called 'Ideas'—shows a spontaneity so pure that it goes far beyond anything sensibility can offer. It manifests its highest function in distinguishing the world of sense

from the intelligible world and thereby prescribing limits to the understanding itself.

Because of this a rational being must regard himself, *as an intelligence* (i.e., not from the perspective of his lower powers), as belonging to the world of the understanding rather than the world of sense. Consequently he has two perspectives from which he can consider himself and from which he can acknowledge the laws governing the use of his powers and consequently governing all his actions. He can consider himself *first* so far as he belongs to the world of sense, under laws of nature (heteronomy); and *secondly*—so far as he belongs to the intelligible world—under laws that are not empirical but being independent of nature, are founded on reason alone.

As a rational being, and consequently as a being who belongs to the intelligible world, a human being can never conceive the causality of his own will except under the Idea of freedom; for independence from the determining causes of the sensible world (and this is what reason must always ascribe to itself) is freedom. To the Idea of freedom there is inseparably attached the concept of *autonomy,* but to the latter in turn the universal principle of morality—a principle which ideally is the ground of all the actions of *rational* beings, just as the law of nature is the ground of all appearances.

We have now removed the suspicion which we raised earlier, namely, that there might be a hidden circle in our reasoning from freedom to autonomy and from autonomy to the moral law, the suspicion that in effect we had perhaps assumed the Idea of freedom only because of the moral law in order later to derive the moral law from freedom; and that we were thus unable to offer any ground at all for the moral law, but had merely begged the question by putting forward a principle which well-meaning souls would gladly concede us, but never as a demonstrable proposition. We see now that when we think of ourselves as free, we transfer ourselves into the world of the understanding as members and we recognize the autonomy of the will together with its consequence, morality; whereas when we think of ourselves as under obligation, we view ourselves as belonging to the world of sense and yet simultaneously to the world of understanding.

3. How Is a Categorical Imperative Possible?

As an intelligence, a rational being counts himself as belonging to the world of the understanding, and simply as an efficient cause belonging to that world, he calls his causality a will. On the other hand, however, he is also conscious of himself as a part of the world of sense, where his actions are encountered as mere appearances of that causality. But we can have no insight into how these actions are possible by means of such a causality, since we have no direct acquaintance with it. Instead, these actions, when viewed as belonging to the world of sense, have to be understood as determined by other appearances—namely, by desires and inclinations. Hence, if I were solely a member of the world of understanding, all my actions would conform perfectly to the principle of the autonomy of a pure will; if I were solely a part of the sensible world, they would have to be taken as conforming completely to the natural law of desires and inclinations, consequently to the heteronomy of nature. (In the first case they would rest on the supreme principle of morality; in the second case on that of happiness.) But since the *world of understanding contains the ground of the world of sense and therefore also of its laws,* it thus gives laws directly to my will (which belongs entirely to the world of understanding) and must be conceived as thus lawgiving. Therefore, although I regard myself from one point of view as a being that belongs to the world of sense, I shall have to recognize that, as an intelligence, I am subject to the law of the world of understanding—that is, of reason, which contains this law in the Idea of freedom, and thus in the autonomy of the will. I must therefore regard the laws of the world of the understanding as imperatives for me and see the actions that conform to this principle as duties.

And thus categorical imperatives are possible, because the Idea of freedom makes me a member of an intelligible world. If I were only that, then all my actions *would* thereby invariably be in accord with the autonomy of the will. But since I see myself at the same time as a member of the world of sense, my

actions *ought* to be in accord with it. This *categorical* 'ought' presents us with a synthetic a priori proposition, since to my will as affected by sensuous desires there is added the Idea of that same will, viewed, however, as a pure will belonging to the world of understanding and active of its own accord—a will which, according to reason, contains the supreme condition of the former, my sensuously affected will. This is similar to the way in which concepts of the understanding, which by themselves signify nothing but lawful form in general, are added to intuitions of the world of sense and so make possible synthetic a priori propositions on which all knowledge of nature is based.

The use of common human reason in matters of conduct confirms the correctness of this deduction. There is no one, not even the most malicious villain, provided only that he is otherwise accustomed to use reason, who, when presented with examples of honesty of purpose, of faithfulness to good maxims, of sympathy, and of general benevolence even when requiring great sacrifice of advantages and comfort, does not wish that he too might have these qualities. He cannot bring this about in himself, only because of his desires and impulses, but at the same time he wishes he could be free from these burdensome inclinations. By such a wish he proves that with a will free from sensuous impulses he transfers himself in thought into an order of things altogether different from that of his desires in the field of sensibility. For he cannot expect that the fulfillment of this wish would gratify any of his sensuous desires, nor that any of his actual or even conceivable inclinations will be satisfied (since such an expectation would cause the very Idea that elicited the wish to forfeit its excellence). All he can expect is a greater inner worth of his own person. He believes himself to be this better person when he transfers himself to the standpoint of a member of the world of understanding. It is the Idea of freedom that involuntarily constrains him to do this—that is, the Idea of being independent of *determining* causes of the world of sense; and from this standpoint he is conscious of possessing a good will which, on his own admission, constitutes the law for his evil will as a member of the world of sense—a law of whose authority he is conscious even while transgressing it. The moral 'I ought' is thus his own necessary 'I will' as a member of the intelligible world; and he thinks of it as an 'I ought' only insofar as he regards himself at the same time to be a member of the world of sense.

4. The Extreme Limit of Practical Philosophy

All human beings think of themselves as having free will. That is the basis of all the judgements of actions that say they *ought to have been done,* although they *were not done.* But this freedom is not an empirical concept, nor can it be, since it still holds although experience shows the contrary of those requirements that are viewed as necessary under the presupposition of freedom. On the other hand, it is equally necessary that everything that takes place should he inexorably determined in accordance with the laws of nature; and this necessity of nature is likewise not an empirical concept, precisely because it carries with it the concept of necessity and thus the concept of an a priori cognition. This concept of a system of nature is, however, confirmed by experience and must unavoidably be presupposed if experience— that is, coherent knowledge of sensible objects in accordance with universal laws—is to be possible. Hence, while freedom is only an Idea of Reason whose objective reality is in itself questionable, nature is a *concept of the understanding,* which proves, and must necessarily prove, its reality in examples from experience.

From this there arises a dialectic of reason, since the freedom ascribed to the will seems to contradict the necessity of nature. Although at this parting of the ways reason, for *cognitive* purposes, finds the path of natural necessity much more beaten and serviceable than that of freedom, yet for *purposes of action* the footpath of freedom is the only one on which we can make use of our reason in our conduct. Hence it is as impossible for the subtlest philosophy as it is for the most common human reason to argue freedom away. Philosophy must therefore presuppose that no genuine contradiction will be found between freedom and natural necessity ascribed to the very same human actions, for it cannot give up the concept of nature any more than that of freedom.

456

All the same, even if we should never be able to grasp how freedom is possible, this seeming contradiction must at least be eradicated convincingly. For if even the thought of freedom contradicts itself or contradicts nature—a concept which is equally necessary—freedom would have to be given up altogether in favour of natural necessity.

It would be impossible to escape from this contradiction if the subject who believes himself free thought of himself *in the same sense,* or *in precisely the same relationship,* when he calls himself free as when he assumes that in the same action he is subject to the law of nature. Hence speculative philosophy has the unavoidable task of showing at least that its illusion about the contradiction rests on our thinking of the human being in one sense and relation when we call him free and in another when we consider him, as a part of nature, to be subject to nature's laws. And philosophy must show not merely that both characteristics *can* very well coexist, but that they must be thought of as *necessarily united* in one and the same subject. For otherwise we could not explain why we should burden reason with an Idea which—even if it can *without contradiction* be united with another concept that has been adequately justified—entangles us in a perplexity that sorely embarrasses reason in its theoretical use. This duty is imposed on speculative philosophy only in order that it may clear a path for practical philosophy. Thus philosophers have no choice as to whether they will remove the seeming contradiction or leave it untouched; for in the latter case the theory on this topic would be *bonum vacans* [unoccupied property—a good that belongs to no one], of which the fatalist can justifiably take possession and can chase all of morality out of its supposed property, which it has no title to hold.

Nevertheless we cannot yet say that at this point the boundary of practical philosophy begins. For the settlement of this controversy is not part of practical philosophy, which merely requires speculative reason to bring to an end the dissension in which it is entangled on theoretical questions, so that practical reason may have peace and security from external attacks which could contest its right to the ground on which it seeks to build.

457

The legitimate title to freedom of the will claimed even by common human reason is grounded on the consciousness and the accepted presupposition that reason is independent of purely subjective determining causes which collectively make up all that belongs to sensation and comes under the general name of sensibility. In thus regarding himself as an intelligence, a human being puts himself into another order of things, and into relation with determining causes of quite another sort, when he thinks of himself as an intelligence endowed with a will and consequently with causality, than he does when he perceives himself as a phenomenon (which he actually is as well) in the world of sense, and sees his causality as the result of external determination in accordance with laws of nature. He then soon realizes that both of these can, and indeed must, take place at the same time. For there is not the slightest contradiction in holding that a thing *as an appearance* (as belonging to the world of sense) is subject to certain laws, laws of which it is independent *as a thing* or a being *in itself.* That he must think and conceive of himself in this twofold way rests, as regards the first way, on the consciousness of himself as an object affected through the senses; as concerns the second way, it rests on the consciousness of himself as an intelligence—that is, as independent of sensible impressions in his use of reason (and so as belonging to the world of understanding).

This is why the human being claims for himself a will that does not allow him to be accountable for anything that belongs merely to his desires and inclinations. Rather, he conceives of actions that can be done only by disregarding all desires and incitements of sense as possible—indeed as necessary—through this will. The causality of such actions lies in him as intelligence and in the laws of effects and actions according to the principles of an intelligible world. Of that world he knows nothing but this—that in that intelligible world, reason alone, and indeed pure reason independent of sensibility, is the source of law; and also that since in that world he is his true self, an intelligence only (while as a human being he is merely an appearance of himself), these laws apply to him directly and categorically. It follows that what desires and impulses (and therefore the whole nature of the sensible world) spur him to do cannot impair the laws of his will as intelligence. Indeed he does not even hold himself responsible for those desires and impulses nor impute them to his true self, that is, to his will, though he does impute to himself the indulgence he would show them if he were to let them influence his maxims to the detriment of the rational laws of his will.

458

Practical reason does not overstep its limits in the least by *thinking* itself into the world of understanding. It would do so only if it sought to *inspect* [*hineinschauen*] *or feel itself* into that world. That thinking is a merely negative thought—that the world of sense gives reason no laws for determining the will. It is a positive thought only in one point: that that freedom, as a negative characteristic, is combined with a (positive) power as well—a causality of reason we call a will—the power to act so that the principle of our actions accords with the essential character of a rational cause, that is, with the condition that the maxim of these actions have the universal validity of a law. But if practical reason were also to take from the intelligible world *an object of the will,* that is, a motivating cause of action, it would overstep its limits and pretend to be acquainted with something of which it knows nothing. The concept of a world of understanding is thus only a *standpoint* that reason finds itself constrained to adopt outside of appearances, *in order to think of itself as practical.* If the influences of sensibility were determining for human beings, this would be impossible. It is nevertheless necessary unless the human being is to be denied the consciousness of himself as an intelligence and consequently as a rational and rationally active cause—that is, a cause that is free in its operation. This thought certainly brings on the Idea of another order and another lawgiving than that of the mechanism of nature, which applies to the world of sense. It makes necessary the concept of an intelligible world (that is, the concept of the totality of rational beings as things in themselves) but it makes not the slightest pretence of doing more than to conceive of such a world with respect to its *formal* condition—that is, as conforming to the condition that the maxim of the will should have the universality of a law, and so as conforming to the autonomy of the will, which alone is compatible with its freedom. In contrast with this, all laws determined by reference to an object give us heteronomy, which can be found only in laws of nature and can apply only to the world of sense.

But reason would overstep all its limits if it took it upon itself to *explain how* pure reason can be practical. This would be exactly the same task as explaining *how freedom is possible.*

For we cannot explain anything unless we can bring it under laws whose object can be given in some possible experience. Freedom, however, is a mere Idea: its objective reality can in no way be exhibited according to laws of nature nor, consequently, in any possible experience. And since no example can ever illustrate it even by analogy, we can have no full comprehension or insight into the Idea of freedom. It holds only as a necessary presupposition of reason in a being that believes itself to be conscious of a will—that is, of a power distinct from the mere faculty of desire (a power, namely, of determining itself to act as intelligence and consequently to act in accordance with laws of reason independently of natural instincts). But where determination by laws of nature comes to an end, all *explanation* comes to an end as well. Nothing remains but *defence*—that is, to repulse the objections of those who pretend to have seen more deeply into the essence of things and therefore boldly declare freedom to be impossible. We can only show them that the contradiction they pretend to have discovered in it consists just in this: in order to make the law of nature apply validly to human actions, they must necessarily consider the human being as an appearance; and now that they are asked to think of him as an intelligence and also as a thing in himself, they persist in looking at him as an appearance in this respect also. In that case, admittedly, to exempt the human being's causality (that is, his will) from all the natural laws of the sensible world, in one and the same subject, would yield a contradiction. But that contradiction would fall away if they were willing to reflect and to admit, as is only fair, that behind appearances there must lie things in themselves as their hidden ground, and that we cannot expect the laws by which things in themselves act to be identical with those laws that govern their appearances.

The subjective impossibility of explaining the freedom of the will is one and the same as the impossibility of locating and making comprehensible an *interest*[19] that a human being can take in moral laws; and yet he does really take such an interest. We call the foundation in us of this interest "moral feeling"—a feeling that has been mistakenly taken by some people to be the standard for our moral judgement. It ought to be regarded rather as the *subjective* effect exercised on our will by the law. It is reason alone that supplies the objective grounds for that law.

In order to will actions that reason by itself prescribes to a rational, yet sensuously affected being as what he ought to do, it is certainly necessary that reason should have a power of *infusing a feeling of pleasure* or a feeling of satisfaction in the fulfilment of duty, and consequently that it should possess a kind of causality by which it can determine sensibility in accordance with rational principles. It is, however, wholly impossible to comprehend—that is, to make intelligible a priori—how a mere thought containing nothing sensible in itself can bring about a sensation of pleasure or displeasure; for there is here a special kind of causality, and—as with all causality—we are totally unable to determine its character a priori. For any knowledge of such a causality, we must consult experience alone. But experience cannot provide us with a relation of cause and effect except between two objects of experience—whereas here pure reason by means of mere Ideas (which furnish absolutely no objects for experience) has to be the cause of an effect admittedly found in experience. Hence for us human beings it is wholly impossible to explain how and why the *universality of a maxim as a law*—and therefore morality—should interest us. This much only is certain; the law is not valid for us *because it interests us* (for this is heteronomy and makes practical reason dependent on sensibility— that is to say, on an underlying feeling—in which case practical reason could never give us moral laws). The law interests us because it is valid for us as human beings in virtue of having sprung from our will as intelligence and so from our true self. *But what belongs to mere appearance is necessarily subordinated by reason to the character of the thing in itself.*

Thus the question 'How is a categorical imperative possible?' can be answered to this extent: We can supply the sole presupposition under which it is possible—namely, the Idea of freedom—and we can discern the necessity of this presupposition. This is sufficient for the *practical use* of reason—that is, to convince us of the *validity of this imperative,* and so too of the moral law. But human reason will forever lack insight into how this presupposition itself is possible. On the presupposition that the will of an intelligence is free, its *autonomy* follows necessarily as the formal condition under which alone it can be determined. It is not only perfectly *possible* to presuppose such freedom of the will (as speculative philosophy can prove, and without contradicting the principle that natural necessity governs the interconnection of appearances in the world of sense); it is also unconditionally *necessary,* that is, necessary in Idea that a rational being conscious of exercising his causality by means of reason and so of having a will (which is distinct from desires) should take such freedom as the fundamental condition of all his voluntary actions. But *how* pure reason can be practical by itself without any further motives drawn from some other source; that is, how the bare principle of *the universal validity of all its maxims as laws* (which would certainly be the form of a pure practical reason) can by itself—without any material (or object) of the will in which we might take some prior interest—how pure reason can supply a motive and create an interest which could be called purely *moral*; or, in other words, *how pure reason can be practical*—all human reason is totally incapable of explaining this, and all the pains and labour to seek such an explanation are wasted.

It is precisely the same as if I sought to fathom how freedom itself as the causality of a will is possible. For in doing this I would abandon the philosophical basis of explanation, and I have no other. I could, no doubt, proceed to daydream in the intelligible world, which still remains to me—the world of intelligences; but although I have a well-founded *Idea* of it, I have not the slightest *knowledge* of it and cannot hope to arrive at any by all the efforts of my natural power of reason. My Idea of this intelligible world signifies only a 'something' that remains when I have excluded from the grounds determining my will everything that belongs to the world of sense; its sole purpose is to restrict the principle of motivating causes [*Bewegursachen*] from the field of sensibility, by setting bounds to this field and by showing that it does not encompass absolutely everything within itself, but that there is still more beyond it; yet with this 'more' I have no further acquaintance. All that remains for me of the pure reason that formulates this ideal, after I have excluded all material—that is, all knowledge of objects—from it, is its form: the practical law that maxims should be universally valid, plus the corresponding conception of reason, in its relation to a purely intelligible world, as a possible efficient cause, that is, as a cause determining the will. Here the sensuous motive [*Triebfeder*] must be entirely absent; for this Idea of an intelligible world would itself have to be the motive or that in which reason took a direct interest. But to make this comprehensible is precisely the problem that we cannot solve.

Here then is the supreme limit of all moral inquiry. To define it is of great importance so that reason may not, on the one hand, hunt around in the sensible world, to the detriment of morality, for the supreme motive and for some comprehensible but empirical interest; and so that it will not, on the other hand, impotently flap its wings in the space (for it, an empty space) of transcendent concepts known as 'the intelligible world', flailing without moving from the spot, and thus losing itself among phantoms of the brain. For the rest, the Idea of a pure world of the understanding, as a whole of all intelligences to which we ourselves belong as rational beings (although from another point of view we are also members of the world of sense), remains always as a useful and permitted Idea for the purposes of a reasonable faith though all knowledge ends at its border. It serves to produce in us a lively interest in the moral law by means of the splendid ideal of a universal kingdom of ends in themselves (rational beings), to which we can belong as members only if we are scrupulous to conduct ourselves in accordance with maxims of freedom, as if they were laws of nature.

Concluding Remark

The speculative use of reason *in regard to nature* leads to the absolute necessity of some supreme cause of the *world;* the practical use of reason *with respect to freedom* leads also to absolute necessity, but only to the absolute necessity *of the laws of actions* for a rational being as such. Now it is an essential *principle* for every use of reason to push its knowledge to a consciousness of its *necessity* (for without necessity it would not be rational knowledge). But it is an equally essential *limitation* of this same reason that it cannot have insight into the necessity either of what is or of what happens, or of what ought to happen, unless a *condition* is presupposed under which it is or happens or ought to happen. In this way, however, by continual asking for the condition, reason's satisfaction is merely postponed again and again. Hence reason restlessly seeks the unconditionally necessary and sees itself compelled to assume it without any means of making it comprehensible, though it is happy enough if only it can find a concept compatible with this presupposition. Thus it is no discredit to our deduction of the supreme principle of morality, but rather a reproach which must be brought against reason as such, that it cannot make comprehensible the absolute necessity of an unconditional practical law (such as the categorical imperative must be). For reason cannot be blamed for its unwillingness to do this by means of a condition—namely, by basing this necessity on some underlying interest—since in that case there would be no moral law, that is, no supreme law of freedom. And thus, while we do not comprehend the practical unconditional necessity of the moral imperative, we do comprehend its *incomprehensibility.* This is all that can fairly be demanded of a philosophy that presses forward in its principles to the very frontier of human reason.

NOTES

1. Kant refers here to the second proposition of morality without having explicitly identified the first proposition as such. Probably what was intended as the first proposition of morality was that only an action done from duty could have moral worth.

2. A *maxim* is the subjective principle of volition: an objective principle (that is, one which would also serve subjectively as a practical principle for all rational beings if reason had full control over the faculty of desire) is a practical *law.*

3. It might be objected that instead of clearly resolving the question by means of a concept of reason I have tried to take refuge in an obscure feeling, under the cover of the word *'respect'* [*Achtung*]. However, though respect is a feeling, it is not a feeling that we are caused to *receive* by some (external) influence: rather, it is a feeling that is *self-generated* by a rational concept, and it is therefore different in kind from feelings of the first sort, all of which can be reduced to inclination or fear. What I recognize directly as a law for myself, I recognize with respect, which means nothing more than the consciousness of my will's *submission* to the law, without the mediation of any other influences on my mind. The direct determination of the will by the law, and the awareness of that determination, is called *'respect'* so we should see respect as the *effect* of the law on a person rather than as what *produces* the law. Actually, respect is the thought of something of such worth that it breaches my self-love. It is neither an object of inclination nor an object of fear, though it is somewhat analogous to both. The sole *object* of respect is the [moral] *law*—that law which we impose *on ourselves* and yet recognize as necessary in itself. As a law, we must submit to it without any consulting of self-love; as self-imposed it is nevertheless a consequence of our will. Considered in the first way, it is analogous to fear: considered in the second way, analogous to inclination. All respect for a person is actually only respect for the law (of righteousness, etc.,) that that person exemplifies. Because we regard the development of our talents as a duty, we see a talented person also as a sort of *example of a law* (to strive to resemble that person), and this is what constitutes our respect. Any moral so-called *interest* consists solely in *respect* for the law.

4. We can, if we wish, distinguish pure moral philosophy (metaphysics) from applied (applied, that is, to human nature—just as pure mathematics is distinguished from applied mathematics and pure logic from applied logic). Using this terminology immediately reminds us that moral principles are not grounded on the peculiarities of human nature, but must be established a priori by themselves, though it must be possible to derive practical rules for human

beings from them as well, just as it is for every kind of rational being.

5. I have a letter from the late, distinguished Professor Sulzer, in which he asks me why moral teachings are so ineffective, even though they contain much that is convincing to reason. My answer was delayed because I wanted it to be complete. Yet it is just this: the teachers themselves fail to make their concepts clear, and they over-do their job by looking for all sorts of inducements to moral goodness, spoiling their medicine altogether by their very attempt to make it really powerful. For the most ordinary observation shows that when a righteous act is represented as being done with a steadfast mind in complete disregard of any advantage in this world or another, and even under the greatest temptations of need or enticement, it far surpasses and eclipses any similar act that was affected even in the slightest by an extraneous incentive; it uplifts the soul and arouses the wish that we too could act in this way. Even children of moderate age feel this impression, and one should never present duties to them in any other way. [Editor's note: Johann Georg Sulzer (1720–79) was a prominent aesthetician and so-called 'popular philosopher', important in Berlin intellectual circles. The only extant letter from Sulzer to Kant does not in fact raise the particular question Kant here ascribes to him.]

6. The dependence of the faculty of desire on sensations is called an inclination, and thus an inclination always indicates a *need*. The dependence of a contingently determinable will on principles of reason is called an *interest*. Hence an interest is found only where there is a dependent will which of itself is not always in accord with reason; to God's will we cannot ascribe any interest. But even the human will can *take an interest* in something without therefore *acting out of interest*. The first expression signifies *practical* interest in the action; the second signifies *pathological* interest in the object of the action. [Editor's note: pathological = a feeling one is *caused* or *made* to have by something outside one's own will.] The first indicates only dependence of the will on principles of reason in themselves; the second its dependence on principles of reason at the service of inclination—that is to say, where reason merely supplies a practical rule for meeting the needs of inclination. In the first case what interests me is the action; in the second case what interests me is the object of the action (so far as this object is pleasant to me). We have seen in Chapter One that in an action done out of duty one must consider not the interest in

the object, but the interest in the action itself and its rational principle (namely, the law).

7. The word 'prudence' (*Klugheit*) is used in two senses; in one sense it can be called 'worldly wisdom' (*Weltklugheit*); in a second sense, 'personal wisdom' (*Privatklugheit*). The first is a person's skill in influencing others in order to use them for his own ends. The second is the ability to combine all of these ends to his own lasting advantage. The latter is properly that to which the value of the former can itself be traced; and if a person is prudent in the first sense, but not in the second, we might better say that he is clever and astute, but on the whole imprudent.

8. It seems to me that the proper meaning of the word 'pragmatic' can be defined most accurately in this way. For *sanctions* that do nor properly speaking spring from the law of states as necessary statutes, but arise from *provision* for the general welfare are called pragmatic. We say that a *history* is written pragmatically when it teaches *prudence*—that is, when it instructs the world how to provide for its interests better than, or at least as well as, the world of other times has done.

9. I connect the deed with the will a priori and thus necessarily, without supposing as a condition that there is any inclination for this deed (although I make this connection only objectively—that is to say, under the Idea of a power of reason that would have complete control over all subjective motives). Hence we have here a practical proposition in which the willing of an action is not derived analytically from some other volition already presupposed (for we do not possess any such perfect will); rather, the willing of the action is connected directly with the concept of the will of a rational being [but] as something that is not contained in this concept.

10. A *maxim* is a subjective principle of action and must be distinguished from an *objective principle*—namely, a practical law. The former contains a practical rule determined by reason in accordance with the conditions of the subject (often his ignorance or his inclinations): it is thus a principle on which the subject *acts*. A law, on the other hand, is an objective principle, valid for every rational being; and it is a principle on which he *ought to act*—that is, an imperative.

11. It should be noted that I reserve the division of duties entirely for a future *Metaphysic of Morals* and that my present division is put forward as an arbitrary one (merely for the purpose of arranging my examples). Further, I understand here by a perfect duty one that

allows no exception in the interests of inclination, and so I recognize among *perfect* duties, both outer and inner duties. This runs contrary to the standard usage in the schools, but I do not intend to justify it here, since for my purpose it makes no difference whether this point is conceded or not.

12. To behold virtue in her true form means nothing other than to show morality stripped of any admixture with what is sensuous and of all the inauthentic adornments of reward or self-love. How much she then casts into the shade all else that appears enticing to the inclinations can be readily perceived by anyone willing to exert his reason in the slightest if it is not entirely spoiled for all abstract thinking.

13. This proposition I put forward here as a postulate. The grounds for it will be found in the final chapter.

14. Let no one think that the trivial *'quod tibi non vis fieri, etc.'* [what you do not want to be done to you, etc.] could here serve as a guide or principle. For it is merely a derivation from our principle, and subject to various qualifications: it cannot be a universal law since it contains the ground neither of duties to oneself nor of duties of kindness to others (for many a man would gladly consent that others should not benefit him if only he could be excused from showing benevolence to them. Nor, finally, does this rule contain the ground of strict duties owed to others; for the criminal would be able to argue on this basis against the judge who sentences him, and so on.

15. I may be excused from citing examples to illustrate this principle, since those that were already used to illustrate the categorical imperative and its formula can all serve the same purpose here.

16. Teleology considers nature as a kingdom of ends, morality considers a possible kingdom of ends as a kingdom of nature. In the former, the kingdom of ends is a theoretical Idea that aims to explain what exists. In the latter, it is a practical Idea, aiming to bring about that which does not exist but which could actually become real through our conduct.

17. I classify the principle of moral feeling with that of happiness because every empirical principle promises a contribution to our well-being merely from the satisfaction that something leads us to expect— whether this satisfaction occurs directly and without any consideration of advantage or with a view to such advantage. Similarly we must, with Hutcheson, classify the principle of sympathy for the happiness of others with the principle of moral sense which he assumed.

18. I use this approach here because I take it as sufficient for our purpose if all rational beings in their actions presuppose freedom merely *as an Idea.* Thus I avoid having to prove freedom also from a theoretical point of view. For even if this latter problem is left unsettled, the laws that would obligate a being who was really free are equally valid for a being who cannot act except under the Idea of his own freedom. In this way we can escape from the burden that weighs upon the theory.

19. An interest is that by which reason becomes practical— that is, becomes a cause determining the will. Therefore only of a rational being can one say that he takes an interest in something: non-rational creatures feel only sensuous impulses. Reason takes a direct interest in an action only when the universal validity of the maxim of the action is a ground sufficient to determine the will. Only such an interest is pure. If reason can motivate the will only by means of some further object of desire or under the presupposition of some special feeling in the subject, then it takes only an indirect interest in the action; and since reason all by itself, without the help of experience, can discover neither objects of the will nor a special feeling underlying the will, the latter interest would be merely empirical, and not a pure rational interest. The logical interest of reason (interest in furthering its insights) is never direct, but presupposes purposes for its use.

STUDY QUESTIONS

1. What is Kant's distinction between a hypothetical and a categorical imperative?
2. According to Kant, why does empirical inquiry not provide a sound basis for morality?
3. Can you imagine circumstances in which lying would be morally acceptable?
4. Does Kant's moral philosophy recognize special duties to relatives or friends?

Kantianism

Shelly Kagan

Shelly Kagan, Professor of Philosophy at Yale University, offers an accessible overview of Kant's moral theory. Kagan finds that its appeal lies in the connections it forges between freedom, reasons, and duties. We are free in virtue of our capacity to act for reasons, and these are universal. Hence we fail to act rationally when we act on non-universalizable reasons. Because acting irrationally is the hallmark of immorality, we have a duty to act only on reasons we can share.

I. AUTONOMY AND THE FORMULA OF UNIVERSAL LAW

Where then should we begin? Kantianism begins with freedom. More particularly, it begins with the fact that we are free, and with an account of that freedom. So we must begin with that account. (It is worth noting, however, that the *Groundwork* itself does not begin with the idea of freedom, but rather works backward toward it, arguing in the first two sections that if there is to be such a thing as morality, then we must be free—that freedom is the basis of morality. Unfortunately, in the *Groundwork* itself Kant says rather little explicitly about how exactly we are supposed to be able to move from the assumption of freedom back "up" to morality (see G 4:446–47). Thus we must depart from Kant exegesis almost immediately.)

Kantianism begins with freedom. But I think we will better understand the relevant notion of freedom if we begin instead with rationality. What, exactly, is it to be rational?

Suppose we start with theoretical rationality. As a theoretically rational being, I am capable of examining my various beliefs and seeing whether it makes sense for me to hold them. Thus, in the first place, I have *standards* for evaluating beliefs, in the light of which I can ask whether or not I am justified in holding a given belief. I might, for example, appeal to various principles of logic, discovering that some of my beliefs commit me to accepting still other beliefs; or I might appeal to various rules of scientific methodology, finding that, given the available evidence, I am unjustified in accepting some further belief. But rationality in the theoretical domain goes beyond the mere *evaluation* of my beliefs: I can *change* my beliefs in light of my judgments concerning the extent to which they meet (or fail to meet) the relevant standards. Normally, that is, when I see that the evidence better supports one claim rather than another, my beliefs change accordingly. Roughly, then, theoretical rationality consists in my ability to evaluate my beliefs in light of the standards relevant for evaluating beliefs, and to alter my beliefs in the light of those evaluations.

From Shelly Kagan, "Kantianism for Consequentialists," in *Groundwork for the Metaphysics of Morals*, edited and translated by A. Wood, Yale University Press, 2002. Reprinted by permission of the publisher.

Practical rationality is similar. As a practically rational being I am capable of examining my various desires, goals, intentions, actions, and the like, so as to see which of these make sense in the circumstances. Here too, then, I have standards in terms of which my plans can be evaluated, goals assessed, actions endorsed or criticized. Nor are these various practical elements merely subject to evaluation; I can *change* my goals, my intentions, and the like, in light of my judgments concerning the extent to which these meet (or fail to meet) the relevant standards. Thus practical rationality consists in my ability to evaluate actions, intentions, and so forth, in light of the standards relevant for these, and to alter these elements in light of those evaluations.

Generalizing, then, we can say that rationality—whether practical or theoretical—consists in the ability to evaluate beliefs and acts (and so forth) with an eye to whether they meet the relevant standards, and to alter our beliefs and acts in light of those evaluations.

In this way rationality goes beyond mere intelligence. Nonhuman animals, I presume, also have beliefs and desires, and act in a way that is often appropriate to their circumstances. Some animals may well be extremely adept at achieving goals and forming appropriate beliefs about their environment. Thus they display varying (and perhaps considerable) degrees of intelligence. We could say that *intelligence* consists in the ability to produce beliefs and actions that in point of fact are appropriate (that is, conform to the relevant standards); animals are often intelligent in this sense. But only rational creatures are capable of *articulating* the standards against which beliefs and actions are to be evaluated, and only rational creatures are capable of consciously *comparing* beliefs and actions (real or imagined) against those same standards (G 4:412, 427).

It is worth emphasizing as well the point that as rational beings we are capable of *rejecting* the beliefs and actions (and the like) that don't meet what we take to be the relevant standards. We modify our behavior and our beliefs in light of what we think appropriate. For example, we are not normally *forced* to act on desires that we happen to have, when we conclude that such desires don't make sense, or that

acting on them in present circumstances would be inappropriate (by whatever standards we here take to be relevant). In this way, too, rational beings are different from merely intelligent animals. For it seems plausible to view animals as mere "playthings" or "puppets" of their desires—incapable of evaluating them, and thus incapable of rejecting them. In contrast, rational beings are in an important sense *free*: if we conclude that a given desire makes no sense (perhaps we recognize that it was based on what we now see to be a mistaken belief) or that a given intention is inappropriate, we are free to step back from that desire or intention, and to refuse to act on it.

Of course, the simple fact of the matter is that humans are not *perfectly* rational. At times we misapply our own standards and fail to see that a belief cannot be justified (given the relevant standards). Or we may find ourselves incapable of *abandoning* certain beliefs, even though we can see that these beliefs are not in fact justified. Similarly, at times we may find ourselves giving in to desires, even though we see full well that acting on this desire, in this situation, doesn't actually make sense, or is otherwise inappropriate. Thus we are, at best, only imperfectly rational. Still, it would be implausible to suggest that we are not rational at all (in this sense), for we clearly are capable of articulating standards for evaluating beliefs and actions, and we are typically capable of evaluating our beliefs and actions in the light of those standards; and often, at least, we are capable of modifying our behavior and beliefs in the light of those evaluations. Humans may not be perfectly rational, but we are rational nonetheless, even if only imperfectly so.

The account of rationality that I have been sketching is, indeed, only a sketch. But even so, it remains significantly incomplete, in that I have not yet drawn attention to an important further fact: not only are we capable of articulating relevant standards, and evaluating and modifying beliefs and actions in light of those standards; the standards *themselves* are things that we can evaluate and modify. That is, for any given standard that I might use to evaluate a belief or an act (or an intention, and so forth), I can ask of the standard itself whether *it* makes sense, whether *it* is indeed an appropriate standard to be used in this way in these circumstances. In effect, I can ask whether the given standard itself meets the standards (whatever they are) relevant for evaluating *standards*. And armed with these evaluations, I can in turn reject any given standard, modify it, or replace it. Thus, as a rational being I am free not only to reject, modify, or endorse my various beliefs and actions—I am also free to reject, modify, or endorse the standards I appeal to in evaluating beliefs and actions. I am not forced to accept and appeal to standards that do not make sense to me or that seem unjustified or inappropriate. I am free to alter the standards as I see fit.

And the same is true, of course, with regard to the "second order" standards that I may use to evaluate the "first order" standards. These higher order standards can themselves be subject to critical evaluation: I can ask whether the standards I use for evaluating standards are themselves appropriate, whether they themselves meet the relevant ("third order") standards (whatever I may take these to be) for evaluating such (second order) standards. And I can modify these higher order standards as seems appropriate in light of these further evaluations. And so on, and so forth, all the way up (or all the way down): no standard is itself forced upon me, no standard is immune to potential criticism or evaluation. I am free, in principle, to evaluate any standard whatsoever, to ask whether it makes sense to me, whether it is indeed an appropriate standard to use. The principles or standards by which I evaluate beliefs and actions are themselves subject to rational assessment and open to modification or rejection. Put another way, the rules of rationality are not forced upon me (against my will, as it were): I need only appeal to standards that make sense to me, that seem appropriate in light of whatever principles, rules, or standards I endorse.

Our examination of the nature of rationality has thus led us to an important insight. The rules or standards to which I appeal in rationally assessing beliefs and actions are themselves subject to rational assessment, and at no point need I simply accept a relevant rule or standard as simply given—from "out there," as it were, forced upon me despite its making no sense. On the contrary, the relevant rules

or standards need only be accepted if they, too, make sense in light of whatever rules and standards I reasonably accept. We could put the point this way: the laws of rationality are not forced upon reason from the outside. Rather, reason is free to reject those standards (at whatever level) that do not make sense to itself. Reason is its own last court of appeal. It chooses what standards to obey. In short: reason is *autonomous* (G 4:440).

The fact that reason is autonomous in this way is certainly not altogether obvious. Indeed, Kant believed that previous moral philosophers had failed to recognize the autonomy of reason, and certainly had failed to appreciate the implications of reason's autonomy for ethics (G 4:432–33). Most moral philosophies have been founded in heteronomous conceptions of reason, where some ultimate principle of reasoning is simply taken as "given" (from outside reason's control) and beyond question (G 4:441–44). But kantians believe that since we are autonomous (insofar as we are rational), all such approaches to ethics must fail. If there is to be any hope for a sound foundation for ethics, it must take account of our autonomy.

In the account I have been sketching, the ideas of reason, freedom, and autonomy are tightly connected. Clearly, much more needs to be said, both in defense of the general kantian picture I have been presenting, and by way of further clarification of the three related concepts. But I am going to restrict myself here to two quick remarks.

First, our analysis of rationality has led us to a picture of rational beings as free. So eventually the kantian must confront the question of whether the freedom that we take ourselves to have (as rational beings) is genuine or a mere illusion. Kant himself postpones the discussion of this issue until the third section of the *Groundwork,* and even there the discussion is cursory. In this essay I shall make no attempt whatsoever to pursue this question.[1] I believe it plausible to hold that we are free, in the relevant sense, but I won't attempt to defend this claim here. And so, along with Kant in the first two sections of the *Groundwork,* we can view the rest of our discussion as taking the form of a conditional: if we *are* free, what follows?

Second, I want to say a word more about the concept of autonomy. Kant typically expresses the thought that reason is autonomous by saying that reason is the *author* or *source* of the rules and standards used by reason (e.g., G 4:431). But it is not clear that our concept of rationality can take us quite this far. Suppose we grant the kantian that the freedom involved in rationality means that there are no sound or valid standards for rational assessment that cannot themselves withstand the scrutiny of rational assessment. This would mean that there are no valid rules of reasoning that reason doesn't itself "accept," or "will," or "approve." We might capture this idea by saying that reason must itself "sign off" on any purported rules of rationality that are themselves to be binding upon reason. (There are no rules binding upon reason that reason wishes itself free of, no rules that it considers unreasonable rules.) But is it also true that we must think of reason as the *author* of these rules (the *ground* of their validity)? Kant apparently thinks so, though it is not clear why. Perhaps (and this is sheer speculation) he believes that it is inexplicable how reason *could* have this kind of veto power over rules of reasoning (so that no rule it disapproves of is valid) unless reason is itself the *source* of the validity of the (valid) rules of reasoning. This claim is not completely unattractive, and so I shall follow Kant here in speaking of reason as the source or author of its own rules. I believe, however, that this further claim is not strictly needed by the kantian. So long as it is conceded that reason's autonomy means that reason must "sign off" on any principles of rationality if they are indeed to be sound—that no standard for rational assessment is valid unless reason itself can approve of it—the kantian has, I believe, all that he needs.

Now kantians believe that *given* the autonomy of reason, certain implications fall out concerning the rules or standards that reason can give to itself. In particular, they believe that once we recognize the autonomy of reason, we are committed to accepting a certain fundamental rule—the *universal law* formulation of the categorical imperative (FUL). Here is a possible reconstruction of the main line of thought.

Whenever I act, my acting presupposes that there is reason to do whatever it is that I am doing,

that my act makes sense in the given circumstances. In effect, each action presupposes some rule or principle (though not necessarily the same rule from act to act) that endorses the act, a rule in the light of which the act can be seen as reasonable. Typically, of course, these underlying principles or rules will only be implicit, but were we to make them explicit, they might say something along the following lines: under such and such circumstances, given such and such desires or such and such goals, there is reason to act in such and such a way. As I say, we rarely make such rules explicit (and even less frequently attempt to state them fully and with care), but whenever I act, I presuppose some such rule—a rule which, if sound, would validate my action, by showing why it is that I have reason to do whatever it is that I am doing. (In many cases, of course, one acts spontaneously, or simply "goes with the flow." But in such cases, presumably, the principle implicit in one's act is precisely one that endorses acting spontaneously in circumstances of this sort.)

So when I act, I presuppose a rule or principle that claims that I have reason to do what I do (given the circumstances, and so forth). But which rules should I act on? This much seems clear: I should only act on rules that are themselves *valid*. (The precise term of commendation used here isn't important for our purposes. We could equally well talk of those rules that are sound, or legitimate, or good, or reasonable.) I should only do what it truly makes sense for me to do; so I should only act on those rules that are themselves correct in their claims about what it is that I have reason to do. I should only act on those principles that are valid.

But given that I am autonomous, the rules are up to me. Valid rules are valid by virtue of my signing off on them, by virtue of my approving of them as a rational being.

So this means: I should only act on rules that I can sign off on. I should only act on rules that I can rationally choose to be rules. Put in slightly different terms: I should act only upon rules that I can (rationally) *will* to be rules.

But rules are *laws*. They tell everyone what to do (or believe, or intend, and so on) in relevant circumstances. They say, for example, that in such and such circumstances, given such and such desires, one has reason to perform an act of such and such a type. But this means (if the given rule is valid) that *everyone* has such a reason—provided that they have the relevant desires and find themselves in the relevant circumstances. Of course not everyone will necessarily find themselves in the relevant circumstances, or with the relevant desires—but it is true of everyone that *if* they were in the relevant circumstances (and so forth) then they *would* have reason to perform an act of the relevant sort. Rules are *universal,* providing the same reasons (under the relevant circumstances) to everyone.

So we can restate our earlier conclusion. Instead of saying that I should act only upon rules that I can (rationally) will to be rules, we can say: I should act only on those rules that I can (rationally) will to be universal laws.

This is Kant's formula of universal law, though his own favored statement of it makes use of a piece of jargon. Kant typically talks about *maxims,* which for our purposes we can take to be first person statements of intentions ("I will perform such and such an act in such and such circumstances, given such and such goals"). Each such maxim corresponds to an implicit principle ("if one is in such and such circumstances, with such and such goals, then one has reason to perform such and such an act"), and so we could restate the formula at which we have arrived as follows: I should act only on those maxims, where I can (rationally) will that the corresponding principle be universal law. Simplifying a bit further still, we can say: act only on those maxims that I can will to be universal laws. And this is exactly what Kant tells us. Here is his own statement of the formula of universal law:

> FUL: "Act only in accordance with that maxim through which you at the same time can will that it become a universal law" (G 4:421).

Kant's decision to state FUL in terms of maxims rather than the corresponding principles carries certain risks, for one can normally state one's intentions in a way that only gives a partial indication of what one takes oneself to be doing, and why it seems to make sense. Thus, for example, if my intention is to close the door to keep out the person attacking me, so as to save my life, it will normally be correct to say, as well, that I intend to close the door. But if we then focus on "I will close the door" as a statement of my maxim, we will have no idea (or at best a poor idea) of why I think it makes sense to do this in the present circumstances, and thus no idea (or at best a poor idea) of just what the corresponding principle is supposed to be that I am to examine so as to see whether I can indeed will it to be universal law. These problems could have been avoided had Kant stated FUL directly in terms of examining complete statements of the underlying principles. But so long as we bear in mind that the real question is always whether a purported reason-giving principle is indeed one that we can rationally will to be universal law, we should be able to make use of Kant's own formulation without too much confusion.

Now the argument I have just sketched moves from our autonomy to FUL, a requirement to act only on certain types of maxims (in Kant's formulation). But if this argument is sound, then the resulting requirement should apply equally to *everyone,* that is, to every rational being. For if reason is autonomous, and autonomy yields FUL, then FUL is binding upon all rational beings. That is to say: all rational beings should obey FUL; they *must* do it if they are to act rationally. We can express this point in kantian jargon by saying that FUL is a *categorical imperative* (one binding upon all rational beings; see, e.g., G 4:432). Of course this does not mean that all rational beings *will* obey FUL. As we have already noted, humans, at least, are only imperfectly rational, and thus may often fail to conform to FUL, sometimes knowingly. But everyone *should* obey FUL: they have reason to do so, based on the mere fact that they are rational. If the argument is sound, then FUL is a categorical imperative.

Kant says there is exactly one categorical imperative, though it has several equivalent formulations (G 4:420–21, 436). FUL is supposedly only one of the different ways of stating this single imperative. Another of the formulations, the formula of autonomy (FA), goes like this:

> FA: "the idea of the will of every rational being as a will giving universal law" (G 4:431).

Note that Kant doesn't even bother to state this version in the form of an imperative at all! Presumably, however, what he is most concerned to impress upon us here is the idea that it is autonomy (the fact that reason is the source of its own laws) that provides the basis for FUL: given the former, we are led to the latter. The argument I have been sketching tries to make good on this thought. (To get full equivalence, of course, we would also need to go on to argue as well that given FUL we can derive an imperative along the lines of "Act autonomously!" or "Act in keeping with your autonomy!" I won't attempt to argue that here.)

But is the argument sound? Can we actually derive FUL from the mere assumption of reason's autonomy? I am not sure. Doubtless several steps of the argument could be questioned, but the most important issue, I believe, is this. Is it really true that the only rules or standards that I could autonomously will are *universal*? Must the reason-giving principles I endorse be principles that would equally give *everyone* a reason? Putting the same point in a slightly different way, is it really true that the only rules that I could freely give to myself are rules that make similar prescriptions for everyone? Unless something like this is true, then all that autonomy will demand is that I act on maxims that I can (autonomously) will. We won't have a requirement that I act only on maxims that I can will to be universal law. And so we won't have made it all the way to FUL. So we need to ask: is it really true that the only principles I can autonomously give myself are universal?

Now it might seem that the answer to this question is obvious. For it seems obvious that I can (and should!) endorse principles that recognize that what *I* have reason to do normally differs from what *you* have reason to do. For example, I may have reason to eat right now, while you do not.

In thinking about this question, however, it is important to bear in mind the point, already noted, that the requirement that the reason-giving principles be (ones that I can will to be) universal laws only amounts to a requirement that people *in the same circumstances* have the same reasons. Thus, universality here only amounts to the requirement

that *if* someone else were in the same circumstances (that is, whatever the principle takes to be the relevant circumstances) then they too would have reason to perform the same kind of act. (And it should be noted that, depending on the given principle, the relevant circumstances may well include a specification of the person's desires or goals as well as more "external" circumstances.) So even if the principles I give myself are universal, this doesn't mean that everyone has reason to do the same specific types of acts, for people will still find themselves in differing circumstances.

In typical cases, at least, when we find ourselves thinking that one person has reason to do something that another person does not, this will be because we think there is some relevant difference in their circumstances—and a full specification of the relevant reason-giving principles will take note of these circumstances. Thus, for example, I may believe that I should eat, while you should not, but this may be because I believe that only hungry people should eat, and I recognize that you are not hungry. (Or perhaps I believe that people on diets shouldn't eat between meals, and you are on a diet and it is between meals; or that you need to get to a class, and I do not, and so on.) Despite initial appearances to the contrary, then, the underlying principle will actually be universal: anyone who is similarly situated (with regard to hunger, dietary needs, availability of food, more pressing demands, and so forth) will have similar reason to eat (or not). If this is right, then at the very least most of the principles I can actually sign off on will indeed be universal laws in the relevant sense.

But is it truly *impossible* for me to autonomously will principles that are not in this way universal? Can't I simply endorse a rule that says that *I* (but not others) should do such and such an act in *this* case (but not in other cases that are otherwise similar)?

Here I can only reply that when I honestly contemplate such irreducibly person specific or irreducibly case specific principles I find them virtually unintelligible. I cannot fathom the idea that I might have reason to do something in a certain kind of case, while you do not—even though there is not a single relevant difference between us. This is not to say that I can't imagine someone "stating" such a principle, nor do I mean to claim that I wouldn't understand what someone affirming such a principle would be attempting to do. Rather, I simply find that I cannot take seriously the possibility that such a principle would be one that merits endorsement. If in the circumstances someone has *reason* to act in a given way, then it seems to me that anyone at all who genuinely found themselves in relevantly *identical* circumstances would have reason to act in the same way. Which is to say, when I ask myself what sorts of reason-giving principles I can truly imagine autonomously giving to myself—fully accepting upon complete rational reflection—the only such principles are ones that are universal.

In my own case, then, if I am indeed to restrict myself to maxims that I can autonomously will, then I must restrict myself to maxims that I can will to be universal laws. Perhaps others differ from me in this regard. The idea seems just barely possible, though, again, I find that I can't take the thought seriously. As far as I can see, *any* rational being would find that the only maxims he could autonomously will would be maxims that he could will to be universal laws. And if this is indeed correct, then given the autonomy of reason something like FUL may well follow for all rational beings whatsoever. In short, FUL may indeed be a categorical imperative.

To be sure, other questions about this step of the argument could be pressed, and other stages of the argument could be challenged as well. So I would not want to claim that the validity of the derivation of FUL (from the assumption of autonomy) has now been established. But I hope that I have said enough at this point to make it clear why the kantian's appeal to FUL is a position worth taking seriously. The claim that reason is autonomous is, I think, a plausible one, and the further claim that autonomy yields FUL is not, I believe, one that can be easily dismissed. If nothing more, these claims are sufficiently plausible (even if one ultimately rejects one or the other of the pair) that what I have said should make it clear why many people have found FUL so compelling.

II. UNDERSTANDING THE FORMULA OF UNIVERSAL LAW

Suppose, then, that we grant the kantians the validity of FUL (if only for the sake of argument). Even if we do this, it is hardly obvious how FUL is to be applied, how it is to be put to work. Nor is it the least bit obvious whether—as kantians believe—FUL has sufficient "bite" that it can be used to generate concrete moral guidance. So let us put aside further questions about the derivation of FUL, and turn instead to the question of what follows from it. Granted that I must only act on maxims that I can will to be universal law, how exactly am I to decide what to do?

The first thing to notice is that FUL itself doesn't actually provide us with maxims; it only serves to rule some of them out. We bring candidate maxims *to* FUL, to see whether they are acceptable. The point here is easy enough to grasp if we recall that maxims are, in effect, statements of what one intends to *do* in a given situation. What we should imagine then is that faced with the given situation, I have come up with some tentative plan of action, something that I propose to do (perhaps to serve some desire or goal I have). Armed with this tentative plan, then, I turn to FUL to see if it is legitimate to act on it. FUL is, in effect, a *test* of maxims: it tells me to act only on maxims that have a certain feature.

For the moment, let's leave the details of that test aside, and focus on the negative form of the imperative. FUL tells me to act only on maxims that pass a certain test. Thus, if some maxim *fails* the test, FUL commands me not to act on it. Notice, however, that although FUL tells me to act *only* on maxims that pass the test, it does not require me to act on all the maxims that *do* pass the test. Apparently, then, if a maxim passes the relevant test you *may* act on it (FUL, at least, won't rule this out); but absent any further argument, it seems, there won't be any *requirement* to act on the maxim. We must restrict ourselves to acting on maxims that pass the test, but among the maxims that do pass, which we choose to act upon is up to us.[2]

Suppose, then, that some maxim fails the FUL test (whatever, exactly, it turns out to be). What can we conclude? If FUL is indeed a categorical imperative, binding upon all rational beings, then we must conclude that it is forbidden to act on that maxim. But what follows in the alternative case, where the given maxim passes the test? Here we have to be more cautious. Obviously enough, if a given maxim passes FUL, then as far as FUL itself is concerned there is nothing objectionable about acting on the maxim. But we cannot yet safely conclude that it is indeed *permissible* to act on the maxim in question, because, for all that we have said so far, there might be some other imperative—beyond FUL— that must be taken into account as well. After all, even if kantians are right in thinking that reason's autonomy supports FUL, it doesn't yet follow that this is the only fundamental principle supported by our autonomy. Perhaps there are *additional* tests that must be passed as well. If so, then passing FUL will be necessary for permissibility but not sufficient.

Presumably Kant means to put this possibility aside with his insistence that FUL is the *only* categorical imperative. (Because of this belief, he typically refers to it simply as "the" categorical imperative, though as we have noted Kant also believes that this imperative can be stated in several different, though equivalent, ways.) But even if Kant *could* prove that FUL (in its various formulations) is indeed the only categorical imperative,[3] that wouldn't necessarily put the worry to rest. For what if there were additional, basic principles (that is, principles not derived from FUL) that, although not categorical, nonetheless validly applied in particular cases? Even if FUL is the only *categorical* imperative, nothing yet rules out the possibility that a maxim might pass FUL but nonetheless fail to pass these further (noncategorical) principles.

What the kantian needs to claim then (*regardless* of whether FUL is the only categorical imperative) is that even if there are any further valid principles (not themselves derived from FUL), it is not actually possible for a maxim to pass FUL but to violate these further principles. Happily, this may not be an implausible claim for the kantian to make. Imagine that a given maxim violates some such principle, P. Now given the autonomy of reason, any

valid principle of reasoning, including P, must be one that I rationally favor. But if I truly continue to endorse P (even in light of its ruling out the maxim in question) then I cannot rationally favor any principle incompatible with P—including, in particular, the underlying principle corresponding to the maxim. Thus, given my acceptance of P, I cannot in fact rationally will the maxim to be universal law. That is, if the maxim violates P, it fails FUL as well.

What this means, then, is that even if there *are* additional principles (not themselves derived from FUL), so long as a given maxim does pass FUL it will pass those additional principles (if any) as well.[4] Thus, provided that a maxim passes FUL, it is indeed permissible to act upon it.

I think, therefore, that we can put aside the potential complications that threatened to arise from the existence of additional tests beyond that provided by FUL. We can say, straightforwardly, that if a maxim passes FUL then it is permissible to act on it. And we can combine this result with a point already made, that if a maxim *fails* FUL it is *forbidden* to act on it. Summing all of this up then we can conclude, quite simply, that it is permissible to act on a maxim if and only if it passes FUL.

It would, however, be easy to become confused about what we have shown so far. Suppose that in some situation I consider a maxim, M, that would permit me to perform an act, A, in those circumstances. And let us suppose, as well, that this maxim fails FUL. It would be natural to think that what this shows me is that it is forbidden to do A (at least, in these circumstances). But in point of fact this doesn't actually follow at all. From the mere fact that M fails FUL, all that immediately follows is that one should not act on M. That is, one should not do A for the particular *reasons* given by M. The maxim M, after all, corresponds to a particular reason-giving principle, and that principle picks out certain features of the situation, and tells me that by virtue of these features I have reason to do A. The fact that M fails FUL shows me that this particular claim about what I have reason to do (and why) is mistaken. Thus, if I *do* have reason to do A it is not for *those* (purported) reasons. But all of this is still compatible with the possibility that there may be other (genuine) reasons to do A—even in this very situation. For there may still be some other reason-giving principle which *is* sound—a principle that focuses on different features of the very same situation, and tells me that by virtue of *those* features I have reason to do A. In short, even though M fails FUL, some other maxim that would permit me to do A may still pass.

Thus, even though M fails FUL, we cannot yet conclude that it is forbidden to do A (in this situation). To reach that conclusion we would need to examine various other maxims as well, that is, the various other maxims that would also instruct me to do A. It is only if *all* such "permission giving" maxims fail FUL as well that we can conclude that doing A is forbidden. (Since I may only act on maxims that do pass FUL, if *all* such permission giving maxims fail, then I am indeed forbidden to do A.)

This is not to say, of course, that before concluding that a given type of act is forbidden in a certain situation one must literally examine a huge (perhaps infinite) number of maxims. It is possible that when a particular maxim fails FUL we will be able to see precisely why it fails, and generalize to other, relevant maxims. In effect, we may be able to test large classes of maxims at (more or less) the same time. But logically speaking the point remains, that the failure of a single maxim does not suffice to establish that a given act is forbidden; that requires, rather, the failure of all maxims that would permit the act (in those circumstances). (Similarly, of course, to establish that a given type of act was forbidden under *all* circumstances, we would need to show that all such permission giving maxims would fail, regardless of what circumstances the maxims specify as relevant.)

In the last few paragraphs I have been freely talking about actions as permissible or forbidden. What kind of permissibility is this? So far, the answer is *rational* permissibility. FUL provides a test for reason-giving principles, allowing us to conclude, in certain cases, that an action is rationally forbidden (say) because no genuinely adequate reason supports doing it. But the kantian believes that FUL captures a central *moral* idea as well. It serves to sort the morally permissible from the morally forbidden. If this is right, then rationality meets

morality here: if the autonomy of reason requires you to conform to FUL, and acts forbidden by FUL are morally forbidden, then reason requires you to obey morality.

To understand why the kantian thinks FUL can plausibly be taken not only as a requirement of rationality but also as the basic principle of morality, it may be helpful to turn to a concrete example. Kant asks us to consider a case where I attempt to borrow some money, promising to pay it back, even though I know full well that I will be unable to keep such a promise. (The same basic example is discussed at two different places—G 4:402–3 and 422—though only the second discussion makes explicit that the case involves money.) Kant supposes that my maxim here tells me that "when I am in a tight spot" I will "make a promise with the intention of not keeping it" (G 4:402). And here is part of Kant's discussion of whether this maxim passes FUL:

> I ask myself: would I be content with it if my maxim (of getting myself out of embarrassment through an untruthful promise) should be valid as a universal law (for myself as well as for others), and would I be able to say to myself that anyone may make an untruthful promise when he finds himself in embarrassment which he cannot get out of in any other way? Then I soon become aware that I can will the lie but not at all a universal law to lie. (G 4:403)

Several details of this argument will require more careful discussion later. Here I only want to draw attention to the plausibility of the idea that FUL is indeed concerned with fundamental moral aspects of the situation. In effect, Kant is telling us that immorality is a matter of cheating—making an exception of oneself (cf. G 4:424). When I tell a lie, or make a promise I don't intend to keep (or butt in line, or kill someone for personal gain, and so forth), I am playing by rules that I don't favor others acting on as well. After all, it is not as though someone who is immoral wants others to act in the same way! On the contrary, what I want when I act immorally is that everyone else should play by one set of rules (the moral rules) while I alone get to act on a *different* set of rules. Here I am, then, proposing to act in a certain way, in a certain situation, but it is perfectly clear that I cannot rationally will that everyone act in the same way in similar situations. There is a (purported) reason-giving principle that I propose to act on, but I can't reasonably favor that others act on it as well. This is the telltale sign of immorality, says the kantian. I want to treat myself differently than everyone else gets treated; I want one set of rules for myself, and another set of rules for everyone else. When I violate FUL, acting on a principle that I cannot will to be universal law, I try to make an exception of myself, even though I see full well that there is nothing at all that I consider a relevant difference between myself and others; and that is the mark of immorality.

That is why FUL is a requirement, not only of rationality, but of morality as well. And so we can conclude: if an act is forbidden by FUL, it is morally forbidden. But can we similarly conclude that if an act is permitted by FUL, it is morally permissible? As before, however, this conclusion assumes that FUL is not only one test among many, but is indeed the only fundamental principle—now, the only fundamental *moral* principle. This, too, is a claim that Kant appears to make (though it is not clearly distinguished from the earlier claim that FUL is the only fundamental rational principle), and for the sake of argument, at least, let us grant it as well (we'll consider its plausibility later). Then we can say that an act is morally permissible if and only if it is permitted by FUL.

Once again, it is important to avoid misunderstanding. We have just concluded that an act will be morally permissible if and only if it is permitted by FUL. And as we have already discussed, an action will be permitted by FUL provided that there is some maxim that passes FUL that permits the action in the circumstances. Note, however, that nothing that we have said requires that this maxim be the one that the person is actually acting upon. Provided that there is *some* permission giving maxim that passes FUL, it will be morally permissible to perform the act in question, even if the person is acting on some *other* maxim, and that maxim *fails* FUL!

Of course, if the person *is* acting on another maxim, and that maxim fails FUL, there will be plenty that is amiss. The person will be acting on a maxim that is unsound, both rationally and morally. That is to say, she will be performing the action for the *wrong* reasons—for "reasons" that are not actually adequate reasons for action at all. What's more, she will be performing the action for reasons that are not morally legitimate. As such, the person may well be open to moral condemnation of one sort or another. But this is not to say that what she is doing is morally *forbidden*. Rather, we will have a case of someone who is doing an action that is perfectly permissible morally, but is doing so for the wrong reason. In kantian jargon we can say that such a person is conforming to the moral law, but not acting for the sake of the moral law (G 4:390).

The distinction being drawn here is a perfectly familiar one. We all have the idea of someone doing the morally right thing, but for the wrong reasons. For example, Kant discusses a shopkeeper who gives correct change to his customers, but does so only out of fear of being caught and having business suffer (G 4:397). Presumably, we will all agree that giving correct change is a morally permissible (indeed morally obligatory) thing to do. And so we would agree that when the shopkeeper does this his action is morally permissible; he is conforming to the moral law. This is true even though he acts out of fear—acts for the morally wrong reasons. Thus, despite the fact that the maxim he acts on is unsound, that it would (as we may suppose) fail FUL, it remains true that the action he performs is morally permissible. And what *makes* it morally permissible is the very fact that some *other* maxim that enjoins giving correct change *would* pass FUL. In short, an act is morally permissible if and only if some permission giving maxim passes FUL, whether or not the person in question is actually acting on that maxim.

Let us now return to the question, earlier set aside, of how exactly we are to determine whether or not a given maxim does pass FUL. The basic idea, of course, is clear: a maxim passes FUL just in case I can will it to be a universal law. But how, exactly, can

I tell whether or not I can "universalize" a maxim in this way? What, exactly, do I do when I try to determine whether a maxim can be universalized?

On what I take to be the standard proposal here, I should begin by trying to imagine a world where everyone *does* in fact conform to the reason-giving principle corresponding to the maxim being tested. If the maxim enjoins me to perform an act of type A, in such and such circumstances, then I am to imagine a world in which *everyone* performs acts of type A when in circumstances of that sort. I attempt to imagine a *full compliance world,* as we might call it, and then I ask myself two questions about this world. First, is such a world truly possible, or does something go wrong in trying to imagine it? Second, assuming that such a world is indeed possible (that nothing goes wrong in the relevant sense), can I rationally will it? The first question, in effect, is supposed to tell me whether the principle corresponding to the maxim could actually *be* a universal law; the second, whether I can *will* it to be such. To pass FUL, I must be able to answer both questions in the affirmative.

According to this interpretation, then, there are two distinct ways in which a maxim could fail to pass FUL, corresponding to the two questions I've just distinguished. In effect, there are two distinct subtests. This seems to be Kant's own view of the matter, in any event: he says that some maxims "cannot even be *thought* without contradiction as a universal law," while other maxims that also fail FUL generate no such "internal impossibility"; for these other maxims, rather, the *will* would "contradict itself" if it attempted to will the maxims to be universal laws (G 4:424).

More significantly, Kant seems to think this distinction picks out something important, generating different types of moral requirements. These are obscure matters, and Kant says little about them in the *Groundwork,* but roughly the picture seems to be this: when maxims fail at the first step, this is supposed to generate "perfect" duties, while "imperfect" duties (which are, despite the name, perfectly genuine duties) are generated by maxims failing at the second step (cf. G 4:424). But it is far from obvious why the two subtests should be invested with

anything like this kind of significance. FUL says that one should not act on maxims that cannot be willed to be universal law. It does *not* say that it matters *why* a given maxim cannot be so willed. So it is far from clear that the kantian should follow Kant in holding it significant at which step a given maxim fails.

For that matter, it must be admitted as well that it is far from clear what precisely we are supposed to be concerned with as we consider the two subtests. In a moment we will turn to an examination of some of Kant's own examples. At the very least this should help us get clearer about what Kant thought could lead to a maxim's failing FUL. Whether, at the end of the day, we agree with Kant that it makes a difference at which step a maxim fails (or whether, indeed, maxims can fail in only two basic ways) is a matter of less importance.

Kant discusses four main examples in the *Groundwork.* I am going to discuss only two of these, but I am going to do so in some detail. (In thinking about these examples, it is also worth bearing in mind the point that Kant is only human. In certain cases he may simply be wrong about what FUL entails. Kantians can embrace FUL while still rejecting one or more of Kant's own views concerning which particular moral requirements emerge from it.)

A. The False Promise

The first example I want to examine is Kant's second, a return to the false promise case that we have already had a look at. Recall that Kant claims that "I can will the lie but not at all a universal law to lie." Here is Kant's initial argument for this claim—that I cannot will the maxim to be a universal law:

> for in accordance with such a law there would properly be no promises, because it would be pointless to avow my will in regard to my future actions to those who would not believe this avowal, or, if they rashly did so, who would pay me back in the same coin; hence my maxim, as soon as it were made into a universal law, would destroy itself. (G 4:403)

And here is the argument the second time around, when Kant returns to the case as one of his four examples:

> Yet I see right away that it [my maxim] could never be valid as a universal law of nature[5] and still agree with itself, but rather it would necessarily contradict itself. For the universality of a law that everyone who believes himself to be in distress could promise whatever occurred to him with the intention of not keeping it would make impossible the promise and the end one might have in making it, since no one would believe that anything has been promised him, but rather would laugh about every such utterance as vain pretense. (G 4:422)

Now the basic line of argument here is clear enough. If we try to imagine a world in which everyone lies, or makes insincere promises, so as to achieve personal goals by deceiving others, we find that something goes wrong. No one would believe you when you tried to make such a promise.

But what, exactly, is it that goes wrong here? Some think that what we find is that it is *literally impossible* for there to be a world in which everyone lies or makes insincere promises. Perhaps in a world where promises are so routinely broken, the very institution of promising would disappear (or, alternatively, would never have come into being). So there cannot be a world in which everyone makes promises they do not intend to keep. The maxim of lying to get out of a tight spot could not be a universal law, because there literally could not be a world in which everyone complies with this maxim. This interpretation sits nicely with Kant's saying that in such a world "there would properly be no promises," that the universality of the law would make such promises "impossible"—that (as he later puts it) the maxim "cannot even be *thought* without contradiction" to be a universal law (G 4:424). If there literally cannot *be* a world in which everyone acts on the maxim, I cannot will it to be universal law, and the maxim fails FUL.

Others interpret the argument somewhat differently. Taking their cue instead from Kant's remarks that making the promise in such a world would be "pointless," that it would be impossible to achieve "the end one might have" in making the promise, they conclude that what actually goes wrong is this: in a world in which promises are routinely broken, it is much more difficult, and perhaps even impossible, to achieve the *goal* specified in the maxim (getting out of a tight spot by deceiving others) by performing the *action* specified in the maxim (making an insincere promise). Insincere promising works more effectively (and perhaps only at all) against a general background in which people keep their promises. Thus, making the maxim be a universal law—one that everyone has reason to act on—undercuts the effectiveness of the maxim itself. And this involves a kind of practical contradiction: if I will my maxim to be universal law, I make it harder to achieve the very goal specified by the maxim by acting on that maxim. From the point of view of someone willing the maxim, then, it is irrational of me to will it to be universal law. So I cannot will the maxim to be universal law, and it fails FUL.[6]

This second interpretation, it should be noted, assumes that it is not rational for someone who accepts the maxim to *will* that everyone act on the maxim, since this makes it harder to achieve the goal specified in the maxim (in the specified manner). The argument thus presupposes some principle to the effect that it is not rational to favor things that make it harder to achieve one's goals. This is not an objection to the argument, of course, for presumably we would indeed want to endorse *some* such principle of instrumental reasoning (although the details of the principle might be a matter of debate). Kant himself, for example, earlier in the *Groundwork* (G 4:417), defends the claim that "Whoever wills the end, also wills (insofar as reason has decisive influence on his actions) the means," and it looks as though, on the second interpretation, this principle, or some near relative of it, is assumed.

Again, this observation is not intended as an objection to the second argument. If we are to sometimes reject maxims on the grounds that we cannot autonomously will them to be universal laws, then presumably one reason this may happen is because we find that willing the maxim to be universal law would be an act that would fall short in terms of one or another standard that we rationally endorse. Thus, if we do rationally endorse some principle of instrumental reasoning, it is not problematic for the kantian to appeal to that principle when arguing that one cannot will a particular maxim to be universal law.

Regardless of which interpretation we accept, it is worth drawing attention to the fact that the argument makes use of various contingent, empirical facts. The argument assumes, for example, that people have memories, and will recognize the fact that promise breaking has become widespread, and that this will result in either a breakdown of promising (on the first interpretation) or a disinclination to trust the promises of others (on the second interpretation). I note this point only to put to rest the widely held belief that kantians think that morality is entirely *a priori,* something that can be established without appeal to empirical facts.[7] At best, FUL itself has this kind of status. As we can see, however, more specific moral conclusions—such as a prohibition against lying or making insincere promises—are derived from FUL through the use of empirical truths.[8]

Suppose we grant, if only for the sake of argument, that Kant has successfully shown that the maxim in question cannot pass FUL. For reasons we have already discussed, however, it won't yet follow that it is morally forbidden to make an insincere promise in this case. To reach that conclusion, after all, we must argue that not only this maxim, but any other maxim that would permit lying here, would fail as well. Kant doesn't try to generalize his argument, to cover the other relevant maxims, but it is easy to see how the attempt might go. The features of the maxim that seem relevant to its failure are ones that would appear in any permission granting maxim relevant to the case at hand. Thus if one maxim that would permit lying here would fail, others should as well. (We'll consider an objection to this claim below.)

Can the argument be generalized even further? Can we derive not only a prohibition against lying in this particular case, but a general prohibition against all lying whatsoever? Kant thought so, and notoriously claimed that it is never morally permissible to

tell a lie. But this is a point at which many kantians part company from Kant himself. To take the standard case, many kantians believe it permissible to lie to a would-be murderer so as to protect his innocent victim hiding in your basement. And it seems at least possible that a maxim that would permit this act could pass FUL. After all, the existence of at least some insincere promising is compatible with the continued existence and effectiveness of promising (for there are, let us admit, insincere promises made in the real world, yet promising has not been rendered impossible or ineffective). Thus it seems possible that a maxim that enjoined promise breaking or lying in sufficiently rare or special circumstances (for example) might yet pass FUL. Perhaps a maxim that permitted lying to the would-be murderer is one such.[9] Kant may have thought that FUL supported an absolute prohibition against lying, but the kantian need not follow him in this regard.

B. The Maxim of Nonaid to Others

Kant's fourth example involves a person who has a chance to aid another in need, but is tempted to pass him by without offering assistance. Kant imagines the person's maxim to be one of complete refusal to provide aid ("I will not take anything from him or even envy him; only I do not want to contribute to his welfare or to his assistance in distress"), and he says of this case:

> But although it is possible that a universal law of nature could well subsist in accordance with that maxim, yet it is impossible *to will* that such a principle should be valid without exception as a natural law. For a will that resolved on this would conflict with itself, since the case could sometimes arise in which he needs the love and sympathetic participation of others, and where, through such a natural law arising from his own will, he would rob himself of all the hope of assistance that he wishes for himself. (G 4:423)

Once again, the basic line of argument is fairly straightforward. Kant says that although there could be a world in which everyone acts on the maxim in question—a world where no one helps others—you cannot will this maxim to be universal law. You cannot rationally will that indifference to the needs of others be universal law, for you might find yourself in a situation where you *need* the help of others. The maxim thus fails at the second subtest: it cannot be willed to be universal law.

The first thing to notice about this argument is that it, too, appeals to empirical facts, here the fact that each of us has needs that we cannot always meet on our own. The second thing to notice is that it, too, makes use of something like the principle of instrumental reasoning. The thought is that each of us has goals of some sort, goals that we will want to achieve. But this makes it irrational to favor things that would make it more difficult to achieve those goals. Yet this is precisely what we will have done, in at least certain logically possible scenarios, if we will that it be *universal law* that no one help another. Once I recognize that I, too, can be in need of the aid of others, I cannot rationally favor a principle that would mean that I not get the help I need.

Notice, as well, that the relevant question is not particularly what I *would* will, *were* I in the situation where I needed help. That is no more relevant than the question of what I would will in the case where I don't need help. Rather, the question is what I am rationally prepared to will *here and now* as a principle to govern the case where I need help. Presumably, it is not rational of me (here and now) to be indifferent to my own need in that possible case. So I cannot (here and now) favor a rule that would mean that that need would go unmet (were it to arise). That is why I cannot will the maxim to be universal law. Thus it fails FUL.

Being clear about this point helps us to understand why it is irrelevant for someone to object that in the actual world they simply do not need anyone's help. Even if that were the case, it would remain a live possibility that the situation could be different: for anyone other than a deity, one *could* find oneself in need. And the thought, then, is that it cannot be rational to will, with regard to such a situation, that one not get the aid one would need.

Sometimes it is thought that whatever the force of this argument, it fails against an imagined "rugged individualist" who truly favors getting by completely on his own. Such a person, it is suggested, can will that the maxim of nonaid be universal law—for when he contemplates the possibility that he would himself be in need of the aid of others, he insists that even in such a case he (here and now) prefers that he die (in the given case) rather than be helped by others. (Of course, were he actually in a position of extreme need, he might lose his resolve and desire help. But as we have seen, that is strictly irrelevant. What matters is that here and now he wills that he not be aided, even in that case.)

I believe, however, that the kantian may have an answer to this objection available to him. For even the rugged individualist wants help of a particular kind—namely, to be left alone. This is easily seen if we imagine someone else bent on "aiding" him, despite his protests. The individualist wants the cooperation of others, just as the rest of us do; it is just that aid and cooperation take an unusual form in his case: leaving him to do things completely by himself. If this is right, then not even the individualist can favor a principle that would enjoin everyone to refuse to provide each with the particular aid that they need, for that would strip the individualist of what he most needs—to be left alone. If this is right, then none of us—not even the rugged individualist—can will a maxim of nonaid to be universal law.

Of course, as always, even if this is right it doesn't yet show us that it is morally forbidden to refuse to aid others. Doing that would require showing that not only this particular maxim but other, similar maxims would fail FUL as well. Once again, Kant doesn't attempt to generalize the argument, but here too it is not difficult to see how that more general argument might go: all humans (at least) are finite in ability, capable, in principle, of needing help (of some sort) from others; thus for any maxim at all that would simply permit disregarding the needs of others, no one can rationally will the maxim to be universal law.

But there remains a further worry. It might be objected that no principle at all could avoid the objection being raised against a principle of nonaid. For if, as the argument claims, it is irrational for me to will a principle (such as a principle of nonaid) that might leave me unable, or less able, to achieve my goals, then won't it be similarly irrational for me to will a principle that *requires* providing aid to others? After all, acting on a requirement to provide aid can itself leave me unable, or less able, to achieve one or another of my goals. Thus, won't the very same principle of instrumental reasoning that supposedly makes it irrational to favor a principle of nonaid also make it irrational to favor a principle *requiring* aid to others? How, then, can any principle at all—whether requiring aid or not—pass FUL?

Presumably the kantian must claim that an adequate answer to this worry involves balancing the various needs and aims I might have that might go unmet under the differing principles. I am looking for a principle that I can will to be universal law. And since, logically speaking, I might find myself in either one of the relevant roles (aid provider or aid recipient), I have to ask myself which costs I would rather endure. But in at least some cases—for example, when the gain to the needy when aid is provided is significantly greater than the loss to the person who actually provides the aid—the answer to this question is clear. Presumably, then, the principle of instrumental reasoning can lead me (here and now) to favor principles that do require providing aid in cases of this sort. But if this is right, then FUL will indeed support some sort of requirement to provide aid after all.

Doubtless, further questions could be raised about both of these examples (and as I have already noted, Kant discusses two other examples in the *Groundwork* as well). But I hope I have said enough to give at least some sense of how FUL is supposed to be used as a test for maxims and for deriving moral obligations.

Our discussion should also put to rest one common objection to FUL, namely, that it has no "bite," that any maxim at all can pass. For as we have now seen, it's not implausible to think that certain maxims do indeed fail FUL. Thus, whatever its other shortcomings may be, at least FUL isn't altogether devoid of content.

There are, however, other general objections to FUL that merit further discussion. Let me quickly mention four. All of them concern the adequacy of FUL from the *moral* point of view. First, it is sometimes objected that FUL is raising a morally irrelevant concern when it asks us to consider a world where everyone acts on the maxim in question. After all (the objection notes), in the *real* world typically it simply isn't going to happen that *everyone* acts on a given maxim. From the moral point of view, then, why should we concern ourselves with such an unrealistic possibility?

Recall, however, that the kantian's position is that if a maxim passes FUL, then it is morally permissible to act on it, indeed, morally permissible for anyone at all to act on it. It hardly seems irrelevant, then, to consider a world in which everyone *does* act on the given maxim. This would simply be a world in which—in the relevant way at least—everyone is acting in a manner that is supposedly morally permissible. Surely it makes sense to insist that it must at least be *possible* for everyone to act in a morally permissible manner, and indeed, to insist further that it must be reasonable to *favor* a world in which everyone acts in a morally permissible manner. (It cannot be preferable, from the moral point of view, that some act in a morally forbidden manner.) A world in which everyone acts morally must be both possible and attractive. Thus, in directing our attention to a full compliance world, FUL is not at all directing our attention to a morally irrelevant possibility.

But this immediately suggests a second objection: even if the full compliance world is indeed a world worth considering when testing maxims from the moral point of view, it is quite another matter to suggest that this is the *only* world worth considering, or even the most important. After all, in the real world not everyone is going to act morally, and so it is important to know how one is permitted (or required) to act in the face of immoral behavior by others. It would seem that the relevant question with regard to such cases of *partial* compliance is what I can will with regard to a world in which *not* everyone is acting on the maxim in question. But FUL apparently never asks us to consider such worlds: it *restricts* our attention to asking whether I can will a given maxim in a world in which everyone is acting on the maxim. Thus FUL inappropriately disregards the very real possibility of immoral behavior (partial compliance). Worse still, because of this neglect, it can generate morally implausible guidance, since acts that might be perfectly attractive were everyone to be acting morally (ones that I can will for the full compliance world) might be catastrophic when done in the face of immoral behavior.

Presumably, this difficulty about how to properly evaluate maxims for dealing with partial compliance might not be particularly worrisome if there were further tests, beyond FUL, that needed to be passed as well before it was permissible to act on a given maxim. If there were such further tests, then they might do a better job of evaluating whether a maxim can properly handle cases of merely partial compliance. We could appeal to these further tests to rule out maxims passed by FUL that were inadequate in this regard. But as we have already noted, Kant believes that FUL (and its equivalent, alternative formulations) is the only fundamental principle needed, and kantians have typically followed him in this. So it is worth asking whether FUL has the ability to handle the problem of imperfect compliance on its own.

I believe that it does. The problem, I think, lies not with FUL itself, but with what I earlier called the "standard proposal" for interpreting FUL. According to this interpretation, recall, to see whether a maxim passes FUL I need only ask whether I can will that the principle corresponding to the maxim be one that everyone acts upon. That is, I need only consider the full compliance world—whether it is possible, and whether I can rationally favor it. But why should we take FUL to be so easily satisfied? According to FUL, after all, I should only act on maxims that I can will to be *universal* law. In particular, then, I have to ask whether the appropriate principle is one that I can rationally will for *all* cases to which it applies. Now one such case, to be sure, may well be the case of full compliance. But often enough the principle in question will apply to other cases as well, cases of imperfect compliance; and so I must ask whether I can rationally will that the principle govern *those* cases as well. Thus, contrary to the claim put forward by the objection (and reinforced by the standard interpretation), FUL does not actually disregard consideration of partial compliance

worlds, worlds where not everyone is acting morally. On the contrary, it demands that we consider such worlds as well, before signing off on a principle. Only if we can will the principle for cases of imperfect compliance as well (assuming that it applies to such cases) is it really true that we can will the maxim to be universal law.

It may also be worth recalling, in this regard, that the principles we favor need not prescribe the same type of action regardless of circumstances. In particular, then, we might favor principles that tell us to act in one way when others are acting similarly, and in quite another way when they are not. Thus the principles that pass FUL may enjoin one kind of behavior when others are acting morally, and quite another in the face of immoral behavior. In short, there is no good reason to believe that FUL will be unable to generate appropriate moral guidance for dealing with cases of noncompliance.

A third objection complains that in point of fact *no* maxims (or perhaps only very few maxims) can actually pass FUL. In particular, perfectly harmless maxims—maxims that intuitively it ought to be permissible to act upon—fail. If this is correct, of course, then we have some reason to reject FUL: if it fails maxims that ought to pass, then it isn't a very good test of the validity of a maxim. Here is an example of the sort of problem that people have in mind when they raise this worry. Suppose that I form the intention of going to the local pizza house, and ask whether my maxim ("I will go to Naples for lunch") can pass FUL. I must ask whether I can will this maxim to be universal law; and apparently this involves trying to imagine a world in which *everyone*— at a minimum, all five billion humans—goes to Naples for lunch! But as soon as I do this I see that either this is literally not possible (not everyone could fit) or it would involve a practical contradiction (it would make it much more difficult to get lunch). Thus my maxim fails FUL. But this—the objection concludes—is absurd. Surely going to the local pizza house is morally permissible (special circumstances aside), and if FUL condemns my maxim, so much the worse for FUL.

In answering this objection, the first thing to remember is that even if this maxim does fail FUL, that doesn't entail that it is morally impermissible to have lunch at Naples. So long as another maxim that permits having lunch at Naples passes FUL, then it will be perfectly permissible to have lunch there. At worst, all that would follow is that the short maxim we are here testing—"I will go to Naples for lunch"—does not provide a completely accurate account of what I have reason to do. And this is not, in fact, an implausible claim. For as a moment's reflection makes clear, whether it makes sense for me to go to Naples depends on any number of factors not mentioned in the maxim as stated, for example, whether or not I am hungry, whether or not I want pizza, whether or not the restaurant is crowded, whether or not it is nearby, and so forth. Presumably I do *not* have reason to go to Naples regardless of how crowded it is, how inconvenient it is to get to it, and so on. Thus the simple maxim "I will go to Naples for lunch" cannot in fact be plausibly taken to be a complete account of what I have reason to do and why. That requires a much fuller statement, one that, for obvious reasons, I rarely have occasion to try to articulate fully. Normally, the relevant extra conditions are left implicit, and so the short maxim is perhaps best understood as a kind of shorthand for that fuller statement.

Once we keep this point in mind, and try to universalize an appropriately full statement of the maxim (or universalize the short maxim, understood to implicitly contain the various necessary qualifications), we find that the maxim can indeed pass FUL. I can certainly will that everyone go to Naples if it is convenient, if it isn't too crowded, if they want pizza, and so forth. After all, obviously enough, one or another of these conditions won't be met for almost any person we might consider (most, for example, are much too far away for it to be convenient). And so, when we imagine a world in which everyone acts on this maxim, we won't imagine a world with billions trying to crowd into the local restaurant. Rather, we imagine a world in which those who want pizza and are nearby (and so forth) go. And this is a world, it appears, that we can readily will.

In short, if we take the simple maxim to be a complete statement, it does fail FUL, but appropriately so, while the fuller maxim passes. And if we take the simple maxim to be shorthand for that fuller maxim, then of course it passes as well. Either way, there will indeed be a maxim that passes FUL that permits me to go to Naples (special circumstances aside), and so, contrary to the claim of the objection, FUL won't forbid this morally innocuous act.

The third objection claimed (albeit incorrectly) that too little passes FUL. The final objection that I want to consider, our fourth, makes the opposite complaint, that too much passes. For as we have just seen, a complete specification of one's maxim might include any number of clauses and conditions. (FUL does not restrict us to testing "simple" maxims: any maxim can be put forward for testing.) The worry, then, is that if one is sufficiently clever in formulating one's maxim, one can always arrive at a version that will pass FUL, no matter how morally unacceptable the act in question. For example, suppose I want to murder you. Even if (as we might suppose) the straightforward maxim "I will murder those I want dead" would fail FUL, I need only propose, instead, a maxim that includes, say, my proper name. Suppose, then, that I try the maxim "If I am named Shelly Kagan then I will murder those I want dead." If this maxim can indeed pass FUL, then I am permitted to murder you (whether or not this is in fact my maxim). But this would clearly be unacceptable. So if the rigged maxim does indeed pass FUL, we will simply have to reject FUL.

The objection then continues by insisting that this maxim does, in fact, pass FUL. After all, there is presumably no impossibility about having a world in which *everyone* named Shelly Kagan kills at will (indeed I may well be the only person named Shelly Kagan in the world), and it certainly seems that I (Shelly Kagan!) can be in favor of a principle that gives me this extra freedom. So it looks as though I can will the maxim to be universal law, and FUL unacceptably permits me to kill at will. (Similar results could presumably be achieved by replacing my name with a definite description that uniquely picks me out, for example, "If I am a professor of philosophy at a midsize university, with three children, and a wife who works as a midwife, etc., etc., . . . then . . ." For simplicity, however, I'll stick to introducing the proper name.)

In fact, however, I think it far from obvious that I can rationally will the maxim in question to be universal law. After all, although I believe that I am one of at best a handful of people named Shelly Kagan—perhaps, indeed, the only one—I could presumably be mistaken about this. Perhaps there is a vast extended clan, currently living peacefully in the jungle, all of whose members are named Shelly Kagan. I can hardly rationally favor a principle that would permit this vast group to kill at will. And even if (as certainly seems likely) this possibility is unrealized in the actual world, there *could* be such a world, and it simply isn't true that I (here and now) am prepared to will with regard to such a world that all the Shelly Kagans in that world be permitted to kill at will. Thus it isn't really true that I can rationally will that the maxim "If I am named Shelly Kagan then I will murder those I want dead" be a universal law. Accordingly, the fourth objection fails as well.

Generalizing from the failure of this particular example, it seems we can say the following. Although nothing in FUL, in and of itself, places restrictions on the content of the maxims that we bring for testing—we can add whatever silly clauses and conditions we'd like—proper application of FUL does have the result of ruling out maxims that introduce irrelevant conditions. If a maxim is couched in terms of conditions that are in point of fact rationally and morally irrelevant, we will discover that we are not genuinely prepared to will that the maxim be a universal law.

But the discussion of the third objection has already suggested a complementary point as well, namely, that proper application of FUL will also have the result of ruling out maxims that *lack* relevant conditions. If a maxim is overly simplistic, we will find that we are not genuinely prepared to will that either. Taking these points together, then, the kantian claims that FUL provides a sufficiently subtle and sophisticated test to guide us toward plausible moral principles, ones that are sensitive to the relevant features of acts and their circumstances while disregarding the irrelevant features.

NOTES

1. I will note, however, that Kant's own discussion of freedom is made complicated by his unargued assumption of incompatibilism—the claim that freedom is incompatible with determinism (see, e.g., G 4:446–47 or 455–56)—and that this is a view that the kantian need not accept.

2. Might the line of thought that leads from autonomy to FUL support an even stronger conclusion? If autonomy requires that I restrict myself to acting on reason-giving principles that I can autonomously will to be universal law, does it also require that I act on all those principles that I *can* so will? This is an important question, but I won't pursue it here (except to note that the distinction between what I can will, and what I do will, will be relevant). For simplicity, let's continue to follow Kant's lead and consider FUL only in its familiar, "negative" formulation.

3. His reasons for claiming this are not altogether clear or persuasive. At G 4:402 and 420–21 he seems to have in mind something like the following disjunctive argument: (1) the validity of imperatives must be based either on their content or on their form. But (2) considerations of content yield no categorical imperatives, and (3) the only categorical imperative based on form is FUL. So (4) the only categorical imperative is FUL. Now one worry about this argument is that it is difficult to see how to reconcile (2) with the later search (at G 4:428–29) for a formulation of the categorical imperative based on its inevitable content, a search that supposedly successfully results in the derivation of the formula of humanity. But since Kant holds that the formula of humanity is itself simply another way of formulating the same imperative as FUL, perhaps (2) could be replaced with (2'): the only categorical imperative derivable from considerations of content is equivalent to FUL. He could then still conclude with (4')—that the only categorical imperative is FUL or its equivalent. The more serious difficulty with the argument, however, is that even if we grant (1) (and it is not clear that we should) neither (2) (or (2')) nor (3) seems adequately defended or obviously correct.

4. Are there any such additional principles—valid, but not derived from FUL? I don't see why the kantian should deny their existence. Indeed, as we will note later, many applications of FUL seem to make use of some sort of principle of instrumental reasoning. Kant defends his own favored version of this principle, but it is noteworthy that this defense doesn't make reference to FUL at all (see G 4:417). So there may be at least one such further principle, and I don't see why there shouldn't be others.

5. Kant speaks here of a universal law "of nature," since his discussion of the four examples actually proceeds in terms of the formula of the law of nature (FLN)—a variant of FUL which he introduces at G 4:421. For our purposes, however, the differences between FUL and FLN are unimportant.

6. See Christine Korsgaard, "Kant's Formula of Universal Law," reprinted in her *Creating the Kingdom of Ends* (New York: Cambridge University Press, 1996), for a fuller discussion of these and other interpretations, including a defense of the second.

7. Unfortunately, Kant seems to be confused on this point, sometimes apparently holding the view just shown to be mistaken—that the familiar moral rules are themselves *a priori* as well. (See, e.g., G 4:389, 408, or 410–12.) In any event, the claim that *FUL* is *a priori* is less clearly mistaken, and Kant certainly believed it too (see, e.g., G 4:419–21), though whether it is correct depends on, among other things, whether the autonomy of reason is something that can be established *a priori*.

8. This has an interesting implication, which I will mention in passing. People often take the familiar moral rules (to keep your promises, to tell the truth, and so forth) as themselves being categorical imperatives, binding upon everyone. But in light of what we have just noted, we must reject this view. (We would need to reject it in any event, if we insisted on taking seriously Kant's claim that FUL and its alternative formulations represent the *only* categorical imperative.) If the derivation of particular moral rules makes essential use of contingent empirical facts, then those rules will themselves only be binding *given* the facts in question. This means that moral rules will not be binding upon *all* rational beings, *regardless* of what else is true. Thus the familiar moral rules are not categorical—since categorical imperatives must be binding upon all rational beings without condition (see G 4:416). What *is* true, of course, is that they *are* binding, nonetheless, for those rational beings for whom the relevant empirical facts do obtain, and in a world like ours that may well mean for all human beings whatsoever. In particular, then, while the familiar moral rules are not categorical, they are not conditional upon the particular desires and goals of the people involved. (It must be admitted, however, that Kant himself seems confused on this point as well, suggesting at various places that the familiar moral rules are indeed categorical. See, e.g., G 4:389, 408, or 410–12.)

9. For one example of an argument to this effect, see Christine Korsgaard, "The Right to Lie: Kant on Dealing with Evil," in *Creating the Kingdom of Ends.*

STUDY QUESTIONS

1. What is practical rationality?
2. According to Kagan, in what sense are people free?
3. Can you think of reasons for action that apply only to you?
4. Is immorality always irrational?

On the Value of Acting from the Motive of Duty

Barbara Herman

Barbara Herman is Professor of Philosophy and Law at the University of California, Los Angeles. She explores the Kantian doctrine that the moral worth of an action requires that it be done from the motive of duty. In her view, an act has moral worth only if it is required by and primarily motivated by duty. If other motives move the agent to act, then whether the agent is acting morally is a matter of luck.

It has quite reasonably been a source of frustration to sympathetic readers that Kant seems to claim that a dutiful action can have moral worth only if it is done from the motive of duty alone. The apparent consequence of this view—that an action cannot have moral worth if there is supporting inclination or desire present—is, at the least, troubling in that it judges a grudging or resentfully performed dutiful act morally preferable to a similar act done from affection or with pleasure. To many, sympathetic or not, it has in addition seemed contrary to ordinary judgment to withhold the accolade of moral worth from actions done from "good" motives other than the motive of duty. These concerns cut deeply, challenging the intuitive basis in ordinary moral knowledge that is essential to Kant's argument.

There are strategies that might be employed to disperse the problem of moral worth. One might note that the discussion of moral worth is brief and unique to the *Groundwork of the Metaphysics of Morals* where it plays a bridging role between the announcement of the unconditioned goodness of the good will and the Categorical Imperative as its principle. Kant may not have accorded moral worth the doctrinal importance we give it and so was not attentive to the kinds of cases that concern us. We might then amend his account. While it is indeed important to locate moral worth in the full argument of the *Groundwork,* Kant seems careful enough about the cases and quite clear about his conclusion: an act has moral worth if and only if it is done from the motive of duty.

Alternatively, one might accept this conclusion but seek to give it diminished importance within the general Kantian argument. It is because one takes the doctrine of moral worth to contain Kant's central claim about the moral goodness of persons that restriction of moral worth to actions done from the motive of duty seems so objectionable. Kant has much to say elsewhere—especially in *The Doctrine of Virtue* and *Religion Within the Limits of Reason Alone*—about virtue and the moral disposition that supports caution about the scope of the doctrine of moral worth. But one cannot, I think, avoid the importance of the idea that *one way* of acting—from one motive—is given moral preeminence. So even if

Barbara Herman. "On the Value of Acting from the Motive of Duty," in *The Philosophical Review*, vol, 90, no. 3. pp. 359–382. Copyright 1981, Cornell University. All rights reserved. Reprinted by permission of the present publisher, Duke University Press.

Kant has an account of moral virtue that makes room for other motives and traits, if the virtuous disposition represents a good will, then it (its virtue) will be expressed in actions done from the motive of duty.

It is best to take a direct approach to the doctrine of moral worth: we need to understand the moral question that Kant thought required "dutiful action done from the motive of duty" as an answer. Both sympathetic and hostile critics of the doctrine take the question to be obvious: What motive (or motives) distinguish the actions of the good moral agent from those of the agent whose actions are merely morally correct? If the dour "the motive of duty alone" is Kant's response to *this* question, it is not surprising that it has provoked harsh reactions.[1] If, however, the question is not the one Kant asked, then these reactions may not be in order. Since we proceed against the grain of traditional interpretation, we will do well to go slowly.

I

Kant introduces the concept of moral worth in the *Groundwork* as part of the opening account of the good will. The paragraphs that precede its introduction present the two basic facts about the good will: it is unqualifiedly good (and the only thing that is), and it is good only because of its willing, not because of its success in producing effects. With this characterization of the good will, what is needed, Kant says, is "to elucidate the concept of a will estimable in itself and good apart from any further end."[2] That is, we need to see what good willing looks like. Kant proceeds by taking up

> the concept of duty, which includes that of a good will, exposed, however, to certain subjective limitations and obstacles. These so far from hiding a good will or disguising it, rather bring it out by contrast and make it shine forth more brightly. (G397)

What follows is the discussion of moral worth and the examples of "acting for the sake of duty."

The way the examples are set up suggests that they are offered as cases in which good willing is perspicuous, rather than as the only kinds of cases in which good willing is present or can be known. If this is correct, and it is good willing in an action that "moral worth" honors, we need to see exactly what the "subjective limitations and obstacles" reveal about good willing (and so about moral worth) before we can generalize to correct conditions of attribution of moral worth.

Staying with Kant's presentation: the key to good willing is to be found in an examination of the motive someone has in performing a dutiful act *for the sake of duty.* Kant seems to think that what is special about this motive is revealed by contrasting it to other motives that, in at least some circumstances, can also lead to dutiful actions. He proceeds by looking at examples of two kinds of action that are "according to duty" but are not performed from the motive of duty, and so are said not to have moral worth: (1) dutiful actions done because they serve the agent's self-interest (the shopkeeper example) and (2) dutiful actions that are just what the agent wants to do—those for which he is said to have an "immediate inclination" or interest (the sympathy, self-preservation, and happiness examples).

The crucial question, obviously, is: *why* is it not possible that these nonmoral motives give dutiful actions moral worth? We will look at the two most famous of Kant's examples to see whether they provide a clue to what Kant thinks is of value in the actions he says have moral worth.

The shopkeeper example. We want to see whether this example makes clear what significant moral difference there is between doing a dutiful action (treating people honestly, giving inexperienced customers the correct change) from the motive of self-interest (or profit) and doing the same action from the motive of duty. One may say: when you do a dutiful action from duty, you do it because it is what duty requires; when you do it from self-interest, you do it for some other reason. This is hardly wrong. But it is uninformative about *why* doing an action "because it is what duty requires" is of any moral importance.

The details of the example are instructive. The dutiful action is not to overcharge inexperienced customers. When there is considerable competition, Kant points out, it is good business not to overcharge, and so the sensible shopkeeper's business interests *require* him to act honestly in such circumstances. The message is plain: while it is *always* morally correct to serve people honestly (we can assume this for the example), acting from an interest in making a profit will require honest actions in only *some* circumstances—there may be times when honesty is not the best policy.

It seems, then, that the moral fault with the profit motive is that it is unreliable. When it leads to dutiful actions, it does so for circumstantial reasons. The businessman's interest in the dutiful action is controlled by (Kant says: mediated by) his interest in his business, and whether he acts well or not depends on the paths that circumstances open for the pursuit of his business goals. This example suggests the need for a motive that will guarantee that the right action will be done. But the sympathy example suggests that this is only part of the story.

The sympathy example.[3] Here is a person who would help others from an *immediate* inclination: he helps others because that is what he wants to do; helping others is not the means to some further end he has. In Kant's words, "there are many spirits of so sympathetic a temper that, *without any further motive of vanity or self-interest,* they find an inner pleasure in spreading happiness around them" (G398, emphasis added). Now if, following the shopkeeper example, the issue here is the reliability of the motive (wanting to help others), we have a problem. In the shopkeeper example it seemed plausible to argue that the interest in profit was inadequate as a moral motive[4] because the likelihood of such a motive producing morally correct action was dependent on contingent and changeable circumstances. But here, where the right action is given as helping another, and that is just what the person has an immediate inclination to do, there can be no complaint that this motive will lead to other sorts of action in changed circumstances. But if the motive of sympathy yields right actions, why isn't it judged to be a motive producing actions with moral worth?

Kant says that such an action,

> however right and amiable it might be, has still no genuinely moral worth. It stands on the same footing as [action from] the other inclinations—for example, the inclination for honor, which if fortunate to hit on something beneficial and right and consequently honorable, deserves praise and encouragement, but not esteem; for its maxim lacks moral content, namely, the performance of such actions, not from inclination, but *from duty*. (G398)

The inclination for honor is criticized in two ways: it is described as only "fortunate" to hit on something right; and the maxim of the action it prompts is said to lack moral content. Is the motive of sympathy only fortunate when it hits on a right action? Doesn't it necessarily prompt a person to help others? Suppose I see someone struggling, late at night, with a heavy burden at the backdoor of the Museum of Fine Arts. Because of my sympathetic temper I feel the immediate inclination to help him out. We need not pursue the example to see its point: the class of actions that follows from the inclination to help others is not a subset of the class of right or dutiful actions.

In acting from immediate inclination, the agent is not concerned with whether his action is morally correct or required. That is why he acts no differently, and in a sense no better, when he saves a drowning child than when he helps the art thief. Of course we are happier to see the child saved, and indeed might well prefer to live in a community of sympathetic persons to most others, but the issue remains. The man of sympathetic temper, while concerned with others, is indifferent to morality. In Kant's language, the maxim of his action—the subjective principle on which the agent acts—has no moral content. If we suppose that the *only* motive the agent has is the desire to help others, then we are imagining someone who would not be concerned with or deterred by the fact that his action is morally wrong. And, correspondingly, the moral rightness of an action is no part of what brings him to act.

On this reading of the sympathy example it would seem that Kant did not reject such emotions as moral motives because they could not be steady and strong, or because they were essentially partial.[5] Even if, for example, sympathy could be strengthened to the force of habit, and trained (as Hume suggests) toward impartial response, it would still generate morally correct actions only by accident. For while sympathy can give an interest in an action that is (as it happens) right, it cannot give an interest in its being right.[6]

I said of the shopkeeper example that the person's motive was to make a profit, and so his hitting upon a right action was also, in this way, a matter of luck. The economic circumstances that happened to prevail required honest actions as the necessary means to business ends. So in this example, too, the denial of moral worth to an action is intended to mark the absence of interest in the morality of the action; that the shopkeeper's action was morally correct and required was not a matter of concern to him.

This suggests a more general thesis. Even if social institutions were arranged to guarantee that profit and honesty went together (through penalties, social sanctions, and so on), the performance of honest actions, so motivated, would still be no more than "fortunate"; that is, dependent on external and contingent circumstances. Maximizing the number of honest transactions is not what moral worth looks to. And a concern with moral worth will not encourage the social manipulation of circumstances so that people just find themselves doing what is right.

What can we conclude? This reading of the two examples does not (and is not intended to) give us an account of what moral worth is or a clear idea of the conditions for its correct attribution. It does suggest why Kant thought that there was something the matter with a dutiful action performed from a nonmoral motive; nonmoral motives may well lead to dutiful actions, and may do this with any degree of regularity desired. The problem is that the dutiful actions are the product of a fortuitous alignment of motives and circumstances. People who act according to duty from such motives may nonetheless remain morally indifferent.

Taking the limits of nonmoral motives as a guide, we can introduce a minimal claim. For a motive to be a moral motive, it must provide the agent with an interest in the moral rightness of his actions. And when we say that an action has moral worth, we mean to indicate (at the very least) that the agent acted dutifully from an interest in the rightness of his action; an interest that therefore makes its being a right action the nonaccidental effect of the agent's concern.

II

If we now see why a dutiful action does not have moral worth when done from a nonmoral motive alone, what can we say of the dutiful actions that *are* done from the motive of duty where the agent *also* has nonmoral interests in the action? This is the problem of the overdetermination of dutiful action.

The overdetermination of actions is a general phenomenon. It is quite common for us to have more than one motive for what we do, and even more than one motive that by itself would be sufficient to produce a particular action. Although Kant never explicitly discusses overdetermined moral cases, where an action is done from the motive of duty and from some other nonmoral motive, there is a tradition of reading Kant—especially the sympathy example—as holding that the mere presence of the nonmoral motive signifies a lack of moral worth. On this reading, the value that moral worth marks depends on the motive of duty acting alone.

The key text is in the second stage of the sympathy example. In the first stage of the example, Kant considers a man of sympathetic temper who does what is right (he helps others where he can) because he finds "an inner satisfaction in spreading joy and rejoice[s] in the contentment which [he has] made possible" (G398). As we have seen, Kant says that while such an action is "dutiful and amiable," it has no moral worth. In the second stage, Kant imagines "this friend of man" so overcome by sorrow that he is no longer moved by the needs of others. Kant continues:

> Suppose that, when no longer moved by any inclination, he tears himself out of this deadly insensibility and does the action without any inclination for the sake of duty alone; then for the first time his action has its genuine moral worth. (G398)

As one commentator responds: "Surely the most obvious way of generalizing from this remark yields the doctrine that only when one acts from duty alone—'without *any* inclination'—does his act have moral worth."[7] If one accepts this generalization—and it is traditional to do so—then one is faced either with the grim interpretation of moral worth or with the need to revise the doctrine to include cooperating nonmoral motives in a less stringent requirement. Although I think the generalization drawn from the passage is neither obvious nor necessary, there is insight to be gained from the difficulties that come with trying to accommodate it.

An instructive example is Richard Henson's attempt to take the sting out of the doctrine of moral worth by diminishing the significance of the *Groundwork* view. Drawing on the account of duties of virtue in the later *Metaphysics of Morals,* Henson argues that Kant can be seen as having another and benign conception of moral worth—he calls it the "fitness-report" model—according to which a dutiful act would have moral worth "provided that respect for duty was present and would have sufficed by itself [to produce the dutiful act], even though (as it happened) other motives were also present and might themselves have sufficed."[8] This is the model that is to do the basic work of crediting moral agents for doing the right thing in the right way. By contrast, Henson suggests we understand the *Groundwork's* conception of moral worth on the analogue of praise acknowledging victory against great odds (say, powerful desires tempting one away from duty), calling it, appropriately, the "battle-citation" model. If the conditions of action include supporting inclinations, and especially if the inclinations are sufficient by themselves to produce the dutiful act, then there is no great victory and no reason for praise. And, as Henson remarks, in honoring a person who has struggled morally and won, "we mean of course to encourage others who find themselves in comparable straits; but we emphatically do not mean to encourage anyone to try to *bring about* such situations"[9] which this sort of praise is appropriate. It need not be a fault if one never earns a battle citation for one's dutiful actions.[10]

The two-model approach to moral worth leaves Kant acquitted of the damaging charge that he believes it morally desirable not to want to do the action you morally ought to do. And each of the models of moral worth captures a natural form of moral praise. But the success of the two-model strategy depends on the adequacy of either model to capture the moral point of Kant's account of moral worth; that a right or dutiful action is performed is the non-accidental effect of the agent's moral concern.

According to the fitness-report model, overdetermined actions can have moral worth so long as the motive of duty is *sufficient by itself* to produce the dutiful action. But what it means for the moral motive to be "sufficient by itself" is unclear. It could mean sufficient if alone—that is, cooperating motives would not be required to bring about the dutiful action. Or it might be a stronger condition: if at the time of the action the agent had some conflicting motives, the moral motive was capable of bringing about the dutiful action without the aid of cooperating motives. Neither of these quite natural interpretations will support a satisfactory account of moral worth. It is instructive to see why they cannot.

Overdetermination involves cooperation between moral and nonmoral motives. Knowing this much does not reveal the conditions of cooperation. For the most part, two motives will cooperate to produce the same action only by accident.[11] As circumstances change, we may expect the actions the two motives require to be different and, at times, incompatible. But then, on either reading of sufficient moral motive, an agent judged morally fit might not have a moral motive capable of producing a required action "by itself" if his *presently* cooperating nonmoral motives were, instead, in conflict with the moral motive.[12] That is, an agent with a sufficient moral motive could, in different circumstances, act contrary to duty, from the *same* configuration of moral and non-moral motives that in felicitous circumstances led him to act morally.

Consider a shopkeeper whose honest actions are overdetermined. On the fitness model, a shopkeeper with a sufficient moral motive will perform honest actions even if the profit motive is absent. But the fact that the moral motive was sufficient by itself in the overdetermined case does not imply that he would perform honest actions when the profit motive clearly indicated that he should *not* act honestly. What does this tell us? Looking at the possible outcome of the original configuration of motives in altered circumstances introduces the suspicion that it might have been an accident that the agent acted as duty required in the *first* case: the explanation of his dutiful action might have been the absence of conflict with the profit motive. In what sense, then, was the shopkeeper morally fit? Surely to say that an action had moral worth we need to know that it was no accident that the agent acted as duty required.

There are two paths that can be taken here. (1) If the moral motive would have prevailed in altered circumstances (where the presently cooperating non-moral motive instead indicated some other, incompatible, course of action), then the success of the moral motive in the case at hand was not dependent on the accident of circumstances that produced cooperation rather than conflict. This suggests a move to a greater-strength interpretation of sufficiency. While such a move solves the problem with the fitness model, it would pose a serious difficulty to an argument like Henson's for two models of moral worth.

On a greater-strength interpretation of the fitness model, an action can have moral worth only if the moral motive is strong enough to prevail over the other inclinations—without concern for whether they in fact cooperate or conflict. Henson's battle-citation model of moral worth differs only in that the moral motive has had to prevail. We do give different praise to the man who we know would be courageous than we do to the man who is (though why we do is a matter of some puzzlement), but there is no difference in the structure and strength of the two men's motives. Henson is right to point out that it is not morally desirable to be in circumstances where the moral motive has to win out, and so we are under no moral requirement to put ourselves in situations where we will earn such praise. But it is hardly plausible to see *this* difference in praise as marking a distinct notion of moral worth—since there is no difference in moral motive or the configuration of

motives in the two cases. The only difference is in the circumstantial accident of cooperation or opposition of the nonmoral motives in the presence of an overpowering moral motive. A greater-strength interpretation of sufficiency would then undermine the claim that there were *two* notions of moral worth in Kant, and leave us with just the battle-citation model's powerful moral motive.

There are more substantive questions raised by a shift to a greater-strength interpretation of sufficiency, however. It is not at all clear that we should require of the moral motive that it be stronger or be able to prevail in altered circumstances in order to attribute moral worth to a given action. Even if circumstances tomorrow are such that the alignment of moral and nonmoral motives breaks down, and the dutiful action is as a result not done, it is surely possible that the dutiful action that *is* done today, when the motives are aligned, has moral worth. (In much the same way, succumbing to temptation only *raises* a question about motives in past cases.) Moral worth is not equivalent to moral virtue.

The problem is this: the experiment of imagining altered circumstances while holding fixed a given configuration of moral and nonmoral motives suggests that a dutiful action's being performed may be an accident of circumstances even with the presence of a sufficient moral motive (in Henson's original sense). While it seems reasonable to credit an action with moral worth only if its performance does not depend on an accident of circumstances, it seems equally reasonable to allow that failure in different circumstances does not require denial of moral worth to the original performance. With strength its only variable, the sufficiency account cannot satisfy both reasonable requirements.

(2) Both conditions could be met by a configuration of moral and nonmoral motives such that in acting dutifully it is the moral motive itself on which the agent acted. When this configuration holds, it would be no accident that the dutiful action was done, since it was just the agent's concern to act as duty required that determined his acting as he did. In different circumstances, if the configuration remains the same, the agent will again act dutifully. If he does not, it can only be from a different configuration of

motives—one in which he is acting from some motive other than the motive of duty. But this failure to act dutifully would provide no reason to discredit the dutiful action in the original case. Thus the difficulties that emerge with the notion of sufficiency support a literal reading of Kant's requirement that dutiful actions be done *from* the motive of duty: the presence of a moral motive sufficient to produce the dutiful action does not show that the interest that in fact determined the action was a moral one.[13]

Support for this third alternative to strength and fitness can be found in the *Critique of Practical Reason* (92–93),[14] where Kant denies any necessary opposition between moral and nonmoral motives, including the "principle of happiness." What is required is that where there is a question of duty, we "take no account" of the claims of happiness; we are not required to renounce them. For an action to have moral worth, the nonmoral motives (which are empirical and therefore belong to the principle of happiness, not the moral law) "must be separated from the supreme practical principle and never be incorporated with it *as a condition*" (emphasis added). It seems natural to conclude that when an action has moral worth nonmoral motives may be present, but they may not be what moves the agent to act. But it is not obvious how a motive could be present and yet not operative. To make sense of the third alternative, we need to complicate our understanding of motives in Kant's theory of action.

From the perspective of a familiar empiricist account of motives, the third alternative is unintelligible. It is easy to see why. If one takes motives to be desires, and desires are a kind of cause, when a motive is present it should have an effect (direct or indirect) on choice or action.[15] In line with this, one would suppose that cooperating motives add force in a given direction of action, and conflicting motives interfere with or even cancel each other (at the extreme). A prudential or a moral motive would be just another kind of desire, distinguished, presumably, by its object. What moves an agent to act is the resultant of these vector-like forces.[16] On such an account of motives, it will seem that the only way to satisfy the moral-worth requirement—that acting from the motive of duty not be an accident—is to require that

the outcome of the agent's present configuration of motives be invariant through changes in circumstances. The implausibility of the latter requirement then counts against the former one. We plainly cannot use this kind of account of motives to make sense of Kant's view.

The key to understanding Kant is in the idea that moral worth does not turn on the presence or absence of inclination supporting an action, but on its inclusion in the agent's maxim *as* a determining ground of action: as a motive. Kantian motives are neither desires nor causes. An agent's motives reflect his *reasons* for acting. An agent may take the presence of a desire to give him a reason for action as he may also find reasons in his passions, principles, or practical interests. All of these, in themselves, are "incentives" (*Triebfedern*), not motives, to action. It is the mark of a rational agent that incentives determine the will only as they are taken up into an agent's maxim. Indeed, it is only when an agent has a maxim that we can talk about his motive.[17]

The man of sympathetic temper responds to suffering *and* takes that response to give him a reason to help. Only then does he act from the motive of sympathy. An action that is done from the motive of duty is performed because the agent finds it to be the right thing to do and takes its rightness or requiredness as his reason for acting. He acts from the motive of duty with a maxim that has moral content.

On this view of motives, an agent could act from more than one motive in more than one way. It may be that neither of two incentives alone gives the agent sufficient reason to act (assuming a "favorable balance of reasons" principle). Then the agent may act from a combined motive. Or an agent may have incentives that provide two independent sufficient reasons for an action. Clearly no dutiful action from a combined motive could have moral worth. The harder question is whether there is anything wrong with taking both moral and nonmoral incentives into one's maxim as independently sufficient motives. Since a dutiful action has moral worth because the agent takes the fact that an action is morally required to be his reason for action—it is morality that guides his will—the presence of a nonmoral motive in his maxim is disqualifying.[18]

What we should now say about the preferred (third) alternative is this: when an action has moral worth, nonmoral *incentives* may be present, but they may not be the agent's motives in acting. If the agent acts from the motive of duty, he acts because he takes the fact that the action is morally required to be the ground of choice. It does not follow from this that the action's moral worth is compromised by the presence of nonmoral feelings or interests, so long as they are not taken by the agent as grounds of choice: as motives. Thus one can say both that an agent's doing the right thing is nonaccidental because he acted from the motive of duty *and* admit that he might not have acted from this motive in altered circumstances. Strictly speaking, the doctrine of moral worth can accept the overdetermination of action with respect to *incentives,* not motives.

One might still object that, on this account of moral worth, it remains a matter of luck or accident that an agent acted in a morally worthy way. The strength of competing inclinations, the presence of circumstances that evoke competition, the strength of the moral motive itself may be affected by chance. The effect of chance, however, is on *who* is able to act in a morally worthy way. It poses a distributive problem that belongs to the theory of moral virtue and not to moral worth. It is *actions* and not agents that are credited with moral worth.[19] And although it may be a matter of luck *whose* actions have moral worth, what moral worth expresses is the relation of a motive to an action (through its maxim). When an agent does act dutifully from the motive of duty, when his maxim of action has moral content, it is not a matter of luck that the *action* has moral worth.[20]

III

The scope of the motive of duty is not restricted to morally worthy actions. It applies as well to actions that are merely correct or permissible: actions whose maxims satisfy the conditions set by the Categorical Imperative. Since it is possible to act in accordance with duty, but not from duty, it is obviously possible to have a morally correct action and only a nonmoral motive for acting on it. But for an action not required

by duty, what can the moral motive add when the maxim already passes the Categorical Imperative's tests?

Our discussion of why *dutiful* actions should be done from the motive of duty suggests an answer: in acting from the motive of duty, the agent sets himself to abide by the moral assessment of his proposed actions. Suppose you have something you want (for whatever reason) to do. What the motive of duty provides is a commitment to do what you want only if the maxim of your action is judged morally satisfactory.[21] If it does pass the test, you are free to act, and the motive of duty as well as your original motive are satisfied. The difference introduced by the motive of duty is that one would *not* have acted on the original (nonmoral) motive had the maxim of action it prompted been morally unsatisfactory (failed the Categorical Imperative tests).

This aspect of the motive of duty fits a general pattern of motives that do not themselves have an object (in the ordinary way), but rather set limits to the ways (and whether) *other motives* may be acted upon. For example, a concern for economy is a motive that, by itself, does not normally lead one to do anything. It leads one to consider whether something that is wanted for other reasons is also a good value. That is, the motive to economy does not have a role to play unless another motive to action is already present. Then it says to act as you plan to only if what you would do is economical (as well as whatever else it is). If there is conflict between my desire for something and my more general concern for economy, that does not indicate what I will do; motives like that for economy may be easily (and sometimes appropriately) set aside for the satisfaction of other desires. (We often experience this as a kind of quasi-moral guilt; sometimes it is a release from inhibition.)

Following Kant, let us say that such motives provide *limiting conditions* on what may be done from other motives (usually primary, or initiating, motives).[22] Cooperation is then seen as the case in which the limiting condition sanctions acting on the primary motive; it does not merely, and independently, push along with it. Similarly, conflict does not consist in opposing tugs, but in the action suiting the primary motive failing to satisfy the limiting condition. What, in the end, will be done does involve an issue of strength. But the strength metaphor alone masks the complexity of the interaction.

When the motive of duty functions as a limiting condition, there is no lessening of the agent's moral commitment if he acts from the motive of duty *and* nonmoral motives, so long as the motive of duty is effective; its satisfaction is decisive in the agent's going on with his proposed action. Rather than posing a moral obstacle, the nonmoral motive is in most cases necessary if the motive of duty (as a limiting condition) is to have an object of interest. As Kant sees it, moral deliberation characteristically begins with a nonmoral interest or motive that prompts consideration of an appropriate course of action.[23] Ordinary moral life is embedded in desires for ordinary things, desires that lead to different kinds of action in different circumstances. My need for money may send me to the bank, to work, or to a deceitful promise, depending on the situation in which I must act to meet my need. Whether I will be tempted to act in a morally impermissible way will likewise depend on contingent and variable circumstances. If we follow Kant, it is what happens next that is the crucial moment for the moral agent. Once I am aware of what I want to do, I must consider whether it is morally permissible. If I have an effective motive of duty. I will act only when I determine that it is. I then act in the presence of more than one motive, satisfying both my nonmoral desire *and* the motive of duty. This is the normal state of affairs for someone with a sincere interest in doing what is right.[24]

Although as a limiting condition the motive of duty can enter only when there is a proposed course of action based on another motive, it is unlike many other motives that impose limiting conditions since it can, by itself, move an agent to act. The clearest case of this is, of course, in morally worthy actions. There are also certain kinds of action that cannot be done at all unless done from the motive of duty (as a primary motive). For example, not every act of bringing aid is a beneficent act. It is beneficent only if the agent conceives of what he is doing as an instance of what *any* moral agent is required to do when he can help another, and acts to help for that reason. For Kant, only

the motive of duty could prompt someone to act on a maxim with such content—for no other motive responds to a conception of action that regards the agent himself impersonally or is impartial in its application.

The motive of duty cannot, by itself (as a primary motive), prompt merely permissible actions, for it is by definition a matter of moral indifference whether they are performed. (We might say, with Kant, that the maxims of permissible actions have no moral content.) The role of the motive of duty here can only be in the background, as an effective limiting condition, requiring that the agent not act contrary to duty. If the agent loses interest in his proposed course of action, the motive of duty can have nothing to say about what he should do until another course of action is proposed (other things morally equal). In other words, permissible actions cannot be done "from the motive of duty." Therefore merely permissible actions, even when they are performed on the condition that they are permissible (that is, even when the motive of duty is effective as a limiting condition in them), cannot have moral worth.[25]

For an action to be a *candidate* for moral worth, it must make a moral difference whether it is performed. (Only then is it even possible for the action to be done from the motive of duty.) For an action to *have* moral worth, moral considerations must determine how the agent conceives of his action (he understands his action to be what morality requires), and this conception of his action must then determine what he does. (It is when this condition is satisfied that a maxim of action has moral content.[26]) That is, an action has moral worth if it is required by duty and has as its primary motive the motive of duty. The motive of duty need not reflect the only interest the agent has in the action (or its effect); it must, however, be the interest that determines the agent's acting as he did.

Earlier we noted that the discussion of moral worth was introduced by Kant to illuminate the nature of good willing (good of itself, without regard to any further end). Now we can see why good willing is found in actions that have moral worth: in them, the agent need not be concerned with anything other than the morality of what he does in order to have sufficient motive to act. If the maxim of an action is an expression of an agent's will in acting, to say that the maxim of a dutiful action done from the motive of duty has moral content is to say of the agent's will that it is ultimately determined by "that preeminent good which we call moral" (G401).

It is clear that the role of the motive of duty is considerably more extensive than the illustrative examples in the *Groundwork* might lead one to believe. This is especially important in providing some idea of the moral cast given to ordinary action in the theory. Although we should never act contrary to duty, the function of the motive of duty is not to press constantly for *more* dutiful actions, or to get us to see the most trivial actions as occasions for virtue: rather it is to keep us free of the effects of temptations in ordinary situations that can suggest morally prohibited courses of action. It is only in its function as a primary motive that one acts *from* the motive of duty at all, and only those actions that are required (by the Categorical Imperative) *can* have the motive of duty as a primary motive. As a limiting condition, the motive of duty can be present in (or satisfied by) an action, and yet that action have no moral import. Thus we can preserve the sense in which, for Kant, the motive of duty is ubiquitous—governing all our actions—without having to accept the view that all of our actions must be seen as matters of duty.

IV

At this point we need to return to the *Groundwork*'s sympathy example to see how our account of moral worth and the moral motive fares interpretively. That is, we want, in its terms, an analysis of the value of acting with moral worth that satisfactorily explains Kant's apparent insistence that only the action done from the motive of duty alone has moral worth.

Earlier I suggested that the problem with the natural motive of sympathy is that the interest it gives an agent in his action is not a moral interest. The man of sympathetic temper is one whose helpful actions, however steady and genuinely beneficial, are motivated by his natural response to the plight of others. He acts because he is moved by

others' distress. As such there is no moral component in his conception of what he does. Therefore nothing in what motivates him would prevent his acting in a morally impermissible way if that were helpful to others, and it is to be regarded as a bit of good luck that he happens to have the inclination to act as morality requires.[27] What is missing is an effective and motivating moral interest in his action: the source of the action is not the moral motive itself (he is not acting beneficently), nor is he committed to refraining from helpful actions that are not permissible. That is to say, his action neither has moral worth nor indicates an attitude of virtue.

If the moral motive *is* effective and motivating, it would seem that the presence of a nonmoral inclination should have no effect on the action's moral worth. That is, even if the moral motive expresses but *one* kind of interest the agent has in the helpful action, so long as it is the moral motive the agent acts on, the action should have moral worth. Indeed, what is morally valuable in actions judged to have moral worth seems prominently displayed in cases of this type: the dutiful act is chosen without concern for its satisfying other incentives the agent may have.

What, then, can we make of Kant's supposed insistence that only when there is no natural inclination to help can the helping action have moral worth? The key to the sympathy example is found in attending to the fact that it describes the moral situation of the *same man* in two different circumstances: the "friend of man," no longer moved by the needs of others, is the man of sympathetic temper with whom the discussion begins. Straightaway we should ask why Kant would think *this* change of circumstances for *this* man is revelatory. At the least, the emphasis on an individual should make us cautious about how we generalize from the case.

Let us follow Kant. The first part of the sympathy example looks at the helping act of the man of sympathetic temper. We concluded that there is good reason to find moral fault in the dutiful action done from inclination alone. Kant says that this action has no moral worth. In the second part of the example, we are to suppose that things change for the man, and his natural concern for others becomes ineffective. We need not imagine that his character changes—he is still a man of sympathetic temper; changed circumstances have called forth other, more powerful inclinations, which have made him unable to feel for others or disinclined to concern himself on their behalf. Looking to inclination *alone* for motivation, then, he cannot act to help. Kant supposes that he does act in the face of this "deadly insensibility," from the motive of duty. That such an action is judged to have moral worth is in no way problematic. What has seemed unwarranted is the claim that in acting "without any inclination—then for the first time the action has its genuine moral worth." And it would be if it were an instance of the generalization "only when there is no inclination to a dutiful action can it have moral worth." We come to a quite different conclusion, however, if we see the passage as a set of remarks about one (kind of) person, a man of sympathetic temper who normally helps others because he is stirred by their need but sometimes, when his feelings are dimmed, helps them because that is what duty requires. Of *him* it is then said: only when the inclination to help others is not available does *his* helping action have moral worth. For of him it was true that when he had the inclination he did not act from the motive of duty. This does not imply that no dutiful action can have moral worth if there is cooperating inclination. Nor does it imply that a sympathetic man could not act from the motive of duty when his sympathy was aroused. The account is of a kind of temperament we are tempted to value morally, designed to show how even dutiful actions done from apparently attractive motives might yet be morally wanting.

We should expect confirmation of this interprétation in the other examples Kant offers in this section, and it will be worth reminding ourselves of their detail to see it.[28] Immediately after the shopkeeper example, which describes an action "done neither from duty nor from immediate inclination." Kant considers the duty of self-preservation;

> to preserve one's life is a duty, and besides this everyone has also an immediate inclination to do so. But on account of this the often anxious precautions taken by the greater part of mankind for this purpose have no inner worth, and

the maxim of their action is without moral content. They do protect their lives in conformity with duty, but not from the motive of duty. When on the contrary, disappointments and hopeless misery have quite taken away the taste for life; when a wretched man, strong in soul and more angered at his fate than fainthearted or cast down, longs for death and still preserves his life without loving it—not from inclination or fear but from duty; then indeed his maxim has a moral content. (G397–398)

I think that one reads this as *obviously* supporting the "no-inclination" generalization only by ignoring what Kant seems to be raking elaborate pains to say; most of the time people act to preserve their lives with no regard to its being a duty (and often with no regard to morality at all), simply because they have an inclination to self-preservation. This seems true enough. *If* it is a duty to preserve one's life, then Kant would surely be right in saying that most self-preserving acts have no moral worth. Here, as before, we could point to a lack of interest in the morality of such actions. There is a willingness, from the point of view of the inclination to self-preservation, to act in a morally impermissible way; and with the absence of such inclination, "when disappointments and hopeless misery have quite taken away the taste for life," no reason remains to preserve the life no longer cared about. The conclusion is that actions motivated by the inclination to self-preservation alone have no moral worth. And since, as a matter of fact, most self-preserving actions come from this source, "the often anxious precautions taken by the greater part of mankind for this purpose have no inner worth."

Now the contrast. We imagine a person who normally acts to preserve his life because he wants to keep living. Circumstances change, his "taste for life," is gone; death appears as a more attractive alternative to continued life.[29] If inclination were all that now prompted his actions, what once led him to self-preserving actions would now lead him to act contrary to duty. He then acts to preserve his life from the motive of duty; *that* self-preserving action has moral worth. The conclusion: for most of us, most of the time, self-preserving actions stem from inclination alone and have no moral worth. Sometimes, some people, when they have no inclination to preserve their lives, may yet do so from the motive of duty. For such a person, only then, and for the first time, would his self-preserving action have moral worth. Nothing in this account speaks against the possibility of an action with more than one incentive having moral worth. As with the sympathy example, what is being examined is the dutiful act done from immediate inclination *alone*. The point of the discussion is to reveal what is added, morally, when a person acts from the motive of duty. It is easier to see what is added when all inclination is taken away.[30]

We can see this structure of argument again in Kant's discussion of the indirect duty we have to promote our happiness. He begins with the observation that the motive for most of the actions that conform to this duty is the ordinary desire to be happy ("the universal inclination towards happiness"). Such actions, plainly, have no moral worth. As with the sympathy and self-preservation examples, the argument looks at the actions of a particular man (in this case someone suffering from gout), whose altered circumstances direct an inclination that ordinarily conforms to duty away from it. The gout sufferer is in the odd situation where he cannot act according to the (indirect) duty to promote his own happiness unless he acts from the motive of duty. This is so because the inclination toward happiness *in him,* in his special circumstances, is distracted by present pleasure, when, for the sake of happiness, he ought to abstain and seek good *health.* If he follows inclination, *in these circumstances,* he will act contrary to duty, although ordinarily he would not. (Pleasure and happiness frequently coincide.) Kant concludes that when the gout sufferer acts to promote his happiness from the motive of duty (choosing health over pleasure), "for the first time his conduct has a real moral worth." Here again the example directs us to refrain from giving moral value to inclination, however likely it is to promote dutiful actions, because of the accidental nature of the connection between *any* inclination and duty. When the inclination alone prompts a morally correct action, there is no moral worth because, in Kant's terms,

there is no moral content or interest in the volition (maxim). Nothing in the example forces the reading that it is the mere *presence* of the inclination that is responsible for the denial of moral worth. The moral failure is seen when, in the absence of the motive of duty, and so of a moral interest in the action, circumstances may be such that inclination alone gives the agent no reason to do the dutiful action. Indeed, in acting from inclination alone, the agent *never had* a reason to do what morality required.

What can be said in summary about these three examples? They concern men motivated to dutiful actions by different kinds of inclination.[31] Exactly what normally motivates their acting according to duty leads them to act impermissibly when changed circumstances direct the inclination to something other than a dutiful action. It is said of *these* men that their dutiful actions have moral worth only when, in the altered circumstances (where inclination does not in fact support a dutiful action), they nonetheless act, from the motive of duty alone. Then, for the first time, they show a moral interest in their action. For it is only then that they act from the motive of duty at all. If there is any obvious generalization to be taken from these cases, it has to do with the moral inadequacy of nonmoral motives.

If an agent does not have an independently effective and motivating moral interest in an action, although he may act as duty requires, there remains a dependence on nonmoral interests that compromises his ability to act morally. One need not be indifferent to the possible satisfactions that a dutiful action may produce. It is just that the presence of such possibilities should not be the ground of the agent's commitment to acting morally. Overdetermined actions *can* have moral worth so long as the moral motive is the determining ground of action—the motive on which the agent acts. Morality is not to he merely one of the things, among others, in which we have an interest.

When someone acts from an effective and primary moral motive, it could well be said that such a person is morally fit. But the nature of this fitness includes more than the presence of a moral motive sufficient to produce a dutiful action. It expresses a kind of independence from circumstances and need, such that in acting from the motive of duty, we are, as Kant saw it, free.

NOTES

1. And the reactions have been extremely harsh; from the mockery of Schiller's verse, to the dismissive arguments of philosophers responsive to the virtues, to the angry contempt of contemporary philosophical feminists. It has seemed incredible that Kant could have held such a view *and* claimed authority for it in ordinary moral knowledge.

2. *Groundwork of the Metaphysics of Morals,* p. 397; Hereafter cited G with page numbers from the Prussian Academy edition.

3. I consider here only the first part of the sympathy example, since it most clearly addresses the question of the moral value of the moral motive. The reading of the whole example comes after this question is resolved, and we have a clearer sense of what it is for an action to have moral worth (see section IV).

4. "The moral motive" and "the motive of duty" I use interchangeably. In asking whether something could be *a* moral motive I am asking whether it could be a motive that gives an action moral worth.

5. A sharply argued version of this criticism can be found in Bernard Williams, "Morality and the Emotions," in *Problems of the Self* (Cambridge: Cambridge University Press, 1973), pp. 226–228.

6. Whether *any* emotion could give an agent a moral interest in an action is a question that must look first to an account of the emotions (of what it is to say of a motive that it is an emotion). For Kant, the answer is clearly no; he holds that no emotion or inclination can make the moral law the determining ground of the will, since they determine the will according to the principle of happiness. See *Critique of Practical Reason* (hereafter cited KpV) 92–93 and G401n.

7. Richard Henson, "What Kant Might Have Said: Moral Worth and the Overdetermination of Dutiful Action." *Philosophical Review 88* (1979). 45.

8. Ibid., p. 48. The original version of this chapter was written in response to Henson's essay.

9. Ibid., p. 50.

10. The battle-citation metaphor suggests powerful, serious, difficult-to-control conflict. But the metaphor exaggerates the case. Dutiful action from a moral motive in the face of temptation is an ordinary and natural part of moral life. Indeed, the introduction of such conflict would be a necessary part of a moral education if its occurrence were not inevitable.

11. Part of the task of moral education is to shape a person's character so that the alignment of moral and non-moral motives can be depended upon.

12. The weaker version may not yield a dutiful action in the presence of any conflicting motive. The stronger version takes care of only motives that in fact conflict with the moral motive at the time of the action. It is not set up to deal with motives that *might have* produced conflict.

13. Henson acknowledges such an account as an alternative to his fitness and battle-citation models of moral worth, but rejects it because he believes there are no adequate criteria for deciding the factual question of which of a number of motives an agent actually acted on (p. 44). By itself this is a weak argument. We often need to insist that although we had a motive we did not act on it. Unless this were so, there would be little room for moral insincerity.

14. See also G400–401 and *Theory and Practice* 278–279.

15. Holly Smith, canvassing this way of understanding moral worth, remarks, "Since I find problems in understanding the idea of a desire that exists but has no connection with the agent's choice, even though it is a desire to perform or to avoid performance of actions available for choice, I shall not discuss this suggestion." See "Moral Worth and Moral Credit," *Ethics 101* (1991), 290–291n. Interestingly, she finds no issue in couching a claim about motives in the language of desires. A similar objection to the idea of motives not acted on can be found in Paul Benson, "Moral Worth," *Philosophical Studies 51* (1987), 365–382.

16. This is of course a crude version of the empiricist view. In particular, it leaves out the complexity of structure that comes with second-order desires. Nevertheless, something very much like the crude version is at work in the critical debate about Kant's doctrine of moral worth.

17. Evidence for this account of motives can be found throughout Kant's practical philosophy. It is perhaps most clearly laid out in the introduction to the *Metaphysics of Morals.*

18. I take the conjunction of motives in one maxim to imply a principle that makes each the condition of acting on the other. More puzzling is the disjunctive motive, "Do the right thing because it is right *or* because it promotes some nonmoral good." Here as well the motive of duty would not be the determining ground of the will, not because of some condition but because the principle is one of indifference.

19. This may not seem so clear, for the moral worth of an action is said to be in its maxim (G399): the expression (in rule form) of an agent's volition (what the agent is moved to do and for what reason). Thus there is a sense in which moral worth *is* about agents—it is about their willings. The point of saying that it is actions that are credited with moral worth is to highlight the relationship between *an* action and *its* motive (via the action's maxim), which is where moral worth resides (and not in the permanent structure of an agent's motives: that is the matter of virtue—see DV46). The opposite view is argued in Keith Simmons, "Kant on Moral Worth," *History of Philosophy Quarterly 6* (1989). 85–100.

20. Here I disagree with Thomas Sorrell, "Kant's Good Will," *Kant-Studien* 78 (1987), 87–101, who argues that if moral worth signifies good willing, and the good will is a will that can never be bad, an action cannot have moral worth unless it is done from a good will. This erases the distinction between moral worth and virtue that I would draw. I see no reason why good willing cannot be present in a will that is not altogether good. We do not always give moral concerns priority—and so our will is not good—but sometimes we do.

21. Motives other than duty can appear to produce this result: someone might believe that the road to salvation lies in satisfying the Categorical Imperative. The only difference here is in the motive: the end (satisfying the Categorical Imperative), and so the actions taken, will be the same. That is, the difference is in the nature of the agent's attachment to his end. In the one case, Kant could argue, it is the realization through the Categorical Imperative of the agent's dignity as a rational being; in the other, the attachment to the Categorical Imperative depends on a desire to be saved. Giving up the idea of an afterlife might require that such a person remotivate his attachment to morality. The attachment to the Categorical Imperative that comes from the motive of duty does not depend on the maintenance of such extramoral beliefs (although such beliefs may be needed to reinforce moral commitment).

22. A primary motive is one that can, by itself, produce action. Limiting conditions may also be directed at other limiting conditions—lexically, or in some other structure (with or without conflict among them). Insofar as a motive functions as a limiting condition, all it can require is that the actions prompted by *other* motives satisfy its condition. The problem of disjunctive motives does not occur here because the moral motive is the condition of acting on the nonmoral motive.

23. This is clear in the way he presents instances of moral deliberation. For example: "[A person] finds himself driven to borrow money because of need. He well knows that he will not be able to pay it back; but he sees too that he will get no loan unless he gives a firm promise to pay it back . . . He is inclined to make such a promise; but he still has enough conscience to ask 'Is it not unlawful and contrary to duty to get out of difficulties in this way?'" (G422).

24. Such actions can be described as overdetermined in the sense that they satisfy more than one motive. They are not overdetermined in Henson's sense, where each motive must be sufficient by itself to produce the action.

25. One might want to say that, in permitting myself to act only when and because my maxim satisfies the Categorical Imperative, I *am* doing an action that has moral worth, since it is done from the motive of duty. But it is the permitting and not the action permitted that would have moral worth. (In permitting myself another glass of wine I am not acting on the same motive I will be acting on when I drink it.) Since it is not clear to me how there can be a *duty* to act on maxims that satisfy the Categorical Imperative (the Categorical Imperative tells you what your duty is), I would rather treat the permitting as acting on the moral motive in its limiting condition function, thereby indicating an attitude of virtue rather than moral worth.

26. Thus a dutiful action performed on the condition that it is permissible (that is, from the motive of duty as a limiting condition only), will not have moral worth, even if it is no accident of circumstances that the dutiful action is done. Its not being an accident is only a necessary condition for moral worth. In the case of a perfect duty, for example, only those maxims of inclination that include the required action will be permissible (G401n). So an agent with a policy of never acting impermissibly will (nonaccidentally) act as perfect duty requires. When inclination and duty coincide, however, he may act with no other conception of his action than as a permissible means of satisfying inclination. That is, he may act dutifully, with no sense that his action is required, from a maxim that has no moral content.

27. One might, of course, cultivate an inclination because of its recognized moral utility. In *Doctrine of Virtue* (hereafter cited DV) 456 Kant distinguishes between what we might call "natural" and "moral" sympathy: the latter appears to be the moral motive making use of our natural propensity to care about the welfare of

others to promote "active and rational benevolence." The message for us is in the clear subordination of the natural to the moral motive. We are not morally better off without natural sympathy.

28. It is unfortunate that such exclusive attention has been lavished on the sympathy example for it is difficult to see its point given the obvious attractiveness of the kind of person it criticizes. The striking similarity of detail in the self-preservation and happiness examples is easily overlooked once one is convinced that Kant has made the argument "if inclination, no moral worth" in the sympathy case.

29. There is surprising subtlety in this example. Why, one might wonder, does Kant insist on someone "strong in soul" and angered by his fate, rather than someone depressed or weak? Is it that a weaker person might turn to morality as a comfort? Or perhaps he is interested in cases where the choice against morality seems strongest, most rational. The resolution of this does not affect the larger interpretive question. The presence and the quality of the detail do suggest a kind of concern with a particular case that should quickly warn one off easy and large generalizations.

30. Beck notes that when Kant discusses the use of examples in *Second Critique* 92–93 he compares himself to a chemist separating a compound (of motives) into its elements: Kant's purpose in using cases that present conflict between moral and nonmoral motives is merely to precipitate the motive of duty, and not to present conflict as a condition for moral worth. See Lewis W. Beck, *A Commentary on Kant's Critique of Practical Reason* (Chicago: University of Chicago Press, 1960), p. 120n.

31. Each of the examples deals with a different category of inclination: the inclination to self-preservation is an instinct; a sympathetic temper is a natural (to human beings) disposition; the desire for happiness is based on an empirically determined Idea.

STUDY QUESTIONS

1. If you visit a friend in the hospital in hope of being financially rewarded, are you acting morally?

2. If you visit a friend in the hospital because of concern for your friend, are you acting morally?

3. If you visit a friend in the hospital not to relieve your friend's distress but because you believe you have a duty to visit, are you acting morally?

4. If you visit a friend in the hospital both to relieve your friend's distress and because you believe you have a duty to visit, are you acting morally?

Kant's Formula of Humanity

Christine M. Korsgaard

Kant claims that the supreme principle of morality is categorical, universal, and unconditional. But he also claims that we are obligated to act only conformity with our own will. How can both claims be true? Christine Korsgaard, Professor of Philosophy at Harvard University, defends a reading of Kant's formula of humanity that she believes provides an answer. Human beings are the source of the value of valuable things. My coffee is conditionally good due to my desire for it. Without me, it is a worthless liquid. I thus am a bestower of value, and in virtue of this status must see myself and also act as having unconditional value. This line of thought, however, is not unique to me but applies to all rational beings. Hence by valuing anything, I am committed to respecting myself and others as ends in themselves. In this way I adhere to Kant's categorical imperative, although the source of the imperative is my own will.

I INTRODUCTION

The Second Section of the *Groundwork of the Metaphysics of Morals* contains three arguments that have the form: if there were a categorical imperative, this is what it would have to be like.[1] Each of these arguments leads to a new set of terms in which the categorical imperative can be formulated. In summarizing these arguments, Kant tells us that universality gives us the form of the moral law; rational nature or humanity as an end in itself gives us the material of the law; and autonomous legislation in a kingdom of ends represents a complete determination of maxims and a totality of ends. The Formula of the Universal Law is to be used in actual decision making, we are told; the other two, which bring the moral law "closer to intuition" and "nearer

to feeling" can be used to "gain a hearing for the moral law" (G 436).

Attention to these remarks about the relations among the three formulas has perhaps obscured the fact that the three formulas represent a progression in the argument that leads from "popular moral philosophy" into "the metaphysics of morals." I think that it is sometimes supposed that Kant's claim that the categorical imperative is a principle of reason rests squarely on the Formula of Universal Law—i.e., on that formula's "formality." The claims of the other two formulas to be rational principles are then taken to be based upon their presumed equivalence to the Formula of Universal Law. Those who make such a supposition err not only by ignoring the fact that the Categorical Imperative is not "deduced" in the *Groundwork* until the Third Section, but also by

From Christine M. Korsgaard, *Creating the Kingdom of Ends*, Cambridge University Press, 1996.
Reprinted by permission of the publisher.

ignoring the fact that each formulation is intended to represent some characteristic feature of rational principles. In particular, "humanity" is argued to be the appropriate material for a rational principle, just as universality is its appropriate form. Furthermore, the addition of each new feature represents a step further into the metaphysics of morals, with the idea of autonomy providing the stepping-stone that will make the transition to a critique of practical reason possible. In this paper, I am concerned with the argument for the Formula of Humanity. Specifically, I want to consider what characteristic feature of "humanity" as Kant thinks of it makes humanity the appropriate material for a principle of practical reason.

At the end of the discussion of the Formula of Universal Law and the examples of its application, Kant claims to have shown that duty must be expressed in categorical imperatives and to have "clearly exhibited the content of the categorical imperative," if there is one (G 425). Having established that a categorical imperative would say that we should act only on such maxims as we can will to be universal laws, Kant raises a new question: "Is it a necessary law for all rational beings that they should always judge their actions by such maxims as they themselves could will to serve as universal laws?" (G 426). To answer this question we must discover an *a priori* connection between the law and the will of a rational being, and in order to discover this connection we will be driven into metaphysics (G 426). That is, we have to investigate the possibility of "reason thus determining conduct" (G 427). This investigation is a motivational one.

Kant proceeds to tell us that what "serves the will as the objective ground of its self-determination" is an end. Ends may be either objective or subjective, depending on whether they are determined by reason or not. A formal principle is one that disregards all subjective ends; not one that disregards ends altogether (G 427). It is Kant's view throughout his moral philosophy that every action "contains" an end; there is no action done without some end in view. The difference between morally worthy action and morally indifferent action is that in the first case the end is adopted because it is dictated by reason

and in the second case the end is adopted in response to an inclination for it. For instance, in the *Groundwork 1* example of the comparison between morally worthy beneficence and morally indifferent beneficence, the difference is found to rest in the different grounds on which each of the two men have adopted the welfare of others as his end. It is a mistake to suppose that Kant is contrasting a man who helps others as a mere means to his own pleasure with a man who does so from duty. Kant says explicitly that the man of sympathetic temperament is "without any motive of vanity of selfishness" (G 398). Each of these characters genuinely has the welfare of others as his end—that is, each values it for its own sake.[2] The difference is that the morally worthy man has adopted this end because it is a duty to have such an end. Of course, in the case of action that promotes the obligatory ends it is obvious that the morally motivated person has an end in view. But is there an end in view in the sort of moral action that is required as strict duty, and does not involve one of the two obligatory ends? Kant's answer is that there is—the end in view is humanity. The difference between the person who acts merely in accordance with duty and the person who acts *from* duty is described, in the *Metaphysical Principles of Virtue,* in terms of this end;

> Although the conformity of actions to right (i.e., being an upright man) is nothing meritorious, yet the conformity to right of the maxim of such actions regarded as duties, i.e., *respect* for right, is meritorious. For by this latter conformity a man makes the right of humanity or of men his end. (MPV 390)

It is important here to keep in mind that there are two different roles an end can play in the determination of conduct; it can serve as a purpose pursued, or it can play a negative role and serve as something one must not act against. To take an ordinary example: we do not often get into situations where self-preservation serves as a positive incentive to any action, but it might quite frequently keep us from taking undue risks in the pursuit of our other ends: without much thought and in an everyday way, one might, under the influence of this end, avoid a dangerous area or going out at night. Kant thinks that the end of humanity functions in this negative way; "the end here is not conceived as one to be effected but as an independent end, and thus merely negatively. It is that which must never be acted against . . ." (G 437). In the *Metaphysical Principles of Virtue* Kant explains the constraining role of humanity as an end this way:

> The doctrine of right had to do merely with the formal condition of external freedom. . . . Ethics, on the other hand, supplies in addition a matter (an object of free choice), namely, an *end* of pure reason which is at the same time represented as an objectively necessary and, i.e., as a duty for man. For since sensible inclinations may misdirect us to ends (the matter of choice) which may be contrary to duty, legislative reason cannot guard against their influence other than, in turn, by means of an opposing moral end, which therefore must be given a priori independently of inclination. (MPV 380–81)

The role that Kant here assigns to this end stands in a specific relation to *human* reason, for it is human reason that has the obstacles provided by sensuous inclination to overcome. The sensuous inclinations present themselves falsely as sufficient reasons for action, because of a tendency in human nature which is described in *Religion Within the Limits of Reason Alone* as a "propensity to evil" (R 34–36), and in the *Critique of Practical Reason* as "self-conceit" (C2 73–74). These obstacles to goodness are controlled by making humanity an unconditional end which must never be acted against; and it is in this that human virtue consists (C2 84–89). There is no contradiction between this view and the many passages where Kant insists that morality needs no end as an incentive. Having humanity as an end is not an incentive for adopting the moral law; rather, the moral law commands that humanity be treated as an end. Although the role of this end in checking the inclinations is specific to human reason, it has a metaphysical point. Human *freedom* is realized in the adoption of humanity as an end in

itself, for the one thing that no one can be compelled to do by another is to adopt a particular end (MPV 381), and this end, freely adopted, checks the power of the inclinations. In the *Groundwork,* the argument for the Formula of Humanity is preceded by warnings that the motive we are seeking not only must not be an empirical or subjective feeling or propensity, but also must not be derived from "a particular tendency of the human reason which might not hold necessarily for the will of every rational being" (G 425). Therefore, it must turn out that freely acting *from* duty and adopting humanity as one's unconditioned end are one and the same thing.

The argument for the Formula of Humanity as an End in Itself has two parts: Kant first argues that there must be an unconditional end; second, that the end must be humanity. The first part of this argument is simple; one can make it in either direction. If there is a necessary end, then there is a categorical imperative, for this end would be "a ground of definite laws" (G 428). If there is a categorical imperative, then there must be some necessary end or ends, for if there is a categorical imperative there are necessary actions, and every action contains an end (MPV 385). In the *Metaphysical Principles of Virtue* this consideration also serves as the basis for what Kant calls a deduction of the duties of virtue from pure practical reason:

> For practical reason to be indifferent to ends, i.e., to take no interest in them, would be a contradiction; for then it would not determine the maxims of actions (and the actions always contain an end) and, consequently, would not be practical reason. (MPV 395)

This shows that if there is a categorical imperative, it must have as its material a necessary end or ends. This end, Kant argues, must be "humanity."

II HUMANITY

Before looking at Kant's argument that the necessary end must be humanity, I want to review the available evidence about what Kant means by that term. The argument itself will show us what Kant has in mind, but preliminary evidence will pave the way for the argument. In the *Groundwork,* Kant interchanges the terms "humanity" and "rational nature." And he tells us that

> Rational nature is distinguished from others in that it proposes an end to itself. (G 437)

The fullest statement of his notion of humanity is found in the *Metaphysical Principles of Virtue*:

> The capacity to propose an end to oneself is the characteristic of humanity (as distinguished from animality). The rational will is therefore bound up with the end of the humanity in our own person, as is also, consequently, the duty to deserve well of humanity by means of culture in general, and to acquire or promote the capacity of carrying out all sorts of ends, as far as this capacity is to be found in man. (MPV 392)

In clarifying the idea of cultivation he has referred to "humanity, by which he alone is capable of setting himself ends" (MPV 387).

As these passages indicate, Kant takes the characteristic feature of humanity, or rational nature, to be the capacity for setting an end. Ends are "set" by practical reason; human beings are distinguished from animals by the fact that practical reason rather than instinct is the determinant of our actions. An end is an object of free choice (MPV 384). A rational being, as possessor of a will, acts on maxims of his or her own choosing; but every maxim contains an end, and in choosing the maxim one also chooses an end. In the case of morally worthy actions, the end is chosen because of the necessity of the principle embodied in the maxim; but it is not only the morally obligatory ends that are freely chosen under the agency of practical reason. All maxims are freely adopted and so all ends are so chosen.

While it will be obvious that Kant thinks that the obligatory ends are objects of reason, the idea that all human ends are in some sense set by reason requires a little more explanation. It might seem to some that it is more natural to say of ends other than the obligatory ends that they are "set" by inclination or "passion," and that reason's only role with respect to these is that of determining the means by which they are to be realized. To see that this is not Kant's view is important for an understanding of the Formula of Humanity: it is the capacity for the rational determination of ends in general, not just the capacity for adopting morally obligatory ends, that the Formula of Humanity orders us to cherish unconditionally. I would therefore like to cite some additional evidence for this point.

First, there are the remarks about reason and happiness in the *Groundwork*. In the teleological argument concerning the purpose of practical reason in Section One, Kant argues that if happiness were nature's end for us, instinct would have been a better guide; nature would have allowed us theoretical reason with which to contemplate out happy state, but

> would have taken care that reason did not break forth into practical use nor have the presumption, with its weak insight, to think out for itself the plan of happiness and the means of attaining it. Nature would have taken over not only the choice of ends but also that of the means, and with wise foresight she would have entrusted both to instinct alone. (G 395)

This remark could be read either as suggesting that nature has the choice of ends but would also have taken over the means as well, or as suggesting that in us nature has relinquished the control of both ends and means (and would not have done so if happiness had been her purpose). The remark that practical reason tries to think out the plan of happiness as well as the means to it, however, suggests the latter reading. The latter remarks to the effect that happiness is an indefinite "ideal of the imagination" support this reading (G 418). If happiness were some plain and obvious thing—for example pleasure as Bentham thought of it—the problem of determining the means to it could be no more serious than the problem of determining the means to anything whatever. The difficulty Kant points to is that in constructing the imperative of prudence reason must specify the end before it can determine the means; but there is no possible rule for specifying "the plan of happiness."[3]

The second and best piece of evidence for the role of reason in the selection of ends in general comes from the essay *Conjectural Beginning of Human History*. In this essay, Kant uses Genesis as the basis for a speculative reconstruction of the steps taken by humanity in its transformation from a creature governed by instinct to a rational being. The first object of free choice is the apple and Kant explains how it comes about. Humans are guided by instinct through the sense of smell and taste to their natural food. But by means of comparison they notice that other foods are visually similar to the things they eat. This operation of comparison is assigned to reason, and it leads to new desires; not only desires that go beyond instinct, but desires that are positively contrary to it (CBHH 111). The result of this event is described by Kant:

> The original occasion for deserting natural instinct may have been trifling. But this was man's first attempt to become conscious of his reason as a power which can extend itself beyond the limits to which all animals are confined . . . this was a sufficient occasion for reason to do violence to the voice of nature (3:1) and, its protest notwithstanding, to make the first attempt at a free choice . . . He discovered in himself a power of choosing for himself a way of life, of not being bound without alternative to a single way, like the animals . . . He stood, as it were, at the brink of an abyss. Until that moment instinct had directed him toward specific objects of desire. But from these now opened up an infinity of such objects, and he did not yet know how to choose between them. (CBHH 111–12)

Kant goes on to trace further steps by which the powers of reason are developed. Reason not only directs the human being to objects around it for which there is no instinctual desire, but leads to the development of specifically human desires, such as love and the taste for beauty, and later concern for the future (CBHH 112–15). Morality comes only at the end of this development. But the development represents a logical or rational completion as well as a

genesis. The possession of practical reason, through such operations as comparison and foresight, directs our desires to an ever-increasing range of objects, but so far it does not teach us how to choose among them. Reason makes it possible to set new ends, but its guidance at this stage is only partial. This is a crucial point, for it is because of this fact that these ends are still "subjective" and not yet "objective" ends. Reason plays a role in determining our interest in them, but they are not dictated by reason. Human reason, by directing us to "an infinity" of new possible objects of desire without determining more definitely which are worthy of choice, sets up a problem. The *Groundwork* argument suggests that the idea of making a plan for happiness will not solve this problem. Rather, it is only through the development of morality that reason can give us *complete* guidance in choosing ends. In any case, there can be no question that in this essay Kant thinks of all human ends as being partially "set" by the operations of reason. They may be objects of desire or inclination, but it is reason that is responsible for the unique human characteristic of having non-instinctual desires.

The third piece of evidence for Kant's views about the specific nature of "humanity" comes from *Religion Within the Limits of Reason Alone*. In a discussion of the question whether human beings are good or evil by nature, Kant describes an "Original Predisposition to Good in Human Nature," divided into three parts: predispositions to animality, humanity, and personality (R 26–27). Of these three predispositions the first is associated with the instinctual desires and the last with respect for the moral law as sufficient incentive of the will. In between them comes the predisposition to humanity which

> can be brought under the general title of self-love which is physical and yet *compares* (for which reason is required); that is to say, we judge ourselves happy or unhappy only by making comparison with others. (R 27)

Kant adds that

> The first requires no reason, the second is based on practical reason, but a reason thereby

subservient to other incentives, while the third alone is rooted in reason which is practical of itself, that is, reason which dictates laws unconditionally. (R 28)

It might be possible to read "practical reason . . . subservient to other incentives" as referring to a "hypothetical" use of practical reason—that is, a discovery of means—except that the role actually assigned to practical reason here is not the discovery of means but "comparison." This is the role of reason in *Conjectural History* as well, although in the *Religion* the comparison is not among possible objects of desire but a comparison of one's own lot with another's. Again, however, the result must be the acquisition of new, specifically human ends, for Kant claims that "nature, indeed, wanted to use the idea of such rivalry . . . only as a spur to culture" (R 27).

Throughout the historical writings, culture represents the development towards the perfect freedom or rule of reason that will only be achieved by morality.

When Kant says that the characteristic of humanity is the power to set an end, then, he is not merely referring to personality, which would encompass the power to adopt an end for moral or sufficient reasons. Rather, he is referring to a more general capacity for choosing, desiring, or valuing ends; ends different from the ones that instinct lays down for us, and to which our interest is directed by the operations of reason. At the same time, of course, it is important to emphasize that this capacity is only completed and perfected when our ends are fully determined by reason, and this occurs only when we respond to moral incentives. Humanity, completed and perfected, becomes personality, so that in treating the first as an end in itself we will inevitably be led to realize the second. Thus, in the *Critique of Practical Reason,* humanity in one's own person and personality are spoken of as if they were the same thing (C2 87). But the distinctive feature of humanity, *as such,* is simply the capacity to take a rational interest in something: to decide, under the influence of reason, that something is desirable, that it is worthy of pursuit or realization, that it is to be deemed important or valuable, not because it contributes to

survival or instinctual satisfaction, but as an end—for its own sake. It is this capacity that the Formula of Humanity commands us never to treat as a mere means, but always as an end in itself.

III THE BASIS OF THE ARGUMENT

But suppose that there were something the existence of which in itself had absolute worth, something which, as an end in itself, could be a ground of definite laws. In it and only in it could lie the ground of a possible categorical imperative, i.e., of a practical law (G 428).

With these words, Kant, in the *Groundwork,* establishes the connection between the existence of a categorical imperative and the existence of an unconditionally valuable end. Immediately after, he asserts, and then argues, that this end must be "man and, in general, every rational being." In the next section, I want to reconstruct that argument in order to show why humanity must be this unconditional end and the material of a rational principle. In this section I want to say something about the theory of rational action upon which that argument is based.

In the discussion of good and evil in the *Critique of Practical Reason* (57–71), Kant discusses what he refers to as an old formula of the schools: *Nihil appetimus, nisi sub ratione boni; nihil aversamur, nisi sub ratione mali.* If this is taken to mean that "we desire nothing except with a view to our weal or woe" it is "at least very doubtful." But if it is read as saying "we desire nothing, under the direction of reason, except in so far as we hold it to be good or bad" it is "indubitably certain" (C2 59–60). Similarly, in the *Groundwork* Kant says that "the will is a faculty of choosing only that which reason, independently of inclination, recognizes as practically necessary, i.e., as good" (G 412–29). Insofar as we are rational agents we will choose what is good—or take what we choose to be chosen as good.

As the identification of "good" with "practically necessary" in the *Groundwork* quotation suggests, Kant takes "good" to be a rational concept.

This means two related things. First, reason must determine what is good. On this basis Kant argues in the *Critique of Practical Reason* that if the end were set by inclination and reason determined only the means, then only the means could be called "good" (C2 62). Thus, if an end is good, it must be set by reason; and if an action is done under the full direction of reason, then the end must be good. Second, and correlatively, if an end is deemed good it provides reasons for action that apply to every rational being:

> What we call good must be, in the judgment of every reasonable man, an object of the faculty of desire, and the evil must be, in everyone's eyes, an object of aversion. Thus, in addition to sense, this judgment requires reason. (C2 60–61)

It is this that gives rise to the *Groundwork* requirement, associated with the Formula of Humanity, that others "must be able to contain in themselves the end of the very same action" (G 430). If one's end cannot be shared, and so cannot be an object of the faculty of desire for everyone, it cannot be good, and the action cannot be rational.

From these considerations it follows that if there are perfectly rational actions, there must be good ends, and that when we act under the direction of reason, we pursue an end that is objectively good. But human beings, who act on their conception of laws, take themselves to act under the direction of reason. In the argument for the Formula of Humanity, as I understand it, Kant uses the premise that when we act we take ourselves to be acting reasonably and so we suppose that our end is, in his sense, objectively good. Perhaps it will at first seem odd that he uses that premise in an argument leading to a formula of the categorical imperative, since only if there is a categorical imperative will anything be in his sense objectively good. Here it is crucial to remember that the arguments leading to the formulations of the categorical imperative all tell us what the imperative will be like *if it exists*. Only *if* there is a categorical imperative will there be perfectly rational action; but if there is perfectly rational action there will be ends that are good.

Since good is a rational concept, a good end will be one for which there is reason—an end whose existence can be *justified*. But this by itself is not enough to establish a categorical imperative, for reasons can be relative: means for example can be called good, but only relatively to a given end (C2 62). If the goodness of an end is only relative, it will not have that claim upon all rational beings that Kant associates with the rationality of the concept "good," and cannot provide the basis for a categorical imperative.

> The ends which a rational being arbitrarily proposes to himself as the consequences of his action are material ends and are without exception only relative, for only their relation to a particularly constituted faculty of desire in the subject gives them their worth. And this worth cannot, therefore, afford any universal principles for all rational beings or valid and necessary principles for every volition. (G 427–28)

What is required for a categorical imperative, therefore, is an end for which there is sufficient reason—an end whose existence can be completely justified, and which therefore has a claim on every rational will. This is why Kant seeks "something the existence of which in itself has absolute worth" or an "end in itself" (G 428). Justification—the giving of practical reasons for ends and actions—is in one sense subject to the same fate as explanation—the giving of theoretical reasons for events. Reason seeks the "unconditioned," as the basis for an account (justification or explanation) that provides a sufficient reason.

As these comparisons suggest, the argument for the Formula of Humanity depends upon the application of the unconditioned/conditioned distinction to the concept of goodness. This follows from the fact that good is a rational concept. In any case where anything is conditioned in any way, reason seeks out its conditions, not resting until the "unconditioned condition" is discovered (if possible). An inquiry in the "analytic" or as Kant in one passage more helpfully calls it the "regressive" style (PFM 276n) is an argument in which something is taken as given or actual and the conditions of its possibility are explored. The arguments of the *Groundwork,* at least in the first two sections, like the arguments of the *Prolegomena,* are "regressive." If there is a categorical imperative, then there is fully rational action. If there is fully rational action, how is it possible? In the case of the Formula of Humanity the material of the law is sought through an investigation of the question: what is capable of fully justifying an end? What is unconditionally good?

In one sense, this question has already been answered in the first section of the book. There, Kant asserts that the only thing that can be conceived to be unconditionally good is a good will. The location of this claim shows us that Kant attributes it to "common rational knowledge of morals." It is used as a starting point for his analysis. In the remarks that follow, Kant elucidates the claim by explaining that the good will is the only thing that has its "full worth in itself" (G 394); and is the only thing whose value is in no way relative to its circumstances or results. Its value is independent of "what it effects or accomplishes" (G 394), it is in the strictest sense *intrinsically* good.

The good will is also said to be the condition of all our other purposes (G 396). This follows from its being the only unconditionally good thing. The value of anything else whatever is dependent upon certain conditions being met. Kant mentions talents of the mind, qualities of temperament, gifts of fortune such as power, wealth, and health, and happiness among the things whose value is conditional. If the value of something is conditional, however, an inquiry into the conditions of its value should lead us eventually to what is unconditioned. This is partly affirmed in these early passages, for Kant tells us that the talents and temperamental qualities must be directed, the advantages used, and the happiness possessed by one with a good will in order that they be good. The good will is, in all cases, the unconditioned condition of the goodness of other things.

As the inclusion of happiness among the conditional goods shows, although Kant is claiming that the good will is the only thing whose value is intrinsic, he is not claiming that the good will is the only thing that is valuable as an end.[4] Means are obviously conditional goods, for their goodness depends upon the goodness of the ends to which they are instrumental. But happiness, although clearly an end, and an end under which Kant thinks all of our other ends are subsumed, is also a conditional good whose value depends upon the good will. So Kant tells us that the good will is not the sole or complete good but "the condition of all others, even of the desire for happiness" (G 396). It is for this reason that "an impartial observer" disapproves "the sight of a being adorned with no feature of a pure and good will, yet enjoying uninterrupted prosperity" (G 393). But the impartial observer is equally dismayed by the idea that the virtuous person be without happiness:

> That virtue (as the worthiness to be happy) is the supreme condition of whatever appears to us to be desirable and thus of all our pursuit of happiness and, consequently, that it is the supreme good have been proved in the Analytic. But these truths do not imply that virtue is the entire and perfect good as the object of the faculty of desire of rational finite beings. For this, happiness is also required, and indeed not merely in the partial eyes of a person who makes himself his end but even in the judgment of an impartial reason, which impartially regards persons in the world as ends-in-themselves. (C2 110)

A thing, then, can be said to be objectively good, either if it is unconditionally good or if it is conditionally good and the condition under which it is good is met. The happiness of the virtuous, for this reason, forms the other part of the "highest good": virtue, and happiness in proportion to virtue, together comprise all that is objectively good. A conditionally good thing, like happiness, is objectively good when its condition is met in the sense that it is fully justified and the reasons for it are sufficient. Every rational being has a reason to bring it about, and it is this that makes it a duty both to pursue the happiness of others and, in general, to make the highest good one's end.

Since all objective value must come from unconditioned value, the good will is the source of all the good in the world. The highest good, as virtue and happiness in proportion to virtue; or the Kingdom of Ends, as "a whole of rational beings as ends in themselves as well as of the particular ends which each may set for himself" (G 433) are representations of a system of ends which can be said to be "synthesized" by the categorical imperative. This system is the totality of all that is objectively good under the unconditioned good; it is the systematic whole or unity formed by practical reason.

> As pure practical reason it likewise seeks the unconditioned for the practically conditioned (which rests on inclinations and natural need); and this unconditioned is not only sought as the determining ground of the will but, even when this is given (in the moral law), is also sought as the unconditioned totality of the object of pure practical reason, under the name of the *highest good*. (C2 108)

I have said that practical reason shares the "fate" of theoretical reason insofar as it, too, is driven to "seek the unconditioned," In an important sense, however, the fate of practical reason is different from that of theoretical reason, this is one of the most central tenets of Kant's philosophy. Theoretical reason, in its quest for the unconditioned, produces antinomies; in the end, the kind of unconditional explanation that would fully satisfy reason is unavailable. Practical reason in its quest for justification is subject to no such limitation.[5] This is part of Kant's doctrine of the primacy of practical reason. The argument for the Formula of Humanity provides an initial access to that doctrine, by showing that Humanity can be regarded as an unconditionally good thing, and a source of justification for things that are only conditionally good.

IV THE ARGUMENT FOR THE FORMULA OF HUMANITY

Having established that if there is a categorical imperative there must be something that is unconditionally valuable, Kant proceeds to argue that it must he humanity. Here is what he says:

All objects of inclinations have only a conditional worth, for if the inclination and the needs founded on them did not exist, their objects would be without worth. The inclinations themselves as sources of needs, however, are so lacking in absolute worth that the universal wish of every rational being must be indeed to free himself completely from them. Therefore, the worth of any objects to be obtained by our actions is at all times conditional. Beings whose existence does not depend on our will but on nature, if they are not rational beings, have only a relative worth as means and are therefore called "things"; on the other hand, rational beings are designated "persons" because their nature indicates that they are ends in themselves, i.e. things which may not be used merely as means. Such a being is thus an object of respect and, so far, restricts all (arbitrary) choice. . . . For, without them, nothing of absolute worth could be found, and if all worth is conditional and thus contingent, no supreme practical principle for reason could be found anywhere. (G 428–29)

In one sense, it seems as if Kant is just reviewing the available options in his search for something unconditionally good; considering objects of inclinations, inclinations, natural beings or "things", and finally persons, that being the one that will serve. But it is also possible to read this passage as at least suggesting a regress towards the unconditioned; moving from the objects of our inclinations, to the inclinations themselves, finally (later) back to ourselves, our rational nature. The final step, that rational nature is itself the objective end, is reinforced by this consideration:

> The ground of this principle is: rational nature exists as an end in itself. Man necessarily thinks of his own existence in this way; thus far it is a subjective principle of human actions. Also every other rational being thinks of his existence by means of the same rational ground which holds also for myself; thus it is at the same time an objective principle from which, as a supreme practical ground, it must be possible to derive all laws of the will. (G 429)

I have quoted these rather long passages because my aim in what follows is to give a reconstruction along these lines—that is, on the assumption that the argument is intended as a regress upon the conditions. The reconstruction depends upon the ideas set forth in the previous sections. A rational action must be done with reference to an end that is good, and a good end is one for which there is a sufficient reason. It must be the object of every rational will, and it must be fully justified. If it is only conditionally good, the unconditioned condition for its goodness must be sought. Although we know already that the good will is this condition, the argument helps to show us what the good will must be, by showing us what will serve as such a condition.

Suppose that you make a choice, and you believe what you have opted for is a good thing. How can you justify it or account for its goodness? In an ordinary case it will be something for which you have an inclination, something that you like or want. Yet it looks as if the things that you want, if they are good at all, are good because you want them—rather than your wanting them because they are good. For "all objects of inclinations have only a conditional worth, for if the inclinations and the needs founded on them did not exist, their objects would be without worth" (G 428). The objects of inclination are in themselves neutral; we are not attracted to them by their goodness; rather their goodness consists in their being the objects of human inclinations.

This, however, makes it sound as if it were our inclinations that made things good. This cannot be right, for "the inclinations themselves, as sources of needs, however, are so lacking in absolute worth that the universal wish of every rational being must be indeed to free himself completely from them" (G 428). Now even without fully endorsing what Kant says here, we can easily agree that there are some inclinations of which we want to be free; namely those whose existence is disruptive to our happiness. Take the case of a bad habit associated with an habitual craving—it would not be right to say that the object craved was good simply because of the existence of the craving when the craving itself is one that you would rather be rid of. So it will not be just

any inclination, but one that we choose to act on, that renders its object good.

Even consistency with our own happiness does not make the objects of inclination good, however. (Now I am, admittedly, departing from the passage I am interpreting—for Kant leaves it at the undesirability of having inclinations at all.) This is partly because we are not certain what our happiness consists in, but more because of a claim that has already been made in the opening lines of the *Groundwork*: we do not believe that happiness is good in the possession of one who does not have a good will. This is, of course, our great temptation—to believe that our own happiness is unconditionally good. But it is not really a tenable attitude. For either one must have the attitude that just one's own happiness is unconditionally good, which is rather a remarkable feat of egocentricism,[6] or one has to have the attitude that each person's happiness is unconditionally good. But since "good" is a rational concept and "what we call good must be, in the judgment of every reasonable man, an object of the faculty of desire" (C2 60–61), we cannot rest with the position that everyone's happiness, whatever it might be, is absolutely good. For:

> Though elsewhere natural laws make everything harmonious, if one here attributed the universality of law to this maxim, there would be the extreme opposite of harmony, the most arrant conflict, and the complete annihilation of the maxim itself and its purpose. For the wills of all do not have one and the same object, but each person has his own. . . . In this way a harmony may result resembling that depicted in a certain satirical poem as existing between a married couple bent on going to ruin. "Oh, marvelous harmony, what be wants is what she wants"; or like the pledge which is said to have been given by Francis I to the Emperor Charles V, "What my brother wants (Milan), that I want too." (C2 28)

Given that the good must be a consistent, harmonious object of rational desire and an object of the faculty of desire for every rational being, one can take neither everyone's happiness nor just one's own happiness to be good without qualification: the former does not form a consistent harmonious object; and the latter cannot plausibly be taken to be the object of every rational will if the former is not. Thus happiness cannot in either form be the "unconditioned condition" of the goodness of the object of your inclination, and the regress upon the conditions cannot rest here. We have not yet discovered what if anything makes the object of your choice good and so your choice rational.

Now comes the crucial step. Kant's answer, as I understand him, is that what makes the object of your rational choice good is that it *is* the object of a rational choice. That is, since we still *do* make choices and have the attitude that what we choose is good in spite of our incapacity to find the unconditioned condition of the object's goodness in this (empirical) regress upon the conditions, it must be that we are supposing that rational choice itself *makes* its object good. His idea is that rational choice has what I will call a value-conferring status. When Kant says: "rational nature exists as an end in itself. Man necessarily thinks of his own existence in this way; thus far it is a subjective principle of human actions" (G 429), I read him as claiming that in our private rational choices and in general in our actions we view ourselves as having a value-conferring status in virtue of our rational nature. We act as if our own choice were the sufficient condition of the goodness of its object: this attitude is built into (a subjective principle of) rational action. When Kant goes on to say: "Also every other rational being thinks of his existence by means of the same rational ground which holds also for myself; thus, it is at the same time an objective principle from which, as a supreme practical ground, it must be possible to derive all laws of the will" (G 429), I read him as making the following argument. If you view yourself as having a value-conferring status in virtue of your power of rational choice, you must view anyone who has the power of rational choice as having, in virtue of that power, a value-conferring status. This will mean that what you make good by means of your rational choice must be harmonious with what another can make good by means of her rational choice—for the good is a consistent, harmonious object shared by all

rational beings. Thus it must always be possible for others "to contain in themselves the end of the very same action" (G 430).[7]

Thus, regressing upon the conditions, we find that the unconditioned condition of the goodness of anything is rational nature, or the power of rational choice. To play this role, however, rational nature must itself be something of unconditional value—an end in itself. This means, however, that you must treat rational nature wherever you find it (in your own person or in that of another) as an end. This in turn means that no choice is rational which violates the status of rational nature as an end: rational nature becomes a limiting condition (G 437–38) of the rationality of choice and action. It is an unconditional end, so you can never act against it without contradiction. If you overturn the *source* of the goodness of your end, neither your end nor the action which aims at it can possibly be good, and your action will not be fully rational.

To say that humanity is of unconditional value might seem, at first sight, somewhat different from the claim with which the *Groundwork* opens: that the good will is of unconditional value. What enables Kant to make both claims without any problem is this: humanity is the power of rational choice, but only when the choice is fully rational is humanity fully realized. Humanity, as I argued in Section III, is completed and perfected only in the realization of "personality," which is the good will. But the possession of humanity and the capacity for the good will, whether or not that capacity is realized, is enough to establish a claim on being treated as an unconditional end.

V TREATING HUMANITY AS AN END IN ITSELF

Readers have often been puzzled by the prescription "treat humanity as an end." Kant's claims that the Humanity formula is closer to intuition (G 436), that the Formula of Universal Law gives the content the categorical imperative (G 420–21; 425), and that the latter ought to be used in actual decision making (G 437), might make it seem as if Kant does not intend this formulation to give definite directions for application, independently of its equivalence with the Formula of Universal Law. In opposition to this is the fact that Kant re-explains his *Groundwork* examples in terms of this formulation; in one case—the suicide example—providing a rather better account in terms of this formulation than he does in terms of universal law. Even more important, however, is the fact that all of the duties described in the *Metaphysical Principles of Virtue* are derived from the idea that humanity must always be treated as unconditionally valuable.

In fact, the argument that reveals the unconditional value of humanity also teaches us how to apply the Formula of Humanity. In order to know what is meant by "treating humanity as an end," we need only consider this argument, and see how humanity got to be an end in itself. What was in question was the source of the goodness of an end—the goodness say, of some ordinary object of inclination. This source was traced to the power of rationally choosing ends, exercised in this case on this end. So when Kant says rational nature or humanity is an end in itself, it is the power of rational choice that he is referring to, and in particular, the power to set an end (to make something an end by conferring the status of goodness on it) and pursue it by rational means.

The question is then: what is involved in treating your own and every other human being's capacity for the rational choice of ends—that is to say, for conferring value—as an end in itself? There are several things that are important to keep in mind. First, Kant thinks that this end functions in our deliberations negatively—as something that is not to be acted against. The capacity for rational choice is not a purpose that we can realize or something for us to bring into existence. Second, it is an unconditional end, and that has two important implications. The first is that as an unconditional end it must *never* be acted against. It is not one end among others, to be weighed along with the rest. The second implication in a sense gives the reason for the first: as an unconditional end it is the condition of the goodness of all our other ends. If humanity is not regarded and treated as unconditionally good then nothing else

can be objectively good. As Kant puts it in the *Groundwork*: "the subject of a possible will which is absolutely good . . . cannot be made secondary to any other object without contradiction" (G 437). No relative end can be pursued as if it were better or more important than humanity itself without a kind of contradiction.

While it would not be feasible to go through all of the many cases Kant gives of duties derived from the Formula of Humanity, I want to say something about the two major kinds of derivations from this formula that exist, and how each is supposed to work. In order to do this, I will concentrate on the *Groundwork* examples.

The first treatment of the examples, used to illustrate the workings of the Formula of Universal Law, divides them into two groups. The duty not to commit suicide because of the prospect of wretchedness, and the duty not to make a false promise because of a financial emergency, illustrate cases in which the maxim cannot be thought as a universal law without contradiction. Under the Formula of Humanity, these are classified as cases in which humanity, in your own person or another, is treated as a mere means. The duties of developing your talents and powers, and of helping others, are classified under Universal Law as cases where the maxim, though thinkable as a universal law, cannot be willed as such. Under the Formula of Humanity, these are classified as cases in which the action is not in conflict with humanity, but fails to "harmonize" with it (G 430). In both cases, what is involved is a failure to properly acknowledge in your conduct the value-conferring status either of another or of yourself. We can make this plausible, and also see why Kant takes the two formulas to be identical, by considering the examples and the way Kant explains them.

In the suicide case, Kant says that "if, in order to escape from burdensome circumstances, he destroys himself, he uses a person merely as a means to maintain a tolerable condition up to the end of life" (G 429). As mentioned before, Kant takes it to be a consequence of his argument that humanity cannot be made secondary to any relative end without contradiction. This is what happens in the case of suicide: the end, in the example, is "a tolerable condition" and the means is the destruction of a rational being—hence a rational being is being used as a mere means to a relative or conditional end. The reason why this is said to be a contradiction rather than merely a case of misordered values is that the relative end must get its value from the thing that is being destroyed for its sake. However obvious it may seem that a "tolerable condition" is a good thing, it is good only because of the value conferred upon it by the choice of a rational being. Destroy the rational being, and you cut off the source of the goodness of this end—it is no longer really an end at all, and it is no longer rational to pursue it.

The false promising case is slightly more complicated, and easier to explain if we use the result of applying the Formula of Universal Law. Because we know from that test that the maxim of false promising in order to escape a financial emergency could not be universalized, we know that false promising could not be the universal method of escaping financial emergencies. From this it follows, because reasons must be universal, that the desire to escape a financial emergency cannot justify (be a sufficient reason for) making a false promise. If you make a false promise, then, you accord to your value-conferring capacity a greater power, so to speak, than you do that of others. You act as if your desire to avoid financial trouble has a justifying power that someone else's exactly similar desire would not have. But this cannot be right: if your desire gets its justifying power from your humanity, then any other person's similar desire would have the same justifying power. If the end of your action is not good because of your humanity, on the other hand, it cannot be good at all, and your action is not rational. There is another way to describe this kind of case that is perhaps even better for bringing out the violation of humanity that is involved. Whenever you violate the first contradiction test under the Formula of Universal Law, and act on a maxim that cannot be universalized, you must be using some method to achieve your end that not everyone could use to achieve that end. The efficacy of your action depends upon the fact that others do not act as you do, and that in a sense means that others are making

your method work. This is characteristic of the kind of violation of duty that is most amenable to treatment under the first contradiction test. For example, when you tell a lie for a certain purpose, the lie works to achieve the purpose only because most people tell the truth. That is why you are believed, and so why the lie achieves its purpose. In such a case it is not just the person to whom you lie that you treat as a means but all of those who tell the truth. This is because you allow their actions to fuel your method, and that is explicitly treating their rational nature as a mere means: indeed it is making a tool of other people's good wills. Whenever you use a method that works only because others do not use it—which is the first contradiction test reveals—you make an instrument of the rational nature of others, and treat them as mere means.

The third and fourth examples, of the duty of self-perfection and the duty to promote the happiness of others, admit of very clear accounts in terms of the idea of acknowledging the value-conferring power of rational beings as ends in themselves. In the case of the duty of self-perfection, it is a question of developing and realizing the capacities which enable you to exercise your power of rational choice—the talents and powers that make it possible for you to set and pursue ends. It is your powers as an agent that are to be promoted. This, indeed, is as close as Kant comes to assigning a positive function to humanity as an end. What makes this possible is the fact that rational nature is a sort of capacity. It is, as Kant says, not an end to be effected (G 437), for rational nature is not something that we can create; nevertheless, we can realize our rational capacities more or less fully, and this is what generates the various positive duties of self-perfecting. In the case of the duty to promote the happiness of others, Kant says:

> For the ends of any person, who is an end in himself, must as far as possible also be my end[s][8] if that conception of an end in itself is to have its full effect on me. (G 430)

This is because the full realization and acknowledgment of the fact that another is an end in itself involves viewing the end upon which this person confers value as *good*—and when one acknowledges that something is good, one acknowledges it to be "in the judgment of every reasonable man, an object of the faculty of desire." To treat another as an end in itself is to treat his or her ends as objectively good, as you do your own. To treat anyone as an end in itself is to regard that person as one who confers value on the objects of his or her choice.

VI CONFERRING VALUE

In this last section I want to bring in as a final piece of support for the reading I have given a set of passages from the *Critique of Judgment*. These passages seem to me to support in a very forceful way the idea that it is our power to confer objective value that Kant thinks of as having unconditional worth.

In the "Methodology of Teleological Judgment," Kant is concerned with the question of what might appropriately play the role of final purpose of creation. He has established the idea of a natural purpose, which provides the basis for a teleological interpretation of nature; but in order to view nature as a teleological *system,* we must discover its final purpose: we must discover, that is, a reason for the existence of nature itself. This will not be a purpose internal to nature, but one outside or independent of it: "an objective supreme purpose, such as the highest reason would require for creation" (C3 436). In carrying out his inquiry, Kant undertakes a familiar sort of regress argument. In this case, the condition of a given thing is its purpose, and the regress must end with something which is in itself a final purpose, "that purpose which needs no other as the condition of its possibility"; something about which "it can no longer be asked why" it exists (C3 434–35). Starting with the idea of a natural purpose, the argument proceeds to what Kant calls an ultimate purpose: this will be that which we judge to be the purpose *within* nature towards which all nature is organized. This ultimate purpose, being as it were nature's contribution to the final purpose, will give us an idea of what the final purpose is.

Beginning with consideration of vegetable nature, we can reason back to the ultimate purpose as follows:

> a more intimate knowledge of its indescribably wise organization does not permit us to hold to this thought (that it is a mere mechanism), but prompts the question: What are these things created for? If it is answered: For the animal kingdom, which is thereby nourished and has thus been able to spread over the earth in genera so various, then the further question comes: What are these plant-devouring animals for? The answer would be something like this: For beasts of prey, which can only be nourished by that which has life. Finally we have the question: What are these last, as well as the first-mentioned natural kingdoms, good for? For man in reference to the manifold use which his understanding teaches him to make of all these creatures. He is the ultimate purpose of creation here on earth, because he is the only being who can form a concept of purposes and who can, by his reason, make out of an aggregate of purposively formed things a system of purposes. (C3 426–27)

Kant then goes on to inquire for the more specific feature of human life that is the purpose of nature—that is to say, for something "found in man himself which is to be furthered as a purpose by means of his connection with nature" (C3 429). This Kant supposes must be either human happiness or human culture (C3 429–30). At this point Kant takes up an argument that is repeated throughout the teleological historical writings and also appears in the teleological argument at the beginning of the *Groundwork*. Happiness does not seem to be something that nature can achieve or aims at achieving: the evidence favors culture. But furthermore, the argument requires that the ultimate purpose of human beings within nature teaches us what the final purpose of nature itself is. And happiness cannot be the final purpose of nature, for the same reasons that we found, in the argument for the Formula of Humanity, that happiness could not be the unconditioned good.

Happiness, on the contrary, as has been shown in the preceding paragraphs by the testimony of experience, is not even a *purpose of nature* in respect of man in preference to other creatures, much less a *final purpose of creation.* Men may of course make it their ultimate subjective purpose. But if I ask, in reference to the final purpose of creation, Why must men exist? then we are speaking of an objective supreme purpose, such as the highest reason would require for creation. If we answer: These beings exist to afford objects for the benevolence of that supreme cause, then we contradict the condition to which the reason of man subjects even his own inmost wish for happiness (viz. the harmony with his own internal moral legislation). (C3 436n)

The answer then will be that the ultimate purpose in nature is "culture" in the specific sense of the development of humanity:

The production of the aptitude of a rational being for arbitrary purposes in general (consequently in his freedom) is *culture.* (C3 431)

Culture, according to Kant, is an appropriate ultimate purpose in nature, for the development of culture is something that "nature can do in regard to the final purpose that lies outside it" (C3 431).

The final purpose of nature, Kant argues, is morality itself. It is in morality that the aptitude of setting purposes before ourselves finds its completion, for an end or purpose must be objectively good, and only in morality do we find the unconditioned condition of its goodness:

Only in man, and only in him as subject of morality, do we meet with unconditioned legislation in respect of purposes, which therefore alone renders him capable of being a final purpose, to which the whole of nature is teleologically subordinated. (C3 435–36)

It is our capacity to set ends—to freely choose what shall be an end by means of reason, that not only makes every rational being an end in itself, but which forms the only possible final purpose of nature, teleologically conceived. It is only this capacity that has its value completely in itself; so that this not only forms the basis of a possible categorical imperative, but also the only possible basis for a complete teleological view of creation.

Without men the whole creation would be a mere waste, in vain, and without final purpose. But it is not in reference to man's cognitive faculty (theoretical reason) that the being of everything else in the world gets its worth; he is not there merely that there may be someone to *contemplate* the world . . . we must presuppose for it a final purpose, in reference to which its contemplation itself has worth. Again it is not in reference to the feeling of pleasure or to the sum of pleasures that we think a final purpose of creation as given, . . . or, in a word, by happiness. For the fact that man, if he exists, takes this for his final design gives us no concept as to why in general he should exist and as to what worth he has in himself. . . . But it is that worth which he alone can give to himself and which consists in what he does, how and according to what principles he acts, and that not as a link in nature's chain but in the *freedom* of his faculty of desire. That is, a good will is that whereby alone his being can have an absolute worth and in reference to which the being of the world can have a *final purpose.* (C3 442–43)

Or as Kant puts it in an earlier footnote:

There remains, then, nothing but the value which we ourselves give our life, . . . in such independence of nature that the existence of nature itself can only be a purpose under this condition. (C3 434n)

On Kant's view it is human beings, with our capacity for valuing things, that bring to the world such value as it has. Even the justification of nature is up to us.

NOTES

1. The three arguments mentioned here are in the *Groundwork* at 420–21; 427–29; 431–32.

2. In fact, the example is explicitly given as one in which the agent has a "direct inclination" to the action and its purpose as opposed to the kind of case (like that of the "honest" grocer) in which the agent has no direct inclination but is "impelled to do [the action] by another inclination." That is, the action with its purpose is an end and not a means (G 397). Admittedly, Kant's discussion of happiness in the *Critique of Practical Reason* (C2 23) suggests a hedonistic view of the inclinations. But though the sympathetic character may value the beneficent action because it is pleasant, this *may* still be taken as an explanation of why he values it rather than a reduction of it to a mere means. (This is the way Mill, as I understand him, proposes to interpret hedonism in Chapter IV of *Utilitarianism*.) However, Kant's language in the *Critique of Practical Reason* is that of the more conventional sort of hedonism which makes pleasure and the avoidance of pain ends to which everything else desired must be regarded as means.

3. If Kant's view of the inclinations in the *Critique of Practical Reason* is understood to be a conventional hedonistic view (see note 2), then the account of happiness given there must count either against my reading of these remarks in the *Groundwork* or against the *Groundwork's* "Ideal of the Imagination" view itself. Beck thinks that the difficulty is in Kant's psychological views. See *A Commentary on Kant's Critique of Practical Reason*, p. 101. I would like to thank a reader for *Kant-Studien* for this reference, as well as for other useful references and comments.

4. A more extended version of some of the arguments of this section appears in my paper *Two Distinctions in Goodness*. In that paper I compare G. E. Moore's conception of intrinsic value as something possessed by all ends that ought to be valued for their own sakes and Kant's conception of unconditional value as possessed only by the good will.

5. Practical reason does of course also have its antinomy, but it results not from a failure to locate the unconditioned as the "determining ground of the will" (the original source of all justification), but rather from the apparent failure of the unconditioned principle to produce the associated unconditioned totality, the highest good, in the natural world (C2 108; 113–14).

6. Some of the standard arguments against the rationality of egoism might be useful in supporting this point; for example, that of G. E. Moore in *Principia Ethica*, Sections 59–61. See also the discussions by Thomas Nagel in *The Possibility of Altruism*, especially Chapter X.

7. The idea that choice in accordance with the moral law is the basis of the concept of "good" (and not the reverse) is also argued in the *Critique of Practical Reason*, in the chapter on "The Concept of an Object of Pure Practical Reason" (57–67).

8. Beck translates this passage "as far as possible also be my end." On my reading, the plural fits the sense of the passage better.

STUDY QUESTIONS

1. Without human beings, would the world be devoid of value?
2. According to Korsgaard, what is the relationship between acting from duty and acting with humanity as one's unconditional end?
3. If you didn't value anything, would you yourself still have value?
4. Can nonhuman animals be unconditionally valuable?

Moral Luck

Thomas Nagel

Thomas Nagel is Professor of Philosophy and Law at New York University. He examines the extent to which factors beyond our control enter into the moral evaluation of our actions. He emphasizes that although we believe our moral assessments are not dependent on luck, in a variety of cases chance plays a significant role in how we are judged. Whether, for example, a driver's negligence results in a deadly accident or merely a dented fire hydrant is beyond the driver's control, yet affects the extent of the driver's moral and legal responsibility. Nagel concludes that the problem of moral luck has no entirely satisfactory solution.

Kant believed that good or bad luck should influence neither our moral judgment of a person and his actions, nor his moral assessment of himself.

> The good will is not good because of what it effects or accomplishes or because of its adequacy to achieve some proposed end; it is good only because of its willing, i.e., it is good of itself. And, regarded for itself, it is to be esteemed incomparably higher than anything which could be brought about by it in favor of any inclination or even of the sum total of all inclinations. Even if it should happen that, by a particularly unfortunate fate or by the niggardly provision of a stepmotherly nature, this will should be wholly lacking in power to accomplish its purpose, and if even the greatest effort should not avail it to achieve anything of its end, and if there remained only the good will (not as a mere wish but as the summoning of all the means in our power), it would sparkle like a jewel in its own right, as something that had its full worth in itself. Usefulness or fruitlessness can neither diminish nor augment this worth.[1]

He would presumably have said the same about a bad will: whether it accomplishes its evil purposes is morally irrelevant. And a course of action that would be condemned if it had a bad outcome cannot be vindicated if by luck it turns out well. There cannot be moral risk. This view seems to be wrong, but it arises in response to a fundamental problem about moral responsibility to which we possess no satisfactory solution.

The problem develops out of the ordinary conditions of moral judgment. Prior to reflection it is intuitively plausible that people cannot be morally assessed for what is not their fault, or for what is due to factors beyond their control. Such judgment is different from the evaluation of something as a good or bad thing, or state of affairs. The latter may be present in addition to moral judgment, but when we

From Thomas Nagel, *Mortal Questions*, Cambridge University Press, 1979. Reprinted by permission of the publisher.

blame someone for his actions we are not merely saying it is bad that they happened, or bad that he exists: we are judging *him,* saying he is bad, which is different from his being a bad thing. This kind of judgment takes only a certain kind of object. Without being able to explain exactly why, we feel that the appropriateness of moral assessment is easily undermined by the discovery that the act or attribute, no matter how good or bad, is not under the person's control. While other evaluations remain, this one seems to lose its footing. So a clear absence of control produced by involuntary movement, physical force, or ignorance of the circumstances, excuses what is done from moral judgment. But what we do depends in many more ways than these on what is not under our control—what is not produced by a good or a bad will, in Kant's phrase. And external influences in this broader range are not usually thought to excuse what is done from moral judgment, positive or negative.

Let me give a few examples, beginning with the type of case Kant has in mind. Whether we succeed or fail in what we try to do nearly always depends to some extent on factors beyond our control. This is true of murder, altruism, revolution, the sacrifice of certain interests for the sake of others—almost any morally important act. What has been done, and what is morally judged, is partly determined by external factors. However jewel-like the good will may be in its own right, there is a morally significant difference between rescuing someone from a burning building and dropping him from a twelfth-story window while trying to rescue him. Similarly, there is a morally significant difference between reckless driving and manslaughter. But whether a reckless driver hits a pedestrian depends on the presence of the pedestrian at the point where he recklessly passes a red light. What we do is also limited by the opportunities and choices with which we are faced, and these are largely determined by factors beyond our control. Someone who was an officer in a concentration camp might have led a quiet and harmless life if the Nazis had never come to power in Germany. And someone who led a quiet and harmless life in Argentina might have become an officer in a concentration camp if he had not left Germany for business reasons in 1930.

I shall say more later about these and other examples. I introduce them here to illustrate a general point. Where a significant aspect of what someone does depends on factors beyond his control, yet we continue to treat him in that respect as an object of moral judgment, it can be called moral luck. Such luck can be good or bad. And the problem posed by this phenomenon, which led Kant to deny its possibility, is that the broad range of external influences here identified seems on close examination to undermine moral assessment as surely as does the narrower range of familiar excusing conditions. If the condition of control is consistently applied, it threatens to erode most of the moral assessments we find it natural to make. The things for which people are morally judged are determined in more ways than we at first realize by what is beyond their control. And when the seemingly natural requirement of fault or responsibility is applied in light of these facts, it leaves few pre-reflective moral judgments intact. Ultimately, nothing or almost nothing about what a person does seems to be under his control.

Why not conclude, then, that the condition of control is false—that it is an initially plausible hypothesis refuted by clear counter-examples? One could in that case look instead for a more refined condition which picked out the *kinds* of lack of control that really undermine certain moral judgments, without yielding the unacceptable conclusion derived from the broader condition, that most or all ordinary moral judgments are illegitimate.

What rules out this escape is that we are dealing not with a theoretical conjecture but with a philosophical problem. The condition of control does not suggest itself merely as a generalization from certain clear cases. It seems *correct* in the further cases to which it is extended beyond the original set. When we undermine moral assessment by considering new ways in which control is absent, we are not just discovering what *would* follow given the general hypothesis, but are actually being persuaded that in itself the absence of control is relevant in these cases too. The erosion of moral judgment emerges not as the absurd consequence of an over-simple theory, but as a natural consequence of the ordinary idea of moral assessment, when it is applied in view of a more complete and precise account of the facts. It would therefore be a mistake to argue from the unacceptability of the conclusions to the need for a different account of the conditions of moral responsibility. The view that moral luck is paradoxical is not a *mistake,* ethical or logical, but a perception of one of the ways in which the intuitively acceptable conditions of moral judgment threaten to undermine it all.

It resembles the situation in another area of philosophy, the theory of knowledge. There too conditions which seem perfectly natural, and which grow out of the ordinary procedures for challenging and defending claims to knowledge, threaten to undermine all such claims if consistently applied. Most skeptical arguments have this quality: they do not depend on the imposition of arbitrarily stringent standards of knowledge, arrived at by misunderstanding, but appear to grow inevitably from the consistent application of ordinary standards.[2] There is a substantive parallel as well, for epistemological skepticism arises from consideration of the respects in which our beliefs and their relation to reality depend on factors beyond our control. External and internal causes produce our beliefs. We may subject these processes to scrutiny in an effort to avoid error, but our conclusions at this next level also result, in part, from influences which we do not control directly. The same will be true no matter how far we carry the investigation. Our beliefs are always, ultimately, due to factors outside our control, and the impossibility of encompassing those factors without being at the mercy of others leads us to doubt whether we know anything. It looks as though, if any of our beliefs are true, it is pure biological luck rather than knowledge.

Moral luck is like this because while there are various respects in which the natural objects of moral assessment are out of our control or influenced by what is out of our control, we cannot reflect on these facts without losing our grip on the judgments.

There are roughly four ways in which the natural objects of moral assessment are disturbingly subject to luck. One is the phenomenon of constitutive luck—the kind of person you are, where this is not just a question of what you deliberately do, but of your inclinations, capacities, and temperament.

Another category is luck in one's circumstances—the kind of problems and situations one faces. The other two have to do with the causes and effects of action: luck in how one is determined by antecedent circumstances, and luck in the way one's actions and projects turn out. All of them present a common problem. They are all opposed by the idea that one cannot be more culpable or estimable for anything than one is for that fraction of it which is under one's control. It seems irrational to take or dispense credit or blame for matters over which a person has no control, or for their influence on results over which he has partial control. Such things may create the conditions for action, but action can be judged only to the extent that it goes beyond these conditions and does not just result from them.

Let us first consider luck, good and bad, in the way things turn out. Kant, in the above-quoted passage, has one example of this in mind, but the category covers a wide range. It includes the truck driver who accidentally runs over a child, the artist who abandons his wife and five children to devote himself to painting,[3] and other cases in which the possibilities of success and failure are even greater. The driver, if he is entirely without fault, will feel terrible about his role in the event, but will not have to reproach himself. Therefore this example of agent-regret[4] is not yet a case of *moral* bad luck. However, if the driver was guilty of even a minor degree of negligence—failing to have his brakes checked recently, for example—then if that negligence contributes to the death of the child, he will not merely feel terrible. He will blame himself for the death. And what makes this an example of moral luck is that he would have to blame himself only slightly for the negligence itself if no situation arose which required him to brake suddenly and violently to avoid hitting a child. Yet the *negligence* is the same in both cases, and the driver has no control over whether a child will run into his path.

The same is true at higher levels of negligence. If someone has had too much to drink and his car swerves on to the sidewalk, he can count himself morally lucky if there are no pedestrians in its path. If there were, he would be to blame for their deaths, and would probably be prosecuted for manslaughter.

But if he hurts no one, although his recklessness is exactly the same, he is guilty of a far less serious legal offense and will certainly reproach himself and be reproached by others much less severely. To take another legal example, the penalty for attempted murder is less than that for successful murder—however similar the intentions and motives of the assailant may be in the two cases. His degree of culpability can depend, it would seem, on whether the victim happened to be wearing a bullet-proof vest, or whether a bird flew into the path of the bullet—matters beyond his control.

Finally, there are cases of decision under uncertainty—common in public and in private life. Anna Karenina goes off with Vronsky, Gauguin leaves his family, Chamberlain signs the Munich agreement, the Decembrists persuade the troops under their command to revolt against the czar, the American colonies declare their independence from Britain, you introduce two people in an attempt at match-making. It is tempting in all such cases to feel that some decision must be possible, in the light of what is known at the time, which will make reproach unsuitable no matter how things turn out. But this is not true; when someone acts in such ways he takes his life, or his moral position, into his hands, because how things turn out determines what he has done. It is possible *also* to assess the decision from the point of view of what could be known at the time, but this is not the end of the story. If the Decembrists had succeeded in overthrowing Nicholas I in 1825 and establishing a constitutional regime, they would be heroes. As it is, not only did they fail and pay for it, but they bore some responsibility for the terrible punishments meted out to the troops who had been persuaded to follow them. If the American Revolution had been a bloody failure resulting in greater repression, then Jefferson, Franklin and Washington would still have made a noble attempt, and might not even have regretted it on their way to the scaffold, but they would also have had to blame themselves for what they had helped to bring on their compatriots. (Perhaps peaceful efforts at reform would eventually have succeeded.) If Hitler had not overrun Europe and exterminated millions, but instead had died of a heart attack after occupying the Sudetenland, Chamberlain's action at Munich would

still have utterly betrayed the Czechs, but it would not be the great moral disaster that has made his name a household word.[5]

In many cases of difficult choice the outcome cannot be foreseen with certainty. One kind of assessment of the choice is possible in advance, but another kind must await the outcome, because the outcome determines what has been done. The same degree of culpability or estimability in intention, motive, or concern is compatible with a wide range of judgments, positive or negative, depending on what happened beyond the point of decision. The *mens rea* which could have existed in the absence of any consequences does not exhaust the grounds of moral judgment. Actual results influence culpability or esteem in a large class of unquestionably ethical cases ranging from negligence through political choice.

That these are genuine moral judgments rather than expressions of temporary attitude is evident from the fact that one can say *in advance* how the moral verdict will depend on the results. If one negligently leaves the bath running with the baby in it, one will realize, as one bounds up the stairs toward the bathroom, that if the baby has drowned one has done something awful, whereas if it has not one has merely been careless. Someone who launches a violent revolution against an authoritarian regime knows that if he fails he will be responsible for much suffering that is in vain, but if he succeeds he will be justified by the outcome. I do not mean that *any* action can be retroactively justified by history. Certain things are so bad in themselves, or so risky, that no results can make them all right. Nevertheless, when moral judgment does depend on the outcome, it is objective and timeless and not dependent on a change of standpoint produced by success or failure. The judgment after the fact follows from an hypothetical judgment that can be made beforehand, and it can be made as easily by someone else as by the agent.

From the point of view which makes responsibility dependent on control, all this seems absurd. How is it possible to be more or less culpable depending on whether a child gets into the path of one's car, or a bird into the path of one's bullet? Perhaps it is true that what is done depends on more than the agent's state of mind or intention. The problem then is, why is it not irrational to base moral assessment on what people do, in this broad sense? It amounts to holding them responsible for the contributions of fate as well as for their own—provided they have made some contribution to begin with. If we look at cases of negligence or attempt, the pattern seems to be that overall culpability corresponds to the product of mental or intentional fault and the seriousness of the outcome. Cases of decision under uncertainty are less easily explained in this way, for it seems that the overall judgment can even shift from positive to negative depending on the outcome. But here too it seems rational to subtract the effects of occurrences subsequent to the choice, that were merely possible at the time, and concentrate moral assessment on the actual decision in light of the probabilities. If the object of moral judgment is the *person,* then to hold him accountable for what he has done in the broader sense is akin to strict liability, which may have its legal uses but seems irrational as a moral position.

The result of such a line of thought is to pare down each act to its morally essential core, an inner act of pure will assessed by motive and intention. Adam Smith advocates such a position in *The Theory of Moral Sentiments,* but notes that it runs contrary to our actual judgments.

> But how well soever we may seem to be persuaded of the truth of this equitable maxim, when we consider it after this manner, in abstract, yet when we come to particular cases, the actual consequences which happen to proceed from any action, have a very great effect upon our sentiments concerning its merit or demerit, and almost always either enhance or diminish our sense of both. Scarce, in any one instance, perhaps, will our sentiments be found, after examination, to be entirely regulated by this rule, which we all acknowledge ought entirely to regulate them.[6]

Joel Feinberg points out further that restricting the domain of moral responsibility to the inner world will not immunize it to luck. Factors beyond the agent's control, like a coughing fit, can interfere

with his decisions as surely as they can with the path of a bullet from his gun.[7] Nevertheless the tendency to cut down the scope of moral assessment is pervasive, and does not limit itself to the influence of effects. It attempts to isolate the will from the other direction, so to speak, by separating out constitutive luck. Let us consider that next.

Kant was particularly insistent on the moral irrelevance of qualities of temperament and personality that are not under the control of the will. Such qualities as sympathy or coldness might provide the background against which obedience to moral requirements is more or less difficult, but they could not be objects of moral assessment themselves, and might well interfere with confident assessment of its proper object—the determination of the will by the motive of duty. This rules out moral judgment of many of the virtues and vices, which are states of character that influence choice but are certainly not exhausted by dispositions to act deliberately in certain ways. A person may be greedy, envious, cowardly, cold, ungenerous, unkind, vain, or conceited, but *behave* perfectly by a monumental effort of will. To possess these vices is to be unable to help having certain feelings under certain circumstances, and to have strong spontaneous impulses to act badly. Even if one controls the impulses, one still has the vice. An envious person hates the greater success of others. He can be morally condemned as envious even if he congratulates them cordially and does nothing to denigrate or spoil their success. Conceit, likewise, need not be displayed. It is fully present in someone who cannot help dwelling with secret satisfaction on the superiority of his own achievements, talents, beauty, intelligence, or virtue. To some extent such a quality may be the product of earlier choices; to some extent it may be amenable to change by current actions. But it is largely a matter of constitutive bad fortune. Yet people are morally condemned for such qualities, and esteemed for others equally beyond control of the will: they are assessed for what they are *like.*

To Kant this seems incoherent because virtue is enjoined on everyone and therefore must in principle be possible for everyone. It may be easier for some than for others, but it must be possible to achieve it by making the right choices, against whatever temperamental background.[8] One may want to have a generous spirit, or regret not having one, but it makes no sense to condemn oneself or anyone else for a quality which is not within the control of the will. Condemnation implies that you should not be like that, not that it is unfortunate that you are.

Nevertheless, Kant's conclusion remains intuitively unacceptable. We may be persuaded that these moral judgments are irrational, but they reappear involuntarily as soon as the argument is over. This is the pattern throughout the subject.

The third category to consider is luck in one's circumstances, and I shall mention it briefly. The things we are called upon to do, the moral tests we face, are importantly determined by factors beyond our control. It may be true of someone that in a dangerous situation he would behave in a cowardly or heroic fashion, but if the situation never arises, he will never have the chance to distinguish or disgrace himself in this way, and his moral record will be different.[9]

A conspicuous example of this is political. Ordinary citizens of Nazi Germany had an opportunity to behave heroically by opposing the regime. They also had an opportunity to behave badly, and most of them are culpable for having failed this test. But it is a test to which the citizens of other countries were not subjected, with the result that even if they, or some of them, would have behaved as badly as the Germans in like circumstances, they simply did not and therefore are not similarly culpable. Here again one is morally at the mercy of fate, and it may seem irrational upon reflection, but our ordinary moral attitudes would be unrecognizable without it. We judge people for what they actually do or fail to do, not just for what they would have done if circumstances had been different.[10]

This form of moral determination by the actual is also paradoxical, but we can begin to see how deep in the concept of responsibility the paradox is embedded. A person can be morally responsible only for what he does; but what he does results from a great deal that he does not do; therefore he is not morally responsible for what he is and is not responsible for. (This is not a contradiction, but it is a paradox.)

It should be obvious that there is a connection between these problems about responsibility and control and an even more familiar problem, that of freedom of the will. That is the last type of moral luck I want to take up, though I can do no more within the scope of this essay than indicate its connection with the other types.

If one cannot be responsible for consequences of one's acts due to factors beyond one's control, or for antecedents of one's acts that are properties of temperament not subject to one's will, or for the circumstances that pose one's moral choices, then how can one be responsible even for the stripped-down acts of the will itself, if *they* are the product of antecedent circumstances outside of the will's control?

The area of genuine agency, and therefore of legitimate moral judgment, seems to shrink under this scrutiny to an extensionless point. Everything seems to result from the combined influence of factors, antecedent and posterior to action, that are not within the agent's control. Since he cannot be responsible for them, he cannot be responsible for their results—though it may remain possible to take up the aesthetic or other evaluative analogues of the moral attitudes that are thus displaced.

It is also possible, of course, to brazen it out and refuse to accept the results, which indeed seem unacceptable as soon as we stop thinking about the arguments. Admittedly, if certain surrounding circumstances had been different, then no unfortunate consequences would have followed from a wicked intention, and no seriously culpable act would have been performed; but since the circumstances were *not* different, and the agent *in fact* succeeded in perpetrating a particularly cruel murder, *that* is what he did, and that is what he is responsible for. Similarly, we may admit that if certain antecedent circumstances had been different, the agent would never have developed into the sort of person who would do such a thing; but since he *did* develop (as the inevitable result of those antecedent circumstances) into the sort of swine he is, and into the person who committed such a murder, *that* is what he is blameable for. In both cases one is responsible for what one actually does—even if what one actually does depends in important ways on what is not within one's control.

This compatibilist account of our moral judgments would leave room for the ordinary conditions of responsibility—the absence of coercion, ignorance, or involuntary movement—as part of the determination of what someone has done; but it is understood not to exclude the influence of a great deal that he has not done.[11]

The only thing wrong with this solution is its failure to explain how skeptical problems arise. For they arise not from the imposition of an arbitrary external requirement, but from the nature of moral judgment itself. Something in the ordinary idea of what someone does must explain how it can seem necessary to subtract from it anything that merely happens—even though the ultimate consequence of such subtraction is that nothing remains. And something in the ordinary idea of knowledge must explain why it seems to be undermined by any influences on belief not within the control of the subject—so that knowledge seems impossible without an impossible foundation in autonomous reason. But let us leave epistemology aside and concentrate on action, character, and moral assessment.

The problem arises, I believe, because the self which acts and is the object of moral judgment is threatened with dissolution by the absorption of its acts and impulses into the class of events. Moral judgment of a person is judgment not of what happens to him, but of him. It does not say merely that a certain event or state of affairs is fortunate or unfortunate or even terrible. It is not an evaluation of a state of the world, or of an individual as part of the world. We are not thinking just that it would be better if he were different, or did not exist, or had not done some of the things he has done. We are judging *him,* rather than his existence or characteristics. The effect of concentrating on the influence of what is not under his control is to make this responsible self seem to disappear, swallowed up by the order of mere events.

What, however, do we have in mind that a person must *be* to be the object of these moral attitudes? While the concept of agency is easily undermined, it is very difficult to give it a positive characterization. That is familiar from the literature on Free Will.

I believe that in a sense the problem has no solution, because something in the idea of agency is incompatible with actions being events, or people being things. But as the external determinants of what someone has done are gradually exposed, in their effect on consequences, character, and choice itself, it becomes gradually clear that actions are events and people things. Eventually nothing remains which can be ascribed to the responsible self, and we are left with nothing but a portion of the larger sequence of events, which can be deplored or celebrated, but not blamed or praised.

Though I cannot define the idea of the active self that is thus undermined, it is possible to say something about its sources. There is a close connection between our feelings about ourselves and our feelings about others. Guilt and indignation, shame and contempt, pride and admiration are internal and external sides of the same moral attitudes. We are unable to view ourselves simply as portions of the world, and from inside we have a rough idea of the boundary between what is us and what is not, what we do and what happens to us, what is our personality and what is an accidental handicap. We apply the same essentially internal conception of the self to others. About ourselves we feel pride, shame, guilt, remorse—and agent-regret. We do not regard our actions and our characters merely as fortunate or unfortunate episodes—though they may also be that. We cannot *simply* take an external evaluative view of ourselves—of what we most essentially are and what we do. And this remains true even when we have seen that we are not responsible for our own existence, or our nature, or the choices we have to make, or the circumstances that give our acts the consequences they have. Those acts remain ours and we remain ourselves, despite the persuasiveness of the reasons that seem to argue us out of existence.

It is this internal view that we extend to others in moral judgment—when we judge *them* rather than their desirability or utility. We extend to others the refusal to limit ourselves to external evaluation, and we accord to themselves like our own. But in both cases this comes up against the brutal inclusion of humans and everything about them in a world from which they cannot be separated and of which they are nothing but contents. The external view forces itself on us at the same time that we resist it. One way this occurs is through the gradual erosion of what we do by the subtraction of what happens.[12]

The inclusion of consequences in the conception of what we have done is an acknowledgment that we are parts of the world, but the paradoxical character of moral luck which emerges from this acknowledgment shows that we are unable to operate with such a view, for it leaves us with no one to be. The same thing is revealed in the appearance that determinism obliterates responsibility. Once we see an aspect of what we or someone else does as something that happens, we lose our grip on the idea that it has been done and that we can judge the doer and not just the happening. This explains why the absence of determinism is no more hospitable to the concept of agency than is its presence—a point that has been noticed often. Either way the act is viewed externally, as part of the course of events.

The problem of moral luck cannot be understood without an account of the internal conception of agency and its special connection with the moral attitudes as opposed to other types of value. I do not have such an account. The degree to which the problem has a solution can be determined only by seeing whether in some degree the incompatibility between this conception and the various ways in which we do not control what we do is only apparent. I have nothing to offer on that topic either. But it is not enough to say merely that our basic moral attitudes toward ourselves and others are determined by what is actual; for they are also threatened by the sources of that actuality, and by the external view of action which forces itself on us when we see how everything we do belongs to a world that we have not created.

NOTES

1. *Foundations of the Metaphysics of Morals*, first section, third paragraph.
2. See Thompson Clark. "The Legacy of Skepticism," *Journal of Philosophy*, LXIX, no. 20 (November 9, 1972), 754–69.
3. Such a case, modelled on the life of Gauguin, is discussed by Bernard Williams in "Moral Luck," *Proceedings of the Aristotelian Society*, supplementary vol. L (1976), 115–35 (to which the original version of this essay was a reply). He points out that though success or failure cannot be predicted in advance, Gauguin's most basic retrospective feelings about the decision will be determined by the development of his talent. My disagreement with Williams is that his account fails to explain why such retrospective attitudes can be called moral. If success does not permit Gauguin to justify himself to others, but still determines his most basic feelings, that shows only that his most basic feelings need not be moral. It does not show that morality is subject to luck. If the retrospective judgment were moral, it would imply the truth of a hypothetical judgment made in advance, of the form "If I leave my family and become a great painter, I will be justified by success; if I don't become a great painter, the act will be unforgivable."
4. Williams' term (ibid.).
5. For a fascinating but morally repellent discussion of the topic of justification by history, see Maurice Merleau-Ponty. *Humanisme et Terreur* (Paris: Gallimard, 1947), translated as *Humanism and Terror* (Boston: Beacon, 1969).
6. Pt. II, sect. 3, Introduction, para. 5.
7. "Problematic Responsibility in Law and Morals," in Joel Feinberg, *Doing and Deserving* (Princeton: Princeton University Press, 1970).
8. "If nature has put little sympathy in the heart of a man, and if he, though an honest man, is by temperament cold and indifferent to the sufferings of others, perhaps because he is provided with special gifts of patience and fortitude and expects or even requires that others should have the same—and such a man would certainly not be the meanest product of nature—would not he find in himself a source from which to give himself a far higher worth than he could have got by having a good-natured temperament?" (*Foundations of the Metaphysics of Morals*, first section, eleventh paragraph).
9. Cf. Thomas Gray, "Elegy Written in a Country Churchyard":

   Some mute inglorious Milton here may rest,
   Some Cromwell, guiltless of his country's blood.

   An unusual example of circumstantial moral luck is provided by the kind of moral dilemma with which someone can be faced through no fault of his own, but which leaves him with nothing to do which is not wrong. See . . . Bernard Williams, "Ethical

Consistency," *Proceedings of the Aristotelian Society,* supplementary vol. xxxix (1965), reprinted in *Problems of the Self* (Cambridge: Cambridge University Press, 1973), pp. 166–86.

10. Circumstantial luck can extend to aspects of the situation other than individual behavior. For example, during the Vietnam War even U.S. citizens who had opposed their country's actions vigorously from the start often felt compromised by its crimes. Here they were not even responsible; there was probably nothing they could do to stop what was happening, so the feeling of being implicated may seem unintelligible. But it is nearly impossible to view the crimes of one's own country in the same way that one views the crimes of another country, no matter how equal one's lack of power to stop them in the two cases. One *is* a citizen of one of them, and has a connection with its actions (even if only through taxes that cannot be withheld)— that one does not have with the other's. This makes it possible to be ashamed of one's country, and to feel a victim of moral bad luck that one was an American in the 1960s.

11. The corresponding position in epistemology would be that knowledge consists of true beliefs formed in certain ways, and that it does not require all aspects of the process to be under the knower's control, actually or potentially. Both the correctness of these beliefs and the process by which they are arrived at would therefore be importantly subject to luck. The Nobel Prize is not awarded to people who turn out to be wrong, no matter how brilliant their reasoning.

12. See P. F. Strawson's discussion of the conflict between the objective attitude and personal reactive attitudes in "Freedom and Resentment," *Proceedings of the British Academy,* 1962, reprinted in *Studies in the Philosophy of Thought and Action,* ed. P. F. Strawson (London: Oxford University Press, 1968), and in P. F. Strawson, *Freedom and Resentment and Other Essays* (London: Methuen, 1974).

STUDY QUESTIONS

1. Do you think that the problem of moral luck is generated with equal force by resultant, circumstantial, constitutive, and causal luck?
2. Is the difference in our moral assessment between a murderer and an attempted murderer explained by our access to different information about each?
3. Explain in your own words the difference between the objective and the subjective point of view.
4. Do you think the problem of moral luck is irresolvable?

Part VII

CONSEQUENTIALISM

An Introduction to the Principles of Morals and Legislation

Jeremy Bentham

Jeremy Bentham (1748–1822) was a British philosopher and social reformer who founded utilitarianism, the theory that an act is morally right when, more than any other, it increases the happiness of the community. By happiness, Bentham means pleasure and the absence of pain, which can be measured quantitatively by such criteria as intensity and duration. In addition to this hedonistic account of the nature of value, Bentham also maintains that pain and pleasure stand as the sole motives behind all human actions. Among the improvements to society Bentham advocated were the abolition of capital punishment, more humane conditions in prisons, and relief programs for the poor.

CHAPTER I

Of the Principle of Utility

1. Nature has placed mankind under the governance of two sovereign masters, *pain* and *pleasure.* It is for them alone to point out what we ought to do, as well as to determine what we shall do. On the one hand the standard of right and wrong, on the other the chain of causes and effects, are fastened to their throne. They govern us in all we do, in all we say, in all we think: every effort we can make to throw off our subjection, will serve but to demonstrate and confirm it. In words a man may pretend to abjure their empire: but in reality he will remain subject to it all the while. The *principle of utility* recognises this subjection, and assumes it for the foundation of that system, the object of which is to rear the fabric of felicity by the hands of reason and of law. Systems which attempt to question it, deal in sounds instead of sense, in caprice instead of reason, in darkness instead of light.

But enough of metaphor and declamation: it is not by such means that moral science is to be improved.

2. The principle of utility is the foundation of the present work: it will be proper therefore at the outset to give an explicit and determinate account of what is meant by it. By the principle of utility is meant that principle which approves or disapproves of every action whatsoever, according to the tendency which it appears to have to augment or diminish the happiness of the party whose interest is in question; or, what is the same thing in other words, to promote or to oppose that happiness. I say of every action whatsoever; and therefore not only of every action of a private individual, but of every measure of government.

3. By utility is meant that property in any object, whereby it tends to produce benefit, advantage,

From *An Introduction to the Principles of Morals and Legislation*, Jeremy Bentham (1789).

pleasure, good, or happiness, (all this in the present case comes to the same thing), or (what comes again to the same thing) to prevent the happening of mischief, pain, evil, or unhappiness to the party whose interest is considered: if that party be the community in general, then the happiness of the community: if a particular individual, then the happiness of that individual.

4. The interest of the community is one of the most general expressions that can occur in the phraseology of morals: no wonder that the meaning of it is often lost. When it has a meaning, it is this. The community is a fictitious *body,* composed of the individual persons who are considered as constituting as it were its *members.* The interest of the community then is, what?—the sum of the interests of the several members who compose it.

5. It is in vain to talk of the interest of the community, without understanding what is the interest of the individual. A thing is said to promote the interest, or to be *for* the interest of an individual, when it tends to add to the sum total of his pleasures: or, what comes to the same thing, to diminish the sum total of his pains.

6. An action then may be said to be conformable to the principle of utility, or, for shortness sake, to utility, (meaning with respect to the community at large) when the tendency it has to augment the happiness of the community is greater than any it has to diminish it.

7. A measure of government (which is but a particular kind of action, performed by a particular person or persons) may be said to be conformable to or dictated by the principle of utility, when in like manner the tendency which it has to augment the happiness of the community is greater than any which it has to diminish it.

8. When an action, or in particular a measure of government, is supposed by a man to be conformable to the principle of utility, it may be convenient, for the purposes of discourse, to imagine a kind of law or dictate, called a law or dictate of utility: and to speak of the action in question, as being conformable to such law or dictate.

9. A man may be said to be a partisan of the principle of utility, when the approbation or disapprobation he annexes to any action, or to any measure, is determined by, and proportioned to the tendency which he conceives it to have to augment or to diminish the happiness of the community: or in other words, to its conformity or unconformity to the laws or dictates of utility.

10. Of an action that is conformable to the principle of utility, one may always say either that it is one that ought to be done, or at least that it is not one that ought not to be done. One may say also, that it is right it should be done; at least that it is not wrong it should be done; that it is a right action; at least that it is not a wrong action. When thus interpreted, the words *ought,* and *right* and *wrong,* and others of that stamp, have a meaning: when otherwise, they have none.

11. Has the rectitude of this principle been ever formally contested? It should seem that it had, by those who have not known what they have been meaning. Is it susceptible of any direct proof? it should seem not: for that which is used to prove every thing else, cannot itself be proved: a chain of proofs must have their commencement somewhere. To give such proof is as impossible as it is needless.

12. Not that there is or ever has been that human creature breathing, however stupid or perverse, who has not on many, perhaps on most occasions of his life, deferred to it. By the natural constitution of the human frame, on most occasions of their lives men in general embrace this principle, without thinking of it: if not for the ordering of their own actions, yet for the trying of their own actions, as well as of those of other men. There have been, at the same time, not many, perhaps, even of the most intelligent, who have been disposed to embrace it purely and without reserve. There are even few who have not taken some occasion or other to quarrel with it, either on account of their not understanding always how to apply it, or on account of some prejudice or other which they were afraid to examine into, or could not bear to part with. For such is the stuff that man is made of: in principle and in practice, in a right track and in a wrong one, the rarest of all human qualities is consistency.

13. When a man attempts to combat the principle of utility, it is with reasons drawn, without his being aware of it, from that very principle itself.

His arguments, if they prove any thing, prove not that the principle is *wrong,* but that, according to the applications he supposes to be made of it, it is *misapplied.* Is it possible for a man to move the earth? Yes; but he must first find out another earth to stand upon.

14. To disprove the propriety of it by arguments is impossible; but, from the causes that have been mentioned, or from some confused or partial view of it, a man may happen to be disposed not to relish it. Where this is the case, if he thinks the settling of his opinions on such a subject worth the trouble, let him take the following steps, and at length, perhaps, he may come to reconcile himself to it.

(1) Let him settle with himself, whether he would wish to discard this principle altogether; if so, let him consider what it is that all his reasonings (in matters of politics especially) can amount to?

(2) If he would, let him settle with himself, whether he would judge and act without any principle, or whether there is any other he would judge and act by?

(3) If there be, let him examine and satisfy himself whether the principle he thinks he has found is really any separate intelligible principle; or whether it be not a mere principle in words, a kind of phrase, which at bottom expresses neither more nor less than the mere averment of his own unfounded sentiments; that is, what in another person he might be apt to call *caprice*?

(4) If he is inclined to think that his own approbation or disapprobation, annexed to the idea of an act, without any regard to its consequences, is a sufficient foundation for him to judge and act upon, let him ask himself whether his sentiment is to be a standard of right and wrong, with respect to every other man, or whether every man's sentiment has the same privilege of being a standard to itself?

(5) In the first case, let him ask himself whether his principle is not despotical, and hostile to all the rest of human race?

(6) In the second case, whether it is not anarchical, and whether at this rate there are not as many different standards of right and wrong as there are men? and whether even to the same man, the same thing, which is right today, may not (without the

least change in its nature) be wrong to-morrow? and whether the same thing is not right and wrong in the same place at the same time? and in either case, whether all argument is not at an end? and whether, when two men have said, 'I like this,' and 'I don't like it', they can (upon such a principle) have any thing more to say?

(7) If he should have said to himself, No; for that the sentiment which he proposes as a standard must be grounded on reflection, let him say on what particulars the reflection is to turn? if on particulars having relation to the utility of the act, then let him say whether this is not deserting his own principle, and borrowing assistance from that very one in opposition to which he sets it up: or if not on those particulars, on what other particulars?

(8) If he should be for compounding the matter, and adopting his own principle in part, and the principle of utility in part, let him say how far he will adopt it?

(9) When he has settled with himself where he will stop, then let him ask himself how he justifies to himself the adopting it so far? and why he will not adopt it any farther?

(10) Admitting any other principle than the principle of utility to be a right principle, a principle that it is right for a man to pursue: admitting (what is not true) that the word *right* can have a meaning without reference to utility, let him say whether there is any such thing as a *motive* that a man can have to pursue the dictates of it: if there is, let him say what that motive is, and how it is to be distinguished from those which enforce the dictates of utility: if not, then lastly let him say what it is this other principle can be good for?

CHAPTER II

Of Principles Adverse to That of Utility

1. If the principle of utility be a right principle to be governed by, and that in all cases, it follows from what has been just observed, that whatever principle differs from it in any case must necessarily be a wrong one. To prove any other principle, therefore, to be a wrong one, there needs no more than just to show it to

be what it is, a principle of which the dictates are in some point or other different from those of the principle of utility: to state it is to confute it.

2. A principle may be different from that of utility in two ways: 1. By being constantly opposed to it: this is the case with a principle which may be termed the principle of *asceticism*. 2. By being sometimes opposed to it, and sometimes not, as it may happen: this is the case with another, which may be termed the principle of *sympathy* and *antipathy*.

3. By the principle of asceticism I mean that principle, which, like the principle of utility, approves or disapproves of any action, according to the tendency which it appears to have to augment or diminish the happiness of the party whose interest is in question; but in an inverse manner: approving of actions in as far as they tend to diminish his happiness; disapproving of them in as far as they tend to augment it. . . .

9. The principle of asceticism seems originally to have been the reverie of certain hasty speculators, who having perceived, or fancied, that certain pleasures, when reaped in certain circumstances, have, at the long run, been attended with pains more than equivalent to them, took occasion to quarrel with every thing that offered itself under the name of pleasure. Having then got thus far, and having forgot the point which they set out from, they pushed on, and went so much further as to think it meritorious to fall in love with pain. Even this, we see, is at bottom but the principle of utility misapplied.

10. The principle of utility is capable of being consistently pursued; and it is but tautology to say, that the more consistently it is pursued, the better it must ever be for human-kind. The principle of asceticism never was, nor ever can be, consistently pursued by any living creature. Let but one tenth part of the inhabitants of this earth pursue it consistently, and in a day's time they will have turned it into a hell.

11. Among principles adverse to that of utility, that which at this day seems to have most influence in matters of government, is what may be called the principle of sympathy and antipathy. By the principle of sympathy and antipathy, I mean that principle which approves or disapproves of certain actions, not on account of their tending to augment the happiness, nor yet on account of their tending to diminish the happiness of the party whose interest is in question, but merely because a man finds himself disposed to approve or disapprove of them: holding up that approbation or disapprobation as a sufficient reason for itself, and disclaiming the necessity of looking out for any extrinsic ground. Thus far in the general department of morals; and in the particular department of politics, measuring out the quantum (as well as determining the ground) of punishment, by the degree of the disapprobation.

12. It is manifest, that this is rather a principle in name than in reality: it is not a positive principle of itself, so much as a term employed to signify the negation of all principle. What one expects to find in a principle is something that points out some external consideration, as a means of warranting and guiding the internal sentiments of approbation and disapprobation: this expectation is but ill fulfilled by a proposition, which does neither more nor less than hold up each of those sentiments as a ground and standard for itself.

13. In looking over the catalogue of human actions (says a partisan of this principle) in order to determine which of them are to be marked with the seal of disapprobation, you need but to take counsel of your own feelings: whatever you find in yourself a propensity to condemn, is wrong for that very reason. For the same reason it is also meet for punishment; in what proportion it is adverse to utility, or whether it be adverse to utility at all, is a matter that makes no difference. In that same *proportion* also is it meet for punishment: if you hate much, punish much: if you hate little, punish little: punish as you hate. If you hate not at all, punish not at all: the fine feelings of the soul are not to be overborne and tyrannized by the harsh and rugged dictates of political utility.

14. The various systems that have been formed concerning the standard of right and wrong, may all be reduced to the principle of sympathy and antipathy. One account may serve for all of them. They consist all of them in so many contrivances for avoiding the obligation of appealing to any external standard, and for prevailing upon the reader to accept of the author's sentiment or opinion as a

reason and that a sufficient one for itself. The phrases different, but the principle the same.

15. It is manifest, that the dictates of this principle will frequently coincide with those of utility, though perhaps without intending any such thing. Probably more frequently than not: and hence it is that the business of penal justice is carried on upon that tolerable sort of footing upon which we see it carried on in common at this day. For what more natural or more general ground of hatred to a practice can there be, than the mischievousness of such practice? What all men are exposed to suffer by, all men will be disposed to hate. It is far yet, however, from being a constant ground: for when a man suffers, it is not always that he knows what it is he suffers by. A man may suffer grievously, for instance, by a new tax, without being able to trace up the cause of his sufferings to the injustice of some neighbour, who has eluded the payment of an old one.

16. The principle of sympathy and antipathy is most apt to err on the side of severity. It is for applying punishment in many cases which deserve none: in many cases which deserve some, it is for applying more than they deserve. There is no incident imaginable, be it ever so trivial, and so remote from mischief, from which this principle may not extract a ground of punishment. Any difference in taste: any difference in opinion: upon one subject as well as upon another. No disagreement so trifling which perseverance and altercation will not render serious. Each becomes in the other's eyes an enemy, and, if laws permit, a criminal. This is one of the circumstances by which the human race is distinguished (not much indeed to its advantage) from the brute creation.

17. It is not, however, by any means unexampled for this principle to err on the side of lenity. A near and perceptible mischief moves antipathy. A remote and imperceptible mischief, though not less real, has no effect. Instances in proof of this will occur in numbers in the course of the work. It would be breaking in upon the order of it to give them here.

18. It may be wondered, perhaps, that in all this while no mention has been made of the *theological* principle; meaning that principle which professes to recur for the standard of right and wrong to the will

of God. But the case is, this is not in fact a distinct principle. It is never any thing more or less than one or other of the three before-mentioned principles presenting itself under another shape. The *will* of God here meant cannot be his revealed will, as contained in the sacred writings: for that is a system which nobody ever thinks of recurring to at this time of day, for the details of political administration: and even before it can be applied to the details of private conduct, it is universally allowed, by the most eminent divines of all persuasions, to stand in need of pretty ample interpretations; else to what use are the works of those divines? And for the guidance of these interpretations, it is also allowed, that some other standard must be assumed. The will then which is meant on this occasion, is that which may be called the *presumptive* will: that is to say, that which is presumed to be his will on account of the conformity of its dictates to those of some other principle. What then may be this other principle? it must be one or other of the three mentioned above: for there cannot, as we have seen, be any more. It is plain, therefore, that, setting revelation out of the question, no light can ever be thrown upon the standard of right and wrong, by any thing that can be said upon the question, what is God's will. We may be perfectly sure, indeed, that whatever is right is conformable to the will of God: but so far is that from answering the purpose of showing us what is right, that it is necessary to know first whether a thing is right, in order to know from thence whether it be conformable to the will of God.

19. There are two things which are very apt to be confounded, but which it imports us carefully to distinguish:—the motive or cause, which, by operating on the mind of an individual, is productive of any act: and the ground or reason which warrants a legislator, or other by-stander, in regarding that act with an eye of approbation. When the act happens, in the particular instance in question, to be productive of effects which we approve of, much more if we happen to observe that the same motive may frequently be productive, in other instances, of the like effects, we are apt to transfer our approbation to the motive itself, and to assume, as the just ground for the approbation we bestow on the act, the

circumstance of its originating from that motive. It is in this way that the sentiment of antipathy has often been considered as a just ground of action. Antipathy, for instance, in such or such a case, is the cause of an action, which is attended with good effects: but this does not make it a right ground of action in that case, any more than in any other. Still farther. Not only the effects are good, but the agent sees beforehand that they will be so. This may make the action indeed a perfectly right action: but it does not make antipathy a right ground of action. For the same sentiment of antipathy, if implicitly deferred to, may be, and very frequently is, productive of the very worst effects. Antipathy, therefore, can never be a right ground of action. No more, therefore, can resentment, which, as will be seen more particularly hereafter, is but a modification of antipathy. The only right ground of action, that can possibly subsist, is, after all, the consideration of utility, which, if it is a right principle of action, and of approbation, in any one case, is so in every other. Other principles in abundance, that is, other motives, may be the reasons why such and such an act *has* been done: that is, the reasons or causes of its being done: but it is this alone that can be the reason why it might or ought to have been done. Antipathy or resentment requires always to be regulated, to prevent its doing mischief: to be regulated by what? always by the principle of utility. The principle of utility neither requires nor admits of any other regulator than itself.

CHAPTER III

Of the Four Sanctions or Sources of Pain and Pleasure

1. It has been shown that the happiness of the individuals, of whom a community is composed, that is their pleasures and their security, is the end and the sole end which the legislator ought to have in view: the sole standard, in conformity to which each individual ought, as far as depends upon the legislator, to be *made* to fashion his behaviour. But whether it be this or any thing else that is to be *done,* there is nothing by which a man can ultimately be *made* to do it, but either pain or pleasure. Having taken a

general view of these two grand objects (viz. pleasure, and what comes to the same thing, immunity from pain) in the character of *final* causes; it will be necessary to take a view of pleasure and pain itself, in the character of *efficient* causes or means.

2. There are four distinguishable sources from which pleasure and pain are in use to flow: considered separately, they may be termed the *physical,* the *political,* the *moral,* and the *religious:* and inasmuch as the pleasures and pains belonging to each of them are capable of giving a binding force to any law or rule of conduct, they may all of them be termed *sanctions.*

3. If it be in the present life, and from the ordinary course of nature, not purposely modified by the interposition of the will of any human being, nor by any extraordinary interposition of any superior invisible being, that the pleasure or the pain takes place or is expected, it may be said to issue from or to belong to the *physical sanction.*

4. If at the hands of a *particular* person or set of persons in the community, who under names correspondent to that of *judge,* are chosen for the particular purpose of dispensing it, according to the will of the sovereign or supreme ruling power in the state, it may be said to issue from the *political sanction.*

5. If at the hands of such *chance* persons in the community, as the party in question may happen in the course of his life to have concerns with, according to each man's spontaneous disposition, and not according to any settled or concerted rule, it may be said to issue from the *moral* or *popular sanction.*

6. If from the immediate hand of a superior invisible being, either in the present life, or in a future, it may be said to issue from the *religious sanction.*

7. Pleasures or pains which may be expected to issue from the *physical, political,* or *moral* sanctions, must all of them be expected to be experienced, if ever, in the *present* life: those which may be expected to issue from the *religious* sanction, may be expected to be experienced either in the *present* life or in a *future.*

8. Those which can be experienced in the present life, can of course be no others than such as human nature in the course of the present life is susceptible of: and from each of these sources may flow all the pleasures or pains of which, in the course of

the present life, human nature is susceptible. With regard to these then (with which alone we have in this place any concern) those of them which belong to any one of those sanctions, differ not ultimately in kind from those which belong to any one of the other three: the only difference there is among them lies in the circumstances that accompany their production. A suffering which befalls a man in the natural and spontaneous course of things, shall be styled, for instance, a *calamity:* in which case, if it be supposed to befall him through any imprudence of his, it may be styled a punishment issuing from the *physical* sanction. Now this same suffering, if inflicted by the law, will be what is commonly called a *punishment;* if incurred for want of any friendly assistance, which the misconduct, or supposed misconduct, of the sufferer has occasioned to be withholden, a punishment issuing from the *moral* sanction; if through the immediate interposition of a particular providence, a punishment issuing from the *religious* sanction.

9. A man's goods, or his person, are consumed by fire. If this happened to him by what is called an accident, it was a *calamity:* if by reason of his own imprudence (for instance, from his neglecting to put his candle out) it may be styled a punishment of the *physical* sanction: if it happened to him by the sentence of the political magistrate, a punishment belonging to the *political* sanction: that is, what is commonly called a *punishment:* if for want of any assistance which his *neighbour* withheld from him out of some dislike to his *moral* character, a punishment of the *moral* sanction: if by an immediate act of *God's* displeasure, manifested on account of some *sin* committed by him, or through any distraction of mind, occasioned by the dread of such displeasure, a punishment of the *religious* sanction.

10. As to such of the pleasures and pains belonging to the religious sanction, as regard a future life, of what kind these may be we cannot know. These lie not open to our observation. During the present life they are matter only of expectation: and, whether that expectation be derived from natural or revealed religion, the particular kind of pleasure or pain, if it be different from all those which lie open to our observation, is what we can have no idea of. The best ideas we can obtain of such pains and pleasures are altogether unliquidated in point of quality. In what other respects our ideas of them *may* be liquidated will be considered in another place.

11. Of these four sanctions the physical is altogether, we may observe, the ground-work of the political and the moral: so is it also of the religious, in as far as the latter hears relation to the present life. It is included in each of those other three. This may operate in any case, (that is, any of the pains or pleasures belonging to it may operate) independently of *them:* none of *them* can operate but by means of this. In a word, the powers of nature may operate of themselves; but neither the magistrate, nor men at large, *can* operate, nor is God in the case in question *supposed* to operate, but through the powers of nature.

12. For these four objects, which in their nature have so much in common, it seemed of use to find a common name. It seemed of use, in the first place, for the convenience of giving a name to certain pleasures and pains, for which a name equally characteristic could hardly otherwise have been found: in the second place, for the sake of holding up the efficacy of certain moral forces, the influence of which is apt not to be sufficiently attended to. Does the political sanction exert an influence over the conduct of mankind? The moral, the religious sanctions do so too. In every inch of his career are the operations of the political magistrate liable to be aided or impeded by these two foreign powers: who, one or other of them, or both, are sure to be either his rivals or his allies. Does it happen to him to leave them out in his calculations? he will be sure almost to find himself mistaken in the result. . . . It behoves him, therefore, to have them continually before his eyes; and that under such a name as exhibits the relation they bear to his own purposes and designs.

CHAPTER IV

Value of a Lot of Pleasure or Pain, How to Be Measured

1. Pleasures then, and the avoidance of pains, are the *ends* which the legislator has in view: it behoves him therefore to understand their *value*. Pleasures and

pains are the *instruments* he has to work with: it behoves him therefore to understand their force, which is again, in another point of view their value.

2. To a person considered *by himself,* the value of a pleasure or pain considered *by itself,* will be greater or less, according to the four following circumstances:

(1) Its *intensity.*
(2) Its *duration.*
(3) Its *certainty* or *uncertainty.*
(4) Its *propinquity* or *remoteness.*

3. These are the circumstances which are to be considered in estimating a pleasure or a pain considered each of them by itself. But when the value of any pleasure or pain is considered for the purpose of estimating the tendency of any *act* by which it is produced, there are two other circumstances to be taken into the account; these are,

(5) Its *fecundity,* or the chance it has of being followed by sensations of the *same* kind: that is, pleasures, if it be a pleasure: pains, if it be a pain.
(6) Its *purity,* or the chance it has of *not* being followed by sensations of the *opposite* kind: that is, pains, if it be a pleasure: pleasures, if it be a pain.

These two last, however, are in strictness scarcely to be deemed properties of the pleasure or the pain itself; they are not, therefore, in strictness to be taken into the account of the value of that pleasure or that pain. They are in strictness to be deemed properties only of the act, or other event, by which such pleasure or pain has been produced; and accordingly are only to be taken into the account of the tendency of such act or such event.

4. To a *number* of persons, with reference to each of whom the value of a pleasure or a pain is considered, it will be greater or less, according to seven circumstances: to wit, the six preceding ones; viz.

(1) Its *intensity.*
(2) Its *duration.*

(3) Its *certainty* or *uncertainty.*
(4) Its *propinquity* or *remoteness.*
(5) Its *fecundity.*
(6) Its *purity.*

And one other; to wit;

(7) Its *extent;* that is, the number of persons to whom it *extends;* or (in other words) who are affected by it.

5. To take an exact account then of the general tendency of any act, by which the interests of a community are affected, proceed as follows. Begin with any one person of those whose interests seem most immediately to be affected by it: and take an account,

(1) Of the value of each distinguishable *pleasure* which appears to be produced by it in the *first* instance.
(2) Of the value of each *pain* which appears to be produced by it in the *first* instance.
(3) Of the value of each pleasure which appears to be produced by it *after* the first. This constitutes the *fecundity* of the first *pleasure* and the impurity of the first *pain.*
(4) Of the value of each *pain* which appears to be produced by it after the first. This constitutes the *fecundity* of the first *pain,* and the *impurity* of the first pleasure.
(5) Sum up all the values of all the *pleasures* on the one side, and those of all the *pains* on the other. The balance, if it be on the side of pleasure, will give the *good* tendency of the act upon the whole, with respect to the interests of that *individual* person; if on the side of pain, the *bad* tendency of it upon the whole.
(6) Take an account of the *number* of persons whose interests appear to be concerned; and repeat the above process with respect to each. *Sum up* the numbers expressive of the degrees of *good* tendency, which the act has, with respect to each individual, in regard to whom the tendency of it is *good* upon the whole: do this again with respect to each individual, in regard to whom the

tendency of it is *good* upon the whole: do this again with respect to each individual, in regard to whom the tendency of it is *bad* upon the whole. Take the *balance:* which, if on the side of *pleasure,* will give the general *good tendency* of the act, with respect to the total number or community of individuals concerned; if on the side of pain, the general *evil tendency,* with respect to the same community.

6. It is not to be expected that this process should be strictly pursued previously to every moral judgment, or to every legislative or judicial operation. It may, however, be always kept in view: and as near as the process actually pursued on these occasions approaches to it, so near will such process approach to the character of an exact one.

7. The same process is alike applicable to pleasure and pain, in whatever shape they appear: and by whatever denomination they are distinguished: to pleasure, whether it be called *good* (which is properly the cause or instrument of pleasure) or *profit* (which is distant pleasure, or the cause or instrument of distant pleasure,) or *convenience,* to *advantage, benefit, emolument, happiness,* and so forth: to pain, whether it be called *evil,* (which corresponds to

good) or *mischief,* or *inconvenience,* or *disadvantage,* or *loss,* or *unhappiness,* and so forth.

8. Nor is this a novel and unwarranted, any more than it is a useless theory. In all this there is nothing but what the practice of mankind, wheresoever they have a clear view of their own interest, is perfectly conformable to. An article of property, an estate in land, for instance, is valuable, on what account? On account of the pleasures of all kinds which it enables a man to produce, and what comes to the same thing the pains of all kinds which it enables him to avert. But the value of such an article of property is universally understood to rise or fall according to the length or shortness of the time which a man has in it: the certainty or uncertainty of its coming into possession: and the nearness or remoteness of the time at which, if at all, it is to come into possession. As to the *intensity* of the pleasures which a man may derive from it, this is never thought of, because it depends upon the use which each particular person may come to make of it: which cannot be estimated till the particular pleasures he may come to derive from it, or the particular pains he may come to exclude by means of it, are brought to view. For the same reason, neither does he think of the *fecundity* or *purity* of those pleasures.

STUDY QUESTIONS

1. Is your reading a novel morally wrong because you could be doing more to enhance the happiness of the community?
2. Is friendship good solely because it brings pleasure?
3. Is punishing the innocent morally right if doing so maximizes the happiness of the community?
4. Are certain sorts of pleasure more worthwhile than others?

Utilitarianism

John Stuart Mill

John Stuart Mill (1806–1873), born in London, received an intense early education from his father, James Mill, a philosophical and political writer. While pursuing a career in the East India Company, Mill published widely in philosophy, political theory, and economics. Harriet Taylor, whom he met in 1831 and married two decades later following the death of her husband, exerted a strong influence on his thought. Mill wrote that she was "the inspirer, and in part the author, of all that is best in my writings." Mill defends utilitarianism, the view that actions are right in proportion as they tend to promote happiness and wrong as they tend to produce the reverse of happiness, each person to be counted equally. By "happiness" Mill means pleasure and the absence of pain. He grants, however, that some pleasures are more valuable than others, and these higher pleasures are those that would be chosen by knowledgeable judges. In response to the criticism that utilitarians do not adequately recognize claims of justice, Mill replies that the pursuit of justice has clear social utility.

CHAPTER I

General Remarks

There are few circumstances among those which make up the present condition of human knowledge more unlike what might have been expected, or more significant of the backward state in which speculation on the most important subjects still lingers, than the little progress which has been made in the decision of the controversy respecting the criterion of right and wrong. From the dawn of philosophy, the question concerning the *summum bonum,* or, what is the same thing, concerning the foundation of morality, has been accounted the main problem in speculative thought, has occupied the most gifted intellects and divided them into sects and schools carrying on a vigorous warfare against one another. And after more than two thousand years the same discussions continue, philosophers are still ranged under the same contending banners, and neither thinkers nor mankind at large seem nearer to being unanimous on the subject than when the youth Socrates listened to the old Protagoras and asserted (if Plato's dialogue be grounded on a real conversation) the theory of utilitarianism against the popular morality of the so-called sophist.

It is true that similar confusion and uncertainty and, in some cases, similar discordance exist respecting the first principles of all the sciences, not excepting that which is deemed the most certain of them—mathematics, without much impairing, generally indeed without impairing at all, the trustworthiness of

From "Utilitarianism," John Stuart Mill (1861).

the conclusions of those sciences. An apparent anomaly, the explanation of which is that the detailed doctrines of a science are not usually deduced from, nor depend for their evidence upon, what are called its first principles. Were it not so, there would be no science more precarious, or whose conclusions were more insufficiently made out, than algebra, which derives none of its certainty from what are commonly taught to learners as its elements, since these, as laid down by some of its most eminent teachers, are as full of fictions as English law, and of mysteries as theology. The truths which are ultimately accepted as the first principles of a science are really the last results of metaphysical analysis practiced on the elementary notions with which the science is conversant; and their relation to the science is not that of foundations to an edifice, but of roots to a tree, which may perform their office equally well though they be never dug down to and exposed to light. But though in science the particular truths precede the general theory, the contrary might be expected to be the case with a practical art, such as morals or legislation. All action is for the sake of some end, and rules of action, it seems natural to suppose, must take their whole character and color from the end to which they are subservient. When we engage in pursuit, a clear and precise conception of what we are pursuing would seem to be the first thing we need, instead of the last we are to look forward to. A test of right and wrong must be the means, one would think, of ascertaining what is right or wrong, and not a consequence of having already ascertained it.

The difficulty is not avoided by having recourse to the popular theory of a natural faculty, a sense of instinct, informing us of right and wrong. For—besides that the existence of such a moral instinct is itself one of the matters in dispute—those believers in it who have any pretensions to philosophy have been obliged to abandon the idea that it discerns what is right or wrong in the particular case in hand, as our other senses discern the sight or sound actually present. Our moral faculty, according to all those of its interpreters who are entitled to the name of thinkers, supplies us only with the general principles of moral judgments; it is a branch of our reason, not of our sensitive faculty, and must be looked to for the abstract doctrines of morality, not for perception of it in the concrete. The intuitive, no less than what may be termed the inductive, school of ethics insists on the necessity of general laws. They both agree that the morality of an individual action is not a question of direct perception, but of the application of a law to an individual case. They recognize also, to a great extent, the same moral laws, but differ as to their evidence and the source from which they derive their authority. According to the one opinion, the principles of morals are evident *a priori,* requiring nothing to command assent except that the meaning of the terms be understood. According to the other doctrine, right and wrong, as well as truth and falsehood, are questions of observation and experience. But both hold equally that morality must be deduced from principles; and the intuitive school affirm as strongly as the inductive that there is a science of morals. Yet they seldom attempt to make out a list of the *a priori* principles which are to serve as the premises of the science; still more rarely do they make any effort to reduce those various principles to one first principle or common ground of obligation. They either assume the ordinary precepts of morals as of *a priori* authority, or they lay down as the common groundwork of those maxims some generality much less obviously authoritative than the maxims themselves, and which has never succeeded in gaining popular acceptance. Yet to support their pretensions there ought either to be some one fundamental principle or law at the root of all morality, or, if there be several, there should be a determinate order of precedence among them; and the one principle, or the rule for deciding between the various principles when they conflict, ought to be self-evident.

To inquire how far the bad effects of this deficiency have been mitigated in practice, or to what extent the moral beliefs of mankind have been vitiated or made uncertain by the absence of any distinct recognition of an ultimate standard, would imply a complete survey and criticism of past and present ethical doctrine. It would, however, be easy to show that whatever steadiness or consistency these moral beliefs have attained has been mainly due to the tacit influence of a standard not recognized. Although the nonexistence of an acknowledged first principle has made ethics not so much a guide as a consecration of men's actual sentiments, still, as men's sentiments, both of favor and of aversion, are greatly influenced by what they suppose to be the effects of things upon their happiness, the principle of utility, or, as Bentham latterly called it, the greatest happiness principle, has had a large share in forming the moral doctrines even of those who most scornfully reject its authority. Nor is there any school of thought which refuses to admit that the influence of actions on happiness is a most material and even predominant consideration in many of the details of morals, however unwilling to acknowledge it as the fundamental principle of morality and the source of moral obligation. I might go much further and say that to all those *a priori* moralists who deem it necessary to argue at all, utilitarian arguments are indispensable. It is not my present purpose to criticize these thinkers; but I cannot help referring, for illustration, to a systematic treatise by one of the most illustrious of them, the *Metaphysics of Ethics* by Kant. This remarkable man, whose system of thought will long remain one of the landmarks in the history of philosophical speculation, does, in the treatise in question, lay down a universal first principle as the origin and ground of moral obligation; it is this: "So act that the rule on which thou actest would admit of being adopted as a law by all rational beings." But when he begins to deduce from this precept any of the actual duties of morality, he fails, almost grotesquely, to show that there would be any contradiction, any logical (not to say physical) impossibility, in the adoption by all rational beings of the most outrageously immoral rules of conduct. All he shows is that the *consequences* of their universal adoption would be such as no one would choose to incur.

On the present occasion, I shall, without further discussion of the other theories, attempt to contribute something toward the understanding and appreciation of the "utilitarian" or "happiness" theory, and toward such proof as it is susceptible of. It is evident that this cannot be proof in the ordinary and popular meaning of the term. Questions of ultimate ends are not amenable to direct proof. Whatever can be proved to be good must be so by being shown to be a means to something admitted to be good without proof. The medical art is proved to be good by its conducing to health; but how is it possible to prove that health is good? The art of music is good, for the reason, among others, that it produces pleasure; but what proof is it possible to give that pleasure is good? If, then, it is asserted that there is a comprehensive formula, including all things which are in themselves good, and that whatever else is good is not so as an end but as a means, the formula may be accepted or rejected, but is not a subject of what is commonly understood by proof. We are not, however, to infer that its acceptance or rejection must depend on blind impulse or arbitrary choice. There is a larger meaning of the word "proof," in which this question is as amenable to it as any other of the disputed questions of philosophy. The subject is within the cognizance of the rational faculty; and neither does that faculty deal with it solely in the way of intuition. Considerations may be presented capable of determining the intellect either to give or withhold its assent to the doctrine; and this is equivalent to proof.

We shall examine presently of what nature are these considerations; in what manner they apply to the case, and what rational grounds, therefore, can be given for accepting or rejecting the utilitarian formula. But it is a preliminary condition of rational acceptance or rejection that the formula should be correctly understood. I believe that the very imperfect notion ordinarily formed of its meaning is the chief obstacle which impedes its reception, and that, could it be cleared even from only the grosser misconceptions, the question would be greatly simplified and a large proportion of its difficulties removed. Before, therefore, I attempt to enter into the philosophical grounds which can be given for assenting to the utilitarian standard, I shall offer some illustrations of the doctrine itself, with the view of showing more clearly what it is, distinguishing it from what it is not, and disposing of such of the practical objections to it as either originate in, or are closely connected with, mistaken interpretations of its meaning. Having thus prepared the ground, I shall afterwards endeavor to throw such light as I can call upon the question considered as one of philosophical theory.

CHAPTER II

What Utilitarianism Is

A passing remark is all that needs to be given to the ignorant blunder of supposing that those who stand up for utility as the test of right and wrong use the term in that restricted and merely colloquial sense in which utility is opposed to pleasure. An apology is due to the philosophical opponents of utilitarianism for even the momentary appearance of confounding them with anyone capable of so absurd a misconception: which is the more extraordinary, inasmuch as the contrary accusation, of referring everything to pleasure, and that, too, in its grossest form, is another of the common charges against utilitarianism: and, as has been pointedly remarked by an able writer, the same sort of persons, and often the very same persons, denounce the theory "as impracticably dry when the word 'utility' precedes the word 'pleasure,' and as too practicably voluptuous when the word 'pleasure' precedes the word 'utility.'" Those who know anything about the matter are aware that every writer, from Epicurus to Bentham, who maintained the theory of utility meant by it, not something to be contradistinguished from pleasure, but pleasure itself, together with exemption from pain; and instead of opposing the useful to the agreeable or the ornamental, have always declared that the useful means these, among other things. Yet the common herd, including the herd of writers, not only in newspapers and periodicals, but in books of weight and pretension, are perpetually falling into this shallow mistake. Having caught up the word "utilitarian," while knowing nothing whatever about it but its sound, they habitually express by it the rejection or the neglect of pleasure in some of its forms: of beauty, of ornament, or of amusement. Nor is the term thus ignorantly misapplied solely in disparagement, but occasionally in compliment, as though it implied superiority to frivolity and the mere pleasures of the moment. And this perverted use is the only one in which the word is popularly known, and the one from which the new generation are acquiring their sole notion of its meaning. Those who introduced the word, but who had for many years discontinued it as a distinctive appellation, may well feel themselves called upon to resume it if by doing so they can hope to contribute anything toward rescuing it from this utter degradation.[1]

The creed which accepts as the foundation of morals "utility" or the "greatest happiness principle" holds that actions are right in proportion as they tend to promote happiness; wrong as they tend to produce the reverse of happiness. By happiness is intended pleasure and the absence of pain; by unhappiness, pain and the privation of pleasure. To give a clear view of the moral standard set up by the theory, much more requires to be said; in particular, what things it includes in the ideas of pain and pleasure, and to what extent this is left an open question. But these supplementary explanations do not affect the theory of life on which this theory of morality is grounded—namely, that pleasure and freedom from pain are the only things desirable as ends; and that all desirable things (which are as numerous in the utilitarian as in any other scheme) are desirable either for pleasure inherent in themselves or as means to the promotion of pleasure and the prevention of pain.

Now such a theory of life excites in many minds, and among them in some of the most estimable in feeling and purpose, inveterate dislike. To suppose that life has (as they express it) no higher end than pleasure—no better and nobler object of desire and pursuit—they designate as utterly mean and groveling, as a doctrine worthy only of swine, to whom the followers of Epicurus were, at a very early period, contemptuously likened; and modern holders of the doctrine are occasionally made the subject of equally polite comparisons by its German, French, and English assailants.

When thus attacked, the Epicureans have always answered that it is not they, but their accusers, who represent human nature in a degrading light, since the accusation supposes human beings to be capable of no pleasures except those of which swine are capable. If this supposition were true, the charge could not be gainsaid, but would then be no longer an imputation; for if the sources of pleasure were precisely the same to human beings and to swine, the rule of life which is good enough for the one would be good enough for the other. The comparison of the Epicurean life to that of beasts is felt as degrading, precisely because a beast's pleasures do not satisfy a human being's conceptions of happiness. Human beings have faculties more elevated than the animal appetites and, when once made conscious of them, do not regard anything as happiness which does not include their gratification. I do not indeed, consider the Epicureans to have been by any means faultless in drawing out their scheme of consequences from the utilitarian principle. To do this in any sufficient manner, many Stoic, as well as Christian, elements require to be included. But there is no known Epicurean theory of life which does not assign to the pleasures of the intellect, of the feelings and imagination, and of the moral sentiments a much higher value as pleasures than to those of mere sensation. It must be admitted, however, that utilitarian writers in general have placed the superiority of mental over bodily pleasures chiefly in the greater permanency, safety, uncostliness, etc., of the former—that is, in their circumstantial advantages rather than in their intrinsic nature. And on all these points utilitarians have fully proved their case; but they might have taken the other and, as it may be called, higher ground with entire consistency. It is quite compatible with the principle of utility to recognize the fact that some kinds of pleasures are more desirable and more valuable than others. It would be absurd that, while in estimating all other things quality is considered as well as quantity, the estimation of pleasure should be supposed to depend on quantity alone.

If I am asked what I mean by difference of quality in pleasures, or what makes one pleasure more valuable than another, merely as a pleasure, except its being greater in amount, there is but one possible answer. Of two pleasures, if there be one to which all or almost all who have experience of both give a decided preference, irrespective of any feeling of moral obligation to prefer it, that is the more desirable pleasure. If one of the two is, by those who are competently acquainted with both, placed so far above the other that they prefer it, even though knowing it to be attended with a greater amount of discontent, and would not resign it for any quantity of the other pleasure which their nature is capable of, we are justified

in ascribing to the preferred enjoyment a superiority in quality so far outweighing quantity as to render it, in comparison, of small account.

Now it is an unquestionable fact that those who are equally acquainted with and equally capable of appreciating and enjoying both do give a most marked preference to the manner of existence which employs their higher faculties. Few human creatures would consent to be changed into any of the lower animals for a promise of the fullest allowance of a beast's pleasures; no intelligent human being would consent to be a fool, no instructed person would be an ignoramus, no person of feeling and conscience would be selfish and base, even though they should be persuaded that the fool, the dunce, or the rascal is better satisfied with his lot than they are with theirs. They would not resign what they possess more than he for the most complete satisfaction of all the desires which they have in common with him. If they ever fancy they would, it is only in cases of unhappiness so extreme that to escape from it they would exchange their lot for almost any other, however undesirable in their own eyes. A being of higher faculties requires more to make him happy, is capable probably of more acute suffering, and certainly accessible to it at more points, than one of an inferior type; but in spite of these liabilities, he can never really wish to sink into what he feels to be a lower grade of existence. We may give what explanation we please of this unwillingness; we may attribute it to pride, a name which is given indiscriminately to some of the most and to some of the least estimable feelings of which mankind are capable; we may refer it to the love of liberty and personal independence, an appeal to which was with the Stoics one of the most effective means for the inculcation of it; to the love of power or to the love of excitement, both of which do really enter into and contribute to it; but its most appropriate appellation is a sense of dignity, which all human beings possess in one form or other, and in some, though by no means in exact, proportion to their higher faculties, and which is so essential a part of the happiness of those in whom it is strong that nothing which conflicts with it could be otherwise than momentarily an object of desire to them. Whoever supposes that this preference takes place at a sacrifice of happiness—that the superior being, in anything like equal circumstances, is not happier than the inferior—confounds the two very different ideas of happiness and content. It is indisputable that the being whose capacities of enjoyment are low has the greatest chance of having them fully satisfied; and a highly endowed being will always feel that any happiness which he can look for, as the world is constituted, is imperfect. But he can learn to bear its imperfections, if they are at all bearable; and they will not make him envy the being who is indeed unconscious of the imperfections, but only because he feels not at all the good which those imperfections qualify. It is better to be a human being dissatisfied than a pig satisfied; better to be Socrates dissatisfied than a fool satisfied. And if the fool, or the pig, are of a different opinion, it is because they only know their own side of the question. The other party to the comparison knows both sides.

It may be objected that many who are capable of the higher pleasures occasionally, under the influence of temptation, postpone them to the lower. But this is quite compatible with a full appreciation of the intrinsic superiority of the higher. Men often, from infirmity of character, make their election for the nearer good, though they know it to be the less valuable; and this no less when the choice is between two bodily pleasures than when it is between bodily and mental. They pursue sensual indulgences to the injury of health, though perfectly aware that health is the greater good. It may be further objected that many who begin with youthful enthusiasm for everything noble, as they advance in years, sink into indolence and selfishness. But I do not believe that those who undergo this very common change voluntarily choose the lower description of pleasures in preference to the higher. I believe that, before they devote themselves exclusively to the one, they have already become incapable of the other. Capacity for the nobler feelings is in most natures a very tender plant, easily killed, not only by hostile influences, but by mere want of sustenance; and in the majority of young persons it speedily dies away if the occupations to which their position in life has devoted them, and the society into which it has thrown them, are not favorable to keeping that higher capacity in exercise. Men lose their high aspirations as they lose their intellectual tastes, because they have not time or opportunity for indulging them; and they addict themselves to inferior pleasures, not because they deliberately prefer them, but because they are either the only ones to which they have access or the only ones which they are any longer capable of enjoying. It may be questioned whether anyone who has remained equally susceptible to both classes of pleasures ever knowingly and calmly preferred the lower, though many, in all ages, have broken down in an ineffectual attempt to combine both.

From this verdict of the only competent judges, I apprehend there can be no appeal. On a question which is the best worth having of two pleasures, or which of two modes of existence is the most grateful to the feelings, apart from its moral attributes and from its consequences, the judgment of those who are qualified by knowledge of both, or, if they differ, that of the majority among them, must be admitted as final. And there needs be the less hesitation to accept this judgment respecting the quality of pleasures, since there is no other tribunal to be referred to even on the question of quantity. What means are there of determining which is the acutest of two pains, or the intensest of two pleasurable sensations, except the general suffrage of those who are familiar with both? Neither pains nor pleasures are homogeneous, and pain is always heterogeneous with pleasure. What is there to decide whether a particular pleasure is worth purchasing at the cost of a particular pain, except the feelings and judgment of the experienced? When, therefore, those feelings and judgment declare the pleasures derived from the higher faculties to be preferable *in kind,* apart from the question of intensity, to those of which the animal nature, disjoined from the higher faculties, is susceptible, they are entitled on this subject to the same regard.

I have dwelt on this point as being a necessary part of a perfectly just conception of utility or happiness considered as the directive rule of human conduct. But it is by no means an indispensable condition to the acceptance of the utilitarian standard; for that standard is not the agent's own greatest happiness, but the greatest amount of happiness altogether; and if it may possibly be doubted whether a noble character is always the happier for its nobleness, there can be no doubt that it makes other people happier, and that the world in general is immensely a gainer by it. Utilitarianism, therefore, could only attain its end by the general cultivation of nobleness of character, even if each individual were only benefited by the nobleness of others, and his own, so far as happiness is concerned, were a sheer deduction from the benefit. But the bare enunciation of such an absurdity as this last renders refutation superfluous.

According to the greatest happiness principle, as above explained, the ultimate end, with reference to and for the sake of which all other things are desirable—whether we are considering our own good or that of other people—is an existence exempt as far as possible from pain, and as rich as possible in enjoyments, both in point of quantity and quality; the test of quality and the rule for measuring it against quantity being the preference felt by those who, in their opportunities of experience, to which must be added their habits of self-consciousness and self-observation, are best furnished with the means of comparison. This, being according to the utilitarian opinion the end of human action, is necessarily also the standard of morality, which may accordingly be defined "the rules and precepts for human conduct." by the observance of which an existence such as has been described might be, to the greatest extent possible, secured to all mankind; and not to them only, but, so far as the nature of things admits to, to the whole sentient creation.

Against this doctrine, however, arises another class of objectors who say that happiness, in any form, cannot be the rational purpose of human life and action; because, in the first place, it is unattainable; and they contemptuously ask, What right hast thou to be happy?—a question which Mr. Carlyle clinches by the addition, What right, a short time ago, hadst thou even *to be?* Next they say that men can do *without* happiness; that all noble human beings have felt this, and could not have become noble but by learning the lesson of *Entsagen,* or renunciation; which lesson, thoroughly learned and submitted to, they affirm to be the beginning and necessary condition of all virtue.

The first of these objections would go to the root of the matter were it well founded; for if no happiness is to be had at all by human beings, the attainment of it cannot be the end of morality or of any rational conduct. Though, even in that case, something might still be said for the utilitarian theory, since utility includes not solely the pursuit of happiness, but the prevention or mitigation of unhappiness; and if the former aim be chimerical, there will be all the greater scope and more imperative need for the latter, so long at least as mankind think fit to live and do not take refuge in the simultaneous act of suicide recommended under certain conditions by Novalis. When, however, it is thus positively asserted to be impossible that human life should be happy, the assertion, if not something like a verbal quibble, is at least an exaggeration. If by happiness be meant a continuity of highly pleasurable excitement, it is evident enough that this is impossible. A state of exalted pleasure lasts only moments or in some cases, and with some intermissions, hours or days, and is the occasional brilliant flash of enjoyment, not its permanent and steady flame. Of this the philosophers who have taught that happiness is the end of life were as fully aware as those who taunt them. The happiness which they meant was not a life of rapture, but moments of such, in an existence made up of few and transitory pains, many and various pleasures, with a decided predominance of the active over the passive, and having as the foundation of the whole not to expect more from life than it is capable of bestowing. A life thus composed, to those who have been fortunate enough to obtain it, has always appeared worthy of the name of happiness. And such an existence is even now the lot of many during some considerable portion of their lives. The present wretched education and wretched social arrangements are the only real hindrance to its being attainable by almost all.

The objectors perhaps may doubt whether human beings, if taught to consider happiness as the end of life, would be satisfied with such a moderate share of it. But great numbers of mankind have been satisfied with much less. The main constituents of a satisfied life appear to be two, either of which by itself is often found sufficient for the purpose: tranquility and excitement. With much tranquility, many find that they can be content with very little pleasure;

with much excitement, many can reconcile themselves to a considerable quantity of pain. There is assuredly no inherent impossibility of enabling even the mass of mankind to unite both, since the two are so far from being incompatible that they are in natural alliance, the prolongation of either being a preparation for, and exciting a wish for, the other. It is only those in whom indolence amounts to a vice that do not desire excitement after an interval of repose; it is only those in whom the need of excitement is a disease that feel the tranquility which follows excitement dull and insipid, instead of pleasurable in direct proportion to the excitement which preceded it. When people who are tolerably fortunate in their outward lot do not find in life sufficient enjoyment to make it valuable to them, the cause generally is caring for nobody but themselves. To those who have neither public nor private affections, the excitements of life are much curtailed, and in any case dwindle in value as the time approaches when all selfish interests must be terminated by death; while those who leave after them objects of personal affection, and especially those who have also cultivated a fellow-feeling with the collective interests of mankind, retain as lively an interest in life on the eve of death as in the vigor of youth and health. Next to selfishness, the principal cause which makes life unsatisfactory is want of mental cultivation. A cultivated mind—I do not mean that of a philosopher, but any mind to which the fountains of knowledge have been opened, and which has been taught, in any tolerable degree, to exercise its faculties—finds sources of inexhaustible interest in all that surrounds it: in the objects of nature, the achievements of art, the imaginations of poetry, the incidents of history, the ways of mankind, past and present, and their prospects in the future. It is possible, indeed, to become indifferent to all this, and that too without having exhausted a thousandth part of it, but only when one has had from the beginning no moral or human interest in these things and has sought in them only the gratification of curiosity.

Now there is absolutely no reason in the nature of things why an amount of mental culture sufficient to give an intelligent interest in these objects of contemplation should not be the inheritance of everyone born in a civilized country. As little is there an inherent necessity that any human being should be a selfish egotist, devoid of every feeling or care but those which center in his own miserable individuality. Something far superior to this is sufficiently common even now, to give ample earnest of what the human species may be made. Genuine private affections and a sincere interest in the public good are possible, though in unequal degrees, to every rightly brought up human being. In a world in which there is so much to interest, so much to enjoy, and so much also to correct and improve, everyone who has this moderate amount of moral and intellectual requisites is capable of an existence which may be called enviable; and unless such a person, through bad laws or subjection to the will of others, is denied the liberty to use the sources of happiness within his reach, he will not fail to find this enviable existence, if he escapes the positive evils of life, the great sources of physical and mental suffering—such as indigence, disease, and the unkindness, worthlessness, or premature loss of objects of affection. The main stress of the problem lies, therefore, in the contest with these calamities from which it is a rare good fortune entirely to escape; which, as things now are, cannot be obviated, and often cannot be in any material degree mitigated. Yet no one whose opinion deserves a moment's consideration can doubt that most of the great positive evils of the world are in themselves removable, and will, if human affairs continue to improve, be in the end reduced within narrow limits. Poverty, in any sense implying suffering, may be completely extinguished by the wisdom of society combined with the good sense and providence of individuals. Even that most intractable of enemies, disease, may be indefinitely reduced in dimensions by good physical and moral education and proper control of noxious influences, while the progress of science holds out a promise for the future of still more direct conquests over this detestable foe. And every advance in that direction relieves us from some, not only of the chances which cut short our own lives, but, what concerns us still more, which deprive us of those in whom our happiness is wrapt up. As for vicissitudes of fortune and other disappointments connected with wordly circumstances, these are principally the effect either of gross imprudence, of ill-regulated desires, or of bad or imperfect social institutions. All the grand sources, in short, of human suffering are in a great degree, many of them almost entirely, conquerable by human care and effort; and though their removal is grievously slow—though a long succession of generations will perish in the breach before the conquest is completed, and this world becomes all that, if will and knowledge were not wanting, it might easily be made—yet every mind sufficiently intelligent and generous to bear a part, however small and inconspicuous, in the endeavour will draw a noble enjoyment from the contest itself, which he would not for any bribe in the form of selfish indulgence consent to be without.

And this leads to the true estimation of what is said by the objectors concerning the possibility and the obligation of learning to do without happiness. Unquestionably it is possible to do without happiness; it is done involuntarily by nineteen-twentieths of mankind, even in those parts of our present world which are least deep in barbarism; and it often has to be done voluntarily by the hero or the martyr, for the sake of something which he prizes more than his individual happiness. But this something, what is it, unless the happiness of others or some of the requisites of happiness? It is noble to be capable of resigning entirely one's own portion of happiness, or chances of it; but, after all, this self-sacrifice must be for some end, it is not its own end; and if we are told that its end is not happiness but virtue, which is better than happiness, I ask, would the sacrifice be made if the hero or martyr did not believe that it would earn for others immunity from similar sacrifices? Would it be made if he thought that his renunciation of happiness for himself would produce no fruit for any of his fellow creatures, but to make their lot like his and place them also in the condition of persons who have renounced happiness? All honor to those who can abnegate for themselves the personal enjoyment of life when by such renunciation they contribute worthily to increase the amount of happiness in the world; but he who does it or professes to do it for any other purpose is no more deserving of admiration than the ascetic mounted on his pillar. He may be an inspiriting proof of what men *can* do, but assuredly not an example of what they *should*.

Though it is only in a very imperfect state of the world's arrangements that anyone can best serve the happiness of others by the absolute sacrifice of his own, yet, so long as the world is in that imperfect state, I fully acknowledge that the readiness to make such a sacrifice is the highest virtue which can be found in man. I will add that in this condition of the world, paradoxical as the assertion may be, the conscious ability to do without happiness gives the best prospect of realizing such happiness as is attainable. For nothing except that consciousness can raise a person above the chances of life by making him feel that, let fate and fortune do their worst, they have not power to subdue him; which, once felt, frees him from excess of anxiety concerning the evils of life and enables him, like many a Stoic in the worst times of the Roman Empire, to cultivate in tranquillity the sources of satisfaction accessible to him, without concerning himself about the uncertainty of their duration any more than about their inevitable end.

Meanwhile, let utilitarians never cease to claim the morality of self-devotion as a possession which belongs by as good a right to them as either to the Stoic or to the Transcendentalist. The utilitarian morality does recognize in human beings the power of sacrificing their own greatest good for the good of others. It only refuses to admit that the sacrifice is itself a good. A sacrifice which does not increase or tend to increase the sum total of happiness, it considers as wasted. The only self-renunciation which it applauds is devotion to the happiness, or to some of the means of happiness, of others, either of mankind collectively or of individuals within the limits imposed by the collective interests of mankind.

I must again repeat what the assailants of utilitarianism seldom have the justice to acknowledge, that the happiness which forms the utilitarian standard of what is right in conduct is not the agent's own happiness but that of all concerned. As between his own happiness and that of others, utilitarianism requires him to be as strictly impartial as a disinterested and benevolent spectator. In the golden rule of Jesus of Nazareth, we read the complete spirit of the ethics of utility. "To do as you would be done by," and "to love your neighbor as yourself," constitute the ideal perfection of utilitarian morality. As the means of making the nearest approach to this ideal, utility would enjoin, first, that laws and social arrangements should place the happiness or (as, speaking practically, it may be called) the interest of every individual as nearly as possible in harmony with the interest of the whole: and, secondly, that education and opinion, which have so vast a power over human character, should so use that power as to establish in the mind of every individual an indissoluble association between his own happiness and the good of the whole, especially between his own happiness and the practice of such modes of conduct, negative and positive, as regard for the universal happiness prescribes; so that not only he may be unable to conceive the possibility of happiness to himself, consistently with conduct opposed to the general good, but also that a direct impulse to promote the general good may be in every individual one of the habitual motives of action, and the sentiments connected therewith may fill a large and prominent place in every human being's sentient existence. If the impugners of the utilitarian morality represented it to their own minds in this its true character, I know not what recommendation possessed by any other morality they could possibly affirm to be wanting to it; what more beautiful or more exalted developments of human nature any other ethical system can be supposed to foster, or what springs of action, not accessible to the utilitarian, such systems rely on for giving effect to their mandates.

The objectors to utilitarianism cannot always be charged with representing it in a discreditable light. On the contrary, those among them who entertain anything like a just idea of its disinterested character sometimes find fault with its standard as being too high for humanity. They say it is exacting too much to require that people shall always act from the inducement of promoting the general interests of society. But this is to mistake the very meaning of a standard of morals and confound the rule of action with the motive of it. It is the business of ethics to tell us what are our duties, or by what test we may know them; but no system of ethics requires that the sole motive of all we do shall be a feeling of duty; on the

contrary, ninety-nine hundredths of all our actions are done from other motives, and rightly so done if the rule of duty does not condemn them. It is the more unjust to utilitarianism that this particular misapprehension should be made a ground of objection to it, inasmuch as utilitarian moralists have gone beyond almost all others in affirming that the motive has nothing to do with the morality of the action, though much with the worth of the agent. He who saves a fellow creature from drowning does what is morally right, whether his motive be duty or the hope of being paid for his trouble; he who betrays the friend that trusts him is guilty of a crime, even if his object be to serve another friend to whom he is under greater obligations.[2] But to speak only of actions done from the motive of duty, and in direct obedience to principle: it is a misapprehension of the utilitarian mode of thought to conceive it as implying that people should fix their minds upon so wide a generality as the world, or society at large. The great majority of good actions are intended not for the benefit of the world, but for that of individuals, of which the good of the world is made up; and the thoughts of the most virtuous man need not on these occasions travel beyond the particular persons concerned, except so far as is necessary to assure himself that in benefiting them he is not violating the rights, that is, the legitimate and authorized expectations, of anyone else. The multiplication of happiness is, according to the utilitarian ethics, the object of virtue: the occasions on which any person (except one in a thousand) has it in his power to do this on an extended scale—in other words, to be a public benefactor—are but exceptional; and on these occasions alone is he called on to consider public utility; in every other case, private utility, the interest or happiness of some few persons, is all he has to attend to. Those alone the influence of whose actions extends to society in general need concern themselves habitually about so large an object. In the case of abstinences indeed—of things which people forbear to do from moral considerations, though the consequences in the particular case might be beneficial—it would be unworthy of an intelligent agent not to be consciously aware that the action is of a class which, if practiced generally, would be generally injurious, and that this is the ground of the obligation to abstain from it. The amount of regard for the public interest implied in this recognition is no greater than is demanded by every system of morals, for they all enjoin to abstain from whatever is manifestly pernicious to society.

The same considerations dispose of another reproach against the doctrine of utility, founded on a still grosser misconception of the purpose of a standard of morality and of the very meaning of the words "right" and "wrong." It is often affirmed that utilitarianism renders men cold and unsympathizing; that it chills their moral feelings toward individuals; that it makes them regard only the dry and hard consideration of the consequences of actions, not taking into their moral estimate the qualities from which those actions emanate. If the assertion means that they do not allow their judgment respecting the rightness or wrongness of an action to be influenced by their opinion of the qualities of the person who does it, this is a complaint not against utilitarianism, but against any standard of morality at all; for certainly no known ethical standard decides an action to be good or bad because it is done by a good or bad man, still less because done by an amiable, a brave, or a benevolent man, or the contrary. These considerations are relevant, not to the estimation of actions, but of persons; and there is nothing in the utilitarian theory inconsistent with the fact that there are other things which interest us in persons besides the rightness and wrongness of their actions. The Stoics, indeed, with the paradoxical misuse of language which was part of their system, and by which they strove to raise themselves above all concern about anything but virtue, were fond of saying that he who has that has everything; that he, and only he, is rich, is beautiful, is a king. But no claim of this description is made for the virtuous man by the utilitarian doctrine. Utilitarians are quite aware that there are other desirable possessions and qualities besides virtue, and are perfectly willing to allow to all of them their full worth. They are also aware that a right action does not necessarily indicate a virtuous character, and that actions which are blamable often proceed from qualities entitled to praise. When this is apparent in any particular case, it modifies their estimation, not certainly of the act, but of the agent. I grant

that they are, notwithstanding, of opinion that in the long run the best proof of a good character is good actions; and resolutely refuse to consider any mental disposition as good of which the predominant tendency is to produce bad conduct. This makes them unpopular with many people, but it is an unpopularity which they must share with everyone who regards the distinction between right and wrong in a serious light; and the reproach is not one which a conscientious utilitarian need be anxious to repel.

If no more be meant by the objection than that many utilitarians look on the morality of actions, as measured by the utilitarian standards, with too exclusive a regard, and do not lay sufficient stress upon the other beauties of character which go toward making a human being lovable or admirable, this may be admitted. Utilitarians who have cultivated their moral feelings, but not their sympathies, nor their artistic perceptions, do fall into this mistake; and so do all other moralists under the same conditions. What can be said in excuse for other moralists is equally available for them, namely, that, if there is to be any error, it is better that it should be on that side. As a matter of fact, we may affirm that among utilitarians, as among adherents of other systems, there is every imaginable degree of rigidity and of laxity in the application of their standard; some are even puritanically rigorous, while others are as indulgent as can possibly be desired by sinner or by sentimentalist. But on the whole, a doctrine which brings prominently forward the interest that mankind have in the repression and prevention of conduct which violates the moral law is likely to be inferior to no other in turning the sanctions of opinion against such violations. It is true, the question "What does violate the moral law?" is one on which those who recognize different standards of morality are likely now and then to differ. But difference of opinion on moral questions was not first introduced into the world by utilitarianism, while the doctrine does supply, if not always an easy, at all events a tangible and intelligible, mode of deciding such differences.

It may not be superfluous to notice a few more of the common misapprehensions of utilitarian ethics, even those which are so obvious and gross that it might appear impossible for any person of candor and intelligence to fall into them; since persons, even of considerable mental endowment, often give themselves so little trouble to understand the bearings of any opinion against which they entertain a prejudice, and men are in general so little conscious of this voluntary ignorance as a defect that the vulgarest misunderstandings of ethical doctrines are continually met with in the deliberate writings of persons of the greatest pretensions both to high principle and to philosophy. We not uncommonly hear the doctrine of utility inveighed against a *godless* doctrine. If it be necessary to say anything at all against so mere an assumption, we may say that the question depends upon what idea we have formed of the moral character of the Deity. If it be a true belief that God desires, above all things, the happiness of his creatures, and that this was his purpose in their creation, utility is not only not a godless doctrine, but more profoundly religious than any other. If it be meant that utilitarianism does not recognize the revealed will of God as the supreme law of morals, I answer that a utilitarian who believes in the perfect goodness and wisdom of *God* necessarily believes that whatever God has thought fit to reveal on the subject of morals must fulfill the requirements of utility in a supreme degree. But others besides utilitarians have been of opinion that the Christian revelation was intended, and is fitted, to inform the hearts and minds of mankind with a spirit which should enable them to find for themselves what is right, and incline them to do it when found, rather than to tell them, except in a very general way, what it is; and that we need a doctrine of ethics, carefully followed out, to *interpret* to us the will of God. Whether this opinion is correct or not, it is superfluous here to discuss; since whatever aid religion, either natural or revealed, can afford to ethical investigation is as open to the utilitarian moralist as to any other. He can use it as the testimony of God to the usefulness or hurtfulness of any given course of action by as good a right as others can use it for the indication of a transcendental law having no connection with usefulness or with happiness.

Again, utility is often summarily stigmatized as an immoral doctrine by giving it the name of "expediency," and taking advantage of the popular use of that term to contrast it with principle. But the expedient, in the sense in which it is opposed to the right, generally means that which is expedient for the particular interest of the agent himself; as when a minister sacrifices the interests of his country to keep himself in place. When it means anything better than this, it means that which is expedient for some immediate object, some temporary purpose, but which violates a rule whose observance is expedient in a much higher degree. The expedient, in this sense, instead of being the same thing with the useful, is a branch of the hurtful. Thus it would often be expedient, for the purpose of getting over some momentary embarrassment, or attaining some object immediately useful to ourselves or others, to tell a lie. But inasmuch as the cultivation in ourselves of a sensitive feeling on the subject of veracity is one of the most useful, and the enfeeblement of that feeling one of the most hurtful, things to which our conduct can be instrumental; and inasmuch as any, even unintentional, deviation from truth does that much toward weakening the trustworthiness of human assertion, which is not only the principal support of all present social well-being, but the insufficiency of which does more than any one thing that can be named to keep back civilization, virtue, everything on which human happiness on the largest scale depends—we feel that the violation, for a present advantage, of a rule of such transcendent expediency is not expedient, and that he who, for the sake of convenience to himself or to some other individual, does what depends on him to deprive mankind of the good, and inflict upon them the evil, involved in the greater or less reliance which they can place in each other's word, acts the part of one of their worst enemies. Yet that even this rule, sacred as it is, admits of possible exceptions is acknowledged by all moralists; the chief of which is when the withholding of some fact (as of information from a malefactor, or of bad news from a person dangerously ill) would save an individual (especially an individual other than oneself) from great and unmerited evil, and when the withholding can only be effected by denial. But in order that the exception may not extend itself beyond the need, and may have the least possible effect in weakening reliance on veracity, it ought to be recognized and, if possible, its limits defined: and, if the principle of utility is good for anything, it must be good for weighing these conflicting utilities against one another and marking out the region within which one or the other preponderates.

Again, defenders of utility often find themselves called upon to reply to such objections as this—that there is not time, previous to action, for calculating and weighing the effects of any line of conduct on the general happiness. This is exactly as if anyone were to say that it is impossible to guide our conduct by Christianity because there is not time, on every occasion on which anything has to be done, to read through the Old and New Testaments. The answer to the objection is that there has been ample time, namely, the whole past duration of the human species. During all that time mankind have been learning by experience the tendencies of actions; on which experience all the prudence as well as all the morality of life are dependent. People talk as if the commencement of this course of experience had hitherto been put off, and as if, at the moment when some man feels tempted to meddle with the property or life of another, he had to begin considering for the first time whether murder and theft are injurious to human happiness. Even then I do not think that he would find the question very puzzling; but, at all events, the matter is now done to his hand. It is truly a whimsical supposition that, if mankind were agreed in considering utility to be the test of morality, they would remain without any agreement as to what *is* useful, and would take no measures for having their notions on the subject taught to the young and enforced by law and opinion. There is no difficulty in proving any ethical standard whatever to work ill if we suppose universal idiocy to be conjoined with it; but on any hypothesis short of that, mankind must by this time have acquired positive beliefs as to the effects of some actions on their happiness; and the beliefs which have thus come down are the rules of morality for the multitude, and for the philosopher until he has succeeded in finding better. That philosophers might easily do this, even now, on many subjects; that the received code of ethics is by no means of divine right; and that mankind have still much to learn as to the effects of actions on the general happiness,

I admit or rather earnestly maintain. The corollaries from the principle of utility, like the precepts of every practical art, admit of indefinite improvement, and, in a progressive state of the human mind, their improvement is perpetually going on. But to consider the rules of morality as improvable is one thing; to pass over the intermediate generalization entirely and endeavor to test each individual action directly by the first principle is another. It is a strange notion that the acknowledgment of a first principle is inconsistent with the admission of secondary ones. To inform a traveler respecting the place of his ultimate destination is not to forbid the use of landmarks and direction-posts on the way. The proposition that happiness is the end and aim of morality does not mean that no road ought to be laid down to that goal, or that persons going thither should not be advised to take one direction rather than another. Men really ought to leave off talking a kind of nonsense on this subject, which they would neither talk nor listen to on other matters of practical concernment. Nobody argues that the art of navigation is not founded on astronomy because sailors cannot wait to calculate the Nautical Almanac. Being rational creatures, they go to sea with it ready calculated; and all rational creatures go out upon the sea of life with their minds made up on the common questions of right and wrong, as well as on many of the far more difficult questions of wise and foolish. And this, as long as foresight is a human quality, it is to be presumed they will continue to do. Whatever we adopt as the fundamental principle of morality, we require subordinate principles to apply it by; the impossibility of doing without them, being common to all systems, can afford no argument against any one in particular; but gravely to argue as if no such secondary principles could be had, and as if mankind had remained till now, and always must remain, without drawing any general conclusions from the experience of human life is as high a pitch. I think, as absurdity has ever reached in philosophical controversy.

The remainder of the stock arguments against utilitarianism mostly consist in laying to its charge the common infirmities of human nature, and the general difficulties which embarrass conscientious persons in shaping their course through life. We are told that a utilitarian will be apt to make his own particular case an exception to moral rules, and, when under temptation, will see a utility in the breach of a rule, greater than he will see in its observance. But is utility the only creed which is able to furnish us with excuses for evil-doing and means of cheating our own conscience? They are afforded in abundance by all doctrines which recognize as a fact in morals the existence of conflicting considerations, which all doctrines do that have been believed by sane persons. It is not the fault of any creed, but of the complicated nature of human affairs, that rules of conduct cannot be so framed as to require no exceptions, and that hardly any kind of action can safely be laid down as either always obligatory or always condemnable. There is no ethical creed which does not temper the rigidity of its laws by giving a certain latitude, under the moral responsibility of the agent, for accommodation to peculiarities of circumstances; and under every creed, at the opening thus made, self-deception and dishonest casuistry get in. There exists no moral system under which there do not arise unequivocal cases of conflicting obligation. These are the real difficulties, the knotty points both in the theory of ethics and in the conscientious guidance of personal conduct. They are overcome practically, with greater or with less success, according to the intellect and virtue of the individual; but it can hardly be pretended that anyone will be the less qualified for dealing with them, from possessing an ultimate standard to which conflicting rights and duties can be referred. If utility is the ultimate source of moral obligations, utility may be invoked to decide between them when their demands are incompatible. Though the application of the standard may be difficult, it is better than none at all; while in other systems, the moral laws all claiming independent authority, there is no common umpire entitled to interfere between them; their claims to precedence one over another rest on little better than sophistry, and, unless determined, as they generally are, by the unacknowledged influence of consideration of utility, afford a free scope for the action of personal desires and partialities. We must remember that only in these cases of conflict between secondary principles is it requisite that first principles should be appealed to. There is no case of moral obligation in which some secondary principle is not involved; and if only one, there can seldom be any real doubt which one it is, in the mind of any person by whom the principle itself is recognized.

CHAPTER III

Of the Ultimate Sanction of the Principle of Utility

The question is often asked, and properly so, in regard to any supposed moral standard—What is its sanction? what are the motives to obey? or, more specifically, what is the source of its obligation? whence does it derive its binding force? It is a necessary part of moral philosophy to provide the answer to this question, which, though frequently assuming the shape of an objection to the utilitarian morality, as if it had some special applicability to that above others, really arises in regard to all standards. It arises, in fact, whenever a person is called on to *adopt* a standard, or refer morality to any basis on which be has not been accustomed to rest it. For the customary morality, that which education and opinion have consecrated, is the only one which presents itself to the mind with the feeling of being *in itself* obligatory; and when a person is asked to believe that this morality *derives* its obligation from some general principle round which custom has not thrown the same halo, the assertion is to him a paradox; the supposed corollaries seem to have a more binding force than the original theorem; the superstructure seems to stand better without than with what is represented as its foundation. He says to himself, I feel that I am bound not to rob or murder, betray or deceive; but why am I bound to promote the general happiness? If my own happiness lies in something else, why may I not give that the preference?

If the view adopted by the utilitarian philosophy of the nature of the moral sense be correct, this difficulty will always present itself until the influences which form moral character have taken the same hold of the principle which they have taken of some of the consequences—until, by the improvement of education, the feeling of unity with our fellow creatures shall be (what it cannot be denied that Christ intended it to be) as deeply rooted in our character, and to our own consciousness as completely a part of our nature, as the horror of crime is in an ordinarily well-brought up young person. In the meantime, however, the difficulty has no peculiar application to the doctrine of utility, but is inherent in every attempt to analyze morality and reduce it to principles; which, unless the principle is already in men's minds invested with as much sacredness as any of its applications, always seems to divest them of a part of their sanctity.

The principle of utility either has, or there is no reason why it might not have, all the sanctions which belong to any other system of morals. Those sanctions are either external or internal. Of the external sanctions it is not necessary to speak at any length. They are the hope of favor and the fear of displeasure from our fellow creatures or from the Ruler of the universe, along with whatever we may have of sympathy or affection for them, or of love and awe of Him, inclining us to do His will independently of selfish consequences. There is evidently no reason why all these motives for observance should not attach themselves to the utilitarian morality as completely and as powerfully as to any other. Indeed, those of them which refer to our fellow creatures are sure to do so, in proportion to the amount of general intelligence; for whether there be any other ground of moral obligation than the general happiness or not, men do desire happiness; and however imperfect may be their own practice, they desire and commend all conduct in others toward themselves by which they think their happiness is promoted. With regard to the religious motive, if men believe, as most profess to do, in the goodness of God, those who think that conduciveness to the general happiness is the essence or even only the criterion of good must necessarily believe that it is also that which God approves. The whole force therefore of external reward and punishment, whether physical or moral, and whether proceeding from God or from our fellow men, together with all that the capacities of human nature admit of disinterested devotion to either, become available to enforce the utilitarian morality, in proportion as that morality is recognized; and the more powerfully, the more the appliances of education and general cultivation are bent to the purpose.

So far as to external sanctions. The internal sanction of duty, whatever our standard of duty may be, is one and the same—a feeling in our own mind; a pain, more or less intense, attendant on violation of duty, which in properly cultivated moral natures rises, in the more serious cases, into shrinking from it as an impossibility. This feeling, when disinterested and connecting itself with the pure idea of duty, and not with some particular form of it, or with any of the merely accessory circumstances, is the essence of conscience; though in that complex phenomenon as it actually exists, the simple fact is in general all encrusted over with collateral associations derived from sympathy, from love, and still more from fear; from all the forms of religious feeling; from the recollections of childhood and of all our past life; from self-esteem, desire of the esteem of others, and occasionally even self-abasement. This extreme complication is, I apprehend, the origin of the sort of mystical character which, by a tendency of the human mind of which there are many other examples, is apt to be attributed to the idea of moral obligation, and which leads people to believe that the idea cannot possibly attach itself to any other objects than those which, by a supposed mysterious law, are found in our present experience to excite it. Its binding force, however, consists in the existence of a mass of feeling which must be broken through in order to do what violates our standard of right, and which, if we do nevertheless violate that standard, will probably have to be encountered afterwards in the form of remorse. Whatever theory we have of the nature or origin of conscience, this is what essentially constitutes it.

The ultimate sanction, therefore, of all morality (external motives apart) being a subjective feeling in our own minds, I see nothing embarrassing to those whose standard is utility in the question, What is the sanction of that particular standard? We may answer, the same as of all other moral standards—the conscientious feelings of mankind. Undoubtedly this sanction has no binding efficacy on those who do not possess the feelings it appeals to; but neither will these persons be more obedient to any other moral principle than to the utilitarian one. On them morality of any kind has no hold but through the external sanctions. Meanwhile the feelings exist, a fact in human nature, the reality of which, and the great power with which they are capable of acting on those in whom they have been duly cultivated, are proved by experience. No reason has ever been shown why they may not be cultivated to as great intensity in connection with the utilitarian as with any other rule of morals.

There is, I am aware, a disposition to believe that a person who sees in moral obligation a transcendental fact, an objective reality belonging to the province of "things in themselves," is likely to be more obedient to it than one who believes it to be entirely subjective, having its seat in human consciousness only. But whatever a person's opinion may be on this point of ontology, the force he is really urged by is his own subjective feeling, and is exactly measured by its strength. No one's belief that duty is an objective reality is stronger than the belief that God is so; yet the belief in God, apart from the expectation of actual reward and punishment, only operates on conduct through, and in proportion to, the subjective religious feeling. The sanction, so far as it is disinterested, is always in the mind itself; and the motion, therefore, of the transcendental moralists must be that this sanction will not exist *in* the mind unless it is believed to have its root out of the mind; and that if a person is able to say to himself, "That which is restraining me and which is called my conscience is only a feeling in my own mind," he may possibly draw the conclusion that when the feeling ceases the obligation ceases, and that if he find the feeling inconvenient, he may disregard it and endeavor to get rid of it. But is this danger confined to the utilitarian morality? Does the belief that moral obligation has its seat outside the mind make the feeling of it too strong to get rid of? The fact is so far otherwise that all moralists admit and lament the ease with which, in the generality of minds, conscience can be silenced or stifled. The question, "Need I obey my conscience?" is quite as often put to themselves by persons who never heard of the principle of utility as by its adherents. Those whose conscientious feelings are so weak as to allow of their asking this question,

if they answer it affirmatively, will not do so because they believe in the transcendental theory, but because of the external sanctions.

It is not necessary, for the present purpose, to decide whether the feeling of duty is innate or implanted. Assuming it to be innate, it is an open question to what objects it naturally attaches itself; for the philosophic supporters of that theory are now agreed that the intuitive perception is of principles of morality and not of the details. If there be anything innate in the matter, I see no reason why the feeling which is innate should not be that of regard to the pleasures and pains of others. If there is any principle of morals which is intuitively obligatory, I should say it must be that. If so, the intuitive ethics would coincide with the utilitarian, and there would be no further quarrel between them. Even as it is, the intuitive moralists, though they believe that there are other intuitive moral obligations, do already believe this to be one; for they unanimously hold that a large *portion* of morality turns upon the consideration due to the interests of our fellow creatures. Therefore, if the belief in the transcendental origin of moral obligation gives any additional efficacy to the internal sanction, it appears to me that the utilitarian principle has already the benefit of it.

On the other hand, if, as is my own belief, the moral feelings are not innate but acquired, they are not for that reason the less natural. It is natural to man to speak, to reason, to build cities, to cultivate the ground, though these are acquired faculties. The moral feelings are not indeed a part of our nature in the sense of being in any perceptible degree present in all of us; but this, unhappily, is a fact admitted by those who believe the most strenuously in their transcendental origin. Like the other acquired capacities above referred to, the moral faculty, if not a part of our nature, is a natural outgrowth from it; capable, like them, in a certain small degree, of springing up spontaneously; and susceptible of being brought by cultivation to a high degree of development. Unhappily it is also susceptible, by a sufficient use of the external sanctions and of the force of early impressions, of being cultivated in almost any direction, so that there is hardly anything so absurd or so mischievous that it may not, by means of these influences, be made to act on the human mind with all the authority of conscience. To doubt that the same potency might be given by the same means to the principle of utility, even if it had no foundation in human nature, would be flying in the face of all experience.

But moral associations which are wholly of artificial creation, when the intellectual culture goes on, yield by degrees to the dissolving force of analysis; and if the feeling of duty, when associated with utility, would appear equally arbitrary; if there were no leading department of our nature, no powerful class of sentiments, with which that association would harmonize, which would make us feel congenial and incline us not only to foster it in ourselves—if there were not, in short, a natural basis of sentiments for utilitarian morality, it might well happen that this association also, even after it had been implanted by education, might be analyzed away.

But there *is* this basis of powerful natural sentiment; and that it is which, when once the general happiness is recognized as the ethical standard, will constitute the strength of the utilitarian morality. This firm foundation is that of the social feelings of mankind—the desire to be in unity with our fellow creatures, which is already a powerful principle in human nature, and happily one of those which tend to become stronger, even without express inculcation, from the influences of advancing civilization. The social state is at once so natural, so necessary, and so habitual to man, that, except in some unusual circumstances or by an effort of voluntary abstraction, he never conceives himself otherwise than as a member of a body; and this association is riveted more and more, as mankind are further removed from the state of savage independence. Any condition, therefore, which is essential to a state of society becomes more and more an inseparable part of every person's conception of the state of things which he is born into, and which is the destiny of a human being. Now society between human beings, except in the relation of master and slave, is manifestly impossible on any other footing than that of the interests of all are to be consulted. Society between equals can only exist on the understanding that the interests of all are to be regarded equally. And since in all states of civilization, every person, except an absolute

monarch, has equals, everyone is obliged to live on these terms with somebody; and in every age some advance is made toward a state in which it will be impossible to live permanently on other terms with anybody. In this way people grow up unable to conceive as possible to them a state of total disregard of other people's interests. They are under a necessity of conceiving themselves as at least abstaining from all the grosser injuries, and (if only for their own protection) living in a state of constant protest against them. They are also familiar with the fact of co-operating with others and proposing to themselves a collective, not an individual, interest as the aim (at least for the time being) of their actions. So long as they are co-operating, their ends are identified with those of others; there is at least a temporary feeling that the interests of others are their own interests. Not only does all strengthening of social ties, and all healthy growth of society, give to each individual a stronger personal interest in practically consulting the welfare of others, it also leads him to identify his *feelings* more and more with their good, or at least with an even greater degree of practical consideration for it. He comes, as though instinctively, to be conscious of himself as a being who *of course* pays regard to others. The good of others becomes to him a thing naturally and necessarily to be attended to, like any of the physical conditions of our existence. Now, whatever amount of this feeling a person has, he is urged by the strongest motives both of interest and of sympathy to demonstrate it, and to the utmost of his power encourage it in others; and even if he has none of it himself, he is as greatly interested as anyone else that others should have it. Consequently, the smaller germs of the feeling are laid hold of and nourished by the contagion of sympathy and the influences of education; and a complete web of corroborative association is woven round it by the powerful agency of the external sanctions. This mode of conceiving ourselves and human life, as civilization goes on, is felt to be more and more natural. Every step in political improvement renders it more so, by removing the sources of opposition of interest and leveling those inequalities of legal privilege between individuals or classes, owing to which there are large portions of mankind whose happiness it is still practicable to disregard. In an improving state of the human mind, the influences are constantly on the increase which tend to generate in each individual a feeling of unity with all the rest; which, if perfect, would make him never think of, or desire, any beneficial condition for himself in the benefits of which they are not included. If we now suppose this feeling of unity to be taught as a religion, and the whole force of education, of institutions, and of opinion directed, as it once was in the case of religion, to make every person grow up from infancy surrounded on all sides both by the profession and the practice of it, I think that no one who can realize this conception will feel any misgiving about the sufficiency of the ultimate sanction for the happiness morality. To any ethical student who finds the realization difficult, I recommend, as a means of facilitating it, the second of M. Comte's two principal works, the *Traité de politique positive*. I entertain the strongest objections to the system of politics and morals set forth in that treatise, but I think it has superabundantly shown the possibility of giving to the service of humanity, even without the aid of belief in a Providence, both the psychological power and the social efficacy of a religion, making it take hold of human life, and color all thought, feeling, and action in a manner of which the greatest ascendancy ever exercised by any religion may be but a type and foretaste; and of which the danger is, not that it should be insufficient, but that it should be so excessive as to interfere unduly with human freedom and individuality.

Neither is it necessary to the feeling which constitutes the binding force of the utilitarian morality on those who recognize it to wait for those social influences which would make its obligation felt by mankind at large. In the comparatively early state of human advancement in which we now live, a person cannot, indeed, feel that entireness of sympathy with all others which would make any real discordance in the general direction of their conduct in life impossible, but already a person in whom the social feeling is at all developed cannot bring himself to think of the rest of his fellow creatures as struggling rivals with him for the means of happiness, whom he must desire to see defeated in their object in order

that he may succeed in his. The deeply rooted conception which every individual even now has of himself as a social being tends to make him feel it one of his natural wants that there should be harmony between his feelings and aims and those of his fellow creatures. If differences of opinion and of mental culture make it impossible for him to share many of their actual feelings—perhaps make him denounce and defy those feelings—he still needs to be conscious that his real aim and theirs do not conflict; that he is not opposing himself to what they really wish for, namely, their own good, but is, on the contrary, promoting it. This feeling in most individuals is much inferior in strength to their selfish feelings, and is often wanting altogether. But to those who have it, it possesses all the characters of a natural feeling. It does not present itself to their minds as a superstition of education or a law despotically imposed by the power of society, but as an attribute which it would not be well for them to be without. This conviction is the ultimate sanction of the greatest happiness morality. This it is which makes any mind of well-developed feelings work with, and not against, the outward motives to care for others, afforded by what I have called the external sanctions; and, when those sanctions are wanting or act in an opposite direction, constitutes in itself a powerful internal binding force, in proportion to the sensitiveness and thoughtfulness of the character, since few but those whose mind is a moral blank could bear to lay out their course of life on the plan of paying no regard to others except so far as their own private interest compels.

CHAPTER IV

Of What Sort of Proof the Principle of Utility Is Susceptible

It has already been remarked that questions of ultimate ends do not admit of proof, in the ordinary acceptation of the term. To be incapable of proof by reasoning is common to all first principles, to the first premises of our knowledge, as well as to those of our conduct. But the former, being matters of fact, may be the subject of a direct appeal to the faculties which judge of fact—namely, our senses and our internal consciousness. Can an appeal be made to the same faculties on questions of practical ends? Or by what other faculty is cognizance taken of them?

Questions about ends are, in other words, questions about what things are desirable. The utilitarian doctrine is that happiness is desirable, and the only thing desirable, as an end; all other things being only desirable as means to that end. What ought to be required of this doctrine, what conditions is it requisite that the doctrine should fulfill—to make good its claim to be believed?

The only proof capable of being given that an object is visible is that people actually see it. The only proof that a sound is audible is that people hear it; and so of the other sources of our experience. In like manner, I apprehend, the sole evidence it is possible to produce that anything is desirable is that people do actually desire it. If the end which the utilitarian doctrine proposes to itself were not, in theory and in practice, acknowledged to be an end, nothing could ever convince any person that it was so. No reason can be given why the general happiness is desirable, except that each person, so far as he believes it to be attainable, desires his own happiness. This, however, being a fact, we have not only all the proof which the case admits of, but all which it is possible to require, that happiness is a good, that each person's happiness is a good to that person, and the general happiness, therefore, a good to the aggregate of all persons. Happiness has made out its title as *one* of the ends of conduct and, consequently, one of the criteria of morality.

But it has not, by this alone, proved itself to be the sole criterion. To do that, it would seem, by the same rule, necessary to show, not only that people desire happiness, but that they never desire anything else. Now it is palpable that they do desire things which, in common language, are decidedly distinguished from happiness. They desire, for example, virtue and the absence of vice no less really than pleasure and the absence of pain. The desire of virtue is not as universal, but it is as authentic a fact as the desire of happiness. And hence the opponents of the utilitarian standard deem that they have a right to infer that there are other ends of human action besides happiness, and that happiness is not the standard of approbation and disapprobation.

But does the utilitarian doctrine deny that people desire virtue, or maintain that virtue is not a thing to be desired? The very reverse. It maintains not only that virtue is to be desired, but that it is to be desired disinterestedly, for itself. Whatever may be the opinion of utilitarian moralists as to the original conditions by which virtue is made virtue, however they may believe (as they do) that actions and dispositions are only virtuous because they promote another end than virtue, yet this being granted, and it having been decided, from considerations of this description, what *is* virtuous, they not only place virtue at the very head of the things which are good as means to the ultimate end, but they also recognize as a psychological fact the possibility of its being, to the individual, a good in itself, without looking to any end beyond it; and hold that the mind is not in a right state, not in a state conformable to utility, not in the state most conducive to the general happiness, unless it does love virtue in this manner—as a thing desirable in itself, even although, in the individual instance, it should not produce those other desirable consequences which it tends to produce, and on account of which it is held to be virtue. This opinion is not, in the smallest degree, a departure from the happiness principle. The ingredients of happiness are very various, and each of them is desirable in itself, and not merely when considered as swelling an aggregate. The principle of utility does not mean that any given pleasure, as music, for instance, or any given exemption from pain, as for example health, is to be looked upon as means to a collective something termed happiness, and to be desired on that account. They are desired and desirable in and for themselves; besides being means, they are a part of the end. Virtue, according to the utilitarian doctrine, is not naturally and originally part of the end, but it is capable of becoming so; and in those who live it disinterestedly it has become so, and is desired and cherished, not as a means to happiness, but as a part of their happiness.

To illustrate this further, we may remember that virtue is not the only thing originally a means, and which if it were not a means to anything else would be and remain indifferent, but which by association with what it is a means to comes to be desired for itself, and that too with the utmost intensity. What, for example, shall we say of the love of money? There is nothing originally more desirable about money than about any heap of glittering pebbles. Its worth is solely that of the things which it will buy; the desires for other things than itself, which it is a means of gratifying. Yet the love of money is not only one of the strongest moving forces of human life, but money is, in many cases, desired in and for itself; the desire to possess it is often stronger than the desire to use it, and goes on increasing when all the desires which point to ends beyond it, to be compassed by it, are falling off. It may, then, be said truly that money is desired not for the sake of an end, but as part of the end. From being a means to happiness, it has come to be itself a principal ingredient of the individual's conception of happiness. The same may be said of the majority of the great objects of human life: power, for example, or fame, except that to each of these there is a certain amount of immediate pleasure annexed, which has at least the semblance of being naturally inherent in them—a thing which cannot be said of money. Still, however, the strongest natural attraction, both of power and of fame, is the immense aid they give to the attainment of our other wishes; and it is the strong association thus generated between them and all our objects of desire which gives to the direct desire of them the intensity it often assumes, so as in some characters to surpass in strength all other desires. In these cases the means have become a part of the end, and a more important part of it than any of the things which they are means to. What was once desired as an instrument for the attainment of happiness has come to be desired for its own sake. In being desired for its own sake it is, however, desired as *part* of happiness. The person is made, or thinks he would be made, happy by its mere possession; and is made unhappy by failure to obtain it. The desire of it is not a different thing from the desire of happiness any more than the love of music or the desire of health. They are included in happiness. They are some of the elements of which the desire of happiness is made up. Happiness is not an abstract idea but a concrete whole; and these are

some of its parts. And the utilitarian standard sanctions and approves their being so. Life would be a poor thing, very ill provided with sources of happiness, if there were not this provision of nature by which things originally indifferent, but conducive to, or otherwise associated with, the satisfaction of our primitive desires, become in themselves sources of pleasure more valuable than the primitive pleasures, both in permanency, in the space of human existence that they are capable of covering, and even in intensity.

Virtue, according to the utilitarian conception, is a good of this description. There was no original desire of it, or motive to it, save its conduciveness to pleasure, and especially to protection from pain. But through the association thus formed it may be felt a good in itself, and desired as such with as great intensity as any other good; and with this difference between it and the love of money, of power, or of fame—that all of these may, and often do, render the individual noxious to the other members of the society to which he belongs, whereas there is nothing which makes him so much a blessing to them as the cultivation of the disinterested love of virtue. And consequently, the utilitarian standard, while it tolerates and approves those other acquired desires, up to the point beyond which they would be more injurious to the general happiness than promotive of it, enjoins and requires the cultivation of the love of virtue up to the greatest strength possible, as being above all things important to the general happiness.

It results from the preceding considerations that there is in reality nothing desired except happiness. Whatever is desired otherwise than as a means to some end beyond itself, and ultimately to happiness, is desired as itself a part of happiness, and is not desired for itself until it has become so. Those who desire virtue for its own sake desire it either because the consciousness of it is a pleasure, or because the consciousness of being without it is a pain, or for both reasons united; as in truth the pleasure and pain seldom exist separately, but almost always together— the same person feeling pleasure in the degree of virtue attained, and pain in not having attained more. If one of these gave him no pleasure, and the other no pain, he would not love or desire virtue, or would desire it only for the other benefits which it might produce to himself or to persons whom he cared for.

We have now, then, an answer to the question, of what sort of proof the principle of utility is susceptible. If the opinion which I have now stated is psychologically true—if human nature is so constituted as to desire nothing which is not either a part of happiness or a means of happiness—we can have no other proof, and we require no other, that these are the only things desirable. If so, happiness is the sole end of human action, and the promotion of it the test by which to judge of all human conduct; from whence it necessarily follows that it must be the criterion of morality, since a part is included in the whole.

And now to decide whether this is really so, whether mankind do desire nothing for itself but that which is a pleasure to them, or of which the absence is a pain, we have evidently arrived at a question of fact and experience, dependent, like all similar questions, upon evidence. It can only be determined by practiced self-consciousness and self-observation, assisted by observation of others. I believe that these sources of evidence, impartially consulted, will declare that desiring a thing and finding it pleasant, aversion to it and thinking of it as painful, are phenomena entirely inseparable or, rather, two parts of the same phenomenon—in strictness of language, two different modes of naming the same psychological fact; that to think of an object as desirable (unless for the sake of its consequences) and to think of it as pleasant are one and the same thing; and that to desire anything except in proportion as the idea of it is pleasant is a physical and metaphysical impossibility.

So obvious does this appear to me that I expect it will hardly be disputed; and the objection made will be, not that desire can possibly be directed to anything ultimately except pleasure and exemption from pain, but that the will is a different thing from desire; that a person of confirmed virtue or any other person whose purposes are fixed carries out his purposes without any thought of the pleasure he has in contemplating them or expects to derive from their fulfillment, and persists in acting on them, even though these pleasures are much diminished by changes in his character or decay of his passive

sensibilities, or are outweighed by the pains which the pursuit of the purposes may bring upon him. All this I fully admit and have stated it elsewhere as positively and emphatically as anyone. Will, the active phenomenon, is a different thing from desire, the state of passive sensibility, and, though originally an offshoot from it, may in time take root and detach itself from the parent stock, so much so that in the case of a habitual purpose, instead of willing the thing because we desire it, we often desire it only because we will it. This, however, is but an instance of that familiar fact, the power of habit, and is nowise confined to the case of virtuous actions. Many indifferent things which men originally did from a motive of some sort they continue to do from habit. Sometimes this is done unconsciously, the consciousness coming only after the action; at other times with conscious volition, but volition which has become habitual and is put in operation by the force of habit, in opposition perhaps to the deliberate preference, as often happens with those who have contracted habits of vicious or hurtful indulgence. Third and last comes the case in which the habitual act of will in the individual instance is not in contradiction to the general intention prevailing at other times, but in fulfillment of it, as in the case of the person of confirmed virtue and of all who pursue deliberately and consistently any determinate end. The distinction between will and desire thus understood is an authentic and highly important psychological fact; but the fact consists solely in this—that will, like all other parts of our constitution, is amenable to habit, and that we may will from habit what we no longer desire for itself, or desire only because we will it. It is not the less true that will, in the beginning, is entirely produced by desire, including in that term the repelling influence of pain as well as the attractive one of pleasure. Let us take into consideration no longer the person who has a confirmed will to do right, but him in whom that virtuous will is still feeble, conquerable by temptation, and not to be fully relied on; by what means can it be strengthened? How can the will to be virtuous, where it does not exist in sufficient force, be implanted or awakened? Only by making the person *desire* virtue—by making him think of it in a pleasurable light, or of its absence in a painful one. It is by associating the doing right with pleasure, or the wrong with pain, or by eliciting and impressing and bringing home to the person's experience the pleasure naturally involved in the one or the pain in the other, that it is possible to call forth that will to be virtuous which, when confirmed, acts without any thought of either pleasure or pain. Will is the child of desire, and passes out of the dominion of its parent only to come under that of habit. That which is the result of habit affords no presumption of being intrinsically good; and there would be no reason for wishing that the purpose of virtue should become independent of pleasure and pain were it not that the influence of the pleasurable and painful associations which prompt to virtue is not sufficiently to be depended on for unerring constancy of action until it has acquired the support of habit. Both in feeling and in conduct, habit is the only thing which imparts certainty; and it is because of the importance to others of being able to rely absolutely on one's feelings and conduct, and to oneself of being able to rely on one's own, that the will to do right ought to be cultivated into this habitual independence. In other words, this state of the will is a means to good, not intrinsically a good; and does not contradict the doctrine that nothing is a good to human beings but in so far as it is either itself pleasurable or a means of attaining pleasure or averting pain.

But if this doctrine be true, the principle of utility is proved. Whether it is so or not must now be left to the consideration of the thoughtful reader.

CHAPTER V

On the Connection Between Justice and Utility

In all ages of speculation one of the strongest obstacles to the reception of the doctrine that utility or happiness is the criteria of right and wrong has been drawn from the idea of justice. The powerful sentiment and apparently clear perception which that word recalls with a rapidity and certainty resembling an instinct have seemed to the majority of thinkers to point to an inherent quality in things; to

show that the just must have an existence in nature as something absolute, generically distinct from every variety of the expedient and, in idea, opposed to it, though (as is commonly acknowledged) never, in the long run, disjoined from it in fact.

In the case of this, as of our other moral sentiments, there is no necessary connection between the question of its origin and that of its binding force. That a feeling is bestowed on us by nature does not necessarily legitimate all its promptings. The feeling of justice might be a peculiar instinct, and might yet require, like our other instincts, to be controlled and enlightened by a higher reason. If we have intellectual instincts leading us to judge in a particular way, as well as animal instincts that prompt us to act in a particular way, there is no necessity that the former should be more infallible in their sphere than the latter in theirs; it may as well happen that wrong judgments are occasionally suggested by those, as wrong actions by these. But though it is one thing to believe that we have natural feelings of justice, and another to acknowledge them as an ultimate criterion of conduct, these two opinions are very closely connected in point of fact. Mankind are always predisposed to believe that any subjective feeling, not otherwise accounted for, is a revelation of some objective reality. Our present object is to determine whether the reality to which the feeling of justice corresponds is one which needs any such special revelation, whether the justice or injustice of an action is a thing intrinsically peculiar and distinct from all its other qualities or only a combination of certain of those qualities presented under a peculiar aspect. For the purpose of this inquiry it is practically important to consider whether the feeling itself, of justice and injustice, is *sui generis* like our sensations of color and taste or a derivative feeling formed by a combination of others. And this it is the more essential to examine, as people are in general willing enough to allow that objectively the dictates of justice coincide with a part of the field of general expediency; but inasmuch as the subjective mental feeling of justice is different from that which commonly attaches to simple expediency, and, except in the extreme cases of the latter, is far more imperative in its demands, people find it difficult to see in justice only a particular kind or branch of general utility, and think that its superior binding force requires a totally different origin.

To throw light upon this question, it is necessary to attempt to ascertain what is the distinguishing character of justice, or of injustice; what is the quality, or whether there is any quality, attributed in common to all modes of conduct designated as unjust (for justice, like many other moral attributes, is best defined by its opposite), and distinguishing them from such modes of conduct as are disapproved, but without having that particular epithet of disapprobation applied to them. If in everything which men are accustomed to characterize as just or unjust some one common attribute or collection of attributes is always present, we may judge whether this particular attribute or combination of attributes would be capable of gathering round it a sentiment of that peculiar character and intensity by virtue of the general laws of our emotional constitution, or whether the sentiment is inexplicable and requires to be regarded as a special provision of nature. If we find the former to be the case, we shall, in resolving this question, have resolved also the main problem; if the latter, we shall have to seek for some other mode of investigating it.

To find the common attributes of a variety of objects, it is necessary to begin by surveying the objects themselves in the concrete. Let us therefore advert successively to the various modes of action and arrangements of human affairs which are classed, by universal or widely spread opinion, as just or as unjust. The things well known to excite the sentiments associated with those names are of a very multifarious character. I shall pass them rapidly in review, without studying any particular arrangement.

In the first place, it is mostly considered unjust to deprive anyone of his personal liberty, his property, or any other thing which belongs to him by law. Here, therefore, is one instance of the application of the terms "just" and "unjust" in a perfectly definite sense, namely, that it is just to respect, unjust to violate, the *legal rights* of anyone. But this judgment admits of several exceptions, arising from the other forms in which the notions of justice and injustice present themselves. For example, the person who suffers the deprivation may (as the phrase is) have *forfeited* the rights which he is so deprived of—a case to which we shall return presently. But also—

Secondly, the legal rights of which he is deprived may be rights which *ought* not to have belonged to him; in other words, the law which confers on him these rights may be a bad law. When it is so or when (which is the same thing for our purpose) it is supposed to be so, opinions will differ as to the justice or injustice of infringing it. Some maintain that no law, however bad, ought to be disobeyed by an individual citizen; that his opposition to it, if shown at all, should only be shown in endeavoring to get it altered by competent authority. This opinion (which condemns many of the most illustrious benefactors of mankind, and would often protect pernicious institutions against the only weapons which, in the state of things existing at the time, have any chance of succeeding against them) is defended by those who hold it on grounds of expediency, principally on that of the importance to the common interest of mankind, of maintaining inviolate the sentiment of submission to law. Other persons, again, hold the directly contrary opinion that any law, judged to be bad, may blamelessly be disobeyed, even though it be not judged to be unjust but only inexpedient, while others would confine the license of disobedience to the case of unjust laws; but, again, some say that all laws which are inexpedient are unjust, since every law imposes some restriction on the natural liberty of mankind, which restriction is an injustice unless legitimated by tending to their good. Among these diversities of opinion it seems to be universally admitted that there may he unjust laws, and that law, consequently, is not the ultimate criterion of justice, but may give to one person a benefit, or impose on another an evil, which justice condemns. When, however, a law is thought to be unjust, it seems always to be regarded as being so in the same way in which a breach of law is unjust, namely, by infringing somebody's right, which, as it cannot in this case he a legal right, receives a different appellation and is called a moral right. We may say, therefore, that a second case of injustice consists in taking or withholding from any person that to which he has a *moral right*.

Thirdly, it is universally considered just that each person should obtain that (whether good or evil) which he *deserves,* and unjust that he should obtain a good or be made to undergo an evil which he does not deserve. This is, perhaps, the clearest and most emphatic form in which the idea of justice is conceived by the general mind. As it involves the notion of desert, the question arises what constitutes desert? Speaking in a general way, a person is understood to deserve good if he does right, evil if he does wrong; and in a more particular sense, to deserve good from those to whom he does or has done good, and evil from those to whom he does or has done evil. The precept of returning good for evil has never been regarded as a case of the fulfillment of justice, but as one in which the claims of justice are waived, in obedience to other considerations.

Fourthly, it is confessedly unjust to *break faith* with anyone: to violate an engagement, either express or implied, or disappoint expectations raised by our own conduct, at least if we have raised those expectations knowingly and voluntarily. Like the other obligations of justice already spoken of, this one is not regarded as absolute, but as capable of being overruled by a stronger obligation of justice on the other side, or by such conduct on the part of the person concerned as is deemed to absolve us from our obligation to him and to constitute a *forfeiture* of the benefit which he has been led to expect.

Fifthly, it is, by universal admission, inconsistent with justice to be *partial*—to show favor or preference to one person over another in matters to which favor and preference do not properly apply. Impartiality, however, does not seem to be regarded as a duty in itself, but rather as instrumental to some other duly; for it is admitted that favor and preference are not always censurable, and, indeed, the cases in which they are condemned are rather the exception than the rule. A person would be more likely to be blamed than applauded for giving his family or friends no superiority in good offices over strangers when he could do so without violating any other duty; and no one thinks it unjust to seek one person in preference to another as a friend, connection, or companion. Impartiality where rights are concerned is of course obligatory, but this is involved in the more general obligation of giving to everyone his right. A tribunal, for example, must be impartial because it is bound to award, without regard to any other consideration, a disputed object to the one of two parties who has the right to it. There are other cases in which impartiality means being solely influenced by desert, as with those who, in the capacity of judges, preceptors, or parents, administer reward and punishment as such. There are cases, again, in which it means being solely influenced by consideration for the public interest, as in making a selection among candidates for a government employment. Impartiality, in short, as an obligation of justice, may be said to mean being exclusively influenced by the considerations which it is supposed ought to influence the particular case in hand, and resisting solicitation of any motives which prompt to conduct different from what those considerations would dictate.

Nearly allied to the idea of impartiality is that of *equality,* which often enters as a component part both into the conception of justice and into the practice of it, and, in the eyes of many persons, constitutes its essence. But in this, still more than in any other case, the notion of justice varies in different persons, and always conforms in its variations to their notion of utility. Each person maintains that equality is the dictate of justice, except where he thinks that expediency requires inequality. The justice of giving equal protection to the rights of all is maintained by those who support the most outrageous inequality in the rights themselves. Even in slave countries it is theoretically admitted that the rights of the slave, such as they are, ought to be as sacred as those of the master, and that a tribunal which fails to enforce them with equal strictness is wanting in justice; while, at the same time, institutions which leave to the slave scarcely any rights to enforce are not deemed unjust because they are not deemed inexpedient. Those who think that utility requires distinctions of rank do not consider it unjust that riches and social privileges should be unequally dispensed; but those who think this inequality inexpedient think it unjust also. Whoever thinks that government is necessary sees no injustice in as much inequality as is constituted by giving to the magistrate powers not granted to other people. Even among those who hold leveling doctrines, there are differences of opinion about expediency. Some communists consider it unjust that the produce of the labor of the community should be shared on any other principle than that of exact equality; others think it just that those should receive most whose wants are greatest; while others hold that those who work harder, or who produce more, or whose services are more valuable to the community, may justly claim a larger quota in the division of the produce. And the sense of natural justice may be plausibly appealed to in behalf of every one of these opinions.

Among so many diverse applications of the term "justice," which yet is not regarded as ambiguous, it is a matter of some difficulty to seize the mental link which holds them together, and on which the moral sentiment adhering to the term essentially depends. Perhaps, in this embarrassment, some help may be derived from the history of the word, as indicated by its etymology.

In most if not in all languages, the etymology of the word which corresponds to "just" points distinctly to an origin connected with the ordinances of law. *Justum* is a form of *jussum,* that which has been ordered. *Dikaion* comes directly from *dike,* a suit at law. *Recht,* from which came *right* and *righteous,* is synonymous with law. The courts of justice, the administration of justice, are the courts and the administration of law. *La justice,* in French, is the established term for judicature. I am not committing the fallacy, imputed with some show of truth to Horne Tooke, of assuming that a word must still continue to mean what it originally meant. Etymology is slight evidence of what the idea now signified is, but the very best evidence of how it sprang up. There can, I think, be no doubt that the *idée mère,* the primitive element, in the formation of the notion of justice was conformity to law. It constituted the entire idea among the Hebrews, up to the birth of Christianity; as might be expected in the case of a people whose laws attempted to embrace all subjects on which precepts were required, and who believed those laws to be a direct emanation from the Supreme Being. But other nations, and in particular the Greeks and Romans, who knew that their laws had been made originally, and still continued to be made, by men,

were not afraid to admit that those men might make bad laws; might do, by law, the same things, and from the same motives, which if done by individuals without the sanction of law would be called unjust. And hence the sentiment of injustice came to be attached, not to all violations of law, but only to violations of such laws as *ought* to exist, including such as ought to exist but do not, and to laws themselves if supposed to be contrary to what ought to be law. In this manner the idea of law and of its injunctions was still predominant in the notion of justice, even when the laws actually in force ceased to be accepted as the standard of it.

It is true that mankind consider the idea of justice and its obligations as applicable to many things which neither are, nor is it desired that they should be, regulated by law. Nobody desires that laws should interfere with the whole detail of private life; yet everyone allows that in all daily conduct a person may and does show himself to be either just or unjust. But even here, the idea of the breach of what ought to be law still lingers in a modified shape. It would always give us pleasure, and chime in with our feelings of fitness, that acts which we deem unjust should be punished, though we do not always think it expedient that this should be done by the tribunals. We forego that gratification on account of incidental inconveniences. We should be glad to see just conduct enforced and injustice repressed, even in the minutest details, if we were not, with reason, afraid of trusting the magistrate with so unlimited an amount of power over individuals. When we think that a person is bound in justice to do a thing, it is an ordinary form of language to say that he ought to be compelled to do it. We should be gratified to see the obligation enforced by anybody who had the power. If we see that its enforcement by law would be inexpedient, we lament the impossibility, we consider the impunity given to injustice as an evil, and strive to make amends for it by bringing a strong expression of our own and the public disapprobation to bear upon the offender. Thus the idea of legal constraint is still the generating idea of the notion of justice, though undergoing several transformations before that notion as it exists in an advanced state of society becomes complete.

The above is, I think, a true account, as far as it goes, of the origin and progressive growth of the idea of justice. But we must observe that it contains as yet nothing to distinguish that obligation from moral obligation in general. For the truth is that the idea of penal sanction, which is the essence of law, enters not only into the conception of injustice, but into that of any kind of wrong. We do not call anything wrong unless we mean to imply that a person ought to be punished in some way or other for doing it—if not by law, by the opinion of his fellow creatures; if not by opinion, by the reproaches of his own conscience. This seems the real turning point of the distinction between morality and simple expediency. It is a part of the notion of duty in every one of its forms that a person may rightfully be compelled to fulfill it. Duty is a thing which may be *exacted* from a person, as one exacts a debt. Unless we think that it may be exacted from him, we do not call it his duty. Reasons of prudence, or the interest of other people, may militate against actually exacting it, but the person himself, it is clearly understood, would not be entitled to complain. There are other things, on the contrary, which we wish that people should do, which we like or admire them for doing, perhaps dislike or despise them for not doing, but yet admit that they are not bound to do; it is not a case of moral obligation; we do not blame them, that is, we do not think that they are proper objects of punishment. How we come by these ideas of deserving and not deserving punishment will appear, perhaps, in the sequel; but I think there is no doubt that this distinction lies at the bottom of the notions of right and wrong; that we call any conduct wrong, or employ, instead, some other term of dislike or disparagement, according as we think that the person ought, or ought not, to be punished for it; and we say it would be right to do so and so, or merely that it would be desirable or laudable, according as we would wish to see the person whom it concerns compelled, or only persuaded and exhorted, to act in that manner.[3]

This, therefore, being the characteristic difference which marks off, not justice, but morality in general from the remaining provinces of expediency and worthiness, the character is still to be sought which distinguishes justice from other branches of morality. Now it is known that ethical writers divide moral duties into two classes, denoted by the ill-chosen expressions, duties of perfect and of imperfect obligation; the latter being those in which, though the act is obligatory, the particular occasions of performing it are left to our choice, as in the case of charity or beneficence, which we are indeed bound to practice but not toward any definite person, nor at any prescribed time. In the more precise language of philosophic jurists, duties of perfect obligation are those duties in virtue of which a correlative *right* resides in some person or persons; duties of imperfect obligation are those moral obligations which do not give birth to any right. I think it will be found that this distinction exactly coincides with that which exists between justice and the other obligations of morality. In our survey of the various popular acceptations of justice, the term appeared generally to involve the idea of a personal right—a claim on the part of one or more individuals, like that which the law gives when it confers a proprietary or other legal right. Whether the injustice consists in depriving a person of a possession, or in breaking faith with him, or in treating him worse than he deserves, or worse than other people who have no greater claims—in each case the supposition implies two things: a wrong done, and some assignable person who is wronged. Injustice may also be done by treating a person better than others; but the wrong in this case is to his competitors, who are also assignable persons. It seems to me that this feature in the case—a right in some person, correlative to the moral obligation—constitutes the specific difference between justice and generosity of beneficence. Justice implies something which it is not only right to do, and wrong not to do, but which some individual person can claim from us as his moral right. No one has a moral right to our generosity or beneficence because we are not morally bound to practice those virtues toward any given individual. And it will be found with respect to this as to every correct definition that the instances which seem to conflict with it are those which most confirm it. For if a moralist attempts, as some have done, to make out that mankind generally, though not any given individual, have a right to all the good we can do them, he at once, by that thesis, includes generosity and beneficence within the category of justice. He is obliged to say that our utmost exertions are *due* to our fellow creatures, thus assimilating them to a debt; or that nothing less can be a sufficient *return* for what society does for us, thus classing the case as one of gratitude; both of which are acknowledged cases of justice, and not of the virtue of beneficence; and whoever does not place the distinction between justice and morality in general, where we have now placed it, will be found to make no distinction between them at all, but to merge all morality in justice.

Having thus endeavored to determine the distinctive elements which enter into the composition of the idea of justice, we are ready to enter on the inquiry whether the feeling which accompanies the idea is attached to it by a special dispensation of nature, or whether it could have grown up, by any known laws, out of the idea itself; and, in particular, whether it can have originated in considerations of general expediency.

I conceive that the sentiment itself does not arise from anything which would commonly or correctly be termed an idea of expediency, but that, though the sentiment does not, whatever is moral in it does.

We have seen that the two essential ingredients in the sentiment of justice are the desire to punish a person who has done harm and the knowledge or belief that there is some definite individual or individuals to whom harm has been done.

Now it appears to me that the desire to punish a person who has done harm to some individual is a spontaneous outgrowth from two sentiments, both in the highest degree natural and which either are or resemble instincts: the impulse of self-defense and the feeling of sympathy.

It is natural to resent and to repel or retaliate any harm done or attempted against ourselves or against those with whom we sympathize. The origin of this sentiment it is not necessary here to discuss. Whether it be an instinct or a result of intelligence, it is, we know, common to all animal nature; for every animal tries to hurt those who have hurt, or who it thinks are about to hurt, itself or its young. Human beings, on this point, only differ from other animals in two particulars. First, in being capable of sympathizing, not solely with their offspring, or, like some of the more noble animals, with some superior animal who is kind to them, but with all human, and even with all sentient, beings; secondly, in having a more developed intelligence, which gives a wider range to the whole of their sentiments, whether self-regarding or sympathetic. By virtue of his superior intelligence, even apart from his superior range of sympathy, a human being is capable of apprehending a community of interest between himself and the human society of which he forms a part, such that any conduct which threatens the security of the society generally is threatening to his own, and calls forth his instinct (if instinct it be) of self-defense. The same superiority of intelligence, joined to the power of sympathizing with human beings generally, enables him to attach himself to the collective idea of his tribe, his country, or mankind in such a manner that any act hurtful to them raises his instinct of sympathy and urges him to resistance.

The sentiment of justice, in that one of its elements which consists of the desire to punish, is thus. I conceive, the natural feeling of retaliation or vengeance, rendered by intellect and sympathy applicable to those injuries, that is, to those hurts, which wound us through, or in common with, society at large. This sentiment, in itself, has nothing moral in it; what is moral is the exclusive subordination of it to the social sympathies, so as to wait on and obey their call. For the natural feeling would make us resent indiscriminately whatever anyone does that is disagreeable to us; but, when moralized by the social feeling, it only acts in the directions conformable to the general good: just persons resenting a hurt to society, though not otherwise a hurt to themselves, and not resenting a hurt to themselves, however painful, unless it be of the kind which society has a common interest with them in the repression of.

It is no objection against this doctrine to say that, when we feel our sentiment of justice outraged, we are not thinking of society at large or of any collective interest, but only of the individual case. It is common enough, certainly, though the reverse of commendable, to feel resentment merely because we have suffered pain; but a person whose resentment is really a moral feeling, that is, who considers whether an act is blamable before he allows himself to resent it—such a person, though he may not say expressly to himself that he is standing up for the interest of society, certainly does feel that he is asserting a rule which is for the benefit of others as well as for his own. If he is not feeling this, if he is regarding the act solely as it affects him individually, he is not consciously just; he is not concerning himself about the justice of his actions. This is admitted even by anti-utilitarian moralists. When Kant (as before remarked) propounds as the fundamental principle of morals, "So act that thy rule of conduct might be adopted as a law by all rational beings," he virtually acknowledges that the interest of mankind collectively, or at least of mankind indiscriminately, must be in the mind of the agent when conscientiously deciding on the morality of the act. Otherwise he uses words without a meaning; for that a rule even of utter selfishness could not *possibly* be adopted by all rational beings—that there is any insuperable obstacle in the nature of things to its adoption—cannot be even plausibly maintained. To give any meaning to Kant's principle, the sense put upon it must be that we ought to shape our conduct by a rule which all rational beings might adopt *with benefit to their collective interest.*

To recapitulate: the idea of justice supposes two things—a rule of conduct and a sentiment which sanctions the rule. The first must be supposed common to all mankind and intended for their good. The other (the sentiment) is a desire that punishment may be suffered by those who infringe the rule. There is involved, in addition, the conception of some definite person who suffers by the infringement, whose rights (to use the expression appropriated to the case) are violated by it. And the sentiment of justice appears to me to be the animal desire to repel or retaliate a hurt or damage to oneself or to those with whom one sympathizes, widened so as to include all persons, by the human capacity of enlarged sympathy and the human conception of intelligent self-interest. From the latter elements the feeling derives its morality; from the former, its peculiar impressiveness and energy of self-assertion.

I have, throughout, treated the idea of a *right* residing in the injured person and violated by the injury, not as a separate element in the composition of the idea and sentiment, but as one of the forms in which the other two elements clothe themselves. These elements are a hurt to some assignable person or persons, on the one hand, and a demand for punishment, on the other. An examination of our own minds, I think, will show that these two things include all that we mean when we speak of violation of a right. When we call anything a person's right, we mean that he has a valid claim on society to protect him in the possession of it, either by the force of law or by that of education and opinion. If he has what we consider a sufficient claim, on whatever account, to have something guaranteed to him by society, we say that he has a right to it. If we desire to prove that anything does not belong to him by right, we think this done as soon as it is admitted that society ought not to take measure for securing it to him, but should leave him to chance or to his own exertions. Thus a person is said to have a right to what he can earn in fair professional competition, because society ought not to allow any other person to hinder him from endeavoring to earn in that manner as much as he can. But he has not a right to three hundred a year, though he may happen to be earning it; because society is not called on to provide that he shall earn that sum. On the contrary, if he owns ten thousand pounds three-percent stock, he *has* a right to three hundred a year because society has come under an obligation to provide him with an income of that amount.

To have a right, then, is, I conceive, to have something which society ought to defend me in the possession of. If the objector goes on to ask why it ought, I can give him no other reason than general utility. If that expression does not seem to convey a sufficient feeling of the strength of the obligation, nor to account for the peculiar energy of the feeling, it is because there goes to the composition of the sentiment, not a rational only but also an animal element—the thirst for retaliation; and this thirst derives its intensity, as well as its moral justification, from the extraordinarily important and impressive kind of utility which is concerned. The interest involved is that of security, to everyone's feelings the most vital of all interests. All other earthly benefits are needed by one person, not needed by another; and many of them can, if necessary, be cheerfully foregone or replaced by something else; but security no human being can possibly do without; on it we depend for all our immunity from evil and for the whole value of all and every good, beyond the passing moment, since nothing but the gratification of the instant could be of any worth to us if we could be deprived of everything the next instant by whoever was momentarily stronger than ourselves. Now this most indispensable of all necessaries, after physical nutriment, cannot be had unless the machinery for providing it is kept unintermittedly in active play. Our notion, therefore, of the claim we have on our fellow creatures to join in making safe for us the very groundwork of our existence gathers feelings around it so much more intense than those concerned in any of the more common cases of utility that the difference in degree (as is often the case in psychology) becomes a real difference in kind. The claim assumes that character of absoluteness, that apparent infinity and incommensurability with all other considerations which constitute the distinction between the feeling of right and wrong and that of ordinary expediency and inexpediency. The feelings concerned are so powerful, and we count so positively on finding a responsive feeling in others (all being alike interested) that *ought* and *should* grow into *must,* and recognized indispensability becomes a moral necessity, analogous to physical, and often not inferior to it in binding force.

If the preceding analysis, or something resembling it, be not the correct account of the notion of justice—if justice be totally independent of utility, and be a standard *per se,* which the mind can recognize by simple introspection of itself—it is hard to understand why that internal oracle is so ambiguous, and why so many things appear either just or unjust, according to the light in which they are regarded.

We are continually informed that utility is an uncertain standard, which every different person interprets differently, and that there is no safety but in the immutable, ineffaceable, and unmistakable dictates of justice, which carry their evidence in themselves and are independent of the fluctuations of opinion. One would suppose from this that on questions of justice there could be no controversy; that, if we take that for our rule, its application to any given case could leave us in as little doubt as a mathematical demonstration. So far is this from being the fact that there is as much difference of opinion, and as much discussion, about what is just as about what is useful to society. Not only have different nations and individuals different notions of justice, but in the mind of one and the same individual, justice is not some one rule, principle, or maxim, but many which do not always coincide in their dictates, and, in choosing between which, he is guided either by some extraneous standard or by his own personal predilections.

For instance, there are some who say that it is unjust to punish anyone for the sake of example to others, that punishment is just only when intended for the good of the sufferer himself. Others maintain the extreme reverse, contending that to punish persons who have attained years of discretion, for their own benefit, is despotism and injustice, since, if the matter at issue is solely their own good, no one has a right to control their own judgment of it; but that they may justly be punished to prevent evil to others, this being the exercise of the legitimate right of self-defense, Mr. Owen, again, affirms that it is unjust to punish at all, for the criminal did not make his own character; his education and the circumstances which surrounded him have made him a criminal, and for these he is not responsible. All these opinions are extremely plausible; and so long as the question is argued as one of justice simply, without going down to the principles which lie under justice and are the source of its authority, I am unable to see how any of these reasoners can be refuted. For in truth every one of the three builds upon rules of justice confessedly true. The first appeals to the acknowledged injustice of singling out an individual and making him a sacrifice, without his consent, for other people's benefit. The second relies on the acknowledged justice of self-defense and the admitted injustice of forcing one person to conform to another's notions of what constitutes his good. The Owenite invokes the admitted principle that it is unjust to punish anyone for what he cannot help. Each is triumphant so long as he is not compelled to take into consideration any other maxims of justice than the one he has selected; but as soon as their several maxims are brought face to face, each disputant seems to have exactly as much to say for himself as the others. No one of them can carry out his own notion of justice without trampling upon another equally binding. These are difficulties; they have always been felt to be such; and many devices have been invented to turn rather than to overcome them. As a refuge from the last of the three, men imagined what they called the freedom of the will—fancying that they could not justify punishing a man whose will is in a thoroughly hateful state unless it be supposed to have come into that state through no influence of anterior circumstances. To escape from the other difficulties, a favorite contrivance has been the fiction of a contract whereby at some unknown period all the members of society engaged to obey the laws and consented to be punished for any disobedience to them, thereby giving to their legislators the right, which it is assumed they would not otherwise have had, of punishing them, either for their own good or for that of society. This happy thought was considered to get rid of the whole difficulty and to legitimate the infliction of punishment, in virtue of another received maxim of justice, *volenti non fit injuria*—that is not unjust which is done with the consent of the person who is supposed to be hurl by it. I need hardly remark that, even if the consent were not a mere fiction, this maxim is not superior in authority to the others which it is brought in to supersede. It is, on the contrary, an instructive specimen of the loose and irregular manner in which supposed principles of justice grow up. This particular one evidently came into use as a help to the coarse exigencies of courts of law, which are sometimes obliged to be content with very uncertain presumptions, on account of the greater evils which would often arise from any attempt on their part to cut finer. But even courts of law are not able to adhere consistently to the maxim, for they allow voluntary engagements to be set aside on the ground of fraud, and sometimes on that of mere mistake or misinformation.

Again, when the legitimacy of inflicting punishment is admitted, how many conflicting conceptions of justice come to light in discussing the proper apportionment of punishments to offenses, No rule on the subject recommends itself so strongly to the primitive and spontaneous sentiment of justice as the *lex talionis,* an eye for an eye and a tooth for a tooth. Though this principle of the Jewish and of the Mohammedan law has been generally abandoned in Europe as a practical maxim, there is, I suspect, in most minds, a secret hankering after it; and when retribution accidentally falls on an offender in that precise shape, the general feeling of satisfaction evinced bears witness how natural is the sentiment to which this repayment in kind is acceptable. With many, the test of justice in penal infliction is that the punishment should be proportioned to the offense, meaning that it should be exactly measured by the moral guilt of the culprit (whatever be their standard for measuring moral guilt), the consideration what amount of punishment is necessary to deter from the offense having nothing to do with the question of justice, in their estimation; while there are others to whom that consideration is all in all, who maintain that it is not just, at least for man, to inflict on a fellow creature, whatever may be his offenses, any amount of suffering beyond the least that will suffice to prevent him from repeating, and others from imitating, his misconduct.

To take another example from a subject already once referred to. In co-operative industrial association, is it just or not that talent or skill should give a title to superior remuneration? On the negative side of the question it is argued that whoever does the best he can deserves equally well, and ought not in justice to be put in a position of inferiority for no fault of his own: that superior abilities have already advantages more than enough, in the admiration they excite, the personal influence they command, and the internal sources of satisfaction attending them, without adding to these a superior share of the world's goods; and that society is bound in justice rather to make compensation to the less favored for this unmerited inequality of advantages than to aggravate it. On the contrary side it is contended that society receives more from the more efficient laborer;

that, his services being more useful, society owes him a larger return for them; that a greater share of the joint result is actually his work, and not to allow his claim to it is a kind of robbery; that, if he is only to receive as much as others, he can only be justly required to produce as much, and to give a smaller amount of time and exertion, proportioned to his superior efficiency. Who shall decide between these appeals to conflicting principles of justice? Justice has in this case two sides to it, which it is impossible to bring into harmony, and the two disputants have chosen opposite sides; the one looks to what it is just that the individual should receive, the other to what it is just that the community should give. Each, from his own point of view, is unanswerable; and any choice between them, on grounds of justice, must be perfectly arbitrary. Social utility alone can decide the preference.

How many, again, and how irreconcilable are the standards of justice to which reference is made in discussing the repartition of taxation. One opinion is that payment to the state should be in numerical proportion to pecuniary means. Others think that justice dictates what they term graduated taxation—taking a higher percentage from those who have more to spare. In point of natural justice a strong case might be made for disregarding means altogether, and taking the same absolute sum (whenever it could be got) from everyone; as the subscribers to a mess or to a club all pay the same sum for the same privileges, whether they can all equally afford it or not. Since the protection (it might be said) of law and government is afforded to and is equally required by all, there is no injustice in making all buy it at the same price. It is reckoned justice, not injustice, that a dealer should charge to all customers the same price for the same article, not a price varying according to their means of payment. This doctrine, as applied to taxation, finds no advocates because it conflicts so strongly with man's feelings of humanity and of social expediency, but the principle of justice which it invokes is as true and as binding to those which can be appealed to against it. Accordingly it exerts a tacit influence on the line of defense employed for other modes of assessing taxation. People feel obliged to argue that the state does more

for the rich man than for the poor, as a justification for its taking more from them, though this is in reality not true, for the rich would be far better able to protect themselves, in the absence of law or government, than the poor, and indeed would probably be successful in converting the poor into their slaves. Others, again, so far defer to the same conception of justice as to maintain that all should pay an equal capitation tax for the protection of their persons (these being of equal value to all), and an unequal tax for the protection of their property, which is unequal. To this others reply that the all of one man is as valuable to him as the all of another. From these confusions there is no other mode of extrication than the utilitarian.

Is, then, the difference between the just and the expedient a merely imaginary distinction? Have mankind been under a delusion in thinking that justice is a more sacred thing than policy, and that the latter ought only to be listened to after the former has been satisfied? By no means. The exposition we have given of the nature and origin of the sentiment recognizes a real distinction; and no one of those who profess the most sublime contempt for the consequences of actions as an element in their morality attaches more importance to the distinction than I do. While I dispute the pretensions of any theory which sets up an imaginary standard of justice not grounded on utility, I account the justice which is grounded on utility to be the chief part, and incomparably the most sacred and binding part, of all morality. Justice is a name for certain classes of moral rules which concern the essentials of human well-being more nearly, and are therefore of more absolute obligation, than any other rules for the guidance of life; and the notion which we have found to be of the essence of the idea of justice—that of a right residing in an individual—implies and testifies to this more binding obligation.

The moral rules which forbid mankind to hurt one another (in which we must never forget to include a wrongful interference with each other's freedom) are more vital to human well-being than any maxims, however important, which only point out the best mode of managing some department of human affairs. They have also the peculiarity that they are the main element in determining the whole of the social feelings of mankind. It is their observance which alone preserves peace among human beings; if obedience to them were not the rule, and disobedience the exception, everyone would see in everyone else an enemy against whom he must be perpetually guarding himself. What is hardly less important, these are the precepts which mankind have the strongest and the most direct inducements for impressing upon one another. By merely giving to each other prudential instruction or exhortation, they may gain, or think they gain, nothing; in inculcating on each other the duty of positive beneficence, they have an unmistakable interest, but far less in degree; a person may possibly not need the benefits of others, but he always needs that they should not do him hurt. Thus the moralities which protect every individual from being harmed by others, either directly or by being hindered in his freedom of pursuing his own good, are at once those which he himself has most at heart and those which he has the strongest interest in publishing and enforcing by word and deed. It is by a person's observance of these that his fitness to exist as one of the fellowship of human beings is tested and decided; for on that depends his being a nuisance or not to those with whom he is in contact. Now it is these moralities primarily which compose the obligations of justice. The most marked cases of injustice, and those which give the tone to the feeling of repugnance which characterizes the sentiment, are acts of wrongful aggression or wrongful exercise of power over someone; the next are those which consist in wrongfully withholding from him something which is his due—in both cases inflicting on him a positive hurt, either in the form of direct suffering or of the privation of some good which he had reasonable ground, either of a physical or of a social kind, for counting upon.

The same powerful motives which command the observance of these primary moralities enjoin the punishment of those who violate them; and as the impulses of self-defense, of defense of others, and of vengeance are all called forth against such persons, retribution, or evil for evil, becomes closely connected with the sentiment of justice, and is universally included in the idea. Good for good is also one of the dictates of justice; and this, though its social utility is evident, and though it carries with it a natural human feeling, has not at first sight that obvious connection with hurt or injury which, existing in the most elementary cases of just and unjust, is the source of the characteristic intensity of the sentiment. But the connection, though less obvious, is not less real. He who accepts benefits and denies a return of them when needed inflicts a real hurt by disappointing one of the most natural and reasonable of expectations, and one which he must at least tacitly have encouraged, otherwise the benefits would seldom have been conferred. The important rank, among human evils and wrongs, of the disappointment of expectation is shown in the fact that it constitutes the principal criminality of two such highly immoral acts as a breach of friendship and a breach of promise. Few hurts which human beings can sustain are greater, and none wound more, than when that on which they habitually and with full assurance relied fails them in the hour of need; and few wrongs are greater than this mere withholding of good; none excite more resentment, either in the person suffering or in a sympathizing spectator. The principle, therefore, of giving to each what they deserve, that is, good for good as well as evil for evil, is not only included within the idea of justice as we have defined it, but is a proper object of that intensity of sentiment which places the just human estimation above the simply expedient.

Most of the maxims of justice current in the world, and commonly appealed to in its transactions, are simply instrumental to carrying into effect the principles of justice which we have now spoken of. That a person is only responsible for what he has done voluntarily, or could voluntarily have avoided, that it is unjust to condemn any person unheard; that the punishment ought to be proportioned to the offense, and the like, are maxims intended to prevent the just principle of evil for evil from being perverted to the infliction of evil without that justification. The greater part of these common maxims have come into use from the practice of courts of justice, which have been naturally led to a more complete recognition and elaboration than was likely to suggest itself to others, of the rules necessary to enable them to fulfill their double function—of inflicting punishment when due, and of awarding to each person his right.

That first of judicial virtues, impartiality, is an obligation of justice, partly for the reason last mentioned, as being a necessary condition of the fulfillment of other obligations of justice. But this is not the only source of the exalted rank, among human obligations, of those maxims of equality and impartiality, which, both in popular estimation and in that of the most enlightened, are included among the precepts of justice. In one point of view, they may be considered as corollaries from the principles already laid down. If it is a duty to do to each according to his deserts, returning good for good, as well as repressing evil by evil, it necessarily follows that we should treat all equally well (when no higher duty forbids) who have deserved equally well of *us,* and that society should treat all equally well who have deserved equally well of *it,* that is, who have deserved equally well absolutely. This is the highest abstract standard of social and distributive justice, toward which all institutions and the efforts of all virtuous citizens should be made in the utmost possible degree to converge. But this great moral duty rests upon a still deeper foundation, being a direct emanation from the first principle of morals, and not a mere logical corollary from secondary or derivative doctrines. It is involved in the very meaning of utility, or the greatest happiness principle. That principle is a mere form of words without rational signification unless one person's happiness, supposed equal in degree (with the proper allowance made for kind), is counted for exactly as much as another's. Those conditions being supplied, Bentham's dictum "everybody to count for one, nobody for more than one," might be written under the principle of utility as an explanatory commentary.[4] The equal claim of everybody to happiness, in the estimation of the moralist and of the legislator, involves an equal claim to all the means of happiness except in so far as the inevitable conditions of human life and the general interest in which that of every individual is included set limits to the maxim; and those limits ought to be strictly construed. As every other maxim of justice, so this is by no means applied or held

applicable universally; on the contrary, as I have already remarked, it bends to every person's ideas of social expediency. But in whatever case it is deemed applicable at all, it is held to be the dictate of justice. All persons are deemed to have a *right* to equality of treatment, except when some recognized social expediency requires the reverse. And hence all social inequalities which have ceased to be considered expedient assume the character, not of simple inexpediency, but of injustice, and appear so tyrannical that people are apt to wonder how they ever could have been tolerated—forgetful that they themselves, perhaps, tolerate other inequalities under an equally mistaken notion of expediency, the correction of which would make that which they approve seem quite as monstrous as what they have at last learned to condemn. The entire history of social improvement has been a series of transitions by which one custom or institution after another, from being a supposed primary necessity of social existence, has passed into the rank of a universally stigmatized injustice and tyranny. So it has been with the distinctions of slaves and freemen, nobles and serfs, patricians and plebeians; and so it will be, and in part already is, with the aristocracies of color, race, and sex.

It appears from what has been said that justice is a name for certain moral requirements which, regarded collectively, stand higher in the scale of social utility, and are therefore of more paramount obligation, than any others, though particular cases may occur in which some other social duty is so important as to overrule any one of the general maxims of justice. Thus, to save a life, it may not only be allowable, but a duty, to steal or take by force the necessary food or medicine, or to kidnap and compel to officiate the only qualified medical practitioner. In such cases, as we do not call anything justice which is not a virtue, we usually say, not that justice must give way to some other moral principle, but that what is just in ordinary cases is, by reason of that other principle, not just in the particular case. By this useful accommodation of language, the character of indefeasibility attributed to justice is kept up, and we are saved from the necessity of maintaining that there can be laudable injustice.

The considerations which have not been adduced resolve, I conceive, the only real difficulty in the utilitarian theory of morals. It has always been evident that all cases of justice are also cases of expediency; the difference is in the peculiar sentiment which attaches to the former, as contradistinguished from the latter. If this characteristic sentiment has been sufficiently accounted for; if there is no necessity to assume for it any peculiarity of origin; if it is simply the natural feeling of resentment, moralized by being made co-extensive with the demands of social good; and if this feeling not only does but ought to exist in all the classes of cases to which the idea of justice corresponds—that idea no longer presents itself as a stumbling block to the utilitarian ethics. Justice remains the appropriate name for certain social utilities which are vastly more important, and therefore more absolute and imperative, than any others are as a class (though not more so than others may be in particular cases): and which, therefore, ought to be, as well as naturally are, guarded by a sentiment, not only different in degree, but also in kind; distinguished from the milder feeling which attaches to the mere idea of promoting human pleasure or convenience at once by the more definite nature of its commands and by the sterner character of its sanctions.

NOTES

1. The author of this essay has reason for believing himself to be the first person who brought the word "utilitarian" into use. He did not invent it, but adopted it from a passing expression in Mr. Galt's *Annals of the Parish*. After using it as a designation for several years, he and others abandoned it from a growing dislike to anything resembling a badge or watchword of sectarian distinction. But as a name for one single opinion, not a set of opinions—to denote the recognition of utility as a standard, not any particular way of applying it—the term supplies a want in the language, and offers, in many cases, a convenient mode of avoiding tiresome circumlocutions.

2. An opponent, whose intellectual and moral fairness it is a pleasure to acknowledge (the Rev. J. Llewellyn Davies), has objected to this passage, saying, "Surely the rightness or wrongness of saving a man from drowning does depend very much upon the motive with which it is done. Suppose that a tyrant, when his enemy jumped into the sea to escape from him, saved him from drowning simply in order that he might inflict upon him more exquisite tortures, would it tend to clearness to speak of that rescue as 'a morally right action'? Or suppose again, according to one of the stock illustrations of ethical inquiries, that a man betrayed a trust received from a friend, because the discharge of it would fatally injure that friend himself or someone belonging to him, would utilitarianism compel one to call the betrayal 'a crime' as much as if it had been done from the meanest motive?"

I submit that he who saves another from drowning in order to kill him by torture afterwards does not differ only in motive from him who does the same thing from duty or benevolence; the act itself is different. The rescue of the man is, in the case supposed, only the necessary first step of an act far more atrocious than leaving him to drown would have been. Had Mr. Davies said, "The rightness or wrongness of saving a man from drowning does depend very much"—not upon the motive, but—"upon the *intention*," no utilitarian would have differed from him. Mr. Davies, by an oversight too common not to be quite venial, has in this case confounded the very different ideas of Motive and Intention. There is no point which utilitarian thinkers (and Bentham preeminently) have taken more pains to illustrate than this. The morality of the action depends entirely upon the intention—that is, upon what the agent *wills to do.* But the motive, that is, the feeling which makes him will so to do, if it makes no difference in the act makes none in the morality: though it makes a great difference in our moral estimation of the agent, especially if it indicates a good or a bad habitual *disposition*—a bent of character from which useful, or from which hurtful actions are likely to arise.

[This note appeared in the second edition of *Utilitarianism* but not in subsequent ones.]

3. See this point enforced and illustrated by Professor Bain, in an admirable chapter (entitled "The Ethical Emotions, or the Moral Sense"), of the second of the two treatises composing his elaborate and profound work on the Mind.

4. This implication, in the first principle of the utilitarian scheme, of perfect impartiality between persons is regarded by Mr. Herbert Spencer (in his *Social Statics*) as a disproof of the pretensions of utility to be a sufficient guide to right; since (he says) the principle of

utility presupposes the anterior principle that everybody has an equal right to happiness. It may be more correctly described as supposing that equal amounts of happiness are equally desirable, whether felt by the same or different persons. This, however, is not a *pre*-supposition, not a premise needful to support the principle of utility, but the very principle itself; for what is the principle of utility if it be not that "happiness" and "desirable" are synonymous terms? If there is any anterior principle implied, it can be no other than this, that the truths of arithmetic are applicable to the valuation of happiness, as of all other measurable quantities.

(Mr. Herbert Spencer, in a private communication on the subject of the preceding note, objects to being considered an opponent of utilitarianism and states that he regards happiness as the ultimate end of morality; but deems that end only partially attainable by empirical generalizations from the observed results of conduct, and completely attainable only by deducing, from the laws of life and the conditions of existence, what kinds of action necessarily tend to produce happiness, and what kinds to produce unhappiness. With the exception of the word "necessarily," I have no dissent to express from this doctrine; and (omitting that word) I am not aware that any modern advocate of utilitarianism is of a different opinion. Bentham, certainly, to whom in the Social Statics Mr. Spencer particularly referred, is, least of all writers, chargeable with unwillingness to deduce the effect of actions on happiness from the laws of human nature and the universal conditions of human life. The common charge against him is of relying too exclusively upon such deductions and declining altogether to be bound by the generalizations from specific experience which Mr. Spencer thinks that utilitarians generally confine themselves to. My own opinion (and, as I collect, Mr. Spencer's) is that in ethics, as in all other branches of scientific study, the consilience of the results of both these processes, each corroborating and verifying the other, is requisite to give to any general proposition the kind and degree of evidence which constitutes scientific proof.)

STUDY QUESTIONS

1. Does utilitarianism judge actions by actual or expected consequences?
2. If people knowledgeable about poetry and video games prefer the latter, are they, therefore, more worthwhile?
3. Does Mill believe the principle of utilitarianism can be proven?
4. Does utilitarianism justify the actions of a professor who awards all students high grades in order to enhance happiness?

The Meaning and Proof of Utilitarianism

Henry Sidgwick

As Bentham was the originator of utilitarianism and Mill its popularizer, so Henry Sidgwick (1838–1900), Professor of Philosophy at the University of Cambridge, presented the doctrine in its most sophisticated form. Sidgwick identified three methods or systems of ethics: egoism, common sense (also known as intuitionism), and utilitarianism. He believes that utilitarianism can be reconciled with common sense though perhaps not with egoism. Yet even if we accept the utilitarian doctrine that the right act is that which will produce the greatest amount of happiness for all affected parties, we still face a number of challenging issues. First, does "greatest amount of happiness" mean the greatest total happiness or the greatest average happiness, in other words, the total divided by the number of persons? Second, does "all affected parties" apply to future persons, whose very existence might be affected by our decisions? Third, should utilitarians make their views publicly known, or does the theory demand secrecy? In short, Sidgwick was a utilitarian, notable for bringing to the fore and analyzing with care the doctrine's numerous complexities.

BOOK IV

Utilitarianism

Chapter I

The Meaning of Utilitarianism

§1. The term Utilitarianism is, at the present day, in common use, and is supposed to designate a doctrine or method with which we are all familiar. But on closer examination, it appears to be applied to several distinct theories, having no necessary connexion with one another, and not even referring to the same subject-matter. It will be well, therefore, to define, as carefully as possible, the doctrine that is to be denoted by the term in the present Book: at the same time distinguishing this from other doctrines to which usage would allow the name to be applied, and indicating, so far as seems necessary, its relation to these.

By Utilitarianism is here meant the ethical theory, that the conduct which, under any given circumstances, is objectively right, is that which will produce the greatest amount of happiness on the whole; that is, taking into account all whose happiness is affected by the conduct. It would tend to clearness if we might call this principle, and the method based upon it, by some such name as "Universalistic Hedonism"; and I have therefore sometimes ventured to use this term, in spite of its cumbrousness.

The first doctrine from which it seems necessary to distinguish this [is] Egoistic Hedonism. . . . The difference, however, between the propositions (1) that

From Henry Sidgwick, *The Methods of Ethics*, 7th ed. (1907).

each ought to seek his own happiness, and (2) that each ought to seek the happiness of all, is so obvious and glaring, that instead of dwelling upon it we seem rather called upon to explain how the two ever came to be confounded, or in any way included under one notion. . . .[1] [T]he confusion between these two ethical theories [is] partly assisted by the confusion with both of the psychological theory that in voluntary actions every agent does, universally or normally, seek his own individual happiness or pleasure. Now there seems to be no necessary connexion between this latter proposition and any ethical theory: but in so far as there is a natural tendency to pass from psychological to ethical Hedonism, the transition must be—at least primarily—to the Egoistic phase of the latter. For clearly, from the fact that every one actually does seek his own happiness we cannot conclude, as an immediate and obvious inference, that he ought to seek the happiness of other people. . . .

Finally, the doctrine that Universal Happiness is the ultimate standard must not be understood to imply that Universal Benevolence is the only right or always best motive of action. For, as we have before observed, it is not necessary that the end which gives the criterion of rightness should always be the end at which we consciously aim: and if experience shows that the general happiness will be more satisfactorily attained if men frequently act from other motives than pure universal philanthropy, it is obvious that these other motives are reasonably to be preferred on Utilitarian principles.

§2. Let us now examine the principle itself somewhat closer. . . . We shall understand . . . that by Greatest Happiness is meant the greatest possible surplus of pleasure over pain, the pain being conceived as balanced against an equal amount of pleasure, so that the two contrasted amounts annihilate each other for purposes of ethical calculation. And of course . . . the assumption is involved that all pleasures included in our calculation are capable of being compared quantitatively with one another and with all pains; that every such feeling has a certain intensive quantity, positive or negative (or, perhaps, zero), in respect of its desirableness, and that this quantity may be to some extent known: so that each

may be at least roughly weighed in ideal scales against any other. This assumption is involved in the very notion of Maximum Happiness; as the attempt to make 'as great as possible' a sum of elements not quantitatively commensurable would be a mathematical absurdity. . . .

We have next to consider who the "all" are, whose happiness is to be taken into account. Are we to extend our concern to all the beings capable of pleasure and pain whose feelings are affected by our conduct? or are we to confine our view to human happiness? The former view is the one adopted by Bentham and Mill, and (I believe) by the Utilitarian school generally: and is obviously most in accordance with the universality that is characteristic of their principle. It is the Good Universal, interpreted and defined as 'happiness' or 'pleasure,' at which a Utilitarian considers it his duty to aim: and it seems arbitrary and unreasonable to exclude from the end, as so conceived, any pleasure of any sentient being.

It may be said that by giving this extension to the notion, we considerably increase the scientific difficulties of the hedonistic comparison, . . . for if it be difficult to compare the pleasures and pains of other men accurately with our own, a comparison of either with the pleasures and pains of brutes is obviously still more obscure. Still, the difficulty is at least not greater for Utilitarians than it is for any other moralists who recoil from the paradox of disregarding altogether the pleasures and pains of brutes. But even if we limit our attention to human beings, the extent of the subjects of happiness is not yet quite determinate. In the first place, it may be asked, How far we are to consider the interests of posterity when they seem to conflict with those of existing human beings? It seems, however, clear that the time at which a man exists cannot affect the value of his happiness from a universal point of view; and that the interests of posterity must concern a Utilitarian as much as those of his contemporaries, except in so far as the effect of his actions on posterity—and even the existence of human beings to be affected—must necessarily be more uncertain. But a further question arises when we consider that we can to some extent influence the number of future human (or sentient) beings. We have to ask how, on Utilitarian principles, this influence is to be exercised. Here I shall assume that, for human beings generally, life on the average yields a positive balance of pleasure over pain. This has been denied by thoughtful persons: but the denial seems to me clearly opposed to the common experience of mankind, as expressed in their commonly accepted principles of action. The great majority of men, in the great majority of conditions under which human life is lived, certainly act as if death were one of the worst of evils, for themselves and for those whom they love: and the administration of criminal justice proceeds on a similar assumption. . . .

Assuming, then, that the average happiness of human beings is a positive quantity, it seems clear that, supposing the average happiness enjoyed remains undiminished, Utilitarianism directs us to make the number enjoying it as great as possible. But if we foresee as possible that an increase in numbers will be accompanied by a decrease in average happiness or vice versa, a point arises which has not only never been formally noticed, but which seems to have been substantially overlooked by many Utilitarians. For if we take Utilitarianism to prescribe, as the ultimate end of action, happiness on the whole, and not any individual's happiness, unless considered as an element of the whole, it would follow that, if the additional population enjoy on the whole positive happiness, we ought to weigh the amount of happiness gained by the extra number against the amount lost by the remainder. So that, strictly conceived, the point up to which, on Utilitarian principles, population ought to be encouraged to increase, is not that at which average happiness is the greatest possible, as appears to be often assumed by political economists . . .—but that at which the product formed by multiplying the number of persons living into the amount of average happiness reaches its maximum. . . .

There is one more point that remains to be noticed. It is evident that there may be many different ways of distributing the same quantum of happiness among the same number of persons; in order, therefore, that the Utilitarian criterion of right conduct may be as complete as possible, we ought to know

which of these ways is to be preferred. This question is often ignored in expositions of Utilitarianism. It has perhaps seemed somewhat idle as suggesting a purely abstract and theoretical perplexity, that could have no practical exemplification; and no doubt, if all the consequences of actions were capable of being estimated and summed up with mathematical precision, we should probably never find the excess of pleasure over pain exactly equal in the case of two competing alternatives of conduct. But the very indefiniteness of all hedonistic calculations . . . renders it by no means unlikely that there may be no cognisable difference between the quantities of happiness involved in two sets of consequences respectively; the more rough our estimates necessarily are, the less likely we shall be to come to any clear decision between two apparently balanced alternatives. In all such cases, therefore, it becomes practically important to ask whether any mode of distributing a given quantum of happiness is better than any other. Now the Utilitarian formula seems to supply no answer to this question: at least we have to supplement the principle of seeking the greatest happiness on the whole by some principle of Just or Right distribution of this happiness. The principle which most Utilitarians have either tacitly or expressly adopted is that of pure equality—as given in Bentham's formula, "everybody to count for one, and nobody for more than one". And this principle seems the only one which does not need a special justification; for, as we saw, it must be reasonable to treat any one man in the same way as any other, if there be no reason apparent for treating him differently. . . .[2]

Chapter II

The Proof of Utilitarianism

. . . [T]he principle of aiming at universal happiness is more generally felt to require some proof, or at least (as Mill puts it) some "considerations determining the mind to accept it", than the principle of aiming at one's own happiness. From the point of view, indeed, of abstract philosophy, I do not see why the Egoistic principle should pass unchallenged any more than the Universalistic. I do not see why the axiom of Prudence should not be questioned, when it conflicts with present inclination, on a ground similar to that on which Egoists refuse to admit the axiom of Rational Benevolence. If the Utilitarian has to answer the question, 'Why should I sacrifice my own happiness for the greater happiness of another?' it must surely be admissible to ask the Egoist, 'Why should I sacrifice a present pleasure for a greater one in the future? Why should I concern myself about my own future feelings any more than about the feelings of other persons?' It undoubtedly seems to Common Sense paradoxical to ask for a reason why one should seek one's own happiness on the whole; but I do not see how the demand can be repudiated as absurd by those who adopt the views of the extreme empirical school of psychologists, although those views are commonly supposed to have a close affinity with Egoistic Hedonism. Grant that the Ego is merely a system of coherent phenomena, that the permanent identical 'I' is not a fact but a fiction, as Hume and his followers maintain; why, then, should one part of the series of feelings into which the Ego is resolved be concerned with another part of the same series, any more than with any other series?

However, I will not press this question now; since I admit that Common Sense does not think it worth while to supply the individual with reasons for seeking his own interest. . . . To this challenge some Utilitarians would reply by saying that it is impossible to "prove" a first principle and this is of course true, if by proof we mean a process which exhibits the principle in question as an inference from premises upon which it remains dependent for its certainty; for these premises, and not the inference drawn from them, would then be the real first principles. Nay, if Utilitarianism is to be proved to a man who already holds some other moral principles,—whether he be an Intuitional moralist, who regards as final the principles of Truth, Justice, Obedience to authority, Purity, etc., or an Egoist who regards his own interest as the ultimately reasonable end of his conduct,—it would seem that the process must be one which establishes a conclusion actually superior in validity to the premises from which it starts. For the Utilitarian prescriptions of duty are *prima facie*

in conflict, at certain points and under certain circumstances, both with rules which the Intuitionist regards as self-evident, and with the dictates of Rational Egoism; so that Utilitarianism, if accepted at all, must be accepted as overruling Intuitionism and Egoism. At the same time, if the other principles are not throughout taken as valid, the so-called proof does not seem to be addressed to the Intuitionist or Egoist at all. How shall we deal with this dilemma? How is such a process—clearly different from ordinary proof—possible or conceivable? Yet there certainly seems to be a general demand for it. Perhaps we may say that what is needed is a line of argument which on the one hand allows the validity, to a certain extent, of the maxims already accepted, and on the other hand shows them to be not absolutely valid, but needing to be controlled and completed by some more comprehensive principle. . . .

If the Egoist strictly confines himself to stating his conviction that he ought to take his own happiness or pleasure as his ultimate end, there seems no opening for any line of reasoning to lead him to Universalistic Hedonism as a first principle; . . . it cannot be proved that the difference between his own happiness and another's happiness is not for him all-important. In this case all that the Utilitarian can do is to effect as far as possible a reconciliation between the two principles, by expounding to the Egoist the sanctions of rules deduced from the Universalistic principle,—i.e. by pointing out the pleasures and pains that may be expected to accrue to the Egoist himself from the observation and violation respectively of such rules. It is obvious that such an exposition has no tendency to make him accept the greatest happiness of the greatest number as his ultimate end; but only as a means to the end of his own happiness. It is therefore totally different from a proof (as above explained) of Universalistic Hedonism. When, however, the Egoist puts forward, implicitly or explicitly, the proposition that his happiness or pleasure is Good, not only for him but from the point of view of the Universe,—as (e.g.) by saying that 'nature designed him to seek his own happiness,'—it then becomes relevant to point out to him that his happiness cannot be a more important part of Good, taken universally, than the equal happiness of any other person. And thus, starting with his own principle, he may be brought to accept Universal happiness or pleasure as that which is absolutely and without qualification Good or Desirable: as an end, therefore, to which the action of a reasonable agent as such ought to be directed. . . .

It should be observed, however, that as addressed to the Intuitionist, this reasoning only shows the Utilitarian first principle to be one moral axiom: it does not prove that it is sole or supreme. The premises with which the Intuitionist starts commonly include other formulae held as independent and self-evident. Utilitarianism has therefore to exhibit itself in the twofold relation above described, at once negative and positive, to these formulae. The Utilitarian must, in the first place, endeavour to show to the Intuitionist that the principles of Truth, Justice, etc. have only a dependent and subordinate validity: arguing either that the principle is really only affirmed by Common Sense as a general rule admitting of exceptions and qualifications, as in the case of Truth, and that we require some further principle for systematising these exceptions and qualifications; or that the fundamental notion is vague and needs further determination, as in the case of Justice; . . . and further, that the different rules are liable to conflict with each other, and that we require some higher principle to decide the issue thus raised; and again, that the rules are differently formulated by different persons, and that these differences admit of no Intuitional solution, while they show the vagueness and ambiguity of the common moral notions to which the Intuitionist appeals. . . .

It remains to supplement this line of reasoning by developing the positive relation that exists between Utilitarianism and the Morality of Common Sense: by showing how Utilitarianism sustains the general validity of the current moral judgments, and thus supplements the defects which reflection finds in the intuitive recognition of their stringency; and at the same time affords a principle of synthesis, and a method for binding the unconnected and occasionally conflicting principles of common moral reasoning into a complete and harmonious system. If systematic reflection upon the morality of Common Sense thus exhibits the Utilitarian principle as that

to which Common Sense naturally appeals for that further development of its system which this same reflection shows to be necessary, the proof of Utilitarianism seems as complete as it can be made. . . .

Chapter III

Relation of Utilitarianism to the Morality of Common Sense

§1. . . . [I]f a list were drawn up of the qualities of character and conduct that are directly or indirectly productive of pleasure to ourselves or to others, it would include all that are commonly known as virtues. Whatever be the origin of our notion of moral goodness or excellence, there is no doubt that "Utility" is a general characteristic of the dispositions to which we apply it: and that, so far, the Morality of Common Sense may be truly represented as at least unconsciously Utilitarian. But it may still be objected, that this coincidence is merely general and qualitative, and that it breaks down when we attempt to draw it out in detail, with the quantitative precision which Bentham introduced into the discussion. And no doubt there is a great difference between the assertion that virtue is always productive of happiness, and the assertion that the right action is under all circumstances that which will produce the greatest possible happiness on the whole. But it must be borne in mind that Utilitarianism is not concerned to prove the absolute coincidence in results of the Intuitional and Utilitarian methods. Indeed, if it could succeed in proving as much as this, its success would be almost fatal to its practical claims; as the adoption of the Utilitarian principle would then become a matter of complete indifference. Utilitarians are rather called upon to show a natural transition from the Morality of Common Sense to Utilitarianism, somewhat like the transition in special branches of practice from trained instinct and empirical rules to the technical method that embodies arid applies the conclusions of science: so that Utilitarianism may be presented as the scientifically complete and systematically reflective form of that regulation of conduct, which through the whole course of human history has always tended substantially in the same direction. For this purpose it is not necessary to prove that existing moral rules are more conducive to the general happiness than any others: but only to point out in each case some manifest felicific tendency which they possess. . . .

In fact, the Utilitarian argument cannot be fairly judged unless we take fully into account the cumulative force which it derives from the complex character of the coincidence between Utilitarianism and Common Sense.

It may be shown, I think, that the Utilitarian estimate of consequences not only supports broadly the current moral rules, but also sustains their generally received limitations and qualifications: that, again, it explains anomalies in the Morality of Common Sense, which from any other point of view must seem unsatisfactory to the reflective intellect; and moreover, where the current formula is not sufficiently precise for the guidance of conduct, while at the same time difficulties and perplexities arise in the attempt to give it additional precision, the Utilitarian method solves these difficulties and perplexities in general accordance with the vague instincts of Common Sense, and is naturally appealed to for such solution in ordinary moral discussions. It may be shown further, that it not only supports the generally received view of the relative importance of different duties, but is also naturally called in as arbiter, where rules commonly regarded as co-ordinate come into conflict: that, again, when the same rule is interpreted somewhat differently by different persons, each naturally supports his view by urging its Utility, however strongly he may maintain the rule to be self-evident and known *a priori*: that where we meet with marked diversity of moral opinion on any point, in the same age and country, we commonly find manifest and impressive utilitarian reasons on both sides: and that finally the remarkable discrepancies found in comparing the moral codes of different ages and countries are for the most part strikingly correlated to differences in the effects of actions on happiness, or in men's foresight of, or concern for, such effects. . . .

But considering the importance of the present question, it may be well to exhibit in systematic detail the cumulative argument which has just been summed up, even at the risk of repeating to some extent the results previously given.

§2. We may begin by replying to an objection which is frequently urged against Utilitarianism. How, it is asked, if the true ground of the moral goodness or badness of actions lies in their utility or the reverse, can we explain the broad distinction drawn by Common Sense between the moral and other parts of our nature? Why is the excellence of Virtue so strongly felt to be different in kind, not merely from the excellence of a machine, or a fertile field, but also from the physical beauties and aptitudes, the intellectual gifts and talents of human beings. I should answer that . . . qualities that are, in the strictest sense of the term, Virtuous, are always such as we conceive capable of being immediately realised by voluntary effort, at least to some extent; so that the prominent obstacle to virtuous action is absence of adequate motive. Hence we expect that the judgments of moral goodness or badness, passed either by the agent himself or by others, will—by the fresh motive which they supply on the side of virtue— have an immediate practical effect in causing actions to be at least externally virtuous: and the habitual consciousness of this will account for almost any degree of difference between moral sentiments and the pleasure and pain that we derive from the contemplation of either extra-human or non-voluntary utilities and inutilities. . . .

. . . [W]e must carefully distinguish between the recognition of goodness in dispositions, and the recognition of rightness in conduct. An act that a Utilitarian must condemn as likely to do more harm than good may yet show a disposition or tendency that will on the whole produce more good than harm. This is eminently the case with scrupulously conscientious acts. However true it may be that unenlightened conscientiousness has impelled men to fanatical cruelty, mistaken asceticism, and other infelicific conduct, I suppose no Intuitionist would maintain that carefulness in conforming to accepted moral rules has not, on the whole, a tendency to promote happiness. It may be observed, however, that when we perceive the effects of a disposition generally felicific to be in any particular case adverse to happiness, we often apply to it, as so operating, some term of condemnation: thus we speak, in the case above noticed, of 'over-scrupulousness' or 'fanaticism'. But in so far as we perceive that the same disposition would generally produce good results, it is not inconsistent still to regard it, abstracting from the particular case, as a good element of character. Secondly, although, in the view of a Utilitarian, only the useful is praiseworthy, he is not bound to maintain that it is necessarily worthy of praise in proportion as it is useful. From a Utilitarian point of view, as has been before said, we must mean by calling a quality 'deserving of praise', that it is expedient to praise it, with a view to its future production: accordingly, in distributing our praise of human qualities, on utilitarian principles, we have to consider primarily not the usefulness of the quality, but the usefulness of the praise: and it is obviously not expedient to encourage by praise qualities which are likely to be found in excess rather than in defect. Hence (e.g.) however necessary self-love or resentment may be to society, it is quite in harmony with Utilitarianism that they should not be recognised as virtues by Common Sense, in so far as it is reasonably thought that they will always be found operating with at least sufficient intensity. We find, however, that when self-love comes into conflict with impulses seen to be on the whole pernicious, it is praised as Prudence: and that when a man seems clearly deficient in resentment, he is censured for tameness: though as malevolent impulses are much more obviously productive of pain than pleasure, it is not unnatural that their occasional utility should be somewhat overlooked. The case of Humility and Diffidence may be treated in a somewhat similar way. As we saw, it is only inadvertently that Common Sense praises the tendency to underrate one's own powers: on reflection it is generally admitted that it cannot be good to be in error on this or any other point. But the desires of Superiority and Esteem are so strong in most men, that arrogance and self-assertion are both much commoner than the opposite defects, and at the same time are faults peculiarly disagreeable to others: so that humility gives us an agreeable surprise, and hence Common Sense is easily led to overlook the more latent and remote bad consequences of undue self-distrust.

We may observe further that the perplexity which we seemed to find in the Morality of Common Sense, as to the relation of moral excellence to moral effort, is satisfactorily explained and removed when we adopt a Utilitarian point of view: for on the one hand it is easy to see how certain acts—such as kind services—are likely to be more felicific when performed without effort, and from other motives than regard for duty: while on the other hand a person who in doing similar acts achieves a triumph of duty over strong seductive inclinations, exhibits thereby a character which we recognise as felicific in a more general way, as tending to a general performance of duty in all departments. So again, there is a simple and obvious utilitarian solution of another difficulty which I noticed, as to the choice between Subjective and Objective rightness in the exceptional case in which alone the two can be presented as alternatives,—i.e. when we are considering whether we shall influence another to act contrary to his conviction as to what is right. A utilitarian would decide the question by weighing the felicific consequences of the particular right act against the infelicific results to be apprehended hereafter from the moral deterioration of the person whose conscientious convictions were overborne by other motives: unless the former effects were very important he would reasonably regard the danger to character as the greater: but if the other's mistaken sense of duty threatened to cause a grave disaster, he would not hesitate to overbear it by any motives which it was in his power to apply. And in practice I think that the Common Sense of mankind would come to similar conclusions by more vague and semi-conscious reasoning of the same kind.

In order, however, to form a precise estimate of the extent to which Utilitarianism agrees or disagrees with Common Sense, it seems best to examine the more definite judgments of right and wrong in conduct, under the particular heads represented by our common notions of virtues and duties. I may begin by pointing out once more that so far as any adequately precise definitions of these notions are found to involve, implicitly or explicitly, the notion of 'good' or of 'right' supposed already determinate, they can afford no ground for opposing a Utilitarian interpretation of these fundamental conceptions. For example, . . . [w]isdom, as commonly conceived, is not exactly the faculty of choosing the right means to the end of universal happiness; rather, as we saw, its notion involves an uncritical synthesis of the different ends and principles that are distinguished and separately examined in the present treatise. But if its import is not distinctly Utilitarian, it is certainly not anything else as distinct from Utilitarian: if we can only define it as the faculty or habit of choosing the right or best means to the right or best end, for that very reason our definition leaves it quite open to us to give the notions 'good' and 'right' a Utilitarian import.

§3. Let us then examine first the group of virtues and duties . . . under the head of Benevolence. As regards the general conception of the duty, there is, I think, no divergence that we need consider between the Intuitional and Utilitarian systems. For though Benevolence would perhaps be more commonly defined as a disposition to promote the Good of one's fellow-creatures, rather than their Happiness (as definitely understood by Utilitarians); still, as the chief element in the common notion of good (besides happiness) is moral good or Virtue, . . . if we can show that the other virtues are—speaking broadly—all qualities conducive to the happiness of the agent himself or of others, it is evident that Benevolence, whether it prompts us to promote the virtue of others or their happiness, will aim directly or indirectly at the Utilitarian end. . . .

It has been said, however, that the special claims and duties belonging to special relations, by which each man is connected with a few out of the whole number of human beings, are expressly ignored by the rigid impartiality of the Utilitarian formula . . . and hence that, though Utilitarianism and Common Sense may agree in the proposition that all right action is conducive to the happiness of some one or other, and so far beneficent, still they are irreconcileably divergent on the radical question of the distribution of beneficence.

Here, however, it seems that even fair-minded opponents have scarcely understood the Utilitarian position. They have attacked Bentham's well-known formula, "every man to count for one, nobody for more than one," on the ground that the general happiness will be best attained by inequality in the distribution of each one's services. But so far as it is

clear that it will be best attained in this way, Utilitarianism will necessarily prescribe this way of aiming at it; and Bentham's dictum must be understood merely as making the conception of the ultimate end precise—laying down that one person's happiness is to be counted for as much as another's (supposed equal in degree) as an element of the general happiness—not as directly prescribing the rules of conduct by which this end will be best attained. And the reasons why it is, generally speaking, conducive to the general happiness that each individual should distribute his beneficence in the channels marked out by commonly recognised ties and claims, are tolerably obvious.

For first, in the chief relations . . . the domestic, and those constituted by consanguinity, friendship, previous kindnesses, and special needs,—the services which Common Sense prescribes as duties are commonly prompted by natural affection, while at the same time they tend to develop and sustain such affection. Now the subsistence of benevolent affections among human beings is itself an important means to the Utilitarian end, because . . . the most intense and highly valued of our pleasures are derived from such affections; for both the emotion itself is highly pleasurable, and it imparts this quality to the activities which it prompts and sustains, and the happiness thus produced is continually enhanced by the sympathetic echo of the pleasures conferred on others. And again, where genuine affection subsists, the practical objections to spontaneous beneficence, which were before noticed, are much diminished in force. For such affection tends to be reciprocated, and the kindnesses which are its outcome and expression commonly win a requital of affection: and in so far as this is the case, they have less tendency to weaken the springs of activity in the person benefited; and may even strengthen them by exciting other sources of energy than the egoistic—personal affection, and gratitude, and the desire to deserve love, and the desire to imitate beneficence. And hence it has been often observed that the injurious effects of almsgiving are at least much diminished if the alms are bestowed with unaffected sympathy and kindliness, and in such a way as to elicit a genuine response of gratitude. And further, the beneficence that springs from affection is less likely to be frustrated from defect of knowledge: for not only are we powerfully stimulated to study the real conditions of the happiness of those whom we love, but also such study is rendered more effective from the sympathy which naturally accompanies affection. . . .

In all such cases there are three distinct lines of argument which tend to show that the commonly received view of special claims and duties arising out of special relations, though *prima facie* opposed to the impartial universality of the Utilitarian principle, is really maintained by a well-considered application of that principle. First, morality is here in a manner protecting the normal channels and courses of natural benevolent affections; and the development of such affections is of the highest importance to human happiness, both as a direct source of pleasure, and as an indispensable preparation for a more enlarged "altruism". And again, the mere fact that such affections are normal, causes an expectation of the services that are their natural expression; and the disappointment of such expectations is inevitably painful. While finally, apart from these considerations, we can show in each care strong utilitarian reasons why, generally speaking, services should be rendered to the persons commonly recognised as having such claims rather than to others.

We have to observe, in conclusion, that the difficulties which we found in the way of determining by the Intuitional method the limits and the relative importance of these duties are reduced in the Utilitarian system, to difficulties of hedonistic comparison. . . . For each of the preceding arguments has shown us different kinds of pleasures gained and pains averted by the fulfilment of the claims in question. There are, first, those which the service claimed would directly promote or avert: secondly, there is the pain and secondary harm of disappointed expectation, if the service be not rendered: thirdly, we have to reckon the various pleasures connected with the exercise of natural benevolent affections, especially when reciprocated, including the indirect effects on the agent's character of maintaining such affections. All these different pleasures and pains combine differently, and with almost infinite variation as circumstances

vary, into utilitarian reasons for each of the claims in question; none of these reasons being absolute and conclusive, but each having its own weight, while liable to be outweighed by others.

§7. The preceding survey has supplied us with several illustrations of the manner in which Utilitarianism is normally introduced as a method for deciding between different conflicting claims, in cases where common sense leaves their relative importance obscure,—as (e.g.) between the different duties of the affections, and the different principles which analysis shows to be involved in our common conception of Justice—: and we have also noticed how, when a dispute is raised as to the precise scope and definition of any current moral rule, the effects of different acceptations of the rule on general happiness or social wellbeing are commonly regarded as the ultimate grounds on which the dispute is to be decided. In fact these two arguments practically run into one; for it is generally a conflict between maxims that impresses men with the need of giving each a precise definition. . . . We may now observe that this hypothesis of 'Unconscious Utilitarianism' explains the different relative importance attached to particular virtues by different classes of human beings, and the different emphasis with which the same virtue is inculcated on these different classes by mankind generally. For such differences ordinarily correspond to variations—real or apparent— in the Utilitarian importance of the virtues under different circumstances. . . . [A] soldier is expected to show a higher degree of courage than (e.g.) a priest. Again, though we esteem candour and scrupulous sincerity in most persons, we scarcely look for them in a diplomatist who has to conceal secrets, nor do we expect that a tradesman in describing his goods should frankly point out their defects to his customers.

Finally, when we compare the different moral codes of different ages and countries, we see that the discrepancies among them correspond, at least to a great extent, to differences either in the actual effects of actions on happiness, or in the extent to which such effects are generally foreseen—or regarded as important—by the men among whom the codes are maintained. Several instances of this have already been noticed: and the general fact, which has been much dwelt upon by Utilitarian writers, is also admitted and even emphasised by their opponents. . . . I conceive that few persons who have studied the subject will deny that there is a certain degree of correlation between the variations in the moral code from age to age, and the variations in the real or perceived effects on general happiness of actions prescribed or forbidden by the code. And in proportion as the apprehension of consequences becomes more comprehensive and exact, we may trace not only change in the moral code handed down from age to age, but progress in the direction of a closer approximation to a perfectly enlightened Utilitarianism. . . .

Chapter V

The Method of Utilitarianism

§3. We have hitherto supposed that the innovator is endeavouring to introduce a new rule of conduct, not for himself only, but for others also, as more conducive to the general happiness than the rule recognised by Common Sense. It may perhaps be thought that this is not the issue most commonly raised between Utilitarianism and Common Sense: but rather whether exceptions should be allowed to rules which both sides accept as generally valid. For no one doubts that it is, generally speaking, conducive to the common happiness that men should be veracious, faithful to promises, obedient to law, disposed to satisfy the normal expectations of others, having their malevolent impulses and their sensual appetites under strict control: but it is thought that an exclusive regard to pleasurable and painful consequences would frequently admit exceptions to rules which Common Sense imposes as absolute. It should, however, be observed that the admission of an exception on general grounds is merely the establishment of a more complex and delicate rule, instead of one that is broader and simpler; for if it is conducive to the general good that such an exception be admitted in one case, it will be equally so in all similar cases. Suppose (e.g.) that a Utilitarian thinks it on general grounds right to answer falsely a question as to the manner in which he has voted at a political election where the voting is by secret ballot.

His reasons will probably be that the Utilitarian prohibition of falsehood is based on (1) the harm done by misleading particular individuals, and (2) the tendency of false statements to diminish the mutual confidence that men ought to have in each other's assertions: and that in this exceptional case it is (1) expedient that the questioner should be misled; while (2), in so far as the falsehood tends to produce a general distrust of all assertions as to the manner in which a man has voted, it only furthers the end for which voting has been made secret. It is evident, that if these reasons are valid for any person, they are valid for all persons; in fact, that they establish the expediency of a new general rule in respect of truth and falsehood, more complicated than the old one; a rule which the Utilitarian, as such, should desire to be universally obeyed.

There are, of course, some kinds of moral innovation which, from the nature of the case, are not likely to occur frequently; as where Utilitarian reasoning leads a man to take part in a political revolution, or to support a public measure in opposition to what Common Sense regards as Justice or Good Faith. Still, in such cases a rational Utilitarian will usually proceed on general principles, which he would desire all persons in similar circumstances to carry into effect.

We have, however, to consider another kind of exceptions, differing fundamentally from this, which Utilitarianism seems to admit; where the agent does not think it expedient that the rule on which he himself acts should be universally adopted, and yet maintains that his individual act is right, as producing a greater balance of pleasure over pain than any other conduct open to him would produce.

Now we cannot fairly argue that, because a large aggregate of acts would cause more harm than good, therefore any single act of the kind will produce this effect. It may even be a straining of language to say that it has a tendency to produce it: no one (e.g.) would say that because an army walking over a bridge would break it down, therefore the crossing of a single traveller has a tendency to destroy it. And just as a prudent physician in giving rules of diet recommends an occasional deviation from them, as more conducive to the health of the body than absolute regularity; so there may be rules of social behaviour of which the general observance is necessary to the well-being of the community, while yet a certain amount of non-observance is rather advantageous than otherwise.

Here, however, we seem brought into conflict with Kant's fundamental principle, that a right action must be one of which the agent could "will the maxim to be law universal" . . . But, as was before noticed in the particular case of veracity, we must admit an application of this principle, which importantly modifies its practical force: we must admit the case where the belief that the action in question will not be widely imitated is an essential qualification of the maxim which the Kantian principle is applied to test. For this principle,—at least so far as I have accepted it as self-evident—means no more than that an act, if right for any individual, must be right on general grounds, and therefore for some class of persons; it therefore cannot prevent us from defining this class by the above-mentioned characteristic of believing that the act will remain an exceptional one. Of course if this belief turns out to be erroneous, serious harm may possibly result; but this is no more than may be said of many other Utilitarian deductions. Nor is it difficult to find instances of conduct which Common Sense holds to be legitimate solely on the ground that we have no fear of its being too widely imitated. Take, for example, the case of Celibacy. A universal refusal to propagate the human species would be the greatest of conceivable crimes from a Utilitarian point of view;—that is, according to the commonly accepted belief in the superiority of human happiness to that of other animals;—and hence the principle in question, applied without the qualification above given, would make it a crime in any one to choose celibacy as the state most conducive to his own happiness. But Common Sense (in the present age at least) regards such preference as within the limits of right conduct; because there is no fear that population will not be sufficiently kept up, as in fact the tendency to propagate is thought to exist rather in excess than otherwise.

In this case it is a non-moral impulse on the average strength of which we think we may reckon: but there does not appear to be any formal or universal

reason why the same procedure should not be applied by Utilitarians to an actually existing moral sentiment. The result would be a discrepancy of a peculiar kind between Utilitarianism and Common-Sense morality; as the very firmness with which the latter is established would be the Utilitarian ground for relieving the individual of its obligations. We are supposed to see that general happiness will be enhanced (just as the excellence of a metrical composition is) by a slight admixture of irregularity along with a general observance of received rules; and hence to justify the irregular conduct of a few individuals, on the ground that the supply of regular conduct from other members of the community may reasonably be expected to be adequate.

It does not seem to me that this reasoning can be shown to be necessarily unsound, as applied to human society as at present constituted: but the cases in which it could really be thought to be applicable, by any one sincerely desirous of promoting the general happiness, must certainly be rare. For it should be observed that it makes a fundamental difference whether the sentiment in mankind generally, on which we rely to sustain sufficiently a general rule while admitting exceptions thereto, is moral or non-moral; because a moral sentiment is inseparable from the conviction that the conduct to which it prompts is objectively right—i.e. right whether or not it is thought or felt to be so—for oneself and all similar persons in similar circumstances; it cannot therefore coexist with approval of the contrary conduct in any one case, unless this case is distinguished by some material difference other than the mere non-existence in the agent of the ordinary moral sentiment against his conduct. Thus, assuming that general unveracity and general celibacy would both be evils of the worst kind, we may still all regard it as legitimate for men in general to remain celibate if they like, on account of the strength of the natural sentiments prompting to marriage, because the existence of these sentiments in ordinary human beings is not affected by the universal recognition of the legitimacy of celibacy: but we cannot similarly all regard it as legitimate for men to tell lies if they like, however strong the actually existing sentiment against lying may be, because as soon as this legitimacy is generally recognised the sentiment must be expected to decay and vanish. If therefore we were all enlightened Utilitarians, it would be impossible for any one to justify himself in making false statements while admitting it to be inexpedient for persons similarly conditioned to make them; as he would have no ground for believing that persons similarly conditioned would act differently from himself. The case, no doubt, is different in society as actually constituted; it is conceivable that the practically effective morality in such a society, resting on a basis independent of utilitarian or any other reasonings, may not be materially affected by the particular act or expressed opinion of a particular individual: but the circumstances are, I conceive, very rare, in which a really conscientious person could feel so sure of this as to conclude that by approving a particular violation of a rule, of which the general (though not universal) observance is plainly expedient, he will not probably do harm on the whole. Especially as all the objections to innovation, noticed in the previous section, apply with increased force if the innovator does not even claim to be introducing a new and better general rule.

It appears to me, therefore, that the cases in which practical doubts are likely to arise, as to whether exceptions should be permitted from ordinary rules on Utilitarian principles, will mostly be those which I discussed in the first paragraph of this section: where the exceptions are not claimed for a few individuals, on the mere ground of their probable fewness, but either for persons generally under exceptional circumstances, or for a class of persons defined by exceptional qualities of intellect, temperament, or character. In such cases the Utilitarian may have no doubt that in a community consisting generally of enlightened Utilitarians, these grounds for exceptional ethical treatment would be regarded as valid; still he may, as I have said, doubt whether the more refined and complicated rule which recognises such exceptions is adapted for the community in which he is actually living; and whether the attempt to introduce it is not likely to do more harm by weakening current morality than good by improving its quality. Supposing such a doubt to arise, either in a case of this kind, or in one of the rare cases

discussed in the preceding paragraph, it becomes necessary that the Utilitarian should consider carefully the extent to which his advice or example are likely to influence persons to whom they would be dangerous: and it is evident that the result of this consideration may depend largely on the degree of publicity which he gives to either advice or example. Thus, on Utilitarian principles, it may be right to do and privately recommend, under certain circumstances, what it would not be right to advocate openly; it may be right to teach openly to one set of persons what it would be wrong to teach to others; it may be conceivably right to do, if it can be done with comparative secrecy, what it would be wrong to do in the face of the world; and even, if perfect secrecy can be reasonably expected, what it would be wrong to recommend by private advice or example. These conclusions are all of a paradoxical character: . . . there is no doubt that the moral consciousness of a plain man broadly repudiates the general notion of an esoteric morality, differing from that popularly taught; and it would be commonly agreed that an action which would be bad if done openly is not rendered good by secrecy. We may observe, however, that there are strong utilitarian reasons for maintaining generally this latter common opinion; for it is obviously advantageous, generally speaking, that acts which it is expedient to repress by social disapprobation should become known, as otherwise the disapprobation cannot operate; so that it seems inexpedient to support by any moral encouragement the natural disposition of men in general to conceal their wrong doings; besides that the concealment would in most cases have importantly injurious effects on the agent's habits of veracity. Thus the Utilitarian conclusion, carefully stated, would seem to be this; that the opinion that secrecy may render an action right which would not otherwise be so should itself be kept comparatively secret; and similarly it seems expedient that the doctrine that esoteric morality is expedient should itself be kept esoteric. Or if this concealment be difficult to maintain, it may be desirable that Common Sense should repudiate the doctrines which it is expedient to confine to an enlightened few. And thus a Utilitarian may reasonably desire, on Utilitarian principles, that some of his conclusions should be rejected by mankind generally; or even that the vulgar should keep aloof from his system as a whole, in so far as the inevitable indefiniteness and complexity of its calculations render it likely to lead to bad results in their hands.

Of course, as I have said, in an ideal community of enlightened Utilitarians this swarm of perplexities and paradoxes would vanish; as in such a society no one can have any ground for believing that other persons will act on moral principles different from those which he adopts. And any enlightened Utilitarian must of course desire this consummation; as all conflict of moral opinion must *pro tanto* be regarded as an evil, as tending to impair the force of morality generally in its resistance to seductive impulses. Still such conflict may be a necessary evil in the actual condition of civilised communities, in which there are so many different degrees of intellectual and moral development. . . .

And so generally it may be best on the whole that there should be conflicting codes of morality in a given society at a certain stage of its development. And, as I have already hinted, the same general reasoning, from the probable origin of the moral sense and its flexible adjustment to the varying conditions of human life, which furnished a presumption that Common-Sense morality is roughly coincident with the Utilitarian code proper for men as now constituted, may be applied in favour of these divergent codes also: it may be said that these, too, form part of the complex adjustment of man to his circumstances, and that they are needed to supplement and qualify the morality of Common Sense.

However paradoxical this doctrine may appear, we can find cases where it seems to be implicitly accepted by Common Sense; or at least where it is required to make Common Sense consistent with itself. Let us consider, for example, the common moral judgments concerning rebellions. It is commonly thought, on the one hand, that these abrupt breaches of order are sometimes morally necessary; and, on the other hand, that they ought always to be vigorously resisted, and in ease of failure punished by extreme penalties inflicted at least on the ring-leaders; for otherwise they would be attempted under circumstances where there was no sufficient justification for them: but it seems evident that, in the actual condition of men's moral sentiments, this vigorous repression requires the support of a strong body of opinion condemning the rebels as wrong, and not merely as mistaken in their calculations of the chances of success. For similar reasons it may possibly be expedient on the whole that certain special relaxations of certain moral rules should continue to exist in certain professions and sections of society, while at the same time they continue to be disapproved by the rest of the society. The evils, however, which must spring from this permanent conflict of opinion are so grave, that an enlightened Utilitarian will probably in most cases attempt to remove it; by either openly maintaining the need of a relaxation of the ordinary moral rule under the special circumstances in question; or, on the other hand, endeavouring to get the ordinary rule recognised and enforced by all conscientious persons in that section of society where its breach has become habitual. And of these two courses it seems likely that he will in most cases adopt the latter; since such rules are most commonly found on examination to have been relaxed rather for the convenience of individuals, than in the interest of the community at large.

BOOK II

Chapter V

Happiness and Duty

§ 1. The belief in the connexion of Happiness with Duty is one to which we find a general tendency among civilised men, at least after a certain stage in civilisation has been reached. But it is doubtful whether it would be affirmed, among ourselves, as a generalisation from experience, and not rather as a matter of direct Divine Revelation, or an inevitable inference from the belief that the world is governed by a perfectly Good and Omnipotent Being. To examine thoroughly the validity of the latter belief is one of the most important tasks that human reason can attempt: but involving as it does an exhaustive inquiry into the evidences of Natural and Revealed Religion, it could hardly be included within the scope of the present treatise. Here, then, I shall only consider the coincidence of Duty and Happiness in so far as it is maintained by arguments drawn from experience and supposed to be realised in our present earthly life. Perhaps, as so restricted, the coincidence can hardly be said to be "currently believed": indeed it may be suggested that the opposite belief is implied in the general admission of the necessity of rewards and punishments in a future state, in order to exhibit and realise completely the moral government of the world. But reflection will show that this implication is not necessary; for it is possible to hold that even here virtue is always rewarded and vice punished, so far as to make the virtuous course of action always the most prudent; while yet the rewards and punishments are not sufficient to satisfy our sense of justice. Admitting that the virtuous man is often placed on earth in circumstances so adverse that his life is not as happy as that of many less virtuous; it is still possible to maintain that by virtue he will gain the maximum of happiness that can be gained under these circumstances, all appearances to the contrary notwithstanding. And this view has certainly been held by moralists of reputation on grounds drawn from actual experience of human life; and seems often to be confidently put forward on similar grounds by popular preachers and moralisers. It appears therefore desirable to subject this opinion to a careful and impartial examination. In conducting this examination, at the present stage of our inquiry, we shall have to use the received notions of Duty without further definition or analysis: but it is commonly assumed by those whose view we are to examine that these conceptions—as they are found in the moral consciousness of ordinary well-meaning persons—are at least approximately valid and trustworthy. . . .

§ 2. Accepting, then, the common division of duties into self-regarding and social, it may be conceded that as far as the first are concerned the view that we are examining is not likely to provoke any controversy: for by "duties towards oneself" are commonly meant acts that tend directly or indirectly to promote one's happiness. We may therefore confine our attention to the social department of Duty, and consider whether by observing the moral rules that prescribe certain modes of behaviour towards others we shall always tend to secure the greatest balance of happiness to ourselves.

Here it will be convenient to adopt with some modification the terminology of Bentham; and to regard the pleasures consequent on conformity to moral rules, and the pains consequent on their violation, as the "sanctions" of these rules. These "sanctions" we may classify as External and Internal. The former class will include both "Legal Sanctions," or penalties inflicted by the authority, direct or indirect, of the sovereign; and "Social Sanctions," which are either the pleasures that may be expected from the approval and goodwill of our fellow-men generally, and the services that they will be prompted to render both by this goodwill and by their appreciation of the usefulness of good conduct, or the annoyance and losses that are to be feared from their distrust and dislike. The internal sanctions of duty— so far as it diverges from the conduct which self-interest apart from morality would dictate—will lie in the pleasurable emotion attending virtuous action, or in the absence of remorse, or will result more indirectly from some effect on the mental constitution of the agent produced by the maintenance of virtuous dispositions and habits. This classification is important for our present purpose, chiefly because the systems of rules to which these different sanctions are respectively attached may be mutually conflicting. The Positive Morality of any community undergoes development, and is thus subject to changes which affect the consciences of the few before they are accepted by the many; so that the rules at any time sustained by the strongest social sanctions may not only fall short of, but even clash with, the intuitions of those members of the community who have most moral insight. For similar reasons Law and Positive Morality may be at variance, in details. For though a law could not long exist, which it was universally thought wrong to obey; there may easily be laws commanding conduct that is considered immoral by some more or less enlightened fraction of the community, especially by some sect or party that has a public opinion of its own: and any individual may be so much more closely connected with this fraction than with the rest of the community, that the social sanction may in his case practically operate against the legal.

This conflict of sanctions is of great importance in considering whether these sanctions, as at present capable of being foreseen, are sufficient in all cases to determine a rational egoist to the performance of social duty: for the more stress we lay on either the legal or the social sanctions of moral conduct, the greater difficulty we shall have in proving the coincidence of duty and self-interest in the exceptional cases in which we find these sanctions arrayed against what we conceive to be duty.

But even if we put these cases out of sight, it still seems clear that the external sanctions of morality alone are not always sufficient to render immoral conduct also imprudent. We must indeed admit that in an even tolerably well-ordered society—i.e., in an ordinary civilised community in its normal condition—all serious open violation of law is contrary to prudence, unless it is an incident in a successful process of violent revolution: and further, that violent revolutions would very rarely—perhaps never—be made by a combination of persons, all perfectly under the control of enlightened self-love; on account of the general and widespread destruction of security and of other means of happiness which such disturbances inevitably involve. Still, so long as actual human beings are not all rational egoists, such times of disorder will be liable to occur: and we cannot say that *under existing circumstances* it is a clear universal precept of Rational Self-love that a man should "seek peace and ensue it"; since the disturbance of political order may offer to a cool and skilful person, who has the art of fishing in troubled waters, opportunities of gaining wealth, fame, and power, far beyond what he could hope for in peaceful times. In short, though we may admit that a society composed entirely of rational egoists would, when once organised, tend to remain in a stable and orderly condition, it does not follow that any individual rational egoist will always be on the side of order in any existing community.

But at any rate, in the most orderly societies with which we are acquainted, the administration of law and justice is never in so perfect a state as to render *secret* crimes always acts of folly, on the score of the legal penalties attached to them. For however much these may outweigh the advantages of crime, cases must inevitably occur in which the risk of discovery is so small, that on a sober calculation the almost certain gain will more than compensate for the slight chance of the penalty. And finally, in no community is the law actually in so perfect a state that there are not certain kinds of flagrantly anti-social conduct which slip through its meshes and escape legal penalties altogether, or incur only such legal penalties as are outweighed by the profit of law-breaking.

§ 3. Let us proceed, then, to consider how far the social sanction in such cases supplies the defects of the legal. No doubt the hope of praise and liking and services from one's fellow-men, and the fear of forfeiting these and incurring instead aversion, refusal of aid, and social exclusion, are considerations often important enough to determine the rational egoist to law-observance, even in default of adequate legal penalties. Still these sanctions are liable to fail just where the legal penalties are defective; social no less than legal penalties are evaded by secret crimes; and in cases of criminal revolutionary violence, the efficacy of the social sanction is apt to be seriously impaired by the party spirit enlisted on the side of the criminal. For it has to be observed that the force of the social sanction diminishes very rapidly, in proportion to the number of dissidents from the common opinion that awards it. Disapprobation that is at once intense and quite universal would be so severe a penalty as perhaps to outweigh any imaginable advantages; since it seems impossible for a human being to live happily, whatever other goods he may enjoy, without the kindly regards of some of his fellows: and so, in contemplating the conventional portrait of the tyrant, who is represented as necessarily suspicious of those nearest him, even of the members of his own family, we feel prepared to admit that such a life must involve the extreme of unhappiness. But when we turn to contemplate the actual tyrannical usurpers, wicked statesmen, successful leaders of unwarranted rebellion, and, speaking generally, the great criminals whose position raises them out of the reach of legal penalties, it does not appear that the moral odium under which they lie must necessarily count for much in an egoistic calculation of the gain and loss resulting from their conduct. For this disesteem is only expressed by a portion of the community: and its utterance is often drowned in the loud-voiced applause of the multitude whose admiration is largely independent of moral considerations. Nor are there wanting philosophers and historians whose judgment manifests a similar independence.

It seems, then, impossible to affirm that the external sanctions of men's legal duties will always be sufficient to identify duty with interest. And a corresponding assertion would be still more unwarranted in respect of moral duties not included within the sphere of Law. In saying this, I am fully sensible of the force of what may be called the Principle of Reciprocity, by which certain utilitarians have endeavoured to prove the coincidence of any individual's interest with his social duties. Virtues (they say) are qualities either useful or directly agreeable to others: thus they either increase the market value of the virtuous man's services, and cause others to purchase them at a higher rate and to allot to him more dignified and interesting functions; or they dispose men to please him, both out of gratitude and in order to enjoy the pleasures of his society in return: and again—since man is an imitative animal—the exhibition of these qualities is naturally rewarded by a reciprocal manifestation of them on the part of others, through the mere influence of example. I do not doubt that the prospect of these advantages is an adequate motive for cultivating many virtues and avoiding much vice. Thus on such grounds a rational egoist will generally be strict and punctual in the fulfilment of all his engagements, and truthful in his assertions, in order to win the confidence of other men; and he will be zealous and industrious in his work, in order to obtain gradually more important and therefore more honourable and lucrative employment; and he will control such of his passions and appetites as are likely to interfere with his efficiency; and will not exhibit violent anger or use unnecessary harshness even towards servants and subordinates; and towards his equals and superiors in rank he will be generally polite and complaisant and good-humoured, and prompt to show them all

such kindness as costs but little in proportion to the pleasure it gives. Still, reflection seems to show that the conduct recommended by this line of reasoning does not really coincide with moral duty. For, first, what one requires for social success is that one should *appear,* rather than *be,* useful to others: and hence this motive will not restrain one from doing secret harm to others, or even from acting openly in a way that is really harmful, though not perceived to be so. And again, a man is not useful to others by his virtue only, but sometimes rather by his vice; or more often by a certain admixture of unscrupulousness with his good and useful qualities. And further, morality prescribes the performance of duties equally towards all, and that we should abstain as far as possible from harming any but on the Principle of Reciprocity we should exhibit our useful qualities chiefly towards the rich and powerful, and abstain from injuring those who can retaliate; while we may reasonably omit our duties to the poor and feeble, if we find a material advantage in so doing, unless they are able to excite the sympathy of persons who can harm us. Moreover, some vices (as for example, many kinds of sensuality and extravagant luxury) do not inflict any immediate or obvious injury on any individual, though they tend in the long-run to impair the general happiness: hence few persons find themselves strongly moved to check or punish this kind of mischief.

Doubtless in the last-mentioned cases the mere disrepute inevitably attaching to open immorality is an important consideration. But I do not think that this will be seriously maintained to be sufficient always to turn the scales of prudence against vice— at least by any one who has duly analysed the turbid and fluctuating streams of social opinion upon which the good or ill repute of individuals mainly depends, and considered the conflicting and divergent elements that they contain. Many moralists have noticed the discrepancy in modern Europe between the Law of Honour (or the more important rules maintained by the social sanction of polite persons) and the morality professed in society at large. This is, however, by no means the only instance of a special code, divergent in certain points from the moral rules generally accepted in the community where it exists. Most religious sects and parties, and probably the majority of trades and professions, exhibit this phenomenon in some degree. I do not mean merely that special rules of behaviour are imposed upon members of each profession, corresponding to their special social functions and relations: I mean that a peculiar moral opinion is apt to grow up, conflicting to a certain extent with the opinion of the general public. The most striking part of this divergence consists generally in the approval or excusal of practices disapproved by the current morality: as (e.g.) licence among soldiers, bribery among politicians in certain ages and countries, unveracity of various degrees among priests and advocates, fraud in different forms among tradesmen. In such cases there are generally strong natural inducements to disobey the stricter rule (in fact it would seem to be to the continual pressure of these inducements that the relaxation of the rule has been due): while at the same time the social sanction is weakened to such an extent that it is sometimes hard to say whether it outweighs a similar force on the other side. For a man who, under these circumstances, conforms to the stricter rule, if he does not actually meet with contempt and aversion from those of his calling, is at least liable to be called eccentric and fantastic: and this is still more the case if by such conformity he foregoes advantages not only to himself but to his relatives or friends or party. Very often this professional or sectarian excusal of immorality of which we are speaking is not so clear and explicit as to amount to the establishment of a rule, conflicting with the generally received rule: but is still sufficient to weaken indefinitely the social sanction in favour of the latter. And, apart from these special divergences, we may say generally that in most civilised societies there are two different degrees of positive morality, both maintained in some sort by common consent; a stricter code being publicly taught and avowed, while a laxer set of rules is privately admitted as the only code which can be supported by social sanctions of any great force. By refusing to conform to the stricter code a man is often not liable to incur exclusion from social intercourse, or any material hindrance to professional advancement, or even serious dislike on the part of any of the persons whose society he will most naturally

seek; and under such circumstances the mere loss of a certain amount of reputation is not likely to be felt as a very grave evil, except by persons peculiarly sensitive to the pleasures and pains of reputation. And there would seem to be many men whose happiness does not depend on the approbation or disapprobation of the moralist—and of mankind in general in so far as they support the moralist—to such an extent as to make it prudent for them to purchase this praise by any great sacrifice of other goods.

§ 4. We must conclude, then, that if the conduct prescribed to the individual by the avowedly accepted morality of the community of which he is a member, can be shown to coincide with that to which Rational Self-love would prompt, it must be, in many cases, solely or chiefly on the score of the internal sanctions. In considering the force of these sanctions, I shall eliminate those pleasures and pains which lie in the anticipation of rewards and punishments in a future life: for as we are now supposing the calculations of Rational Egoism to be performed without taking into account any feelings that are beyond the range of experience, it will be more consistent to exclude also the pleasurable or painful anticipations of such feelings.

Let us, then, contemplate by itself the satisfaction that attends the performance of duty as such (without taking into consideration any ulterior consequences), and the pain that follows on its violation. . . . I shall not of course attempt to weigh exactly these pleasures and pains against others; but I see no empirical grounds for believing that such feelings are always sufficiently intense to turn the balance of prospective happiness in favour of morality. This will hardly be denied if the question is raised in respect of isolated acts of duty. Let us take an extreme case, which is yet quite within the limits of experience. The call of duty has often impelled a soldier or other public servant, or the adherent of a persecuted religion, to face certain and painful death, under circumstances where it might be avoided with little or no loss even of reputation. To prove such conduct always reasonable from an egoistic point of view, we have to assume that, in all cases where such a duty could exist and be recognised, the mere pain that would follow on evasion of duty would be so great as to render the whole remainder of life hedonistically worthless. Surely such an assumption would be paradoxical and extravagant. Nothing that we know of the majority of persons in any society would lead us to conclude that their moral feelings taken alone form so preponderant an element of their happiness. And a similar conclusion seems irresistible even in more ordinary cases, where a man is called on to give up, for virtue's sake, not life, but a considerable share of the ordinary sources of human happiness. Can we say that all, or even most, men are so constituted that the satisfactions of a good conscience are certain to repay them for such sacrifices, or that the pain and loss involved in them would certainly be outweighed by the remorse that would follow the refusal to make them?

Perhaps, however, so much as this has scarcely ever been expressly maintained. What Plato in his *Republic* and other writers on the same side have rather tried to prove, is not that at any particular moment duty will be, to every one on whom it may devolve, productive of more happiness than any other course of conduct; but rather that it is every one's interest on the whole to choose the life of the virtuous man. But even this it is very difficult even to render probable: as will appear, I think, if we examine the lines of reasoning by which it is commonly supported.

To begin with Plato's argument. He represents the soul of the virtuous man as a well-ordered polity of impulses, in which every passion and appetite is duly obedient to the rightful sovereignty of reason, and operates only within the limits laid down by the latter. He then contrasts the tranquil peace of such a mind with the disorder of one where a succession of baser impulses, or some ruling passion, lords it over reason: and asks which is the happiest, even apart from external rewards and punishments. But we may grant all that Plato claims, and yet be no further advanced towards the solution of the question before us. For here the issue does not lie between Reason and Passion, but rather—in Butler's language—between Rational Self-love and Conscience. We are supposing the Egoist to have all his impulses under control, and are only asking how this control is to be exercised. Now we have seen

that the regulation and organisation of life best calculated to attain the end of self-interest appears prima facie divergent at certain points from that to which men in general are prompted by a sense of duty. In order to maintain Plato's position it has to be shown that this appearance is false; and that a system of self-government, which under certain circumstances leads us to pain, loss, and death, is still that which self-interest requires. It can scarcely be said that our nature is such that only this anti-egoistic kind of regulation is possible; that the choice lies between this and none at all. It is easy to imagine a rational egoist, strictly controlling each of his passions and impulses—including his social sentiments—within such limits that its indulgence should not involve the sacrifice of some greater gratification: and experience seems to show us many examples of persons who at least approximate as closely to this type as any one else does to the ideal of the orthodox moralist. Hence if the regulation of Conscience be demonstrably the best means to the individual's happiness, it must be because the order kept by Self-love involves a sacrifice of pleasure on the whole, as compared with the order kept by Conscience. And if this is the case, it would seem that it can only be on account of the special emotional pleasure attending the satisfaction of the moral sentiments, or special pain or loss of happiness consequent on their repression and violation.

Before, however, we proceed further, a fundamental difficulty must be removed which has probably some time since suggested itself to the reader. If a man thinks it reasonable to seek his own interest, it is clear that he cannot himself disapprove of any conduct that comes under this principle or approve of the opposite. And hence it may appear that the pleasures and pains of conscience cannot enter into the calculation whether a certain course of conduct is or is not in accordance with Rational Egoism, because they cannot attach themselves in the egoist's mind to any modes of action which have not been already decided, on other grounds, to be reasonable or the reverse. And this is to a certain extent true; but we must here recur to the distinction . . . between the general impulse to do what we believe to be reasonable, and special sentiments of liking or aversion for special kinds of conduct, independent of their reasonableness. In the moral sentiments as they exist in ordinary men, these two kinds of feeling are indistinguishably blended; because it is commonly believed that the rules of conduct to which the common moral sentiments are attached are in some way or other reasonable. We can, however, conceive the two separated: and in fact, as was before said, we have experience of such separation whenever a man is led by a process of thought to adopt a different view of morality from that in which he has been trained; for in such a case there will always remain in his mind some quasi-moral likings and aversions, no longer sustained by his deliberate judgment of right and wrong. And thus there is every reason to believe that most men, however firmly they might adopt the principles of Egoistic Hedonism, would still feel sentiments prompting to the performance of social duty, as commonly recognised in their society, independently of any conclusion that the actions prompted by such sentiments were reasonable and right. For such sentiments would always be powerfully supported by the sympathy of others, and their expressions of praise and blame, liking and aversion: and since it is agreed that the conduct commonly recognised as virtuous is *generally* coincident with that which enlightened self-love would dictate, a rational egoist's habits of conduct will be such as naturally to foster these (for him) "quasi-moral" feelings. The question therefore arises—not whether the egoist should cherish and indulge these sentiments up to a certain point, which all would admit—but whether he can consistently encourage them to grow to such a pitch that they will always prevail over the strongest opposing considerations; or, to put it otherwise, whether prudence requires him to give them the rein and let them carry him whither they will. We have already seen ground for believing that Rational Self-love will best attain its end by limiting its conscious operation and allowing free play to disinterested impulses: can we accept the further paradox that it is reasonable for it to abdicate altogether its supremacy over some of these impulses?

On a careful consideration of the matter, it will appear, I think, that this abdication of self-love is not really a possible occurrence in the mind of a sane person, who still regards his own interest as the reasonable ultimate end of his actions. Such a man may, no doubt, resolve that he will devote himself unreservedly to the practice of virtue, without any particular consideration of what appears to him to be his interest: he may perform a series of acts in accordance with this resolution, and these may gradually form in him strong habitual tendencies to acts of a similar kind. But it does not seem that these habits of virtue can ever become so strong as to gain irresistible control over a sane and reasonable will. When the occasion comes on which virtue demands from such a man an extreme sacrifice— the imprudence of which must force itself upon his notice, however little he may be in the habit of weighing his own pleasures and pains—he must always be able to deliberate afresh, and to act (as far as the control of his will extends) without reference to his past actions. It may, however, be said that, though an egoist retaining his belief in rational egoism cannot thus abandon his will to the sway of moral enthusiasm, still, supposing it possible for him to change his conviction and prefer duty to interest,—or supposing we compare him with another man who makes this choice,—we shall find that a gain in happiness on the whole results from this preference. It may be held that the pleasurable emotions attendant upon such virtuous or quasi-virtuous habits as are compatible with adhesion to egoistic principles are so inferior to the raptures that attend the unreserved and passionate surrender of the soul to virtue, that it is really a man's interest—even with a view to the present life only—to obtain, if he can, the convictions that render this surrender possible; although under certain circumstances it must necessarily lead him to act in a manner which, considered by itself, would be undoubtedly imprudent. This is certainly a tenable proposition, and I am quite disposed to think it true of persons with specially refined moral sensibilities. But—though from the imperfections of the hedonistic calculus the proposition cannot in any case be conclusively disproved— it seems, as I have said, to be opposed to the broad results of experience, so far as the great majority of mankind are concerned. Observation would lead me to suppose that most men are so constituted as to feel far more keenly pleasures (and pains) arising from some other source than the conscience; either from the gratifications of sense, or from the possession of power and fame, or from strong human affections, or from the pursuit of science, art, etc.; so that in many cases perhaps not even early training could have succeeded in giving to the moral feelings the requisite predominance: and certainly where this training has been wanting, it seems highly improbable that a mere change of ethical conviction could develop their moral susceptibilities so far as to make it clearly their earthly interest to resolve on facing all sacrifices for the fulfilment of duty.

To sum up: although the performance of duties towards others and the exercise of social virtue seem to be *generally* the best means to the attainment of the individual's happiness, and it is easy to exhibit this coincidence between Virtue and Happiness rhetorically and popularly; still, when we carefully analyse and estimate the consequences of Virtue to the virtuous agent, it appears improbable that this coincidence is complete and universal. We may conceive the coincidence becoming perfect in a Utopia where men were as much in accord on moral as they are now on mathematical questions, where Law was in perfect harmony with Moral Opinion, and all offences were discovered and duly punished: or we may conceive the same result attained by intensifying the moral sentiments of all members of the community, without any external changes (which indeed would then be unnecessary). But just in proportion as existing societies and existing men fall short of this ideal, rules of conduct based on the principles of Egoistic Hedonism seem liable to diverge from those which most men are accustomed to recognise as prescribed by Duty and Virtue.

NOTES

1. It may be worth while to notice, that in Mill's well-known treatise on Utilitarianism this confusion, though expressly deprecated, is to some extent encouraged by the authors treatment of the subject.
2. It should be observed that the question here is as to the distribution of *Happiness,* not the *means of happiness.* If more happiness on the whole is produced by giving the same means of happiness to B rather than to A, it is an obvious and incontrovertible deduction from the Utilitarian principle that it ought to be given to B, whatever inequality in the distribution of the *means* of happiness this may involve.

STUDY QUESTIONS

1. Should a utilitarian take into account the happiness of future generations?
2. Would utilitarians ever be justified in keeping secret their commitment to utilitarianism?
3. Would a utilitarian be justified in sacrificing the lives of a few people in order to maximize the happiness of many others?
4. Might being moral lead to unhappiness?

Well-Being

Shelly Kagan

Many consequentialists hold that the only good to be maximized is well-being. But what makes someone's life go well? Shelly Kagan, Professor of Philosophy at Yale University, provides an overview of the three most prominent theories of well-being: attaining pleasures, satisfying desires, and obtaining objective goods. Kagan considers each view in turn and concludes that none is without serious problems.

. . . [W]hat, exactly, is well-being? What is it for someone's life to go better or worse? What does someone's being better or worse off consist in?

It is important to understand what we are *not* asking in raising these questions. We are not asking what sorts of things may have a causal impact on well-being. Obviously enough, almost anything at all might, in the right circumstances, affect someone's level of well-being. And certain things will have an effect in almost all circumstances: money, a job, and opportunities, for example, will almost always raise your level of well-being; and poverty, disease, and enemies will almost always lower your well-being. But these things are only a means to raising or lowering your level of well-being. They have instrumental value (or disvalue) because of the impact they can have on how well off you are. But they are not themselves what well-being (or ill-being) *consists* in. What we want to know, then, is what is it that *constitutes* being well off? (Not: what are the *means* to being well off?) We want to know: what are the "components" of well-being?

One important and popular answer is this: well-being consists in the presence of pleasure and

the absence of pain. The more pleasure and the less pain that a life contains, the better the life. Increase the amount of pleasure that a person experiences (or decrease the amount of pain), and you make that person better off; increase the pain (or decrease the pleasure), and you make her worse off.

Now in point of fact, pretty much everyone believes at least this much: the presence of pleasure and the absence of pain is at least one component of well-being. (It is quite hard to deny this. The value of pleasure and the disvalue of pain seem virtually self-evident to anyone experiencing them.) But the particular view I have in mind makes a bolder claim; it holds that well-being consists *solely* in the presence of pleasure and the absence of pain. Pleasure and pain are the *only* elements that directly constitute how well off a person is.

We can put this same point another way. If we ask ourselves what are the intrinsic goods by virtue of which a life worth living *is* a life worth living, the answer—according to this view—is pleasure, and only pleasure. Similarly, the only intrinsic evil by virtue of which a life is less worth living is pain. This view—that well-being consists solely in the

From Shelly Kagan, *Normative Ethics*, Westview Press, 1998. Reprinted by permission of the publisher.

presence of pleasure and the absence of pain—might be called *welfare hedonism.*

Actually, there are at least four different hedonistic views that need to be distinguished. *Psychological hedonism* is the claim that—as a matter of empirical, psychological fact—everyone's ultimate goal is to pursue their own pleasure and minimize their own pain. *Ethical hedonism* is the claim that—as a matter of normative ethics—what everyone *should* do morally is to try to maximize pleasure and minimize pain. From a logical standpoint, at least, since these two views make no claims about what has or lacks intrinsic value, they need to be distinguished from *value hedonism,* which is the claim that pleasure is the only intrinsic good and pain the only intrinsic evil. But even this last view needs to be distinguished from welfare hedonism, which limits itself to the somewhat more modest claim that *well-being* consists solely in the presence of pleasure and the absence of pain. (After all, one might accept welfare hedonism and yet still believe that there are other intrinsic goods that have nothing to do with well-being.)

Some people are attracted to all four hedonistic claims. But it is only welfare hedonism with which we are concerned here, since it is only welfare hedonism that purports to be and limits itself to being a theory about the nature of well-being. So, for our purposes, we can put these other versions of hedonism aside and use the term "hedonism" to refer to welfare hedonism.

Of course, the fact of the matter is that life is not one unending run of intense pleasure, unblemished by any pain, and so the hedonist needs to tell us how to rank lives that are mixtures of various sorts of pleasures and pains. However, the basic idea here is fairly simple and obvious: add up the pleasures and subtract the pains. The greater the "sum" (that is, the higher the net balance of pleasure minus pain), the better the life. But since not all pleasures are equally good, and not all pains are equally bad, the view needs to be made somewhat more complicated. Still, a solution is not beyond our reach. Intuitively, it seems, the longer a pleasure lasts, the better; and the more intense the pleasure is, the better as well. So by multiplying intensity times duration, we can calculate the quantity of pleasure a given pleasant experience

contains. Similarly, we can calculate the quantity of pain by multiplying the intensity of the pain times the duration of the pain. By adding up the total quantity of pleasure and then subtracting from this the total quantity of pain, we arrive at a measure of how good a life someone has had as a whole—their overall level of well-being. (Different calculations, but along similar lines, will allow us to make judgments about how well off a person is at a time, or during a certain period, or how much a person's level of well-being would vary under different outcomes.)

Advocates of such *quantitative hedonism* need not believe that we can actually make the relevant calculations, at least not with very much precision. But they can still claim that the basic ideas expressed here capture real and important insights into the nature of well-being: well-being is simply a matter of pleasure and pain; and the value or disvalue of pleasures and pains is simply a matter of their intensity and duration.

One important implication of quantitative hedonism is that quantity for quantity, all pleasures are equally valuable. Of course, people will differ from one another with regard to what sorts of things *give* them pleasure: you may derive great pleasure from listening to opera, while I find the experience painful; I may enjoy bird-watching, while you find it boring. From a practical standpoint, therefore, it will clearly be important to get our facts straight about what exactly gives pleasure to whom. But so long as we are indeed talking about equal quantities of pleasure, it doesn't matter where the pleasure comes from. Similarly, some things (such as great art) may be rich and fruitful sources of large quantities of intense and abiding pleasure, while other things (such as watching television) are at best sources of minimal, mild, and fleeting pleasure. So from a practical standpoint it may well be rational to invest more energy in contemplating art than in watching television. But so long as we are talking about equal quantities of pleasure, it doesn't matter where the pleasure comes from: a unit of art-based pleasure is of no greater value than a unit of television-based pleasure.

This, at any rate, is the view of quantitative hedonism. But it is at just this point that some think quantitative hedonism goes astray. Many find it very hard to believe that one kind of pleasure is no more valuable than another (unit for unit). After all, if *quantity* of pleasure is all that matters, this seems to lead to some pretty bizarre conclusions. Consider the life of a contented pig, wallowing in the mud: it might be filled with pleasure, a far greater quantity of pleasure than can be found in the life of a person. Yet who would want to trade places with the pig? Who thinks that the pig has a better life?

Pressed to defend our preference for a human life over a porcine existence, a natural suggestion is this: pigs might have a greater quantity of pleasure, but humans can have pleasures of a much more valuable *kind*. Unlike pigs, humans can experience love, friendship, and art; they can have the pleasures of discovery, creativity, and understanding. We seem drawn to the thought that such "spiritual" or "mental" pleasures are simply of a higher quality than the mere "physical" or "bodily" pleasures that are all that are available to the pig—and that these "higher" pleasures are of greater intrinsic value than the "lower" pleasures. If this is right, then when judging the level of well-being of some individual (whether human or non-human) we must take into account not only quantity but also *quality*. (Perhaps a new formula could achieve this by multiplying intensity times duration times a "quality rating"—but we need not pursue this question. We can also put aside, for the sake of simplicity, the question of whether quality can also affect the value of *pains,* as well as pleasures.)

Such *qualitative hedonism* will be resisted by advocates of quantitative hedonism, who may claim that the appeal of qualitative hedonism is based on a simple mistake. As we have already observed, and as the quantitative hedonists themselves would stress, the sources of the so-called higher pleasures typically lead to far greater *quantities* of pleasure than do the sources of the so-called lower pleasures. So from a practical point of view, it typically makes sense to prefer the experiences of the higher pleasures—for these experiences will simply contain more pleasure! But this doesn't show that a given quantity of higher pleasure is any more valuable than the *same* quantity of lower pleasure. In and of itself, quality just doesn't make a difference to the intrinsic value of (a unit of) pleasure.

In reply, the qualitative hedonists will simply deny that they are making any such mistake. Admittedly, sources of higher pleasures typically yield far greater quantities of pleasure than do sources of lower pleasures; but even when we take this into account— even when we focus on similar quantities of pleasure—we still find ourselves attracted to the thought that a given quantity of higher pleasure is more valuable than the same quantity of lower pleasure. . . .

Of course, even if we agree with the qualitative hedonist, that higher pleasures are more valuable than lower pleasures, we are still in need of some test to tell which of two pleasures is the more valuable (that is, higher in quality). The most plausible suggestion that has been made is this: ask the experts. That is, ask those who have experience with both sorts of pleasures. If those who have experience with both pleasure X and pleasure Y prefer to have X rather than Y (given a choice between equal quantities of either), then we can reasonably conclude that X is the more valuable pleasure.

It must be admitted that applying this test is not without its difficulties. As often as not, it may be impossible to find someone who genuinely has first-hand experience with both kinds of pleasures. How many lovers of opera really know what it is like to be totally absorbed watching game shows on television? And what human being has had the experience of being a pig wallowing in the mud? Still, the qualitative hedonist can admit these practical difficulties while insisting that the basic idea behind the test is correct: pleasures can differ as to their quality; and these differences in quality would be reflected in the preferences of those who had experienced them.

A remaining worry is this. Is qualitative hedonism genuinely a form of *hedonism?* The welfare hedonist claims that pleasure (and the absence of pain) is all that matters intrinsically for well-being. If one holds that quantity of pleasure is not all that matters, but that quality matters too, has one abandoned the commitment to hedonism? People's intuitions on this question seem to differ, although it is not clear what turns on the answer other than the label. Even if the so-called qualitative hedonist is not genuinely a hedonist, the position she holds might still be the truth.

However, pushed this far, we might want to go farther. If the value of our various experiences can vary—depending on what *kind* of pleasures they are—perhaps other experiences may have value, too, even though they are not pleasures at all! Perhaps certain experiences have a high quality and contribute to our well-being, even though it would be stretching things to say they are pleasant. At the very least, it might be grossly misleading to focus on whatever pleasure they contain, as this might be quite irrelevant to their value.

Perhaps, then, the position we should actually accept is this: all that intrinsically matters for determining one's level of well-being are the various experiences one has—one's mental states. Some mental states are more valuable than others, and pleasure is presumably one such kind of valuable experience (or one aspect of an experience that may make it valuable). But it is not the only kind of valuable experience (or the only aspect of an experience that can give it value). In short, perhaps we should simply accept a *mental slate* theory of well-being.

Strictly speaking, of course, hedonism is a version of a mental state theory (or perhaps: it is a family of mental state theories). It agrees that your mental states are what determine your level of well-being, and it holds a particular view as to which mental states have value (namely, the pleasant ones). But we are now considering the possibility of theories that move beyond hedonism in allowing other kinds of experiences to have value as well. Of course, any fully specified mental state theory would need to tell us exactly what kinds of experiences have what kind of value. And it should be noted that, other than hedonism, there have been relatively few attempts to do this. But even if one is uncertain as to exactly which kinds of experiences contribute to well-being, and by how much, one might be quite convinced as to the fundamental truth of mental statism: your mental states are the only things that directly determine your level of well-being.

Many people find the idea of mental statism quite compelling. It lies behind the common saying that "What you don't know can't hurt you." What else *could* constitute well-being other than having the right mental states? Yet mental state theories seem to leave something important out, for there are cases in which all mental state theories lead to answers that are difficult to accept.

Imagine a man who dies contented, thinking he has achieved everything he wanted in life: his wife and family love him, he is a respected member of the community, and he has founded a successful business. Or so he thinks. In reality, however, he has been completely deceived: his wife cheated on him, his daughter and son were only nice to him so that they would be able to borrow the car, the other members of the community only pretended to respect him for the sake of the charitable contributions he sometimes made, and his business partner has been embezzling funds from the company, which will soon go bankrupt.

In thinking about this man's life, it is difficult to believe that it is all a life could be, that this life has gone about as well as a life could go. Yet this seems to be the very conclusion mental state theories must reach! For from the "inside"—looking only at the man's experiences—everything was perfect. We can imagine that the man's mental states were *exactly* the same as the ones he would have had if he had actually been loved and respected. So if mental states are all that matter, then—since this man got the mental states right—there is nothing missing from this man's life at all. It is a picture of a life that has gone well. But this seems quite an unacceptable thing to say about this life; it is surely not the kind of life we would want for ourselves. So mental state theories must be wrong.

A defender of the mental state approach might insist that the businessman's life must have gone well, since he was happy. But those who think something important was missing from this man's life need not be impressed by this answer. Some will deny that the man was genuinely happy: he *thought* he was, but in reality, he was not; perhaps the example shows that there is more to happiness than having the right sorts of mental states. Others will agree that the businessman was indeed happy; but they will argue that this only shows that there is more to well-being than happiness, since something is certainly less than ideal about the deceived man's life. In short, whatever we feel about the correct account of happiness, the example still seems to show that mental state theories are wrong: having the best kind of mental states is just not enough.

To be fair, some mental state theorists may not think that our deceived businessman had the very best kinds of experiences—perhaps it would be better to have experiences of adventure or discovery. But it seems we could compose a comparable story whichever mental states are best. Indeed, if we want, we can imagine an "experience machine" that electronically stimulates your brain, giving you whatever experiences you think most valuable. The effect is so perfect that it will feel ("from the inside") *exactly* as though you were climbing mountains, composing symphonies, or what have you. In reality, you are simply floating in a tank in the scientist's lab—but once you are hooked up, all memory of this will disappear, and you will have exactly the mental states endorsed by your favorite mental state theory.

Would you want to spend your life hooked up to an experience machine? If not, then it seems that mental state theories must be wrong—all of them. For life on the experience machine gets the mental states exactly right; so if something is missing from a life on the experience machine—if it is not the best kind of life imaginable—then there must be more to well-being than having the right kind of experiences.

But what is missing? A natural response to these examples—the deceived businessman, the experience machine—is that these people don't really have what they *want.* They *think* they do, but they don't. The businessman wanted to be loved and respected. He thought he was—from the inside it *seemed* that he was, he had the same mental states as someone who was—but still he wasn't *really* loved and respected, even though that was what he *wanted.* Similarly, the person on the experience machine may, say, have the very same mental states as someone who is climbing a mountain, and climbing a mountain may be what he most wants to do. But since he obviously is not really climbing any mountains, he doesn't truly have what he wants—to climb mountains! In short, what is missing from all of these examples is that the person's preferences are not actually satisfied; things are not in fact the way they want them to be.

The point could be put this way: what we want out of life is to have what we *want* out of life, and what we want is almost always far more than merely having certain kinds of experiences. For example, if

you want to be a great and famous novelist, then your desire is only satisfied if you have in fact written a great novel, and your work is well-known by others. Merely having the experiences is not enough to actually satisfy the desire. (It should be noted that "satisfy" is being used here in a somewhat technical sense: a desire is satisfied, in this sense, if and only if the very thing that is desired actually occurs. This concept should not be confused with the *feeling* of satisfaction that often accompanies our believing that our desires have been met.)

These thoughts suggest a desire-based or a *preference* theory of well-being. According to the preference theory, well-being consists in having one's preferences satisfied. To the extent that your preferences or desires are satisfied, you are better off; to the extent that your preferences or desires are not satisfied, you are less well off. (Of course not all of your preferences are equally important to you, so we would probably want to make the view more complicated, holding that the stronger the desire, the greater the contribution to well-being made by the satisfaction of that desire. But we won't pursue these details here.)

Not surprisingly, mental state theorists will argue that the attractiveness of the preference theory is based on a confusion. Unlike our make-believe examples, they will note, in real life there is actually only one way to achieve the very same mental stares one would have if the corresponding "external" states of affairs really existed—and that is to actually bring about the external states of affairs. For example, the only way to have the very same experiences as someone climbing a mountain is to actually climb a mountain. So from a practical standpoint, we are justified in simply aiming at the *external* states, knowing that, if we can achieve these, the mental states will follow. Thus, aiming at the external states has instrumental value; it is the best means to the mental states. But this should not mislead us into thinking that the external states have *intrinsic* value, making a direct contribution to well-being; only the mental states themselves do that.

Preference theorists, however, may not be impressed by this argument. They will, of course, admit that in real life a given set of experiences and the corresponding external states of affairs go pretty much hand in hand—we don't get the one without the other. But this doesn't show that it is the former and not the latter that matters. We may have to think about various kinds of make-believe examples to find cases where we would have the mental states without the corresponding external reality; but when we do think about such cases, we see quite clearly that what we value is *more* than merely having the right mental states. Our preferences concern external reality, too, and not only experiences. Of course, it is certainly true that *one* of the things we all have preferences about is having the right mental states. (I want to experience pleasures and not pain; I want to have the experiences of loving and being loved; I want to experience the accomplishment of my various goals; and so on.) So a preference theory will certainly recognize that my mental states are one of the things that help determine my level of well-being. But mental state theories go wrong in claiming that mental states are the only thing that directly determine my level of well-being. My other preferences matter too; and they must be satisfied as well if I am to be completely well off.

Once more, I won't try to settle this dispute. But I do want to consider two other possible objections to the preference theory. Both try to show that the theory yields unacceptable results. The first objection notes that, according to the preference theory, I am made better off by the satisfaction of my various desires, regardless of the subject matter of the given desire. Suppose, then, that I am a fan of large prime numbers, and so I hope and desire that the total number of atoms in the universe is a prime. Imagine, furthermore, that the total number of atoms is, in point of fact, prime. Since this desire is satisfied, the preference theory must say that I am better off for it, that my life is the better for it. (I don't *know* that my desire is satisfied, of course. But as already noted, the question of whether a desire is satisfied should not be confused with the question of whether one realizes it and consequently has a feeling of satisfaction.)

But this is absurd! The number of atoms in the universe has nothing at all to do with the quality of my life. It makes no difference at all to my level of well-being. (Were the number really even, this would not leave me *worse* off!) So the preference theory must be false.

One possible explanation of what has gone wrong is this. My preferences can range over anything at all—including things that have nothing to do with me or my life. But the brute satisfaction of *these* preferences cannot plausibly be claimed to make me better off; so an *unrestricted* preference theory is unacceptable. The only plausible approach will be in terms of a *restricted* preference theory: we will have to find the particular subset of my desires that concern my life, and claim that it is only the satisfaction of *those* desires that constitutes my well-being.

(The mental state theorist, of course, will insist that this misdiagnoses the problem. The real source of the absurdity is in thinking that the mere satisfaction of a desire—any desire—can, in and of itself, make me better off, even if I never know about it, and so even if it never has any effect on my mental states. But the preference theorist may reply that she has already admitted that one of the things we care about are our mental states, in particular knowing that our desires have been satisfied. So the preference theorist can acknowledge that if one of my desires is satisfied without my knowing about it, I am still not as well off as I might have been—since my desire to *know* about it is not satisfied.)

The second objection to the preference theory—even in its restricted form—is this. Many of my desires, including desires about my life, are based on misinformation, sloppy thinking, inexperience, prejudice, bias, and various other kinds of error or irrationality. I might want something, for example, because I am misinformed as to its nature, and I falsely believe I will enjoy having it. It seems implausible to claim that giving me what I want in a case like this makes me better off. (Well, strictly speaking, knowing that I had gotten my way might give me some mild feeling of satisfaction, and this would presumably make me slightly better off; but what seems implausible is the claim that satisfying this mistaken desire leaves me better off in and of itself.) Yet I do in fact have such mistaken (or crazy, or irrational) desires among my desires, and so the preference theory apparently has to say that satisfying these desires does indeed improve my level of well-being.

To avoid this result, we need to distinguish between *actual* preference theories and *ideal* preference theories. As the name suggests, actual preference theories claim that well-being is a matter of the satisfaction of your actual desires—the desires you do in fact have, whatever their basis. As we have just seen, this has the counterintuitive implication that satisfying even your irrational or misinformed desires leaves you better off. In contrast, ideal preference theories claim that well-being is a matter of the satisfaction of your "ideal" desires—that is, the desires you *would* have if you were fully informed, thinking clearly, free from prejudice and bias, and so on. Since you would not have misinformed, crazy, or irrational desires under such ideal conditions, they are not among your ideal desires; so, on this view, satisfaction of such desires does not contribute to your well-being. It seems, then, that preference theorists who want to avoid the second objection should embrace an *ideal* preference theory. (Of course, assuming that they want to avoid the first objection as well, they will actually need to embrace a *restricted* ideal preference theory.)

But once we have made the move to an ideal preference theory, we may want to move even further. After all, what exactly is it that explains why it is only ideal desires whose satisfaction will contribute to well-being? Why does having what we want leave us better off in those cases—but only in those cases—where the desires in question are ideal desires? We cannot say: having what we want makes us better off by virtue of the very fact that these are the things we want. For this view actually supports the *actual* preference theory, rather than the ideal preference theory. (The things we want include everything that we *do* want—not just those things we would want if informed; and some of the things we *would* want if we had ideal preferences we do nor in fact already want.)

A tempting thought is this. Having the things we would want—if only we were fully informed, rational, free from bias, and so forth—is valuable, because these are the things that are truly worth having! That is, if we were fully informed, and so on, we would be in an ideal position to *recognize* which things have value and which things do not. And then our preferences would follow accordingly: we would prefer to have what has more value over what has less.

But this means that the appeal to preferences is not doing any actual work in explaining the source of the value. It is not that the various goods that we would want were we ideally informed are valuable because we would desire them; rather, we would want these goods because we would be able to *see* that they are indeed valuable, *independently* of our wanting them.

Thus we are led to *objective* theories of well-being, theories that hold that being well off is a matter of having certain goods in one's life, goods that are simply worth having, objectively speaking. Similarly, there may be certain objective bads or evils, the having of which simply leaves one worse off. Possession of the relevant goods and the absence of the relevant evils is what constitutes well-being. And the goods and evils themselves have intrinsic value or disvalue independently of our desires (actual or ideal); indeed, they have the particular value they have regardless of whether anyone is in a position to realize this.

Of course, any fully specified objective theory will need to provide us with a list of the various objective goods and evils that together determine one's level of well-being. Different objective theories will provide different lists. Indeed, it is possible to view hedonism as a kind of objective theory—one with a very short list! (Pleasure is the only objective good; pain the only objective evil.) But most objective theories will go beyond hedonism in offering longer lists—lists that include other mental states, and indeed include various external states of affairs as well (that is, they will include more than mental states alone). Typical goods on such lists might include accomplishment, creativity, health, knowledge, friendship, freedom, fame, and respect.

The preference theorist will hasten to point out that goods like these are typically desired by us (and certainly would be desired under ideal conditions), so the preference theory too can recognize the contribution these things make to well-being. And the hedonist will hasten to point out that goods like these are typically of crucial instrumental value in achieving the most pleasant mental states, so hedonism too will recognize the contribution these things make to well-being. The objective theorist, however, thinks that both these approaches miss the mark: the hedonist goes wrong in failing to recognize that these goods have intrinsic value, and not merely instrumental value; the preference theorist goes wrong in failing to see that the intrinsic value these goods possess is had objectively—it is not based on or somehow derived from the fact that we do or would desire them.

Yet if desire is not the basis of the value of these goods, what is? And what is it, if anything, that unifies the various items on the list? Why do these things, and only these things, have objective value? Not surprisingly, answers to these questions are difficult to come by, and different objective theorists offer different answers. Many proposals take the form of *perfectionism:* the objective goods are those that are elements in an ideal or perfect human life, one which fully realizes the distinctive and essential characteristics of human nature. Of course, even within a broadly perfectionist approach there is room for considerable disagreement, both with regard to what constitutes human nature and—accordingly—what goods are elements in the perfect human life.

But however we settle these questions, a difficulty remains. As we have seen, the objective theorist holds that possession of the objective goods makes one better off—regardless of whether or not one realizes this. This seems to have the implication that your life could be made better off by the possession of some "good" even though you yourself dislike it and would greatly prefer to be without it: since the good possesses objective value, your own opinion on the subject is quite irrelevant. Your life could be going well even though you are unhappy with almost all its central features! Thus, like the other theories of well-being, the objective theory too seems to lead to unacceptable results.

Some objective theorists may be willing to live with this implication of their theory. Others, however, may try to resist it, by claiming that although the value of the objective goods is not *based* on one's preferences or pleasure, nonetheless it is true for each objective good that if one possessed it, one would be glad to have it. But it is hard to see what could guarantee the truth of this fortunate convergence of objective value and desire or enjoyment. Indeed, critics of objective theories may well think that there simply *is* no way to guarantee this result: if we want convergence of goodness and desire or enjoyment, then we must build desire or enjoyment right into the definition of goodness. That is to say, we must appeal to either hedonism or a preference theory.

This then brings us full circle. Each theory of well-being has its attractive features, but none is without its drawbacks. Although there is considerable agreement that well-being is a central factor in determining the goodness of an outcome, there is nothing approaching agreement as to what exactly well-being consists in. As always, this does not mean that no single view is correct; it does, however, mean that each of us will have to decide for himself or herself which view is the most plausible one on balance—once all of the arguments of each side have been considered.

It is worth noting, finally, that despite this philosophical disagreement as to the precise theoretical basis of well-being, there is in fact a considerable consensus concerning most real-life cases. Advocates of the various theories may differ as to whether various goods are merely instrumental to well-being or are instead directly constitutive of well-being. But when considering realistic cases, we find that most plausible views are in a fair amount of agreement as to who is well off and who is not. So from a practical standpoint, at least, our inability to resolve the theoretical dispute may not be debilitating.

STUDY QUESTIONS

1. What is the distinction between *quantitative* and *qualitative* hedonism?
2. If you mistakenly believe you have satisfied your preferences, might you still achieve well-being?
3. Do you enhance your well-being by succeeding in your chosen endeavors?
4. If you are happy without harming others, have you achieved well-being?

Objective and Subjective Consequentialism

Julia Driver

We are limited in how much information we have when deciding to act. Should this limitation matter? Consequentialists are divided. Objectivists maintain that the right act is the one that brings about the best consequences. Subjectivists hold that the right act is the one the agent expects will produce the best consequences. Julia Driver, Professor of Philosophy at Washington University in St. Louis, defends objective consequentialism, arguing that we should separate the assessment of acts from the assessment of agents.

Consequentialists disagree amongst themselves about whether it is the actual consequences produced by an action that matter morally, or the intended (or expected, or foreseen) consequences. Those who believe that it is the actual consequences, independent of the agent's psychological states, which determine moral quality are objective consequentialists. Those who hold that it is the intended or foreseen consequences are subjective consequentialists, since they tie the moral quality to the agent's psychology—what the agent believes and/or desires. . . .

Subjective consequentialism can be spelled out, in principle, in a variety of ways. One *could* hold that the right action is the action the agent hopes produces the best outcome, or doubts will produce the best outcome, or fears will produce the best outcome. But none of these is at all plausible. They define right action in terms of the agent having a certain subjective mental state with respect to optimal outcomes, but, we know, empirically, that the relevant psychological state has to do with the agent's expectations, or what the agent actually foresees will produce the best outcome. Thus, the following general formulation is often given as an account that is a fairly good example of subjective consequentialism with respect to act evaluation:

> (EUS) The right action is the action the agent *expects* will produce the most good and/or least bad among the agent's alternatives.

Note that in (EUS) what determines the rightness of the action is the agent's subjective state. (EUS) can be formulated either so that the agent needs to be consciously trying to maximize the good, or simply so that the agent's expectations about what will happen in the future, plus her normative commitments, determine the right action. . . .

How can we spell out the difference between subjective and objective? We can contrast objective with subjective by holding that the right action is the one that actually produces the most good, regardless of whether the agent is trying to do so. This is the actual outcomes formulation:

> (AO) The right action is the action that produces the most good and/or the least bad amongst the options open to the agent at the time of action.

From Julia Driver, *Consequentialism*, Routledge, 2012. Reprinted by permission of the publisher.

Or the contrast is that the objective consequentialist holds that the right action is determined by factors independent of the agent's actual psychology—so the contrast is between a criterion that is *actually* subjective and one that is not. For example, the foreseeable consequences formulation holds that:

> (FO) The right action is the action that produces the most foreseeable good and/or least bad amongst the options open to the agent at the time of action. . . .

. . . [T]he subjective version can be spelled out in a wide variety of ways. Do we formulate the criterion on the basis of what the agent actually expects, or what the agent, given her actual beliefs, should expect? We can draw on the literature on epistemic possibility to highlight what is at stake. Consider this case . . .

> (S) Steve is searching for a sunken ship. He has copies of the ship's log, and on the basis of the information in the log calculates the location of the wreck as lying in a bay to the north. However, Steve has made a miscalculation, and in reality the wreck is over 30 miles from the bay in which he expects to find the ship.[1]

Steve certainly believes it is possible that the ship is in the northern bay, and, more than that, he fully expects it to be there. Indeed, he has this expectation on the basis of what he considers good evidence, but he simply makes a miscalculation on the basis of that evidence and comes to a conclusion regarding the location of the ship that is not, in fact, a possible location.[2] On the basis of what Steve expects, he is right to go to the northern bay; on the basis of what he expects, given consideration of the evidence, he is right to go to the northern bay; but on the basis of the evidence as it should have been utilized, using proper calculations, and thus, on the basis of what he should have expected given his actual evidence, he is wrong to go to the northern bay.

The general issue is that, in order for the subjective view to remain a plausible account of 'right' it needs *some* constraint on the basis of evidence, on the basis of what is reasonable for the agent to believe. Otherwise, people with extremely unreasonable views that are not at all supported by the evidence available to *them* end up acting rightly. Suppose Alex believes that the best use of her charitable contributions is to support groups that condone the killing of all persons who disagree with her political views. She is seriously mistaken about this, there is no evidence that this would be good, and plenty of evidence that it would be bad. But if the final court of moral appeal is just what Alex happens to believe, then on the radical subjective view this course of action is 'right'. But this, at least intuitively, seems incorrect, although some theorists seem willing to condone this since they view 'right' as what is 'right' in the agent's own eyes. But even writers who make this move, such as Frank Jackson, note they have a problem with cases of negligent ignorance. Usually, then, they add a duty to acquire reliable information to the account, so that the person who is negligent may be said to, strictly speaking, act rightly, but in a way that is still blameworthy if he fails to exert himself to acquire reliable information.

Another way to go, that doesn't tag on this extra duty, is to make some reference to conformity to evidence in the account of right action itself. This would be an *evidence-sensitive* subjective account of right action. Again, there are different levels of sensitivity. If the account ties 'right' to evidence the agent actually is aware of, then some of the counterintuitive implications of the simple subjective view can be avoided, but not all. However, if the account ties 'right' to evidence the agent isn't actually aware of, but which is available to her—for example, if only she were to read the newspaper, or be minimally attentive to the world around her—then the account is moving further away from the spirit of the subjective approach, which was to capture the sense of 'right' by 'the agent's own lights' . . .

Why would anyone choose (FO) over (AO)? (AO), after all, seems much more theoretically pure. (FO), however, is tempting because it solves a major problem for the theory—the problem of how to restrict the scope of the relevant consequences. If we don't do this somehow, then really there's never been a right action, let alone a right action that we actually know about. James Lenman pushes this objection to objective consequentialism.[3] Lenman notes that many of our moral decisions will have 'identity'-affecting outcomes. Thus, if a company, for example, decides to reduce the amount of pollution it offloads into a river, this decision will affect the identities of those living in the future. Different people will exist than otherwise would have existed, and these people will in turn make different decisions. This means that—given enough time—we won't be able to predict outcomes, and thus won't be able to know what action amongst the options open to us is the best outcome. Of course, the full problem with objective consequentialism is more severe: it would follow from that view that there is no right action *so far,* which seems very implausible. However, if we argue that the right action is that action that produces the best in terms of foresee*able* outcomes, then this doesn't follow. The scope of relevant outcomes is fixed by what is foreseeable for the agent. This is one reason, then, for opting for (FO) over (AO).

But this problem loses its bite when we consider that the future is real, not something which, at this point, is not real. The view that holds that on the (AO) view there are no right actions because there is no future would be undercut. So, (AO) can avoid this particular criticism. Often those who make this criticism are really worried about the epistemological concern that we won't be able to tell which action really is the right action because of our epistemic limitations: we are not able to see into the future, certainly not able to infer into the future with perfect accuracy. But this is a separate worry. (AO) is giving an account of what 'right action' means, either a semantic account or a metaphysical one, about what right actions *are.* How we go about figuring out which action is right is a different, though interesting, issue. Further, (FO) itself does not offer a perfect solution to the epistemological worries. There will still be the problem of how to figure out the 'foreseeable'—people will often make mistakes that affect their judgment about which action is the right action. That doesn't make it the case that there is no right action, however.

Thus, these worries about (AO) can be met. . . .

There is another problem for objective consequentialism, the *action ownership problem.* Frank Jackson is critical of the objective approach because it divorces rightness from the agent too much:

> We need, if you like, a story from the inside of an agent to be part of any theory which is

properly a theory in ethics, and having the best consequences is a story from the outside. It is fine for a theory in physics to tell us about its central notions in a way which leaves it obscure how to move from those notions to action, for that passage can be left to something which is not physics: but the passage to action is the very business of ethics.[4]

Further, it leads to ridiculous conclusions about right action, since on Jackson's view the right one is at least in some cases not the best one.

He asks us to consider the case of Jill and John: Jill is a doctor, John her patient with a skin problem. Jill has two drugs available to treat the skin problem, X and Y. Drug X has a 90 percent chance of curing John, but a 10 percent chance of killing him. Drug Y has only a 50 percent chance of curing him, but no chance at all of killing him. Which should Jill prescribe?

> Railton's proposal is, I take it, that the moral decision problem should be approached by setting oneself the goal of doing what is objectively right—the action that in fact has the best consequences—and then performing the action which the empirical evidence suggests is most likely to have this property.[5]

Given this understanding of what the objective consequentialist is committed to, Jackson argues that the objective consequentialist will give the wrong answer in cases like the Jill and John case. Going for the best is a mistake. If one went with the option that had the highest probability of the best outcome it would be to give John drug X, which would be a terrible mistake. It is much too risky. Instead, we need to go with the action that has the best expected utility. That would be to prescribe drug Y, since drug Y has the best expected payoff. Often we need, morally, to 'play it safe' and this means that under conditions of uncertainty we don't opt for the course of action that is likeliest to have the best outcome. In unpacking 'maximize the good', it may be that the correct standard involves production of good, yes, but also avoidance of bad effects. In the case above, while the mistake involves opting for the option with the best outcome in terms of positive effects, Railton, or any objective consequentialist, would also consider in practical deliberation what is least likely to lead to bad effects. This does not mean that there is no truth of the matter as to which action is best given full information.

Jackson himself offers a view in which the right action is a function of what the agent actually believes and what the agent would desire given that he had the right set of values. So, what is right by the agent's own lights is what the agent would believe to be right given his own actual assessment of the probable outcomes and given that he had the right conception of value, the consequentialist conception of value. It is a function of what Jackson terms 'expected moral value', and in the above medicine case the *expected moral value*—due to moral safety considerations—is lower for drug X than for drug Y.

There are several things to note here. First, whatever the advantages of the decision-theoretic approach, it is not an alternative to objective consequentialism. For Jackson, it isn't the agent's *actual* psychology that determines the rightness of the action, since the agent needs to have the correct consequentialist value function—i.e. the right view of value, whatever that view is. Jackson's account is 'subjective' only in the sense that it ties rightness to the agent's actual beliefs.

Jackson also has a problem with negligent, or culpable, ignorance cases. The only way to deal with these cases is to idealize not just the agent's value function, but also the agent's beliefs—so the right action is understood relative to what the agent ought to believe. But Jackson wants to resist this, because it will not solve the action ownership problem, as it makes the standard too remote. He believes the culpable ignorance cases can be handled in the following way:

> Getting more information and then doing what has greatest moral utility has itself greatest moral utility provided the possible change in utility consequent on the new information when weighed by the probability of getting that new information is great enough to compensate for the effort and cost of getting the new information. Thus, working solely with a person's subjective probability function, with what he or she

actually believes, we can distinguish plausibly between cases where more information ought to be obtained and where we may legitimately rest content with what we have.[6]

This doesn't fully solve the problem. There will be very many cases where the agent misjudges how much information is relevant, and makes the misjudgment sincerely, due to some other lack of information. A doctor may not order an extra test, thinking that a patient's cough is a cold when in fact it is pneumonia. And the doctor may be genuinely surprised later to find out the illness was much more serious than he thought. Assuming the extra test was called for as part of routine diagnostic procedures, we would, I think, view the doctor as having acted wrongly even if his actual subjective beliefs were—*in his own mind*—well founded.

Given the above arguments, we have at best a very strong *preliminary* case for the objective form of consequentialism that restricts the scope of consequences to what is foreseeable. In disagreement with Jackson, this involves idealizing the beliefs, since the agent may not actually foresee what is foreseeable. To fully develop this we need an account of 'foreseeable'. A good first run is to maintain that foreseeable effects are the ones a reasonably well-informed person at that time would be aware of or anticipate. This ties the rightness of the action to evidence that a reasonably well-informed person would be cognizant of.

This doesn't capture intuitions about cases where the agent doesn't know what a reasonable person would know, but through no fault of his own. Imagine a variation on Jackson's case. Suppose that a week before she treated John, there was a seminar at Jill's hospital on the very disease that John was suffering from. In the seminar new research was presented that demonstrated that John fell into a reference class for patients in which drug X would be a perfectly safe drug to use. Knowing this, of course, we would argue that she should prescribe drug X, because for patients like John there was virtually no risk of death and that drug would cure him. Jill failed to make it to the seminar, and thus ended up prescribing the wrong drug. She was not reasonably well informed. But our intuitions shift in Jill's favor if we discover that her colleague, Sam, who is normally extremely reliable and trustworthy, told her that she shouldn't bother going to the seminar that week—that it wouldn't be informative. In this case we don't view her failure to acquire relevant information as blameworthy, and this tends to reflect on how we view her subsequent action. Given what she knew, and what we think she should have known under the circumstances, she did do the right thing. Thus, when it comes to spelling out 'foreseeable' the more plausible characterization would involve relativizing it to what the reasonably attentive agent would know under the circumstances. Jill is attentive, and Sam misled her, something that was not her fault.

All of these reasons are ones that have been given for preferring subjective over objective. But which version of objective is best? My claim is that (AO) is the correct account of 'right action' but that (FO) tracks much of our practice of praise and blame. . . .

Consider the following case:

(M) Mary is trying to decide whether or not she should make her charitable donation to Oxfam or to her local community charity, Gofam, which provides counseling to troubled teenagers. She decides, after careful reflection, that she will give to Gofam. It is a local charity, and thus she will be in a better position, she thinks, to determine its success. She also feels that counseling teenagers is an important intervention that can do a great deal to promote their long-term happiness.

Let's suppose that the facts are as Mary thinks they are in (M). Counseling has long-term positive effects and it is good that people give to local charities (perhaps because, as in (M) they can gauge success better, perhaps because of the psychological connections, etc.). But suppose that there is more that Mary doesn't know, and could not reasonably be expected to know. Suppose that the director of Gofam is going through a difficult time. He is addicted to gambling and has run out of money. One night, two months after Mary has made her donation, he takes all of Gofam's money and leaves for Las Vegas. He squanders the money gambling. The money never makes it to the counseling centers that depend upon it. After reading of the scandal in the newspaper Mary may well decide that she did the 'wrong' thing by not giving the money to Oxfam, where she is fairly confident it would be well spent, even though she will never know exactly where. Subjective consequentialists argue that when Mary makes this judgment she is not judging that she did something morally wrong. She is simply making the judgment that it would have been better had she given the money to Oxfam. . . .

I don't think this is true, however. Mary is likely to feel very badly about not giving the money to Oxfam. She failed to succeed. Granted, it is not her fault that she failed to succeed, so she isn't blameworthy for the failure. Her action satisfies the praiseworthy standard even if it does not succeed. Mary *tried* to do what she thought was best, but she didn't. She failed. . . .

NOTES

1. Ian Hacking, "Possibility," *Philosophical Review* 76 (1967), 143–68.
2. Here, of course, we are not speaking of metaphysical possibility, but, rather, physical possibility.
3. James Lenman,"Consequentialism and Cluelessness," *Philosophy & Public Affairs* 29 (2000), 242–70.
4. Frank Jackson, "Decision-Theoretic Consequentialism and the Nearest and Dearest Objection," *Ethics* 101 (1991), 461–82.
5. Jackson, "Decision-Theoretic," 467.
6. Jackson, "Decision-Theoretic," 467.

STUDY QUESTIONS

1. What is the distinction between objective and subjective consequentialism?
2. What lessons does Driver draw from the case of Steve?
3. What lessons does Driver draw from the case of Mary?
4. Because the consequences of any act continue forever, can objective consequentialists ever be sure that anyone has acted rightly?

Rule-consequentialism versus Act-consequentialism

Brad Hooker

Consequentialism judges actions by their consequences, but are acts to be judged individually (act-consequentialism) or by classes (rule-consequentialism)? In other words, if you consider telling a lie, are you to judge the consequences of that one lie or, instead, the consequences of lying in general? Brad Hooker, Professor of Philosophy at University of Reading, argues that the rightness or wrongness of acts is to be judged by their conformity with rules whose general internalization would be for the best.

1. FORMULATIONS OF THE TWO THEORIES

... Act-consequentialism is normally characterized as the view that the rightness or wrongness of any act is a matter of a comparison of that act's consequences with the consequences of alternative acts. Act-consequentialism, as normally characterized, does not hold the absurd view that agents should always decide how to act by surveying the possible alternatives and choosing the act with the highest expected value. Act-consequentialists instead hold that people should generally decide how to act by fairly automatically following rules that generally have the best consequences.

What are these rules? The ones usually mentioned first are rules against killing or maiming innocent people. Other central prohibitions are ones against stealing or damaging others' property and rules against breaking promises or telling lies. Positive requirements include a duty to pay special attention to the welfare of one's family and friends when one is deciding how to allocate one's own time, energy, or other resources. There is also a more general rule requiring one to help others with morally innocent projects. (I have listed these tried and tested rules here merely so as to make the discussion less abstract. I do not mean to suggest that this list is complete).

Let us consider what act-consequentialism and rule-consequentialism would prescribe for a policy-making group or legislative body. Should the policy be that doctor-assisted suicide is "tolerated"? Should the law explicitly permit it? The usual act-consequentialist answer is that the policy-making group or legislative body should choose whatever policies and laws have the greatest expected value. If a policy of tolerating doctor-assisted suicide would result in the best consequences on the whole, then consequentialists would favour this selection. If refusing to legalize doctor-assisted suicide would result in the best consequences, then consequentialists would favour refusing to legalize it.

From Brad Hooker, "Rule-consequentialism versus Act-consequentialism," *Politeia*, vol. 24, 2008. Reprinted by permission of the journal.

Should there be a policy of protecting whistle blowers from corporate punishment? Should stem-cell research be illegal? Should surrogacy contracts be legally enforceable? What should be the sanction against illegally obtained evidence—e.g. should the sanction be that the evidence is inadmissible in court or should the sanction be instead that those who obtained the evidence be demoted or fired? In answering all questions of policy and rule selection, act-consequentialism and rule-consequentialism have the same focus.

Of course, different consequentialists might disagree about what policy or law would have the best consequences. But this disagreement would come from disagreement about what the consequences of this or that policy or law would be, or from disagreement about the value of the consequences. Such disagreement would not come from the difference between act-consequentialism and rule-consequentialism. At the level of assessing policies, laws, and rules, there is no significant difference between act-consequentialism and rule-consequentialism.

Many people only rarely assess policies, laws, and rules. But everyone has to decide what to do. As I remarked earlier, act-consequentialism and rule-consequentialism pretty much agree how agents should decide what to do—namely, by fairly automatically following certain tried and tested rules.

So for act-consequentialism and rule-consequentialism to be different, rule-consequentialism must be conceived of as holding not only that people should generally decide how to act by reference to rules but also that rules that are justified by their consequences determine which acts are right or wrong. Act-consequentialism and rule-consequentialism disagree about what makes acts right or wrong. For act-consequentialism, what makes acts wrong is a fact about how their consequences compare with the consequences of alternative acts. For rule-consequentialism, what makes acts wrong is that they conflict with rules justified by their consequences. . . .

Textbooks sometimes say rule-consequentialism holds that what makes wrong acts wrong is that they are forbidden by rules *compliance* with which by everyone would produce the most good, or

greatest expected value. The consequences of people's complying with rules are of course hugely important. But the acceptance of rules can have consequences apart from those that come from compliance. Accepting some rules might make people happy, though they never find themselves in circumstances where they ought to comply with the rules. Accepting other rules might make people sad, though again they happen never to have occasion to comply with these rules. Since the consequences of accepting rules incorporate the consequences of complying with them but not vice versa, we should frame rule-consequentialism in terms of the more inclusive category, i.e., in terms of the consequences of accepting rules.

An even broader perspective would take into consideration not only the consequences of compliance plus the consequences of acceptance that do not come from compliance but also the "transition" costs of getting rules deeply embedded in people's characters so that people are very strongly motivated to comply with the rules and to judge others by them. Suppose the benefits of people's accepting and complying with a certain rule R would greatly outweigh the costs of their accepting and complying with it. Nevertheless, the costs incurred during the period of getting people to accept R may outweigh whatever eventual benefits result from their coming to accept R.

The best version of rule-consequentialism must consider these transition costs. Perhaps the term "internalization costs" is a more revealing name for the costs involved in getting rules deeply embedded in people's characters so that people are very strongly motivated to comply with the rules and to judge others by them. So I shall refer to these costs as internalization costs.

The internalization costs of a rule might be different from one person to another. Suppose Francesco has already internalized a rule requiring one not to discriminate against homosexuals. Suppose Sophia has meanwhile internalized a rule requiring one to discriminate against homosexuals. Then the effort that will be needed to get Francesco to internalize a rule forbidding discrimination against trans-gendered people will probably be less than the effort needed to get Sophia to internalize a rule forbidding discrimination against trans-gendered people.

If rule-consequentialism is formulated so as to count the costs of getting rules internalized by people who have already internalized quite different rules, then which rules rule-consequentialism will end up favouring will be influenced by which rules happen to have already been internalized. This seems to me to enable the past internalization of misconceived or even ridiculous rules to infect rule-consequentialist assessment of new rules. The question should *not* be: "What would be the net expected value of the internalization of a set of rules S by people who have already internalized some other set in conflict with S?" The question should instead be: "What would be the net expected value of S's internalization by people who have not already internalized rules?". So I think that the best formulation of rule-consequentialism is framed in terms of the internalization of rules by new (as yet uncorrupted) generations of humans.

A final matter to be resolved is how idealistic rule-consequentialism should be. In an ideal world, there are no attacks, no robberies, no broken contracts, etc. Thus, in an ideal world, there is no need for rules about how and when deterrence and punishment are appropriate. A code of rules *for an ideal world* would lack rules concerning many of the moral *problems of the real world*.

The way to frame rule-consequentialism so that it doesn't define real moral problems out of existence is for it to be formulated in terms of internalization by less [than] 100% of everyone. So we might point to a form of rule-consequentialism that assesses the internalization of rules by a percentage of everyone in new (as yet uncorrupted) generations that is less than 100%. Exactly what percentage is appropriate to use here? The answer is controversial. But I have followed Richard Brandt in suggesting 90% in each new generation.[1] (The 90% figure cuts across socio-economic groups. The assessment of rules is run on the basis that they are to be internalized by 90% of the rich, 90% of the middle classes, 90% of the poor, etc.)

To say that a consequentialist assessment should be directed at rules with the assumption that they are to be internalized by 90% of everyone in each generation is *not* to hope or desire that only 90% of everyone accepts rules. Of course we should welcome rules' internalization by 100%. Still, the test for which set of moral rules is justified focuses on the net expected consequences of rules' internalization by 90% of everyone in each new generation.

Thus, my own preferred formulation of rule-consequentialism is as follows. What makes wrong acts wrong is that they are forbidden by a code of rules whose internalization by 90% of each future generation either (a) would have either greater expected value than any other code or (b) would have at least as much as any other code and is closer to conventionally accepted morality than other codes with the same expected value. . . .

2. CONFLICT BETWEEN THE THEORIES

Maximizing act-consequentialism and rule-consequentialism disagree about why wrong acts are wrong. According to maximizing act-consequentialism, they are wrong because they fail to maximize the good, or the expected good. According to rule-consequentialism, they are wrong because they are forbidden by a code of rules whose internalization by 90% of each future generation either would have either greater expected value than any other code or would have at least as much as any other code and is closer to conventionally accepted morality than other codes with the same expected value.

But while act-consequentialism and rule-consequentialism disagree about why wrong acts are wrong, circumstances *might* be such that they agree about which acts are wrong. In fact, circumstances are often such that act-consequentialism and rule-consequentialism do agree about which acts are wrong.

And yet circumstances are often such that the two theories disagree not only in principle but also in practice—that is, disagree not only about why wrong acts are wrong but also about which acts are wrong. We can illustrate this with examples of many kinds. Some of these involve physical harm. Others involve property. Others involve promise keeping. Others involve benefiting family or friends. Still others involve doing good generally. To avoid being tedious, I will go through examples of only three kinds: physical harm, promises, and doing good generally.

Here is an example involving physical harm. Suppose Fabio physically harms Antonio but the benefit to Fabio is for some reason slightly larger than the harm to Antonio. In this case, maximizing act-consequentialism holds that Fabio was not wrong to injure Antonio.

However, the consequences of widespread internalization of rule permitting agents to physically harm others whenever they think this will produce a little greater aggregate good would be, on balance, bad. Agents would too often convince themselves that at least a little more impartial good would be produced by physically harming others. And if everyone knew that others accepted a rule allowing physical harm to be inflicted whenever the agent thought that at least a little more impartial good would come from doing the harm than from not doing it, people would be fearful of one another. So rule-consequentialism favours a rule forbidding the infliction of physical harm in the sort of cases we have been considering.

Here now is an example concerning promises. Suppose Ronaldo breaks a solemn promise and this produces a little more impartial good than his keeping the promise would have produced. In this case, maximizing act-consequentialism holds that Ronaldo was not wrong to break the solemn promise.

But the consequences of widespread internalization of [a] rule permitting agents to break solemn promises whenever they think this will produce a little more impartial good would not be good on balance. Agents would far too often convince themselves that at least a little more impartial good would be produced by breaking their promises. And if everyone knew that others accepted a rule allowing promises to be broken whenever the agent thought that at least a little more impartial good would come from breaking the promise than from keeping it, people would have very little trust in promises. If promises provide too little trust, society loses out on one of the main enablers of social cooperation. So rule-consequentialism favours a rule about promise

breaking that will conflict with the dictates of maximizing act-consequentialism in those cases where breaking a promise will produce a little more good than keeping it would.

Finally, I turn to an example concerning doing good for others generally. Suppose Maria is in a situation where she could make a sacrifice that would maximize aggregate good. However, she refuses because in the circumstances this sacrifice would benefit someone else only slightly more than she would lose and the other person has no particular connection with her. Act-consequentialism holds that Maria did something morally wrong here.

Again, rule-consequentialism disagrees. Consider the internalization costs of a rule requiring people to make sacrifices for others whenever the benefit to those others is even just slightly greater than the sacrifice. This rule would require people to go so much against their natural inclinations that very considerable time, energy, attention, and psychological conflict would be required to get new generations to internalize the rule. To be sure, benefits would flow after the rule had been internalized. But those benefits would be outweighed by the costs associated with getting such a demanding rule internalized.[2] Hence, rule-consequentialism endorses a rule requiring people to make some sacrifices for the benefit of others but does not require so much as act-consequentialism does. According to rule-consequentialism's rule about aiding others, Maria's refusal to make the sacrifice was not wrong.

I have run through examples where act-consequentialism and rule-consequentialism disagree about whether some acts of physical harm, promise breaking, and refusing to make sacrifices for others are wrong. In each of the examples I have just discussed, rule-consequentialism generates a more intuitively plausible answer than act-consequentialism does.

Most people believe that many kinds of act that are normally wrong are instead right when necessary to prevent a *huge* loss in aggregate good. The idea here is that inflicting physical harm on someone, stealing, breaking promises, directing benefits to strangers rather than to one's family and friends, or making personal sacrifices can be morally required *in extreme circumstances.* Act-consequentialism definitely agrees with such judgements. Rule-consequentialism presumably agrees as well. Hence these sorts of "extreme" cases are not helpful in deciding between act-consequentialism and rule-consequentialism.

The cases involving Fabio, Ronaldo, and Maria above, however, are not extreme cases and do separate act-consequentialism and rule-consequentialism. In these not-extreme cases, acts of physical harm, promise breaking, and refusing to make sacrifices for marginally greater gains to others are wrong according to act-consequentialism but not wrong according to rule-consequentialism. These are precisely the sorts of cases that show rule-consequentialism to accord better with ordinary moral opinion than act-consequentialism does.

NOTES

1. See Hooker, 2000, section 3.3; Hooker and Fletcher, 2008.
2. See Hooker, 2000, sections 4.2, 6.5, and 8.5; and Hooker, 2007.

REFERENCES

Hooker, B. (2000), *Ideal Code, Real World: A Rule-consequentialist Theory of Morality,* Oxford: Oxford University Press.

Hooker, B. (2007), "Rule-consequentialism and Internal Consistency: A Reply to Card," *Utilitas,* 19, pp. 514–19.

Hooker, B. and Fletcher, G. (2008), "Variable versus Fixed-rate Rule-utilitarianism," *Philosophical Quarterly,* 58, pp. 344–52.

STUDY QUESTIONS

1. What is the distinction between act-consequentialism and rule-consequentialism?
2. What does Hooker mean by "internalization costs"?
3. If breaking a promise usually leads to unfortunate consequences but on one occasion would result in good consequences, should that promise be broken?
4. Does a rule-consequentialist test rules differently than a Kantian does?

A Critique of Utilitarianism

Bernard Williams

Bernard Williams (1929–2003), born in England, was Professor of Philosophy at the University of California, Berkeley. He argues that utilitarianism presents an impoverished view of our moral lives, reducing agents to mere instruments for maximizing overall happiness and overlooking the importance of the agents' own projects and sense of self. Thus because utilitarianism holds us responsible both for what we do and for what we fail to prevent, the doctrine poses a serious threat to our most deeply held commitments. In short, Williams argues that utilitarianism renders the value of integrity unintelligible.

. . . [L]et us look . . . at two examples, to see what utilitarianism might say about them, what we might say about utilitarianism and, most importantly of all, what would be implied by certain ways of thinking about the situations. The examples are inevitably schematized, and they are open to the objection that they beg as many questions as they illuminate. There are two ways in particular in which examples in moral philosophy tend to beg important questions. One is that, as presented, they arbitrarily cut off and restrict the range of alternative courses of action—this objection might particularly be made against the first of my two examples. The second is that they inevitably present one with the situation as a going concern, and cut off questions about how the agent got into it, and correspondingly about moral considerations which might flow from that: this objection might perhaps specially arise with regard to the second of my two situations. These difficulties, however, just have to be accepted, and if anyone finds these

examples cripplingly defective in this sort of respect, then he must in his own thought rework them in richer and less question-begging form. If he feels that no presentation of any imagined situation can ever be other than misleading in morality, and that there can never be any substitute for the concrete experienced complexity of actual moral situations, then this discussion, with him, must certainly grind to a halt: but then one may legitimately wonder whether every discussion with him about conduct will not grind to a halt, including any discussion about the actual situations, since discussion about how one would think and feel about situations somewhat different from the actual (that is to say, situations to that extent imaginary) plays an important role in discussion of the actual.

(1) George, who has just taken his Ph.D. in chemistry, finds it extremely difficult to get a job. He is not very robust in health, which cuts down the number of jobs he might be able to do satisfactorily. His wife has to go out to work to keep them,

From J. J. C. Smart and Bernard Williams, *Utilitarianism: For and Against*, Cambridge University Press, 1973. Reprinted by permission of the publisher.

which itself causes a great deal of strain, since they have small children and there are severe problems about looking after them. The results of all this, especially on the children, are damaging. An older chemist, who knows about this situation, says that he can get George a decently paid job in a certain laboratory, which pursues research into chemical and biological warfare. George says that he cannot accept this, since he is opposed to chemical and biological warfare. The older man replies that he is not too keen on it himself, come to that, but after all George's refusal is not going to make the job or the laboratory go away; what is more, he happens to know that if George refuses the job, it will certainly go to a contemporary of George's who is not inhibited by any such scruples and is likely if appointed to push along the research with greater zeal than George would. Indeed, it is not merely concern for George and his family, but (to speak frankly and in confidence) some alarm about this other man's excess of zeal, which has led the older man to offer to use his influence to get George the job . . . George's wife, to whom he is deeply attached, has views (the details of which need not concern us) from which it follows that at least there is nothing particularly wrong with research into CBW. What should he do?

(2) Jim finds himself in the central square of a small South American town. Tied up against the wall are a row of twenty Indians, most terrified, a few defiant, in front of them several armed men in uniform. A heavy man in a sweat-stained khaki shirt turns out to be the captain in charge and, after a good deal of questioning of Jim which establishes that he got there by accident while on a botanical expedition, explains that the Indians are a random group of the inhabitants who, after recent acts of protest against the government, are just about to be killed to remind other possible protestors of the advantages of not protesting. However, since Jim is an honoured visitor from another land, the captain is happy to offer him a guest's privilege of killing one of the Indians himself. If Jim accepts, then as a special mark of the occasion, the other Indians will be let off. Of course, if Jim refuses, then there is no special occasion, and Pedro here will do what he was about to do when Jim arrived, and kill them all. Jim, with some desperate recollection of schoolboy fiction, wonders whether if he got hold of a gun, he could hold the captain, Pedro and the rest of the soldiers to threat, but it is quite clear from the set-up that nothing of that kind is going to work: any attempt at that sort of thing will mean that all the Indians will be killed, and himself. The men against the wall, and the other villagers, understand the situation, and are obviously begging him to accept. What should he do?

To these dilemmas, it seems to me that utilitarianism replies, in the first case, that George should accept the job, and in the second, that Jim should kill the Indian. Not only does utilitarianism give these answers but, if the situations are essentially as described and there are no further special factors, it regards them, it seems to me, as *obviously* the right answers. But many of us would certainly wonder whether, in (1), that could possibly be the right answer at all; and in the case of (2), even one who came to think that perhaps that was the answer, might well wonder whether it was obviously the answer. Nor is it just a question of the rightness or obviousness of these answers. It is also a question of what sort of considerations come into finding the answer. A feature of utilitarianism is that it cuts out a kind of consideration which for some others makes a difference to what they feel about such cases: a consideration involving the idea, as we might first and very simply put it, that each of us is specially responsible for what *he* does, rather than for what other people do. This is an idea closely connected with the value of integrity. It is often suspected that ultilitarianism, at least in its direct forms, makes integrity as a value more or less unintelligible. I shall try to show that this suspicion is correct. Of course, even if that is correct, it would not necessarily follow that we should reject utilitarianism; perhaps, as utilitarians sometimes suggest, we should just forget about integrity, in favour of such things as a concern for the general good. However, if I am right, we cannot merely do that, since the reason why utilitarianism cannot understand integrity is that it cannot coherently describe the relations between a man's projects and his actions.

TWO KINDS OF REMOTE EFFECT

A lot of what we have to say about this question will be about the relations between my projects and other people's projects. But before we get on to that, we should first ask whether we are assuming too hastily what the utilitarian answers to the dilemmas will be. In terms of more direct effect of the possible decisions, there does not indeed seem much doubt about the answer in either case; but it might be said that in terms of more remote or less evident effects counterweights might be found to enter the utilitarian scales. Thus the effect on George of a decision to take the job might be invoked, or its effect on others who might know of his decision. The possibility of there being more beneficent labours in the future from which he might be barred or disqualified, might be mentioned; and so forth. Such effects—in particular, possible effects on the agent's character, and effects on the public at large—are often invoked by utilitarian writers dealing with problems about lying or promise-breaking, and some similar considerations might be invoked here.

There is one very general remark that is worth making about arguments of this sort. The certainty that attaches to these hypotheses about possible effects is usually pretty low; in some cases, indeed, the hypothesis invoked is so implausible that it would scarcely pass if it were not being used to deliver the respectable moral answer, as in the standard fantasy that one of the effects of one's telling a particular lie is to weaken the disposition of the world at large to tell the truth. The demands on the certainty or probability of these beliefs as beliefs about particular actions are much milder than they would be on beliefs favouring the unconventional course. It may be said that this is as it should be, since the presumption must be in favour of the conventional course: but that scarcely seems a *utilitarian* answer, unless utilitarianism has already taken off in the direction of not applying the consequences to the particular act at all.

Leaving aside that very general point, I want to consider now two types of effect that are often invoked by utilitarians, and which might be invoked in connexion with these imaginary cases. The attitude or tone involved in invoking these effects may sometimes seem peculiar; but that sort of peculiarity soon becomes familiar in utilitarian discussions, and indeed it can be something of an achievement to retain a sense of it.

First, there is the psychological effect on the agent. Our descriptions of these situations have not so far taken account of how George or Jim will be after they have taken the one course or the other; and it might be said that if they take the course which seemed at first the utilitarian one, the effects on them will be in fact bad enough and extensive enough to cancel out the initial utilitarian advantages of that course. Now there is one version of this effect in which, for a utilitarian, some confusion must be involved, namely that in which the agent feels bad, his subsequent conduct and relations are crippled and so on, *because he thinks that he has done the wrong thing*—for if the balance of outcomes was as it appeared to be *before* invoking this effect, then he has not (from the utilitarian point of view) done the wrong thing. So that version of the effect, for a rational and utilitarian agent, could not possibly make any difference to the assessment of right and wrong. However, perhaps he is not a thoroughly rational agent, and is disposed to have bad feelings, whichever he decided to do. Now such feelings, which are from a strictly utilitarian point of view irrational—nothing, a utilitarian can point out, is advanced by having them—cannot, consistently, have any great weight in a utilitarian calculation. I shall consider in a moment an argument to suggest that they should have no weight at all in it. But short of that, the utilitarian could reasonably say that such feelings should not be encouraged, even if we accept their existence, and that to give them a lot of weight is to encourage them. Or, at the very best, even if they are straightforwardly and without any discount to be put into the calculation, their weight must be small: they are after all (and at best) one man's feelings.

That consideration might seem to have particular force in Jim's case. In George's case, his feelings represent a larger proportion of what is to be weighed, and are more commensurate in character with other items in the calculation. In Jim's case, however, his feelings might seem to be of very little weight compared with other things that are at stake. There is a powerful and recognizable appeal that can be made on this point: as that a refusal by Jim to do what he has been invited to do would be a kind of self-indulgent squeamishness. That is an appeal which can be made by other than utilitarians—indeed, there are some uses of it which cannot be consistently made by utilitarians, as when it essentially involves the idea that there is something dishonourable about such self-indulgence. But in some versions it is a familiar, and it must be said a powerful, weapon of utilitarianism. One must be clear, though, about what it can and cannot accomplish. The most it can do, so far as I can see, is to invite one to consider how seriously, and for what reasons, one feels that what one is invited to do is (in these circumstances) wrong, and in particular, to consider that question from the utilitarian point of view. When the agent is not seeing the situation from a utilitarian point of view, the appeal cannot force him to do so; and if he does come round to seeing it from a utilitarian point of view, there is virtually nothing left for the appeal to do. If he does not see it from a utilitarian point of view, he will not see his resistance to the invitation, and the unpleasant feelings he associates with accepting it, *just* as disagreeable experiences of his; they figure rather as emotional expressions of a thought that to accept would be wrong. He may be asked, as by the appeal, to consider whether he is right, and indeed whether he is fully serious, in thinking that. But the assertion of the appeal, that he is being self-indulgently squeamish, will not itself answer that question, or even help to answer it. since it essentially tells him to regard his feelings just as unpleasant experiences of his, and he cannot, by doing that, answer the question they pose when they are precisely not so regarded, but are regarded as indications of what he thinks is right and wrong. If he does come round fully to the utilitarian point of view then of course he will regard these feelings just as unpleasant experiences of his. And once Jim—at least—has come to see them in that light, there is nothing left for the appeal to do, since *of course* his feelings, so regarded, are of virtually no weight at all in relation to the

other things at stake. The "squeamishness" appeal is not an argument which adds in a hitherto neglected consideration. Rather, it is an invitation to consider the situation, and one's own feelings, from a utilitarian point of view.

The reason why the squeamishness appeal can be very unsettling, and one can be unnerved by the suggestion of self-indulgence in going against utilitarian considerations, is not that we are utilitarians who are uncertain what utilitarian value to attach to our moral feelings, but that we are partially at least not utilitarians, and cannot regard our moral feelings merely as objects of utilitarian value. Because our moral relation to the world is partly given by such feelings, and by a sense of what we can or cannot "live with," to come to regard those feelings from a purely utilitarian point of view, that is to say, as happenings outside one's moral self, is to lose a sense of one's moral identity; to lose, in the most literal way, one's integrity. At this point utilitarianism alienates one from one's moral feelings; we shall see a little later how, more basically, it alienates one from one's actions as well.

If, then, one is really going to regard one's feelings from a strictly utilitarian point of view, Jim should give very little weight at all to his; it seems almost indecent, in fact, once one has taken that point of view, to suppose that he should give any at all. In George's case one might feel that things were slightly different. It is interesting, though, that one reason why one might think that—namely that one person principally affected is his wife—is very dubiously available to a utilitarian. George's wife has some reason to be interested in George's integrity and his sense of it; the Indians, quite properly, have no interest in Jim's. But it is not at all clear how utilitarianism would describe that difference.

There is an argument, and a strong one, that a strict utilitarian should give not merely small extra weight, in calculations of right and wrong, to feelings of this kind, but that he should give absolutely no weight to them at all. This is based on the point, which we have already seen, that if a course of action is, before taking these sorts of feelings into account, utilitarianly preferable, then bad feelings about that kind of action will be from a utilitarian point of view irrational. Now it might be thought that even if that is so, it would not mean that in a utilitarian calculation such feelings should not be taken into account; it is after all a well-known boast of utilitarianism that it is a realistic outlook which seeks the best in the world as it is, and takes any form of happiness or unhappiness into account. While a utilitarian will no doubt seek to diminish the incidence of feelings which are utilitarianly irrational—or at least of disagreeable feelings which are so—he might be expected to take them into account while they exist. This is without doubt classical utilitarian doctrine, but there is good reason to think that utilitarianism cannot stick to it without embracing results which are startlingly unacceptable and perhaps self-defeating.

Suppose that there is in a certain society a racial minority. Considering merely the ordinary interests of the other citizens, as opposed to their sentiments, this minority does no particular harm; we may suppose that it does not confer any very great benefits either. Its presence is in those terms neutral or mildly beneficial. However, the other citizens have such prejudices that they find the sight of this group, even the knowledge of its presence, very disagreeable. Proposals are made for removing in some way this minority. If we assume various quite plausible things (as that programmes to change the majority sentiment are likely to be protracted and ineffective) then even if the removal would be unpleasant for the minority, a utilitarian calculation might well end up favouring this step, especially if the minority were a rather small minority and the majority were very severely prejudiced, that is to say, were made very severely uncomfortable by the presence of the minority.

A utilitarian might find that conclusion embarrassing; and not merely because of its nature, but because of the grounds on which it is reached. While a utilitarian might be expected to take into account certain other sorts of consequences of the prejudice, as that a majority prejudice is likely to be displayed in conduct disagreeable to the minority, and so forth, he might be made to wonder whether the unpleasant experiences of the prejudiced people should be allowed, *merely as such,* to count. If he does count them, merely as such, then he has once more separated himself from a body of ordinary moral thought

which he might have hoped to accommodate; he may also have started on the path of defeating his own view of things. For one feature of these sentiments is that they are from the utilitarian point of view itself irrational, and a thoroughly utilitarian person would either not have them, or if he found that he did tend to have them, would himself seek to discount them. Since the sentiments in question are such that a rational utilitarian would discount them in himself, it is reasonable to suppose that he should discount them in his calculations about society; it does seem quite unreasonable for him to give just as much weight to feelings—considered just in themselves, one must recall, as experiences of those that have them—which are essentially based on views which are from a utilitarian point of view irrational, as to those which accord with utilitarian principles. Granted this idea, it seems reasonable for him to rejoin a body of moral thought in other respects congenial to him, and discount those sentiments, just considered in themselves, totally, on the principle that no pains or discomforts are to count in the utilitarian sum which their subjects have just because they hold views which are by utilitarian standards irrational. But if he accepts that, then in the cases we are at present considering no extra weight at all can be put in for bad feelings of George or Jim about their choices, if those choices are, leaving out those feelings, on the first round utilitarianly rational.

The psychological effect on the agent was the first of two general effects considered by utilitarians, which had to be discussed. The second is in general a more substantial item, but it need not take so long, since it is both clearer and has little application to the present cases. This is the *precedent effect.* As Burke rightly emphasized, this effect can be important: that one morally *can* do what someone has actually done, is a psychologically effective principle, if not a deontically valid one. For the effect to operate, obviously some conditions must hold on the publicity of the act and on such things as the status of the agent (such considerations weighed importantly with Sir Thomas More); what these may be will vary evidently with circumstances.

In order for the precedent effect to make a difference to a utilitarian calculation, it must be based upon a confusion. For suppose that there is an act which would be the best in the circumstances, except that doing it will encourage by precedent other people to do things which will not be the best things to do. Then the situation of those other people must be relevantly different from that of the original agent; if it were not, then in doing the same as what would be the best course for the original agent, they would necessarily do the best thing themselves. But if the situations are in this way relevantly different, it must be a confused perception which takes the first situation, and the agent's course in it, as an adequate precedent for the second.

However, the fact that the precedent effect, if it really makes a difference, is in this sense based on a confusion, does not mean that it is not perfectly real, nor that it is to be discounted: social effects are by their nature confused in this sort of way. What it does emphasize is that calculations of the precedent effect have got to be realistic, involving considerations of how people are actually likely to be influenced. In the present examples, however, it is very implausible to think that the precedent effect could be invoked to make any difference to the calculation. Jim's case is extraordinary enough, and it is hard to imagine who the recipients of the effect might be supposed to be; while George is not in a sufficiently public situation or role for the question to arise in that form, and in any case one might suppose that the motivations of others on such an issue were quite likely to be fixed one way or another already.

No appeal, then, to these other effects is going to make a difference to what the utilitarian will decide about our examples. Let us now look more closely at the structure of those decisions.

INTEGRITY

The situations have in common that if the agent does not do a certain disagreeable thing, someone else will, and in Jim's situation at least the result, the state of affairs after the other man has acted, if he does, will be worse than after Jim has acted, if Jim does. The same, on a smaller scale, is true of George's case. . . . [It] is inherent in consequentialism that it offers a strong

doctrine of negative responsibility: if I know that if I do X, O_1 will eventuate, and if I refrain from doing X, O_2 will, and that O_2 is worse than O_1, then I am responsible for O_2 if I refrain voluntarily from doing X. "You could have prevented it," as will he said, and truly, to Jim, if he refuses, by the relatives of the other Indians. . . .

In the present cases, the situation of O_2 includes another agent bringing about results worse than O_1. So far as O_2 has been identified up to this point— merely as the worse outcome which will eventuate if I refrain from doing X—we might equally have said that what that other brings about is O_2; but that would be to underdescribe the situation. For what occurs if Jim refrains from action is not solely twenty Indians dead, but *Pedro's killing twenty Indians,* and that is not a result which Pedro brings about, though the death of the Indians is. We can say: what one does is not included in the outcome of what one does, while what another does can be included in the outcome of what one does. For that to be so, as the terms are now being used, only a very weak condition has to be satisfied: for Pedro's killing the Indians to be the outcome of Jim's refusal, it only has to be causally true that if Jim had not refused, Pedro would not have done it.

That may be enough for us to speak, in some sense, of Jim's responsibility for that outcome, if it occurs; but it is certainly not enough, it is worth noticing, for us to speak of Jim's *making* those things happen. For granted this way of their coming about, he could have made them happen only by making Pedro shoot, and there is no acceptable sense in which his refusal makes Pedro shoot. If the captain had said on Jim's refusal, "you leave me with no alternative," he would have been lying, like most who use that phrase. While the deaths, and the killing, may be the outcome of Jim's refusal, it is misleading to think, in such a case, of Jim having an *effect* on the world through the medium (as it happens) of Pedro's acts; for this is to leave Pedro out of the picture in his essential role of one who has intentions and projects, projects for realizing which Jim's refusal would leave an opportunity. Instead of thinking in terms of supposed effects of Jim's projects on Pedro, it is more revealing to think in terms of the effects of

Pedro's projects on Jim's decision. This is the direction from which I want to criticize the notion of negative responsibility. . . .

What projects does a utilitarian agent have? As a utilitarian, he has the general project of bringing about maximally desirable outcomes; how he is to do this at any given moment is a question of what causal levers, so to speak, are at that moment within reach. The desirable outcomes, however, do not just consist of agents carrying out *that* project; there must be other more basic or lower-order projects which he and other agents have, and the desirable outcomes are going to consist, in part, of the maximally harmonious realization of those projects ("in part," because one component of a utilitarianly desirable outcome may be the occurrence of agreeable experiences which are not the satisfaction of anybody's projects). Unless there were first-order projects, the general utilitarian project would have nothing to work on, and would be vacuous. What do the more basic or lower-order projects comprise? Many will be the obvious kinds of desires for things for oneself, one's family, one's friends, including basic necessities of life, and in more relaxed circumstances, objects of taste. Or there may be pursuits and interests of an intellectual, cultural or creative character. I introduce those as a separate class not because the objects of them lie in a separate class, and provide—as some utilitarians, in their churchy way, are fond of saying—"higher" pleasures. I introduce them separately because the agent's identification with them may be of a different order. It does not have to be: cultural and aesthetic interests just belong, for many, along with any other taste; but some people's commitment to these kinds of interests just is at once more thoroughgoing and serious than their pursuit of various objects of taste, while it is more individual and permeated with character than the desire for the necessities of life.

Beyond these, someone may have projects connected with his support of some cause: Zionism, for instance, or the abolition of chemical and biological warfare. Or there may be projects which flow from some more general disposition towards human conduct and character, such as a hatred of injustice, or of cruelty, or of killing.

It may be said that this last sort of disposition and its associated project do not count as (logically) "lower-order" relative to the higher-order project of maximizing desirable outcomes; rather, it may be said, it is itself a "higher-order" project. The vital question is not, however, how it is to be classified, but whether it and similar projects are to count among the projects whose satisfaction is to be included in the maximizing sum, and, correspondingly, as contributing to the agent's happiness. If the utilitarian says "no" to that, then he is almost certainly committed to a version of utilitarianism as absurdly superficial and shallow as Benthamite versions have often been accused of being. For this project will be discounted, presumably, on the ground that it involves, in the specification of its object, the mention of other people's happiness or interests: thus it is the kind of project which (unlike the pursuit of food for myself) presupposes a reference to other people's projects. But that criterion would eliminate any desire at all which was not blankly and in the most straightforward sense egoistic.[1] Thus we should be reduced to frankly egoistic first-order projects, and—for all essential purposes—the one second-order utilitarian project of maximally satisfying first-order projects. Utilitarianism has a tendency to slide in this direction, and to leave a vast hole in the range of human desires, between egoistic inclinations and necessities at one end, and impersonally benevolent happiness-management at the other. But the utilitarianism which has to leave this hole is the most primitive form, which offers a quite rudimentary account of desire. Modern versions of the theory are supposed to be neutral with regard to what sorts of things make people happy or what their projects are. Utilitarianism would do well then to acknowledge the evident fact that among the things that make people happy is not only making other people happy, but being taken up or involved in any of a vast range of projects, or—if we waive the evangelical and moralizing associations of the word—commitments. One can be committed to such things as a person, a cause, an institution, a career, one's own genius, or the pursuit of danger.

Now none of these is itself the *pursuit of happiness:* by an exceedingly ancient platitude, it is not at all clear that there could be anything which was just that, or at least anything that had the slightest chance of being successful. Happiness, rather, requires being involved in, or at least content with, something else.[2] It is not impossible for utilitarianism to accept that point: it does not have to be saddled with a naïve and absurd philosophy of mind about the relation between desire and happiness. What it does have to say is that if such commitments are worth while, then pursuing the projects that flow from them, and realizing some of those projects, will make the person for whom they are worth while, happy. It may be that to claim that is still wrong: it may well be that a commitment can make sense to a man (can make sense to his life) without his supposing that it will make him *happy*.[3] But that is not the present point; let us grant to utilitarianism that all worthwhile human projects must conduce, one way or another, to happiness. The point is that even if that is true, it does not follow, nor could it possibly be true, that those projects are themselves projects of pursuing happiness. One has to believe in, or at least want, or quite minimally, be content with, other things, for there to be anywhere that happiness can come from.

Utilitarianism, then, should be willing to agree that its general aim of maximizing happiness does not imply that what everyone is doing is just pursuing happiness. On the contrary, people have to be pursuing other things. What those other things may be, utilitarianism, sticking to its professed empirical stance, should be prepared just to find out. No doubt some possible projects it will want to discourage, on the grounds that their being pursued involves a negative balance of happiness to others: though even there, the unblinking accountant's eye of the strict utilitarian will have something to put in the positive column, the satisfactions of the destructive agent. Beyond that, there will be a vast variety of generally beneficent or at least harmless projects; and some no doubt, will take the form not just of tastes or fancies, but of what I have called "commitments." It may even be that the utilitarian researcher will find that many of those with commitments, who have really identified themselves with objects outside themselves, who are thoroughly involved with other persons, or institutions, or activities or causes, are

actually happier than those whose projects and wants are not like that. If so, that is an important piece of utilitarian empirical lore. . . .

Let us now go back to the agent as utilitarian, and his higher-order project of maximizing desirable outcomes. At this level, he is committed only to that: what the outcome will actually consist of will depend entirely on the facts, on what persons with what projects and what potential satisfactions there are within calculable reach of the causal levers near which he finds himself. His own substantial projects and commitments come into it, but only as one lot among others—they potentially provide one set of satisfactions among those which he may be able to assist from where he happens to be. He is the agent of the satisfaction system who happens to be at a particular point at a particular time: in Jim's case, our man in South America. His own decisions as a utilitarian agent are a function of all the satisfactions which he can affect from where he is: and this means that the projects of others, to an indeterminately great extent, determine his decision.

This may be so either positively or negatively. It will be so positively if agents within the causal field of his decision have projects which are at any rate harmless, and so should be assisted. It will equally be so, but negatively, if there is an agent within the causal field whose projects are harmful, and have to be frustrated to maximize desirable outcomes. So it is with Jim and the soldier Pedro. On the utilitarian view, the undesirable projects of other people as much determine, in this negative way, one's decisions as the desirable ones do positively: if those people were not there, or had different projects, the causal nexus would be different, and it is the actual state of the causal nexus which determines the decision. The determination to an indefinite degree of my decisions by other people's projects is just another aspect of my unlimited responsibility to act for the best in a causal framework formed to a considerable extent by their projects.

The decision so determined is, for utilitarianism, the right decision. But what if it conflicts with some project of mine? This, the utilitarian will say, has already been dealt with; the satisfaction to you of fulfilling your project, and any satisfactions to others of your so doing, have already been through the calculating device and have been found inadequate. Now in the case of many sorts of projects, that is a perfectly reasonable sort of answer. But in the case of projects of the sort I have called "commitments," those with which one is more deeply and extensively involved and identified, this cannot just by itself be an adequate answer, and there may be no adequate answer at all. For, to take the extreme sort of case, how can a man, as a utilitarian agent, come to regard as one satisfaction among others, and a dispensable one, a project or attitude round which he has built his life, just because someone else's projects have so structured the causal scene that that is how the utilitarian sum comes out?

The point here is not, as utilitarians may hasten to say, that if the project or attitude is that central to his life, then to abandon it will be very disagreeable to him and great loss of utility will be involved. I have already argued in [the previous] section that it is not like that; on the contrary, once he is prepared to look at it like that, the argument in any serious case is over anyway. The point is that he is identified with his actions as flowing from projects and attitudes which in some cases he takes seriously at the deepest level, as what his life is about (or, in some cases, this section of his life—seriousness is not necessarily the same as persistence). It is absurd to demand of such a man, when the sums come in from the utility network which the projects of others have in part determined, that he should just step aside from his own project and decision and acknowledge the decision which utilitarian calculation requires. It is to alienate him in a real sense from his actions and the source of his action in his own convictions. It is to make him into a channel between the input of everyone's projects, including his own, and an output of optimific decision; but this is to neglect the extent to which *his* actions and *his* decisions have to be seen as the actions and decisions which flow from the projects and attitudes with which he is most closely identified. It is thus, in the most literal sense, an attack on his integrity.

NOTES

1. On the subject of egoistic and non-egoistic desires, see "Egoism and altruism," in *Problems of the Self* (Cambridge University Press, London, 1973).
2. This does not imply that there is no such thing as the project of pursuing pleasure. Some writers who have correctly resisted the view that all desires are desires for pleasure, have given an account of pleasure so thoroughly adverbial as to leave it quite unclear how there could be a distinctively hedonist way of life at all. Some room has to be left for that, though there are important difficulties both in defining it and living it. Thus (particularly in the case of the very rich) it often has highly ritual aspects, apparently part of a strategy to counter boredom.
3. For some remarks on this possibility, see *Morality* section on "What is morality about?" [*Morality: An Introduction to Ethics* (Harper and Row, New York, 1972).]

STUDY QUESTIONS

1. What is the right action for George to perform?
2. What is the right action for Jim to perform?
3. What does Williams mean by "integrity"?
4. Why does Williams believe that utilitarianism renders integrity unintelligible?

Part VIII

PLURALISM

The Right and the Good

W. D. Ross

William David Ross (1877–1971) was Professor of Philosophy at the University of Oxford. He argues that neither utilitarianism nor Kantianism captures the special relationships we may have with others, such as gratitude to a benefactor. These give rise to prima facie duties, those we ought to do unless they are outweighed by conflicting prima facie duties. How to take them all into account is a matter of judgment in particular cases. Ross maintains that prima facie duties are self-evident, known by intuition just like logical or mathematical truths.

The real point at issue between hedonism and utilitarianism on the one hand and their opponents on the other is not whether "right" means "productive of so and so"; for it cannot with any plausibility be maintained that it does. The point at issue is that to which we now pass, viz, whether there is any general character which makes right acts right, and if so, what it is. Among the main historical attempts to state a single characteristic of all right actions which is the foundation of their rightness are those made by egoism and utilitarianism. But I do not propose to discuss these, not because the subject is unimportant, but because it has been dealt with so often and so well already, and because there has come to be so much agreement among moral philosophers that neither of these theories is satisfactory. A much more attractive theory has been put forward by Professor Moore: that what makes actions right is that they are productive of more *good* than could have been produced by any other action open to the agent.[1]

This theory is in fact the culmination of all the attempts to base rightness on productivity of some sort of result. The first form this attempt takes is the attempt to base rightness on conduciveness to the advantage or pleasure of the agent. This theory comes to grief over the fact, which stares us in the face, that a great part of duty consists in an observance of the rights and a furtherance of the interests of others, whatever the cost to ourselves may be. Plato and others may be right in holding that a regard for the rights of others never in the long run involves a loss of happiness for the agent, that "the just life profits a man." But this, even if true, is irrelevant to the rightness of the act. As soon as a man does an action *because* he thinks he will promote his own interests thereby, he is acting not from a sense of its rightness but from self-interest.

To the egoistic theory hedonistic utilitarianism supplies a much-needed amendment. It points out correctly that the fact that a certain pleasure will be enjoyed by the agent is no reason why he *ought* to bring it into being rather than an equal or greater pleasure to be enjoyed by another, though, human nature being what it is, it makes it not unlikely that he *will* try to

Reprinted from W. D. Ross, *The Right and the Good*, Oxford University Press, 1930. Reprinted by permission of the publisher.

bring it into being. But hedonistic utilitarianism in its turn needs a correction. On reflection it seems clear that pleasure is not the only thing in life that we think good in itself, that for instance we think the possession of a good character, or an intelligent understanding of the world, as good or better. A great advance is made by the substitution of "productive of the greatest good" for "productive of the greatest pleasure."

Not only is this theory more attractive than hedonistic utilitarianism, but its logical relation to that theory is such that the latter could not be true unless *it* were true, while it might be true though hedonistic utilitarianism were not. It is in fact one of the logical bases of hedonistic utilitarianism. For the view that what produces the maximum pleasure is right has for its bases the views (1) that what produces the maximum good is right, and (2) that pleasure is the only thing good in itself. If they were not assuming that what produces the maximum *good* is right, the utilitarians' attempt to show that pleasure is the only thing good in itself, which is in fact the point they take most pains to establish, would have been quite irrelevant to their attempt to prove that only what produces the maximum *pleasure* is right. If, therefore, it can be shown that productivity of the maximum good is not what makes all right actions right, we shall *a fortiori* have refuted hedonistic utilitarianism.

When a plain man fulfils a promise because he thinks he ought to do so, it seems clear that he does so with no thought of its total consequences, still less with any opinion that these are likely to be the best possible. He thinks in fact much more of the past than of the future. What makes him think it right to act in a certain way is the fact that he has promised to do so—that and, usually, nothing more. That his act will produce the best possible consequences is not his reason for calling it right. What lends colour to the theory we are examining, then, is not the actions (which form probably a great majority of our actions) in which some such reflection as "I have promised" is the only reason we give ourselves for thinking a certain action right, but the exceptional cases in which the consequences of fulfilling a promise (for instance) would be so disastrous to others that we judge it right not to do so. It must of course be admitted that such cases exist. If I

have promised to meet a friend at a particular time for some trivial purpose, I should certainly think myself justified in breaking my engagement if by doing so I could prevent a serious accident or bring relief to the victims of one. And the supporters of the view we are examining hold that my thinking so is due to my thinking that I shall bring more good into existence by the one action than by the other, A different account may, however, be given of the matter, an account which will, I believe, show itself to be the true one. It may be said that besides the duty of fulfilling promises I have and recognize a duty of relieving distress,[2] and that when I think it right to do the latter at the cost of not doing the former, it is not because I think I shall produce more good thereby but because I think it the duty which is in the circumstances more of a duty. This account surely corresponds much more closely with what we really think in such a situation. If, so far as I can see, I could bring equal amounts of good into being by fulfilling my promise and by helping some one to whom I had made no promise, I should not hesitate to regard the former as my duty. Yet on the view that what is right is right because it is productive of the most good I should not so regard it.

There are two theories, each in its way simple, that offer a solution of such cases of conscience. One is the view of Kant, that there are certain duties of perfect obligation, such as those of fulfilling promises, of paying debts, of telling the truth, which admit of no exception whatever in favour of duties of imperfect obligation, such as that of relieving distress. The other is the view of, for instance, Professor Moore and Dr. Rashdall, that there is only the duty of producing good, and that all "conflicts of duties" should be resolved by asking "by which action will most good be produced?" But it is more important that our theory fit the facts than that it be simple, and the account we have given above corresponds (it seems to me) better than either of the simpler theories with what we really think, viz. that normally promise-keeping, for example, should come before benevolence, but that when and only when the good to be produced by the benevolent act is very great and the promise comparatively trivial, the act of benevolence becomes our duty.

In fact the theory of "ideal utilitarianism," if I may for brevity refer so to the theory of Professor Moore, seems to simplify unduly our relations to our fellows. It says, in effect, that the only morally significant relation in which my neighbours stand to me is that of being possible beneficiaries by my action.[3] They do stand in this relation to me, and this relation is morally significant. But they may also stand to me in the relation of promisee to promiser, of creditor to debtor, of wife to husband, of child to parent, of friend to friend, of fellow countryman to fellow countryman, and the like; and each of these relations is the foundation of a *prima facie* duty, which is more or less incumbent on me according to the circumstances of the case. When I am in a situation, as perhaps I always am, in which more than one of these *prima facie* duties is incumbent on me, what I have to do is to study the situation as fully as I can until I form the considered opinion (it is never more) that in the circumstances one of them is more incumbent than any other; then I am bound to think that to do this *prima facie* duty is my duty *sans phrase* in the situation.

I suggest "*prima facie* duty" or "conditional duty" as a brief way of referring to the characteristic (quite distinct from that of being a duty proper) which an act has, in virtue of being of a certain kind (e.g. the keeping of a promise), of being an act which would be a duty proper if it were not at the same time of another kind which is morally significant. Whether an act is a duty proper or actual duty depends on *all* the morally significant kinds it is an instance of. The phrase "*prima facie* duty" must be apologized for, since (1) it suggests that what we are speaking of is a certain kind of duty, whereas it is in fact not a duty, but something related in a special way to duty. Strictly speaking, we want not a phrase in which duty is qualified by an adjective, but a separate noun. (2) "*Prima*" *facie* suggests that one is speaking only of an appearance which a moral situation presents at first sight, and which may turn out to be illusory; whereas what I am speaking of is an objective fact involved in the nature of the situation, or more strictly in an element of its nature, though not, as duty proper does, arising from its *whole* nature. I can, however, think of no term which fully meets the case. "Claim" has been suggested by Professor Prichard. The word "claim" has the advantage of being quite a familiar one in this connexion, and it seems to cover much of the ground. It would be quite natural to say, "a person to whom I have made a promise has a claim on me," and also, "a person whose distress I could relieve (at the cost of breaking the promise) has a claim on me." But (1) while "claim" is appropriate from *their* point of view, we want a word to express the corresponding fact from the agent's point of view—the fact of his being subject to claims that can be made against him; and ordinary language provides us with no such correlative to "claim." And (2) (what is more important) "claim" seems inevitably to suggest two persons, one of whom might make a claim on the other; and while this covers the ground of social duty, it is inappropriate in the case of that important part of duty which is the duty of cultivating a certain kind of character in oneself. It would be artificial, I think, and at any rate metaphorical, to say that one's character has a claim on oneself.

There is nothing arbitrary about these *prima facie* duties. Each rests on a definite circumstance which cannot seriously be held to be without moral significance. Of *prima facie* duties I suggest, without claiming completeness or finality for it, the following division.[4]

(1) Some duties rest on previous acts of my own. These duties seem to include two kinds, (*a*) those resting on a promise or what may fairly be called an implicit promise, such as the implicit undertaking not to tell lies which seems to be implied in the act of entering into conversation (at any rate by civilized men), or of writing books that purport to be history and not fiction. These may be called the duties of fidelity. (*b*) Those resting on a previous wrongful act. These may be called the duties of reparation. (2) Some rest on previous acts of other men, i.e. services done by them to me. These may be loosely described as the duties of gratitude. (3) Some rest on the fact or possibility of a distribution of pleasure or happiness (or of the means thereto) which is not in accordance with the merit of the persons concerned; in such cases there arises a duty to upset or prevent such a distribution. These are the duties of justice. (4) Some

rest on the mere fact that there are other beings in the world whose condition we can make better in respect of virtue, or of intelligence, or of pleasure. These are the duties of beneficence. (5) Some rest on the fact that we can improve our own condition in respect of virtue or of intelligence. These are the duties of self-improvement. (6) I think that we should distinguish from (4) the duties that may be summed up under the title of "not injuring others." No doubt to injure others is incidentally to fail to do them good; but it seems to me clear that non-maleficence is apprehended as a duty distinct from that of beneficence, and as a duty of a more stringent character. It will be noticed that this alone among the types of duty has been stated in a negative way. An attempt might no doubt be made to state this duty, like the others, in a positive way. It might be said that it is really the duty to prevent ourselves from acting either from an inclination to harm others or from an inclination to seek our own pleasure, in doing which we should incidentally harm them. But on reflection it seems clear that the primary duty here is the duty not to harm others, this being a duty whether or not we have an inclination that if followed would lead to our harming them; and that when we have such an inclination the primary duty not to harm others gives rise to a consequential duty to resist the inclination. The recognition of this duty of non-maleficence is the first step on the way to the recognition of the duty of beneficence; and that accounts for the prominence of the commands "thou shalt not kill," "thou shalt not commit adultery," "thou shalt not steal," "thou shalt not bear false witness," in so early a code as the Decalogue. But even when we have come to recognize the duty of beneficence, it appears to me that the duty of non-maleficence is recognized as a distinct one, and as *prima facie* more binding. We should not in general consider it justifiable to kill one person in order to keep another alive, or to steal from one in order to give alms to another.

The essential defect of the "ideal utilitarian" theory is that it ignores, or at least does not do full justice to, the highly personal character of duty. If the only duty is to produce the maximum of good, the question who is to have the good—whether it is myself, or my benefactor, or a person to whom I have made a promise to confer that good on him, or a mere fellow man to whom I stand in no such special relation—should make no difference to my having a duty to produce that good. But we are all in fact sure that it makes a vast difference.

One or two other comments must be made on this provisional list of the divisions of duty. (1) The nomenclature is not strictly correct. For by "fidelity" or "gratitude" we mean, strictly, certain states of motivation; and, as I have urged, it is not our duty to have certain motives, but to do certain acts. By "fidelity," for instance, is meant, strictly, the disposition to fulfil promises and implicit promises *because we have made them*. We have no general word to cover the actual fulfilment of promises and implicit promises *irrespective of motive:* and I use "fidelity," loosely but perhaps conveniently, to fill this gap. So too I use "gratitude" for the returning of services, irrespective of motive. The term "justice" is not so much confined, in ordinary usage, to a certain state of motivation, for we should often talk of a man as acting justly even when we did not think his motive was the wish to do what was just simply for the sake of doing so. Less apology is therefore needed for our use of "justice" in this sense. And I have used the word "beneficence" rather than "benevolence," in order to emphasize the fact that it is our duty to do certain things, and not to do them from certain motives.

(2) If the objection be made, that this catalogue of the main types of duty is an unsystematic one resting on no logical principle, it may be replied, first, that it makes no claim to being ultimate. It is a *prima facie* classification of the duties which reflection on our moral convictions seems actually to reveal. And if these convictions are, as I would claim that they are, of the nature of knowledge, and if I have not misstated them, the list will be a list of authentic conditional duties, correct as far as it goes though not necessarily complete. The list of *goods* put forward by the rival theory is reached by exactly the same method—the only sound one in the circumstances—viz. that of direct reflection on what we really think. Loyalty to the facts is worth more than a symmetrical architectonic or a hastily reached simplicity. If further reflection discovers a perfect

logical basis for this or for a better classification, so much the better.

(3) It may, again, be objected that our theory that there are these various and often conflicting types of *prima facie* duty leaves us with no principle upon which to discern what is our actual duty in particular circumstances. But this objection is not one which the rival theory is in a position to bring forward. For when we have to choose between the production of two heterogeneous goods, say knowledge and pleasure, the "ideal utilitarian" theory can only fall back on an opinion, for which no logical basis can be offered, that one of the goods is the greater; and this is no better than a similar opinion that one of two duties is the more urgent. And again, when we consider the infinite variety of the effects of our actions in the way of pleasure, it must surely be admitted that the claim which *hedonism* sometimes makes, that it offers a readily applicable criterion of right conduct, is quite illusory.

I am unwilling, however, to content myself with an *argumentum ad hominem,* and I would contend that in principle there is no reason to anticipate that every act that is our duty is so for one and the same reason. Why should two sets of circumstances, or one set of circumstances, *not* possess different characteristics, any one of which makes a certain act our *prima facie* duty? When I ask what it is that makes me in certain cases sure that I have a *prima facie* duty to do so and so, I find that it lies in the fact that I have made a promise; when I ask the same question in another case, I find the answer lies in the fact that I have done a wrong. And if on reflection I find (as I think I do) that neither of these reasons is reducible to the other, I must not on any *a priori* ground assume that such a reduction is possible.

An attempt may be made to arrange in a more systematic way the main types of duty which we have indicated. In the first place it seems self-evident that if there are things that are intrinsically good, it is *prima facie* a duty to bring them into existence rather than not to do so, and to bring as much of them into existence as possible. . . . [T]here are three main things that are intrinsically good—virtue, knowledge, and, with certain limitations, pleasure. And since a given virtuous disposition, for instance, is

equally good whether it is realized in myself or in another, it seems to be my duty to bring it into existence whether in myself or in another. So too with a given piece of knowledge.

The case of pleasure is difficult; for while we clearly recognize a duty to produce pleasure for others, it is by no means so clear that we recognize a duty to produce pleasure for ourselves. This appears to arise from the following facts. The thought of an act as our duty is one that presupposes a certain amount of reflection about the act; and for that reason does not normally arise in connexion with acts towards which we are already impelled by another strong impulse. So far, the cause of our thinking of the promotion of our own pleasure as a duty is analogous to the cause which usually prevents a highly sympathetic person from thinking of the promotion of the pleasure of others as a duty. He is impelled so strongly by direct interest in the well-being of others towards promoting their pleasure that he does not stop to ask whether it is his duty to promote it; and we are all impelled so strongly towards the promotion of our own pleasure that we do not stop to ask whether it is a duty or not. But there is a further reason why even when we stop to think about the matter it does not usually present itself as a duty: viz. that, since the performance of most of our duties involves the giving up of some pleasure that we desire, the doing of duty and the getting of pleasure for ourselves come by a natural association of ideas to be thought of as incompatible things. This association of ideas is in the main salutary in its operation, since it puts a check on what but for it would be much too strong, the tendency to pursue one's own pleasure without thought of other considerations. Yet if pleasure is good, it seems in the long run clear that it is right to get it for ourselves as well as to produce it for others, when this does not involve the failure to discharge some more stringent *prima facie* duty. The question is a very difficult one, but it seems that this conclusion can be denied only on one or other of three grounds: (1) that pleasure is not *prima facie* good (i.e. good when it is neither the actualization of a bad disposition nor undeserved), (2) that there is no *prima facie* duty to produce as much that is good as we can, or (3) that though there is a *prima facie* duty to produce other things that are good, there is no *prima facie* duty to produce pleasure which will be enjoyed by ourselves. I give reasons later for not accepting the first contention. The second hardly admits of argument but seems to me plainly false. The third seems plausible only if we hold that an act that is pleasant or brings pleasure to ourselves must for that reason not be a duty; and this would lead to paradoxical consequences, such as that if a man enjoys giving pleasure to others or working for their moral improvement, it cannot be his duty to do so. Yet it seems to be a very stubborn fact, that in our ordinary consciousness we are not aware of a duty to get pleasure for ourselves; and by way of partial explanation of this I may add that though, as I think, one's own pleasure is a good and there is a duty to produce it, it is only if we *think* of our own pleasure not as simply our own pleasure, but as an objective good, something that an impartial spectator would approve, that we can think of the getting it as a duty; and we do not habitually think of it in this way.

If these contentions are right, what we have called the duty of beneficence and the duty of self-improvement rest on the same ground. No different principles of duty are involved in the two cases. If we feel a special responsibility for improving our own character rather than that of others, it is not because a special principle is involved, but because we are aware that the one is more under our control than the other. It was on this ground that Kant expressed the practical law of duty in the form "seek to make yourself good and other people happy." He was so persuaded of the internality of virtue that he regarded any attempt by one person to produce virtue in another as bound to produce, at most, only a counterfeit of virtue, the doing of externally right acts not from the true principle of virtuous action but out of regard to another person. It must be admitted that one man cannot compel another to be virtuous; compulsory virtue would just not be virtue. But experience clearly shows that Kant overshoots the mark when he contends that one man cannot do anything to *promote* virtue in another, to bring such influences to bear upon him that his own response to them is more likely to be virtuous than his response to other influences would have been. And our duty to do this is not different in kind from our duty to improve our own characters.

It is equally clear, and clear at an earlier stage of moral development, that if there are things that are bad in themselves we ought, *prima facie,* not to bring them upon others; and on this fact rests the duty of non-maleficence.

The duty of justice is particularly complicated, and the word is used to cover things which are really very different—things such as the payment of debts, the reparation of injuries done by oneself to another, and the bringing about of a distribution of happiness between other people in proportion to merit. I use the word to denote only the last of these three. In the fifth chapter I shall try to show that besides the three (comparatively) simple goods, virtue, knowledge, and pleasure, there is a more complex good, not reducible to these, consisting in the proportionment of happiness to virtue. The bringing of this about is a duty which we owe to all men alike, though it may be reinforced by special responsibilities that we have undertaken to particular men. This, therefore, with beneficence and self-improvement, comes under the general principle that we should produce as much good as possible, though the good here involved is different in kind from any other.

But besides this general obligation, there are special obligations. These may arise, in the first place, incidentally, from acts which were not essentially meant to create such an obligation, but which nevertheless create it. From the nature of the case such acts may be of two kinds—the infliction of injuries on others, and the acceptance of benefits from them. It seems clear that these put us under a special obligation to other men, and that only these acts can do so incidentally. From these arise the twin duties of reparation and gratitude.

And finally there are special obligations arising from acts the very intention of which, when they were done, was to put us under such an obligation. The name for such acts is "promises"; the name is wide enough if we are willing to include under it implicit promises, i.e. modes of behaviour in which without explicit verbal promise we intentionally create an expectation that we can be counted on to behave in a certain way in the interest of another person.

These seem to be, in principle, all the ways in which *prima facie* duties arise. In actual experience they are compounded together in highly complex ways. Thus, for example, the duty of obeying the laws of one's country arises partly (as Socrates contends in the *Crito*) from the duty of gratitude for the benefits one has received from it; partly from the implicit promise to obey which seems to be involved in permanent residence in a country whose laws we know we are *expected* to obey, and still more clearly involved when we ourselves invoke the protection of its laws (this is the truth underlying the doctrine of the social contract); and partly (if we are fortunate in our country) from the fact that its laws are potent instruments for the general good.

Or again, the sense of a general obligation to bring about (so far as we can) a just apportionment of happiness to merit is often greatly reinforced by the fact that many of the existing injustices are due to a social and economic system which we have, not indeed created, but taken part in and assented to; the duty of justice is then reinforced by the duty of reparation.

It is necessary to say something by way of clearing up the relation between *prima facie* duties and the actual or absolute duty to do one particular act in particular circumstances. If, as almost all moralists except Kant are agreed, and as most plain men think, it is sometimes right to tell a lie or to break a promise, it must be maintained that there is a difference between *prima facie* duty and actual or absolute duty. When we think ourselves justified in breaking, and indeed morally obliged to break, a promise in order to relieve some one's distress, we do not for a moment cease to recognize a *prima facie* duty to keep our promise, and this leads us to feel, not indeed shame or repentance, but certainly compunction, for behaving as we do: we recognize, further, that it is our duty to make up somehow to the promisee for the breaking of the promise. We have to distinguish from the characteristic of being our duty that of tending to be our duty. Any act that we do contains various elements in virtue of which it falls under various categories. In virtue of being the breaking of a promise, for instance, it tends to be wrong; in virtue of being an instance of relieving distress it tends to be right. Tendency to be one's

duty may be called a parti-resultant attribute, i.e. one which belongs to an act in virtue of some one component in its nature. *Being* one's duty is a toti-resultant attribute, one which belongs to an act in virtue of its whole nature and of nothing less than this. This distinction between parti-resultant and toti-resultant attributes is one which we shall meet in another context also.

Another instance of the same distinction may be found in the operation of natural laws. *Qua* subject to the force of gravitation towards some other body, each body tends to move in a particular direction with a particular velocity; but its actual movement depends on *all* the forces to which it is subject. It is only by recognizing this distinction that we can preserve the absoluteness of laws of nature, and only by recognizing a corresponding distinction that we can preserve the absoluteness of the general principles of morality. But an important difference between the two cases must be pointed out. When we say that in virtue of gravitation a body tends to move in a certain way, we are referring to a causal influence actually exercised on it by another body or other bodies. When we say that in virtue of being deliberately untrue a certain remark tends to be wrong, we are referring to no causal relation, to no relation that involves succession in time, but to such a relation as connects the various attributes of a mathematical figure. And if the word "tendency" is thought to suggest too much a causal relation, it is better to talk of certain types of act as being *prima facie* right or wrong (or of different persons as having different and possibly conflicting claims upon us), than of their tending to be right or wrong.

Something should be said of the relation between our apprehension of the *prima facie* rightness of certain types of act and our mental attitude towards particular acts. It is proper to use the word "apprehension" in the former case and not in the latter. That an act, *qua* fulfilling a promise, or *qua* effecting a just distribution of good, or *qua* returning services rendered, or *qua* promoting the good of others, or *qua* promoting the virtue or insight of the agent, is *prima facie* right, is self-evident; not in the sense that it is evident from the beginning of our lives, or as soon as we attend to the proposition for the first time, but in the sense that when we have reached sufficient mental maturity and have given sufficient attention to the proposition it is evident without any need of proof, or of evidence beyond itself. It is self-evident just as a mathematical axiom, or the validity of a form of inference, is evident. The moral order expressed in these propositions is just as much part of the fundamental nature of the universe (and, we may add, of any possible universe in which there were moral agents at all) as is the spatial or numerical structure expressed in the axioms of geometry or arithmetic. In our confidence that these propositions are true there is involved the same trust in our reason that is involved in our confidence in mathematics; and we should have no justification for trusting it in the latter sphere and distrusting it in the former. In both cases we are dealing with propositions that cannot be proved, but that just as certainly need no proof.

Some of these general principles of *prima facie* duty may appear to be open to criticism. It may be thought, for example, that the principle of returning good for good is a falling off from the Christian principle, generally and rightly recognized as expressing the highest morality, of returning good for evil. To this it may be replied that I do not suggest that there is a principle commanding us to return good for good and forbidding us to return good for evil, and that I do suggest that there is a positive duty to seek the good of all men. What I maintain is that an act in which good is returned for good is recognized as *specially* binding on us just because it is of that character, and that *ceteris paribus* any one would think it his duty to help his benefactors rather than his enemies, if he could not do both; just as it is generally recognized that *ceteris paribus* we should pay our debts rather than give our money in charity, when we cannot do both. A benefactor is not only a man, calling for our effort on his behalf on that ground, but also our benefactor, calling for our *special* effort on *that* ground.

Our judgements about our actual duty in concrete situations have none of the certainty that attaches to our recognition of the general principles of duty. A statement is certain, i.e. is an expression of knowledge, only in one or other of two cases; when

it is either self-evident, or a valid conclusion from self-evident premises. And our judgements about our particular duties have neither of these characters. (1) They are not self-evident. Where a possible act is seen to have two characteristics, in virtue of one of which it is *prima facie* right, and in virtue of the other *prima facie* wrong, we are (I think) well aware that we are not certain whether we ought or ought not to do it; that whether we do it or not, we are taking a moral risk. We come in the long run, after consideration, to think one duty more pressing than the other, but we do not feel certain that it is so. And though we do not always recognize that a possible act has two such characteristics, and though there *may* be cases in which it has not, we are never certain that any particular possible act has not, and therefore never certain that it is right, nor certain that it is wrong. For, to go no further in the analysis, it is enough to point out that any particular act will in all probability in the course of time contribute to the bringing about of good or of evil for many human beings, and thus have a *prima facie* rightness or wrongness of which we know nothing. (2) Again, our judgements about our particular duties are not logical conclusions from self-evident premises. The only possible premises would be the general principles stating their *prima facie* rightness or wrongness *qua* having the different characteristics they do have; and even if we could (as we cannot) apprehend the extent to which an act will tend on the one hand, for example, to bring about advantages for our benefactors, and on the other hand to bring about disadvantages for fellow men who are not our benefactors, there is no principle by which we can draw the conclusion that it is on the whole right or on the whole wrong. In this respect the judgement as to the rightness of a particular act is just like the judgement as to the beauty of a particular natural object or work of art. A poem is, for instance, in respect of certain qualities beautiful and in respect of certain others not beautiful, and our judgement as to the degree of beauty it possesses on the whole is never reached by logical reasoning from the apprehension of its particular beauties or particular defects. Both in this and in the moral case we have more or less probable opinions which are not logically justified conclusions from the general principles that are recognized as self-evident.

There is therefore much truth in the description of the right act as a fortunate act. If we cannot be certain that it is right, it is our good fortune if the act we do is the right act. This consideration does not, however, make the doing of our duty a mere matter of chance. There is a parallel here between the doing of duty and the doing of what will be to our personal advantage. We never *know* what act will in the long run be to our advantage. Yet it is certain that we are more likely in general to secure our advantage if we estimate to the best of our ability the probable tendencies of our actions in this respect, than if we act on caprice. And similarly we are more likely to do our duty if we reflect to the best of our ability on the *prima facie* rightness or wrongness of various possible acts in virtue of the characteristics we perceive them to have, than if we act without reflection. With this greater likelihood we must be content.

Many people would be inclined to say that the right act for me is not that whose general nature I have been describing, viz. that which if I were omniscient I should see to be my duty, but that which on all the evidence available to me I should think to be my duty. But suppose that from the state of partial knowledge in which I think act *A* to be my duty, I could pass to a state of perfect knowledge in which I saw act *B* to be my duty should I not say "act *B* was the right act for me to do"? I should no doubt add "though I am not to be blamed for doing act *A*." But in adding this am I not passing from the question "what is right" to the question "what is morally good"? At the same time I am not making the *full* passage from the one notion to the other: for in order that the act should be morally good, or an act I am not to be blamed for doing, it must not merely be the act which it is reasonable for me to think my duty; it must also be done for that reason, or from some other morally good motive. Thus the conception of the right act as the act which it is reasonable for me to think my duty is an unsatisfactory compromise between the true notion of the right act and the notion of the morally good action.

The general principles of duty are obviously not self-evident from the beginning of our lives. How do they come to be so? The answer is, that they come to be self-evident to us just as mathematical axioms do. We find by experience that this couple of matches and that couple make four matches, that this couple of balls on a wire and that couple make four balls; and by reflection on these and similar discoveries we come to see that it is of the nature of two and two to make four. In a precisely similar way, we see the *prima facie* rightness of an act which would be the fulfilment of a particular promise, and of another which would be the fulfilment of another promise, and when we have reached sufficient maturity to think in general terms, we apprehend *prima facie* rightness to belong to the nature of any fulfilment of promise. What comes first in time is the apprehension of the self-evident *prima facie* rightness of an individual act of a particular type. From this we come by reflection to apprehend the self-evident general principle of *prima facie* duty. From this, too, perhaps along with the apprehension of the self-evident *prima facie* rightness of the same act in virtue of its having another characteristic as well, and perhaps in spite of the apprehension of its *prima facie* wrongness in virtue of its having some third characteristic, we come to believe something not self-evident at all, but an object of probable opinion, viz. that this particular act is (not *prima facie* but) actually right.

In this respect there is an important difference between rightness and mathematical properties. A triangle which is isosceles necessarily has two of its angles equal, whatever other characteristics the triangle may have—whatever, for instance, be its area, or the size of its third angle. The equality of the two angles is a parti-resultant attribute. And the same is true of all mathematical attributes. It is true, I may add, of *prima facie* rightness. But no act is ever, in virtue of falling under some general description, necessarily actually right; its rightness depends on its whole nature[5] and not on any element in it. The reason is that no mathematical object (no figure, for instance, or angle) ever has two characteristics that tend to give it opposite resultant characteristics, while moral acts often (as every one knows) and indeed always (as on reflection we must admit) have different characteristics that tend to make them at the same time *prima facie* right and *prima facie* wrong; there is probably no act, for instance, which does good to any one without doing harm to some one else, and *vice versa*.

NOTES

1. I take the theory which, as I have tried to show, seems to be put forward in *Ethics* rather than the earlier and less plausible theory put forward in *Principia Ethica*.
2. These are not strictly speaking duties, but things that tend to be our duty, or *prima facie* duties.
3. Some will think it, apart from other considerations, a sufficient refutation of this view to point out that I also stand in that relation to myself, so that for this view the distinction of oneself from others is morally insignificant.
4. I should make it plain at this stage that I am *assuming* the correctness of some of our main convictions as to *prima facie* duties, or, more strictly, am claiming that we *know* them to be true. To me it seems as self-evident as anything could be, that to make a promise, for instance, is to create a moral claim on us in someone else. Many readers will perhaps say that they do *not* know this to be true. If so, I certainly cannot prove it to them; I can only ask them to reflect again, in the hope that they will ultimately agree that they also know it to be true. The main moral convictions of the plain man seem to me to be, not opinions which it is for philosophy to prove or disprove, but knowledge from the start; and in my own case I seem to find little difficulty in distinguishing these essential convictions from other moral convictions which I also have, which are merely fallible opinions based on an imperfect study of the working for good or evil of certain institutions or types of action.
5. To avoid complicating unduly the statement of the general view I am putting forward, I have here rather overstated it. Any act is the origination of a great variety of things many of which make no difference to its rightness or wrongness. But there are always many elements in its nature (i.e. in what it is the origination of) that make a difference to its rightness or wrongness, and no element in its nature can be dismissed without consideration as indifferent.

STUDY QUESTIONS

1. According to Ross, what is a prima facie duty?
2. Does Ross believe you are ever justified in telling a lie?
3. How do we decide if a duty is self-evident?
4. Might a self-evident claim be mistaken?

An Unconnected Heap of Duties?

David McNaughton

Moral theories are supposed to provide simplicity, not offer a new principle for every circumstance. Intuitionism, the moral theory defended by Ross, leaves us with a long list of basic principles. Thus we might wonder whether it even qualifies as a theory. David McNaughton, Professor of Philosophy at Florida State University, argues that we seek a moral theory, however simple, that fits the facts and offers explanatory power. McNaughton maintains that intuitionism meets these tests at least as well if not better than its rivals.

Despite its name, the school of ethical intuitionism which flourished between the world wars, and whose greatest proponents were H.A. Prichard and W.D. Ross, was not distinguished from its competitors by a distinctive epistemology. The dispute between intuitionism and its main rival, the utilitarian tradition, revolved around the issue of whether there was more than one fundamental moral principle. The utilitarian tradition in ethical thought can be represented as holding that there is just one fundamental duty or moral principle: the duty of beneficence. In the hands of G.E. Moore, whom Ross and Prichard saw as their main opponent, the theory had developed into a sophisticated consequentialism which subscribed to a pluralist account of the good. Even so, in determining which action is right, only one consideration is relevant: which action will produce the most good? Ethical intuitionism rejected this monism about what makes right actions right as over-simple, and insisted that there are a number of distinct and irreducible basic duties or moral principles, all of which can be relevant in determining

whether some action is right. Both parties to this debate were taken to agree that an ethical theory rests on intuition, by which was meant no more than that the most basic ethical principles, since they could not be inferred from more basic ones, must be self-evident.

It has become commonplace to dismiss the deontic pluralism of an ethical intuitionist such as Ross fairly briskly. . . . In this paper I examine the charge that . . . intuitionism is . . . unsystematic, offering us merely a 'heap of unconnected duties' with no unifying rationale. . . . I shall argue . . . that Ross has an entire answer to those who maintain that his theory is unsystematic. . . .

We can expand this complaint as follows. Common-sense morality appeals to a large variety of moral principles, which have no discernible structure. Intuitionism does not attempt to systematize ordinary morality, but simply mirrors it. An intuitionist, such as Ross, merely presents us with a more or less arbitrarily selected list of the more common (*prima facie*) duties, and announces them to be self-evident.

Reprinted from David McNaughton, "An Unconnected Heap of Duties?" *The Philosophical Quarterly*, vol. 46, no. 185, 1996. Reprinted by permission of the journal.

Since there is no structure to this list, there seems to be no explanation of why some items are on the list and not others, and therefore no room for rational debate in the event of disagreement about what should be included. Given the unavailability of reasoned discussion we simply have one bare intuition pitted against another. Even a philosopher who admits that we may eventually have to appeal to intuition may rightly feel that this is too quick. Moral theory should facilitate reasoned debate, not forestall it. Indeed, in the absence of such a structure it is doubtful whether intuitionism, unlike utilitarianism, can lay claim to be a moral *theory* at all.

Such a criticism fails to recognize that philosophical intuitionism does seek to systematize common-sense morality, and in much the same way as many utilitarians have tried to do. For it seeks to show that the plethora of precepts which constitutes common-sense morality can be derived from a very small number of self-evident basic duties. According to Ross, 'The general principles which [intuitionism] regards as intuitively seen to be true are very few in number and very general in character'. Sidgwick also saw this as the aim of philosophical intuitionism.[1] Both utilitarianism and intuitionism can therefore be seen as sharing the theoretical goal of explaining and justifying our everyday moral judgements by appeal to the smallest number of most general principles. In this sense, intuitionism is as much engaged as is utilitarianism in constructing a moral theory; they only differ over how many basic principles they need to accomplish the task.

In fairness to his critics it must be admitted that Ross does not explicitly state in his famous exposition of his theory in . . . *The Right and the Good* that his theory has this explanatory structure, but it is implicit throughout his long and detailed discussion.[2] He begins by offering a categorization or division of *prima facie* duties, for which he does not claim 'completeness or finality', but which he maintains is not 'arbitrary' because 'Each rests on a definite circumstance which cannot seriously be held to be without moral significance'. Subsequent discussion makes it clear that this list of *prima facie* duties is a first shot at a complete list of basic and underivative duties.[3] As he points out, it is misleading to

think of these as distinct or fundamental *duties,* since on his account *prima facie* duties are not strictly duties at all, 'but something related in a special kind of way to duty'. One's duty proper is what one ought actually to do, all things considered, in some particular situation. The list might more accurately be thought of as a list of fundamental morally relevant characteristics of actions—of features of actions which are right- or wrong-making characteristics and which always carry weight when we are considering whether a particular action is right or wrong. With that proviso, here is my summary of Ross's original list.

(1) Duties resting on a previous act of my own. These in turn divide into two main categories:
   (a) duties of *fidelity*; these result from my having made a promise or something like a promise;
   (b) duties of *reparation*; these stem from my having done something wrong so that I am now required to make amends.
(2) Duties resting on previous acts of others; these are duties of *gratitude,* which I owe to those who have helped me.
(3) Duties to prevent (or overturn) a distribution of benefits and burdens which is not in accordance with the merit of the persons concerned; these are duties of *justice.*
(4) Duties which rest on the fact that there are other people in the world whose condition we could make better; these are duties of *beneficence.*
(5) Duties which rest on the fact that I could better myself; these are duties of *self-improvement.*
(6) Duties of not injuring others; these are duties of *non-maleficence.*

This list is only provisional: Ross goes on to discuss whether it can be further reduced by showing that some of these duties are not really basic. Since the dialectic of the argument dictates that a duty cannot remain on the list if it can be shown to be derivative, we need to know what it is for one duty to be derived from another.

Unfortunately, Ross gives no systematic account of the relation of derivation, but one can be gleaned from scattered remarks throughout the text. After reviewing and revising his list of basic duties, he writes:

> These seem to be, in principle, all the ways in which *prima facie* duties arise. In actual experience they are compounded together in highly complex ways.[4]

He then gives as an example one's duty as a citizen to obey the laws of one's country. That duty 'arises from' (at least in the ideal case) three basic duties: gratitude, fidelity and beneficence. We should be grateful for the benefits we have received from the state; we have made an implicit promise to obey by retaining permanent residence in a country whose laws we know we are expected to obey; beneficence also requires us to obey the laws because they are 'a potent instrument for the general good'. Ross later gives a similar account of the duty not to lie. He claims that this duty, which he does not sharply distinguish from the duty of veracity, stems from two of the basic duties on his list: those of non-maleficence and fidelity. To lie to someone is (normally) to do an injury to that person (and perhaps to others). In addition, Ross holds that communication standardly presupposes an implicit mutual undertaking by all parties that they will use language to convey their real opinions. In such cases, to lie is to breach this implicit promise. We show what is wrong with law-breaking and lying by showing that to act in these ways is, normally, to be in breach of more than one of our fundamental duties.

In his discussion of both these cases, Ross makes it clear that there can be special circumstances in which some of the considerations which count against acting in these ways do not apply. In such cases, the force or bindingness of the duty in question may be weakened. For example, a very bad government will not be promoting the general good, and then there will be no duty arising from considerations of beneficence to support it. In the case of lying, the presupposition that there is a mutual agreement to make true assertions can lapse. People who are habitual liars have announced by their actions their refusal to be bound by this implicit

contract, thus releasing others from their own obligation to honour it. Similarly, if I am in a strange society and know nothing of its social practices, not even whether they are friendly or hostile, then there is no such implicit understanding. In Ross's opinion, a large part of the stringency of the duty not to lie stems from the supposed implicit promise; where it is not present then the obligation not to lie is much weakened.

Although Ross does not discuss this point, it seems perfectly possible that there might be cases where none of the considerations which normally make law-breaking or lying wrong applies. For example, if I play a game of Cheat with my children, I must lie, because that is part of the game. On Ross's account of what makes lying wrong, it may be that there is absolutely nothing wrong with lying in such cases. The tacit agreement to tell the truth is explicitly cancelled in such games and it is at least arguable that I am, in this context, doing no harm whatever to my children in lying to them.[5] Similarly, there can surely be governments so bad that there is nothing to be said in favour of obeying them, and everything to be said against. If there are circumstances, such as playing Cheat, where the fact that saying something would be a lie does not furnish any reason whatever for not saying it, then in what sense can it be said, as Ross says, that there is a duty not to lie? On Ross's official account of *prima facie* duty, refraining from lying cannot be such a duty because, as we saw, that would imply that lying was universally a wrong-making characteristic—that it always counted against an action that it involved lying. But this claim is arguably false; it does not count at all against my playing Cheat with my children that we shall all lie as hard as we can. In the case of derivative duties, such as the duty not to lie or to obey the law, we must say rather that it is only normally or standardly that we have a *prima facie* duty to act in this way.

If the duty not to lie is understood in this way, can we still maintain *of a particular act* that it is *prima facie* wrong in virtue of being a lie? We might be tempted to interpret Ross's account of lying as holding that in a normal case, where it does count against an action that it would involve lying, the act is *prima facie* wrong, *not* in virtue of being a lie, but in virtue of its being a case of promise-breaking and causing harm. But this, I think, is a false contrast. Acts can get to be instances of promise-breaking or maleficence in a number of ways. It may be true of some particular act that it is in virtue of its being a lie (rather than, for example, the non-payment of a debt) that it is an instance of promise-breaking and maleficence. If this is right, then the fact that *this* act is a lie may make it *prima facie* wrong, even though there can be acts which, though they involve lying, are not made *prima facie* wrong by that fact. On this interpretation, lying is not a fundamental moral consideration (which is why it does not occur on the list of basic duties), but not all morally relevant considerations need be fundamental. The fact that some act is a lie can still be a reason why that act is *prima facie* wrong.

The examples of derivative duties we have so far considered are cases where our *prima facie* duties are, in Ross's words, 'compounded together in highly complex ways'. But derivative duties need not be complex in this manner. For some kind of action may be a derivative duty in virtue of its falling, in standard cases, under just one basic duty. The duty a child has to honour its parents, for instance: it might plausibly be claimed that this duty rests on the single basic duty of gratitude. As in the previous examples, there could be exceptional cases where there was not even a *prima facie* duty to honour one's parents. Where the child had received nothing from its parents there would be, on this view, no duty to honour them. Ross gives another example himself in his discussion of punishment. He dissents from the common intuitionist view that there is 'a fundamental and underivative duty' to reward the virtuous and punish the guilty. Rather, he claims, the state of affairs in which the good are happy and the bad unhappy is better than the reverse. Since we have a general duty of beneficence, we have a duty to bring about the better state of affairs: 'The duty of reward and punishment seems to me to be . . . derivative. It can be subsumed under the duty of producing as much good as we can'.[6] There may be cases where no good would come of punishing (perhaps because the wrongdoer has suffered enough) and here punishing would not be even *prima facie* right.

In sum, derivative duties are not on the list of basic duties because the characteristic by which they are picked out is not itself morally fundamental, nor does it entail the presence of a morally fundamental characteristic. They still count as duties, however, because acts having that character normally or standardly have one or more of the morally fundamental characteristics that figure on Ross's basic list.

Being underivative is not, however, sufficient for inclusion in Ross's list of basic duties, for he is also striving for as high a level of generality as possible. Thus there may be duties which are not derivative in the sense just defined, but are not on the list because insufficiently general. Thus it is plausible to hold that the fact that an act would be the paying of a debt always counts in its favour. The reason why we are unable to imagine a particular case where debt-paying is not *prima facie* right may be supposed to lie in the fact that one could not be in debt unless one had made an (implicit) promise to repay. That an act is a paying of a debt thus entails that it is the keeping of a promise. The duty to pay debts will then not appear on the list of basic duties because it is only a specific instance of the more general duty of fidelity.

I am not here concerned to defend Ross's analysis of any of these duties; I cite them merely to illustrate his general approach. With the two distinctions between derivative and underivative duties and between more and less general underivative duties in place, we can now see how one might make a case for amending Ross's list. Challenges can come from one of two directions. It may be claimed either that the list needs shortening because it contains some duty that is not really basic, or that the list needs lengthening because it leaves out a basic duty.

The list needs shortening if it can be shown to contain duties that are either derivable from other duties on the list, or are insufficiently general in form. The latter challenge will have been made out if it can be shown either that one duty on the list is just a specific instance of a more general basic duty, or that two of the putative basic duties are just specific instances of one wider inclusive basic duty. Immediately after drawing up his initial list Ross embarks on a discussion to see if it can be made more 'systematic'. His conclusion is that the list does need shortening, and his discussion provides two examples of the latter kind of challenge at work.

First he considers whether beneficence and self-improvement are distinct duties. The main reason for thinking that they are lies in the fact that, while we have a duty to give others pleasure, as well as to make them knowledgeable and virtuous, we normally think we have no corresponding obligation to give ourselves pleasure. Ross discusses whether the belief that we have no duty to give ourselves pleasure arises merely from the fact that it is redundant to require us to do something which we are already (too) strongly motivated to do. If we think, as he is inclined to, that there is in fact a duty to give ourselves pleasure, a duty which it is rarely if ever necessary to invoke, then categories (4) and (5) can be merged under the wider head of universal beneficence.

Second, Ross argues that the duty of justice is simply a specific instance of the general duty to bring about the good, since as we saw when discussing punishment his view is that the distribution of goods in accord with merit is a specific kind of good. So his final list is whittled down to five: the duty to bring about as much good as possible, under which now fall justice, beneficence and self-improvement, and the distinct duties of non-maleficence, fidelity, gratitude and reparation.

The other way to criticize the list would be to claim that it is too short, because there are underivative moral considerations which have not been included. We should note that in order to exclude some putative basic duty from the list we would have to show that it is *wholly* derivative. Thus lying should only be excluded if our moral objection to lying rests solely on the fact that lying would normally involve us in breaching other duties, such as fidelity and non-maleficence; the claim must be that the mere fact that an act is a lie carries no independent moral weight, however slight.

Critics of intuitionism are wont to point out that different intuitionist philosophers cannot agree about which are the basic duties, as if this were itself a sufficient refutation of the theory. But this would only be an objection to intuitionism if the theory held that the contents of the list should be immediately obvious, which it does not. What is important is that there

should be some rational and principled way to settle such disputes, and this is what I have tried to show. There is no need to resort to a blank appeal to intuition. Nor, as Ross points out . . . , should we imagine that intuitionism of this stripe need be conservative. Nothing in Ross's procedure prevents moral criticism of the prevailing *mores* of a society.

It may, of course, be that there is no one way of structuring these duties which will be uncontroversially the right one. That is not, however, a matter that can be determined in advance. Moreover, the discovery that there were several possible ways of carving up the territory between which it was hard to decide would itself constitute important philosophical progress.

A critic of Rossian intuitionism might now complain, rather more cautiously, that while Ross's list is by no means an arbitrary heap, the basic duties are still unconnected, and that this is a weakness in his theory. But why might one think it a weakness? One suggestion might be that the simpler a theory is, the better; and, all else being equal, the fewer independent axioms, postulates or underived principles to which it appeals, the better. Intuitionists need not deny this, but will point out that there are other desiderata for a theory, among which fitting the facts and explanatory adequacy rank highly. Ross's main complaint about consequentialist theories is that they oversimplify and thus fail to account convincingly for the nature of our moral thought. By this he means not only that they deliver counter-intuitive verdicts in particular cases, but that they give a distorted account of the reasons we would offer for the verdicts. Nor is it always the case that the theory with the fewest underived principles is the simplest; for simplicity at the level of principle may lead to complexity at a higher level.

The second suggestion might be that a theory which admits the existence of distinct and irreducible moral principles gains in systematic unity if those principles are generated by some unitary justificatory procedure, as is the case perhaps with Kantianism, or with rule-consequentialism. To this Ross might reply that he also offers a single test. The difference between his test and the Kantian one is that the latter is atomistic, generating each principle independently of the others, whereas his is holistic, testing each principle by seeing whether it can be derived from the others. But why should a holistic test be less systematic than an atomistic one? The real worry here, I suspect, may not be about the lack of systematic unity in Ross's theory, but about the perceived need for a justificatory grounding for each duty. But that is, of course, just to beg the question against the intuitionist who maintains that these basic duties stand in no need of grounding.

A third worry might be that duties which are distinct and irreducible may also be disparate, having nothing significant in common except that they are all duties. But of course they may have a great deal in common, and if they do then the theory would have a further unity. Ross in fact seems to suggest at various points that at least some of and perhaps all of our duties, both basic and derivative, do have something in common: they rest on relationships between persons, each different relationship generating a different duty. Positional duties, contractual duties and duties of special relationship are the model here. Of the seven basic duties which Ross has on his original list, three—fidelity, gratitude and reparation—seem to fit this description neatly. The others, however, raise problems. In order for me to have a duty of beneficence, non-maleficence or justice towards some particular person or group, it does not have to be the case that I previously stood in any particular relationship to them; it is enough that they are in need, or that they could be harmed, or that goods are unjustly distributed among them. Nor, in the case of duties of self-improvement, is it clear what it means to talk about my relationship with myself. These difficulties may or may not be soluble; my only purpose here was to illustrate how it might be that distinct duties may yet have some common structural element which gives them a unity.

My conclusion is that intuitionism, at least in Ross's version, is not systematically less unified than its major rivals. If there are objections to it, they lie elsewhere.

NOTES

1. W.D. Ross, *The Foundations of Ethics* (Oxford: Clarendon Press, 1939), p. 190; H. Sidgwick, *The Methods of Ethics,* 7th edn (London: Macmillan, 1967), p. 102.
2. W.D. Ross, *The Right and the Good* (Oxford: Clarendon Press, 1930).
3. That Ross admits any *basic* principles is denied by Jonathan Dancy, in 'An Ethic of *Prima Facie* Duties', in P. Singer (ed.), *A Companion to Ethics* (Oxford: Basil Blackwell, 1991), p. 219.
4. W.D. Ross, *The Right and Good* (Oxford: Clarendon Press, 1930): 27.
5. For a different account of why there is nothing wrong with lying in these cases, see J. Dancy, *Moral Reasons* (Oxford: Basil Blackwell, 1993), pp. 60–1.
6. W.D. Ross, *The Right and the Good* (Oxford: Clarendon Press, 1930): 58.

STUDY QUESTIONS

1. Is a simpler theory always a better theory?
2. Is moral theory supposed to justify our commonsense moral judgments?
3. What is the distinction between derived and underived duties?
4. In what sense might a moral theory "fit the facts"?

How Strong Is This Obligation?

Walter Sinnott-Armstrong

On Ross's theory, we have various morally relevant relations with others, thereby giving rise to prima facie duties. But which is strongest? The matter is undetermined. Yet, as Walter Sinnott-Armstrong, Professor of Philosophy at Duke University, argues, the strength of our obligations varies with the bad results of our failing to fulfill them. For example, a promise to meet someone for lunch is less compelling than a promise to drive someone to an airport in time for a flight. Consequentialism can easily explain this difference, whereas Ross's pluralism cannot.

The rule 'Keep your promises' (or, more accurately, 'Don't break your promises') is often presented as a challenge to consequentialism, because the ground of your moral obligation not to break a promise seems to lie in the past fact that you made the promise, which is not a consequence of the act. A different picture emerges, however, when we move beyond the question of whether you have any moral obligation at all to the related question of how strong that obligation is.

If I promise to meet you and some other mutual friends for a casual lunch, then my moral obligation to meet you is not as strong as when I promise to drive you to the airport to catch an important flight. Why not? The natural answer is that, if I break the lunch promise, not much bad will happen. You will still have a pleasant lunch with our other friends, and you and I can still have lunch some other time. I have some moral obligation to meet you, but not a very strong one. In contrast, if I break my driving promise, then my failure will cause much more harm, assuming that you will not find another way to get to the

airport in time for your flight. These harmful consequences to you seem to be what give strength to my moral obligation to keep this promise.

The relevant kind of strength is measured by how much is needed to override the obligation. I would need much stronger reasons to justify breaking my promise to drive you to the airport than to justify breaking my promise to meet you for lunch. The fact that my teenage child is sick at home might be enough to justify missing the lunch, even if the teenager would be safe at home for an hour without me. In contrast, I should leave my sick teenager at home while I drive you to the airport if I promise to drive you (again assuming that you will miss your flight if I do not drive you). The fact that some such reasons justify violating the lunch obligation but do not justify violating the driving obligation is what makes the driving obligation stronger.

The source of strength is not the solemn tone in which I made the promise. Even if I explicitly and solemnly promise to meet you for lunch, if nothing much bad will happen if I fail to show up, then I still

From Walter Sinnott-Armstrong, "How strong is this obligation? An argument for consequentialism from concomitant variation," *Analysis*, vol. 69, no. 3, 2009. Reprinted by permission of the journal.

do not have a very strong obligation to meet. In contrast, if I casually promise to drive you to your important flight, then, as long as I know that you are counting on me and will suffer significant harm if I fail, my obligation to drive you is strong. The strength of the moral obligation to keep a promise, thus, does not depend on solemnity while promising.

The source of strength is also not detrimental reliance, at least in one sense that is common in law. Suppose you spent a long time putting together the lunch with friends, and this effort had direct costs (phone bills) as well as opportunity costs (of not doing what you would have done if you had not put the lunch together). In contrast, you spent no time at all in response to my promise to drive you to the airport (other than getting ready for your trip, which you would have done anyway). Nonetheless, my driving promise still generates a stronger moral obligation to keep it if breaking it has worse consequences, as above. (I might have a secondary obligation to compensate you for direct and opportunity costs, but these can be seen as consequences of my joint act of making and then breaking a promise, and the strength of this compensatory obligation depends on consequences of that act.) Admittedly, by not seeking another ride to the airport, you did rely on my driving promise to your detriment, if I break it. Thus, regardless of effort and time lost, the driving promise creates more detrimental reliance of a separate kind: losses that occur only if I break the promise. However, this new kind of detrimental reliance clearly depends on the bad consequences of breaking the promise, so the strength of an obligation varies with the consequences if it varies with detrimental reliance of this new kind.

The strength of an obligation to keep a promise also might seem to be affected by pre-existing relationships, such as friendships, between promissor and promissee. However, if we are equally close friends in the lunch and driving examples, then the driving obligation is stronger than the lunch obligation. The lunch obligation might even be stronger if I am a stranger than if I am a close friend, since close friends are more likely to forgive missing lunch and strangers might jump to conclusions about unreliability that make these strangers reluctant to become friends.

Friendship between promissor and promissee can, thus, make the moral obligation to keep the promise either stronger or weaker, depending on how friendship affects the consequences of breaking the promise.

Of course, the strength of a moral obligation to keep a promise can also vary with factors other than consequences. In some circumstances, an obligation to keep a promise to a friend creates a stronger obligation because breaking it will risk destroying a beautiful friendship. Sometimes the fact that a person is needy or fragile or suspicious increases the strength of a moral obligation not to break a promise to that person. Sometimes the fact that a promise was made in an official or public setting can lead more people to rely on it and can thereby increase the strength of the moral obligation to keep it. Sometimes the solemn tone of a promise makes the promissee more likely to rely on it in a way that makes breaking it more harmful. The other factors in such cases affect the strength of the moral obligation indirectly by means of affecting the consequences of breaking the promise. Hence, when the strength of a promissory obligation varies with these other factors, it also still varies with the consequences of breaking (or keeping) the promise.

Now simply apply John Stuart Mill's method of concomitant variation. If lung cancer rates go up and down when smoking rates go up and down, but lung cancer rates do not change when atmospheric humidity goes up or down, then these data support the hypothesis that smoking rather than humidity causes lung cancer, at least if we can rule out the alternatives that cancer causes smoking, that some third factor causes both smoking and cancer, and that the correlation is accidental. Analogously, since the strength of a moral obligation goes up and down as the harms in violating it go up and down, this correlation supports the hypothesis that the harms of violating it are what make the moral obligation as strong as it is. This argument assumes that (i) the strength of the moral obligation does not explain the degree of harm (it cannot explain, for example, why it is so bad to miss this flight), (ii) no third factor explains the strength, the harm, and their correlation (what would that third factor be?), and (iii) the correlation is not accidental (because consequences are at least part of what matters in morality). Thus, Mill's method of concomitant variation supports a consequentialist account of the strength of moral obligations to keep promises.

This conclusion extends as well to the existence of such moral obligations. There are two main options: we can say either (i) consequences determine both the existence and the strength of the moral obligation not to break the promise or (ii) what determines the existence of the moral obligation is simply that the agent made the promise in the past, whereas what determines the strength of the moral obligation is, instead, the consequences of breaking (or keeping) the promise. Option (i) is clearly simpler and more coherent. Why would one factor determine whether any moral obligation at all exists, while a completely separate factor (in the future rather than the past) determines how strong that moral obligation is? That would be like postulating that the force of a golf club hitting a golf ball is what causes the ball to move but a different factor determines how fast or far the ball moves. Of course, dense air or a tree might explain why the ball did not go as fast or far as otherwise expected. However, in the absence of any such additional force, it would be implausible to postulate separate causes for the existence and degree of the ball's motion. Analogously, we should reject the moral theory that one factor determines the existence of a moral obligation and a separate factor determines its strength. There might be conflicting moral reasons of all sorts (analogous to the dense air and tree), but they do not explain the existence or the strength of the original moral obligation itself. Thus, the better alternative is the consequentialist theory that one factor—the harm caused by violating the obligation—explains both the existence and the strength of the moral obligation not to break promises.

Critics might object that I have a moral obligation not to break my promise even if breaking it will not cause any harm at all. Imagine that you will have a better time at lunch with your other friends without me rather than with me. Still, I seem to have *some* (weak) moral obligation to keep my promise to meet you and them for lunch. However, consequentialists

can explain that weak moral obligation by weak side-consequences. If I break my promise, you will lose trust in me, which will complicate or even prevent later mutual arrangements and will create a risk of undermining our friendship. The risk of such side effects also explains why I need to apologize if I break my promise, since apologies reduce some harmful side effects. Even in the case of a proverbial deathbed promise, breaking it will not harm the promissee (who is dead), but will create risks of harm to my character and of more harmful promise breaking in the future. In the very odd cases where even these effects are ruled out (such as when I will die right after breaking my promise to a dying person), then I doubt that I really do have any moral obligation to keep my promise. Why not? Because nobody at all is harmed if I break this promise in these circumstances. Besides, I am about to die, so give me a break! In any case, we should not trust our moral intuitions in such odd cases, because they did not evolve to fit such weird circumstances.

For these reasons, the best explanation of both the existence and the strength of the moral obligation to keep promises is consequentialist. Moreover, this argument applies as well to other apparently non-consequentialist obligations.

Consider the obligation not to lie. Some lies (such as telling a friend that you like his or her new haircut) are white lies, because they harm nobody, at least directly. As a result, they violate little or no moral obligation. Other lies (such as Bill Clinton's lie about Monica Lewinsky) have very bad consequences, so they violate a very strong moral obligation. The strength of the obligation not to lie varies with the harms caused by lying. Thus, again, Mill's method of concomitant variation suggests that the ground of the moral obligation not to lie is [the] harmful consequences of lying.

Next consider the moral obligation to obey the law. There is a strong moral obligation not to drive on the left side of a crowded two-way road in the USA, even if the violated law happened to be passed by a very slim majority, and even if I never benefited in the past from the law requiring right-side driving rather than left-side driving. In contrast, even if I have some moral obligation not to pass a stop sign without coming to a complete stop in the middle of the night on a clearly deserted road, that moral obligation is very weak, because violating it causes no harm or risk of harm to others, even if the law that I violated was passed unanimously and even if I benefited in the past from other people stopping at that stop sign (at least during the day). Thus, as with promises and lies, the strength of the moral obligation not to break the law varies with the harms caused by breaking that law, so Mill's method of concomitant variation again suggests that the ground of the moral obligation to obey the law is harmful consequences of breaking the law.

All of this suggests a new question and a new method in moral philosophy. Most moral philosophers and common folk have focused on the dichotomous questions of whether or not an act is right or wrong and whether or not someone has a moral obligation to act or not to act in a certain way. Those are important questions, but they are not the only ones worth asking. A moral theory also needs to answer the question of how strong a moral obligation is. When we ask this question, we find correlations between the strength of moral obligations and various factors that, together with Mill's method of concomitant variation, reveal the ground of those moral obligations. This brief note has tried to suggest both that this method is fruitful and also that, when we apply it, consequentialism comes out on top.

To respond, deontologists need to explain why some moral obligations are stronger than others without invoking the harmful consequences of violating those moral obligations. I would like to see them try.

STUDY QUESTIONS

1. Does the strength of an obligation to keep a promise depend on the consequences of breaking it?
2. Does the strength of an obligation not to murder depend on the consequences of murdering?
3. Do any explanations other than harmful consequences explain the varying strength of our obligations?
4. How would you determine the relative strength of your obligations to keep an appointment with your physician, your professor, or your brother?

Part IX

SOCIAL CONTRACT THEORY

Leviathan

Thomas Hobbes

Thomas Hobbes (1588–1679) was an English philosopher who played a crucial role in the history of social thought. He develops a moral and political theory that views justice and other ethical ideals as resting on an implied agreement among individuals. Hobbes argues that reason requires that we should relinquish the right to do whatever we please in exchange for all others limiting their rights in a similar manner, thus achieving security for all. Outside the social order, the good is whatever anyone desires and the evil whatever anyone hates, and each human life is, as Hobbes famously puts it, "solitary, poor, nasty, brutish, and short."

CHAPTER XIII

Of the Natural Condition of Mankind as Concerning Their Felicity, and Misery

Nature hath made men so equal, in the faculties of the body, and mind; as that though there be found one man sometimes manifestly stronger in body, or of quicker mind than another; yet when all is reckoned together, the difference between man, and man, is not so considerable, as that one man can thereupon claim to himself any benefit, to which another may not pretend, as well as he. For as to the strength of body, the weakest has strength enough to kill the strongest, either by secret machination, or by confederacy with others, that are in the same danger with himself.

And as to the faculties of the mind, setting aside the arts grounded upon words, and especially that skill of proceeding upon general, and infallible rules, called science; which very few have, and but in few things; as being not a native faculty, born with us; nor attained, as prudence, while we look after somewhat else, I find yet a greater equality amongst men, than that of strength. For prudence, is but experience; which equal time, equally bestows on all men, in those things they equally apply themselves unto. That which may perhaps make such equality incredible, is but a vain conceit of one's own wisdom, which almost all men think they have in a greater degree, than the vulgar; that is, than all men but themselves, and a few others, whom by fame, or for concurring with themselves, they approve. For such is the nature of men, that howsoever they may acknowledge many others to be more witty, or more eloquent, or more learned; yet they will hardly believe there be many so wise as themselves; for they see their own wit at hand, and other men's at a distance. But this proveth rather that men are in that point equal, than unequal. For there is not ordinarily a greater sign of the equal distribution of any thing, than that every man is contented with his share.

From this equality of ability, ariseth equality of hope in the attaining of our ends. And therefore if any

Reprinted from Thomas Hobbes, *Leviathan* (1660).

two men desire the same thing, which nevertheless they cannot both enjoy, they become enemies; and in the way to their end, which is principally their own conservation, and sometimes their delectation only, endeavour to destroy, or subdue one another. And from hence it comes to pass, that where an invader hath no more to fear, than another man's single power; if one plant, sow, build, or possess a convenient seat, others may probably be expected to come prepared with forces united, to dispossess, and deprive him, not only of the fruit of his labour, but also of his life, or liberty. And the invader again is in the like danger of another.

And from this diffidence of one another, there is no way for any man to secure himself, so reasonable, as anticipation; that is, by force, or wiles, to master the persons of all men he can, so long, till he see no other power great enough to endanger him: and this is no more than his own conservation requireth, and is generally allowed. Also because there be some, that taking pleasure in contemplating their own power in the acts of conquest, which they pursue farther than their security requires; if others, that otherwise would be glad to be at case within modest bounds, should not by invasion increase their power, they would not be able, long time, by standing only on their defence, to subsist. And by consequence, such augmentation of dominion over men being necessary to a man's conservation, it ought to be allowed him.

Again, men have no pleasure, but on the contrary a great deal of grief, in keeping company, where there is no power able to over-awe them all. For every man looketh that his companion should value him, at the same rate he sets upon himself: and upon all signs of contempt, or undervaluing, naturally endeavours, as far as he dares, (which amongst them that have no common power to keep them in quiet, is far enough to make them destroy each other), to extort a greater value from his contemners, by damage; and from others, by the example.

So that in the nature of man, we find three principal causes of quarrel. First, competition; secondly, diffidence; thirdly, glory.

The first, maketh man invade for gain; the second, for safety; and the third, for reputation. The first use

violence, to make themselves masters of other men's persons, wives, children, and cattle; the second, to defend them; the third, for trifles, as a word, a smile, a different opinion, and any other sign of undervalue, either direct in their persons, or by reflection in their kindred, their friends, their nation, their profession, or their name.

Hereby it is manifest, that during the time men live without a common power to keep them all in awe, they are in that condition which is called war; and such a WAR, as is of every man, against every man. For war, consisteth not in battle only, or the act of fighting; but in a tract of time, wherein the will to contend by battle is sufficiently known: and therefore the notion of *time,* is to be considered in the nature of war; as it is in the nature of weather. For as the nature of foul weather, lieth not in a shower or two of rain; but in an inclination thereto of many days together: so the nature of war, consisteth not in actual fighting; but in the known disposition thereto, during all the time there is no assurance to the contrary. All other time is PEACE.

Whatsoever therefore is consequent to a time of war, where every man is enemy to every man; the same is consequent to the time, wherein men live without other security, than what their own strength, and their own invention shall furnish them withal. In such condition, there is no place for industry; because the fruit thereof is uncertain: and consequently no culture of the earth; no navigation nor use of the commodities that may be imported by sea; no commodious building: no instruments of moving, and removing, such things as require much force; no knowledge of the face of the earth; no account of time; no arts; no letters; no society; and which is worst of all, continual fear, and danger of violent death; and the life of man, solitary, poor, nasty, brutish, and short.

It may seem strange to some man, that has not well weighed these things; that nature should thus dissociate, and render men apt to invade, and destroy one another: and he may therefore, not trusting to this inference, made from the passions, desire perhaps to have the same confirmed by experience. Let him therefore consider with himself, when taking a journey, he arms himself, and seeks to go well accompanied; when going to sleep, he locks his doors; when even in his house he locks his chests; and this when he knows there be laws, and public offices, armed, to revenge all injuries shall be done him; what opinion he has of his fellow-subjects, when he rides armed; of his fellow citizens, when he locks his doors; and of his children, and servants, when he locks his chests. Does he not there as much accuse mankind by his actions, as I do by my words? But neither of us accuse man's nature in it. The desires, and other passions of man, are in themselves no sin. No more are the actions, that proceed from those passions, till they know a law that forbids them: which till laws be made they cannot know: nor can any law be made, till they have agreed upon the person that shall make it.

It may peradventure be thought, there was never such a time, nor condition of war as this; and I believe it was never generally so, over all the world: but there are many places, where they live so now. For the savage people in many places of America, except the government of small families, the concord whereof dependeth on natural lust, have no government at all; and live at this day in that brutish manner, as I said before. Howsoever, it may be perceived what manner of life there would be, where there were no common power to fear, by the manner of life, which men that have formerly lived under a peaceful government, use to degenerate into, in a civil war.

But though there had never been any time, wherein particular men were in a condition of war one against another; yet in all times, kings, and persons of sovereign authority, because of their independency, are in continual jealousies, and in the state and posture of gladiators; having their weapons pointing, and their eyes fixed on one another; that is, their forts, garrisons, and guns upon the frontiers of their kingdoms; and continual spies upon their neighbours; which is a posture of war. But because they uphold thereby, the industry of their subjects; there does not follow from it, that misery, which accompanies the liberty of particular men.

To this war of every man, against every man, this also is consequent; that nothing can be unjust. The notions of right and wrong, justice and injustice have there no place, where there is no common power, there is no law: where no law, no injustice. Force, and fraud, are in war the two cardinal virtues. Justice, and injustice are none of the faculties neither of the body, nor mind. If they were, they might be in a man that were alone in the world, as well as his senses, and passions. They are qualities, that relate to men in society, not in solitude. It is consequent also to the same condition, that there be no propriety, no dominion, no *mine* and *thine* distinct; but only that to be every man's, that he can get: and for so long, as he can keep it. And thus much for the ill condition, which man by mere nature is actually placed in; though with a possibility to come out of it, consisting partly in the passions, partly in his reason.

The passions that incline men to peace, are fear of death; desire of such things as are necessary to commodious living; and a hope by their industry to obtain them. And reason suggesteth convenient articles of peace, upon which men may be drawn to agreement. These articles, are they, which otherwise are called the Laws of Nature: whereof I shall speak more particularly, in the two following chapters.

CHAPTER XIV

Of the First and Second Natural Laws, and of Contracts

The RIGHT OF NATURE, which writers commonly call *jus naturale,* is the liberty each man hath, to use his own power, as he will himself, for the preservation of his own nature; that is to say, of his own life; and consequently, of doing any thing, which in his own judgment, and reason, he shall conceive to be the aptest means thereunto.

By LIBERTY, is understood, according to the proper signification of the word, the absence of external impediments: which impediments, may oft take away part of a man's power to do what he would; but cannot hinder him from using the power left him, according as his judgment, and reason shall dictate to him.

A LAW OF NATURE, *lex naturalis,* is a precept or general rule, found out by reason, by which a man is forbidden to do that, which is destructive of his life, or taketh away the means of preserving the same; and to omit that, by which he thinketh it may be best preserved. For though they that speak of this subject, use to confound *jus,* and *lex, right* and *law:* yet they ought to be distinguished; because right, consisteth in liberty to do, or to forbear: whereas LAW, determineth, and bindeth to one of them: so that law, and right, differ as much, as obligation, and liberty; which in one and the same matter are inconsistent.

And because the condition of man, as hath been declared in the precedent chapter, is a condition of war of every one against every one; in which case every one is governed by his own reason; and there is nothing he can make use of, that may not be a help unto him, in preserving his life against his enemies; it followeth, that in such a condition, every man has a right to every thing; even to one another's body. And therefore, as long as this natural right of every man to every thing endureth, there can be no security to any man, how strong or wise soever he be, of living out the time, which nature ordinarily alloweth men to live. And consequently it is a precept, or general rule of reason, *that every man, ought to endeavour peace, as far as he has hope of obtaining it; and when he cannot obtain it, that he may seek, and use, all helps, and advantages of war.* The first branch of which rule, containeth the first, and fundamental law of nature; which is, to *seek peace, and follow it.* The second, the sum of the right of nature; which is, *by all means we can, to defend ourselves.*

From this fundamental law of nature, by which men are commanded to endeavour peace, is derived this second law; *that a man be willing, when others are so too, as far-forth, as for peace, and defence of himself, he shall think it necessary, to lay down this right to all things; and be contented with so much liberty against other men; as he would allow other men against himself.* For as long as every man holdeth this right, of doing any thing he liketh; so long are all men in the condition of war. But if other men will not lay down their right, as well as he; then there is no reason for any one, to divest himself of his; for that were to expose himself to prey, which no man is bound to, rather than to dispose himself to peace. This is that law of the Gospel; *whatsoever you require that others should do to you, that do ye to them. . . .*

To *lay down* a man's *right* to any thing, is to *divest* himself of the *liberty,* of hindering another of the benefit of his own right to the same. For he that renounceth, or passeth away his right, giveth not to any other man a right which he had not before; because there is nothing to which every man had not right by nature: but only standeth out of his way, that he may enjoy his own original right, without hindrance from him: not without hindrance from another. So that the effect which redoundeth to one man, by another man's defect of right, is but so much diminution of impediments to the use of his own right original. Right is laid aside, either by simply renouncing it; or by transferring it to another. By *simply* RENOUNCING; when he cares not to whom the benefit thereof redoundeth. By TRANSFERRING; when he intendeth the benefit thereof to some certain person, or persons. And when a man hath in either manner abandoned, or granted away his right; then he is said to be OBLIGED, or BOUND, not to hinder those, to whom such right is granted, or abandoned, from the benefit of it; and that he *ought,* and it is his DUTY, not to make void that voluntary act of his own: and that such hindrance is INJUSTICE, and INJURY, as being *sine jure;* the right being before renounced, or transferred. So that *injury,* or *injustice,* in the controversies of the world, is somewhat like to that, which in the disputations of scholars is called absurdity. For as it is there called an *absurdity,* to contradict what one maintained in the beginning: so in the world, it is called injustice, and injury, voluntarily to undo that, which from the beginning he had voluntarily done. The way by which a man either simply renounceth, or transferreth his right, is a declaration, or signification, by some voluntary and sufficient sign, or signs, that he doth so renounce, or transfer; or hath so renounced, or transferred the same, to him that accepteth it. And these signs are either words only, or actions only; or, as it happeneth most often, both words, and actions. And the same are the BONDS, by which men are bound, and obliged; bonds, that have their strength, not from their own nature, for nothing is more easily broken than a man's word, but from fear of some evil consequences upon the rupture.

Whensoever, a man transferreth his right, or renounceth it; it is either in consideration of some right reciprocally transferred to himself; or for some other good he hopeth for thereby. For it is a voluntary act: and of the voluntary acts of every man, the object is some *good to himself.* And therefore there be some rights, which no man can be understood by any words, or other signs, to have abandoned, or transferred. As first a man cannot lay down the right of resisting them, that assault him by force, to take away his life; because he cannot be understood to aim thereby, at any good to himself. The same may be said of wounds, and chains, and imprisonment; both because there is no benefit consequent to such patience; as there is to the patience of suffering another to be wounded, or imprisoned; as also because a man cannot tell, when he seeth men proceed against him by violence, whether they intend his death or not. And lastly the motive, and end for which this renouncing, and transferring of right is introduced, is nothing else but the security of a man's person, in his life, and in the means of so preserving life, as not to be weary of it. And therefore if a man by words, or other signs, seem to despoil himself of the end, for which those signs were intended; he is not to be understood as if he meant it, or that it was his will; but that he was ignorant of how such words and actions were to be interpreted.

The mutual transferring of right, is that which men call CONTRACT. . . .

CHAPTER XV

Of Other Laws of Nature

From that law of nature, by which we are obliged to transfer to another, such rights, as being retained, hinder the peace of mankind, there followeth a third; which is this, *that men perform their covenants made:* without which, covenants are in vain, and but empty words; and the right of all men to all things remaining, we are still in the condition of war.

And in this law of nature, consisteth the fountain and original of JUSTICE. For where no covenant hath preceded, there hath no right been transferred, and every man has right to every thing; and consequently, no action can be unjust. But when a covenant is made, then to break it is *unjust:* and the definition of INJUSTICE, is no other than *the not performance of covenant.* And whatsoever is not unjust, is *just.*

But because covenants of mutual trust, where there is a fear of not performance on either part, as hath been said in the former chapter, are invalid; though the original of justice be the making of covenants; yet injustice actually there can be none, till the cause of such fear be taken away; which while men are in the natural condition of war, cannot be done. Therefore before the names of just, and unjust can have place, there must be some coercive power, to compel men equally to the performance of their covenants, by the terror of some punishment, greater than the benefit they expect by the breach of their covenant; and to make good that propriety, which by mutual contract men acquire, in recompense of the universal right they abandon: and such power there is none before the erection of a commonwealth. And this is also to be gathered out of the ordinary definition of justice in the Schools: for they say, that *justice is the constant will of giving to every man his own.* And therefore where there is no *own,* that is no propriety, there is no injustice; and where there is no coercive power erected, that is, where there is no commonwealth, there is no propriety; all men having right to all things: therefore where there is no commonwealth, there nothing is unjust. So that the nature of justice, consisteth in keeping of valid covenants: but the validity of covenants begins not but with the constitution of a civil power, sufficient to compel men to keep them: and then it is also that propriety begins.

The fool hath said in his heart, there is no such thing as justice; and sometimes also with his tongue; seriously alleging, that every man's conservation, and contentment, being committed to his own care, there could be no reason, why every man might not do what he thought conduced thereunto: and therefore also to make, or not make; keep, or not keep covenants, was not against reason, when it conduced to one's benefit. He does not therein deny, that there be covenants; and that they are sometimes broken, sometimes kept; and that such breach of them may be called injustice, and the observance of them justice: but he questioneth, whether injustice, taking away the fear of God, (for the same fool hath said in his heart there is no God,) may not sometimes stand with that reason, which dictateth to every man his own good; and particularly then, when it conduceth to such a benefit, as shall put a man in a condition, to neglect not only the dispraise, and revilings, but also the power of other men. The kingdom of God is gotten by violence; but what if it could be gotten by unjust violence? were it against reason so to get it, when it is impossible to receive hurt by it? and if it be not against reason, it is not against justice; or else justice is not to be approved for good. From such reasoning as this, successful wickedness hath obtained the name of virtue: and some that in all other things have disallowed the violation of faith; yet have allowed it, when it is for the getting of a kingdom. . . . This specious reasoning is nevertheless false.

For the question is not of promises mutual, where there is no security of performance on either side; as when there is no civil power erected over the parties promising; for such promises are no covenants: but either where one of the parties has performed already; or where there is a power to make him perform; there is the question whether it be against reason, that is, against the benefit of the other to perform, or not. And I say it is not against reason. For the manifestation whereof, we are to consider; first, that when a man doth a thing, which notwithstanding any thing can be foreseen, and reckoned on, tendeth to his own destruction, howsoever some accident which he could not expect, arriving may turn it to his benefit; yet such events do not make it reasonably or wisely done. Secondly, that in a condition of war, wherein every man to every man, for want of a common power to keep them all in awe, is an enemy, there is no man can hope by his own strength, or wit, to defend himself from destruction, without the help of confederates; where every one expects the same defence by the confederation, that any one else does: and therefore he which declares he thinks it reason to deceive those that help him, can in reason expect no other means of safety, than what can be had from his own single power. He therefore that breaketh his covenant, and consequently declareth that he thinks he may with reason do so, cannot be received into any society, that unite themselves for peace and defence, but by the error of them that receive him; nor when he is received, be retained in it, without seeing the danger of their error; which errors a man cannot reasonably reckon upon as the means of his security: and therefore if he be left, or cast out of society, he perisheth; and if he live in society, it is by the errors of other men, which he could not foresee, nor reckon upon; and consequently against the reason of his preservation; and so, as all men that contribute not to his destruction, forbear him only out of ignorance of what is good for themselves.

STUDY QUESTIONS

1. Without government to enforce laws, would life be, as Hobbes says, "nasty, brutish, and short"?
2. What does Hobbes mean by "a law of nature"?
3. According to Hobbes, what does the "fool" believe?
4. Does Hobbes provide a satisfying response to the fool?

A Theory of Justice

John Rawls

John Rawls (1921–2002) was Professor of Philosophy at Harvard University. He proposes that justice is the social arrangement that would be chosen by the members of society if they did not know either their individual places in that society or their own personal characteristics, such as race, gender, or class. Rawls claims that in "the original position" in which all are behind "a veil of ignorance," the parties would choose two fundamental principles: first, equality of rights and liberties for all; and second, the arrangement of social and economic inequalities so that both are (a) to the greatest benefit of the least advantaged, "the difference principle," and (b) attached to positions and offices open to all, a condition that has not received the extensive attention given to the difference principle.

THE MAIN IDEA OF THE THEORY OF JUSTICE

. . . [T]he principles of justice . . . are the principles that free and rational persons concerned to further their own interests would accept in an initial position of equality. . . .

[T]he original position of equality corresponds to the state of nature in the traditional theory of the social contract. This original position is not, of course, thought of as an actual historical state of affairs, much less as a primitive condition of culture. It is understood as a purely hypothetical situation. . . . Among the essential features of this situation is that no one knows his place in society, his class position or social status, nor does any one know his fortune in the distribution of natural assets and abilities, his intelligence, strength, and the like. I shall even assume that the parties do not know their conceptions of the good or their special psychological propensities. The principles of justice are chosen behind a veil of ignorance. This ensures that no one is advantaged or disadvantaged in the choice of principles by the outcome of natural chance or the contingency of social circumstances. Since all are similarly situated and no one is able to design principles to favor his particular condition, the principles of justice are the result of a fair agreement or bargain. For given the circumstances of the original position, the symmetry of everyone's relations to each other, this initial situation is fair between individuals as moral persons, that is, as rational beings with their own ends and capable, I shall assume, of a sense of justice. The original position is, one might say, the appropriate initial status quo, and thus the fundamental agreements reached in it are fair. This explains the propriety of the name

Reprinted by permission of the publisher from *A Theory of Justice* by John Rawls, pp. 10–11, 13–14, 16–17, 52–54, 119–121, Cambridge, MA: The Belknap Press of Harvard University Press. Copyright © 1971, 1999 by the President and Fellows of Harvard College.

"justice as fairness": it conveys the idea that the principles of justice are agreed to in an initial situation that is fair. . . .

I shall maintain . . . that the persons in the initial situation would choose two . . . principles: the first requires equality in the assignment of basic rights and duties, while the second holds that social and economic inequalities, for example inequalities of wealth and authority, are just only if they result in compensating benefits for everyone, and in particular for the least advantaged members of society. These principles rule out justifying institutions on the grounds that the hardships of some are offset by a greater good in the aggregate. It may be expedient but it is not just that some should have less in order that others may prosper. But there is no injustice in the greater benefits earned by a few provided that the situation of persons not so fortunate is thereby improved. The intuitive idea is that since everyone's well-being depends upon a scheme of cooperation without which no one could have a satisfactory life, the division of advantages should be such as to draw forth the willing cooperation of everyone taking part in it, including those less well situated. The two principles mentioned seem to be a fair basis on which those better endowed, or more fortunate in their social position, neither of which we can be said to deserve, could expect the willing cooperation of others when some workable scheme is a necessary condition of the welfare of all. Once we decide to look for a conception of justice that prevents the use of the accidents of natural endowment and the contingencies of social circumstance as counters in a quest of political and economic advantage, we are led to these principles. They express the result of leaving aside those aspects of the social world that seem arbitrary from a moral point of view. . . .

THE ORIGINAL POSITION AND JUSTIFICATION

. . . One should not be misled . . . by the somewhat unusual conditions which characterize the original position. The idea here is simply to make vivid to ourselves the restrictions that it seems reasonable to impose on arguments for principles of justice, and therefore on these principles themselves. Thus it seems reasonable and generally acceptable that no one should be advantaged or disadvantaged by natural fortune or social circumstances in the choice of principles. It also seems widely agreed that it should be impossible to tailor principles to the circumstances of one's own case. We should insure further that particular inclinations and aspirations, and persons' conceptions of their good, do not affect the principles adopted. The aim is to rule out those principles that it would be rational to propose for acceptance, however little the chance of success, only if one knew certain things that are irrelevant from the standpoint of justice. For example, if a man knew that he was wealthy, he might find it rational to advance the principle that various taxes for welfare measures be counted unjust; if he knew that he was poor, he would most likely propose the contrary principle. To represent the desired restrictions one imagines a situation in which everyone is deprived of this sort of information. One excludes the knowledge of those contingencies which sets men at odds and allows them to be guided by their prejudices. In this manner the veil of ignorance is arrived at in a natural way. This concept should cause no difficulty if we keep in mind the constraints on arguments that it is meant to express. At any time we can enter the original position, so to speak, simply by following a certain procedure, namely, by arguing for principles of justice in accordance with these restrictions.

It seems reasonable to suppose that the parties in the original position are equal. That is, all have the same rights in the procedure for choosing principles; each can make proposals, submit reasons for their acceptance, and so on. Obviously the purpose of these conditions is to represent equality between human beings as moral persons, as creatures having a conception of their good and capable of a sense of justice. The basis of equality is taken to be similarity in these two respects. Systems of ends are not ranked in value; and each man is presumed to have the requisite ability to understand and to act upon whatever principles are adopted. Together with the veil of ignorance, these conditions define the principles of justice as those which rational persons concerned to advance their interests would consent to as equals when none are known to be advantaged or disadvantaged by social and natural contingencies. . . .

TWO PRINCIPLES OF JUSTICE

I shall now state in a provisional form the two principles of justice that I believe would be chosen in the original position. . . .

The first statement of the two principles reads as follows.

First: each person is to have an equal right to the most extensive scheme of equal basic liberties compatible with a similar scheme of liberties for others.

Second: social and economic inequalities are to be arranged so that they are both (a) reasonably expected to be to everyone's advantage, and (b) attached to positions and offices open to all. . . .

These principles primarily apply . . . to the basic structure of society and govern the assignment of rights and duties and regulate the distribution of social and economic advantages. . . . [I]t is essential to observe that the basic liberties are given by a list of such liberties. Important among these are political liberty (the right to vote and to hold public office) and freedom of speech and assembly; liberty of conscience and freedom of thought; freedom of the person, which includes freedom from psychological oppression and physical assault and dismemberment (integrity of the person); the right to hold personal property and freedom from arbitrary arrest and seizure as defined by the concept of the rule of law. These liberties are to be equal by the first principle.

The second principle applies . . . to the distribution of income and wealth and to the design of organizations that make use of differences in authority and responsibility. While the distributions of wealth and income need not be equal, it must be to everyone's advantage, and at the same time, positions of authority and responsibility must be accessible to all. One applies the second principle by holding positions open, and then, subject to this constraint, arranges social and economic inequalities so that everyone benefits.

These principles are to be arranged in a serial order with the first principle prior to the second. This ordering means that infringements of the basic equal liberties protected by the first principle cannot be justified, or compensated for, by greater social and economic advantages. . . .

[I]n regard to the second principle, the distribution of wealth and income, and positions of authority and responsibility, are to be consistent with both the basic liberties and equality of opportunity. . . .

[T]hese principles are a special case of a more general conception of justice that can be expressed as follows.

> All social values—liberty and opportunity, income and wealth, and the social bases of self-respect—are to be distributed equally unless an unequal distribution of any, or all, of these values is to everyone's advantage.

Injustice, then, is simply inequalities that are not to the benefit of all. . . .

THE VEIL OF IGNORANCE

. . . The notion of the veil of ignorance raises several difficulties. Some may object that the exclusion of nearly all particular information makes it difficult to grasp what is meant by the original position. Thus it may be helpful to observe that one or more persons can at any time enter this position, or perhaps better, simulate the deliberations of this hypothetical situation, simply by reasoning in accordance with the appropriate restrictions. . . .

It may be protested that the condition of the veil of ignorance is irrational. Surely, some may object, principles should be chosen in the light of all the knowledge available. There are various replies to this contention. . . . To begin with, it is clear that since the differences among the parties are unknown to them, and everyone is equally rational and similarly situated, each is convinced by the same arguments. Therefore, we can view the agreement in the original position from the standpoint of one person selected at random. If anyone after due reflection prefers a conception of justice to another, then they all do, and a unanimous agreement can be reached. We can, to make the circumstances more vivid, imagine that the parties are required to communicate with each other through a referee as intermediary, and that he is to announce which alternatives have been suggested and the reasons offered in their support. He forbids the attempt to form coalitions, and he informs the parties when they have come to an understanding. But such a referee is actually superfluous, assuming that the deliberations of the parties must be similar.

Thus there follows the very important consequence that the parties have no basis for bargaining in the usual sense. No one knows his situation in society nor his natural assets, and therefore no one is in a position to tailor principles to his advantage. We might imagine that one of the contractees threatens to hold out unless the others agree to principles favorable to him. But how does he know which principles are especially in his interests? The same holds

for the formation of coalitions: if a group were to decide to band together to the disadvantage of the others, they would not know how to favor themselves in the choice of principles. Even if they could get everyone to agree to their proposal, they would have no assurance that it was to their advantage, since they cannot identify themselves either by name or description. . . .

The restrictions on particular information in the original position are, then, of fundamental importance. Without them we would not be able to work out any definite theory of justice at all. We would have to be content with a vague formula stating that justice is what would be agreed to without being able to say much, if anything, about the substance of the agreement itself. . . . The veil of ignorance makes possible a unanimous choice of a particular conception of justice. Without these limitations on knowledge the bargaining problem of the original position would be hopelessly complicated.

STUDY QUESTIONS

1. What does Rawls mean by "the original position"?
2. According to Rawls, what two principles would be chosen in the original position?
3. Are Rawls's two principles shown to be just by being chosen in the original position, or are they chosen in the original position because they are just?
4. If you were in the original position, what principles would you choose?

Why Contractarianism?

David Gauthier

David Gauthier is Emeritus Professor of Philosophy at the University of Pittsburgh. He argues that, due to the conflict between what morality presupposes and our present worldview, morality faces a crisis. Yet we can salvage morality by incorporating it into a mode of justification we already accept: namely, the maximization of our own considered preferences. In this view, morality is to be identified with the constraints rational persons would agree upon when choosing the terms of their interactions. This perspective, now known as "contractarianism," thus sees morality as cooperation among people for their mutual benefit, and ethics can thereby be justified without any need to appeal to independent moral values.

I

As the will to truth thus gains self-consciousness— there can be no doubt of that—morality will gradually perish *now: this is the great spectacle in a hundred acts reserved for the next two centuries in Europe—the most terrible, most questionable, and perhaps also the most hopeful of all spectacles.*
—*Nietzsche*[1]

Morality faces a foundational crisis. Contractarianism offers the only plausible resolution of this crisis. These two propositions state my theme. What follows is elaboration.

Nietzsche may have been the first, but he has not been alone, in recognizing the crisis to which I refer. Consider these recent statements. "The hypothesis which I wish to advance is that in the actual world which we inhabit the language of morality is in . . . [a] state of grave disorder . . . we have—very largely, if not entirely—lost our comprehension,

both theoretical and practical, of morality" (Alasdair MacIntyre).[2] "The resources of most modern moral philosophy are not well adjusted to the modern world" (Bernard Williams).[3] "There are no objective values. . . . [But] the main tradition of European moral philosophy includes the contrary claim" (J. L. Mackie).[4] "Moral hypotheses do not help explain why people observe what they observe. So ethics is problematic and nihilism must be taken seriously. . . . An extreme version of nihilism holds that morality is simply an illusion. . . . In this version, we should abandon morality, just as an atheist abandons religion after he has decided that religious facts cannot help explain observations" (Gilbert Harman).[5]

I choose these statements to point to features of the crisis that morality faces. They suggest that moral language fits a world view that we have abandoned—a view of the world as purposively ordered. Without this view, we no longer truly understand the moral claims we continue to make.

Reprinted from David Gauthier, "Why Contractarianism?" from *Contractarianism and Rational Choice*, ed. P. Vallentyne, Cambridge University Press, 1991. Reprinted by permission of the publisher.

They suggest that there is a lack of fit between what morality presupposes—objective values that help explain our behavior, and the psychological states—desires and beliefs—that, given our present world view, actually provide the best explanation. This lack of fit threatens to undermine the very idea of a morality as more than an anthropological curiosity. But how could this be? How could morality *perish*?

II

To proceed, I must offer a minimal characterization of the morality that faces a foundational crisis. And this is the morality of justified constraint. From the standpoint of the agent, moral considerations present themselves as constraining his choices and actions, in ways independent of his desires, aims, and interests. Later, I shall add to this characterization, but for the moment it will suffice. For it reveals clearly what is in question—the ground of constraint. This ground seems absent from our present world view. And so we ask, what reason can a person have for recognizing and accepting a constraint that is independent of his desires and interests? He may agree that such a constraint would be *morally* justified; he would have a reason for accepting it *if* he had a reason for accepting morality. But what justifies paying attention to morality, rather than dismissing it as an appendage of outworn beliefs? We ask, and seem to find no answer. . . .

Fortunately, I do not have to defend *normative* foundationalism. One problem with accepting moral justification as part of our ongoing practice is that, as I have suggested, we no longer accept the world view on which it depends. But perhaps a more immediately pressing problem is that we have, ready to hand, an alternative mode for justifying our choices and actions. In its more austere and, in my view, more defensible form, this is to show that choices and actions maximize the agent's expected utility, where utility is a measure of considered preference. In its less austere version, this is to show that choices and actions satisfy, not a subjectively defined requirement such as utility, but meet the agent's objective interests. Since I do not believe that we have

objective interests, I shall ignore this latter. But it will not matter. For the idea is clear; we have a mode of justification that does not require the introduction of moral considerations.[6]

Let me call this alternative nonmoral mode of justification, neutrally, deliberative justification. Now moral and deliberative justification are directed at the same objects—our choices and actions. What if they conflict? And what do we say to the person who offers a deliberative justification of his choices and actions and refuses to offer any other? We can say, of course, that his behavior lacks *moral* justification, but this seems to lack any hold, unless he chooses to enter the moral framework. And such entry, he may insist, lacks any deliberative justification, at least for him.

If morality perishes, the justificatory enterprise, in relation to choice and action, does not perish with it. Rather, one mode of justification perishes, a mode that, it may seem, now hangs unsupported. But not only unsupported, for it is difficult to deny that deliberative justification is more clearly basic, that it cannot be avoided insofar as we are rational agents, so that if moral justification conflicts with it, morality seems not only unsupported but opposed by what is rationally more fundamental.

Deliberative justification relates to our deep sense of self. What distinguishes human beings from other animals, and provides the basis for rationality, is the capacity for semantic representation. You can, as your dog on the whole cannot, represent a state of affairs to yourself, and consider in particular whether or not it is the case, and whether or not you would want it to be the case. You can represent to yourself the contents of your beliefs, and your desires or preferences. But in representing them, you bring them into relation with one another. You represent to yourself that the Blue Jays will win the World Series, and that a National League team will win the World Series, and that the Blue Jays are not a National League team. And in recognizing a conflict among those beliefs, you find rationality thrust upon you. Note that the first two beliefs could be replaced by preferences, with the same effect.

Since in representing our preferences we become aware of conflict among them, the step from representation to choice becomes complicated. We must, somehow, bring our conflicting desires and preferences into some sort of coherence. And there is only one plausible candidate for a principle of coherence—a maximizing principle. We order our preferences, in relation to decision and action, so that we may choose in a way that maximizes our expectation of preference fulfillment. And in so doing, we show ourselves to be rational agents, engaged in deliberation and deliberative justification. There is simply nothing else for practical rationality to be.

The foundational crisis of morality thus cannot be avoided by pointing to the existence of a practice of justification within the moral framework, and denying that any extramoral foundation is relevant. For an extramoral mode of justification is already present, existing not side by side with moral justification, but in a manner tied to the way in which we unify our beliefs and preferences and so acquire our deep sense of self. We need not suppose that this deliberative justification is itself to be understood foundationally. All that we need suppose is that moral justification does not plausibly survive conflict with it.

III

In explaining why we may not dismiss the idea of a foundational crisis in morality as resulting from a misplaced appeal to a philosophically discredited or suspect idea of foundationalism, I have begun to expose the character and dimensions of the crisis. I have claimed that morality faces an alternative, conflicting, deeper mode of justification, related to our deep sense of self, that applies to the entire realm of choice and action, and that evaluates each *action* in terms of the reflectively held concerns of its *agent*. The relevance of the agent's concerns to practical justification does not seem to me in doubt. The relevance of anything else, except insofar as it bears on the agent's concerns, does seem to me very much in doubt. If the agent's reflectively endorsed concerns, his preferences, desires, and aims, are, with his considered beliefs, constitutive of his self-conception, then I can see no remotely plausible way of arguing from their relevance to that of anything else that is not similarly related to his sense of self. And, indeed,

I can see no way of introducing anything as relevant to practical justification except through the agent's self-conception. My assertion of this practical individualism is not a conclusive argument, but the burden of proof is surely on those who would maintain a contrary position. Let them provide the arguments—if they can.

Deliberative justification does not refute morality. Indeed, it does not offer morality the courtesy of a refutation. It ignores morality, and seemingly replaces it. It preempts the arena of justification, apparently leaving morality no room to gain purchase. . . .

There would seem to be three ways for morality to escape. . . . One would be to find, for moral facts or moral properties, an explanatory role that would entrench them prior to any consideration of justification.[7] One could then argue that any mode of justification that ignored moral considerations would be ontologically defective. I mention this possibility only to put it to one side. No doubt there are persons who accept moral constraints on their choices and actions, and it would not be possible to explain those choices and actions were we to ignore this. But our explanation of their behavior need not commit us to their view. . . . [T]o characterize what a moral agent is doing as, say, fulfilling a duty does not commit us to supposing that there are any duties, though it does commit us to supposing that he believes that there are duties. . . . But to establish an explanatory role for morality, one must first demonstrate its justificatory credentials. One may not assume that it has a prior explanatory role.

The second way would be to reinterpret the idea of justification, showing that, more fully understood, deliberative justification is incomplete, and must be supplemented in a way that makes room for morality. There is a long tradition in moral philosophy, deriving primarily from Kant, that is committed to this enterprise. This is not the occasion to embark on a critique of what, in the hope again of achieving a neutral characterization, I shall call universalistic justification. But critique may be out of place. The success of deliberative justification may suffice. For theoretical claims about its incompleteness seem to fail before the simple practical recognition that it works. Of course, on the face of it, deliberative justification does not work to provide a place for morality. But to suppose that it must, if it is to be fully adequate or complete as a mode of justification, would be to assume what is in question, whether moral justification is defensible.

If, independent of one's actual desires, and aims, there were objective values, and if, independent of one's actual purposes, one were part of an objectively purposive order, then we might have reason to insist on the inadequacy of the deliberative framework. An objectively purposive order would introduce considerations relevant to practical justification that did not depend on the agent's self-conception. But the supplanting of teleology in our physical and biological explanations closes this possibility. . . .

I turn then to the third way of resolving morality's foundational crisis. The first step is to embrace deliberative justification, and recognize that morality's place must be found within, and not outside, its framework. Now this will immediately raise two problems. First of all, it will seem that the attempt to establish any constraint on choice and action, within the framework of a deliberation that aims at the maximal fulfillment of the agent's considered preferences, must prove impossible. But even if this be doubted, it will seem that the attempt to establish a constraint *independent of the agent's preferences,* within such a framework, verges on lunacy. Nevertheless, this is precisely the task accepted by my third way. . . .

I shall not rehearse at length an argument. . . . But let me sketch briefly those features of deliberative rationality that enable it to constrain maximizing choice. The key idea is that in many situations, if each person chooses what, given the choices of the others, would maximize her expected utility, then the outcome will be mutually disadvantageous in comparison with some alternative—everyone could do better.[8] Equilibrium, which obtains when each person's action is a best response to the others' actions, is incompatible with (Pareto-) optimality, which obtains when no one could do better without someone else doing worse. Given the ubiquity of such situations, each person can see the benefit, to herself, of participating with her fellows in practices requiring each to refrain from the direct endeavor to maximize her own utility,

when such mutual restraint is mutually advantageous. No one, of course, can have reason to accept any unilateral constraint on her maximizing behavior; each benefits from, and only from, the constraint accepted by her fellows. But if one benefits more from a constraint on others than one loses by being constrained oneself, one may have reason to accept a practice requiring everyone, including oneself, to exhibit such a constraint. We may represent such a practice as capable of gaining unanimous agreement among rational persons who were choosing the terms on which they would interact with each other. And this agreement is the basis of morality.

Consider a simple example of a moral practice that would command rational agreement. Suppose each of us were to assist her fellows only when either she could expect to benefit herself from giving assistance, or she took a direct interest in their well-being. Then, in many situations, persons would not give assistance to others, even though the benefit to the recipient would greatly exceed the cost to the giver, because there would be no provision for the giver to share in the benefit. Everyone would then expect to do better were each to give assistance to her fellows, regardless of her own benefit or interest, whenever the cost of assisting was low and the benefit of receiving assistance considerable. Each would thereby accept a constraint on the direct pursuit of her own concerns, not unilaterally, but given a like acceptance by others. Reflection leads us to recognize that those who belong to groups whose members adhere to such a practice of mutual assistance enjoy benefits in interaction that are denied to others. We may then represent such a practice as rationally acceptable to everyone.

This rationale for agreed constraint makes no reference to the content of anyone's preferences. The argument depends simply on the *structure* of interaction, on the way in which each person's endeavor to fulfill her own preferences affects the fulfillment of everyone else. Thus, each person's reason to accept a mutually constraining practice is independent of her particular desires, aims and interests, although not, of course, of the fact that she has such concerns. The idea of a purely rational agent, moved to act by reason alone, is not, I think, an intelligible one. Morality is not to be understood as a constraint arising from reason alone on the fulfillment of nonrational preferences. Rather, a rational agent is one who acts to achieve the maximal fulfillment of her preferences, and morality is a constraint on the manner in which she acts, arising from the effects of interaction with other agents.

Hobbes's Foole now makes his familiar entry onto the scene, to insist that however rational it may be for a person to agree with her fellows to practices that hold out the promise of mutual advantage, yet it is rational to follow such practices only when so doing directly conduces to her maximal preference fulfillment.[9] But then such practices impose no real constraint. The effect of agreeing to or accepting them can only be to change the expected payoffs of her possible choices, making it rational for her to choose what in the absence of the practice would not be utility maximizing. The practices would offer only true prudence, not true morality.

The Foole is guilty of a twofold error. First, he fails to understand that real acceptance of such moral practices as assisting one's fellows, or keeping one's promises, or telling the truth is possible only among those who are disposed to comply with them. If my disposition to comply extends only so far as my interests or concerns at the time of performance, then you will be the real fool if you interact with me in ways that demand a more rigorous compliance. If, for example, it is rational to keep promises only when so doing is directly utility maximizing, then among persons whose rationality is common knowledge, only promises that require such limited compliance will be made. And opportunities for mutual advantage will be thereby forgone.

Consider this example of the way in which promises facilitate mutual benefit. Jones and Smith have adjacent farms. Although neighbors, and not hostile, they are also not friends, so that neither gets satisfaction from assisting the other. Nevertheless, they recognize that, if they harvest their crops together, each does better than if each harvests alone. Next week, Jone's crop will be ready for harvesting; a fortnight hence, Smith's crop will be ready. The harvest in, Jones is retiring, selling his farm, and moving to Florida, where he is unlikely to encounter

Smith or other members of their community. Jones would like to promise Smith that, if Smith helps him harvest next week, he will help Smith harvest in a fortnight. But Jones and Smith both know that in a fortnight, helping Smith would be a pure cost to Jones. Even if Smith helps him, he has nothing to gain by returning the assistance, since neither care for Smith nor, in the circumstances, concern for his own reputation, moves him. Hence, if Jones and Smith know that Jones acts straightforwardly to maximize the fulfillment of his preferences, they know that he will not help Smith. Smith, therefore, will not help Jones even if Jones pretends to promise assistance in return. Nevertheless, Jones would do better could he make and keep such a promise—and so would Smith.

The Foole's second error, following on his first, should be clear; he fails to recognize that in plausible circumstances, persons who are genuinely disposed to a more rigorous compliance with moral practices that would follow from their interests at the time of performance can expect to do better than those who are not so disposed. For the former, constrained maximizers as I call them, will be welcome partners in mutually advantageous cooperation, in which each relies on the voluntary adherence of the others, from which the latter, straightforward maximizers, will be excluded. Constrained maximizers may thus expect more favorable opportunities than their fellows. Although in assisting their fellows, keeping their promises, and complying with other moral practices, they forgo preference fulfillment that they might obtain, yet they do better overall than those who always maximize expected utility, because of their superior opportunities.

In identifying morality with those constraints that would obtain agreement among rational persons who were choosing their terms of interaction. I am engaged in rational reconstruction. I do not suppose that we have actually agreed to existent moral practices and principles. Nor do I suppose that all existent moral practices would secure our agreement, were the question to be raised. Not all existent moral practices need be justifiable—need be ones with which we ought willingly to comply. Indeed, I do not even suppose that the practices with which we ought willingly to comply need be those that would secure our present agreement. I suppose that justifiable moral practices are those that would secure our agreement ex ante, in an appropriate premoral situation. They are those to which we should have agreed as constituting the terms of our future interaction, had we been, per impossible, in a position to decide those terms. Hypothetical agreement thus provides a test of the justifiability of our existent moral practices.

IV

Many questions could be raised about this account, but here I want to consider only one. I have claimed that moral practices are rational, even though they constrain each person's attempt to maximize her own utility, insofar as they would be the objects of unanimous ex ante agreement. But to refute the Foole, I must defend not only the rationality of agreement, but also that of compliance, and the defense of compliance threatens to preempt the case for agreement, so that my title should be "Why Constraint?" and not "Why Contractarianism?" It is rational to dispose oneself to accept certain constraints on direct maximization in choosing and acting, if and only if so disposing oneself maximizes one's expected utility. What then is the relevance of agreement, and especially of hypothetical agreement? Why should it be rational to dispose oneself to accept only those constraints that would be the object of mutual agreement in an appropriate premoral situation, rather than those constraints that are found in our existent moral practices? Surely it is acceptance of the latter that makes a person welcome in interaction with his fellows. For compliance with existing morality will be what they expect, and take into account in choosing partners with whom to cooperate.

I began with a challenge to morality—how can it be rational for us to accept its constraints? It may now seem that what I have shown is that it is indeed rational for us to accept constraints, but to accept them whether or not they might be plausibly considered moral. Morality, it may seem, has nothing to do with my argument; what I have shown is that it is rational to be disposed to comply with whatever

constraints are generally accepted and expected, regardless of their nature. But this is not my view.

To show the relevance of agreement to the justification of constraints, let us assume an ongoing society in which individuals more or less acknowledge and comply with a given set of practices that constrain their choices in relation to what they would be did they take only their desires, aims, and interests directly into account. Suppose that a disposition to conform to these existing practices is prima facie advantageous, since persons who are not so disposed may expect to be excluded from desirable opportunities by their fellows. However, the practices themselves have, or at least need have, no basis in agreement. And they need satisfy no intuitive standard of fairness or impartiality, characteristics that we may suppose relevant to the identification of the practices with those of a genuine morality. Although we may speak of the practices as constituting the morality of the society in question, we need not consider them morally justified or acceptable. They are simply practices constraining individual behavior in a way that each finds rational to accept.

Suppose now that our persons, as rational maximizers of individual utility, come to reflect on the practices constituting their morality. They will, of course, assess the practices in relation to their own utility, but with the awareness that their fellows will be doing the same. And one question that must arise is: Why these practices? For they will recognize that the set of actual moral practices is not the only possible set of constraining practices that would yield mutually advantageous, optimal outcomes. They will recognize the possibility of alternative moral orders. At this point it will not be enough to say that, as a matter of fact, each person can expect to benefit from a disposition to comply with existing practices. For persons will also ask themselves: Can I benefit more, not from simply abandoning any morality, and recognizing no constraint, but from a partial rejection of existing constraints in favor of an alternative set? Once this question is asked, the situation is transformed; the existing moral order must be assessed, not only against simple noncompliance, but also against what we may call alternative compliance.

To make this assessment, each will compare her prospects under the existing practices with those she would anticipate from a set that, in the existing circumstances, she would expect to result from bargaining with her fellows. If her prospects would be improved by such negotiation, then she will have a real, although not necessarily sufficient, incentive to demand a change in the established moral order. More generally, if there are persons whose prospects would be improved by renegotiation, then the existing order will be recognizably unstable. No doubt those whose prospects would be worsened by renegotiation will have a clear incentive to resist, to appeal to the status quo. But their appeal will be a weak one, especially among persons who are not taken in by spurious ideological considerations, but focus on individual utility maximization. Thus, although in the real world, we begin with an existing set of moral practices as constraints on our maximizing behavior, yet we are led by reflection to the idea of an amended set that would obtain the agreement of everyone, and this amended set has, and will be recognized to have, a stability lacking in existing morality.

The reflective capacity of rational agents leads them from the given to the agreed, from existing practices and principles requiring constraint to those that would receive each person's assent. The same reflective capacity, I claim, leads from those practices that would be agreed to, in existing social circumstances, to those that would receive ex ante agreement, premoral and presocial. As the status quo proves unstable when it comes into conflict with what would be agreed to, so what would be agreed to proves unstable when it comes into conflict with what would have been agreed to in an appropriate presocial context. For as existing practices must seem arbitrary insofar as they do not correspond to what a rational person would agree to, so what such a person would agree to in existing circumstances must seem arbitrary in relation to what she would accept in a presocial condition.

What a rational person would agree to in existing circumstances depends in large part on her negotiating position vis-à-vis her fellows. But her negotiating position is significantly affected by the existing social institutions, and so by the currently accepted moral practices embodied in those institutions. Thus, although agreement may well yield practices differing from those embodied in existing social institutions, yet it will be influenced by those practices, which are not themselves the product of rational agreement. And this must call the rationality of the agreed practices into question. The arbitrariness of existing practices must infect any agreement whose terms are significantly affected by them. Although rational agreement is in itself a source of stability, yet this stability is undermined by the arbitrariness of the circumstances in which it takes place. To escape this arbitrariness, rational persons will revert from actual to hypothetical agreement, considering what practices they would have agreed to from an initial position not structured by existing institutions and the practices they embody.

The content of a hypothetical agreement is determined by an appeal to the equal rationality of persons. Rational persons will voluntarily accept an agreement only insofar as they perceive it to be equally advantageous to each. To be sure, each would be happy to accept an agreement more advantageous to herself than to her fellows, but since no one will accept an agreement perceived to be less advantageous, agents whose rationality is a matter of common knowledge will recognize the futility of aiming at or holding out for more, and minimize their bargaining costs by coordinating at the point of equal advantage. Now the extent of advantage is determined in a twofold way. First, there is advantage internal to an agreement. In this respect, the expectation of equal advantage is assured by procedural fairness. The step from existing moral practices to those resulting from actual agreement takes rational persons to a procedurally fair situation, in which each perceives the agreed practices to be ones that it is equally rational for all to accept, given the circumstances in which agreement is reached. But those circumstances themselves may be called into question insofar as they are perceived to be arbitrary—the result, in part, of compliance with constraining practices that do not themselves ensure the expectation of equal advantage, and so do not reflect the equal rationality of the complying parties. To neutralize this arbitrary element, moral practices to be fully acceptable must be conceived as constituting a possible outcome of a hypothetical agreement under circumstances that are unaffected by social institutions that themselves lack full acceptability. Equal rationality demands consideration of external circumstances as well as internal procedures.

But what is the practical import of this argument? It would be absurd to claim that mere acquaintance with it, or even acceptance of it, will lead to the replacement of existing moral practices by those that would secure presocial agreement. It would be irrational for anyone to give up the benefits of the existing moral order simply because he comes to realize that it affords him more than he could expect from pure rational agreement with his fellows. And it would be irrational for anyone to accept a long-term utility loss by refusing to comply with the existing moral order, simply because she comes to realize that such complicance affords her less than she could expect from pure rational agreement. Nevertheless, these realizations do transform, or perhaps bring to the surface, the character of the relationships between persons that are maintained by the existing constraints, so that some of these relationships come to be recognized as coercive. . . . Without an argument to defend themselves in open dialogue with their fellows, those who are more than equally advantaged can hope to maintain their privileged position only if they can coerce their fellows into accepting it. And this, of course, may be possible. But coercion is not agreement, and it lacks any inherent stability.

Stability plays a key role in linking compliance to agreement. Aware of the benefits to be gained from constraining practices, rational persons will seek those that invite stable compliance. Now compliance is stable if it arises from agreement among persons each of whom considers both that the terms of agreement are sufficiently favorable to herself that it is rational for her to accept them, and that they are not so favorable to others that it would be rational for them to accept terms less favorable to them and more favorable to herself. An agreement affording equally favorable terms to all thus invites, as no other can, stable compliance.

V

In defending the claim that moral practices, to obtain the stable voluntary compliance of rational individuals, must be the objects of an appropriate hypothetical agreement, I have added to the initial minimal characterization of morality. Not only does morality constrain our choices and actions, but it does so in an impartial way, reflecting the equal rationality of the persons subject to constraint. . . .

The foundational crisis of morality is thus resolved by exhibiting the rationality of our compliance with mutual, rationally agreed constraints on the pursuit of our desires, aims, and interests. Although bereft of a basis in objective values or an objectively purposive order, and confronted by a more fundamental mode of justification, morality survives by incorporating itself into that mode. Moral considerations have the same status, and the same role in explaining behavior, as the other reasons acknowledged by a rational deliberator. We are left with a unified account of justification, in which an agent's choices and actions are evaluated in relation to his preferences—to the concerns that are constitutive of his sense of self. But since morality binds the agent independently of the particular content of his preferences, it has the prescriptive grip with which the Christian and Kantian views have invested it.

In incorporating morality into deliberative justification, we recognize a new dimension to the agent's self-conception. For morality requires that a person have the capacity to commit himself, to enter into agreement with his fellows secure in the awareness that he can and will carry out his part of the agreement without regard to many of those considerations that normally and justifiably would enter into his future deliberations. And this is more than the capacity to bring one's desires and interests together with one's beliefs into a single coherent whole. Although this latter unifying capacity must extend its attention to past and future, the unification it achieves may itself be restricted to that extended present within which a person judges and decides. But in committing oneself to future action in accordance with one's agreement, one must fix at least a subset of one's desires and beliefs to hold in that future. The self that agrees and the self that complies must be one. "Man himself must first of all have become *calculable, regular, necessary,* even in his own image of himself, if he is to be able to stand security for *his own future,* which is what one who promises does!"[10]

In developing *"the right to make promises,"*[11] we human beings have found a contractarian bulwark against the perishing of morality.

NOTES

1. *On the Genealogy of Morals,* trans. by Walter Kaufmann and R. J. Hollingdale (New York: Random House, 1967), third essay, sec. 27, p. 161.
2. *After Virtue* (Notre Dame, IN: University of Notre Dame Press, 1981), p. 2.
3. *Ethics and the Limits of Philosophy* (Cambridge, MA: Harvard University Press, 1985), p. 197.
4. *Ethics: Inventing Right and Wrong* (Harmondsworth: Penguin, 1977), pp. 15, 30.
5. *The Nature of Morality* (New York: Oxford University Press, 1977), p. 11.
6. To be sure, if we think of morality as expressed in certain of our affections and/or interests, it will incorporate moral considerations to the extent that they actually are present in our preferences. But this would be to embrace the naturalism that I have put to one side as inadequate.
7. This would meet the challenge to morality found in my previous quotation from Gilbert Harman.
8. The now-classic example of this type of situation is the Prisoner's Dilemma; see *Morals by Agreement,* pp. 79–80. More generally, such situations may be said, in economists' parlance, to exhibit market failure. See, for example, "Market Contractarianism" in Jules Coleman, *Markets, Morals, and the Law* (Cambridge: Cambridge University Press, 1988), chap. 10.
9. See Hobbes, *Leviathan,* London, 1651, chap. 15.
10. Nietzsche, *On the Genealogy of Morals,* trans. by Walter Kaufmann and R. J. Hollingdale (New York: Random House, 1967), second essay, sec. 1, p. 58.
11. Ibid., p. 57.

STUDY QUESTIONS

1. According to Gauthier, why does morality face a foundational crisis?
2. Does contractarianism provide a means to avoid this foundational crisis?
3. Can you provide a case in which acting morally is not in your long-term self-interest?
4. If you could provide such a case, would it undermine Gauthier's theory?

What We Owe to Each Other

T. M. Scanlon

Whereas contractarianism holds that rational self-interest can provide a basis for morality, contractualism maintains that rationality requires respect for persons, thereby providing a foundation for cooperation among equals. T. M. Scanlon, Professor of Philosophy at Harvard University, offers a defense of contractualism, maintaining that an act is wrong if it would be disallowed by a set of principles that no one could reasonably reject as the basis of informed, unforced general agreement. In short, wrong acts are acts that cannot be justified to all others.

1. INTRODUCTION

The idea that an act is right if and only if it can be justified to others is one that even a noncontractualist might accept. Utilitarians, for example, who hold that an act is right only if it would produce a greater balance of happiness than any alternative available to the agent at the time, presumably also believe that an act is justifiable to others just in case it satisfies this utilitarian formula, so they too will hold that an act is right if and only if it is justifiable to others on terms they could not reasonably reject. For utilitarians, however, what makes an action right is having the best consequences; justifiability is merely a consequence of this.

What is distinctive about my version of contractualism is that it takes the idea of justifiability to be basic in two ways: this idea provides both the normative basis of the morality of right and wrong and the most general characterization of its content. According to contractualism, when we address our minds to a question of right and wrong, what we are trying to decide is, first and foremost, whether certain principles are ones that no one, if suitably motivated, could reasonably reject. In order to make the content of my view clearer I need to say more about the ideas of justifiability and reasonable rejection on which it rests. . . .

2. REASONABLENESS

Why speak of "principles which no one could reasonably reject" rather than "principles which no one could rationally reject"? The "reasonableness" formulation seems more obscure. Why use it, then, especially in view of the fact that I add the rider "given the aim of finding principles which others, insofar as they share this aim, could not reasonably reject"? Why not rely upon the idea of what would be *rational* for a person who has this aim? . . .

"[R]ationality" can be understood in a number of different ways. But in recent years "the (most) rational thing to do" has most commonly been taken

From T. M. Scanlon, *What We Owe to Each Other*, Harvard University Press, 1998. Reprinted by permission of the publisher.

to mean "what most conduces to the fulfillment of the agent's aims." . . .

"Reasonable" also has an established meaning, which is much closer to what I take to be basic to moral thinking. A claim about what it is reasonable for a person to do presupposes a certain body of information and a certain range of reasons which are taken to be relevant, and goes on to make a claim about what these reasons, properly understood, in fact support. In the contractualist analysis of right and wrong, what is presupposed first and foremost is the aim of finding principles that others who share this aim could not reasonably reject. This aim then brings other reasons in its train. Given this aim, for example, it would be unreasonable to give the interests of others no weight in deciding which principles to accept. For why should they accept principles arrived at in this way? This then leads to further, more complicated questions about how, more exactly, we can be asked to "take others' interests into account" in various situations.

The distinction between what it would be reasonable to do in this sense and what it would be rational to do is not a technical one, but a familiar distinction in ordinary language. Suppose, for example, that we are negotiating about water rights in our county, and that there is one landowner who already controls most of the water in the vicinity. This person has no need for our cooperation. He can do as he pleases, and what he chooses to do will largely determine the outcome of the negotiations. Suppose also that while he is not ungenerous (he would probably provide water from his own wells for anyone who desperately needed it) he is extremely irritable and does not like to have the legitimacy of his position questioned. In such a situation, it would not be unreasonable for one of us to maintain that each person is entitled to at least a minimum supply of water, and to reject any principle of allocation which does not guarantee this. But it might not be rational to make this claim or to reject such principles, since this is very likely to enrage the large landholder and lead to an outcome that is worse for almost everyone. Moreover, it is natural to say that it would be unreasonable of the large landholder to reject our request for principles guaranteeing minimum water

rights. What it would be rational for him to do (in the most common understanding of that term) is a different question, and depends on what his aims are.

There is, then, a familiar distinction between reasonableness and rationality. . . .

[H]owever, I want to say more about how the idea of reasonableness figures in the process of deciding whether or not an action is wrong. According to contractualism, in order to decide whether it would be wrong to do X in circumstances C, we should consider possible principles governing how one may act in such situations, and ask whether any principle that permitted one to do X in those circumstances could, for that reason, reasonably be rejected. In order to decide whether this is so, we need first to form an idea of the burdens that would be imposed on some people in such a situation if others were permitted to do X. Call these the objections to permission. We then need, in order to decide whether these objections provide grounds for reasonably rejecting the proposed principle, to consider the ways in which others would be burdened by a principle forbidding one to do X in these circumstances. Suppose that, compared to the objections to permission, the objections to prohibition are not significant, and that it is therefore reasonable to reject any principle that would permit one to do X in the circumstances in question. This means that this action is wrong, according to the contractualist formula. Alternatively, if there were some principle for regulating behavior in such situations that would permit one to do X and that it would not be reasonable to reject, then doing X would not be wrong: it could be justified to others on grounds that they could not reasonably refuse to accept.

Returning to the former case for the moment, if it would be reasonable to reject any principle that permitted one to do X in circumstances C, then it would seem that there must be some principle that it would not be reasonable to reject that would disallow doing X in these circumstances. One would expect this to be true because of the comparative nature of the question of reasonable rejection. If the objections to permission are strong enough, *compared to the objections to prohibition,* to make it reasonable to reject any principle permitting doing X in C, then one would not expect the objections to prohibition to be strong enough, *compared to the objections to permission,* to make it reasonable to reject any principle that forbids doing X in C.

But it may seem that there could be cases in which this might be true.[1] Consider, for example, the case of two people swimming from a sinking ship, one of whom finds a life jacket floating in the water. May the other person take the jacket by force? It might seem that, even though any principle that permitted this could reasonably be rejected, any principle forbidding it could also be rejected, since taking the jacket is the only way for the other person to avoid drowning. Put in a general form, the idea might be that there is a threshold of reasonable rejection: a level of cost such that it is reasonable to reject any principle that would lead to one's suffering a cost that great, and reasonable to do this no matter what objections others might have to alternative principles. It does not seem to me that there is such a threshold. It does not seem, for example, that the fact that a principle would forbid one to do something that was necessary in order to save one's life always makes it reasonable to reject that principle. The reasonableness of rejecting such a principle will depend not only on the costs that alternative principles would impose on others but also on how those costs would be imposed. This reflects the general fact, which I will discuss later in this chapter, that the strength of a person's objection to a principle is not determined solely by the difference that the acceptance of that principle would make to that person's welfare. In the shipwreck case, for example, the costs of the two principles to the parties may be the same (one will drown if not permitted to seize the life jacket, and the other will drown if it is taken from him). But it may still make a difference to the force of their objections that one of them now has the jacket (perhaps he has looked hard to find it) and is therefore not now at risk.

Even if the general idea of a threshold of reasonable rejection is incorrect, however, there could still be cases in which opposing parties have strong objections that are evenly balanced. Suppose, for example, that the two swimmers, one of whom is much stronger than the other, arrive at the life jacket at the same moment. May each use force to try to seize it? It might seem that if a principle permitting this could reasonably be rejected then so too could a principle forbidding it, since the considerations on the two sides are the same. This conclusion depends on an overly simple view of the alternatives. A principle permitting each to struggle for the jacket at least has the merit of recognizing the symmetry of their claims and the need for some decisive solution. It would be reasonable to reject this principle if, but only if, there were some alternative that did this better (such as a principle requiring them to take turns or, unrealistic as it may seem, to draw lots). Similarly, a principle forbidding the use of force could not reasonably be rejected if there were some other (nonrejectable) method for resolving the matter.

It thus does not follow, from the fact that the situations of the people who would suffer from an action's being permitted and those who would suffer from its being forbidden are virtually the same, that if any principle that permits the action can reasonably be rejected then so too can any principle that forbids it. The very fact that these objections are symmetrical may point the way toward a class of principles that are not rejectable.

4. STANDPOINTS

The aim of finding and acting on principles that no one similarly motivated could reasonably reject leads us to take other people's interests into account in deciding what principles to follow. More exactly, we have reason to consider whether there are standpoints other than our own present standpoint from which the principles we are considering could reasonably be rejected. I want now to consider what these "standpoints" are.

According to contractualism, our concern with right and wrong is based on a concern that our actions be justifiable to others on grounds that they could not reasonably reject insofar as they share this concern. "Others" figure twice in this schema: as those to whom justification is owed, and as those who might or might not be able reasonably to reject certain principles. When we think of those to whom justification is owed, we naturally think first of the specific individuals who are affected by specific actions. But when we are deciding whether a given principle is one that could reasonably be rejected we must take a broader and more abstract perspective. This perspective is broader because, when we are considering the acceptability or rejectability of a principle, we must take into account not only the consequences of particular actions, but also the consequences of general performance or nonperformance of such actions and of the other implications (for both agents and others) of having agents be licensed and directed to think in the way that that principle requires. So the points of view that the question of reasonable rejectability requires us to take into account are not limited to those of the individuals affected by a particular action. This is so for several reasons, which are worth spelling out.

First and most obviously, widespread performance of acts of a given kind can have very different effects from isolated individual instances. Slightly less obviously, perhaps, the general authorization or prohibition of a class of actions can have significance that goes beyond the consequences of the actions that are performed or not performed as a result. This can be seen both from the point of view of agents and from that of the people who may be affected by these actions. As agents, if we know that we must stand ready to perform actions of a certain kind should they be required, or that we cannot count on being able to perform acts of another kind should we want to, because they are forbidden, these things have important effects on our planning and on the organization of our lives whether or not any occasions of the relevant sort ever actually present themselves. If, for example, I lived in a desert area and were obligated to provide food for strangers in need who came by my house, then I would have to take account of this possibility in my shopping and consumption, whether or not anyone ever asked me for this kind of help; and if I am not entitled to photocopy articles at will when they turn out to be useful in my course, then I have reason to order a more inclusive anthology to begin with, even though this may prove to have been unnecessary. The same is true from the point of view of those affected by

actions. Our need for privacy, for example, is not met simply because, as a matter of fact, other people do not listen in on our phone calls and go through our personal files. In order to have the benefits of privacy we need to have assurance that this will not happen, and this is something that general acceptance of a principle can provide.

These points could be summarized by saying that general prohibitions and permissions have effects on the liberty, broadly construed, of both agents and those affected by their actions. But the acceptance of principles has other implications beyond these effects. Because principles constrain the reasons we may, or must, take into account, they can affect our relations with others and our view of ourselves in both positive and negative ways. . . . The case of privacy offers a . . . positive example. The fact that others recognize reasons to restrain themselves so that I may be free from observation and inquiry when I wish to be is important in defining my standing as an independent person who can enter into relations with others as an equal. If the principles we all accepted did not recognize these reasons, this would crucially alter my relations with other people, and even my view of myself. (Principles defining my distinctive rights over my own body—rights to say who can even touch it, let alone claim its parts for other purposes—are an even clearer example.)

As this discussion of the points of view that must be considered in deciding whether a principle could reasonably be rejected brings out, an assessment of the rejectability of a principle must take into account the consequences of its acceptance in general, not merely in a particular case that we may be concerned with. Since we cannot know, when we are making this assessment, which particular individuals will be affected by it in which ways (who will be affected as an agent required to act a certain way, who as a potential victim, who as a bystander, and so on), our assessment cannot be based on the particular aims, preferences, and other characteristics of specific individuals. We must rely instead on commonly available information about what people have reason to want. I will refer to this as information about generic reasons.

Some examples: We commonly take it that people have strong reasons to want to avoid bodily injury, to be able to rely on assurances they are given, and to have control over what happens to their own bodies. We therefore think it reasonable to reject principles that would leave other agents free to act against these important interests. Similarly, as agents we typically have reason to want to give special attention to our own projects, friends, and family, and thus have reason to object to principles that would constrain us in ways that would make these concerns impossible.

Generic reasons are reasons that we can see that people have in virtue of their situation, characterized in general terms, and such things as their aims and capabilities and the conditions in which they are placed. Not everyone is affected by a given principle in the same way, and generic reasons are not limited to reasons that the majority of people have. If even a small number of people would be adversely affected by a general permission for agents to act a certain way, then this gives rise to a potential reason for rejecting that principle. (This is a generic reason since it is one that we can see people have in virtue of certain general characteristics; it is not attributed to specific individuals.)

Whether such a reason is a ground for reasonably rejecting the principle will depend, of course, on the costs this would involve for others, and these will depend on what alternatives there are. One alternative, if a principle granting general permission to act a certain way is rejected, is a general prohibition against so acting. This may be very costly from the point of view of potential agents, and may be reasonably rejected on that account. A second possibility is a principle in which the permission is qualified, by specific exceptions or by a more open-ended requirement that there be no countervailing considerations. . . .

My purpose is . . . to illustrate the general point that we bring to moral argument a conception of generic points of view and the reasons associated with them which reflects our general experience of life, and that this conception is subject to modification under the pressures of moral thought and argument. Some of the most common forms of moral bias involve failing to think of various points of view which we have not occupied, underestimating the reasons associated with them, and overestimating the costs to us of accepting principles that recognize the force of those reasons.[2]

It is commonly said that one important role of moral theory is to provide a way of correcting these biases. In one respect this is true. The pressure to be able to justify our actions to others, on terms that they could not reasonably reject, can help to reveal biases of this kind and press us to overcome them. But the process of doing this is one of gradually refining our intuitive moral categories under conflicting pressures of the kind I have just described, drawing on our expanding experience of others' points of view. I doubt that it is possible for theory to "correct biases" in a more radical way by specifying once and for all what the outcome of this process should be—for example, by specifying in advance the terms in which all "reasonable rejections" must be defended.

6. REASONABLE REJECTION

In order to decide whether a principle could reasonably be rejected, we need to consider it from a number of standpoints. From the point of view of those who will be its main beneficiaries, there may be strong generic reasons to insist on the principle and to reject anything that offers less. From the point of view of the agents who will be constrained by it, or of those who would be beneficiaries of an alternative principle, there may be reason to reject it in favor of something different or less demanding. In order to decide whether the principle could reasonably be rejected we need to decide whether it would be reasonable to take any of these generic reasons against it to prevail, given the reasons on the other side and given the aim of finding principles that others also could not reasonably reject. What can we say, in general, about the kinds of considerations that count as generic reasons and about how conflicting reasons are to be assessed? . . .

If we were to appeal to a prior notion of rightness to tell us which considerations are morally relevant and which are entitled to prevail in cases of conflict, then the contractualist framework would be unnecessary, since all the work would already have been done by this prior notion. It may seem, then, that when we apply the contractualist test we need to set aside any claims of rights or entitlement, or to focus on cases in which no such claims exist. This appears to mean that the relative strength of various generic reasons for and against a principle must be a function of the effects that that principle, or its absence, would have on the well-being of people in various positions. The crucial questions then would be how this notion of well-being is to be understood, and how the strength of a reason is related to well-being in this sense: Does the strongest objection belong to those whose level of well-being would be lowest if they lose out? or to those to whom the principle would make the greatest difference? Or does it depend on more complicated factors such as some combination of difference and level of well-being?

This is an appealing line of thought, but a mistaken one. While it would be objectionably circular to make "reasonable rejection" turn on presumed entitlements of the very sort that the principle in question is supposed to establish, it is misleading to suggest that when we are assessing the "reasonable rejectability" of a principle we must, or even can, set aside assumptions about other rights and entitlements altogether. Even in those cases that come closest to being decided on the basis of a principle's implications for the welfare of individuals in various positions, many other moral claims must be presupposed in order to provide a context in which that principle can be understood.

Suppose, for example, that we are considering a principle defining our obligations to help those in need. This would seem to be a case in which considerations of welfare are most likely to be predominant. But in order to be in a position to aid someone, an agent must be entitled to dispose of the resources that are needed, and must be free from any obligation that would prevent him or her from acting in the way required to give aid. Similarly, being in need of aid is in part a matter of not being entitled simply to take what one needs, perhaps by force if necessary. So in order

to understand the scope of the proposed principle (the range of actions it might require) we need to presuppose a framework of entitlements. What this illustrates is that a sensible contractualism, like most other plausible views, will involve a holism about moral justification: in assessing one principle we must hold many others fixed. This does not mean that these other principles are beyond question, but just that they are not being questioned at the moment.

Contractualism is not based on the idea that there is a "fundamental level" of justification at which only well-being (conceived in some particular way) matters and the comparison of magnitudes of well-being is the sole basis for assessing the reasonableness of rejecting principles of right and entitlement. Even though components of well-being figure prominently as grounds for reasonable rejection, the idea of such a fundamental level is misleading on two counts. First, the claim that the possibility of suffering a loss in well-being is something that has force in moral argument is a substantive moral claim. By concealing or minimizing this fact, the idea of a fundamental level has the effect of giving these claims a privileged status over other moral considerations. In many cases, gains and losses in well-being (relief from suffering, for example) are clearly the most relevant factors determining whether a principle could or could not be reasonably rejected. And in some cases of this kind questions of responsibility—such as whether the sufferer's claim to aid might be undermined by the fact that it was his or her own fault—do not arise, either because it so obviously was not the person's fault or because it would not matter if it were. But (and this is the second way in which the idea of a fundamental level can be misleading) to identify a case as of this kind is to place it within a specific moral framework, not to view it without any moral assumptions.

It may seem that contractualism becomes viciously circular if it does not take well-being as the basic coin in which reasonable rejection is measured (if, for example, it gives independent weight to considerations such as responsibility). But this is so only if the claims of well-being are unique among moral claims in needing no further justification, and well-being is therefore uniquely suited to serve as the basis in terms of which other moral notions are explained. I believe that something like this is frequently assumed, not only by utilitarians but also by others, like me, who look to views such as contractualism specifically as ways of avoiding utilitarianism. It is therefore worth considering why this assumption should seem so plausible, especially in the context of a contractualist theory of the kind I am trying to present.

There are two directions from which one might challenge the claim that a generic reason arising from a certain standpoint is a relevant, perhaps even decisive ground for rejecting a principle. First, one might question whether the consideration in question is a generic reason at all—whether it is something that people in that situation would have reason to care about. Second, one might question whether this reason has weight in moral argument as contractualism describes it (whether it would have to be recognized as having weight by others who shared a concern with mutual justifiability).

These two challenges correspond to two possible charges of "circularity." If, for example, I were to claim that it would be reasonable to reject a certain principle because it was unfair, this might be challenged as "circular" in two different ways. One might claim that it is circular to assume that people in the situation in question would have reason to object to unfairness per se. Why should they care about it if it does not involve some loss in well-being? Alternatively, it might be held to be circular to assume that an objection on grounds of "unfairness" would have moral force—that if anyone were to have reason to raise it, then others would have reason to accept it insofar as they are concerned with mutual justifiability.

Why might it be thought that objections arising from concerns with well-being are particularly immune to charges of circularity of these two kinds? To begin with charges of the first kind, it is no doubt particularly clear that individuals typically have strong reason to want to have certain benefits, and to want to avoid pain and injury. Perhaps this claim can be generalized to cover anything that affects "how well one's life goes." But these are not the only things that people have reason to want and to object to being deprived of. I argued above, for example, that it is

reasonable to object to principles that favor others arbitrarily. A principle that favors some in this way will often deprive others of benefits and opportunities they have reason to want. But why should these concrete disadvantages be the only grounds for objecting to such a principle? It would be circular for contractualism to cite, as the reason that people have for objecting to such principles, the fact that they are wrong according to some noncontractualist standard. But we need not choose between objections of this kind and objections based on loss of well-being. We have reason to object to principles simply because they arbitrarily favor the claims of some over the identical claims of others: that is to say, because they are unfair. In the process of moral reflection that contractualism describes, this provides a perfectly understandable reason for finding partial principles objectionable, a reason that does not depend on a prior idea that such principles, or the practices they would permit, are wrong.

It seems to me an important strength of contractualism that, in contrast to utilitarianism and other views which make well-being the only fundamental moral notion, it can account for the significance of different moral notions, within a unified moral framework, without reducing all of them to a single idea. What is necessary in order to do this is to show in each case why people would have reason to insist upon principles incorporating these notions (why principles that did not do this would be ones that could reasonably be rejected). I have just indicated how this can be done in the case of fairness. . . .

Let me turn now to charges of circularity of the second kind. These claim that if we count generic reasons not arising from effects on well-being as relevant objections to a principle, this can only reflect a substantive moral judgment and is therefore objectionably circular. This challenge might be based on the idea that (apart from an appeal to some substantive moral doctrine) there *are* no generic reasons for objecting to a principle other than those arising from its effects on how well people's lives go. So understood, it is just a restatement of a challenge of the first kind, to which I have already responded. So I will take the challenge to be not to the existence of certain generic reasons for objecting to a principle but rather to the legitimacy of counting these reasons as morally significant—as relevant grounds for rejecting that principle.

Here my response is that, as I have already mentioned, the judgment that *any* consideration constitutes a relevant, possibly conclusive, reason for rejecting a principle in the context of contractualist moral thinking as I am describing it is a judgment with moral content. This may be easy to overlook when the reason in question is based on the impact that a principle would typically have on "how well life would go" for a person in a certain position, but it is no less true in that case than in any other. . . .

Even if it would not be uniquely immune to charges of circularity, however, a form of contractualism (what might be called "welfarist contractualism") that took a specified conception of well-being as the sole standard for assessing all putative reasons for rejecting proposed principles would represent a particularly strong claim about the nature of right and wrong. It might seem that any interesting form of contractualism would have to be similarly structured: that is, it would have to begin with a clear specification of the possible grounds for reasonably rejecting a principle (whether this is given in terms of a conception of well-being or in some other way) and with a specified method for determining the relative strength of these grounds that allow us to reach conclusions about reasonable rejectability without appeals to judgment.

The version of contractualism that I am defending does not take this form. Its first aim is to provide a unified account of the subject matter of this part of morality and of its normative basis. This account also has some clear substantive implications: the rationale it offers for taking "justifiability to others on grounds they could not reasonably reject" as the central idea of the morality of obligation supports definite conclusions about the grounds of reasonable rejection: it rules out certain considerations and identifies others as definitely relevant. . . . But even if they are accepted, much more is left open than under a contractualism of the kind just mentioned. Of course, even welfarist contractualism would require us to rely on our judgment as to whether a given loss of well-being would, under certain circumstances,

count as grounds for reasonable rejection of a principle. On the version I am defending, however, we must sometimes exercise judgment as to whether certain considerations are or are not relevant to the reasonable rejectability of a principle, since these grounds are not completely specified in advance. There is, of course, the possibility of tightening contractualism by specifying more explicitly the grounds of reasonable rejection and the method to be used in balancing these grounds against one another. I believe that although this is a feasible aim with respect to some specific areas of morality it is not likely to succeed at the level of generality of the theory I am currently offering here—that is to say, at the level of an account that is intended to cover, if not all of "morality," then that large part of it that has to do with what we owe to each other. . . .

7. IMPERSONAL VALUES

In order for a principle to be reasonably rejectable there must be some relevant standpoint from which people typically have good reason either to refuse to accept that principle as part of their own practical thinking or to refuse to recognize it as a ground that others may use to justify their conduct. Reasons for rejecting a principle need not be based on the consequences of the actions that principle would license, or even on the consequences of those actions if performed generally. It can be good grounds for rejecting a principle that accepting it would make it impossible to recognize other values that one has good reason to recognize. For example, a principle requiring strict neutrality between friends and strangers would be unacceptable simply because it would be incompatible with the attitudes and values of friendship.

I have also argued that people's reasons for rejecting a principle need not be based on the effects that accepting it or having others accept it would have on their well-being. In discussing fairness, . . . it is sufficient ground for rejecting a principle that it singles others out, without justification, for a privileged moral status. Even if these reasons do not have to do with well-being, however, they are still what might be called *personal* reasons, since they have to do with the claims and status of individuals in certain positions. The question I want now to address is whether a principle might also be rejected on *impersonal* grounds—that is to say, for reasons that are not tied to the well-being, claims, or status of individuals in any particular position.

It might seem that impersonal reasons for rejection must be allowed, at least in principle. For it does not seem that all the reasons we have are grounded in the moral claims or the well-being of individuals, either ourselves or others. Many people, for example, believe that we have reason not to flood the Grand Canyon, or to destroy the rain forests, or to act in a way that threatens the survival of a species (our own or some other), simply because these things are valuable and ought to be preserved and respected, and not just because acting in these ways would be contrary to the claims or interests of individuals. Whether they are correct in thinking this is not, however, a question to be settled by an account of the morality of right and wrong; it belongs to morality in the wider sense and to the broader subjects of reasons and value. But if there are impersonal reasons of this kind why should they not count as possible grounds for reasonably rejecting principles? If the value of the Grand Canyon gives me reason to want it to be preserved, for example, why does it not also give me a good reason to reject a principle that would license others to neglect this value in deciding whether or not to build a dam on the Colorado River?

In answering this question it is important to bear in mind the limited range of the part of morality we are trying to characterize. The contractualist formula is meant to describe one category of moral ideas: the requirements of "what we owe to each other." Reasons for rejecting a principle thus correspond to particular forms of concern that we owe to other individuals. By definition, impersonal reasons do not represent forms of such concern. They flow from the value of those objects themselves, not (at least in the first instance) from anything having to do with my relation to other people.

To claim this—to claim, for example, that in destroying an ancient monument or tree I do no wrong to anyone—is not to claim that we have no reason (or even no moral reason in the broadest sense) not to commit such acts. It would even be natural to say that it would be wrong to destroy these things, using 'wrong' in the broad sense in which something is wrong if there is a very serious reason against doing it. But insofar as the value of these objects provides me with a reason to preserve them, it would be a misrepresentation of this reason to say that it is grounded in what I owe to others.

Impersonal reasons do not, themselves, provide grounds for reasonably rejecting a principle. But these reasons do play a significant role in determining other grounds for reasonable rejection. This happens in a number of ways. One concerns the benefits, for individuals, of being able to engage in valuable activities. So, for example, part of what it means to say that the Grand Canyon is of value is that visiting and enjoying it is worthwhile. From the point of view of those who might engage in these activities in the future, then, there is reason to reject a principle that would allow someone to decide to flood the Grand Canyon without taking these benefits into account. These reasons for rejecting a principle are what I called above personal reasons, but their force as reasons depends in part on further judgments of impersonal value, namely the judgment that these objects are worth seeing and should be admired.

Generic reasons for rejecting a principle can also arise from the fact that the constraints that it would impose on practical reasoning are incompatible with other values that one has reason to recognize. It may seem that there is reason of this kind to reject principles that simply neglect impersonal reasons, for if I regard something as valuable and believe that its value gives people reason not to destroy it, how can I accept a principle that licenses me and others to neglect this value in deciding what to do?

But as long as a principle only *permits* one to neglect impersonal reasons, there is no ground of this kind for rejecting it. Since a principle of right and wrong specifies only those constraints on our practical thinking that are imposed by what we owe to others, the sense in which such a principle can "license" us to decide what to do in a way that neglects the value of an object is a limited one: it can say that we do not owe it to each other to take this value into account. This is something that one could well accept while regarding that value as important. Indeed, as I have noted above, it would be implausible in most such cases to hold that the reason why others should recognize an impersonal value is that they owe it to us to do so. . . .

9. AGGREGATION

All the grounds for rejecting a principle that I have so far considered arise from generic reasons that an individual would have who occupied a certain position in the situations to which that principle applies. This suggests what Parfit has called the Complaint Model.[3] On this interpretation of contractualism, a person's complaint against a principle must have to do with its effects on him or her, and someone can reasonably reject a principle if there is some alternative to which no other person has a complaint that is as strong. There are, however, two ways in which what I have already said about reasonable rejection departs from this model. First, if a principle's "effects on a person," in the sense intended in the statement of the Complaint Model, include only effects on that person's well-being, then I have departed from that model in allowing that a person could reasonably reject a principle on the grounds that it treated him or her unfairly, as I have interpreted that notion, even if this treatment did not make the person worse off. Second, the Complaint Model appears to suggest that each principle is to be tested by appealing directly to its effects on the well-being of individuals in various standpoints, leaving aside any questions of rights or entitlements, whereas I have maintained that in many cases principles must be considered within the framework of other principles which are, for the moment, being held constant, and that possible grounds for rejection are shaped by these background principles.

These departures aside, the Complaint Model calls attention to a central feature of contractualism that I would not want to give up: its insistence that the justifiability of a moral principle depends only on various *individuals'* reasons for objecting to that principle and alternatives to it. This feature is

central to the guiding idea of contractualism, and is also what enables it to provide a clear alternative to utilitarianism and other forms of consequentialism. These theories are appealing partly because of their simple structure, but more because of the substantive appeal of the particular forms of value—such as the happiness or welfare of sentient creatures—on which they are based. But utilitarianism, and most other forms of consequentialism, have highly implausible implications, which flow directly from the fact that their mode of justification is, at base, an aggregative one: the *sum* of a certain sort of value is to be maximized. Whether this standard is applied directly to actions or to rules governing actions, it remains true in principle that imposing high costs on a few could always be justified by the fact that this brought benefits to others, no matter how small these benefits may be as long as the recipients are sufficiently numerous. A contractualist theory, in which all objections to a principle must be raised by individuals, blocks such justifications in an intuitively appealing way. It allows the intuitively compelling complaints of those who are severely burdened to be heard, while, on the other side, the sum of the smaller benefits to others has no justificatory weight, since there is no individual who enjoys these benefits and would have to forgo them if the policy were disallowed.

The problem is, however, that contractualism appears to go too far in the opposite direction, disallowing any appeal to aggregative benefits even in cases in which the right thing to do does seem to depend not only on the impact that various actions would have on particular individuals but also on the number of individuals who would be so affected. For example, in a situation in which we must choose between saving two different groups of people from the same loss or injury, it seems that it would be wrong, absent some special justification, simply to choose the course of action that leads to more people's being killed or injured. This appears to pose a problem for contractualism, since, assuming that the losses or injuries to all the parties are the same and that their grounds for rejecting a principle depend solely on these losses, the generic reasons for rejecting a principle permitting us to save the smaller number will, it seems, be evenly balanced by the generic individual reasons for rejecting a principle requiring one to save the greater number. It therefore seems that as long as it confines itself to reasons for rejection arising from individual stand-points contractualism will be unable to explain how the number of people affected by an action can ever make a moral difference. . . .

The argument leading to the conclusion that aggregation presents an acute problem for contractualism relies on the assumption that the strength of individuals' complaints against a principle are a function solely of the cost to them of that principle's being accepted. But, as indicated at the outset of this section, I have already departed from the Complaint Model in this respect, by allowing that individuals' reasons for rejecting a principle can depend on factors other than effects on their well-being. We should see, then, whether this divergence provides room for an explanation of how what is right can sometimes depend on aggregative considerations.

[O]n contractualist grounds, . . . there can be a duty in certain situations to prevent injury or loss of life. This would be required, for example, by principles of mutual aid, requiring one to prevent injury or death when one can easily do so, and also by more specific principles, such as one requiring anyone who operates an automobile, or other potentially dangerous machine, to prevent others from being injured or killed by it, insofar as he can do this. But now consider a principle which, in cases in which one has a duty of this kind and one has to choose between preventing a certain level of injury to either a larger or a smaller group of people, permits one to save either the greater or the smaller number (assuming that one is not bound by any other duties or obligations to members of either group).

What objection could be raised to this principle from the point of view of someone in the larger group? The principle would permit someone, faced with the choice between saving one stranger from injury or death and saving two other strangers from the same fate, to save only the one. In such a case, either member of the larger group might complain that this principle did not take account of the value of saving his life, since it permits the agent to decide

what to do in the very same way that it would have permitted had he not been present at all, and there was only one person in each group. The fate of the single person is obviously being given positive weight, he might argue, since if that person were not threatened then the agent would have been required to save the two. And the fact that there is one other person who can be saved if and only if the first person is not saved is being given positive weight to balance the value of saving the one. The presence of the additional person, however, makes no difference to what the agent is required to do or to how she is required to go about deciding what to do. This is unacceptable, the person might argue, since his life should be given the same moral significance as anyone else's in this situation (which is, by stipulation, a situation in which no one has a special moral claim).[4]

This line of reasoning seems to me to have great force. The conclusion it supports is that any principle dealing with cases of this kind would be reasonably rejectable if it did not require agents to treat the claims of each person who could be saved as having the same moral force. Since there is, we are supposing, a positive duty to save in cases in which only one person is present, this means that any nonrejectable principle must direct an agent to recognize a positive reason for saving each person. Since a second reason of this kind can balance the first—turning a situation in which one must save one into one in which it is permissible to save either of two people—the reason presented by the needs of a second person in one of these two groups must at least have the power to break this tie. The principle stated above fails to meet these requirements and is reasonably rejectable. The same objection would also apply to a principle that directed an agent faced with a choice between saving one and saving two in such a situation to decide by flipping a fair coin.

Consider, then, a principle requiring one to save the greater number in situations of the kind described. What objection could be raised to this principle from the standpoint of those in the smaller group? Such a person could not claim that his life was not taken into account in the way that those of others were. He might say that he would have been better off under a principle permitting one to save the smaller number, and might have been better off under a principle requiring the agent to flip a coin. But these are not, by themselves, grounds for reasonable rejection. It will be true of almost any principle that someone would have been better off if some other principle were in effect. And, as we have seen, these particular alternatives are subject to a strong objection that does not apply to the one now under consideration.

It would be reasonable to reject a principle for deciding what to do in these cases that did not give positive weight to each person's life. It would also be reasonable to reject a principle that did not give each person's life the same importance.[5] The principle requiring one to save the greater number in these cases satisfies these two requirements, but it might be claimed that it is not the only principle that does so. Consider, for example, the principle of proportional chances, directing one to decide which group to save by means of a weighted lottery. According to this principle, if one had to choose between saving group A, containing four people, and group B, containing five, then one should use a procedure that has a four-ninths chance of favoring A and a five-ninths chance of favoring B. This principle gives everyone's life a positive weight (it would not call for the same procedure in a case of one versus one as in a case of one versus two). And although the members of the larger group have a greater chance of being saved than those in the smaller group, the presence of each person changes the procedure in the same way. Moreover, it might be argued that the strongest grounds for rejecting this principle are weaker than the strongest grounds for rejecting the principle of saving the greater number, since whoever loses out under this principle has at least been given a chance of being saved.

This argument is not persuasive, however, Whichever of these principles is followed, the ultimate stakes for the people affected are the same: some will suffer severe harm, the others will be saved. So the argument within contractualism for the principle of proportional chances is not that it makes some people better off than they would be under the alternative principle, but rather that it is a better *procedure* for deciding which people will be saved, and that the members of the smaller group could reasonably reject the alternative procedure that requires one always to save the greater number. But it is not clear that they can reasonably reject this principle. In any class of cases in which we must decide between providing a good to one group and providing it to another, if a given principle would decide the matter in favor of one group, then the members of the other have a reason to prefer that the matter be settled by a lottery (even one weighted against them). They have this reason no matter how strong the case for the given principle may be, but it does not follow that they have reasonable grounds for rejecting the principle. This depends on whether there are good substantive reasons supporting that principle, and in this case it seems that there are such reasons.

As argued above, in a case in which we must choose between saving one person and saving two, a principle that did not recognize the presence of the second person on the latter side as making a moral difference, counting in favor of saving that group, could reasonably be rejected. The case for using a weighted lottery acknowledges this, since the reason for *weighting* the lottery rather than using one that gives everyone an equal chance of being saved is that this reflects the positive value of saving each person: everyone's presence makes a difference to the procedure that is followed, counting in favor of the action that would lead to his or her being saved. Why, then, doesn't this settle the matter? If there is a strong reason, other things being equal, to save this additional person, then deciding on this ground to save the two-person group is not *unfair* to the person who is not saved, since the importance of saving him or her has been fully taken into account. There is no reason, at this point, to reshuffle the moral deck by holding a weighted lottery, or an unweighted one.

I conclude that it would not be reasonable to reject a principle requiring one to save the greater number in rescue situations of the kind described. The argument I have given departs from the Complaint Model, but it preserves the individualistic basis of contractualism. The principle just defended directs an agent, under the specified conditions, to choose the course of action that yields the greater benefit, but the argument for the principle considered only objections that could be raised from the standpoints of the individuals involved. Admitting this argument does not, I believe, open the door to implausible forms of aggregation. To see this, we need to consider some examples.

Suppose that Jones has suffered an accident in the transmitter room of a television station. Electrical equipment has fallen on his arm, and we cannot rescue him without turning off the transmitter for fifteen minutes. A World Cup match is in progress, watched by many people, and it will not be over for an hour. Jones's injury will not get any worse if we wait, but his hand has been mashed and he is receiving extremely painful electrical shocks. Should we rescue him now or wait until the match is over? Does the right thing to do depend on how many people are watching—whether it is one million or five million or a hundred million? It seems to me that we should not wait, no matter how many viewers there are, and I believe that contractualism can account for this judgment while still allowing aggregative principles of the kind defended above.

Consider a principle requiring one to save a person in a situation like Jones's. This principle might hold that if one can save a person from serious pain and injury at the cost of inconveniencing others or interfering with their amusement, then one must do so no matter how numerous these others may be. Could this principle reasonably be rejected? I do not believe that it could. No one in the class of people whose enjoyment of the match would be interrupted could make an argument like the one I gave above against the principle allowing one to save the smaller number of people in a case in which everyone is threatened with the same serious loss. That argument relied on the fact that if one of the members of the two-person group were absent then the positive reason for saving the one person would be balanced by an identical reason for saving the remaining member of the pair, thus creating a tie, which is broken by the claims of the other member of the pair, if there is one. But when the harms in question are unequal, we cannot create such a tie simply by imagining some of the people in the larger group to be absent. To claim that there is a tie in such a case

would be already to claim that the fact that there are more people in one group makes it reasonable to reject a principle requiring one to help the smaller number, each of whom would suffer the greater harm. So we cannot use this "tie-breaking" argument to justify the selection of a principle requiring one to save the greater number in such cases.

It might be claimed that my argument goes too far in rejecting aggregative reasoning. Other cases might be cited in which, it is alleged, we do or should "sum up" similar benefits and use them to offset larger costs to individuals. Suppose, for example, that we are deciding whether to build a new system of transmitting towers that will improve the quality of reception for many television viewers. It may be highly probable that in the course of this project a number of workers will suffer harms at least as great as Jones's. Yet we do not think that it is therefore wrong to go ahead. Much the same thing might be said about many other public projects, such as building a bridge, road, or tunnel that will make travel more convenient for many people. So an adequate account of the role of aggregation in our thinking about right and wrong needs to explain the difference between these two kinds of cases.

It is important in understanding our reaction to these cases to note that they involve failing to prevent accidental injuries rather than either intentionally inflicting serious harm on a few people, or withholding aid from people who need it, in order to bring small benefits to others. They differ in this respect from my original television studio example, and if they did not differ in this way our reaction to them would be very different. Our sense that it is permissible to undertake these projects also depends crucially on the assumption that precautions have been taken to make the work safe and that, in addition, workers have the choice of whether or not to undertake the risks involved. So the question in these cases is whether these precautions are adequate—whether, having taken them, it is permissible to proceed—or whether a higher level of caution is required.

This question is properly addressed in two stages. In the first, we ask what level of care is adequate; in the second, we ask whether this standard has been met in the case of a particular project. No doubt there are many actual projects in which this standard has not been met. But the question of whether it has been met (in cases in which the harms in question are serious ones and the gains to each beneficiary are small) does not depend on the number of people who will benefit. (We do not think that a higher level of safety must be provided for workers on a building that will benefit only one family as opposed to an apartment house or a public bridge.)[6]

The first question is a general one, and the answer to it affects our lives in many ways, since there are many things that we do or depend on that involve risk of serious harm to others. Suppose, then, that we are considering a principle that allows projects to proceed, even though they involve risk of serious harm to some, provided that a certain level of care has been taken to reduce these risks. It is obvious what the generic reason would be for rejecting such a principle from the standpoint of someone who is seriously injured despite the precautions that have been taken. On the other side, however, those who would benefit, directly or indirectly, from the many activities that the principle would permit may have good generic reason to object to a more stringent requirement. In meeting the level of care demanded by the principle, they might argue, they have done enough to protect others from harm. Refusing to allow activities that meet this level of care would, they could claim, impose unacceptable constraint on their lives.

My purpose here is not to argue that one or the other of these grounds for reasonable rejection should be decisive. (Since I have not stated the principle in question with any precision it is impossible to tell which side has the stronger claim.) It may be that the views we commonly hold about this matter are mistaken, because they involve exaggerating the sacrifice that would be involved if a higher level of caution were required. My present point concerns the form that such arguments should take rather than the substantive question of what their outcome should be. The contractualist argument I have just stated includes a form of aggregation, but it is aggregation *within* each person's life, summing up all the

ways in which a principle demanding a certain level of care would constrain that life, rather than aggregation *across* lives, adding up the costs or benefits to different individuals. My claim is that once the arguments are properly understood it is apparent that only the first form of aggregation is needed in cases of the kind I am presently considering (that is to say, cases in which practices which benefit many people in relatively small ways will very likely involve serious accidental harm to a few). It is tempting to think that our conclusions about the moral permissibility of these practices depend on summing up the small benefits to many individuals to reach a sum that outweighs the serious losses to a few, but this is in fact an illusion.

The argument just concluded relied upon "intrapersonal aggregation" of the consequences, for an individual, of a principle's being generally accepted and acted upon. This is not an ad hoc move, but is in accord with the point, made several times above, that generic reasons for rejecting a principle can include these general effects as well as the costs and benefits of someone's abiding by the principle in a particular case. Having appealed to such general consequences in this case, however, I should reexamine my television studio example to see whether a similar appeal would have led to a different conclusion in that case. The principle in question was one that required an agent to save one person from an hour of extreme pain even at the cost of inconvenience to others, regardless of the number of people so inconvenienced. The question now is whether, if that principle were generally followed, the consequences for some individuals (intrapersonally aggregated) would be so great as to make it reasonable to reject the principle. I do not believe this is so. It seems to me that we currently follow something close to this principle and that the occasions to which it applies seem sufficiently rare that the costs on each of us are not very significant. I may of course be wrong in thinking this. Perhaps if we realized how much each of us is sacrificing for rescues of this general kind we would conclude correctly that it would not be unreasonable to refuse to pay this price (even though we might want to bear it anyway, since failing to rescue such people would be inhumane even if it were not actually wrong). My point is that, whatever the correct substantive judgment may be in this case, contractualism provides a framework which allows the relevant factors to be considered and leads to plausible conclusions.

I have argued that contractualism supports a principle according to which, in situations in which aid is required and in which one must choose between aiding a larger or a smaller number of people all of whom face harms of comparable moral importance, one must aid the larger number. On the other hand, contractualism does not require, or even permit, one to save a larger number of people from minor harms rather than a smaller number who face much more serious injuries. This distinction, between one class of cases, in which the number of people who can be saved is morally relevant, and all others, in which it is not, is subject to at least two objections. The first concerns the way in which a distinction is drawn between the moral significance of different harms. It seems implausible that in one case, in which we must choose between saving one person and saving ten from harms of the same degree of seriousness, we are required to save the ten, but that in a case that was otherwise identical except for the fact that the harm faced by the one was *slightly* worse we would be required to save the one instead. The proper reply here, I believe, is that the distinctions on which the principles I have argued for rely are distinctions between broad categories of moral seriousness. Slight differences in what happens, such as a pain's lasting a little longer or a person's losing two fingers rather than three, do not make the difference between a very serious loss and a moderate one, and the differences between these moral categories are not "slight."

The second objection is that although the principles I have argued for may seem correct in cases in which the harms in question are serious and all of the same degree of seriousness (as in the choice between saving one life or many) and in cases involving harms of very different degrees of seriousness (as in the television studio example), there are intermediate cases in which they lead to less plausible results. It may be clear that preventing one person from drowning takes priority over warning a whole beach full of

people not to go into the water, which is polluted and will cause them several days of vomiting and diarrhea. In this case it may not matter how many people are on the beach. But this becomes less clear as we modify the example, increasing the seriousness of the harm that the many will suffer to, say, the loss of a limb, or blindness, or paralysis. On the account I have offered of how aggregative principles can be justified within contractualism, the number of people affected does not become relevant until the harm the members of the larger group suffer reaches the same degree of moral seriousness as that suffered by those in the smaller group (in this case, drowning). But it may seem that there are harms such that, although it would not be permissible to save one person from this harm rather than to save someone from drowning, nonetheless an agent would be permitted, perhaps even required, to prevent a very large number of people from suffering it, even if that meant that she would be unable to save a drowning person. As I have said, perhaps blindness and total paralysis are examples of such harms.

This might be questioned. If it is clear that, faced with a choice between saving one person's life and saving another from complete paralysis (where no other factors are relevant), we must choose the former, then is it so clear that we would be required to let one person die in order to save a very large number from being paralyzed? If, as many believe, this is clear, and yet there are other cases, such as that of Jones in the television station, in which aggregative arguments are not appropriate, then it seems that our intuitive moral thinking is best understood in terms of a relation of "relevance" between harms. If one harm, though not as serious as another, is nonetheless serious enough to be morally "relevant" to it, then it is appropriate, in deciding whether to prevent more serious harms at the cost of not being able to prevent a greater number of less serious ones, to take into account the number of harms involved on each side. But if one harm is not only less serious than, but not even "relevant to," some greater one, then we do not need to take the number of people who would suffer these two harms into account in deciding which to prevent, but should always prevent the more serious harm. Thus it might be claimed, for example, that missing half an hour of exciting television is not relevant when we are deciding whether to save a person in front of us who is in extreme pain, but that total paralysis or blindness is relevant to the even more serious harm of loss of life. So it could be wrong to save one person's life when we could instead have prevented a million people from going blind or becoming paralyzed. (Or, at least, it would be permissible to prevent this harm to the greater number of people even though it would not have been permissible to prevent this lesser harm rather than the greater if the numbers involved had been the same.)

Could such a distinction be incorporated into contractualist argument? I am not certain about the answer to this question, but I will consider one possibility, drawing on some points made earlier in this section. I said earlier that a principle permitting us to save one person rather than two might reasonably be rejected, from the point of view of one of the two, on the ground that this principle did not take his or her life into account at all as a reason for choosing one course of action rather than the other. It should, I argued, at least count as a tie-breaker. The same might be said for lesser, but still serious harms, such as blindness or paralysis. It would be reasonable to reject, on this same ground, a principle that permitted one (in absence of any special justification) to save one stranger's life rather than following another course of action that would save a different life and also prevent someone from being blinded or paralyzed for life.

This is still a tie-breaking argument, but it might be extended beyond that, employing the idea of relevance just mentioned. Consider cases in which the choice is between preventing one more serious harm and a greater number of less serious ones. It might be claimed that if the less serious harms are nonetheless morally relevant to the more serious ones this means that a principle requiring (or perhaps even permitting) one always to prevent the more serious harms in such a case could reasonably be rejected from the point of view of someone in the other group on the ground that it did not give proper consideration to his admittedly less serious, but still morally relevant, loss. One might then argue that

such an individual's claim to have his or her harm taken into account can be met only by a principle that is sensitive to the numbers of people involved on each side. I am not certain how such an argument would go, but it does not seem to me to be excluded in advance by the general idea of contractualism.

This rather long discussion of aggregation can be summarized as follows. The most familiar rationale for principles that make the rightness of actions depend on the number of people who will be affected by them appeals to the idea that what morality is most fundamentally concerned with is producing the greatest total benefit. On a contractualist account of right and wrong this rationale is ruled out, because the rightness of actions depends only on the rejectability of principles from various individual standpoints. This emphasis on the claims of individuals is, at least for me, one of the most appealing features of such a view, and it avoids implausible cases of aggregation in what seems, intuitively, to be the right way. But this restriction to the claims of individuals can be construed more broadly or more narrowly, depending on how these "claims" are understood. Even when this notion is construed very narrowly, contractualism can explain (by appeal to the tie-breaking argument) how the number of people affected can make a difference to the rightness or wrongness of an action in certain special cases. It is possible that a less tightly constrained version of contractualism, which gives more structure to the idea of how individuals can demand that their interests be taken into account, might yield aggregative principles that would apply to a wider range of cases, in which the harms on each side were not equally serious. I have not shown that this is the case, but my argument does not exclude it.

NOTES

1. Thomas Nagel discusses this possibility in *Equality and Partiality* (New York: Oxford University Press, 1991).
2. Feminist writers have called attention to important biases of these kinds. See, for example, Catharine MacKinnon, "Sex Equality: On Difference and Domination," in *Toward a Feminist Theory of the State,*

(Cambridge, Mass. Harvard University Press, 1989), pp. 215–34.

3. Derek Parfit, *Equality or Priority?* The Lindley Lecture (Lawrence: University of Kansas, 1991).

4. Francis Kamm considers a similar argument for aggregation in *Morality, Mortality,* 2 vols. (Oxford: Oxford University Press, 1993), ch. 6, esp. pp. 116–17.

5. I should emphasize that the cases in question here are ones that do not involve special ties. As I have said, I think that it would be reasonable to reject principles that required us always to give the same weight to the lives and interests of strangers as to those of our loved ones or, for that matter, our own.

6. . . . Perhaps there are cases (such as protecting a town from being washed away by a flash flood) in which the urgency of the project is so great as to justify risks to workers that would normally not be allowed. But the urgency of these cases is a matter of the greater costs or benefits that are involved for individuals, not simply of the fact that greater numbers are affected.

STUDY QUESTIONS

1. In what ways, if any, does Scanlon's version of contractualism differ from rule utilitarianism?

2. According to Scanlon, who is included in the general agreement to which contractualism refers?

3. Is any test available to determine whether everyone could reasonably reject a particular moral rule?

4. Is morality best understood as a means to our mutual protection?

Can Contract Theory Ground Morality?

Philip Pettit

According to Scanlon's version of contractualism, an action is wrong if it is disallowed by principles for the regulation of behavior that no one could reasonably reject. However, Philip Pettit, Professor of Philosophy at Princeton University, argues that Scanlon's contractualism fails to explain why specific acts are immune to reasonable rejection. Pettit maintains that, unlike consequentialism, contractualism lacks the explanatory resources to provide such a rationale. He concludes, therefore, that contractualism is at best a partial theory.

INTRODUCTION

The contractualist theory of morality that has recently been developed by T. M. Scanlon (1982, 1998), building on the work of John Rawls (1971, 1993), represents a new departure in ethical thought, and an advance on pre-existing ways of thinking. True, it has some structural affinity with the mutual-advantage theory of morality developed by David Gauthier (1986). . . . But it is not clear how deep these go. In any case I shall concentrate on Scanlon's version of contractualism in this chapter.

Although it is original and imaginative, I do not think that contractualism succeeds, at least not in its own terms. More particularly, I do not think that it succeeds in displacing consequentialism as a grounding theory of moral rightness. The goal of displacing consequentialism in that role goes back to Scanlon's (1982) first statement of the doctrine, and it is a centerpiece of the Rawlsian theory of justice on which he builds. I am a consequentialist myself, and it may not be surprising that I take issue with contractualism at

this point (Pettit 1991, 1997). But though I take issue there, I still think that the doctrine is of immense interest and I hope that this will come through in what follows.

This chapter is in three sections. In the first I offer a characterization of contractualism, explaining along the way that under this representation it is proof against two more or less obvious consequentialist objections. In the second section I argue that even when characterized in this manner, however, there remains an attractive and plausible way of taking contractualism that would make it consistent with consequentialism; this would cast it as a theory of the relatively right—the right relative to a practice—rather than the absolutely right. And then in the third section I show that even if this relativized way of taking it is rejected, as Scanlon himself would certainly reject it, there is a second way in which contractualism can in principle be rendered consistent with consequentialism; it may be cast as a partial rather than a complete theory of the absolutely right. Under neither of these ways of taking the doctrine would contractualism ground

Reprinted from Philip Pettit, "Can Contract Theory Ground Morality?" from *Contemporary Debates in Moral Theory,* ed. J. Dreier, Blackwell, 2006. Reprinted by permission of the publisher.

morality—not at least in every relevant sense—but under each it would retain a significant place in moral theory.

THE CHARACTERIZATION OF CONTRACTUALISM

The main points in contractualist doctrine are the following (Pettit 2000):

(1) The central sense of 'right' and 'wrong' derives from what we owe to others, and it is this interpersonal sense that is explicated in contractualism. It contrasts with the intrapersonal sense associated with talk of what I owe to myself and the impersonal sense associated with talk of how to improve the world or society (Scanlon 1998: 6).

(2) 'Wrong' is the primary moral predicate; 'right' is defined simply as 'not wrong'. That an option is right will mean that it is permitted, not that it is mandatory, though of course a right option will be mandatory in the special event that it is the only option permitted—the only option that is not wrong.

(3) An action is wrong in the central, interpersonal sense just in case it is disallowed by principles for the regulation of conduct that no one could reasonably reject as part of an informed, unforced agreement with others (Scanlon 1998: 153, 202); it is wrong, intuitively, just so far as it is unjustifiable from the point of view of others—just so far as it is exposed to reasonable complaint on the part of others (ibid. 229).

(4) This is a contractualist account of wrongness and rightness, because a principle will be compelling under Scanlon's approach, and will serve to justify actions, if and only if no one could reasonably reject it as a general principle of cooperation: if and only if it is, in that sense, contractually irresistible (ibid. 197).

(5) There is no simple algorithm for deciding which principles could not be reasonably rejected. The matter can only be determined by reflection on the sorts of personal reasons—reasons are taken to form a more or less autonomous, cognitively accessible domain (ibid. ch. 1)—to which we would give relevance and weight in thinking about what cooperative life with others requires (ibid. 225, 246).

(6) An action that is wrong and unjustifiable to someone will always be unjustifiable for a reason—because he or she finds it unfair, or unkind, or insensitive, or whatever. But the wrongness is not to be equated with any such lower-order basis of unjustifiability; it is just the higher-order property of being, on whatever basis, unjustifiable (ibid. 5, 155–6).

(7) The wrongness of an action, understood in this way, explains why wrong actions have an aspect under which they are inherently unattractive. We shrink from acting in a way that is unjustifiable in the light of others' claims quite independently of shrinking—as we do also shrink—from doing something that has an unjustifiablity-producing feature: doing something that is unfair or insensitive or whatever (ibid. 11).

(8) This is the primary reason, so it is said, why the contractualist theory of rightness and wrongness is persuasive. As Scanlon puts it: "I myself accept contractualism largely because the account it offers of moral motivation is phenomenologically more accurate than any other I know of" (ibid. 187; cf. 153, 163).

(9) A second reason that allegedly supports such contractualism, however, is that avoiding the unjustifiable in Scanlon's sense necessarily involves "respecting the value of human (rational) life" (ibid. 106). If people avoid the unjustifiable in this sense then they will treat one another in a way that acknowledges their individual capacities for assessing and acting on reasons. By doing right, then, they will also do good: they will give rise to a palpably desirable form of community.

The notion at the centre of this theory is that of unjustifiability to others. The theory identifies the central property of wrongness—the "normative kind" (ibid. 12) that such wrongness constitutes—with the property of being unjustifiable in that sense. Unjustifiability to others means unjustifiability-to-any-other-individual, not unjustifiability-to-others-generally. That is why the doctrine can be said to equate what is wrong with what is open to reasonable complaint on the part of any other. As Scanlon himself says: "The Complaint Model calls attention to a central feature of contractualism that I would not want to give up: its insistence that the justifiability of a moral principle depends only on various *individuals'* reasons for objecting to that principle and alternatives to it" (ibid. 229).

The striking novelty in the contractualist approach, so understood, is that it switches the traditionally recognized priority of rightness and justifiability, or indeed wrongness and unjustifiability (Scanlon 2003: 183–7). Everyone will agree that in some sense of 'justifiable' any right action will be justifiable so far as it is right or because it is right. But contractualists hold that there is an interpersonal sense of justification to others such that the reverse can also be true. An action can be right because it is justifiable to others; it is right because it is allowed under the principles for regulating behaviour that no one could reasonably reject—because it is not exposed to any reasonable complaint on the part of others.

There are two important ambiguities to resolve, however, in the formulation offered of contractualism. It is important to resolve these, because otherwise the approach will seem to be vulnerable to two fairly straightforward consequentialist objections.

First Objection, First Ambiguity

The first objection that may be made to the doctrine is premised on the assumption that the reasons that are supposed to move contractors in rejecting or not rejecting a principle are impersonal values such as justice or kindness or happiness or whatever. The objection is that if contractors find a principle unrejectable—and therefore the actions it disallows wrong—because of such values, then what ultimately makes the principle unrejectable is that it satisfies those values. This means, in a consequentialist version of what satisfaction of values requires, that the principle has its unrejectable status because it maximizes expected neutral value.

Suppose, for example, that contractors were moved only by considerations to do with what was for the maximization of happiness overall; suppose

they were consequentialists of a utilitarian stamp. In that case, so the objection goes, the right would be determined for them by reference to the utilitarian criterion. But if, by their lights, the right just was whatever maximized happiness overall, then why should contractualism suggest that it was determined rather by reference to what they, the utilitarian contractors, found reasonably unrejectable? The utilitarian criterion of right would surely be basic, the contractualist derived.

A number of authors, myself included, took contractualism under earlier formulations to collapse in this manner into an independent—most plausibly, a consequentialist—theory of rightness (Pettit 1993: 302; 1997). But . . . I think that Scanlon's 1998 book *What We Owe To Each Other* makes it clear that his doctrine can avoid that quick collapse.

Scanlon is explicit in that book that the reasons that are to count with people in identifying unrejectable principles are "personal" reasons (1998: 219) or "agent-relative" reasons (Ridge 2001); reasons, in a phrase he takes from Allan Gibbard, that you have "on your own behalf" (Scanlon 2003: 185). As he explicitly says, "impersonal values do not provide, in themselves, reason for rejecting principles of right and wrong" (1998: 222).

Under this construal of contractualism, you or I might reasonably reject a principle for the personal reason that it would serve our interests or projects or friends badly. And while you or I may not reasonably reject a principle for an impersonal reason, we might do so on a personal basis that is tied indirectly to the impersonal reasons that weigh with us. Seeing the principle as offending against a certain strongly held impersonal value—seeing it, say, as licensing cruelty to animals—I might reasonably reject it because of the personal affront or difficulty associated with having to live with the flouting of that value: having to live as if animal pain did not concern me. "If the pain of an animal is something we have strong reason to prevent, then we have good reason to reject a principle that would prevent us from acting on this reason, by requiring us to give animal suffering no more weight than personal inconvenience as a factor affecting our obligations" (Scanlon 1998: 222).

Contractualist principles are selected for not activating any personal reasons for complaint, by this account, not for promoting the expected realization of impersonal values, or any condition of that kind. They will have to pass the hurdle of my reasonable complaint, the hurdle of your reasonable complaint, the hurdle of yet another person's, and so on. But they may do this without having any profile in the space of impersonal values. There need be nothing that characterizes them in our ways of actively representing them over and beyond the fact of that they surmount those personal-level tests. . . .

What makes an action wrong in the sense that Scanlon targets, then, is the fact that it flouts a principle for regulating behavior that no one finds good personal reason to reject—that no one finds a good reason to complain about. What makes it wrong, in other words, is that someone is bound to have a reason to complain about it, given that it flouts such a principle. Being personal in character, the reasonable complaints that show an action to be wrong in this way may be various, being backed here on this basis, there on that. What matters to the action's being wrong—what makes the action wrong (Stratton-Lake 2003)—is not the diverse bases behind the complaints but just the simple fact that the complaints can be reasonably made. Being wrong involves being such as to occasion reasonable complaint from one or another person, on one or another personal basis. Being right involves being immune to that sort of complaint: being justifiable in that sense to others.

Second Objection, Second Ambiguity

In the presentation of contractualism above, it is said that an action is wrong in the central, interpersonal sense just in case it is disallowed by principles for the regulation of conduct that no one could reasonably reject as part of an informed, unforced agreement with others. A very natural way of taking that claim allows of the following explication:

> An action is wrong in a situation R (for Real-world) just in case it is disallowed by principles for the regulation of conduct that no one could reasonably

reject in a situation I (for Ideal-world) of informed, unforced agreement with others about how to behave in I.

This is a natural way of taking contractualism, since many of Scanlon's own formulations suggest something on these lines, and none of them rules it out. He says, for example: "An act is wrong if its performance under the circumstances would be disallowed by any set of principles for the general regulation of behavior that no one could reasonably reject as a basis for informed, unforced general agreement" (1998: 153).

To speak of the principles that no one could reasonably reject as a basis for informed, unforced general agreement is very strongly to suggest that the ideal conditions of informed, unforced agreement are relevant, not just when people are given the chance to reject a principle, but also when they implement them in their own behavior. The suggestion is that the circumstances for which the principles are to be designed, as well as the circumstances in which they are examined and selected, are ones where informed, unforced agreement—for short, cooperation—rules. . . .

If contractualism is taken in this way, then it is construed in a manner that makes it akin to rule-consequentialism and, on some interpretations, Kantianism. Those doctrines hold that we need to identify certain privileged rules or maxims before we can tell whether an action is right or wrong. We identify in the one case the rules such that it would be for the best overall if people were generally to internalize them or act on them or whatever (Hooker 2000); in the other the maxims such that everyone can treat them—treat them simultaneously—as general laws: the maxims satisfied by everyone in the kingdom of ends. We then say that an action is wrong—wrong in the actual, non-ideal world—if it flouts one of those ideal rules, or one of those ideal maxims, right if it does not do so.

But there is a long-standing tradition, at least within consequentialist circles, of criticizing approaches of this kind to the characterization of right and wrong action. The criticism is that while acting on a certain rule or maxim may be for the best in a world of total compliance with those principles—a world like the kingdom of ends—it need not be for the best in a world where not everyone complies: a world of merely partial compliance. It may amount in that world to a waste of effort, or it may be downright counterproductive. Let no one else do anything for the environment, for example, and it is not clear that I achieve anything other than wasted effort by making my lone attempts to be ecologically sound. Let some other people be willing to impose violence on their fellows and my eschewal of violence, admirable though it would be in the kingdom of ends, may be actively counterproductive, ensuring that there is more violence overall, not less. . . .

But while I think that the idealized mode of interpretation is natural in some respects, I am now persuaded that it is not the construal intended by Scanlon. What he has in mind, I think, is better rendered in a formula that exchanges the second reference to situation I for a reference—a second reference—to situation R (Scanlon 1982: 111).

> An action is wrong in a situation R just in case it is disallowed by principles for the regulation of conduct that no one could reasonably reject in a situation I of informed, unforced agreement with others about how to behave in R.

The shift here is very small but it is of great significance (cf. Smith 1994). The real-world situation may vary greatly. At one highly unlikely extreme it may involve circumstances where others display informed, unforced cooperation and comply with the principles suited to ideal circumstances. But it is much more likely to involve some others defecting, whether out of ignorance, weakness, or malice, and of course it is much more likely to be a situation where cooperation is going to require a degree of force or coercion. This being the case, the people in situation I will have to agree, not just about principles that are to rule in situations of ideal cooperation, but also about the principles that are to apply in situations where some or even all others fail to comply fully with ideal principles. . . .

Scanlon intends his contractualist theory of the right to be a theory that is liable to pick out a different action as right, depending on the circumstances prevailing in the real world; or at least he intends it to do this within intuitive limits on how fine-tuned to circumstances principles may be (1998: 205). He does not envisage it as an ideal-world theory according to which the right action in any circumstance is the action that is identified as right in ideal circumstances of cooperation. And so he is not open to the consequentialist objection that where that action might have been for the best in the ideal world, it is likely to occasion very undesirable consequences in real-world situations: in particular, consequences so undesirable as to make the theory counterintuitive.

A COMPLETE OR PARTIAL THEORY OF THE RIGHT?

Let us suppose . . . that we go along with Scanlon and adopt his more radical reading of contractualism as a theory of what is absolutely right—right in the interpersonal sense of the term—not just right according to a practice. Does this mean that there is no room left for the possibility that it is consistent with consequentialism? I argue in this section that it does not. Were contractualism in this sense sound, it would still have to be construed so as to leave open the possibility that there is truth in consequentialism; it would call on a second front for a modest rather than a radical reading. The modest reading would construe it as a partial theory of the right and the wrong, the radical as a complete theory (cf. Pettit 2000).

As we use the terms 'right' and 'wrong' in ordinary language, we load them with a variety of connotations. Plausibly, for example, we expect any option that deserves to be called 'right':

- to be an option that we desire or would desire in the absence of failures of will;
- to be an option that we would be prepared to prescribe for any agent, not just ourselves, in the situation on hand;
- to be an option that has rightness-making properties of a familiar kind, such as fairness or kindness or just being for the best;

- to be an option that virtuous agents might choose;
- and of course to be an option that we could justify to others, being able to answer any objections they might make.

Any philosophical theory as to what rightness is will seek to marshall such connotations (Jackson and Pettit 1995; Pettit 2001b). It must select out the allegedly crucial candidate or candidates and try to show that they on their own capture the essential character of rightness: they explain the "observed normative features," as Scanlon (1998: 12) puts it, of the property. . . . A consequentialist theory will hold that it is the option that best promotes neutral goods or values: say, fairness and kindness and happiness and so on (Pettit 1997). And a 'virtue-ethical' theory might declare that it is the option that would prove eligible for the virtuous agent. Each of these theories orders the ordinary connotations of the word 'right' in different ways: it gives axiomatic status to one or more connotations and—assuming it is not a revisionary doctrine—derives other plausible connotations as theorems.

The theories mentioned are all familiar stories about the nature of rightness and under the interpretation of contractualism as a theory of what is absolutely right, it constitutes a further story in this vein: a rival axiomatization of rightness and, more fundamentally, wrongness. Among the connotations of rightness, it privileges the linkage with justifiability—specifically, with justifiability to others in the sense characterized in the first section—and argues that all we know and need to know is that in the relevant interpersonal sense of the term, rightness is justifiability, justifiability rightness.

The fact that contractualism is a theory of rightness in this sense, however, is quite consistent with its not being a complete theory of rightness and, more specifically, with consequentialism supplying the complementary component required for a full theory. . . .

Take the contractualist test of looking at the options that would survive reasonable complaint on anyone's part: the option that would not be disallowed under any principle for regulating behavior that no one could reasonably reject. Why can't we treat that test . . . as a filter that we may expect to sift out options with a certain independent character: a character that makes them fit to survive reasonable complaint? And why then shouldn't we be open to the thought that as we survey the actions likely to survive reasonable complaint, we may find reason to think that they will have a certain consequentialist character?

The suggestion is not, notice, that there is a quick argument to this conclusion, as there might be under the first objection considered in the opening section. That objection was that the potential complainants we envisage will always base their complaints on considerations of impersonal value and that anything that survives those complaints, therefore, will do so by serving the cause of impersonal value: say, in the consequentialist formula, by maximizing the expected realization of such value. The response to that objection was that people are only allowed to complain about actions and principles on the basis of personal reasons—reasons that they hold on their own behalf.

But consistently with complainants only being allowed to invoke personal reasons in rejecting a principle for the general regulation of behavior, it may still be the case that the principles and actions that are going to be proof against reasonable complaints must have an independent character; that character would explain why precisely they are proof against complaint. And it may still be that the independent character that they have is of a consequentialist cast. In other words, it may be that from contractualism as an upstream theory we may hope to be able to derive a downstream consequentialism.

There is good reason to think that those actions that receive a contractualist blessing must indeed have an independent character, though no ready argument for why that character must be consequentialist. Consider the contrast between the contractualist formula and the majoritarian formula—as it happens, an objectionable one—according to which an action is right if and only if it has majority support among those in the society where it occurs. It is clearly possible for just about any type of action to pass the majoritarian test, given the assumption that there's naught so queer as folk, in the old Yorkshire saying, and that there's no saying in advance where the folk may go. Thus it may be that the only commonality to be found in the various actions that satisfy the majoritarian formula will be that, well, they satisfy the formula. Their each being endorsed by the majority may be the only property that they possess in common. There may be no character that they have, independent of that property.

Might something similar be true of the options that pass the contractualist test? Surely not. What is required of those options is not just that they should happen to escape complaint as a matter of fact, but that they should be proof against complaint, in particular reasonable complaint. But how could they be proof against reasonable complaint without their being complaint-proof in virtue of their inherent nature? After all, there must be something about the options, some independent character, in virtue of which no one can raise a reasonable complaint against them.

Won't that independent character, then, be the ultimate ground or explanation of their being right options to choose? Won't it be a property that unites right options at a more basic level than that at which they display contractual, counterfactual unity: the unity associated with the fact that no one could reasonably object to them? The word 'right' may be used of those option-types because of their contractual unity—it may be, for all we have said, that this is what guides ordinary speakers in the use of the term—but it will still be the case that contractualism is not the whole story about rightness. . . .

Just to illustrate the point, suppose that ordinary people were . . . disposed to treat as reasonable all and only complaints that this or that principle, this or that option-type, would reduce the complainant to a relatively low level of happiness. People would not think of the principles they were reasonably disposed to reject in any common, impersonal terms, as utilitarians might do; they would each make their complaints on a personal, particularistic basis. But still, the principles or options that prove immune to their diverse, personal complaints would prove immune in virtue of an independent character; it is that character that would explain why they and they only enjoy such immunity. Can we say

anything about that character? We certainly can. On the supposition with which we are working, the complaint-proof principles and option-types would have in common the fact of ensuring a certain relative level of happiness for the worst off in the population: a level that would silence complaint even from those in that quarter. Did people in that society not recognize this feature of the options regarded as right amongst them—were they sensitive only to the contractualist truth that obtains in the scenario imagined—then there would be something important that they were missing in their understanding of rightness.

Does this line of reasoning establish definitively, then, that contractualism is at best a partial theory of rightness? Does it demonstrate that contractualism calls or at least allows for supplementation by a theory—perhaps a downstream consequentialism, perhaps a downstream non-consequentialism—that identifies the independent character of rightness? Not quite.

Contractualists might say in response that while there is always going to be an explanation as to why any particular category of option, A, is complaint-proof—it will consist in the character of the A-option in question—there need not be any general explanation as to why options in categories A, B, C . . . are complaint-proof. There may be no independent pattern in the different categories of option, and the associated principles, that pass the contractualist filter. The A option-type may prove complaint-proof because of having an independent a-character, the B-type because of having an independent b-character, and so on. Yet there need be nothing in common to those characters: nothing binding them into a pattern (cf. Jackson et al. 1999).

This response cannot be right, however. Presumably it is by thinking about the possible realization of this or that option-type, independently characterized, that you or I or a third party is put in a position to determine, however fallibly, that no one could reasonably object to it: the type is such that we can envisage no objection that would count as reasonable. But this means that in principle we should be capable of reviewing the various option-types relevant and of fixing on the character shared by those types to which we can imagine no reasonable objection. . . .

What sort of understanding will this independent. . . . characterization of right option-types provide? It will give us an insight into the substantial "suchness" that we are directed to when we are told that an option-type is right if it is *such* that no one could reasonably object to anyone else's enacting it. There may be no substantial suchness shared by all the measures that are such as to attact or to have attracted majority support, given people vote in any old way. But there is bound to be a substantial suchness shared by those option-types that are such that no one could reasonably complain about them. It is going to be that suchness, that inherent character, that explains why they resist *reasonable* complaint. It is going to be that suchness that unites right option-types in themselves, explaining the unity that they have in relation to us: the unity which consists in the fact they resist reasonable complaint. . . .

Assuming that contractualism is intended as an absolute theory of rightness—rightness in the interpersonal sense of the term—and assuming that it serves well in this role, how damaging is the claim that it cannot be a complete theory: that it calls or allows for supplementation by an independent characterization of right option-types? The claim is consistent, as already mentioned, with conceding that what guides ordinary people in the use of the word 'right'. . . . is a sense that the option-types to which it is applied satisfy the contractualist formula, being such as to resist reasonable complaint. And it is consistent with thinking that we do better in reflecting on practical questions of ethical judgment to concentrate mainly on where that formula leads; doing this may be heuristically more valuable than trying to extrapolate from the inherent character of option-types that we do regard as right or wrong. In these ways, then, the partiality of contractualist theory will not matter greatly.

Where it will matter, however, is in consideration of the question raised in the title of this chapter. It will mean that there is a sense in which the fact that an option-type is morally right is grounded, not merely in the subjunctive fact that it would resist reasonable objection, but in the categorical fact that it is of a certain independent type: the type that ensures it would resist reasonable objection. It is because right option-types have that categorical character that they would resist contractual complaint, even if it is the fact that they resist such complaint that prompts us to think of them as right.

There is an important sense, then, in which the normative kind associated with rightness will not, contrary to Scanlon's claims (1998: 12), be fully and properly characterized in contractualist terms. Contract theory identifies a role that right option-types will play. . . . this is the role of proving immune to reasonable complaint. But it tends to ignore the issue, presumably amenable to philosophical, a priori specification, of what sort of property fills or realizes that role. . . . Thus there is a sense in which contractualism does not take us to rock bottom. Under the absolute construal of the doctrine that Scanlon endorses, as under the relativized construal that I myself find attractive, contract theory fails to provide a complete grounding for morality.

REFERENCES

Gauthier, D. (1986). *Morals by Agreement*. Oxford: Oxford University Press.

Hooker, B. (2000). *Ideal Code, Real World*. Oxford: Oxford University Press.

Jackson, F. and Pettit, P. (1995). "Moral functionalism and moral motivation." *Philosophical Quarterly*, 45: 20–40.

Jackson, F., Pettit, P., and Smith, M. (1999). "Ethical particularism and patterns." In B. Hooker and M. Little (eds.), *Moral Particularism*. Oxford: Clarendon Press.

Pettit, P. (1991). "Consequentialism." In P. Singer (ed.), *A Companion to Ethics*. Oxford: Blackwell.

Pettit, P. (1993). *The Common Mind: An Essay on Psychology, Society and Politics*. New York: Oxford University Press.

Pettit, P. (1997). "A consequentialist perspective on ethics." In Pettit, *Three Methods of Ethics: A Debate*. Oxford: Blackwell.

Pettit, P. (2000). "Two construals of Scanlon's contractualism." *Journal of Philosophy*, 97: 148–64.

Pettit, P. (2001). "Embracing objectivity in ethics." In B. Leiter (ed.), *Objectivity in Law and Morals*. Cambridge: Cambridge University Press.

Rawls, J. (1971). *A Theory of Justice*. Oxford: Oxford University Press.

Rawls, J. (1993). *Political Liberalism*. New York: Columbia University Press.

Ridge, M. (2001). "Saving Scanlon: contractualism and agent-relativity." *Journal of Political Philosophy,* 9: 472–81.

Scanlon, T. M. (1982). "Contractualism and utilitarianism." In B. Williams (ed.), *Utilitarianism and Beyond*. Cambridge: Cambridge University Press.

Scanlon, T. M. (1998). *What We Owe To Each Other*. Cambridge, Mass.: Harvard University Press.

Scanlon, T. M. (2003). "Reply to Gauthier and Gibbard." *Philosophy and Phenomenological Research,* 66: 176–89.

Smith, M. (1994). *The Moral Problem*. Oxford: Blackwell.

Stratton-Lake, P. (2003). "Scanlon's contractualism and the redundancy objection." *Analysis,* 63: 70–5.

STUDY QUESTIONS

1. According to Pettit, what are contractualism's main points?
2. What is Pettit's main criticism of Scanlon's contractualism?
3. According to Pettit, why is Scanlon's theory incomplete?
4. If a theory is incomplete, is it wholly unacceptable?

Part X

VIRTUE ETHICS

Nicomachean Ethics

Aristotle

Aristotle (384–322 B.C.E.) made extraordinary contributions in virtually every area of philosophy, and the *Nicomachean Ethics,* named after Aristotle's son Nicomachus, is widely regarded as one of the great books of moral philosophy. Aristotle grounds morality in human nature, viewing the good as the fulfillment of the human potential to live well. To live well is to live in accordance with virtue. But how does one acquire virtue? Aristotle's answer depends on his distinction between moral and intellectual virtue. Moral virtue, which we might call "goodness of character," is formed by habit. One becomes good by doing good. Repeated acts of justice and self-control result in a just, self-controlled person who not only performs just, self-controlled actions but does so from a fixed character. Intellectual virtue, on the other hand, which we might refer to as "wisdom," requires sophisticated intelligence and is acquired by teaching. Virtuous activities are those that avoid the two extremes of excess and deficiency. For example, if you fear too much, you become cowardly; if you fear too little, you become rash. The mean is courage. To achieve the mean, you need to make a special effort to avoid the extremes to which you are prone. Thus if you tend to be foolhardy, aim at timidity, and you will achieve the right measure of boldness.

BOOK I · THE HUMAN GOOD

Subject of Our Inquiry

All human activities aim at some good: some goods subordinate to others

94a 1. Every art and every inquiry, and similarly every action and choice, is thought to aim at some good; and for this reason the good has rightly been declared to be that at which all things aim. But a certain differ-

5 ence is found among ends; some are activities, others

are products apart from the activities that produce them. Where there are ends apart from the actions, it is the nature of the products to be better than the activities. Now, as there are many actions, arts, and sciences, their ends also are many; the end of the 10 medical art is health, that of shipbuilding a vessel, that of strategy victory, that of economics wealth. But where such arts fall under a single capacity—as bridle-making and the other arts concerned with the equipment of horses fall under the art of riding, and 15 this and every military action under strategy, in the

Reprinted from Aristotle, *Aristotle's Nicomachean Ethics,* translated by W. D. Ross, revised by J. L. Ackrill and J. O. Urmson, Oxford University Press, 1925; 1980. Reprinted by permission of the publisher.

same way other arts fall under yet others—in all of these the ends of the master arts are to be preferred to all the subordinate ends; for it is for the sake of
20 the former that the latter are pursued. It makes no difference whether the activities themselves are the ends of the actions, or something else apart from the activities, as in the case of the sciences just mentioned.

The science of the human good is politics

25 2. If, then, there is some end of the things we do, which we desire for its own sake (everything else being desired for the sake of this), and if we do not choose everything for the sake of something else (for at that rate the process would go on to infinity,
30 so that our desire would be empty and vain), clearly this must be the good and the chief good. Will not the knowledge of it, then, have a great influence on life? Shall we not, like archers who have a mark to aim at, be more likely to hit upon what is right? If
35 so, we must try, in outline at least, to determine what it is, and of which of the sciences or capacities it is the object. It would seem to belong to the most authoritative art and that which is most truly the master art. And politics appears to be of this nature;
1094b for it is this that ordains which of the sciences should be studied in a state, and which each class of citizens should learn and up to what point they should learn them; and we see even the most highly
5 esteemed of capacities to fall under this, e.g. strategy, economics, rhetoric; now, since politics uses the rest of the sciences, and since, again, it legislates as to what we are to do and what we are to abstain from, the end of this science must include
10 those of the others, so that this end must be the human good. For even if the end is the same for a single man and for a state, that of the state seems at all events something greater and more complete whether to attain or to preserve; though it is worth
15 while to attain the end merely for one man, it is finer and more godlike to attain it for a nation or for city-states. These, then, are the ends at which our inquiry aims, since it is political science, in one sense of that term.

Nature of the Science

We must not expect more precision than the subject-matter admits of. The student should have reached years of discretion

3. Our discussion will be adequate if it has as much 20 clearness as the subject-matter admits of, for precision is not to be sought for alike in all discussions, any more than in all the products of the crafts. Now noble and just actions, which political science investigates, exhibit much variety and fluctuation, so that 25 they may be thought to exist only by convention, and not by nature. But goods exhibit a similar fluctuation because they bring harm to many people; for before now men have been undone by reason of their wealth, and others by reason of their courage. We 30 must be content, then, in speaking of such subjects and with such premises to indicate the truth roughly and in outline, and in speaking about things which are only for the most part true, and with premises of the same kind, to reach conclusions that are no 35 better. In the same spirit, therefore, should each type of statement be *received*; for it is the mark of an educated man to look for precision in each class of things just so far as the nature of the subject admits; it is evidently equally foolish to accept probable rea- 40 soning from a mathematician and to demand from a rhetorician demonstrative proofs.

Now each man judges well the things he knows, and of these he is a good judge. And so the man who has been educated in a subject is a good judge of that 1095 subject, and the man who has received an all-round education is a good judge in general. Hence a young man is not a proper hearer of lectures on political science; for he is inexperienced in the actions that 5 occur in life, but its discussions start from these and are about these; and, further, since he tends to follow his passions, his study will be vain and unprofitable, because the end aimed at is not knowledge but action. And it makes no difference whether he is 10 young in years or youthful in character; the defect does not depend on time, but on his living, and pursuing each successive object, as passion directs. For to such persons, as to the incontinent, knowledge

15 brings no profit; but to those who desire and act in accordance with reason, knowledge about such matters will be of great benefit.

These remarks about the student, the sort of treatment to be expected, and the purpose of the in
20 quiry, may be taken as our preface.

What is the Human Good?

It is generally agreed to be happiness, but there are various views as to what happiness is. What is required at the start is an unreasoned conviction about the facts, such as is produced by a good upbringing

4. Let us resume our inquiry and state, in view of the fact that all knowledge and every pursuit aims at some good, what it is that we say political science aims at and what is the highest of all goods achiev-
25 able by action. Verbally there is very general agreement; for both the general run of men and people of superior refinement say that it is happiness, and identify living well and faring well with being happy; but with regard to what happiness is they
30 differ, and the many do not give the same account as the wise. For the former think it is some plain and obvious thing, like pleasure, wealth, or honour; they differ, however, from one another—and often even the same man identifies it with different things, with
35 health when he is ill, with wealth when he is poor; but, conscious of their ignorance, they admire those who proclaim some great thing that is above their comprehension. Now some thought that apart from these many goods there is another which is good in
40 itself and causes the goodness of all these as well. To examine all the opinions that have been held were perhaps somewhat fruitless; enough to examine those that are most prevalent or that seem to be arguable.
45 Let us not fail to notice, however, that there is a difference between arguments from and those to the first principles. For Plato, too, was right in raising this question and asking, as he used to do, 'Are we
95b on the way from or to the first principles?' There is a difference, as there is in a racecourse between the

course from the judges to the turning-point and the way back. For, while we must begin with what is evident, things are evident in two ways—some to 5 us, some without qualification. Presumably, then, *we* must begin with things evident to *us*. Hence anyone who is to listen intelligently to lectures about what is noble and just and, generally, about the subjects of political science must have been brought up in good 10 habits. For the fact is a starting-point, and if this is sufficiently plain to him, he will not need the reason as well; and the man who has been well brought up has or can easily get starting-points. And as for him who neither has nor can get them, let him hear the 15 words of Hesiod:

Far best is he who knows all things himself;
Good, he that hearkens when men counsel right;
But he who neither knows, nor lays to heart
Another's wisdom, is a useless wight.   20

Discussion of the popular views that the good is pleasure, honour, wealth; a fourth kind of life, that of contemplation, deferred for future discussion

5. Let us, however, resume our discussion from the point at which we digressed. To judge from the lives that men lead, most men, and men of the most vulgar type, seem (not without some ground) to identify the good, or happiness, with pleasure; which is the 25 reason why they love the life of enjoyment. For there are, we may say, three prominent types of life—that just mentioned, the political, and thirdly the contemplative life. Now the mass of mankind are evidently quite slavish in their tastes, preferring a life suitable 30 to beasts, but they get some ground for their view from the fact that many of those in high places share the tastes of Sardanapallus. A consideration of the prominent types of life shows that people of superior refinement and of active disposition identify happi- 35 ness with honour; for this is, roughly speaking, the end of the political life. But it seems too superficial to be what we are looking for, since it is thought to depend on those who bestow honour rather than on him who receives it, but the good we divine to be 40

something of one's own and not easily taken from one. Further, men seem to pursue honour in order that they may be assured of their merit; at least it is by men of practical wisdom that they seek to be hon-
45 oured, and among those who know them, and on the ground of their virtue; clearly, then, according to them, at any rate, virtue is better. And perhaps one might even suppose this to be, rather than honour,the end of the political life. But even this appears some-
50 what incomplete; for possession of virtue seems actually compatible with being asleep, or with lifelong inactivity, and, further, with the greatest sufferings
1096a and misfortunes; but a man who was living so no one would call happy, unless he were maintaining a thesis at all costs. But enough of this; for the subject has been sufficiently treated even in the popular dis-
5 cussions. Third comes the contemplative life, which we shall consider later.

The life of money-making is one undertaken under compulsion, and wealth is evidently not the good we are seeking; for it is merely useful and for
10 the sake of something else. And so one might rather take the aforenamed objects to be ends; for they are loved for themselves. But it is evident that not even these are the end; yet many arguments have been wasted on the support of them. Let us leave this sub-
15 ject, then. . . .

The good must be something final and self-sufficient. Definition of happiness reached by considering the characteristic function of man

7. Let us again return to the good we are seeking, and ask what it can be. It seems different in different actions and arts; it is different in medicine, in strategy, and in the other arts likewise. What then is the
20 good of each? Surely that for whose sake everything else is done. In medicine this is health, in strategy victory, in architecture a house, in any other sphere something else, and in every action and pursuit the end; for it is for the sake of this that all men do whatever else they do. Therefore, if there is an end for all
25 that we do, this will be the good achievable by action, and if there are more than one, these will be the goods achievable by action.

So the argument has by a different course reached the same point; but we must try to state this
30 reached the same point; but we must try to state this

even more clearly. Since there are evidently more than one end, and we choose some of these (e.g. wealth, flutes, and in general instruments) for the sake of something else, clearly not all ends are final ends; but the chief good is evidently something final. 35
Therefore, if there is only one final end, this will be what we are seeking, and if there are more than one, the most final of these will be what we are seeking. Now we call that which is in itself worthy of pursuit more final than that which is worthy of pursuit for 40 the sake of something else, and that which is never desirable for the sake of something else more final than the things that are desirable both in themselves and for the sake of that other thing, and therefore we call final without qualification that which is always 45 desirable in itself and never for the sake of something else.

Now such a thing happiness, above all else, is 1097 held to be; for this we choose always for itself and never for the sake of something else, but honour, pleasure, reason, and every virtue we choose indeed for themselves (for if nothing resulted from them we 5 should still choose each of them), but we choose them also for the sake of happiness, judging that through them we shall be happy. Happiness, on the other hand, no one chooses for the sake of these, nor, in general, for anything other than itself. 10

From the point of view of self-sufficiency the same result seems to follow; for the final good is thought to be self-sufficient. Now by self-sufficient we do not mean that which is sufficient for a man by himself, for one who lives a solitary life, but also for 15 parents, children, wife, and in general for his friends and fellow citizens, since man is born for citizenship. But some limit must be set to this; for if we extend our requirement to ancestors and descendants and friends' friends we are in for an infinite 20 series. Let us examine this question, however, on another occasion; the self-sufficient we now define as that which when isolated makes life desirable and lacking in nothing; and such we think happiness to be; and further we think it most desirable of all 25 things, not a thing counted as one good thing among others—if it were so counted it would clearly be made more desirable by the addition of even the least of goods; for that which is added becomes an

30   excess of goods, and of goods the greater is always more desirable. Happiness, then, is something final and self-sufficient, and is the end of action.

Presumably, however, to say that happiness is the chief good seems a platitude, and a clearer ac-
35   count of what it is is still desired. This might perhaps be given, if we could first ascertain the function of man. For just as for a flute-player, a sculptor, or any artist, and, in general, for all things that have a func-tion or activity, the good and the 'well' is thought to
40   reside in the function, so would it seem to be for man, if he has a function. Have the carpenter, then, and the tanner certain functions or activities, and has man none? Is he born without a function? Or as eye, hand, foot, and in general each of the parts evi-
45   dently has a function, may one lay it down that man similarly has a function apart from all these? What then can this be? Life seems to belong even to plants, but we are seeking what is peculiar to man. Let us exclude, therefore, the life of nutrition and growth.
50   Next there would be a life of perception, but *it* also
98a   seems to be shared even by the horse, the ox, and every animal. There remains, then, an active life of the element that has reason; of this, one part has it in the sense of being obedient to reason, the other in
5   the sense of possessing reason and exercising thought. And, as 'life of the rational element' also has two meanings, we must state that life in the sense of activity is what we mean; for this seems to be the more proper sense of the term. Now if the
10   function of man is an activity of soul which follows or implies reason, and if we say 'a so-and-so' and 'a good so-and-so' have a function which is the same in kind, e.g. a lyre-player and a good lyre-player, and so without qualification in all cases, eminence in
15   respect of goodness being added to the name of the function (for the function of a lyre-player is to play the lyre, and that of a good lyre-player is to do so well): if this is the case [and we state the function of man to be a certain kind of life, and this to be an
20   activity or actions of the soul implying a rational principle, and the function of a good man to be the good and noble performance of these, and if any action is well performed when it is performed in ac-cordance with the appropriate virtue: if this is the
25   case], human good turns out to be activity of soul

exhibiting virtue, and if there are more than one virtue, in accordance with the best and most complete.

But we must add 'in a complete life'. For one swallow does not make a summer, nor does one day;   30
and so too one day, or a short time, does not make a man blessed and happy.

Let this serve as an outline of the good; for we must presumably first sketch it roughly, and then later fill in the details. But it would seem that any   35
one is capable of carrying on and articulating what has once been well outlined, and that time is a good discoverer or partner in such a work; to which facts the advances of the arts are due; for any one can add what is lacking. And we must also remember what   40
has been said before, and not look for precision in all things alike, but in each class of things such preci-sion as accords with the subject-matter, and so much as is appropriate to the inquiry. For a carpenter and a geometer investigate the right angle in different   45
ways; the former does so in so far as the right angle is useful for his work, while the latter inquires what it is or what sort of thing it is; for he is a spectator of the truth. We must act in the same way, then, in all other matters as well, that our main task may not be   50
subordinated to minor questions. Nor must we demand the cause in all matters alike; it is enough in   1098b
some cases that the *fact* be well established, as in the case of the first principles; the fact is a primary thing and first principle. Now of first principles we see some by induction, some by perception, some by a   5
certain habituation, and others too in other ways. But each set of principles we must try to investigate in the natural way, and we must take pains to deter-mine them correctly, since they have a great influ-ence on what follows. For the beginning is thought   10
to be more than half of the whole, and many of the questions we ask are cleared up by it.

Our definition is confirmed by current beliefs about happiness

8. But we must consider happiness in the light not only of our conclusion and our premises, but also of what is commonly said about it; for with a true view   15
all the data harmonize, but with a false one the facts soon clash. Now goods have been divided into three

classes, and some are described as external, others as relating to soul or to body; we call those that relate to soul most properly and truly goods, and psychical actions and activities we class as relating to soul. Therefore our account must be sound, at least according to this view, which is an old one and agreed on by philosophers. It is correct also in that we identify the end with certain actions and activities; for thus it falls among goods of the soul and not among external goods. Another belief which harmonizes with our account is that the happy man lives well and fares well; for we have practically defined happiness as a sort of living and faring well. The characteristics that are looked for in happiness seem also, all of them, to belong to what we have defined happiness as being. For some identify happiness with virtue, some with practical wisdom, others with a kind of philosophic wisdom, others with these, or one of these, accompanied by pleasure or not without pleasure; while others include also external prosperity. Now some of these views have been held by many men and men of old, others by a few eminent persons; and it is not probable that either of these should be entirely mistaken, but rather that they should be right in at least some one respect, or even in most respects.

With those who identify happiness with virtue or some one virtue our account is in harmony; for to virtue belongs virtuous activity. But it makes, perhaps, no small difference whether we place the chief good in possession or in use, in state of mind or in activity. For the state of mind may exist without producing any good result, as in a man who is asleep or in some other way quite inactive, but the activity cannot; for one who has the activity will of necessity be acting, and acting well. And as in the Olympic Games it is not the most beautiful and the strongest that are crowned but those who compete (for it is some of these that are victorious), so those who act win, and rightly win, the noble and good things in life.

Their life is also in itself pleasant. For pleasure is a state of *soul,* and to each man that which he is said to be a lover of is pleasant; e.g. not only is a horse pleasant to the lover of horses, and a spectacle to the lover of sights, but also in the same way just acts are pleasant to the lover of justice and in general virtuous acts to the lover of virtue. Now for most men their pleasures are in conflict with one another because these are not by nature pleasant, but the lovers of what is noble find pleasant the things that are by nature pleasant; and virtuous actions are such, so that these are pleasant for such men as well as in their own nature. Their life, therefore, has no further need of pleasure as a sort of adventitious charm, but has its pleasure in itself. For, besides what we have said, the man who does not rejoice in noble actions is not even good; since no one would call a man just who did not enjoy acting justly, nor any man liberal who did not enjoy liberal actions; and similarly in all other cases. If this is so, virtuous actions must be in themselves pleasant. But they are also *good* and *noble,* and have each of these attributes in the highest degree, since the good man judges well about these attributes; his judgement is such as we have described. Happiness then is the best, noblest, and most pleasant thing in the world, and these attributes are not severed as in the inscription at Delos—

> Most noble is that which is justest, and best is
> health; But most pleasant it is to win what we
> love.

For all these properties belong to the best activities; and these, or one—the best—of these, we identify with happiness.

Yet evidently, as we said, it needs the external goods as well; for it is impossible, or not easy, to do noble acts without the proper equipment. In many actions we use friends and riches and political power as instruments; and there are some things the lack of which takes the lustre from happiness—good birth, goodly children, beauty; for the man who is very ugly in appearance or ill-born or solitary and childless is not very likely to be happy, and perhaps a man would be still less likely if he had thoroughly bad children or friends or had lost good children or friends by death. As we said, then, happiness seems to need this sort of prosperity in addition; for which reason some identify happiness with good fortune, though others identify it with virtue.

BOOK II · MORAL VIRTUE

Moral Virtue, How It Is Acquired

Moral virtue, like the arts, is acquired by repetition of the corresponding acts

1. Virtue, then, being of two kinds, intellectual and moral, intellectual virtue in the main owes both its birth and its growth to teaching (for which reason it requires experience and time), while moral virtue comes about as a result of habit, whence also its name (*ēthikē*) is one that is formed by a slight variation from the word *ethos* (habit). From this it is also plain that none of the moral virtues arises in us by nature; for nothing that exists by nature can form a habit contrary to its nature. For instance the stone which by nature moves downwards cannot be habituated to move upwards, not even if one tries to train it by throwing it up ten thousand times; nor can fire be habituated to move downwards, nor can anything else that by nature behaves in one way be trained to behave in another. Neither by nature, then, nor contrary to nature do the virtues arise in us; rather we are adapted by nature to receive them, and are made perfect by habit.

Again, of all the things that come to us by nature we first acquire the potentiality and later exhibit the activity (this is plain in the case of the senses; for it was not by often seeing or often hearing that we got these senses, but on the contrary we had them before we used them, and did not come to have them by using them); but the virtues we get by first exercising them, as also happens in the case of the arts as well. For the things we have to learn before we can do them, we learn by doing them, e.g. men become builders by building and lyre-players by playing the lyre; so too we become just by doing just acts, temperate by doing temperate acts, brave by doing brave acts.

This is confirmed by what happens in states; for legislators make the citizens good by forming habits in them, and this is the wish of every legislator, and those who do not effect it miss their mark, and it is in this that a good constitution differs from a bad one.

Again, it is from the same causes and by the same means that every virtue is both produced and destroyed, and similarly every art; for it is from playing the lyre that both good and bad lyre-players are produced. And the corresponding statement is true of builders and of all the rest; men will be good or bad builders as a result of building well or badly. For if this were not so, there would have been no need of a teacher, but all men would have been born good or bad at their craft. This, then, is the case with the virtues also; by doing the acts that we do in our transactions with other men we become just or unjust, and by doing the acts that we do in the presence of danger, and by being habituated to feel fear or confidence, we become brave or cowardly. The same is true of appetites and feelings of anger; some men become temperate and good-tempered, others self-indulgent and irascible, by behaving in one way or the other in the appropriate circumstances. Thus, in one word, states of character arise out of like activities. This is why the activities we exhibit must be of a certain kind; it is because the states of character correspond to the differences between these. It makes no small difference, then, whether we form habits of one kind or of another from our very youth; it makes a very great difference, or rather *all* the difference.

These acts cannot be prescribed exactly, but must avoid excess and defect

2. Since, then, the present inquiry does not aim at theoretical knowledge like the others (for we are inquiring not in order to know what virtue is, but in order to become good, since otherwise our inquiry would have been of no use), we must examine the nature of actions, namely how we ought to do them; for these determine also the nature of the states of character that are produced, as we have said. Now, that we must act in accordance with correct reason is a common principle and must be assumed—it will be discussed later, i.e. both what correct reason is, and how it is related to the other virtues. But this must be agreed upon beforehand, that the whole account of matters of conduct must be given in outline and not precisely, as we said at the very beginning that the accounts we demand must be in accordance with the subject-matter; matters concerned with conduct and questions of what is good for us have no

fixity, any more than matters of health. The general account being of this nature, the account of particular cases is yet more lacking in exactness; for they do not fall under any art or precept, but the agents themselves must in each case consider what is appropriate to the occasion, as happens also in the art of medicine or of navigation.

But though our present account is of this nature we must give what help we can. First, then, let us consider this, that it is the nature of such things to be destroyed by defect and excess, as we see in the case of strength and of health (for to gain light on things imperceptible we must use the evidence of sensible things); exercise either excessive or defective destroys the strength, and similarly drink or food which is above or below a certain amount destroys the health, while that which is proportionate both produces and increases and preserves it. So too is it, then, in the case of temperance and courage and the other virtues. For the man who flies from and fears everything and does not stand his ground against anything becomes a coward, and the man who fears nothing at all but goes to meet every danger becomes rash; and similarly the man who indulges in every pleasure and abstains from none becomes self-indulgent, while the man who shuns every pleasure, as boors do, becomes in a way insensible; temperance and courage, then, are destroyed by excess and defect, and preserved by the mean.

But not only are the sources and causes of their origination and growth the same as those of their destruction, but also the sphere of their actualization will be the same; for this is also true of the things which are more evident to sense, e.g. of strength; it is produced by taking much food and undergoing much exertion, and it is the strong man that will be most able to do these things. So too is it with the virtues; by abstaining from pleasures we become temperate, and it is when we have become so that we are most able to abstain from them; and similarly too in the case of courage; for by being habituated to despise things that are fearful and to stand our ground against them we become brave, and it is when we have become so that we shall be most able to stand our ground against them.

Pleasure in doing virtuous acts is a sign that the virtuous disposition has been acquired: a variety of considerations show the essential connection of moral virtue with pleasure and pain

3. We must take as a sign of states of character the pleasure or pain that supervenes upon acts; for the man who abstains from bodily pleasures and delights in this very fact is temperate, while the man who is annoyed at it is self-indulgent, and he who stands his ground against things that are terrible and delights in this or at least is not pained is brave, while the man who is pained is a coward. For moral virtue is concerned with pleasures and pains; it is on account of the pleasure that we do bad things, and on account of the pain that we abstain from noble ones. Hence we ought to have been brought up in a particular way from our very youth, as Plato says, so as both to delight in and to be pained by the things that we ought; this is the right education.

Again, if the virtues are concerned with actions and passions, and every passion and every action is accompanied by pleasure and pain, for this reason also virtue will be concerned with pleasures and pains. This is indicated also by the fact that punishment is inflicted by these means; for it is a kind of cure, and it is the nature of cures to be effected by contraries.

Again, as we said but lately, every state of soul has a nature relative to and concerned with the kind of things by which it tends to be made worse or better; but it is by reason of pleasures and pains that men become bad, by pursuing and avoiding these—either the pleasures and pains they ought not or when they ought not or as they ought not, or by going wrong in one of the other similar ways that may be distinguished. Hence men even define the virtues as certain states of impassivity and tranquility; not well, however, because they speak absolutely, and do not say 'as one ought' and 'as one ought not' and 'when one ought or ought not', and the other things that may be added. We assume, then, that this kind of virtue tends to do what is best with regard to pleasures and pains, and vice does the contrary.

The following facts also may show us that virtue and vice are concerned with these same things.

There being three objects of choice and three of avoidance, the noble, the advantageous, the pleasant, and their contraries, the base, the injurious, the pain-
50 ful, about all of these the good man tends to go right and the bad man to go wrong, and especially about pleasure; for this is common to the animals, and also it accompanies all objects of choice; for even the
05a noble and the advantageous appear pleasant.

Again, it has grown up with us all from our in-fancy; this is why it is difficult to rub off this passion, engrained as it is in our life. And we measure even our
5   actions, some of us more and others less, by the rule of pleasure and pain. For this reason, then, our whole in-quiry must be about these; for to feel delight and pain rightly or wrongly has no small effect on our actions.

Again, it is harder to fight against pleasure than
10 anger, to use Heraclitus' phrase, but both art and virtue are always concerned with what is harder; for even the good is better when it is harder. Therefore for this reason also the whole concern both of virtue and of political science is with pleasures and pains;
15 for the man who uses these well will be good, he who uses them badly bad.

That virtue, then, is concerned with pleasures and pains, and that by the acts from which it arises it is both increased and, if they are done differently,
20 destroyed, and that the acts from which it arose are those in which it actualizes itself—let this be taken as said.

An objection to the view that one acquires virtues by doing virtuous acts; and a reply: the conditions needed to possess virtue and act from it

4. The question might be asked, what we mean by saying that we must become just by doing just acts,
25 and temperate by doing temperate acts; for if men do just and temperate acts, they are already just and temperate, exactly as, if they do what is grammatical or musical, they are grammarians and musicians.

Or is this not true even of the arts? It is possible
30 to do something grammatical, either by chance or under the guidance of another. A man will be a grammarian, then, only when he has both done something grammatical and done it grammatically;

and this means doing it in accordance with the
35 grammatical knowledge in himself.

Again, the case of the arts and that of the virtues are not similar; for the products of the arts have their goodness in themselves, so that it is enough that they should have a certain character, but if the acts that
40 are in accordance with the virtues have themselves a certain character it does not follow that they are done justly or temperately. The agent also must be in a cer-tain condition when he does them; in the first place he must have knowledge, secondly he must choose
45 the acts, and choose them for their own sakes, and thirdly his action must proceed from a firm and un-changeable character. These are not reckoned in as
1105b conditions of the possession of the arts, except the bare knowledge; but as a condition of the possession of the virtues knowledge has little or no weight, while the other conditions count not for a little but for
5   everything, i.e. the very conditions which result from often doing just and temperate acts.

Actions, then, are called just and temperate when they are such as the just or the temperate man would do, but it is not the man who does these that is
10 just and temperate, but the man who also does them *as* just and temperate men do them. It is well said, then, that it is by doing just acts that the just man is produced, and by doing temperate acts the temper-ate man; without doing these no one would have
15 even a prospect of becoming good.

But most people do not do these, but take refuge in theory and think they are being philosophers and will become good in this way, behaving somewhat like patients who listen attentively to their doctors,
20 but do none of the things they are ordered to do. As the latter will not be made well in body by such a course of treatment, the former will not be made well in soul by such a course of philosophy.

Definition of Moral Virtue

The genus of moral virtue: it is a state of character, not a passion, nor a capacity

5. Next we must consider what virtue is. Since things that are found in the soul are of three kinds—pas-
25 sions, capacities, states of character—virtue must be

one of these. By passions I mean appetite, anger, fear, confidence, envy, joy, friendly feeling, hatred, longing, emulation, pity, and in general the feelings

30   that are accompanied by pleasure or pain; by capacities the things in virtue of which we are said to be capable of feeling these, e.g. of becoming angry or being pained or feeling pity; by states of character the things in virtue of which we stand well or badly

35   with reference to the passions, e.g. with reference to anger we stand badly if we feel it violently or too weakly, and well if we feel it in an intermediate way; and similarly with reference to the other passions.

Now neither the virtues nor the vices are *pas-*

40   *sions,* because we are not called good or bad on the ground of our passions, but are so called on the ground of our virtues and our vices, and because we are neither praised nor blamed for our passions (for the man who feels fear or anger is not praised, nor is

45   the man who simply feels anger blamed, but the man
1106a   who feels it in a certain way), but for our virtues and our vices we *are* praised or blamed.

Again, we feel anger and fear without choice, but the virtues are modes of choice or involve choice.

5   Further, in respect of the passions we are said to be moved, but in respect of the virtues and the vices we are said not to be moved but to be disposed in a particular way.

For these reasons also they are not *capacities*;

10   for we are neither called good or bad, nor praised or blamed, for the simple capacity of feeling the passions; again, we have the capacities by nature, but we are not made good or bad by nature; we have spoken of this before.

15   If, then, the virtues are neither passions nor capacities, all that remains is that they should be *states of character.*

Thus we have stated what virtue is in respect of its genus.

The differentia of moral virtue: it is a disposition to choose the 'intermediate'. Two kinds of intermediate distinguished

20   6. We must, however, not only describe virtue as a state of character, but also say what sort of state it is. We may remark, then, that every virtue or excellence both brings into good condition the thing of

which it is the excellence and makes the work of that thing be done well; e.g. the excellence of the eye   25
makes both the eye and its work good; for it is by the excellence of the eye that we see well. Similarly the excellence of the horse makes a horse both good in itself and good at running and at carrying its rider and at awaiting the attack of the enemy. Therefore, if   30
this is true in every case, the virtue of man also will be the state of character which makes a man good and which makes him do his own work well.

How this is to happen we have stated already, but it will be made plain also by the following con-   35
sideration of the specific nature of virtue. In everything that is continuous and divisible it is possible to take more, less, or an equal amount, and that either in terms of the thing itself or relatively to us; and the equal is an intermediate between excess and defect.   40
By the intermediate in the object I mean that which is equidistant from each of the extremes, which is one and the same for all; by the intermediate relatively to us that which is neither too much nor too little—and this is not one, nor the same for all. For   45
instance, if ten is many and two is few, six is the intermediate, taken in terms of the object; for it exceeds and is exceeded by an equal amount; this is intermediate according to arithmetical proportion. But the intermediate relatively to us is not to be   50
taken so; if ten pounds is too much for a particular person to eat and two too little, it does not follow   110
that the trainer will order six pounds; for this also is perhaps too much for the person who is to take it, or too little—too little for Milo, too much for the beginner in athletic exercises. The same is true of run-   5
ning and wrestling. Thus a master of any art avoids excess and defect, but seeks the intermediate and chooses this—the intermediate not in the object but relatively to us.

If it is thus, then, that every art does its work   10
well—by looking to the intermediate and judging its works by this standard (so that we often say of good works of art that it is not possible either to take away or to add anything, implying that excess and defect destroy the goodness of works of art, while the mean   15
preserves it; and good artists, as we say, look to this in their work), and if, further, virtue is more exact and better than any art, as nature also is, then virtue

must have the quality of aiming at the intermediate. I
mean moral virtue; for it is this that is concerned
with passions and actions, and in these there is
excess, defect, and the intermediate. For instance,
both fear and confidence and appetite and anger and
pity and in general pleasure and pain may be felt both
too much and too little, and in both cases not well;
but to feel them at the right times, with reference to
the right objects, towards the right people, with the
right motive, and in the right way, is what is both intermediate and best, and this is characteristic of
virtue. Similarly with regard to actions also there is
excess, defect, and the intermediate. Now virtue is
concerned with passions and actions, in which excess
is a form of failure, and so is defect, while the intermediate is praised and is a form of success; and being
praised and being successful are both characteristics
of virtue. Therefore virtue is a kind of mean, since,
as we have seen, it aims at what is intermediate.

Again, it is possible to fail in many ways (for
evil belongs to the class of the unlimited, as the Py-
thagoreans conjectured, and good to that of the limited), while to succeed is possible only in one way
(for which reason also one is easy and the other difficult—to miss the mark easy, to hit it difficult); for
these reasons also, then, excess and defect are char
acteristic of vice, and the mean of virtue;

For men are good in but one way, but bad in
many.

Virtue, then, is a state of character concerned
with choice, lying in a mean, i.e. the mean relative to
us, this being determined by reason, and by that
reason by which the man of practical wisdom would
determine it. Now it is a mean between two vices,
that which depends on excess and that which depends on defect; and again it is a mean because the
vices respectively fall short of or exceed what is
right in both passions and actions, while virtue both
finds and chooses that which is intermediate. Hence
in respect of what it is, i.e. the definition which states
its essence, virtue is a mean, with regard to what is
best and right an extreme.

But not every action nor every passion admits of
a mean; for some have names that already imply

badness, e.g. spite, shamelessness, envy, and in the
case of actions adultery, theft, murder; for all of
these and suchlike things imply by their names that
they are themselves bad, and not the excesses or deficiencies of them. It is not possible, then, ever to be
right with regard to them; one must always be wrong.
Nor does goodness or badness with regard to such
things depend on committing adultery with the right
woman, at the right time, and in the right way, but
simply to do any of them is to go wrong. It would be
equally absurd, then, to expect that in unjust, cowardly, and self-indulgent action there should be a
mean, an excess, and a deficiency; for at that rate
there would be a mean of excess and of deficiency,
an excess of excess, and a deficiency of deficiency.
But as there is no excess and deficiency of temperance and courage because what is intermediate is in
a sense an extreme, so too of the actions we have
mentioned there is no mean nor any excess and deficiency, but however they are done they are wrong;
for in general there is neither a mean of excess and
deficiency, nor excess and deficiency of a mean.

The above proposition illustrated by reference to particular virtues

7. We must, however, not only make this general
statement, but also apply it to the individual facts.
For among statements about conduct those which are
general apply more widely, but those which are particular are more true, since conduct has to do with
individual cases, and our statements must harmonize
with the facts in these cases. We may take these cases
from our table. With regard to feelings of fear and
confidence courage is the mean; of the people who
exceed, he who exceeds in fearlessness has no name
(many of the states have no name), while the man
who exceeds in confidence is rash, and he who exceeds in fear and falls short in confidence is a coward.
With regard to pleasures and pains—not all of them,
and not so much with regard to the pains—the mean
is temperance, the excess self-indulgence. Persons
deficient with regard to the pleasures are not often
found; hence such persons also have received no
name. But let us call them 'insensible'.

With regard to giving and taking of money
the mean is liberality, the excess and the defect

prodigality and meanness. In these actions people exceed and fall short in contrary ways; the prodigal exceeds in spending and falls short in taking, while the mean man exceeds in taking and falls short in spending. . . . With regard to money there are also other dispositions—a mean, magnificence (for the magnificent man differs from the liberal man; the former deals with large sums, the latter with small ones), an excess, tastelessness and vulgarity, and a deficiency, niggardliness; these differ from the states opposed to liberality. . . .

With regard to honour and dishonour the mean is proper pride, the excess is known as a sort of 'empty vanity', and the deficiency is undue humility; and as we said liberality was related to magnificence, differing from it by dealing with small sums, so there is a state similarly related to proper pride, being concerned with small honours while that is concerned with great. For it is possible to desire honour as one ought, and more than one ought, and less, and the man who exceeds in his desires is called ambitious, the man who falls short unambitious, while the intermediate person has no name. The dispositions also are nameless, except that that of the ambitious man is called ambition. Hence the people who are at the extremes lay claim to the middle place; and we ourselves sometimes call the intermediate person ambitious and sometimes unambitious, and sometimes praise the ambitious man and sometimes the unambitious. The reason of our doing this will be stated in what follows; but now let us speak of the remaining states according to the method which has been indicated.

With regard to anger also there is an excess, a deficiency, and a mean. Although they can scarcely be said to have names, yet since we call the intermediate person good-tempered let us call the mean good temper; of the persons at the extremes let the one who exceeds be called irascible, and his vice irascibility, and the man who falls short an unirascible sort of person, and the deficiency unirascibility.

There are also three other means, which have a certain likeness to one another, but differ from one another: for they are all concerned with intercourse in words and actions, but differ in that one is concerned with truth in this sphere, the other two with pleasantness; and of this one kind is exhibited in giving amusement, the other in all the circumstances of life. We must therefore speak of these too, that we may the better see that in all things the mean is praiseworthy, and the extremes neither praiseworthy nor right, but worthy of blame. Now most of these states also have no names, but we must try, as in the other cases, to invent names ourselves so that we may be clear and easy to follow. With regard to truth, then, the intermediate is a truthful sort of person and the mean may be called truthfulness, while the pretence which exaggerates is boastfulness and the person characterized by it a boaster, and that which understates is mock modesty and the person characterized by it mock-modest. With regard to pleasantness in the giving of amusement the intermediate person is ready-witted and the disposition ready wit, the excess is buffoonery and the person characterized by it a buffoon, while the man who falls short is a sort of boor and his state is boorishness. With regard to the remaining kind of pleasantness, that which is exhibited in life in general, the man who is pleasant in the right way is friendly and the mean is friendliness, while the man who exceeds is an obsequious person if he has no end in view, a flatterer if he is aiming at his own advantage, and the man who falls short and is unpleasant in all circumstances is a quarrelsome and surly sort of person.

There are also means in the passions and concerned with the passions; since shame is not a virtue, and yet praise is extended to the modest man. For even in these matters one man is said to be intermediate, and another to exceed, as for instance the bashful man who is ashamed of everything; while he who falls short or is not ashamed of anything at all is shameless, and the intermediate person is modest. Righteous indignation is a mean between envy and spite, and these states are concerned with the pain and pleasure that are felt at the fortunes of our neighbours; the man who is characterized by righteous indignation is pained at undeserved good fortune, the envious man, going beyond him, is pained at all good fortune, and the spiteful man falls so far short of being pained that he even rejoices. . . .

Characteristics of the Extreme and Mean States: Practical Corollaries

The extremes are opposed to each other and to the mean

8. There are three kinds of disposition, then, two of them vices, involving excess and deficiency respectively, and one a virtue, namely, the mean, and all are in a sense opposed to all; for the extreme states are contrary both to the intermediate state and to each other, and the intermediate to the extremes; as the equal is greater relatively to the less, less relatively to the greater, so the middle states are excessive relatively to the deficiencies, deficient relatively to the excesses, both in passions and in actions. For the brave man appears rash relatively to the coward, and cowardly relatively to the rash man; and similarly the temperate man appears self-indulgent relatively to the insensible man, insensible relatively to the self-indulgent, and the liberal man prodigal relatively to the mean man, mean relatively to the prodigal. Hence also the people at the extremes push the intermediate man each over to the other, and the brave man is called rash by the coward, cowardly by the rash man, and correspondingly in the other cases.

These states being thus opposed to one another, the greatest contrariety is that of the extremes to each other, rather than to the intermediate; for these are further from each other than from the intermediate, as the great is further from the small and the small from the great than both are from the equal. Again, to the intermediate some extremes show a certain likeness, as that of rashness to courage and that of prodigality to liberality; but the extremes show the greatest unlikeness to each other; now contraries are defined as the things that are furthest from each other, so that things that are further apart are more contrary.

To the intermediate in some cases the deficiency, in some the excess, is more opposed; e.g. it is not rashness, which is an excess, but cowardice, which is a deficiency, that is more opposed to courage, and not insensibility, which is a deficiency, but self-indulgence, which is an excess, that is more opposed to temperance. This happens from two reasons, one being drawn from the thing itself; for because one extreme is nearer and liker to the intermediate, we oppose not this but rather its contrary to the intermediate. For example, since rashness is thought more like and nearer to courage, and cowardice more unlike, we oppose rather the latter to courage; for things that are further from the intermediate are thought more contrary to it. This, then, is one cause, drawn from the thing itself; another is drawn from ourselves; for the things to which we ourselves more naturally tend seem more contrary to the intermediate. For instance, we ourselves tend more naturally to pleasures, and hence are more easily carried away towards self-indulgence than towards propriety. We describe as contrary to the mean, then, rather the directions in which we more often go to great lengths; and therefore self-indulgence, which is an excess, is the more contrary to temperance.

The mean is hard to attain, and is grasped by perception, not by reasoning

9. That moral virtue is a mean, then, and in what sense it is so, and that it is a mean between two vices, the one involving excess, the other deficiency, and that it is such because its character is to aim at what is intermediate in passions and in actions, has been sufficiently stated. Hence also it is no easy task to be good. For in everything it is no easy task to find the middle, e.g. to find the middle of a circle is not for everyone but for him who knows; so, too, anyone can get angry—that is easy—or give or spend money; but to do this to the right person, to the right extent, at the right time, with the right motive, and in the right way, *that* is not for everyone, nor is it easy; wherefore goodness is both rare and laudable and noble.

Hence he who aims at the intermediate must first depart from what is the more contrary to it, as Calypso advises—

Hold the ship out beyond that surf and spray.

45 For of the extremes one is more erroneous, one less so; therefore, since to hit the intermediate is hard in the extreme, we must as a second best, as people say,
1109b take the least of the evils; and this will be done best in the way we describe.

But we must consider the things towards which we ourselves also are easily carried away; for some
5 of us tend to one thing, some to another; and this will be recognizable from the pleasure and the pain we feel. We must drag ourselves away to the contrary extreme; for we shall get into the intermediate state by drawing well away from error, as people do
10 in straightening sticks that are bent.

Now in everything the pleasant or pleasure is most to be guarded against; for we do not judge it impartially. We ought, then, to feel towards pleasure as the elders of the people felt towards Helen, and in
15 all circumstances repeat their saying; for if we dismiss pleasure thus we are less likely to go astray. It is by doing this, then, (to sum the matter up) that we shall best be able to hit the intermediate.

But this is no doubt difficult, and especially in
20 individual cases; for it is not easy to determine both how and with whom and on what provocation and how long one should be angry; for we too sometimes praise those who fall short and call them good-tempered, but sometimes we praise those who get angry
25 and call them manly.

The man, however, who deviates little from goodness is not blamed, whether he do so in the direction of the more or of the less, but only the man who deviates more widely; for *he* does not fail to be
30 noticed. But up to what point and to what extent a man must deviate before he becomes blameworthy it is not easy to determine by reasoning, any more than anything else that is perceived by the senses; such things depend on particular facts, and the decision
35 rests with perception. So much, then, is plain, that the intermediate state is in all things to be praised, but that we must incline sometimes towards the excess,

sometimes towards the deficiency; for so shall we most easily hit the intermediate and what is right. . . .

BOOK III · MORAL VIRTUE

Courage

Courage concerned with the feelings of fear and confidence—strictly speaking, with the fear of death in battle

6. That it is a mean with regard to feelings of fear   40
and confidence has already been made evident; and plainly the things we fear are fearful things, and these are, to speak without qualification, evils; for which reason people even define fear as expectation of evil. Now we fear all evils, e.g. disgrace, poverty,   45
disease, friendlessness, death, but the brave man is not thought to be concerned with all; for to fear some things is even right and noble, and it is base not to fear them—e.g. disgrace; he who fears this is good and modest, and he who does not is shameless. He is,   50
however, by some people called brave, by a transference of the word to a new meaning; for he has in him something which is like the brave man, since the brave man also is a fearless person. Poverty and disease we perhaps ought not to fear, nor in general the   55
things that do not proceed from vice and are not due to a man himself. But not even the man who is fearless of these is brave. Yet we apply the word to him also in virtue of a similarity; for some who in the dangers of war are cowards are liberal and are con-   60
fident in face of the loss of money. Nor is a man a coward if he fears insult to his wife and children or envy or anything of the kind; nor brave if he is confident when he is about to be flogged. With what sort of fearful things, then, is the brave man concerned?   65
Surely with the greatest; for no one is more likely than he to stand his ground against what is awe-inspiring. Now death is the most fearful of all things; for it is the end, and nothing is thought to be any longer either good or bad for the dead. But the brave   70
man would not seem to be concerned even with death in *all* circumstances, e.g. at sea or in disease. In what circumstances, then? Surely in the noblest. Now such deaths are those in battle; for these take

75 place in the greatest and noblest danger. And these are correspondingly honoured in city-states and at the courts of monarchs. Properly, then, he will be called brave who is fearless in face of a noble death, and of all emergencies that involve death; and the

80 emergencies of war are in the highest degree of this

15b kind. Yet at sea also, and in disease, the brave man is fearless, but not in the same way as the seamen; for he has given up hope of safety, and is disliking the thought of death in this shape, while they are hope-

5 ful because of their experience. At the same time, we show courage in situations where there is the opportunity of showing prowess or where death is noble; but in these forms of death neither of these conditions is fulfilled.

The motive of courage is the noble: characteristics of the opposite vices, cowardice and rashness

10 7. What is fearful is not the same for all men; but we say there are things fearful even beyond human strength. These, then, are fearful to everyone—at least to every sensible man; but the fearful things that are *not* beyond human strength differ in magni-

15 tude and degree, and so too do the things that inspire confidence. Now the brave man is as dauntless as man may be. Therefore, while he will fear even the things that are not beyond human strength, he will face them as he ought and as reason directs, for the

20 sake of the noble; for this is the end of virtue. But it is possible to fear these more, or less, and again to fear things that are not fearful as if they were. Of the faults that are committed, one consists in fearing what we should not, another in fearing as we should

25 not, another in fearing when we should not, and so on; and so too with respect to the things that inspire confidence. The man, then, who faces and who fears the right things and from the right motive, in the right way and at the right time, and who feels confi-

30 dence under the corresponding conditions, is brave; for the brave man feels and acts according to the merits of the case and in whatever way reason directs. Now the end of every activity is conformity to the corresponding state of character. This is true,

35 therefore, of the brave man as well as of others. But

courage is noble. Therefore the end also is noble; for each thing is defined by its end. Therefore it is for a noble end that the brave man endures and acts as courage directs.

Of those who go to excess he who exceeds in 40 fearlessness has no name (we have said previously that many states of character have no names), but he would be a sort of madman or insensitive to pain if he feared nothing, neither earthquakes nor the waves, as they say the Celts do not; while the man who exceeds 45 in confidence about what really is fearful is rash. The rash man, however, is also thought to be boastful and only a pretender to courage; at all events, as the brave man *is* with regard to what is fearful, so the rash man wishes to *appear*; and so he imitates him 50 in situations where he can. Hence also most of them are a mixture of rashness and cowardice; for, while in these situations they display confidence, they do not hold their ground against what is really fearful. The man who exceeds in fear is a coward; for he fears 55 both what he ought not and as he ought not, and all the similar characterizations attach to him. He is lacking also in confidence; but he is more conspicuous for his excess of fear in painful situations. The 1116a coward, then, is a despairing sort of person; for he fears everything. The brave man, on the other hand, has the opposite disposition; for confidence is the mark of a hopeful disposition. The coward, the rash 5 man, and the brave man, then, are concerned with the same objects but are differently disposed towards them; for the first two exceed and fall short, while the third holds the middle, which is the right, position; and rash men are precipitate, and wish for dangers 10 beforehand but draw back when they are in them, while brave men are excited in the moment of action, but collected beforehand.

As we have said, then, courage is a mean with respect to things that inspire confidence or fear, in 15 the circumstances that have been stated; and it chooses or endures things because it is noble to do so, or because it is base not to do so. But to die to escape from poverty or love or anything painful is not the mark of a brave man, but rather of a coward; 20 for it is softness to fly from what is troublesome, and such a man endures death not because it is noble but to fly from evil. . . .

BOOK VI · INTELLECTUAL VIRTUE

Introduction

Reasons for studying intellectual virtue: intellect divided into the contemplative and the calculative

1. Since we have previously said that one ought to choose that which is intermediate, not the excess nor the defect, and that the intermediate is determined by reason, let us discuss this. In all the states of character we have mentioned, as in all other matters, there is a mark to which the man who has reason looks, and heightens or relaxes his activity accordingly, and there is a standard which determines the mean states which we say are intermediate between excess and defect, being in accordance with correct reason. But such a statement, though true, is by no means clear; for not only here but in all other pursuits which are objects of knowledge it is indeed true to say that we must not exert ourselves nor relax our efforts too much or too little, but to an intermediate extent and as correct reason dictates; but if a man had only this knowledge he would be none the wiser—e.g. we should not know what sort of medicines to apply to our body if someone were to say 'all those which the medical art prescribes, and which agree with the practice of one who possesses the art'. Hence it is necessary with regard to the states of the soul also, not only that this true statement should be made, but also that it should be determined what correct reason is and what is the standard that fixes it.

We divided the virtues of the soul and said that some are moral virtues and others virtues of intellect. Now we have discussed in detail the moral virtues; with regard to the others let us express our view as follows, beginning with some remarks about the soul. We said before that there are two parts of the soul—that which grasps a rational principle, and the non-rational; let us now draw a similar distinction within the part which grasps a rational principle. And let it be assumed that there are two parts which grasp a rational principle—one by which we contemplate the kind of things whose originative causes are invariable, and one by which we contemplate variable things; for where objects differ in kind the part of the soul answering to each of the two is different in kind, since it is in virtue of a certain likeness and kinship with their objects that they have the knowledge they have. Let one of these parts be called the scientific and the other the calculative; for to deliberate and to calculate are the same thing, but no one deliberates about the invariable. Therefore the calculative is one part of the faculty which grasps a rational principle. We must, then, learn what is the best state of each of these two parts; for this is the virtue of each.

The object of contemplation is truth; that of calculation is truth corresponding with right desire

2. The virtue of a thing is relative to its proper work. Now there are three things in the soul which control action and truth—perception, reason, desire.

Of these perception originates no action; this is plain from the fact that the lower animals have perception but no share in action.

What affirmation and negation are in thinking, pursuit and avoidance are in desire; so that since moral virtue is a state of character concerned with choice, and choice is deliberate desire, therefore both the reasoning must be true and the desire right, if the choice is to be good, and the latter must pursue just what the former asserts. Now this kind of intellect and of truth is practical; of the intellect which is contemplative, not practical nor productive, the good and the bad state are truth and falsity respectively (for this is the work of everything intellectual); while of the part which is practical and intellectual the good state is truth in agreement with right desire.

The origin of action—its efficient, not its final cause—is choice, and that of choice is desire and reasoning with a view to an end. This is why choice cannot exist either without reason and intellect or without a moral state; for good action and its opposite cannot exist without a combination of intellect and character. Intellect itself, however, moves nothing, but only the intellect which aims at an end and is practical; for this rules the productive intellect as well, since everyone who makes makes for an end, and that which is made is not an end in the unqualified sense (but only an end in a particular relation, and the end of

5 a particular operation)—only that which is *done* is that; for good action is an end, and desire aims at this. Hence choice is either desiderative reason or ratiocinative desire, and such an origin of action is a man. (It is to be noted that nothing that is past is an object of

10 choice, e.g. no one chooses to have sacked Troy; for no one *deliberates* about the past, but about what is future and capable of being otherwise, while what is past is not capable of not having taken place; hence Agathon is right in saying:

15   For this alone is lacking even to god,
     To make undone things that have once been
     done.)

The work of both the intellectual parts, then, is truth. Therefore the states that are most strictly those

20 in respect of which each of these parts will reach truth are the virtues of the two parts. . . .

Practical wisdom—knowledge of how to secure the ends of human life

5. Regarding *practical wisdom* we shall get at the truth by considering who are the persons we credit with it. Now it is thought to be a mark of a man of

25 practical wisdom to be able to deliberate well about what is good and expedient for himself, not in some particular respect, e.g. about what sorts of thing conduce to health or to strength, but about what sorts of thing conduce to the good life in general. This is

30 shown by the fact that we credit men with practical wisdom in some particular respect when they have calculated well with a view to some good end which is one of those that are not the object of any art. It follows that in the general sense also the man who is

35 capable of deliberating has practical wisdom. Now no one deliberates about things that are invariable, or about things that it is impossible for him to do. Therefore, since scientific knowledge involves demonstration, but there is no demonstration of

40 things whose first principles are variable (for all such things might actually be otherwise), and since

it is impossible to deliberate about things that are of 1140b necessity, practical wisdom cannot be scientific knowledge or art; not science because that which can be done is capable of being otherwise, not art because action and making are different kinds of 5 thing. The remaining alternative, then, is that it is a true and reasoned state of capacity to act with regard to the things that are good or bad for man. For while making has an end other than itself, action cannot; for good action itself is its end. It is for this reason 10 that we think Pericles and men like him have practical wisdom, namely, because they can see what is good for themselves and what is good for men in general; we consider that those can do this who are good at managing households or states. (This is why 15 we call temperance (*sōphrosunē*) by this name; we imply that it preserves one's practical wisdom (*sōzousa tēn phronēsin*). Now what it preserves is a judgement of the kind we have described. For it is not any and every judgement that pleasant and pain- 20 ful objects destroy and pervert, e.g. the judgement that the triangle has or has not its angles equal to two right angles, but only judgements about what is to be done. For the originating causes of the things that are done consist in the end at which they are aimed; 25 but the man who has been ruined by pleasure or pain forthwith fails to see any such originating cause—to see that for the sake of this or because of this he ought to choose and do whatever he chooses and does; for vice is destructive of the originating cause 30 of action.)

Practical wisdom, then, must be a reasoned and true state of capacity to act with regard to human goods. But further, while there is such a thing as excellence in art, there is no such thing as excellence in 35 practical wisdom; and in art he who errs willingly is preferable, but in practical wisdom, as in the virtues, he is the reverse. Plainly, then, practical wisdom is a virtue and not an art. There being two parts of the soul that can follow a course of reasoning, it must be a 40 virtue of one of the two, i.e. of that part which forms opinions; for opinion is about the variable and so is practical wisdom. But yet it is not only a reasoned state; this is shown by the fact that a state of that sort may be forgotten but practical wisdom cannot. . . . 45

BOOK X · PLEASURE, HAPPINESS

The contemplative life is the happiest

7. If happiness is activity in accordance with virtue, it is reasonable that it should be in accordance with the highest virtue; and this will be that of the best thing in us. Whether it be reason or something else 50 that is this element which is thought to be our natural ruler and guide and to take thought of things noble and divine, whether it be itself also divine or only the most divine element in us, the activity of this in accordance with its proper virtue will be per- 55 fect happiness. That this activity is contemplative we have already said.

Now this would seem to be in agreement both with what we said before and with the truth. For, firstly, this activity is the best (since not only is 60 reason the best thing in us, but the objects of reason are the best of knowable objects); and, secondly, it is the most continuous, since we can contemplate truth more continuously than we can *do* anything. And we think happiness ought to have pleasure mingled 65 with it, but the activity of philosophic wisdom is admittedly the pleasantest of virtuous activities; at all events the pursuit of it is thought to offer pleasures marvellous for their purity and their enduringness, and it is to be expected that those who know will 70 pass their time more pleasantly than those who inquire. And the self-sufficiency that is spoken of must belong most to the contemplative activity. For while a philosopher, as well as a just man or one possessing any other virtue, needs the necessaries of life, 75 when they are sufficiently equipped with things of that sort the just man needs people towards whom and with whom he shall act justly, and the temperate man, the brave man, and each of the others is in the same case, but the philosopher, even when by him- 80 self, can contemplate truth, and the better the wiser he is; he can perhaps do so better if he has fellow 1177b workers, but still he is the most self-sufficient. And this activity alone would seem to be loved for its own sake; for nothing arises from it apart from the contemplating, while from practical activities 5 we gain more or less apart from the action. And

happiness is thought to depend on leisure; for we are busy that we may have leisure, and make war that we may live in peace. Now the activity of the practical virtues is exhibited in political or military affairs, but the actions concerned with these seem to be un- 10 leisurely. Warlike actions are completely so (for no one chooses to be at war, or provokes war, for the sake of being at war; anyone would seem absolutely murderous if he were to make enemies of his friends in order to bring about battle and slaughter); but the 15 action of the statesman also is unleisurely, and aims—beyond the political action itself—at despotic power and honours, or at all events happiness, for him and his fellow citizens—a happiness different from political action, and evidently sought as 20 being different. So if among virtuous actions political and military actions are distinguished by nobility and greatness, and these are unleisurely and aim at an end and are not desirable for their own sake, but the activity of reason, which is contemplative, 25 seems both to be superior in serious worth and to aim at no end beyond itself, and to have its pleasure proper to itself (and this augments the activity), and the self-sufficiency, leisureliness, unweariedness (so far as this is possible for man), and all the other attri- 30 butes ascribed to the supremely happy man are evidently those connected with this activity, it follows that this will be the complete happiness of man, if it be allowed a complete term of life (for none of the attributes of happiness is incomplete). 35

But such a life would be too high for man; for it is not in so far as he is man that he will live so, but in so far as something divine is present in him; and by so much as this is superior to our composite nature is its activity superior to that which is the exercise of 40 the other kind of virtue. If reason is divine, then, in comparison with man, the life according to it is divine in comparison with human life. But we must not follow those who advise us, being men, to think of human things, and, being mortal, of mortal things, 45 but must, so far as we can, make ourselves immortal, and strain every nerve to live in accordance with the best thing in us; for even if it be small in bulk, much more does it in power and worth surpass ev- 117 erything. And this would seem actually to *be* each man, since it is the authoritative and better part of him. It would be strange, then, if he were to choose not the life of himself but that of something else. And what we said before will apply now: that which is proper to each thing is by nature best and most pleasant for each thing; for man, therefore, the life according to reason is best and pleasantest, since reason more than anything else *is* man. This life therefore is also the happiest.

STUDY QUESTIONS

1. What is Aristotle's distinction between moral and intellectual virtue?
2. According to Aristotle, how do people become courageous?
3. According to Aristotle, what is "practical wisdom"?
4. What moral rules, if any, does Aristotle offer?

Virtue Ethics

Julia Annas

Virtue ethics focuses on understanding moral character rather than formulating rules for right action. As Julia Annas, Professor of Philosophy at the University of Arizona, maintains, moral inquiry is not a search for a formula that provides the right answer to every moral problem. Instead, the development of ethical understanding is akin to mastering a practical skill, such as playing music, that we acquire by emulating people who are more expert. They know how to respond appropriately to the particularities of complex situations, and we should seek to act likewise.

In the tradition of Western philosophy since the fifth century B.C., the default form of ethical theory has been some version of what is nowadays called virtue ethics; real theoretical alternatives emerge only with Kant and with consequentialism. This continued dominance is not very surprising, given that concern with virtue is a concern with the kind of person you are, and that this has always been important to real-life ethical matters in Western societies. (And, as is becoming increasingly familiar, this is also true of some non-Western societies and philosophical traditions, particularly Asian ones.)

The tradition has taken several different forms, and sorting these out is useful for finding the underlying structure. I shall also say a little about the way that virtue ethics has been ignored or trivialized by analytical ethical philosophy for about a hundred years, only to reemerge vigorously during the last forty.

Virtue ethics is best approached by looking at the central features of what I shall call the classical version of the tradition. Its theoretical structure is first clearly stated by Aristotle, but it is wrong to think of it as peculiarly Aristotelian, since it underlies all of ancient ethical theory (Annas, 1993, 1999). The classical version is our best entry-point into the subject, because we have a large amount of material that was developed and refined over hundreds of years by extensive debate and that contains resources for establishing the whole theoretical structure, and for understanding what in it is basic and what more parochial. Modern virtue ethical theories have not yet achieved such a critical mass of argument and theory, and most are as yet partial or fragmentary. As I will show, it is only when we have this whole picture in view that we can understand other theories that call themselves virtue ethics. So I shall first build up, cumulatively, a picture of the entire structure of classical virtue ethics, and then see how different versions of it result from ignoring or rejecting parts of that structure. The result, while unavoidably schematic, should help to clarify the various debates that are growing up in virtue ethics, and help to orient those who are less familiar with the terrain and are sometimes puzzled

From Julia Annas, "Virtue Ethics," in D. Copp, ed., *The Oxford Handbook of Ethical Theory*, Oxford University Press, 2006. Reprinted by permission of the publisher.

by the recent proliferation of theories with the name *virtue ethics*.

1. VIRTUE ETHICS: THE WHOLE PICTURE

1.1. The Central Role of Practical Reasoning

A virtue is a state or disposition of a person. This is a reasonable intuitive claim; if someone is generous, say, then she has a character of a certain sort; she is dispositionally, that is, habitually and reliably, generous. A virtue, though, is not a habit in the sense in which habits can be mindless, sources of action in the agent that bypass her practical reasoning. A virtue is a disposition *to act,* not an entity built up within me and productive of behavior; it is my disposition to act in certain ways and not others. A virtue, unlike a mere habit, is a disposition to act *for reasons,* and so a disposition that is exercised through the agent's practical reasoning; it is built up by making choices and exercised in the making of further choices. When an honest person decides not to take something to which he is not entitled, this is not the upshot of a causal buildup from previous actions but a *decision,* a choice that endorses his disposition to be honest.

The exercise of the agent's practical reasoning is thus essential to the way a virtue is both built up and exercised. Because of this feature, classical virtue ethics has been criticized as being overly intellectualist (even "elitist") on this basis (Driver, 2001). However, the reasoning in question is just what everyone does, so it is hard to see how a theory that appeals to what is available to everyone is elitist. Different virtue theories offer us differing ways of making our reflections more theoretically sophisticated, but virtue ethics tries to improve the reasoning we all share, rather than replacing it by a different kind.

What is the role of the agent's practical reasoning? Virtue is the disposition to do the right thing for the right reason, in the appropriate way—honestly, courageously, and so on. This involves two aspects, the affective and the intellectual.

What is the affective aspect of virtue? The agent may do the right thing and have a variety of feelings and reactions to it. She may hate doing the right thing but do it anyway; do the right thing but with conflicted feelings or with difficulty; do the right thing effortlessly and with no internal opposition. One feature of the classical version of virtue ethics is to regard doing the right thing with no contrary inclination as a mark of the virtuous person, as opposed to the merely self-controlled. Mere performance of the right action still leaves open the issue of the agent's overall attitude; virtue requires doing the right thing for the right reason without serious internal opposition, as a matter of character. This is, after all, just one implication of the thought that in an ethics of virtue it matters what kind of person you are. Of course, what it takes to develop your character in such a way that you are wholehearted about being generous, act fairly without regrets, and so on is a large matter. There is no single unified theory of our affective nature that all virtue theories share, and so there is a variety of views as to how we are to become virtuous, rather than merely doing the right thing for the right reason. All theories in the classical tradition, however, accept and emphasize the point, familiar from common sense, that there is an important moral difference between the person who merely acts rightly and the person who is wholehearted in what she does. Some modern theories implicitly deny the importance of this distinction, without giving a reason for this.

The virtuous agent, then, does the right thing, undividedly, for the right reason—he understands, that is, that this is the right thing to do. What is this understanding? In classical virtue ethics, we start our moral education by learning from others, both in making particular judgments about right and wrong, and in adopting some people as role models or teachers or following certain rules. At first, as pupils, we adopt these views because we were told to, or they seemed obvious, and we acquire a collection of moral views that are fragmented and accepted on the authority of others. For virtue ethics, the purpose of good moral education is to get the pupil to think for himself about the reasons on which he acts, and so the content of what he has been taught. Ideally, then, the learner will begin to reflect for himself on what he has accepted, will detect and deal with inconsistencies, and will try to make his judgments and practice coherent in terms of a wider understanding which enables him to unify, explain and justify the particular decisions he makes. This is a process that requires the agent at every stage to use his mind, to think about what he is doing and to try to achieve understanding of it (Annas, 2001).

We can see this from an example. In many modern societies, the obvious models for courage are macho ones focusing on sports and war movies. A boy may grow up thinking that these are the paradigmatic contexts for courage, and have various views about courage and cowardice that presuppose this. But if he reflects about the matter, he may come to think that he is also prepared to call people in other, quite different contexts brave—a child struggling with cancer, someone standing up for an unpopular person in high school, and so on. Further reflection will show that the macho grasp of courage was inadequate, and will drive him to ask what links all these very diverse cases of bravery; this will lead him to ask what the reasons are on which brave people act, rather than to continue uncritically with the views and attitudes he initially found obvious.

The development of ethical understanding, leading the agent to develop a disposition that is a virtue, is in the classical tradition standardly taken to proceed like the acquisition of a practical skill or expertise. As Aristotle says, becoming just is like becoming a builder. With a practical skill, there is something to learn, something conveyable by teaching; the expert is the person who understands through reflection what she has been taught, and thinks for herself about it. We are familiar with the notion of practical expertise in mundane contexts like that of car repair, plumbing, and so on. In the classical tradition of virtue ethics, this is an important analogy, because ethical development displays something that we can see more clearly in these more limited contexts: There is a progress from the mechanical rule- or model-following of the learner to the greater understanding of the expert, whose responses are sensitive to the particularities of situations, as well as expressing learning and general reflection.

The skill analogy brings out two important points about ethical understanding: It requires both that you learn from others and that you come to think and understand for yourself. (The all-important progress from the learner to the expert is lost in the modern tendency to reduce all practical knowledge to 'knowing how', as opposed to 'knowing that'.) Ethical reflection begins from what you have learned in your society; but it requires you to progress from that. Virtue begins from following rules or models in your social and cultural context; but it requires that you develop a disposition to decide and act that involves the kind of understanding that only you can achieve in your own case.

Virtue is like a skill in its structure. But the skill analogy, of course, has limits. One is that practical skills are devoted to achieving ends from which we can detach ourselves if we cease to want them, whereas virtue is devoted to achieving our final end, which, as I will show, is not in this way an end we can just cease to want. Another limit is that the development of practical understanding in a skill can be relatively independent of emotion and feeling, whereas the development of practical understanding goes along with a development in the virtuous person's affect and response.

Some modern theorists have difficulty grasping the role of practical reasoning in the classical version of virtue ethics because it offends against a common modern dogma to the effect that reason functions only instrumentally, to fulfill whatever desires we happen to have. The issue is too large to discuss here, but it is important to notice that the classical theory of practical reasoning is a theoretical rival to this account, so that assuming it against the classical version of virtue ethics is begging the question. (One of the most interesting and fruitful modern debates in ethics is opening up the question of the tenability of the instrumentalist account.) The classical account can be shown to be empirically well supported, and this makes it easier to show that virtue ethics of the classical kind is not vulnerable to some criticisms that assume the truth of an account of practical reasoning that it rejects (Annas, 2001).

The classical account has also been criticized because of the notions of disposition and character that are central to it. Some modern theories object to making character basic to ethical discourse, as

opposed to single actions; this reflects a difference between types of ethical theory that focus on actions in
isolation and types that emphasize the importance of
the agent's life as a whole, and, relatedly, the importance of moral education and development. Recently,
virtue ethics of the classical kind has been attacked
on the ground that its notion of a disposition is unrealistic. These attacks rely on some work in 'situation-
ist' social psychology that claims that unobvious
aspects of particular situations have a large role in
explaining our actions. Some philosophers have
claimed from this that we are not justified in thinking
that people have robust character traits; for, if they
did, these would explain their actions reliably and
across a wide variety of types of situation, excluding
this kind of influence (Doris, 2002; Harman, 1999).

However, these studies assume a notion of disposition that is defined solely in terms of frequency
of actions, where the actions in question are defined
with no reference to the agent's own reasons for
acting. For virtue ethics, however, a virtue is a disposition to act *for reasons,* and claims about frequency of action are irrelevant to this, until some
plausible connection is established with the agent's
reasons, something none of the situationists have
done (Sreenivasan, 2002).

1.2. Virtues and My Flourishing

Virtues, then, are character traits of the kind discussed. There are character traits, however, which
are not virtues. To qualify as a virtue, a character
trait must embody a commitment to some ethical
value, such as justice, or benevolence. Moreover,
this commitment is not merely a matter of performing actions that happen to be just, benevolent or
whatever; a disposition, as already stressed, works
through the agent's practical reasoning. The virtues
are dispositions *to be* just, benevolent and so on, to
give others their fair share, treat others in considerate ways, stand up for others' rights.

So far I have talked of virtue, but of course in
everyday life we encounter a number of different virtues—fairness, generosity, courage and so on. The
virtues, as we ordinarily think of them, embody commitments to a number of values, and this comes out in

the ways in which different kinds of situation are typically thought of as requiring different virtues.

What makes such diverse virtues as courage and
generosity *virtues,* dispositions that it is ethically admirable to have? Any theory of virtue will have
something to say about the way the different virtues
are valuable. Since the virtues are dispositions of me,
they are ways that I am, traits of my character; so
they contribute to my living my life as a whole in a
certain way. So thinking about the virtues leads to
thinking of *my life as a whole.* This notion is crucial,
and is prominent in all forms of classical virtue
ethics, because the virtues make sense only within a
conception of living that takes the life I live to be an
overall unity, rather than a succession of more or less
unconnected states. And further, cultivating the virtues is worthwhile because living virtuously will
constitute my living my life as a whole in a way that
lives it *well,* in a way that it is valuable to live.

The final end to which the virtues contribute is
often called *eudaimonia,* since this is the term found
in ancient Greek theories (that are hence, unsurpris-
ingly, called eudaimonist). The least unsatisfactory
modern English equivalent is *flourishing,* which I
shall use. *Happiness* would be in many ways better,
but unfortunately runs into two problems. One is that
the modern philosophical notion of happiness has
been influenced by utilitarian ideas, leading easily to
the trivializing thought that happiness is pleasure.
And while the idea that happiness is flourishing—a
well-lived life—does have a place in everyday ideas
of happiness, it is often held together with implicitly
conflicting ideas, such as that happiness is having a
good time, or being prosperous. Modern analogues
of ancient eudaimonist theories have, moreover,
come to be called virtue ethics, not happiness ethics.
Virtue is the concept that has become the central one
in recent philosophy, sometimes obscuring the importance of the idea of the agent's overall flourishing
to which the virtues contribute.

Do we have such a final end? It is important to
note here that the idea is not a philosophers' demand
brought in from outside everyday ethical reasoning.
It is just a very ordinary and everyday way of thinking of our lives. We get to it simply by reflecting that
our actions can be thought of not just in a linear way,

as we perform one action after another: They can also be thought of in a nested way, as happens whenever we ask *why* we are doing something, for the answer will typically make reference to some broader concern, and this in turn to one even broader. Given that I have only one life to lead, I will eventually come up with some very broad conception of my life as a whole, as what makes sense of all my actions at any given point. I cannot escape the fact that at any given point, my actions reflect and express the kind of person I am, and the nature of my ends and priorities. This is a very ordinary way of thinking, one in which everybody engages. (People who are severely conflicted about their aims, or in denial about the way their actions fit into broader patterns in their lives, appear to be exceptions to this; but note that we think of them as having *damaged* lives, not as showing us alternative ways of living *well*.)

Thinking in this way, we come up with the notion of my living my life as a whole, and living it well. This is not yet specific as to its content. (For Aristotle, it is trivial that my final end is *eudaimonia* or happiness, but this link is not obvious for us, and even for Aristotle this was the start, not the finish, of debate as to what living well consists in.) But it is not a trivial result. For one thing, my final end must meet the formal constraint of being *complete*—all my actions are done for its sake, while I do not seek it for the sake of anything further. This at once rules out some instrumental ends, such as money or fame, which always raise the question of what they are sought *for,* what part they play in the living of a flourishing life. For another thing, my final end, flourishing, cannot consist in things, stuff, or passive states like pleasure. I am aiming at *living* in a certain way, being active where my life is concerned rather than letting it drift along. One major difference from many modern theories is that I am aiming at living my life in a way that only I can do, by developing the way I reason about it; I am not aiming at stuff, or states that other people could just as well provide for me.

How do the virtues contribute to my flourishing? Classical theories of virtue ethics claim that virtue is, more weakly, necessary, or, more strongly, sufficient for flourishing. How is this to be understood? Classical virtue theories reject the idea that

flourishing can be specified right at the start, in a way that is both substantive and makes no reference to the virtues. Someone who supposes that flourishing can be defined as feeling good, or getting whatever you want, has given an account of it that is unacceptable to a virtue theory even before we get to the virtues. Rather, virtue ethics tells us that a life lived in accordance with the virtues is the *best specification* of what flourishing is. This claim in turn is not neutral ground between the virtue ethicist and the person who thinks that flourishing is getting whatever you want. Rather, we have already got *rival specifications* of what it is to flourish, to lead a good life. And this is exactly what we would expect, given that the issue of what it is to lead a flourishing life is not one that we could expect to be decided at the *start* of ethical investigation, *before* we try to spell out what is involved in living a life in which you try to live fairly, courageously, and so on, as opposed to living a life in which you aim to get whatever you want. It is a theoretical advantage of classical virtue ethics that it respects a fundamental point about our ethical discussions. When people disagree as to whether someone did or did not ruin his life by performing an action that is honest but loses him a job he has aimed for, we do not expect them to resolve the dispute by appeal to some neutral list of indicators that a way of life is worth living. We recognize that this kind of dispute is not a simple disagreement about rival means to an agreed-upon end. It is a complex kind of dispute that brings in a wide range of issues, because what is in dispute just is what kind of life constitutes a flourishing one, as opposed to a failure.

Many modern critics have objected to the claim that virtue is even necessary for flourishing, on the grounds that not everybody thinks that it matters to be fair or brave, and that some of these people appear to be flourishing by conventional standards. It is clear, however, that this kind of objection misses the point that virtue ethics does not begin from any specification of flourishing that is substantive and independent of the virtues. Virtue ethicists are often accused of naivete in thinking that being virtuous is a good bet if you want to flourish, where flourishing is understood independently of the virtues; but virtue ethics rejects this conception of flourishing. Each of us begins with an unspecific notion of living his life well as a whole, and different theories within virtue ethics give us differing answers as to the importance of virtue in giving us a right specification of living well, and so of flourishing. Virtue ethics begins from the point that we do attach value to being virtuous, as well as to having money, a family life, and so on. (It is exceptional, not standard, as some modern critics think, to be cynical about the value of the virtues in life; this is not what we teach our children, or assume in most ethical discourse.) The argument proceeds by getting us to see that virtue is not just one value in life, which could reasonably be outweighed by others, such as money; it has a special status such that, on the weaker version, those without it do not flourish, whatever else they have, and, on the stronger version, virtue is necessary and sufficient for a flourishing life. Different theories press different points, and no complete range of positive arguments can be given here, but it can be stressed that most classical theories emphasize the point that virtue is like a skill exercised on the materials of your life. Acting virtuously is not an *alternative* to making money, for example. Rather, making money is one of the things you have to do, one of the circumstances of your life, and you can do this either virtuously or not; which of the two it is makes all the difference to the place and significance in your life of making money.

The point that flourishing, as the aim of the virtues, is not antecedently specified independently of living virtuously is also important in defusing various objections to the effect that classical virtue ethics is egoistic. Sometimes it is claimed that someone who lives virtuously as a way of aiming at flourishing is acting for egoistic reasons. But this is a confusion. The person who aims at living a flourishing life by living in a fair, generous, and brave way is not aiming at *her* good, as opposed to the good of others. Still less is she aiming at some *state* of herself. Living in a flourishing way is an activity, the ongoing activity of a life, and living in a brave, generous, and so on way is a specification of what that is.

Hence it is a mistake to claim that the virtuous person's motivation is egoistic because it is aimed at her flourishing and not mine, or yours. She aims at her own flourishing and not mine just in the sense that she is living her life and not mine. There is no implication

that she is furthering her own interests at the expense of mine. It would be odd to do this by acting fairly, being generous, courageously standing up for others! Still less is it plausible to think that the agent who thinks that living virtuously is the best specification of a flourishing life will be acting for egoistic reasons. This objection simply misconstrues what a virtue is. Courage, for example, is the disposition to stand up for what is right, among other things, whether or not this benefits me or others. Courage is not a disposition that can be switched off when my own interests, as opposed to those of others, are not at stake. Someone who has dispositions that further only his own interests in a way that could conflict with those of others is not even a minimal candidate for being virtuous.

The complaint that virtue ethics is egoistic is surprisingly stubborn. It seems to depend partly on the assumption that flourishing must be specified independently of the practice of the virtues, so that they are just means to it as an independently agreed end, and partly on the assumption that ethical disputes about lives are disputes about alternative means to agreed-upon ends. But neither assumption is shared by virtue ethics, so these objections miss their target. And in any case, they are false.

1.3. Living Virtuously

How does virtue ethics explicate the notion that I have just made use of so far, of the *right thing to do?* It is clearly important for the theory, since a virtue is a disposition built up by doing the right thing and acquiring increasing understanding of what this is, and why.

Virtue ethics makes the realistic assumption that by the time you come to think about ethics and want to develop or improve your life as a whole, you already *have a life.* You already have a social position, a cultural education, a family, a job, and so on. These are all factors that have contributed to your ethical development, for good or for ill. Because for virtue ethics it matters what kind of person you are, it takes into account the importance of the person you already are when you begin to think about being virtuous. It is unrealistic to think that your ethical views are all completely disposable, and that you can come to be a better person by overnight conversion. By the time you think for yourself about what it is to be brave, just, and so on, you already have developed views and attitudes.

However, classical virtue ethics always assumes that reflection about our ethical views will reveal them to be inadequate to the way we want to be. As Aristotle says, "In general everyone seeks not the traditional but the good" (*Politics* 1269a3–4). All classical virtue ethics assumes, in a way oddly absent from many modern theories, that ethical thought essentially includes an *aspiration* to be better than we are. Classical virtue theories are marked both by realistic recognition of the socially embedded nature of our ethical life, and by insistence that if we are thinking ethically, we are striving to be better, to reach an ideal that is not already attained. And all classical virtue theories are very demanding in this regard (Annas, 2002). It is therefore irrelevant to point out that the specific classical theories were produced for audiences in societies very different from ours. Virtue ethics gets a grip whenever we realize that the ethical beliefs we live by are inadequate, that, for example, they may imply sexist and racist attitudes, and that we need to become *better people*. Virtue ethics develops from the reasonable thought that *I* have to improve myself; no teacher or book can do the job.

None of this is incompatible with our recognizing that there are some judgments about action that are not only widely shared but not negotiable when we think about virtue and the good life. This is just part of the background from which we all begin. What is important, however, is that this cannot be developed into a theory telling people what it is right and wrong to do in a way that pays no attention to the fact that they are aspiring to ideals from within different contexts and at very different stages of their own ethical development. Some modern theories have thought that there is such a thing as a 'theory of right action', which will tell us which actions are right, or give us an account of what makes an action right, and can be used by anyone, at any stage of moral development, with any level of interest in being a good person. This would make ethical thinking about how to act like using a computer manual. As has been forcefully pointed out (Hursthouse, 1991, 1999), this is a completely unrealistic view of ethical thinking. It is not plausible to suppose that a bright eighteen-year-old could by reading a book become an ethically wise person, an excellent source of ethical advice as to what to do. Nor can we realistically separate the questions of whether we respect someone's advice as to what to do, and our attitude to what they find admirable in life. We cannot take someone's 'theory of right action' seriously if they have appalling priorities in their life—even if they claim, on theoretical grounds, that the two are unrelated.

The answer that virtue ethics offers to the question what is the right thing to do denies that there is any such thing as a 'theory of right action' in this abstract sense. In explaining what is the right thing to do, virtue ethics appeals to the idea of what would be done by the virtuous person. This is not a definition in which the virtuous person is independently defined and right actions derived from this. For virtue ethics appreciates that 'the virtuous person' cannot be defined in a void and then used to derive right actions in a void. Rather, the thought is that what I should do, in my situation, is what I would do if I were brave (generous, fair, etc.), where this is taken to mean: braver than I am, nearer the ideal of the brave person. Working out the answer is complex, because, as we have seen, it requires thinking about both what matters in this situation, and what bravery demands. This in turn requires reflection on what the relevant factors in question are, and whether the conception of bravery I have acquired thus far is adequate; perhaps I need now to think harder about the brave person's reasoning. Obviously, no simple universally applicable formula will result from this.

Virtue ethics' commitment to the position that acting rightly should be understood as acting as the virtuous person acts has led to a number of different objections. One simply restates that this is not a 'theory of right action' available to all, regardless of what they are like. We can see by now that there is no way that virtue ethics could produce such a theory, so the issue moves to whether this is an advantage or not. So far, advocates of such a 'theory of right action' have failed to produce any arguments for thinking that this is the form that ethics should take, mostly because it has been until recently an unchallenged assumption. Here the recent resurgence of virtue ethics has opened up a much-needed debate.

Another objection, increasingly fading as virtue ethics becomes better understood, is that it is ethically conservative, since it begins from our embedded lives, rather than assuming that we are blank slates receptive of a 'theory of right action' telling us what to do. These charges come from noticing only half the theory's concern with action, its recognition of embeddedness. They ignore the theory's commitment to virtue as an *ideal,* and the insistence that ethics involves *aspiration* to an ideal. In the classical tradition, different theories make more or less stringent demands on us as we aspire to the ideal. The most stringent demand, that of the Stoics, is that to be virtuous I must think of myself as just one among other rational humans, one member of the moral community, with no special standing because of my individual achievements and relationships. Other theories make less stringent demands. No classical virtue theory takes seriously the idea that virtue could be achieved by conforming to your society's conventions; this would leave out what ethics is all about—aspiration to an ideal, trying to live better.

At the beginning of its recent revival, virtue ethics was sometimes accused of not being "applicable" to moral problems; telling us what kind of person to be, it was thought, would not help us with problems like the ethical status of abortion and euthanasia and other difficult moral problems that we would expect ethical theory to help us with. At this point, it is clear that all that virtue ethics cannot provide is an all-purpose 'theory of right action' that will mechanically give anybody the answers to these problems in any context. But it is also clear that virtue ethics rejects this view of a 'theory of right action' in favor of an account that does more justice to our moral discourse and moral psychology. Meanwhile, virtue ethics has been applied to a gamut of such problems, with spectacular effectiveness, judging by the level of interest. There is now a wealth of virtue ethical approaches in every branch of applied ethics, so the facts are by now on the ground. A virtue ethics approach to abortion in particular has been extremely influential.[1]

1.4. Virtue and Nature

It is often assumed that virtue ethics is naturalistic—that is, that its claims about our final end and virtues depend on a particular view of nature, especially human nature, understood in a broadly scientific way independent of the ethical claims themselves. Sometimes this theory is called 'Aristotelian'.

It is actually not true that virtue ethics is bound to be naturalistic. In the ancient world, we find versions of virtue ethics that incorporate Jewish and Christian beliefs, and Christian virtue theories were standard during the mediaeval period and, in a different form, in the eighteenth century. Even among the ancient pagans there is a minority tradition, deriving from passages in Plato, taking virtue to be 'becoming like God'. Thus aspiring to the ideal of virtue may be understood in terms of a radically otherworldly theory, metaphysical or religious, that tells us to find out about our human nature only to transcend it.

However, the most developed and influential classical theories of virtue were naturalistic, and so are most modern versions (with the exception of a revival of Christian virtue ethics, as in Porter, 2001). The best known modern virtue theories . . . characterize themselves as neo-Aristotelian, and this is the form of naturalism most commonly associated with classical virtue ethics. It is Aristotelian in spirit, in that the claim that the virtues benefit me, by constituting my flourishing, is supported by the claim that having the virtues benefits me as a human being. I flourish only if I am virtuous, because human nature is such that flourishing, for humans, requires us humans to live in a virtuous way.

This is, obviously, a definite and bold claim. It has often been criticized on mistaken grounds. It is sometimes, for example, thought that it depends on a 'metaphysical biology' peculiar to Aristotle and long since refuted. However, classical virtue theory does not depend on biology, or any science, in the way that modern philosophers have often demanded of a theory that is naturalistic. Virtue ethics is not derived from science or any other field; as we have seen, it emerges as a theoretical version (ultimately, several theoretical versions) of reflective thoughts that we all have. There is no question of ethics being "reduced" to some nonethical level, or emerging as the result of the analysis of the vocabulary of some other field. Ethics, in this tradition, emerges from our reflections on how to live, and, when developed in a theoretically rigorous way, guides us in how to live better.

Nonetheless, an ethical theory is weakened if the best contemporary science conflicts with its claims or makes it hard to see how they could be true. In the ancient world, classical forms of virtue ethics appealed to what they considered to be the best science available, which is why Aristotle reasonably thinks that his ethics is supported by his biological account of human nature: It explains and supports the moral psychology that the ethics presupposes. However, can contemporary forms of virtue ethics appeal to human nature, scientifically considered, in the same way? Some have tried to resuscitate particular features of Aristotle's own biological outlook, such as teleology, but this has not been found very convincing.

Contemporary virtue ethics with the ambitions of the classical theories, of which the most powerful example is that of Hursthouse, does in contemporary terms what the classical theories do in theirs. It looks at human nature as we find out about that from the best contemporary science. Here the relevant sciences are biology, ethology, and psychology, studies of humans and other animals as parts of the life on our planet. When we look at other species, it has long been clear that we can discern patterns of flourishing particular to the species. There has been reluctance to extend this to humans, on the grounds that we, unlike other animals, can choose and create different patterns of living, and evaluate them, sometimes rejecting and changing them as a result. It is only recently that it has been realized that this is not a reason for rejecting naturalism. For this fact about our species is, precisely, a *fact* about our *species*. It is because we are rational beings that we can create and evaluate different ways of living, rather than carrying on in the set patterns that members of other species follow. And this is a fact about us of the same sort as the facts about other species on the basis of which we study them. Human rationality is not something that cuts us off from the rest of the biological universe; it is just what is most distinctive about us as a species. If we take this point seriously, then a naturalistic account of humans needs to come up with patterns of flourishing as we do for other species, but specific to humans, thus taking account of the way our life patterns are dominated by the fact that we are rational beings.

Virtue theory takes advantage of the fact that human rationality has been the subject of scientific study by psychologists for quite some time now, though it has only recently been recognized that it is this, rather than some outdated Aristotelian ideas, that forms the basis of a naturalistic support for virtue theory.

Neo-Aristotelian kinds of virtue theory claim not only that it benefits me as an individual to be virtuous, but also that it benefits humans to have the virtues because of the kind of animals that we are. This is obviously a large claim, and it has been found contentious. But it is important to note that it is a claim based on accepting and studying the best science. It does not depend on ignoring biology, or on 'moralizing' biological claims. It comes from taking seriously the fact that we are rational animals, *as a natural fact*. Here, again, virtue ethics has opened up a fruitful new set of issues. One of them is whether, when we do give due weight to our rationality as determining the way we live, we will end up with something nearer to a Stoic than to an Aristotelian view; this is explored by Becker (1998).

This has been a highly schematic and bare account of the major structural features of classical virtue ethics. I have not been able even to touch on some of the many rich areas that have been explored by modern as well as ancient writers. To mention but a few: The importance of practical reasoning in a virtue raises the issue of the degree to which the virtues are unified by the reasoning they share. This in turn highlights the importance of the affective element in virtue, and of exploring the moral psychology of the emotions, and of pleasure. The social embeddedness of the virtues raises issues of social and political cooperation, and the kind of theory of justice a virtue ethics requires. It also foregrounds the kind of demand that the ideal of virtue must make if a virtue ethics is to have the kind of universality that we commonly demand from an ethical theory. All these issues are now reemerging as subjects of lively discussion. . . .

2. CONCLUSION

Why has virtue ethics been so neglected for so much of the last hundred years? One influence has been consequentialism, which has recognized only a reduced notion of virtue as instrumental to the achievement of some independently defined good. There has also been a general focus on actions at the expense of agents; the dominant forms of Kantian ethics have until recently been narrowly obsessed by rules and principles. Indeed, until recently, it was assumed that the only two major forms of ethical theory were consequentialism and deontology—an assumption that clearly takes it for granted that the central concern of ethics is action in isolation from agents. The resurgence of virtue ethics has not merely provided a "third way"; it has challenged this underlying assumption, and thus it not only provides an alternative to the other forms of theory but provides resources from which they have been enriched. . . .

Virtue ethics receives far more bitter and hostile criticism than other forms of ethical theory, and this seems to be because it challenges assumptions that have grounded ethics for much of the last hundred years, and thus is rightly perceived to be a radical and unsettling force. Once we look beyond reduced conceptions of virtue, we can see why virtue ethics has been so uncomfortable for the previous settled academic orthodoxy. Ethics now has to consider rival accounts of practical reasoning; pay attention to moral psychology; ask seriously what is involved in giving a unifying justification to our uses of a moral concept; question whether an ethical theory can churn out a one-size-fits-all decision procedure to settle all ethical problems; take seriously the ethical role of our lives as wholes and the living of a life as activity rather than passive slate. There is enough here to keep the pot boiling for years.

REFERENCES

Annas, Julia. 1993. *The Morality of Happiness.* Oxford: Oxford University Press.

———. 1999. *Platonic Ethics Old and New.* Ithaca, N.Y.: Cornell University Press.

———. 2001. "Moral Knowledge as Practical Knowledge." In *Moral Knowledge,* ed. E. E. Paul, F. D. Miller and J. Paul, 236–256. Cambridge: Cambridge University Press.

———. 2002. "My Station and Its Duties: Ideal and the Social Embeddedness of Virtue." *Proceedings of the Aristotelian Society* n.s., 102: 109–123.

Becker, Lawrence. 1998. *A New Stoicism.* Princeton, N.J.: Princeton University Press.

Doris, John M. 2002. *Lack of Character.* Cambridge: Cambridge University Press.

Driver, Julia. 2001. *Uneasy Virtue.* Cambridge: Cambridge University Press.

Harman, Gilbert. 1999. "Moral Philosophy Meets Social Psychology: Virtue Ethics and the Fundamental Attribution Error." *Proceedings of the Aristotelian Society,* new series, 119: 315–331.

Hursthouse, Rosalind. 1991. "Virtue Theory and Abortion." *Philosophy and Public Affairs* 20: 223–246.

———. 1999. *On Virtue Ethics.* Oxford: Oxford University Press.

Porter, Jean. 2001. "Virtue Ethics." In *The Cambridge Companion to Christian Ethics,* ed. Robin Gill, 96–111. Cambridge: Cambridge University Press.

Sreenivasan, Gopal. 2002. "Errors about Errors: Virtue Theory and Trait Attribution." *Mind* 111: 47–68.

NOTE

1. Hursthouse, 1991, has been reprinted in a large number of anthologies.

STUDY QUESTIONS

1. When you make a moral judgment, should you ask "What should I do?" or "What sort of person should I be?"
2. Should moral decisions always be based on rules?
3. How is a person's character revealed?
4. Do exemplars play a significant role in your moral reasoning?

Normative Virtue Ethics

Rosalind Hursthouse

Kantianism and consequentialism provide specific answers as to how we ought to act. Rosalind Hursthouse, Professor of Philosophy at the University of Auckland, maintains that virtue ethics does the same. It holds that an action is right if and only if is in accord with what a virtuous agent would do in the circumstances. Applying this test in each case leads to the right action. Thus Hursthouse finds that offering guides to action presents no more problem for virtue ethics than for other moral theories.

A common belief concerning virtue ethics is that it does not tell us what we should do. This belief is sometimes manifested merely in the expressed assumption that virtue ethics, in being 'agent-centred' rather than 'act-centred', is concerned with Being rather than Doing, with good (and bad) character rather than right (and wrong) action, with the question 'What sort of person should I be?' rather than the question 'What should I do?' On this assumption, 'virtue ethics' so-called does not figure as a normative rival to utilitarian and deontological ethics; rather, its (fairly) recent revival is seen as having served the useful purpose of reminding moral philosophers that the elaboration of a normative theory may fall short of giving a full account of our moral life. Thus prompted, deontologists have turned to Kant's long neglected 'Doctrine of Virtue', and utilitarians, largely abandoning the old debate about rule- and act-utilitarianism, are showing interest in the general-happiness-maximizing consequences of inculcating such virtues as friendship, honesty, and loyalty.

On this assumption, it seems that philosophers who 'do virtue ethics', having served this purpose, must realize that they have been doing no more than supplementing normative theory, and should now decide which of the two standard views they espouse. Or, if they find that too difficult, perhaps they should confine themselves to writing detailed studies of particular virtues and vices, indicating where appropriate that 'a deontologist would say that an agent with virtue X will characteristically . . . , whereas a utilitarian would say that she will characteristically . . .' But anyone who wants to espouse virtue ethics as a rival to deontological or utilitarian ethics (finding it distinctly bizarre to suppose that Aristotle espoused either of the latter) will find this common belief voiced against her as an objection: 'Virtue ethics does not, because it cannot, tell us what we should do. Hence it cannot be a normative rival to deontology and utilitarianism.'

This paper is devoted to defending virtue ethics against this objection.

Reprinted from Rosalind Hursthouse, "Normative Virtue Ethics," in Roger Crisp, ed., *How Should One Live?*, Oxford University Press, 1996. Reprinted by permission of the publisher.

1. RIGHT ACTION

What grounds might someone have for believing that virtue ethics cannot tell us what we should do? It seems that sometimes the ground is no more than the claim that virtue ethics is concerned with good (and bad) character rather than right (and wrong) action. But that claim does no more than highlight an interesting contrast between virtue ethics on the one hand, and deontology and utilitarianism on the other; the former is agent-centred, the latter (it is said) are act-centred. It does not entail that virtue ethics has nothing to say about the concept of right action, nor about which actions are right and which wrong. Wishing to highlight a different contrast, the one between utilitarianism and deontology, we might equally well say, 'Utilitarianism is concerned with good (and bad) states of affairs rather than right (and wrong) action', and no one would take that to mean that utilitarianism, unlike deontology, had nothing to say about right action, for what utilitarianism does say is so familiar.

Suppose an act-utilitarian laid out her account of right action as follows:

U1. An action is right iff it promotes the best consequences.

This premiss provides a specification of right action, forging the familiar utilitarian link between the concepts of *right action* and *best consequences,* but gives one no guidance about how to act until one knows what to count as the best consequences. So these must be specified in a second premiss, for example:

U2. The best consequences are those in which happiness is maximized,

which forges the familiar utilitarian link between the concepts of *best consequences* and *happiness.*

Many different versions of deontology can be laid out in a way that displays the same basic structure. They begin with a premiss providing a specification of right action:

D1. An action is right iff it is in accordance with a correct moral rule or principle.

Like the first premiss of act-utilitarianism, this gives one no guidance about how to act until, in this case, one knows what to count as a correct moral rule (or principle). So this must be specified in a second premiss which begins

D2. A correct moral rule (principle) is one that . . . ,

and this may be completed in a variety of ways, for example:

  (i) is on the following list (and then a list does follow)
or
 (ii) is laid on us by God
or
(iii) is universalizable
or
(iv) would be the object of choice of all rational beings and so on.

Although this way of laying out fairly familiar versions of utilitarianism and deontology is hardly controversial, it is worth noting that it suggests some infelicity in the slogan 'Utilitarianism begins with (or takes as its fundamental concept etc.) the Good, whereas deontology begins with the Right.' If the concept a normative ethics 'begins with' is the one it uses to specify right action, then utilitarianism might be said to begin with the Good (if we take this to be the 'same' concept as that of the *best*), but we should surely hasten to add 'but only in relation to consequences; not, for instance, in relation to *good* agents, or to living *well'.* And even then, we shall not be able to go on to say that most versions of deontology 'begin with' the Right, for they use the concept of moral rule or principle to specify right action. . . .

And if the dictum is supposed to single out, rather vaguely, the concept which is 'most important', then the concepts of *consequences* or *happiness* seem as deserving of mention as the concept of the Good for utilitarianism, and what counts as most important (if any one concept does) for deontologists would surely vary from case to case. For some it would be God, for others universalizability, for others the Categorical Imperative, for others rational acceptance, and so on.

It is possible that too slavish an acceptance of this slogan, and the inevitable difficulty of finding a completion of and virtue ethics begins with . . .' which does not reveal its inadequacy, has contributed to the belief that virtue ethics cannot provide a specification of right action. I have heard people say, 'Utilitarianism defines the Right in terms of the Good, and deontology defines the Good in terms of the Right; but how can virtue ethics possibly define both in terms of the (virtuous) Agent?', and indeed, with no answer forthcoming to the questions 'Good *what?* Right *what?*', I have no idea. But if the question is 'How can virtue ethics specify right action?', the answer is easy:

V1. An action is right iff it is what a virtuous agent would characteristically (i.e. acting in character) do in the circumstances.

This specification rarely, if ever, silences those who maintain that virtue ethics cannot tell us what we should do. On the contrary, it tends to provoke irritable laughter and scorn. *'That*'s no use', the objectors say. 'It gives us no guidance whatsoever. Who are the virtuous agents?' But if the failure of the first premiss of a normative ethics which forges a link between the concept of right action and a concept distinctive of that ethics may provoke scorn because it provides no practical guidance, why not direct a similar scorn at the first premisses of act-utilitarianism and deontology in the form in which I have given them? Of each of them I remarked, apparently *en passant* but with intent, that they gave us no guidance. Utilitarianism must specify what are to count as the best consequences, and deontology what is to count as a correct moral rule, producing a second premiss, before any guidance is given. And similarly, virtue ethics must specify who is to count as a virtuous agent. So far, the three are all in the same position.

Of course, if the virtuous agent can only be specified as an agent disposed to act in accordance with moral rules, as some have assumed, then virtue ethics collapses back into deontology and is no rival to it. So let us add a subsidiary premiss to this

skeletal outline, with the intention of making it clear that virtue ethics aims to provide a non-deontological specification of the virtuous agent via a specification of the virtues, which will be given in its second premiss:

V1a. A virtuous agent is one who acts virtuously, that is, one who has and exercises the virtues.

V2. A virtue is a character trait that . . .

This second premiss of virtue ethics might, like the second premiss of some versions of deontology, be completed simply by enumeration ('a virtue is one of the following', and then the list is given). Or we might, not implausibly, interpret the Hume of the second *Enquiry* as espousing virtue ethics. According to him, a virtue is a character trait (of human beings) that is useful or agreeable to its possessor or to others (inclusive 'or' both times). The standard neo Aristotelian completion claims that a virtue is a character trait a human being needs for *cudaimonia,* to flourish or live well.

Here, then, we have a specification of right action, whose structure closely resembles those of act-utilitarianism and many forms of deontology. Given that virtue ethics can come up with such a specification, can it still be maintained that it, unlike utilitarianism and deontology, cannot tell us what we should do? Does the specification somehow fail to provide guidance in a way that the other two do not?

At this point, the difficulty of identifying the virtuous agent in a way that makes V1 action-guiding tends to be brought forward again. Suppose it is granted that deontology has just as much difficulty in identifying the correct moral rules as virtue ethics has in identifying the virtues and hence the virtuous agent. Then the following objection may be made.

'All the same,' it may be said, 'if we imagine that that has been achieved—perhaps simply by enumeration—deontology yields a set of clear prescriptions which are readily applicable ("Do not lie", "Do not steal", "Do not inflict evil or harm on others", "Do help others", "Do keep promises", etc.). But virtue ethics yields only the prescription "Do what the virtuous agent (the one who is honest, charitable, just, etc.) would do in these circumstances." And this gives me no guidance unless I am (and know I am) a virtuous agent myself (in which case I am hardly in need of it). If I am less than fully virtuous, I shall have no idea what a virtuous agent would do, and hence cannot apply the only prescription that virtue ethics has given me. (Of course, act-utilitarianism also yields a single prescription, "Do what maximises happiness", but there are no *parallel* difficulties in applying that.) So there is the way in which V1 fails to be action-guiding where deontology and utilitarianism succeed.'

It is worth pointing out that, if I acknowledge that I am far from perfect, and am quite unclear what a virtuous agent would do in the circumstances in which I find myself, the obvious thing to do is to go and ask one, should this be possible. This is far from being a trivial point, for it gives a straightforward explanation of an aspect of our moral life which should not be ignored, namely the fact that we do seek moral guidance from people who we think are morally better than ourselves. When I am looking for an excuse to do something I have a horrid suspicion is wrong, I ask my moral inferiors (or peers if I am bad enough), 'Wouldn't you do such and such if you were in my shoes?' But when I am anxious to do what is right, and do not see my way clear, I go to people I respect and admire—people who I think are kinder, more honest, more just, wiser, than I am myself—and ask them what they would do in my circumstances. How utilitarianism and deontology would explain this fact, I do not know; but, as I said, the explanation within the terms of virtue ethics is straightforward. If you want to do what is right, and doing what is right is doing what a virtuous agent would do in the circumstances, then you should find out what she would do if you do not already know.

Moreover, seeking advice from virtuous people is not the only thing an imperfect agent trying to apply the single prescription of virtue ethics can do. For it is simply false that, in general, 'if I am less than fully virtuous, then I shall have no idea what a virtuous agent would do', as the objection claims. Recall that we are assuming that the virtues have been enumerated, as the deontologist's rules have been. The latter have been enumerated as, say, 'Do

not lie', 'Do not inflict evil or harm', etc.; the former as, say, honesty, charity, justice, etc. So, *ex hypothesi,* a virtuous agent is one who is honest, charitable, just, etc. So what she characteristically does is act honestly, charitably, justly, etc., and not dishonestly, uncharitably, unjustly. So given an enumeration of the virtues, I may well have a perfectly good idea of what the virtuous person would do in my circumstances despite my own imperfection. Would she lie in her teeth to acquire an unmerited advantage? No, for that would be to act both dishonestly and unjustly. Would she help the naked man by the roadside or pass by on the other side? The former, for she acts charitably. Might she keep a deathbed promise even though living people would benefit from its being broken? Yes, for she acts justly. And so on.

2. MORAL RULES

The above response to the objection that V1 fails to be action-guiding clearly amounts to a denial of the oft-repeated claim that virtue ethics does not come up with any rules (another version of the thought that it is concerned with Being rather than Doing and needs to be supplemented with rules). We can now see that it comes up with a large number; not only does each virtue generate a prescription—act honestly, charitably, justly—but each vice a prohibition—do not act dishonestly, uncharitably, unjustly. Once this point about virtue ethics is grasped (and it is remarkable how often it is overlooked), can there remain any reason for thinking that virtue ethics cannot tell us what we should do? Yes. The reason given is, roughly, that rules such as 'Act honestly', 'Do not act uncharitably', etc. are, like the rule 'Do what the virtuous agent would do', still the wrong sort of rule, still somehow doomed to fail to provide the action guidance supplied by the rules (or rule) of deontology and utilitarianism.

But how so? It is true that these rules of virtue ethics (henceforth 'v-rules') are couched in terms, or concepts, which are certainly 'evaluative' in *some* sense, or senses, of that difficult word. Is it this which dooms them to failure? Surely not, unless many forms of deontology fail too.[1] If we concentrate on the single example of lying, defining lying to be 'asserting what you believe to be untrue, with the intention of deceiving your hearer(s)', then we might, for a moment, preserve the illusion that a deontologist's rules do not contain 'evaluative' terms. But as soon as we remember that few deontologists will want to forgo principles of non-maleficence or beneficence, the illusion vanishes. For those principles, and their corresponding rules ('Do no evil or harm to others', 'Help others', 'Promote their well-being'), rely on terms or concepts which are at least as 'evaluative' as those employed in the v-rules. Few deontologists rest content with the simple quasi-biological 'Do not kill', but more refined versions of that rule such as 'Do not murder', or 'Do not kill the innocent', once again employ 'evaluative' terms, and 'Do not kill unjustly' is itself a particular instantiation of a v-rule.

Supposing this point were granted, a deontologist might still claim that the v-rules are markedly inferior to deontological rules as far as providing guidance for children is concerned. Granted, adult deontologists must think hard about what really constitutes harming someone, or promoting their well-being, or respecting their autonomy, or murder, but surely the simple rules we learnt at our mothers knee are indispensable? How could virtue ethics plausibly seek to dispense with these and expect toddlers to grasp 'Act charitably, honestly, and kindly', 'Don't act unjustly', and so on? Rightly are these concepts described as 'thick'! Far too thick for a child to grasp.

Strictly speaking, this claim about learning does not really support the *general* claim that v-rules fail to provide action-guidance, but the claim about learning, arising naturally as it does in the context of the general claim, is one I am more than happy to address. For it pinpoints a condition of adequacy that any normative ethics must meet, namely that such an ethics must not only come up with action guidance for a clever rational adult but also generate some account of moral education, of how one generation teaches the next what they should do. But an ethics inspired by Aristotle is unlikely to have forgotten the question of moral education, and the objection fails

to hit home. First, the implicit empirical claim that toddlers are taught *only* the deontologist's rules, not the 'thick' concepts, is false. Sentences such as 'Don't do that, it hurts, you mustn't be *cruel'*, 'Be *kind* to your brother, he's only little', 'Don't be so *mean, so greedy'* are commonly addressed to toddlers. Secondly, why should a proponent of virtue ethics deny the significance of such mother's-knee rules as 'Don't lie', 'Keep promises', 'Don't take more than your fair share', 'Help others'? Although it is a mistake, I have claimed, to define a virtuous agent simply as one disposed to act in accordance with moral rules, it is a very understandable mistake, given the obvious connection between, for example, the exercise of the virtue of honesty and refraining from lying. Virtue ethicists want to emphasize the fact that, if children are to be taught to be honest, they must be taught to prize the truth, and that *merely* teaching them not to lie will not achieve this end. But they need not deny that to achieve this end teaching them not to lie is useful, even indispensable.

So we can see that virtue ethics not only comes up with rules (the v-rules, couched in terms derived from the virtues and vices), but further, does not exclude the more familiar deontologists' rules. The theoretical distinction between the two is that the familiar rules, and their applications in particular cases, are given entirely different backings. According to virtue ethics, I must not tell this lie, since it would be dishonest, and dishonesty is a vice; must not break this promise, since it would be unjust, or a betrayal of friendship, or, perhaps (for the available virtue and vice terms do not neatly cover every contingency), simply because no virtuous person would.

However, the distinction is not merely theoretical. It is, indeed, the case that, with respect to a number of familiar examples, virtue ethicists and deontologists tend to stand shoulder to shoulder against utilitarians, denying that, for example, this lie can be told, this promise broken, this human being killed because the consequences of so doing will be generally happiness-maximizing. But, despite a fair amount of coincidence in action-guidance between deontology and virtue ethics, the latter has its own distinctive approach to the practical problems involved in dilemmas.

3. THE CONFLICT PROBLEM

It is a noteworthy fact that, in support of the general claim that virtue ethics cannot tell us what we should do, what is often cited is the 'conflict problem'. The requirements of different virtues, it is said, can point us in opposed directions. Charity prompts me to kill the person who would (truly) be better off dead, but justice forbids it. Honesty points to telling the hurtful truth, kindness and compassion to remaining silent or even lying. And so on. So virtue ethics lets us down just at the point where we need it, where we are faced with the really difficult dilemmas and do not know what to do.

In the mouth of a utilitarian, this may be a comprehensible criticism, for, as is well known, the only conflict that classical utilitarianism's one rule can generate is the tiresome logical one between the two occurrences of 'greatest' in its classical statement. But it is strange to find the very same criticism coming from deontologists, who are notoriously faced with the same problem. 'Don't kill', 'Respect autonomy', 'Tell the truth', 'Keep promises' may all conflict with 'Prevent suffering' or 'Do no harm', which is precisely why deontologists so often reject utilitarianism's deliverances on various dilemmas. Presumably, they must think that deontology can solve the 'conflict problem' and, further, that virtue ethics cannot. Are they right?

With respect to a number of cases, the deontologist's strategy is to argue that the 'conflict' is merely apparent, or *prima facie*. The proponent of virtue ethics employs the same strategy: according to her, many of the putative conflicts are merely apparent, resulting from a misapplication of the virtue or vice terms. Does kindness require not telling hurtful truths? Sometimes, but in *this* case, what has to be understood is that one does people no kindness by concealing this sort of truth from them, hurtful as it may be. Or, in a different case, the importance of the truth in question puts the consideration of hurt feelings out of court, and the agent does not show herself to be unkind, or callous, by speaking out. Does charity require that I kill the person who would be better off dead but who wants to stay alive, thereby conflicting with justice? . . .

One does not have to agree with the . . . judgements expressed here to recognize this as a *strategy* available to virtue ethics, any more than one has to agree with the particular judgements of deontologists who, for example, may claim that one rule outranks another, or that a certain rule has a certain exception clause built in, when they argue that a putative case of conflict is resolvable. Whether an individual has resolved a putative moral conflict or dilemma rightly is one question; whether a normative ethics has the wherewithal to resolve it is an entirely different question, and it is the latter with which we are concerned here.

The form the strategy takes within virtue ethics provides what may plausibly be claimed to be the deep explanation of why, in some cases agents do not know the answer to 'What should I do in these circumstances?' despite the fact that there *is* an answer. Trivially, the explanation is that they lack moral knowledge of what to do in this situation; but why? In what way? The lack, according to virtue ethics strategy, arises from lack of moral wisdom, from an inadequate grasp of what is involved in acting *kindly* (unkindly) or *charitably* (uncharitably), in being *honest*, or *just*, or *lacking in charity*, or, in general, of how the virtue (and vice) terms are to be correctly applied.

Here we come to an interesting defence of the v-rules, often criticized as being too difficult to apply for the agent who lacks moral wisdom. The defence relies on an (insufficiently acknowledged) insight of Aristotle's—namely that moral knowledge, unlike mathematical knowledge, cannot be acquired merely by attending lectures and is not characteristically to be found in people too young to have much experience of life.[2] Now *if* right action were determined by rules that any clever adolescent could apply correctly, how could this be so? Why are there not moral whiz-kids, the way there are mathematical (or quasi-mathematical) whiz-kids? But if the rules that determine right action are, like the v-rules, very difficult to apply correctly, involving, for instance, a grasp of the *sort* of truth that one does people no kindness by concealing, the explanation is readily to hand. Clever adolescents do not, in general, have a good grasp of that sort of thing. And *of course* I have to say 'the sort of truth that . . .' and 'that sort of thing', relying on my readers' knowledgeable uptake. For if I could define either sort, then, once again, clever adolescents could acquire moral wisdom from textbooks.

So far, I have described one strategy available to virtue ethics for coping with the 'conflict problem', a strategy that consists in arguing that the conflict is merely apparent, and can be resolved. According to one—only one of many—versions of 'the doctrine of the unity of the virtues', this is the only possible strategy (and ultimately successful), but this is not a claim I want to defend. One general reason is that I still do not know what I think about 'the unity of the virtues' (all those different versions!); a more particular, albeit related, reason is that, even if I were (somehow) sure that the requirements of the particular virtues could never conflict, I suspect that I would still believe in the possibility of moral dilemmas. I have been talking so far as though examples of putative dilemmas and examples of putative conflict between the requirements of different virtues (or deontologists' rules) coincided. But it may seem to many, as it does to me, that there are certain (putative) dilemmas which can only be described in terms of (putative) conflict with much artifice and loss of relevant detail.

Let us, therefore, consider the problem of moral dilemmas without bothering about whether they can be described in the simple terms of a conflict between the requirements of two virtues (or two deontologists' rules). Most of us, it may be supposed, have our own favoured example(s), either real or imaginary, of the case (or cases) where we see the decision about whether to do A or B as a very grave matter, have thought a great deal about what can be said for and against doing A, and doing B, and have still not managed to reach a conclusion which we think is the right one. How, if at all, does virtue ethics direct us to think about such cases?

4. DILEMMAS AND NORMATIVE THEORY

As a preliminary to answering that question, we should consider a much more general one, namely 'How should any normative ethics direct us to think about such cases?' This brings us to the topic of normative theory.

It is possible to detect a new movement in moral philosophy, a movement which has already attracted the name 'anti-theory in ethics'. Its various representatives have as a common theme the rejection of normative ethical theory; but amongst them are numbered several philosophers usually associated with virtue ethics. . . . This does not mean that they maintain what I have been denying, namely that virtue ethics is not normative; rather, they assume that it does not constitute a normative *theory* (and, mindful of this fact, I have been careful to avoid describing virtue ethics as one). What is meant by a 'normative theory' in this context is not easy to pin down, but, roughly, a normative theory is taken to be a set (possibly one-membered in the case of utilitarianism) of general principles which provide a *decision procedure* for all questions about how to act morally.

Part of the point of distinguishing a normative ethics by calling it a normative 'theory' is that a decent theory, as we know from science, enables us to answer questions that we could not answer before we had it. It is supposed to resolve those difficult dilemmas in which, it is said, our moral intuitions clash, and, prior to our grasp of the theory, we do not know what we should do. And a large part of the motivation for subscribing to 'anti-theory in ethics' is the belief that we should not be looking to science to provide us with our model of moral knowledge. Our 'intuitions' in ethics do not play the same role *vis-à-vis* the systematic articulation of moral knowledge as our 'observations' play *vis-à-vis* the systematic articulation of scientific knowledge; many of the goals appropriate to scientific knowledge—universality, consistency, completeness, simplicity—are not appropriate to moral knowledge; the acquisition of moral knowledge involves the training of the emotions in a way that the acquisition of scientific knowledge does not; and so on.

Clearly, many different issues are involved in the question of the extent to which moral knowledge should be modelled on scientific knowledge. The one I want to focus on here is the issue of whether a normative ethics should provide a decision procedure which enables us to resolve all moral dilemmas. Should it, to rephrase the question I asked above, (1) direct us to think about moral dilemmas in the belief that they *must* have a resolution, and that it is the business of the normative ethics in question to provide one? Or should it (2) have built into it the possibility of there being, as David Wiggins puts it, some 'absolutely undecidable questions—e.g. cases where . . . nothing could count as *the* reasonable practical answer',[3] counting questions about dilemmas of the sort described as amongst them? Or should it (3) be sufficiently flexible to allow for a comprehensible disagreement on this issue between two proponents of the normative ethics in question?

If we are to avoid modelling normative ethics mindlessly on scientific theory, we should not simply assume that the first position is the correct one. But rejection of such a model is not enough to justify the second position either. Someone might believe that for *any* dilemma there must be something that counts as the right way out of it, without believing that normative ethics remotely resembles scientific theory, perhaps because they subscribe to a version of realism. . . . More particularly, someone might believe on religious grounds that if I find myself, through no fault of my own, confronted with a dilemma (of the sort described), there must be something that counts as the right way out of it. . . . It seems to me that a normative ethics should be able to accommodate such differences, and so I subscribe to the third position outlined above.

Which position utilitarians and deontologists might espouse is not my concern here; I want to make clear how it is that virtue ethics is able to accommodate the third.

Let us return to V1—'An action is right iff it is what a virtuous agent would characteristically do in the circumstances.' This makes it clear that if two people disagree about the possibility of irresolvable moral dilemmas, their disagreement will manifest itself in what they say about the virtue of agents. So let us suppose that two candidates for being virtuous agents are each faced with their own case of the same dilemma. (I do not want to defend the view that each situation is unique in such a way that nothing would count as two agents being in the same circumstances

and faced with the same dilemma.) And, after much thought, one does A and the other does B.

Now, those who believe that there cannot be irresolvable dilemmas (of the sort described) can say that, in the particular case, at least one agent, say the one who did A, thereby showed themselves to be lacking in virtue, perhaps in that practical wisdom which is an essential aspect of each of the 'non-intellectual' virtues. . . . Or they can say that at least one agent must have been lacking in virtue, without claiming to know which.

But those who believe that there are, or may be, irresolvable dilemmas can suppose that both agents are not merely candidates for being, but actually are, virtuous agents. For to believe in such dilemmas is to believe in cases in which even the perfect practical wisdom that the most idealized virtuous agent has does not direct her to do, say, A rather than B. And then the fact that these virtuous agents acted differently, despite being in the same circumstances, *determines* the fact that there is no answer to the question 'What is *the* right thing to do in these circumstances?' For if it is true both that *a* virtuous agent would do A, and that *a* virtuous agent would do B (as it is, since, *ex hypothesi,* one did do A and the other B), then both A and B are, in the circumstances, right, according to V1.

The acceptance of this should not be taken as a counsel of despair, nor as an excuse for moral irresponsibility. It does not license coin-tossing when one is faced with a putative dilemma, for the moral choices we find most difficult do not come to us conveniently labelled as 'resolvable' or 'irresolvable'. I was careful to specify that the two candidates for being virtuous agents acted only 'after much thought'. It will always be necessary to think very hard before accepting the idea that a particular moral decision does not have one right issue, and, even on the rare occasions on which she eventually reached the conclusion that this is such a case, would the virtuous agent toss a coin? Of course not.

No doubt someone will say, 'Well, if she really thinks the dilemma is irresolvable, why not, according to virtue ethics?', and the answer must, I think, be *ad hominem. If* their conception of the virtuous agent—of someone with the character traits of justice, honesty, compassion, kindness, loyalty, wisdom, etc.—really is of someone who would resort to coin-tossing when confronted with what she believed to be an irresolvable dilemma, then that is the bizarre conception they bring to virtue ethics, and they must, presumably, think that there is nothing morally irresponsible or light-minded about coin-tossing in such cases. So they should not want virtue ethics to explain 'why not'. But if their conception of the virtuous agent does not admit of her acting thus—if they think such coin-tossing would be irresponsible, or light-minded, or indeed simply insane—then they have no need to ask the question. *My* question was, 'Would the virtuous agent toss a coin?'; they agree that of course she would not. Why not? Because it would be irresponsible, or light-minded, or the height of folly.

The acceptance of the possibility of irresolvable dilemmas within virtue ethics (by those of us who do accept it) should not be seen in itself as conceding much to 'pluralism'. If I say that I can imagine a case in which two virtuous agents are faced with a dilemma, and one does A while the other does B, I am not saying that I am imagining a case in which the two virtuous agents each think that what the other does is wrong (vicious, contrary to virtue) because they have radically different views about what is required by a certain virtue, or about whether a certain character trait is a vice, or about whether something is to be greatly valued or of little importance. I am imagining a case in which my two virtuous agents have the same 'moral views' about everything, up to and including the view that, in this particular case, neither decision is *the* right one, and hence neither is wrong. Each recognizes the propriety of the other's reason for doing what she did—say, 'To avoid *that* evil', 'To secure *this* good'—for her recognition of the fact that this is as good a moral reason as her own (say, 'To avoid *this* evil', 'To secure *that* good') is what forced each to accept the idea that the dilemma was irresolvable in the first place. Though each can give such a reason for what they did (A in one case, B in the other), neither attempts to give 'the moral reason' why they did one *rather than* the other. The 'reason' for or explanation of *that* would be, if available at all, in terms of psychological autobiography ('I decided to sleep on it, and when I woke up I just found myself thinking in terms of doing A', or 'I just felt terrified at the thought of doing A: I'm sure this was totally irrational, but I did, so I did B').[4]

The topic of this chapter has been the view that virtue ethics cannot be a normative rival to utilitarianism and deontology because 'it cannot tell us what we should do'. In defending the existence of normative virtue ethics I have not attempted to argue that it can 'tell us what we should do' in such a way that the difficult business of acting well is made easy for us. I have not only admitted but welcomed the fact that, in some cases, moral wisdom is required if the v-rules are to be applied correctly and apparent dilemmas thereby resolved (or indeed identified, since a choice that may seem quite straightforward to the foolish or wicked may rightly appear difficult, calling for much thought, to the wise). Nor have I attempted to show that virtue ethics is guaranteed to be able to resolve every dilemma. It seems bizarre to insist that a normative ethics must be able to do this prior to forming a reasonable belief that there cannot be irresolvable dilemmas, but those who have formed such a belief may share a normative ethics with those who have different views concerning realism, or the existence of God. A normative ethics, I suggested, should be able to accommodate both views on this question, as virtue ethics does, not model itself mindlessly on scientific theory.

NOTES

1. Forms of utilitarianism which aim to be entirely value-free or empirical, such as those which define happiness in terms of the satisfaction of actual desires or preferences, regardless of their content, or as a mental state whose presence is definitively established by introspection, seem to me the least plausible, but I accept that anyone who embraces them may consistently complain that v-rules give inferior action-guidance in virtue of containing 'evaluative' terms. But any utilitarian who wishes to employ any distinction between the higher and lower pleasures, or rely on some list of goods (such as autonomy, friendship, knowledge of important matters) in defining happiness, must grant that even her single rule is implicitly 'evaluative'.

2. *Nicomachean Ethics* 1142a 12–16.
3. D. Wiggins, 'Truth, Invention and the Meaning of Life', *Proceedings of the British Academy* 62 (1976), 371, my italics.

4. It must be remembered that, *ex hypothesi,* these are things said by virtuous agents about what they did when confronted with an irresolvable dilemma. Of course they would be very irresponsible accounts of why one had done A rather than B in a resolvable case.

STUDY QUESTIONS

1. Does virtue ethics tell us what we should do?
2. Does virtue ethics share the same structure as Kantianism and consequentialism?
3. According to Hursthouse, what is the "conflict problem"?
4. Do genuine moral dilemmas exist?

Virtue and Right

Robert N. Johnson

According to virtue ethics, the right act is the one a completely virtuous person would perform. But Robert Johnson, Professor of Philosophy at the University of Missouri, argues that a completely virtuous person wouldn't waste time performing self-improving acts. Thus they cannot be right. Yet for most of us they are precisely the right acts to perform. Johnson thus concludes that the account of right actions offered by proponents of virtue ethics should be rejected.

Is the morally right action the action that a virtuous person would perform? Many may think so, even that this is an uninteresting truism. The only question of consequence may seem to be whether moral philosophy does best to begin by theorizing about right actions or about the virtues. But the claim that right actions are those of a virtuous person is so far from being an uninteresting truism as to be utterly false, or so I believe. In particular, I think that it is inconsistent with the commonsense idea that we ought to become better people. If I am right, then not only is this claim about virtue and right action false, but any theory that relies on it to construct a virtue-oriented theory of right action will be unable to explain moral distinctions we regularly make regarding behavior appropriate for those who could better themselves.

In what follows, I begin by discussing views espoused by Rosalind Hursthouse. . . . I describe in broad strokes . . . [her] account of right action . . . based on the idea that right actions are those characteristic of the virtuous. I then give three examples of right conduct that would be utterly uncharacteristic

of the virtuous and argue that this shows that the account should be rejected. . . .

Although I argue that these virtue-oriented accounts of right action in their current forms are unsatisfactory, I stop short of claiming that no virtue-oriented account can work. As Swanton points out, "virtue ethics in modern guise is still in its infancy,"[1] and so it would be premature to conclude that the whole project must founder on the problems I discuss. My message is in fact broader than this: however an ethical theory combines its account of the virtues with its account of right action, it must make room for a genuine moral obligation to improve your character and to act in other ways that are appropriate only because you could be a better person than you are.

I

Why construct a theory of right action out of a conception of virtue in the first place? After all, some who have favored a virtue-oriented approach to

From Robert N. Johnson, "Virtue and Right," *Ethics*, vol. 113, no. 4, 2003. Reprinted by permission of the journal.

ethics have resisted doing so on the grounds that moral philosophy does better simply to stick with virtue concepts. Such concepts are too "thick," they think, and virtuous behavior too "uncodifiable" to make such a project profitable. But even so there is also a strong interest among many other virtue ethicists in developing an account of right action that is a genuine alternative to standard deontological and consequentialist theories.[2] On a virtue-oriented alternative, "a conception of right conduct is grasped, as it were, from the inside out," as McDowell has put it.[3] . . . Hursthouse's view . . . is the most fully developed account of this kind. In summary, her view is:

> V: An action A is right for S in circumstances C if and only if a completely virtuous agent would characteristically A in C.[4]

A few remarks about V. First, V states that right actions are those characteristic of a completely virtuous agent. This avoids complications arising from the possibility that in the absence of the other virtues, a courageous person, say, might be led by his courage to act unjustly; a just person might be led by her justice to act unkindly; and so on. Virtue ethicists often argue that there is a "unity of the virtues." Claim V renders this explicit, however, by presenting in summary form the idea that a genuinely right action would express or be brought about by a virtuous character trait but at the same time would not express or be brought about by any vices, and so it will be an action *characteristic* of an agent possessing *all* of the virtues *completely.*

Second, there is, naturally, more than one way to conceive of a "completely virtuous person," depending on, for instance, our list of virtues and our optimism about how much perfection a human being can achieve.[5] Certainly any conception of a completely virtuous agent should be a human, rather than an impossibly god-like, ideal. Nevertheless, the conception of complete virtue in V will be an idealization. For one thing, it is likely that complete virtue will be very rare on any theory of the virtues. For another, even if all of the virtues were completely exemplified by some actual person, the extent of the actual and possible circumstance in which we need to speak of

the right or wrong thing to do is far greater than the range of circumstances any actual person will have faced. Hence, in order to speak of right actions outside of that range, we will have to speak of the characteristic actions of someone whose character will be better, perhaps quite a bit better, than that of any actual persons in that circumstance.

Third, by referring to "characteristic" actions of a virtuous person, V excludes those actions that would be for some reason out of character for such a person. This is not to say that no situations can exist in which one ought to perform an action that may seem uncharacteristic of a virtuous person. Circumstances can sometimes force one's hand, so that one must do what is terrible in the face of the even more terrible. But this raises no special problem for V. What the virtuous person would do in these conditions is what would be uncharacteristic of the virtuous person in others. It might be misleading to speak of the actions that a virtuous person would perform in such dilemmas as "right" or even to focus on the action at all rather than the way in which the virtuous would perform it. But V will at least provide an action-guiding answer, or range of answers, to the question of what would be characteristic of a completely virtuous person in such circumstances.[6] . . .

No doubt there are other virtues of V, and clearly many more details need to be filled in. But the basic ideas behind the theory, along with some of its most desirable features, should now be in place. What V offers us is the means to construct a theory of right conduct out of a conception of virtue and, thus, a desirable alternative to the standard utilitarian and deontological theories. One begins by developing an account of the virtues independently of a conception of right action. One then conceives of right actions as first and foremost virtuous actions, or actions characteristic of an agent possessed of the virtues. Moreover, one represents moral facts as being necessarily practical, in that they are themselves at bottom constituted (even if not wholly or even primarily) by dispositions to action. Finally, these facts are themselves constituted by ordinary natural facts, for instance, psychological states of a human being. Let us now turn to the plight of the less than fully virtuous.

II

A

Consider this person: he is mendacious, lying even about unimportant things such as the films he has seen or books he has read. The lies cause little harm, nor are they meant to, and he doesn't lie merely to extricate himself out of difficult situations. That is, lying is not a means by which he expresses other vices such as malice or cowardice. Rather, it is a habit operating more or less independently of other vices, engendered by an insufficient appreciation of the value of truthfulness. Indeed, he occasionally rationalizes lies to himself as a "social lubricant" to keep those around him happy, or perhaps as a way of "getting things done." Even so, often lies pass his lips almost without his notice.

Suppose now that a friend calls him on the carpet for lying, and as a result he decides that he must change. He must change, he thinks, not to avoid further embarrassment or because it would be "the best policy," but because it is after all rotten to behave in the way that he has. His task will not be simple. Lying has become habitual and has permeated his attitudes so deeply that no "decision to do better" can by itself change him. What sorts of steps might he take?

Some virtue theorists, including Aristotle himself, tend to be pessimistic about the possibility of character change.[7] But I will assume for the sake of argument that this person's character is within the range of those that are changeable. With enough effort and persistence he could change. Given this, there are many things he might do, but again for the sake of argument, suppose he does the following: he begins by resolving to tell the truth and exerting his will in that direction. But he soon caves in to temptation, given that lying is so easy and "natural." So after consulting with a therapist he decides to begin writing down lies that he tells, no matter how insignificant, to become more aware of his habits and to keep track of improvements. Further, whenever he is aware of temptations to lie, he tries to develop a concrete idea of what would happen if he told the truth. Who, exactly, is protected by my lie? Why do I want

to protect her? Who, exactly, would be dismayed if my lie were discovered? He also tries to remind himself that people often do not react badly to the person who tells them unpleasant truths. Finally, since he suspects that his mendacity may have something to do with low self-esteem, he engages in activities that enhance it.

The above sketches a range of kinds of actions: "self-monitoring" and keeping track of one's progress toward becoming a better person, trying to change one's thinking about one's situation and the consequences of one's actions, enhancing one's self-esteem, and so on. Common sense would regard these kinds of things as what he morally ought to do in circumstances such as these, at least insofar as they will improve his character. Yet all are utterly uncharacteristic of completely virtuous agents. Note well: it makes absolutely no difference whether these particular things are what this particular person ought to do. Perhaps there are better ways to improve himself. But surely he ought to do things of this sort, things over and above simply "deciding to tell the truth from now on." This would in large part consist in behavior that a completely virtuous person would not characteristically engage in. That he ought to do such things goes directly counter to the claim that right conduct is conduct characteristic of the virtuous.

Or so it seems. For some might think that Aristotle has a ready reply: it is by performing the very same actions that a virtuous person would characteristically perform, he argued, that we cultivate the virtues in ourselves and, hence, better ourselves. In summary, the argument would be:

(1) Virtues are states of character arising in the novice "neither by nor against nature."[8]
(2) "A state results from similar activities."[9] Therefore,
(3) "We become just by doing just actions, temperate by doing temperate actions, brave by doing brave actions."[10]

The first premise ensures that virtues are the sorts of things—states—that can and must be cultivated in a person over time, ideally from child-hood. The second is a general claim about how states develop, so, applying this to the virtues qua states, the virtues arise from performing similar actions. Hence, it is by acting as the virtuous agent acts that we develop the states that the virtuous agent possesses. It may seem to follow, then, that there are no actions other than simply acting as the virtuous person himself acts that develop the virtues, and so no set of right actions uncharacteristic of the virtuous.

But this does not follow. The argument only implies that acting as the virtuous agent acts does produce them. But, even were this true, V is vulnerable *merely if there are actions producing the virtues that one morally ought to perform, and these actions are not part of the characteristic behavior of virtuous persons.* I think that common sense recognizes many such actions.

One might, of course, insist that they are only exceptions. "Sure, one might stick one's finger in a socket and change forever after from coward to hero. But that makes no difference to the general theory of virtue and moral development. What is important is that *in general* one becomes virtuous by acting as the virtuous person acts." But just how plausible is it that as a general rule it is by performing the actions characteristic of the virtuous that we become virtuous ourselves? Not very, at least for many stages of moral development and for many people trying to better themselves. It certainly isn't plausible with regard to the reforming liar. Strategies of the sort my mendacious person employs are far more realistic than simply doing what is characteristic of the truthful person, whatever that may be beyond simply telling the truth. Hence, if the above argument entails that as a general rule one becomes virtuous simply by acting as the virtuous person acts (and, hence, that as a general rule there are no right actions that are uncharacteristic of the virtuous) it is unsound.

It is worth pointing out that what Aristotle himself actually says about those who are not yet completely virtuous takes into account the sorts of actions of which I am thinking. It is difficult to hit the mean, he argues, since "different people have different natural tendencies toward different goals," and "we are already biased in [pleasure's] favor."[11] So we—the not-yet-virtuous—should "steer clear of the more contrary extreme . . . and take the lesser of the evils," "drag ourselves off" in the direction that is contrary to our natural tendencies, and "beware above all of pleasure and its sources."[12] This creates a puzzle: according to the above argument, a person who does what Aristotle says to do would develop the traits of taking the lesser evil, acting contrary to his natural tendencies and avoiding what is pleasant. Yet virtue does not, at least for Aristotle, consist of possessing the traits of taking the lesser evil, acting contrary to natural tendencies, and avoiding the pleasant. The virtuous take pleasure in doing what is best, from a settled disposition that is as if it were a second nature. Now given that Aristotle thought that these strategies would, rather than create dispositions at odds with virtue, help to promote it, then he himself also thought that simply acting as the virtuous act is not necessarily the only, or even best, way to acquire virtue.[13] I think that he is right about this. Whether it can be squared with the above argument, though, is not crucial here. My point is only that if Aristotle's argument regarding the development of virtue is read in such a way that its conclusions are incompatible with the advice that he himself gives us, its implications are false.

There is, in any case, a second problem with V that I want to discuss. Even if there were no obligation to improve ourselves morally, there certainly is one at least to take account of: our shortcomings when we act. In particular, the novice at virtue ought to perform self-controlling acts. But these acts will again be utterly uncharacteristic of the virtuous, who, by contrast, are temperate. As Bernard Williams notes, . . . "If I know that I fall short of temperance and am unreliable with respect even to some kinds of self-control, I shall have good reason not to do some things that a temperate person would properly and safely do." Indeed, as we shall see, I will also have good reason to do some things that a temperate person would not do. My next example develops these points.

B

Imagine someone whose moral upbringing was inadequate, but after many years of lessons learned the hard way manages to keep his life in moral order. To put it simply, he struggles to do what he should. Most who know him would agree that his character lacks grace. His day-to-day life reveals a pattern of behavior characteristic of a person who is at war with malicious and cowardly desires. One might even think less of him for this, but we would find it difficult to fault his actions themselves. He never intentionally harms others, nor does he evade worthy tasks or causes because of risks to himself.

He is able to overcome his unsavory desires not because of any special inner surge of motivation that he is able to muster at the instant duty calls. Far from it. Since he knows that he will fail if he leaves it to a fortuitous surge, he plans ahead when he foresees potential struggles. He thinks of ways to avoid behaving badly for those times when he thinks that temptation may strike, such as alternative ways of phrasing difficult truths that he must tell others. Further, he tries to create social support for behaving well. For example, when he decided to help move his elderly mother across town one weekend, he didn't simply make a private inner "decision to help." He told friends ahead of time that he was going to do it, that he had the free time to help, that he thought he ought to help, that he wouldn't be around to go out with them, and so on.

He also tries to be specific about exactly what he should do, so that he knows exactly what counts as movement toward fulfilling obligations. Instead of meditating on puerile aphorisms such as "I ought to help others in need" and then leaving it to impulse to determine what he will do and when and where he will do it, he brainstorms about exactly where, how, when, and to what he can contribute. Indeed, he does this in part to avoid projects that will require him to rely too heavily on the weaknesses in his character. This of course helps to create the very pattern of action that reveals that character to those who know him. No doubt, he would like to be more "natural" and admires those who are. And although he often must work around his weaknesses, he tries hard not to pander to them. He just has come to know himself well enough to know that, at least in certain situations, he is not at his best.

In order to perform a just, brave, kind, or otherwise virtuous action, a nonvirtuous person will have to control himself in many ways. Indeed, if he didn't have to, he would already possess the kind of psychological makeup that would make virtuous action second nature. In other words, he would not be a novice at all. Notice in particular that a novice's virtuous action is typically embedded in a web of self-controlling actions. That makes the virtuous action itself shrink in significance when viewed within this web. By contrast, a temperate person performs none of these acts of self-control. The virtuous act for the virtuous is not embedded in any such web. Again, how one ought to behave is here utterly uncharacteristic of the virtuous.

The virtuous would also characteristically behave in a fair number of further ways, and not in others, that are at odds with how it seems most of us should. Consider, for instance, this final example.

C

Imagine a person who lacks moral sensitivity in some area. The problem is not that he faces more than his share of dilemmas. Nor is it that he is so malicious that he runs roughshod over the interests, rights, and feelings of others with pleasure. Rather, he faces most of the same sorts of moral situations as the rest of us and means well, but, perhaps because of his upbringing or culture, he has a moral blind spot. Suppose, however, that he possesses enough self-awareness to know this. Therefore, when he has reason to doubt his perception he asks for guidance from a friend who is in these respects more virtuous and whose vision is in these respects unhindered. The friend, by contrast, is able to see precisely what these situations call for. The person I want you to imagine, however, first tries to rely on his own judgment and is determined not to be dependent on his friend's perception. Indeed, given enough time, he might be able to work out many of the problems for himself. But many situations call for immediate steps. In these situations, he surely ought to ask for guidance.

The virtuous are supposed to appreciate fully their circumstances—who has been harmed and how, what is called for in terms of a response, and so on. Indeed, some even think of moral education as itself mostly a matter of perceptual improvement. In any case, the less sensitive ought to try to improve their moral perception and in particular seek guidance from the more sensitive. Hence, what one morally ought to do—seek guidance and try to improve one's perceptual capacities—is again utterly uncharacteristic of the completely virtuous. It would not be plausible to reply here that there is nothing a person can do to improve her perception other than to develop the virtues. One can and should do many things, things other than simply developing virtues, given that one's moral perception is imperfect. One is to seek counsel.[14] This is not to deny that constantly doing so could make one dependent on others rather than possessed of better vision. But in reasonable amounts this can sharpen one's perception or at least help one in difficult situations to discover the right thing to do.

Let me point out, since it will become important in what follows, that it is sensible to ask for guidance only from those who are in a good position to give it, those who are in some way better placed than you, or those who are experts relative to your area of concern. A virtuous person may often be a good source of guidance about what is to be done in this or that situation. But her expertise, if we should call it that, would be much like that of the native speaker of a language. The native speaker can just hear what does or doesn't fit grammatically; likewise, a virtuous agent can just perceive what does or doesn't fit morally, at least so far as her own actions go. Thus, if one wants guidance on how to say such and such in a given language, it may make sense to ask a native speaker. Typically, one should ask what the right thing to say would be in the circumstances. But a native speaker will probably lack explicit knowledge of grammatical rules and, more important, will have little idea how best to learn her language. Anyone who has tried to teach her mother tongue knows just how difficult, how far beyond simply having mastery of the language, it is. Rather, the native speaker knows what sounds right, what she would say, and when and how she would say it.

Similarly, there is nothing in the idea of a virtuous person requiring her to have any explicit knowledge of moral rules (if there are any), much less of moral psychology or education. The virtuous, simply in virtue of their virtues, may be said to know how they are to respond, what they are to feel, what they are to look for, and what they are to do and why. To that limited extent, they may well have good, perhaps even principled and general, counsel to give. But a wide range of situations would remain in which you would have no reason at all to think that a virtuous person will have advice worth following, that she will be any better placed to give answers than are you. For from the fact that the virtuous know how to behave in any given circumstance, it just doesn't follow that they are in a position to tell the less virtuous how to behave. For one thing, whether they would be depends on whether they would also be good predictors of their own behavior, which they need not be to be completely virtuous. For another, there will be no more reason to think that they have worthwhile guidance concerning how to become virtuous than there is to think that the native speaker of a language has worthwhile guidance concerning learning that language. Of course, she may well perceive that, in a given situation, you ought to improve your character, much as a native speaker can just hear that you ought to improve your grammar. But there is no reason to think that either will have much of interest to say about what to do beyond that.

In my example, asking for guidance is sensible, even admirable. The person who has the moral blind spot is asking the person who lacks it to point out anything he might have missed, and this is the sort of thing that is called for. The person, however, does not ask how to improve his moral perception. He just wants to know what he's missing, if there are facts that a better placed person would not have missed. As can often be the case, what the person who lacks sensitivity should do as a result then may well be what the virtuous themselves would characteristically do.[15] What such a person should do, in addition, however, is something quite uncharacteristic of the virtuous, namely, ask for guidance.

The above, I think, oversimplifies things in one respect. For compensating for one's moral blind spots, if such there be, is often compatible with complete virtue. After all, we think better of those who acknowledge their social or cultural biases and trust the insights of those who are in a better position to see what they may have difficulty seeing. And even a completely virtuous person in certain kinds of circumstances might lack the emotional responsiveness required for accurate moral perception. A recent death in the family, a harrowing brush with death, or the birth of a child can and should affect one, no matter how virtuous, so deeply that one's emotional state will make one unresponsive to moral facts to which one would otherwise be perfectly attuned. Hence, a virtuous person would ask for guidance in these cases. But many other blind spots in moral vision are not at all compatible with virtue. Their most common source is neither cultural bias nor emotional upheaval but, if Aristotle is to be believed, the lack of virtue itself. Each and every character flaw brings with it a failure of moral vision: the coward sees the courageous as foolhardy, the miser views the generous person as vulgar or as a spendthrift, to the malicious the benevolent appear weak, and so on. So even if blind spots caused by cultural difference or emotional upheaval are consistent with virtue, there are vastly many more such failures which are not. And in each such case, it will be true that such a person should ask for guidance from those better placed. . . .

V

If self-improvement and other actions of the sort that I have discussed are genuinely morally right, then no ethical theory should accept V, whether to generate a theory of right action out of an account of the virtues or, indeed, to generate a theory of the virtues out of a theory of right action. Further, any alternative virtue-oriented theory of right action must take account of the fact that many actions are morally required of us only because we fail to possess the character traits or motives that we ought to possess. But, again, my argument leaves untouched the

position of virtue ethicists who make no claim to offer any conception of right action. It also leaves a large question about how to combine right and virtue in such a way that it takes seriously the thought that we have a moral obligation to better ourselves. But I must leave that question for another time.

NOTES

1. Christine Swanton, "A Virtue Ethical Account of Right Action," *Ethics* 112 (2001): 32.
2. Bernard Williams, though not a virtue theorist himself, argues this in his *Ethics and the Limits of Philosophy* (Cambridge, Mass.: Harvard University Press, 1985), pp. 140–45; see also Elizabeth Anscombe, "Modern Moral Philosophy," in *Virtue Ethics,* eds. Roger Crisp and Michael Slote (Oxford: Oxford University Press, 1997), pp. 26–44, pp. 37–40; and John McDowell, "Virtue and Reason," in Crisp and Slote, eds., pp. 147–54.
3. John McDowell, "Virtue and Reason," in Crisp and Slote, eds., p. 141.
4. Hursthouse, *On Virtue Ethics* (Oxford: Oxford University Press, 2000), p. 28, and her "Virtue Ethics and Abortion," in Crisp and Slote, eds., pp. 217–38.
5. On the Aristotelian view, the ideal of complete virtue also includes many "intellectual" virtues. However, since it is dubious that complete moral virtue requires possession of literally all of the intellectual virtues, I will just assume that complete virtue that is humanly attainable requires no intellectual facility beyond what one must possess to be "practically wise."
6. See Hursthouse's illuminating discussion of dilemmas in chap. 3 of *On Virtue Ethics.*
7. See Aristotle, *Nicomachean Ethics*, 1114a1–1114b25.
8. Ibid., 1103a25.
9. Ibid., 1103b21.
10. Ibid., 1103b1.
11. Ibid., 1109a20–1109b20.
12. Ibid., 1009b7–1109b12.
13. Also, passages from the *Politics*, 1260a20–1260b7, 1340b10–19, and 1342a5–1342b33, reflect Aristotle's awareness that how one improves character depends on the state of one's character here and now and so is not simply developed by "acting as the fully virtuous characteristically acts."
14. Compare Hursthouse (*On Virtue Ethics,* pp. 35–37), who explicitly endorses the idea that seeking such guidance from the virtuous is what we ought to do in

such situations, without noticing the implications of this for V.

15. There are many other things a novice who lacks sensitivity can and should also do: take longer than may seem necessary to decide on his course of action, not rely on how things seem to be, try to stimulate his imagination, and use ever more of it when reviewing the facts. These also are not characteristic of virtuous persons, since they already use their imagination fully, and given that what is good is what appears good to the man of practical wisdom (*Nicomachean Ethics*, 1113a32–1113b2).

STUDY QUESTIONS

1. What is a self-improving action?
2. What does being completely virtuous require?
3. Would a completely virtuous person perform self-improving actions?
4. Is Johnson's objection to virtue theory decisive?

Part XI

THE ETHICS OF CARE

Moral Orientation and Moral Development

Carol Gilligan

Carol Gilligan, University Professor at New York University, maintains that moral concepts and theories have been constructed from a male perspective, leading to an exaggerated focus on justice. Drawing on her empirical research, she argues for the inclusion of a female moral perspective, one that places an emphasis on care. She does not view the two perspectives as rivals but as different moral orientations.

When one looks at an ambiguous figure like the drawing that can be seen as a young or old woman, or the image of the vase and the faces, one initially sees it in only one way. Yet even after seeing it in both ways, one way often seems more compelling. This phenomenon reflects the laws of perceptual organization that favor certain modes of visual grouping. But it also suggests a tendency to view reality as unequivocal and thus to argue that there is one right or better way of seeing.

The experiments of the Gestalt psychologists on perceptual organization provide a series of demonstrations that the same proximal pattern can be organized in different ways so that, for example, the same figure can be seen as a square or a diamond, depending on its orientation in relation to a surrounding frame. Subsequent studies show that the context influencing which of two possible organizations will be chosen may depend not only on the features of the array presented but also on the perceiver's past experience or expectation. Thus, a bird-watcher and a rabbit-keeper are likely to see the duck-rabbit figure in different ways; yet this difference does not imply that one way is better or a higher form of perceptual organization. It does, however, call attention to the fact that the rabbit-keeper, perceiving the rabbit, may not see the ambiguity of the figure until someone points out that it can also be seen as a duck.

This paper presents a similar phenomenon with respect to moral judgment, describing two moral perspectives that organize thinking in different ways. The analogy to ambiguous figure perception arises from the observation that although people are aware of both perspectives, they tend to adopt one or the other in defining and resolving moral conflict. Since moral judgments organize thinking about choice in difficult situations, the adoption of a single perspective may facilitate clarity of decision. But the wish for clarity may also imply a compelling human need for resolution or closure, especially in the face of decisions that give rise to discomfort or unease. Thus, the search for clarity in seeing may blend with a search for justification, encouraging the position that there is one right or better way to think about moral problems. This question, which has been the subject of intense theological and philosophical debate,

From Carol Gilligan, "Moral Orientation and Moral Development," in *Women and Moral Theory*, eds. E. F. Kittay and D. Meyers, Rowman & Littlefield, 1987. Reprinted by permission of the publisher.

becomes of interest to the psychologist not only because of its psychological dimensions—the tendency to focus on one perspective and the wish for justification—but also because one moral perspective currently dominates psychological thinking and is embedded in the most widely used measure for assessing the maturity of moral reasoning.

In describing an alternative standpoint, I will reconstruct the account of moral development around two moral perspectives, grounded in different dimensions of relationship that give rise to moral concern. The justice perspective, often equated with moral reasoning, is recast as one way of seeing moral problems and a care perspective is brought forward as an alternate vision or frame. The distinction between justice and care as alternative perspectives or moral orientations is based empirically on the observation that a shift in the focus of attention from concerns about justice to concerns about care changes the definition of what constitutes a moral problem, and leads the same situation to be seen in different ways. Theoretically, the distinction between justice and care cuts across the familiar divisions between thinking and feeling, egoism and altruism, theoretical and practical reasoning. It calls attention to the fact that all human relationships, public and private, can be characterized *both* in terms of equality and in terms of attachment, and that both inequality and detachment constitute grounds for moral concern. Since everyone is vulnerable both to oppression and to abandonment, two moral visions—one of justice and one of care—recur in human experience. The moral injunctions, not to act unfairly toward others, and not to turn away from someone in need, capture these different concerns.

The conception of the moral domain as comprised of at least two moral orientations raises new questions about observed differences in moral judgment and the disagreements to which they give rise. Key to this revision is the distinction between differences in developmental stage (more or less adequate positions within a single orientation) and differences in orientation (alternative perspectives or frameworks). The findings reported in this paper of an association between moral orientation and gender speak directly to the continuing controversy over sex differences in moral reasoning. In doing so, however, they also offer an empirical explanation for why previous thinking about moral development has been organized largely within the justice framework.

My research on moral orientation derives from an observation made in the course of studying the relationship between moral judgment and action. Two studies, one of college students describing their experiences of moral conflict and choice, and one of pregnant women who were considering abortion, shifted the focus of attention from the ways people reason about hypothetical dilemmas to the ways people construct moral conflicts and choices in their lives. This change in approach made it possible to see what experiences people define in moral terms, and to explore the relationship between the understanding of moral problems and the reasoning strategies used and the actions taken in attempting to resolve them. In this context, I observed that women, especially when speaking about their own experiences of moral conflict and choice, often define moral problems in a way that eludes the categories of moral theory and is at odds with the assumptions that shape psychological thinking about morality and about the self.[1] This discovery, that a different voice often guides the moral judgments and the actions of women, called attention to a major design problem in previous moral judgment research: namely, the use of all-male samples as the empirical basis for theory construction. . . .

An analysis of the language and logic of men's and women's moral reasoning about a range of hypothetical and real dilemmas underlies the distinction elaborated in this paper between a justice and a care perspective. The empirical association of care reasoning with women suggests that discrepancies observed between moral theory and the moral judgments of girls and women may reflect a shift in perspective, a change in moral orientation. Like the figure-ground shift in ambiguous figure perception, justice and care as moral perspectives are not opposites or mirror-images of one another, with justice uncaring and care unjust. Instead, these perspectives denote different ways of organizing the basic elements of moral judgment: self, others, and the relationship between them. With the shift in perspective from justice to care, the organizing dimension of relationship changes from inequality/equality to attachment/detachment, reorganizing thoughts, feelings, and language so that words connoting relationship like "dependence" or "responsibility" or even moral terms such as "fairness" and "care" take on different meanings. To organize relationships in terms of attachment rather than in terms of equality changes the way human connection is imagined, so that the images or metaphors of relationship shift from hierarchy or balance to network or web. In addition, each organizing framework leads to a different way of imagining the self as a moral agent.

From a justice perspective, the self as moral agent stands as the figure against a ground of social relationships, judging the conflicting claims of self and others against a standard of equality or equal respect (the Categorical Imperative, the Golden Rule). From a care perspective, the relationship becomes the figure, defining self and others. Within the context of relationship, the self as a moral agent perceives and responds to the perception of need. The shift in moral perspective is manifest by a change in the moral question from "What is just?" to "How to respond?"

For example, adolescents asked to describe a moral dilemma often speak about peer or family pressure in which case the moral question becomes how to maintain moral principles or standards and resist the influence of one's parents or friends. "I have a right to my religious opinions," one teenager explains, referring to a religious difference with his parents. Yet, he adds, "I respect their views." The same dilemma, however, is also construed by adolescents as a problem of attachment, in which case the moral question becomes: how to respond both to oneself and to one's friends or one's parents, how to maintain or strengthen connection in the face of differences in belief. "I understand their fear of my new religious ideas," one teenager explains, referring to her religious disagreement with her parents, "but they really ought to listen to me and try to understand my beliefs."

One can see these two statements as two versions of essentially the same thing. Both teenagers

present self-justifying arguments about religious disagreement; both address the claims of self and of others in a way that honors both. Yet each frames the problem in different terms, and the use of moral language points to different concerns. The first speaker casts the problem in terms of individual rights that must be respected within the relationship. In other words, the figure of the considering is the self looking on the disagreeing selves in relationship, and the aim is to get the other selves to acknowledge the right to disagree. In the case of the second speaker, figure and ground shift. The relationship becomes the figure of the considering, and relationships are seen to require listening and efforts at understanding differences in belief. Rather than the rights to disagree, the speaker focuses on caring to hear and to be heard. Attention shifts from the grounds for agreement (rights and respect) to the grounds for understanding (listening and speaking, hearing and being heard). This shift is marked by a change in moral language from the stating of separate claims to rights and respect ("I have a right . . . I respect their views.") to the activities of relationship—the injunction to listen and try to understand ("I understand . . . they ought to listen . . . and try to understand."). The metaphor of moral voice itself carries the terms of the care perspective and reveals how the language chosen for moral theory is not orientation neutral.

The language of the public abortion debate, for example, reveals a justice perspective. Whether the abortion dilemma is cast as a conflict of rights or in terms of respect for human life, the claims of the fetus and of the pregnant woman are balanced or placed in opposition. The morality of abortion decisions thus construed hinges on the scholastic or metaphysical question as to whether the fetus is a life or a person, and whether its claims take precedence over those of the pregnant woman. Framed as a problem of care, the dilemma posed by abortion shifts. The connection between the fetus and the pregnant woman becomes the focus of attention and the question becomes whether it is responsible or irresponsible, caring or careless, to extend or to end this connection. In this construction, the abortion dilemma arises because there is no way not to act, and no way of acting that does not alter the connection between self and others. To ask what actions constitute care or are more caring directs attention to the parameters of connection and the costs of detachment, which become subjects of moral concern.

Finally, two medical students, each reporting a decision not to turn in someone who has violated the school rules against drinking, cast their decision in different terms. One student constructs the decision as an act of mercy, a decision to override justice in light of the fact that the violator has shown "the proper degrees of contrition." In addition, this student raises the question as to whether or not the alcohol policy is just, i.e., whether the school has the right to prohibit drinking. The other student explains the decision not to turn in a proctor who was drinking on the basis that turning him in is not a good way to respond to this problem, since it would dissolve the relationship between them and thus cut off an avenue for help. In addition, this student raises the question as to whether the proctor sees his drinking as a problem.

This example points to an important distinction, between care as understood or construed within a justice framework and care as a framework or a perspective on moral decision. Within a justice construction, care becomes the mercy that tempers justice; or connotes the special obligations or supererogatory duties that arise in personal relationships; or signifies altruism freely chosen—a decision to modulate the strict demands of justice by considering equity or showing forgiveness; or characterizes a choice to sacrifice the claims of the self. All of these interpretations of care leave the basic assumptions of a justice framework intact: the division between the self and others, the logic of reciprocity or equal respect.

As a moral perspective, care is less well elaborated, and there is no ready vocabulary in moral theory to describe its terms. As a framework for moral decision, care is grounded in the assumption that self and other are interdependent, an assumption reflected in a view of action as responsive and, therefore, as arising in relationship rather than the view of action as emanating from within the self and, therefore, "self governed." Seen as responsive,

the self is by definition connected to others, responding to perceptions, interpreting events, and governed by the organizing tendencies of human interaction and human language. Within this framework, detachment, whether from self or from others, is morally problematic, since it breeds moral blindness or indifference—a failure to discern or respond to need. The question of what responses constitute care and what responses lead to hurt draws attention to the fact that one's own terms may differ from those of others. Justice in this context becomes understood as respect for people in their own terms.

The medical student's decision not to turn in the proctor for drinking reflects a judgment that turning him in is not the best way to respond to the drinking problem, itself seen as a sign of detachment or lack of concern. Caring for the proctor thus raises the question of what actions are most likely to ameliorate this problem, a decision that leads to the question of what are the proctor's terms.

The shift in organizing perspective here is marked by the fact that the first student does not consider the terms of the other as potentially different but instead assumes one set of terms. Thus the student alone becomes the arbiter of what is *the* proper degree of contrition. The second student, in turn, does not attend to the question of whether the alcohol policy itself is just or fair. Thus each student discusses an aspect of the problem that the other does not mention.

These examples are intended to illustrate two cross-cutting perspectives that do not negate one another but focus attention on different dimensions of the situation, creating a sense of ambiguity around the question of what is the problem to be solved. Systematic research on moral orientation as a dimension of moral judgment and action initially addressed three questions: (1) Do people articulate concerns about justice and concerns about care in discussing a moral dilemma? (2) Do people tend to focus their attention on one set of concerns and minimally represent the other? and (3) Is there an association between moral orientation and gender? Evidence from studies that included a common set of questions about actual experiences of moral conflict and matched samples of males and females provides affirmative answers to all three questions.

When asked to describe a moral conflict they had faced, 55 out of 80 (69 percent) educationally advantaged North American adolescents and adults raised considerations of both justice and care. Two-thirds (54 out of 80) however, focused their attention on one set of concerns, with focus defined as 75 percent or more of the considerations raised pertaining either to justice or to care. Thus the person who presented, say, two care considerations in discussing a moral conflict was more likely to give a third, fourth, and fifth than to balance care and justice concerns—a finding consonant with the assumption that justice and care constitute organizing frameworks for moral decision. The men and the women involved in this study (high school students, college students, medical students, and adult professionals) were equally likely to demonstrate the focus phenomenon (two-thirds of both sexes fell into the outlying focus categories). There were, however, sex differences in the direction of focus. With one exception, all of the men who focused, focused on justice. The women divided, with roughly one third focusing on justice and one third on care.[2]

These findings clarify the different voice phenomenon and its implications for moral theory and for women. First, it is notable that if women were eliminated from the research sample, care focus in moral reasoning would virtually disappear. Although care focus was by no means characteristic of all women, it was almost exclusively a female phenomenon in this sample of educationally advantaged North Americans. Second, the fact that the women were advantaged means that the focus on care cannot readily be attributed to educational deficit or occupational disadvantage—the explanation Kohlberg and others have given for findings of lower levels of justice reasoning in women.[3] Instead, the focus on care in women's moral reasoning draws attention to the limitations of a justice-focused moral theory and highlights the presence of care concerns in the moral thinking of both women and men. In this light, the Care/Justice group composed of one third of the women and one third of the men becomes of particular interest, pointing to the need for further research that attends to the way people organize justice and care in relation to one another—whether, for example, people alternate perspectives, like seeing the rabbit and the duck in the rabbit-duck figure, or integrate the two perspectives in a way that resolves or sustains ambiguity.

Third, if the moral domain is comprised of at least two moral orientations, the focus phenomenon suggests that people have a tendency to lose sight of one moral perspective in arriving at moral decision—a liability equally shared by both sexes. The present findings further suggest that men and women tend to lose sight of different perspectives. The most striking result is the virtual absence of care-focus reasoning among the men. Since the men raised concerns about care in discussing moral conflicts and thus presented care concerns as morally relevant, a question is why they did not elaborate these concerns to a greater extent.

In summary, it becomes clear why attention to women's moral thinking led to the identification of a different voice and raised questions about the place of justice and care within a comprehensive moral theory. It also is clear how the selection of an all-male sample for research on moral judgment fosters an equation of morality with justice, providing little data discrepant with this view. In the present study, data discrepant with a justice-focused moral theory comes from a third of the women. Previously, such women were seen as having a problem understanding "morality." Yet these women may also be seen as exposing the problem in a justice-focused moral theory. This may explain the decision of researchers to exclude girls and women at the initial stage of moral judgment research. If one begins with the premise that "all morality consists in respect for rules,"[4] or "virtue is one and its name is justice,"[5] then women are likely to appear problematic within moral theory. If one begins with women's moral judgments, the problem becomes how to construct a theory that encompasses care as a focus of moral attention rather than as a subsidiary moral concern.

NOTES

1. Gilligan, C. (1977). "In a Different Voice: Women's Conceptions of Self and of Morality." *Harvard Educational Review* 47 (1982):481–517; *In a Different Voice: Psychological Theory and Women's Development*. Cambridge, Mass.: Harvard University Press.

2. Gilligan, C. and J. Attanucci. (1986). *Two Moral Orientations.* Harvard University, unpublished manuscript.

3. See Kohlberg, L. (1984). *The Psychology of Moral Development*. San Francisco, Calif.: Harper & Row, Publishers, Inc.; also Walker, L. (1984), "Sex Differences in the Development of Moral Reasoning: A Critical Review of the Literature," *Child Development* 55 (3): 677–91.

4. Piaget, J. (1965). *The Moral Judgment of the Child*. New York, N.Y.: The Free Press Paperback Edition, pp. 76–84.

5. Kohlberg, L., *op. cit.*

STUDY QUESTIONS

1. According to Gilligan, what is the "perspective of justice"?
2. According to Gilligan, what is the "perspective of care"?
3. According to Gilligan, can either of these perspectives be subsumed by the other?
4. How, if at all, can people with different perspectives reach agreement?

Beyond Caring

Marilyn Friedman

Marilyn Friedman, Professor Emerita of Philosophy at Vanderbilt University, questions the sharp distinction between notions of care and justice. Drawing attention to the moral defects in caring relationships that lack justice, she maintains that care alone fails to provide an adequate account of morality. In short, without justice the care perspective is incomplete.

INTRODUCTION

Carol Gilligan heard a 'distinct moral language' in the voices of women who were subjects in her studies of moral reasoning.[1] Though herself a developmental psychologist, Gilligan has put her mark on contemporary feminist moral philosophy by daring to claim the competence of this voice and the worth of its message. Her book, *In a Different Voice,* which one theorist has aptly described as a bestseller,[2] explored the concern with care and relationships which Gilligan discerned in the moral reasoning of women and contrasted it with the orientation toward justice and rights which she found to typify the moral reasoning of men.

According to Gilligan, the standard (or 'male') moral voice articulated in moral psychology derives moral judgments about particular cases from abstract, universalized moral rules and principles which are substantively concerned with justice and rights. For justice reasoners: the major moral imperative enjoins respect for the rights of others (100); the concept of duty is limited to reciprocal noninterference (147); the motivating vision is one of the equal worth of self and other (63); and one important underlying presupposition is a highly individuated conception of persons.

By contrast, the other (or 'female') moral voice which Gilligan heard in her studies eschews abstract rules and principles. This moral voice derives moral judgments from the contextual detail of situations grasped as specific and unique (100). The substantive concern for this moral voice is care and responsibility, particularly as these arise in the context of interpersonal relationships (19). Moral judgments, for care reasoners, are tied to feelings of empathy and compassion (69); the major moral imperatives center around caring, not hurting others, and avoiding selfishness (90); and the motivating vision of this ethic is 'that everyone will be responded to and included, that no one will be left alone or hurt' (63).

While these two voices are not necessarily contradictory in all respects, they seem, at the very least, to be different in their orientation. Gilligan's writings about the differences have stimulated extensive feminist reconsideration of various ethical themes.[3] In this paper, I use Gilligan's work as a springboard for extending certain of those themes in new directions. My discussion has three parts. In the first part, I will

From Marilyn Friedman, "Beyond Caring: The De-moralization of Gender," *Canadian Journal of Philosophy*, vol. 17, Supplement, 1987. Reprinted by permission of the journal.

address the unresolved question of whether or not a gender difference in moral reasoning is empirically confirmed. I will propose that even if actual statistical differences in the moral reasoning of women and men cannot be confirmed, there is nevertheless a real difference in the moral norms and values culturally associated with each gender. The genders are 'moralized' in distinctive ways. Moral norms about appropriate conduct, characteristic virtues and typical vices are incorporated into our conceptions of femininity and masculinity, female and male. The result is a dichotomy which exemplifies what may be called a 'division of moral labor'[4] between the genders.

In the second part of the paper, I will explore a different reason why actual women and men may not show a divergence of reasoning along the care-justice dichotomy, namely, that the notions of care and justice overlap more than Gilligan, among others, has realized. I will suggest, in particular, that morally adequate care involves considerations of justice. Thus, the concerns captured by these two moral categories do not define necessarily distinct moral perspectives, in practice.

Third, and finally, I propose that, even if care and justice do not define distinct moral perspectives, nevertheless, these concepts do point to other important differences in moral orientation. One such difference has to do with the nature of relationship to other selves, and the underlying form of moral commitment which is the central focus of that relationship and of the resulting moral thought. In short, the so-called 'care' perspective emphasizes responsiveness to particular persons, in their uniqueness, and commitment to them as such. By contrast, the so-called 'justice' perspective emphasizes adherence to moral rules, values and principles, and an abstractive treatment of individuals, based on the selected categories which they instantiate.

Let us turn first to the issue of gender difference.

I. THE GENDER DIFFERENCE CONTROVERSY

Gilligan has advanced at least two different positions about the care and the justice perspectives. One is that the care perspective is distinct from the moral perspective which is centered on justice and rights. Following Gilligan,[5] I will call this the 'different voice' hypothesis about moral reasoning. Gilligan's other hypothesis is that the care perspective is typically, or characteristically, a *woman's* moral voice, while the justice perspective is typically, or characteristically a *man's* moral voice. Let's call this the 'gender difference' hypothesis about moral reasoning.

The truth of Gilligan's gender difference hypothesis has been questioned by a number of critics who cite what seems to be disconfirming empirical evidence.[6] This evidence includes studies by the psychologist Norma Haan, who has discerned two distinct moral voices among her research subjects, but has found them to be utilized to approximately the same extent by both females and males.[7]

In an attempt to dismiss the research-based objections to her gender difference hypothesis, Gilligan now asserts that her aim was not to disclose a statistical gender difference in moral reasoning, but rather simply to disclose and interpret the differences in the two perspectives.[8] Psychologist John Broughton has argued that if the gender difference is not maintained, then Gilligan's whole explanatory framework is undermined.[9] However, Broughton is wrong. The different voice hypothesis has a significance for moral psychology and moral philosophy which would survive the demise of the gender difference hypothesis. At least part of its significance lies in revealing the lopsided obsession of contemporary theories of morality, in both disciplines, with universal and impartial conceptions of justice and rights and the relative disregard of *particular,* interpersonal relationships based on partiality and affective ties.[10] (However, the different voice hypothesis is itself also suspect if it is made to depend on a dissociation of justice from care, a position which I shall challenge in Part II of this paper.)

But *what about* that supposed empirical disconfirmation of the gender difference hypothesis? Researchers who otherwise accept the disconfirming evidence have nevertheless noticed that many women readers of Gilligan's book find it to 'resonate . . . thoroughly with their own experience.'[11] Gilligan notes that it was precisely one of her purposes to expose the gap between women's experience and the findings of psychological research,[12] and, we may suppose, to critique the latter in light of the former.

These unsystematic, anecdotal observations that females and males do differ in ways examined by Gilligan's research should lead us either: (1) to question, and examine carefully, the methods of that empirical research which does not reveal such differences; or (2) to suspect that a gender difference exists but in some form which is not, strictly speaking, a matter of statistical differences in the moral reasoning of women and men. Gilligan has herself expressed the first of these alternatives. I would like to explore the second possibility.

Suppose that there were a gender difference of a sort, but one which was not a simple matter of differences among the form or substance of women's and men's moral reasonings. A plausible account might take this form. Among the white middle classes of such western industrial societies as Canada and the United States, women and men are associated with different moral norms and values at the level of the stereotypes, symbols, and myths which contribute to the social construction of gender. One might say that morality is 'gendered' and that the genders are 'moralized.' Our very conceptions of femininity and masculinity, female and male, incorporate norms about appropriate behavior, characteristic virtues, and typical vices.

Morality, I suggest, is fragmented into a 'division of moral labor' along the lines of gender, the rationale for which is rooted in historic developments pertaining to family, state, and economy. The tasks of governing, regulating social order, and managing other 'public' institutions have been monopolized by men as their privileged domain, and the tasks of sustaining privatized personal relationships have been imposed on, or left to, women.[13] The genders have thus been conceived in terms of special and distinctive moral projects. Justice and rights have structured male moral norms, values, and virtues, while care and responsiveness have defined female moral norms, values, and virtues. The division of moral labor has had the dual function both of preparing us each for our respective socially defined domains and of rendering us incompetent to manage the affairs of the realm from which we have been excluded. That justice is symbolized in our culture by the figure of a woman is a remarkable irony; her blindfold hides more than the scales she holds.

To say that the genders are moralized is to say that specific moral ideals, values, virtues, and practices are culturally conceived as the special projects or domains of specific genders. These conceptions would determine which commitments and behaviors were to be considered normal, appropriate, and expected of each gender, which commitments and behaviors were to be considered remarkable or heroic, and which commitments and behaviors were to be considered deviant, improper, outrageous, and intolerable. Men who fail to respond to the cry of a baby, fail to express tender emotions, or fail to show compassion in the face of the grief and sorrow of others, are likely to be tolerated, perhaps even benignly, while women who act similarly can expect to be reproached for their selfish indifference. However, women are seldom required to devote themselves to service to their country or to struggles for human rights. Women are seldom expected to display any of the special virtues associated with national or political life. At the same time, women still carry the burden of an excessively restrictive and oppressive sexual ethic; sexual aggressiveness and promiscuity are vices for which women in all social groups are roundly condemned, even while many of their male counterparts win tributes for such 'virility.'

Social science provides ample literature to show that gender differences are alive and well at the level of popular perception. Both men and women, on average, still conceive women and men in a moralized fashion. For example, expectations and perceptions of women's greater empathy and altruism are expressed by both women and men.[14] The gender stereotypes of women center around qualities which some authors call 'communal.' These include: a concern for the welfare of others; the predominance of caring and nurturant traits; and, to a lesser extent, interpersonal sensitivity, emotional expressiveness, and a gentle personal style.[15]

By contrast, men are stereotyped according to what are referred to as 'agentic' norms.[16] These norms center primarily around assertive and controlling tendencies. The paradigmatic behaviors are self-assertion, including forceful dominance, and independence from other people. Also encompassed by these norms are patterns of self-confidence, personal efficacy, and a direct, adventurous personal style.

If reality failed to accord with myth and symbol, if actual women and men did not fit the traits and dispositions expected of them, this might not necessarily undermine the myths and symbols, since perception could be selective and disconfirming experience reduced to the status of 'occasional exceptions' and 'abnormal, deviant cases.' 'Reality' would be misperceived in the image of cultural myth, as reinforced by the homogenizing tendencies of mass media and mass culture, and the popular imagination would have little foothold for the recognition that women and men were not as they were mythically conceived to be.

If I am right, then Gilligan has discerned the *symbolically* female moral voice, and has disentangled it from the *symbolically* male moral voice. The moralization of gender is more a matter of how we *think* we reason than of how we actually reason, more a matter of the moral concerns we *attribute* to women and men than of true statistical differences between women's and men's moral reasoning. Gilligan's findings resonate with the experiences of many people because those experiences are shaped, in part, by cultural myths and stereotypes of gender which even feminist theorizing may not dispel. Thus, both women and men in our culture *expect* women and men to exhibit this moral dichotomy, and, on my hypothesis, it is this expectation which has shaped both Gilligan's observations and the plausibility which we attribute to them. Or, to put it somewhat differently, *whatever* moral matters men concern themselves with are categorized, estimably, as matters of 'justice and rights,' whereas the moral concerns of women are assigned to the devalued categories of 'care and personal relationships.'

It is important to ask why, if these beliefs are so vividly held, they might, nevertheless, still not produced a reality in conformity with them.[17] How could those critics who challenge Gilligan's gender hypothesis be right to suggest that women and men show no significant differences in moral reasoning,

if women and men are culturally educated, trained, pressured, expected, and perceived to be so radically different?[18]

Philosophy is not, by itself, capable of answering this question adequately. My admittedly *partial* answer to it depends upon showing that the care/justice dichotomy is rationally implausible and that the two concepts are conceptually compatible. This conceptual compatibility creates the empirical possibility that the two moral concerns will be intermingled in practice. That they are actually intermingled in the moral reasonings of real women and men is, of course, not determined simply by their conceptual compatibility, but requires as well the wisdom and insight of those women and men who comprehend the relevance of both concepts to their experiences.[19] Philosophy does not account for the actual emergence of wisdom. That the genders do not, in reality, divide along those moral lines is made *possible,* though not inevitable, by the conceptual limitations of both a concept of care dissociated from considerations of justice and a concept of justice dissociated from considerations of care. Support for this partial explanation requires a reconceptualization of care and justice—the topic of the next part of my discussion.

II. SURPASSING THE CARE/JUSTICE DICHOTOMY

I have suggested that if women and men do not show statistical differences in moral reasoning along the lines of a care/justice dichotomy, this should not be thought surprising since the concepts of care and justice are mutually compatible. People who treat each other justly can also care about each other. Conversely, personal relationships are arenas in which people have rights to certain forms of treatment, and in which fairness can be reflected in ongoing interpersonal mutuality. It is this latter insight—the relevance of justice to close personal relationships—which I will emphasize here.

Justice, at the most general level, is a matter of giving people their due, of treating them appropriately. Justice is relevant to personal relationships and to care precisely to the extent that considerations of justice itself determine appropriate ways to treat friends or intimates. Justice as it bears on relationships among friends or family, or on other close personal ties, might not involve duties which are universalizable, in the sense of being owed to all persons simply in virtue of shared moral personhood. But this does not entail the irrelevance of justice among friends or intimates.

Moral thinking has not always dissociated the domain of justice from that of close personal relationships. The earliest Greek code of justice placed friendship at the forefront of conditions for the realization of justice, and construed the rules of justice as being coextensive with the limits of friendship. The reader will recall that one of the first definitions of justice which Plato sought to contest, in the *Republic,* is that of 'helping one's friends and harming one's enemies.'[20] Although the ancient Greek model of justice among friends reserved that moral privilege for free-born Greek males, the conception is, nevertheless, instructive for its readiness to link the notion of justice to relationships based on affection and loyalty. This provides an important contrast to modern notions of justice which are often deliberately constructed so as to avoid presumptions of mutual concern on the parts of those to whom the conception is to apply.

As is well known, John Rawls, for one, requires that the parties to the original position in which justice is to be negotiated be mutually disinterested.[21] Each party is assumed, first and foremost, to be concerned for the advancement of her own interests, and to care about the interests of others only to the extent that her own interests require it. This postulate of mutual disinterestedness is intended by Rawls to ensure that the principles of justice do not depend on what he calls 'strong assumptions,' such as 'extensive ties of natural sentiment.'[22] Rawls is seeking principles of justice which apply to everyone in all their social interrelationships, *whether or not* characterized by affection and a concern for each other's well-being. While such an account promises to disclose duties of justice owed to all other parties to the social contract, it may fail to uncover *special* duties of justice which arise in close personal relationships

the foundation of which is affection or kinship, rather than contract. The methodological device of assuming mutual disinterest might blind us to the role of justice among mutually interested and/or intimate parties.

Gilligan herself has suggested that mature reasoning about care incorporates considerations of justice and rights. But Gilligan's conception of what this means is highly limited. It appears to involve simply the recognition 'that self and other are equal,' a notion which serves to override the problematic tendency of the ethic of care to become *self-sacrificing* care in women's practices. However, important as it may be, this notion hardly does justice to justice.

There are several ways in which justice pertains to close personal relationships. The first two ways which I will mention are largely appropriate only among friends, relatives, or intimates who are of comparable development in their realization of moral personhood, for example, who are both mature responsible adults. The third sort of relevance of justice to close relationships, which I will discuss shortly, pertains to families, in which adults often interrelate with children—a more challenging domain for the application of justice. But first the easier task.

One sort of role for justice in close relationships among people of comparable moral personhood may be discerned by considering that a personal relationship is a miniature social system, which provides valued mutual intimacy, support, and concern for those who are involved. The maintenance of a relationship requires effort by the participants. One intimate may bear a much greater burden for sustaining a relationship than the other participant(s) and may derive less support, concern, and so forth than she deserves for her efforts. Justice sets a constraint on such relationships by calling for an appropriate sharing, among the participants, of the benefits and burdens which constitute their relationship.

Marilyn Frye, for example, has discussed what amounts to a pattern of *violation* of this requirement of justice in heterosexual relationships. She has argued that women of all races, social classes, and societies can be defined as a coherent group in terms of a distinctive function which is culturally assigned to them. This function is, in Frye's words, 'the service of men and men's interests as men define them.'[23] This service work includes personal service (satisfaction of routine bodily needs, such as hunger, and other mundane tasks), sexual and reproductive service, and ego service. Says Frye, '. . . at every race/class level and even across race/class lines men do not serve women as women serve men.'[24] Frye is, of course, generalizing over society and culture, and the sweep of her generalization encompasses both ongoing close personal relationships as well as other relationships which are not close or are not carried on beyond specific transactions, for example, that of prostitute to client. By excluding those latter cases for the time being, and applying Frye's analysis to familial and other close ties between women and men, we may discern the sort of one-sided relational exploitation, often masquerading in the guise of love or care, which constitutes this first sort of injustice.

Justice is relevant to close personal relationships among comparable moral persons in a second way as well. The trust and intimacy which characterize special relationships create special vulnerabilities to harm. Commonly recognized harms, such as physical injury and sexual assault, become more feasible; and special relationships, in corrupt, abusive, or degenerate forms, make possible certain uncommon emotional harms not even possible in impersonal relationships. When someone is harmed in a personal relationship, she is owed a rectification of some sort, a righting of the wrong which has been done her. The notion of justice emerges, once again, as a relevant moral notion.

Thus, in a close relationship among persons of comparable moral personhood, care may degenerate into the injustices of exploitation, or oppression. Many such problems have been given wide public scrutiny recently as a result of feminist analysis of various aspects of family life and sexual relationships. Woman-battering, acquaintance rape, and sexual harassment are but a few of the many recently publicized injustices of 'personal' life. The notion of distributive or corrective injustice seems almost too mild to capture these indignities, involving, as they do, violation of bodily integrity and an assumption of the right to assault and injure. But to call these

harms injustices is certainly not to rule out impassioned moral criticism in other terms as well.

The two requirements of justice which I have just discussed exemplify the standard distinction between distributive and corrective justice. They illustrate the role of justice in personal relationships regarded in abstraction from a social context. Personal relationships may also be regarded in the context of their various institutional settings, such as marriage and family. Here justice emerges again as a relevant ideal, its role being to define appropriate institutions to structure interactions among family members other household cohabitants, and intimates in general. The family, for example,[25] is a miniature society, exhibiting all the major facets of large-scale social life: decision-making affecting the whole unit; executive action; judgments of guilt and innocence; reward and punishment; allocation of responsibilities and privileges, of burdens and benefits; and monumental influences on the life-chances of both its maturing and its matured members. Any of these features *alone* would invoke the relevance of justice; together, they make the case overwhelming.

Women's historically paradigmatic role of mothering has provided a multitude of insights which can be reconstructed as insights about the importance of justice in family relationships, especially those relationships involving remarkable disparities in maturity, capability, and power.[26] In these familial relationships, one party grows into moral personhood over time, gradually acquiring the capacity to be a responsible moral agent. Considerations of justice pertain to the mothering of children in numerous ways. For one thing, there may be siblings to deal with, whose demands and conflicts create the context for parental arbitration and the need for a fair allotment of responsibilities and privileges. Then there are decisions to be made, involving the well-being of all persons in the family unit, whose immature members become increasingly capable over time of participating in such administrative affairs. Of special importance in the practice of raising children are the duties to nurture and to promote growth and maturation. These duties may be seen as counterparts to the welfare rights viewed by many as a matter of social justice.[27] Motherhood continually presents its practitioners with moral problems best seen in terms of a complex framework which integrates justice with care, even though the politico-legal discourse of justice has not shaped its domestic expression.[28]

I have been discussing the relevance of justice to close personal relationships. A few words about my companion thesis—the relevance of care to the public domain—is also in order.[29] In its more noble manifestation, care in the public realm would show itself, perhaps, in foreign aid, welfare programs, famine or disaster relief, or other social programs designed to relieve suffering and attend to human needs. If untempered by justice in the public domain, care degenerates precipitously. The infamous 'boss' of Chicago's old-time Democratic machine, Mayor Richard J. Daley, was legendary for his nepotism and political partisanship; he cared extravagantly for his relatives, friends, and political cronies.[30]

In recounting the moral reasoning of one of her research subjects, Gilligan once wrote that the 'justice' perspective fails 'to take into account the reality of relationships' (147). What she meant is that the 'justice' perspective emphasizes a self's various rights to noninterference by others. Gilligan worried that if this is all that a concern for justice involved, then such a perspective would disregard the moral value of positive interaction, connection, and commitment among persons.

However, Gilligan's interpretation of justice is far too limited. For one thing, it fails to recognize positive rights, such as welfare rights, which may be endorsed from a 'justice' perspective. But beyond this minor point, a more important problem is Gilligan's failure to acknowledge the potential for *violence and harm* in human interrelationships and human community.[31] The concept of justice, in general, arises out of relational conditions in which most human beings have the capacity, and many have the inclination, to treat each other badly.

Thus, notions of distributive justice are impelled by the realization that people who together comprise a social system may not share fairly in the benefits and burdens of their social cooperation. Conceptions of rectificatory, or corrective, justice are founded on the concern that when harms are done, action should be taken either to restore those

harmed as fully as possible to their previous state, or to prevent further similar harm, or both. And the specific rights which people are variously thought to have are just so many manifestations of our interest in identifying ways in which people deserve protection against harm by others. The complex reality of social life encompasses the human potential for helping, caring for, and nurturing others *as well as* the potential for harming, exploiting, and oppressing others. Thus, Gilligan is wrong to think that the justice perspective completely neglects 'the reality of relationships.' Rather, it arises from a more complex, and more realistic estimate of the nature of human interrelationship.

In light of these reflections, it seems wise both to reconsider the seeming dichotomy of care and justice, and to question the moral adequacy of either orientation dissociated from the other. Our aim would be to advance 'beyond caring,' that is, beyond *mere* caring dissociated from a concern for justice. In addition, we would do well to progress beyond gender stereotypes which assign distinct and different moral roles to women and men. Our ultimate goal should be a non-gendered, non-dichotomized, moral framework in which all moral concerns could be expressed. We might, with intentional irony, call this project, 'de-moralizing the genders.'

III. COMMITMENTS TO PARTICULAR PERSONS

Even though care and justice do not define mutually exclusive moral frameworks, it is still too early to dispose of the 'different voice hypothesis.' I believe that there is something to be said for the thesis that there are different moral orientations, even if the concepts of care and justice do not capture the relevant differences and even if the differences do not correlate statistically with gender differences.

My suggestion is that one important distinction has to do with the nature and focus of what may be called 'primary moral commitments.' Let us begin with the observation that, from the so-called 'care standpoint,' responsiveness to other persons in their wholeness and their particularity is of singular importance. This idea, in turn, points toward a notion of moral commitment which takes *particular persons* as its primary focus.[32] A form of moral commitment which contrasts with this is one which involves a focus on general and abstract rules, values, or principles. It is no mere coincidence, I believe, that Gilligan found the so-called 'justice' perspective to feature an emphasis on *rules* (e.g., p. 73).

In Part II of this paper, I argued that the concepts of justice and care are mutually compatible and, to at least some extent, mutually dependent. Based on my analysis, the 'justice perspective' might be said to rest, at bottom, on the assumption that the best way to *care* for persons is to respect their rights, and to accord them their due, both in distribution of the burdens and benefits of social cooperation, and in the rectification of wrongs done. But to uphold these principles, it is not necessary to respond with emotion, feeling, passion, or compassion to other persons. Upholding justice does not require the full range of mutual responsiveness which is possible between persons.

By contrast, the so-called 'ethic of care' stresses an ongoing responsiveness. This ethic is, after all, the stereotypic moral norm for women in the domestic role of sustaining a family in the face of the harsh realities of a competitive marketplace and an indifferent polis. The domestic realm has been idealized as the realm in which people, as specific individuals, were to have been nurtured, cherished, and succored. The 'care' perspective discussed by Gilligan is a limited one; it is not really about care in all its complexity, for, as I have argued, that notion *includes* just treatment. But it *is* about the nature of relationships to particular persons grasped as such. The key issue is the sensitivity and responsiveness to another person's emotional states, individuating differences, specific uniqueness, and whole particularity. The 'care' orientation focuses on whole persons and de-emphasizes adherence to moral rules.

Thus, the important conception which I am extracting from the so-called 'care' perspective is that of commitment to particular persons. What is the nature of this form of moral commitment? Commitment to a specific person, such as a lover, child, or friend, takes as its primary focus the needs, wants, attitudes, judgments, behavior, and overall way of being of that particular person. It is specific to that individual and is not generalizable to others. We show a commitment to someone whenever we attend to her needs, enjoy her successes, defer to her judgment, and find inspiration in her values and goals, simply because they are *hers.* If it is *who she is,* and not her actions or traits subsumed under general rules, which matters as one's motivating guide, then one's responsiveness to her reflects a person-oriented, rather than a rule-based, moral commitment.

Thus, the different perspectives which Gilligan called 'care' and 'justice' do point toward substantive differences in human interrelationship and commitment. Both orientations take account of relationships in some way; both may legitimately incorporate a concern for justice and for care, and both aim to avoid harm to others and (at the highest stages) to the self. But from the standpoint of 'care,' self and other are conceptualized in their *particularity* rather than as instances for the application of generalized moral notions. This difference ramifies into what appears to be a major difference in the organization and focus of moral thought.

This analysis requires a subtle expansion. Like care and justice, commitments to particular persons and commitments to values, rules, and principles are not mutually exclusive within the entire panorama of one person's moral concerns. Doubtless, they are intermingled in most people's moral outlooks. Pat likes and admires Mary because of Mary's resilience in the face of tragedy, her intelligent courage, and her good-humored audacity. Pat thereby shows a commitment *in general* to resilience, courage, and good-humored audacity as traits of human personality.

However, in Mary, these traits coalesce in a unique manner: perhaps no one will stand by a friend in deep trouble quite so steadfastly as Mary; perhaps no one petitions the university president as effectively as Mary. The traits which Pat likes, in general, converge to make *Mary,* in Pat's eyes, an especially admirable human individual, a sort of moral exemplar. In virtue of Pat's loyalty to her, Mary may come to play a role in Pat's life which exceeds, in its weightiness, the sum total of the values which Pat sees in Mary's virtues, taken individually and in abstraction from any particular human personality.

Pat is someone with commitments both to moral abstractions and to particular persons. Pat is, in short, like most of us. When we reason morally, we can take up a stance which makes either of these forms of commitment the focal point of our attention. The choice of which stance to adopt at a given time is probably, like other moral alternatives, most poignant and difficult in situations of moral ambiguity or uncertainty when we don't know how to proceed. In such situations, one can turn *either* to the guidance of principled commitments to values, forms of conduct, or human virtues, *or* one can turn to the guidance which inheres in the example set by a trusted friend or associate—the example of how *she* interprets those same moral ambiguities, or how *she* resolves those same moral uncertainties.

Of course, the commitment to a particular person is evident in more situations than simply those of moral irresolution. But the experience of moral irresolution may make clearer the different sorts of moral commitment which structure our thinking. Following cherished values will lead one out of one's moral uncertainties in a very different way than following someone else's example.

Thus, the insight that each person needs some others in her life who recognize, respect, and cherish her particularity in its richness and wholeness is the distinctive motivating vision of the 'care' perspective.[33] The sort of respect for persons which grows out of this vision is not the abstract respect which is owed to all persons in virtue of their common humanity, but a respect for individual worth, merit, need, or, even, idiosyncrasy. It is a form of respect which involves admiration and cherishing, when the distinctive qualities are valued intrinsically, and which, at the least, involves toleration when the distinctive qualities are not valued intrinsically.

Indeed, there is an apparent irony in the notion of personhood which underlies some philosophers' conceptions of the universalized moral duties owed to all persons. The rational nature which Kant, for example, takes to give each person dignity and to make each of absolute value, and, therefore, irreplaceable,[34] is no more than an abstract rational nature in virtue of which we are all alike. But if we are all alike in this respect, it is hard to understand why we would be irreplaceable. Our common rational nature would seem to make us indistinguishable and, therefore, mutually interchangeable. Specific identity would be a matter of indifference, so far as our absolute value is concerned. Yet it would seem that only in *virtue* of our distinctive particularity could we each be truly irreplaceable.

Of course, our particularity does not *exclude* a common nature, conceptualized at a level of suitable generality. We still deserve equal respect in virtue of our common humanity. But we are also *more* than abstractly and equivalently human. It is this 'more' to which we commit ourselves when we care for others in their particularity.

Thus, as I interpret it, there is at least one important difference in moral reasoning brought to our attention by Gilligan's 'care' and 'justice' frameworks. This difference hinges on the primary form of moral commitment which structures moral thought and the resulting nature of the response to other persons. For so-called 'care' reasoners, recognition of, and commitment to, persons in their particularity is an overriding moral concern.[35]

Unlike the concepts of justice and care, which admit of a mutual integration, it is less clear that these two distinct forms of moral commitment can jointly comprise the focus of one's moral attention, in any single case. Nor can we respond to all other persons equally well in either way. The only integration possible here may be to seek the more intimate, responsive, committed relationships with people who are known closely, or known in contexts in which differential needs are important and can be known with some reliability, and to settle for rule-based equal respect toward that vast number of others whom one cannot know in any particularity.

At any rate, to tie together the varied threads of this discussion, we may conclude that nothing intrinsic to gender demands a division of moral norms which assigns particularized, personalized commitments to women and universalized, rule-based commitments to men. We need nothing less than to 'demoralize' the genders, advance beyond the dissociation of justice from care, and enlarge the symbolic access of each gender to all available conceptual and social resources for the sustenance and enrichment of our collective moral life.

NOTES

1. *In a Different Voice* (Cambridge, MA: Harvard University Press 1982), 73. More recently, the following works by Gilligan on related issues have also appeared: 'Do the Social Sciences Have an Adequate Theory of Moral Development?' in Norma Haan, Robert N. Bellah, Paul Rabinow and William M. Sullivan, eds., *Social Science as Moral Inquiry* (New York: Columbia University Press 1983), 33–51; 'Reply,' *Signs* 11 (1986), 324–33; and 'Remapping the Moral Domain: New Images of the Self in Relationship,' in Thomas C. Heller, Morton Sosna and David E. Wellberry, eds., *Reconstructing Individualism* (Stanford, CA: Stanford University Press 1986) 237–52. Throughout this paper, all page references inserted in the text are to *In a Different Voice*.

2. Frigga Haug, 'Morals Also Have Two Genders,' trans. Rodney Livingstone, *New Left Review* 143 (1984), 55.

3. These sources include: Owen J. Flanagan, Jr. and Jonathan E. Adler, 'Impartiality and Particularity,' *Social Research* 50 (1983), 576–96; Nel Noddings, *Caring* (Berkeley: University of California Press 1984); Claudia Card, 'Virtues and Moral Luck' (unpublished paper presented at American Philosophical Association, Western Division Meetings, Chicago, IL, April 1985, and at the Conference on Virtue Theory, University of San Diego, San Diego, CA, February 1986); Marilyn Friedman, *Care and Context in Moral Reasoning*, MOSAIC Monograph #1 (Bath, England: University of Bath 1985), reprinted in Carol Harding, ed., *Moral Dilemmas* (Chicago: Precedent 1986), 25–42, and in Diana T. Meyers and Eva Feder Kittay, eds., *Women and Moral Theory* (Totowa, NJ: Rowman and Littlefield 1987), 190–204; all the papers in Meyers and Kittay; Linda K. Kerber, 'Some Cautionary Words for Historians,' *Signs* 11 (1986), 304–10; Catherine G. Greeno and Eleanor E. Maccoby, 'How Different Is the "Different Voice?,"' *Signs* 11 (1986) 310–16; Zella Luria, 'A Methodological Critique,' *Signs* 11 (1986), 316–21; Carol B. Stack, 'The Culture of Gender: Women and Men of Color,' *Signs* 11 (1986), 321–4; Owen Flanagan and Kathryn Jackson, 'Justice, Care, and Gender: The Kohlberg-Gilligan Debate Revisited,' *Ethics* 97 (1987), 622–37. An analysis of this issue from an ambiguously feminist standpoint is to be found in: John M. Broughton, 'Women's Rationality and Men's Virtues,' *Social Research* 50 (1983), 597–642. For a helpful review of some of these issues, cf. Jean Grimshaw, *Philosophy and Feminist Thinking* (Minneapolis: University of Minnesota Press 1986), esp. chs. 7 and 8.

4. This term is used by Virginia Held to refer, in general, to the division of moral labor among the multitude of professions, activities, and practices in culture and society, though not specifically to gender roles. Cf. *Rights and Goods* (New York: The Free Press 1984), ch. 3. Held is aware that gender roles are part of the division of moral labor but she mentions this topic only in passing, p. 29.

5. Gilligan, 'Reply,' 326.

6. Research on the 'gender difference' hypothesis is very mixed. The studies which appear to show gender differences in moral reasoning for one or more age levels include: Norma Haan, M. Brewster-Smith and Jeanne Block, 'Moral Reasoning of Young Adults: Political-social Behavior, Family Background, and Personality Correlates,' *Journal of Personality and Social Psychology* 10 (1968), 183–201; James Fishkin, Kenneth Keniston and Catharine MacKinnon, 'Moral Reasoning and Political Ideology,' *Journal of Personality and Social Psychology* 27 (1973), 109–19; Norma Haan, 'Hypothetical and Actual Moral Reasoning in a Situation of Civil Disobedience,' *Journal of Personality and Social Psychology* 32 (1975), 255–70; Constance Holstein, 'Development of Moral Judgment: A Longitudinal Study of Males and Females,' *Child Development* 47 (1976), 51–61 (showing gender differences in middle adulthood but not for other age categories; see references below); Sharry Langdale, 'Moral Orientations and Moral Development: The Analysis of Care and Justice Reasoning across Different Dilemmas in Females and Males from Childhood through Adulthood' (Ed.D. diss., Harvard Graduate School of Education 1983); Kay Johnston, 'Two Moral Orientations—Two Problem-solving Strategies: Adolescents' Solutions to Dilemmas in Fables,' (Ed.D. diss., Harvard Graduate School of Education 1985). The last two sources are cited by Gilligan, 'Reply,' p. 330.

Among the studies which show no gender differences in moral reasoning at one or more age levels are: E. Turiel, 'A Comparative Analysis of Moral Knowledge and Moral Judgment in Males and Females,' *Journal of Personality* 44 (1976), 195–208; C. B. Holstein, 'Irreversible Stepwise Sequence in the Development of Moral Judgment: A Longitudinal Study of Males and Females' (showing no differences in childhood or adolescence but showing differentiation in middle adulthood; see reference above); N. Haan, et al., 'Family Moral Patterns,' *Child Development* 47 (1976), 1204–6; M. Berkowitz, et al., 'The Relation of Moral Judgment

Stage Disparity to Developmental Effects of Peer Dialogues,' *Merrill-Palmer Quarterly* 26 (1980), 341–57; and Mary Brabeck, 'Moral Judgment: Theory and Research on Differences between Males and Females,' *Developmental Review* 3 (1983), 274–91.

Lawrence J. Walker surveyed all the research to date and claimed that rather than showing a gender-based difference in moral reasoning, it showed differences based on occupation and education: 'Sex Differences in the Development of Moral Reasoning,' *Child Development* 55 (1984), 677–91. This 'meta-analysis' has itself recently been disputed: Norma Haan, 'With Regard to Walker (1984) on Sex "Differences" in Moral Reasoning' (University of California, Berkeley, Institute of Human Development mimeograph 1985); Diana Baumrind, 'Sex Differences in Moral Reasoning: Response to Walker's (1984) Conclusion That There Are None,' *Child Development* (in press). The last two sources are cited by Gilligan, 'Reply,' p. 330.

7. Norma Haan, 'Two Moralities in Action Contexts,' *Journal of Personality and Social Psychology* 36 (1978), 286–305. Also cf. Norma Haan, 'Moral Reasoning in a Hypothetical and an Actual Situation of Civil Disobedience,' *Journal of Personality and Social Psychology* 32 (1975), 255–70; and Gertrud Nunner-Winkler, 'Two Moralities? A Critical Discussion of an Ethic of Care and Responsibility versus an Ethic of Rights and Justice,' in William M. Kurtines and Jacob L. Gewirtz, *Morality, Moral Behavior, and Moral Development* (New York: John Wiley & Sons 1984), 348–61.

8. Gilligan, 'Reply,' 326.

9. Broughton, 'Women's Rationality and Men's Virtues,' 636.

10. Gilligan's work arose largely as a critical reaction to the studies of moral reasoning carried on by Lawrence Kohlberg and his research associates. For the reaction by those scholars to Gilligan's work and their assessment of its importance to moral psychology, see Lawrence Kohlberg, 'A Reply to Owen Flanagan and Some Comments on the Puka-Goodpaster Exchange,' *Ethics* 92 (1982), 513–28; and Lawrence Kohlberg, Charles Levine and Alexandra Hewer, *Moral Stages: A Current Reformulation and Response to Critics* (Basel: Karger 1983), 20–7, 121–50.

In philosophy, themes related to Gilligan's concerns have been raised by, among others: Michael Stocker, 'The Schizophrenia of Modern Ethical Theories,' *Journal of Philosophy* 63 (1976) 453–66: Bernard Williams, 'Persons, Character and Morality,' in Amelie O. Rorty, ed., *The Identities of Persons* (Berkeley: University of California 1976), reprinted in Bernard Williams, *Moral Luck* (New York: Cambridge University Press 1982), 1–19; Lawrence Blum, *Friendship, Altruism and Morality* (London: Routledge & Kegan Paul 1980); Alasdair MacIntyre, *After Virtue* (Notre Dame, IN: University of Notre Dame 1981), esp. Ch. 15; Michael Stocker, 'Values and Purposes: The Limits of Teleology and the Ends of Friendship,' *Journal of Philosophy* 78 (1981), 747–65; Owen Flanagan, 'Virtue, Sex and Gender: Some Philosophical Reflections on the Moral Psychology Debate,' *Ethics* 92 (1982), 499–512; Michael Slote, 'Morality Not a System of Imperatives,' *American Philosophical Quarterly* 19 (1982), 331–40; and Christina Hoff Sommers, 'Filial Morality,' *Journal of Philosophy* 83 (1986), 439–56

11. Greeno and Maccoby, 'How Different Is the "Different Voice"?' 314–15.

12. Gilligan, 'Reply,' 325.

13. For a discussion of this historical development, cf. Linda Nicholson, 'Women, Morality and History,' *Social Research* 50 (1983) 514–36; and her *Gender and History* (New York: Columbia University Press 1986) esp. chs. 3 and 4.

14. Cf. Nancy Eisenberg and Roger Lennon, 'Sex Differences in Empathy and Related Capacities,' *Psychological Bulletin* 94 (1983), 100–31.

15. Cf. Alice H. Eagly, 'Sex Differences and Social Roles' (unpublished paper presented at Experimental Social Psychology, Tempe, AZ, October 1986), esp. p. 7. Also cf. Alice H. Eagly and Valerie J. Steffen, 'Gender Stereotypes Stem From the Distribution of Women and Men Into Social Roles,' *Journal of Personality and Social Psychology* 46 (1984), 735–54.

16. The stereotypes of men are not obviously connected with justice and rights, but they are connected with the excessive individualism which Gilligan takes to underlie the justice orientation. Cf. Eagly, 'Sex Differences and Social Roles,' 8.

17. Eagly argues both that people do show a tendency to conform to shared and known expectations, on the parts of others, about their behavior, and that a division of labor which leads people to develop different skills also contributes to differential development; 'Sex Differences and Social Roles,' *passim*. It follows from Eagly's view that if the genders are stereotypically 'moralized,' they would then be likely to develop so as to conform to those different expectations.

18. Eagly and Steffen have found that stereotypic beliefs that women are more 'communal' and less 'agentic' than men, and that men are more 'agentic' and less 'communal' than women are based more deeply on occupational role stereotypes than on gender stereotypes;

'Gender Stereotypes Stem From the Distribution of Women and Men Into Social Roles,' *passim.* In this respect, Eagly and Steffen force us to question whether the gender categorization which pervades Gilligan's analysis really captures the fundamental differentiation among persons. I do not address this question in this paper.

19. In correspondence, Marcia Baron has suggested that a factor accounting for the actual emergence of 'mixed' perspectives on the parts of women and men may have to do with the instability of the distinction between public and private realms to which the justice/care dichotomy corresponds. Men have always been recognized to participate in both realms and, in practice, many women have participated, out of choice or necessity, in such segments of the public world as that of paid labor. The result is a blurring of the experiential segregation which otherwise might have served to reinforce distinct moral orientations.

20. Book I, 322–35. A thorough discussion of the Greek conception of justice in the context of friendship can be found in Horst Hutter, *Politics as Friendship* (Waterloo, ON: Wilfrid Laurier University Press 1978).

21. Rawls, *Theory of Justice,* 13 and elsewhere.

22. Ibid., 129.

23. *The Politics of Reality* (Trumansburg. NY: The Crossing Press 1983) 9.

24. Ibid., 10.

25. For an important discussion of the relevance of justice to the family, cf. Susan Moller Okin, 'Justice and Gender,' *Philosophy and Public Affairs* 16 (1987), 42–72.

26. For insightful discussions of the distinctive modes of thought to which mothering gives rise, cf. Sara Ruddick, 'Maternal Thinking,' *Feminist Studies* 6 (1980) 342–67; and her 'Preservative Love and Military Destruction: Some Reflections on Mothering and Peace,' in Joyce Trebilcot, ed., *Mothering: Essays in Feminism Theory* (Totowa, NJ: Rowman & Allanheld 1983) 231–62; also Virginia Held, 'The Obligations of Mothers and Fathers,' in Trebilcot, ed. 7–20.

27. This point was suggested to me by L. W. Sumner.

28. John Broughton also discusses the concern for justice and rights which appears in women's moral reasoning as well as the concern for care and relationships featured in men's moral reasoning; 'Women's Rationality and Men's Virtues,' esp. 603–22. For a historical discussion of male theorists who have failed to hear the concern for justice in women's voices, cf. Carole Pateman, '"The Disorder of Women": Women, Love, and the Sense of Justice,' *Ethics* 91 (1980), 20–34.

29. This discussion owes a debt to Francesca M. Cancian's warning that we should not narrow our conception of love to the recognized ways in which women love, which researchers find to center around the expression of feelings and verbal disclosure. Such a conception ignores forms of love which are stereotyped as characteristically male, including instrumental help and the sharing of activities. Cf. 'The Feminization of Love,' *Signs* 11 (1986), 692–709.

30. Cf. Mike Royko, *Boss: Richard J. Daley of Chicago* (New York: New American Library 1971).

31. Claudia Card has critiqued Gilligan's work for ignoring, in particular, the dismaying harms to which women have historically been subjected in heterosexual relationships, including, but by no means limited to, marriage ('Virtues and Moral Luck,' 15–17).

32. Discussion in part III of my paper draws upon the insights of Claudia Card, 'Virtues and Moral Luck' and Seyla Benhabib, 'The Generalized and the Concrete Other; Visions of the Autonomous Self,' in Meyers and Kittay, eds., *Women and Moral Theory,* 154–77.

33. This part of my discussion owes a debt to Claudia Card.

34. Cf. Immanuel Kant, *Groundwork of the Metaphysics of Morals,* trans. Lewis White Beck (Indianapolis: Bobbs-Merrill 1959), 46–7, 53–4.

35. For a helpful discussion on this topic, cf. Margaret Walker, 'Moral Particularism,' unpublished manuscript presented at the Pacific Division Meetings of the American Philosophical Association, March 1987.

STUDY QUESTIONS

1. What limitations does Friedman find in Gilligan's approach to moral reasoning?
2. Are justice and care both necessary for understanding morality?
3. What is the distinction between distributive and corrective justice?
4. Does your view of morality depend on your gender?

The Ethics of Care

Virginia Held

Virginia Held is Professor Emerita of Philosophy at Hunter College and the Graduate Center of the City University of New York. She develops what she terms "the ethics of care," which some philosophers have viewed as one form of virtue ethics. She emphasizes, however, that while the two are in some ways similar, virtue ethics focuses on the character of individuals, whereas the ethics of care is concerned especially with fostering connectedness among people.

1

The Ethics of Care as Moral Theory

The ethics of care is only a few decades old. Some theorists do not like the term 'care' to designate this approach to moral issues and have tried substituting 'the ethic of love,' or 'relational ethics,' but the discourse keeps returning to 'care' as the so far more satisfactory of the terms considered, though dissatisfactions with it remain. The concept of care has the advantage of not losing sight of the work involved in caring for people and of not lending itself to the interpretation of morality as ideal but impractical to which advocates of the ethics of care often object. . . .

Features of the Ethics of Care

. . . I think one can discern among various versions of the ethics of care a number of major features.

First, the central focus of the ethics of care is on the compelling moral salience of attending to and meeting the needs of the particular others for whom we take responsibility. Caring for one's child, for instance, may well and defensibly be at the forefront of a person's moral concerns. The ethics of care recognizes that human beings are dependent for many years of their lives, that the moral claim of those dependent on us for the care they need is pressing, and that there are highly important moral aspects in developing the relations of caring that enable human beings to live and progress. All persons need care for at least their early years. Prospects for human progress and flourishing hinge fundamentally on the care that those needing it receive, and the ethics of care stresses the moral force of the responsibility to respond to the needs of the dependent. Many persons will become ill and dependent for some periods of their later lives, including in frail old age, and some who are permanently disabled will need care the whole of their lives. Moralities built on the image of the independent, autonomous, rational individual largely overlook the reality of human dependence and the morality for which it calls. The ethics of care attends to this central concern of human life and delineates the moral values involved. It refuses to relegate care to a realm "outside morality." How caring

Reprinted from Virginia Held, *The Ethics of Care: Personal, Political and Global*, Oxford University Press, 2006. Reprinted by permission of the publisher.

for particular others should be reconciled with the claims of, for instance, universal justice is an issue that needs to be addressed. But the ethics of care starts with the moral claims of particular others, for instance, of one's child, whose claims can be compelling regardless of universal principles.

Second, in the epistemological process of trying to understand what morality would recommend and what it would be morally best for us to do and to be, the ethics of care values emotion rather than rejects it. Not all emotion is valued, of course, but in contrast with the dominant rationalist approaches, such emotions as sympathy, empathy, sensitivity, and responsiveness are seen as the kind of moral emotions that need to be cultivated not only to help in the implementation of the dictates of reason but to better ascertain what morality recommends. Even anger may be a component of the moral indignation that should be felt when people are treated unjustly or inhumanely, and it may contribute to (rather than interfere with) an appropriate interpretation of the moral wrong. This is not to say that raw emotion can be a guide to morality; feelings need to be reflected on and educated. But from the care perspective, moral inquiries that rely entirely on reason and rationalistic deductions or calculations are seen as deficient.

The emotions that are typically considered and rejected in rationalistic moral theories are the egoistic feelings that undermine universal moral norms, the favoritism that interferes with impartiality, and the aggressive and vengeful impulses for which morality is to provide restraints. The ethics of care, in contrast, typically appreciates the emotions and relational capabilities that enable morally concerned persons in actual interpersonal contexts to understand what would be best. Since even the helpful emotions can often become misguided or worse—as when excessive empathy with others leads to a wrongful degree of self-denial or when benevolent concern crosses over into controlling domination—we need an *ethics* of care, not just care itself. The various aspects and expressions of care and caring relations need to be subjected to moral scrutiny and *evaluated*, not just observed and described.

Third, the ethics of care rejects the view of the dominant moral theories that the more abstract the reasoning about a moral problem the better because the more likely to avoid bias and arbitrariness, the more nearly to achieve impartiality. The ethics of care respects rather than removes itself from the claims of particular others with whom we share actual relationships. It calls into question the universalistic and abstract rules of the dominant theories. When the latter consider such actual relations as between a parent and child, if they say anything about them at all, they may see them as permitting and cultivating them a preference that a person may have. Or they may recognize a universal obligation for all parents to care for their children. But they do not permit actual relations ever to take priority over the requirements of impartiality. . . .

The ethics of care may seek to limit the applicability of universal rules to certain domains where they are more appropriate, like the domain of law, and resist their extension to other domains. Such rules may simply be inappropriate in, for instance, the contexts of family and friendship, yet relations in these domains should certainly be *evaluated,* not merely described, hence morality should not be limited to abstract rules. We should be able to give moral guidance concerning actual relations that are trusting, considerate, and caring and concerning those that are not.

Dominant moral theories tend to interpret moral problems as if they were conflicts between egoistic individual interests on the one hand, and universal moral principles on the other. The extremes of "selfish individual" and "humanity" are recognized, but what lies between these is often overlooked. The ethics of care, in contrast, focuses especially on the area between these extremes. Those who conscientiously care for others are not seeking primarily to further their own *individual* interests; their interests are intertwined with the persons they care for. Neither are they acting for the sake of *all others* or *humanity in general*; they seek instead to preserve or promote an actual human relation between themselves and *particular others*. Persons in caring relations are acting for self-and-other together. Their characteristic stance is neither egoistic nor altruistic; these are the options in a conflictual situation, but the well-being of a caring relation involves the cooperative well-being of those in the relation and the well-being of the relation itself. . . .

A fourth characteristic of the ethics of care is that like much feminist thought in many areas, it reconceptualizes traditional notions about the public and the private. The traditional view, built into the dominant moral theories, is that the household is a private sphere beyond politics into which government, based on consent, should not intrude. Feminists have shown how the greater social, political, economic, and cultural power of men has structured this "private" sphere to the disadvantage of women and children, rendering them vulnerable to domestic violence without outside interference, often leaving women economically dependent on men and subject to a highly inequitable division of labor in the family. The law has not hesitated to intervene into women's private decisions concerning reproduction but has been highly reluctant to intrude on men's exercise of coercive power within the "castles" of their homes.

Dominant moral theories have seen "public" life as relevant to morality while missing the moral significance of the "private" domains of family and friendship. Thus the dominant theories have assumed that morality should be sought for unrelated, independent, and mutually indifferent individuals assumed to be equal. They have posited an abstract, fully rational "agent as such" from which to construct morality, while missing the moral issues that arise between interconnected persons in the contexts of family, friendship, and social groups. In the context of the family, it is typical for relations to be between persons with highly unequal power who did not choose the ties and obligations in which they find themselves enmeshed. For instance, no child can choose her parents yet she may well have obligations to care for them. Relations of this kind are standardly noncontractual, and conceptualizing them as contractual would often undermine or at least obscure the trust on which their worth depends. The ethics of care addresses rather than neglects moral issues arising in relations among the unequal and dependent, relations that are often laden with emotion and involuntary, and then notices how often these attributes apply not only in the household but in the wider society as well. For instance, persons do

not choose which gender, racial, class, ethnic, religious, national, or cultural groups to be brought up in, yet these sorts of ties may be important aspects of who they are and how their experience can contribute to moral understanding.

A fifth characteristic of the ethics of care is the conception of persons with which it begins. This will be dealt with in the next section.

The Critique of Liberal Individualism

The ethics of care usually works with a conception of persons as relational, rather than as the self-sufficient independent individuals of the dominant moral theories. The dominant theories can be interpreted as importing into moral theory a concept of the person developed primarily for liberal political and economic theory, seeing the person as a rational, autonomous agent, or a self-interested individual. . . .

The ethics of care, in contrast, characteristically sees persons as relational and interdependent, morally and epistemologically. Every person starts out as a child dependent on those providing us care, and we remain interdependent with others in thoroughly fundamental ways throughout our lives. That we can think and act as if we were independent depends on a network of social relations making it possible for us to do so. And our relations are part of what constitute our identity. This is not to say that we cannot become autonomous; feminists have done much interesting work developing an alternative conception of autonomy in place of the liberal individualist one. Feminists have much experience rejecting or reconstituting relational ties that are oppressive. But it means that from the perspective of an ethics of care, to construct morality *as if* we were Robinson Crusoes . . . is misleading. And it obscures the innumerable ways persons and groups are interdependent in the modern world.

Not only does the liberal individualist conception of the person foster a false picture of society and the persons in it, it is, from the perspective of the ethics of care, impoverished also as an ideal. The ethics of care values the ties we have with particular other persons and the actual relationships that partly constitute our identity. Although persons often may and should reshape their relations with others—distancing themselves from some persons and groups and developing or strengthening ties with others—the autonomy sought within the ethics of care is a capacity to reshape and cultivate new relations, not to ever more closely resemble the unencumbered abstract rational self of liberal political and moral theories. Those motivated by the ethics of care would seek to become more admirable relational persons in better caring relations. . . .

Justice and Care

Some conceptions of the ethics of care see it as contrasting with an ethic of justice in ways that suggest one must choose between them. Carol Gilligan's suggestion of alternative perspectives in interpreting and organizing the elements of a moral problem lent itself to this implication. . . .

An ethic of justice focuses on questions of fairness, equality, individual rights, abstract principles, and the consistent application of them. An ethic of care focuses on attentiveness, trust, responsiveness to need, narrative nuance, and cultivating caring relations. Whereas an ethic of justice seeks a fair solution between competing individual interests and rights, an ethic of care sees the interests of carers and cared-for as importantly intertwined rather than as simply competing. Whereas justice protects equality and freedom, care fosters social bonds and cooperation.

These are very different emphases in what morality should consider. Yet both deal with what seems of great moral importance. This has led many to explore how they might be combined in a satisfactory morality. One can persuasively argue, for instance, that justice is needed in such contexts of care as the family, to protect against violence and the unfair division of labor or treatment of children. One can also persuasively argue that care is needed in such contexts of justice as the streets and the courts, where persons should be treated humanely, and in the way education and health and welfare should be dealt with as social responsibilities. . . .

Few would hold that considerations of justice have no place at all in care. One would not be caring well for two children, for instance, if one showed a persistent favoritism toward one of them that could not be justified on the basis of some such factor as greater need. The issues are rather what constellation of values have priority and which predominate in the practices of the ethics of care and the ethics of justice. It is quite possible to delineate significant differences between them. In the dominant moral theories of the ethics of justice, the values of equality, impartiality, fair distribution, and noninterference have priority; in practices of justice, individual rights are protected, impartial judgments are arrived at, punishments are deserved, and equal treatment is sought. In contrast, in the ethics of care, the values of trust, solidarity, mutual concern, and empathetic responsiveness have priority; in practices of care, relationships are cultivated, needs are responded to, and sensitivity is demonstrated. . . .

The question remains, however, whether justice should be thought to be incorporated into any ethic of care that will be adequate or whether we should keep the notions of justice and care and their associated ethics conceptually distinct. There is much to be said for recognizing how the ethics of care values interrelatedness and responsiveness to the needs of particular others, how the ethics of justice values fairness and rights, and how these are different emphases. Too much integration will lose sight of these valid differences. I am more inclined to say that an adequate, comprehensive moral theory will have to include the insights of both the ethics of care and the ethics of justice, among other insights, rather than that either of these can be incorporated into the other in the sense of supposing that it can provide the grounds for the judgments characteristically found in the other. Equitable caring is not necessarily better caring, it is fairer caring. And humane justice is not necessarily better justice, it is more caring justice. . . .

My own suggestions for integrating care and justice are to keep these concepts conceptually distinct and to delineate the domains in which they should have priority. In the realm of law, for instance, justice and the assurance of rights should have priority, although the humane considerations of care should not be absent. In the realm of the family and among friends, priority should be given to expansive care, though the basic requirements of justice surely should also be met. . . .

Care is probably the most deeply fundamental value. There can be care without justice: There has historically been little justice in the family, but care and life have gone on without it. There can be no justice without care, however, for without care no child would survive and there would be no persons to respect.

Care may thus provide the wider and deeper ethics within which justice should be sought, as when persons in caring relations may sometimes compete and in doing so should treat each other fairly, or, at the level of society, within caring relations of the thinner kind we can agree to treat each other for limited purposes as if we were the abstract individuals of liberal theory. But although care may be the more fundamental value, it may well be that the ethics of care does not itself provide adequate theoretical resources for dealing with issues of justice. Within its appropriate sphere and for its relevant questions, the ethics of justice may be best for what we seek. What should be resisted is the traditional inclination to expand the reach of justice in such a way that it is mistakenly imagined to be able to give us a comprehensive morality suitable for all moral questions. . . .

The Ethics of Care and Virtue Ethics

Insofar as the ethics of care wishes to cultivate in persons the characteristics of a caring person and the skills of activities of caring, might an ethic of care be assimilated to virtue theory? . . .

Certainly there are some similarities between the ethics of care and virtue theory. Both examine practices and the moral values they embody. Both see more hope for moral development in reforming practices than in reasoning from abstract rules. Both understand that the practices of morality must be cultivated, nurtured, shaped.

Until recently, however, virtue theory has not paid adequate attention to the practices of caring in which women have been so heavily engaged. Although this might be corrected, virtue theory has characteristically seen the virtues as incorporated in various traditions or traditional communities. In contrast, the ethics of care as a feminist ethic is wary of existing traditions and traditional communities:

Virtually all are patriarchal. The ethics of care envisions caring not as practiced under male domination, but as it should be practiced in postpatriarchal society, of which we do not yet have traditions or wide experience. Individual egalitarian families are still surrounded by inegalitarian social and cultural influences.

In my view, although there are similarities between them and although to be caring is no doubt a virtue, the ethics of care is not simply a kind of virtue ethics. Virtue ethics focuses especially on the states of character of individuals, whereas the ethics of care concerns itself especially with caring *relations*. Caring relations have primary value. . . .

2

Care as Practice and Value

What *is* care? What do we mean by the term 'care'? Can we define it in anything like a precise way? There is not yet anything close to agreement among those writing on care on what exactly we should take the meaning of this term to be, but there have been many suggestions, tacit and occasionally explicit.

For over two decades, the concept of care as it figures in the ethics of care has been assumed, explored, elaborated, and employed in the development of theory. But definitions have often been imprecise, or trying to arrive at them has simply been postponed (as in my own case), in the growing discourse. Perhaps this is entirely appropriate for new explorations, but the time may have come to seek greater clarity. Some of those writing on care have attempted to be precise, with mixed results, whereas others have proceeded with the tacit understanding that of course to a considerable extent we know what we are talking about when we speak of taking care of a child or providing care for the ill. But care has many forms, and as the ethics of care evolves, so should our understanding of what care is.

Taking Care

The last words I spoke to my older brother after a brief visit and with special feeling were: "take care." He had not been taking good care of himself, and I hoped he would do better; not many days later he died, of problems quite possibly unrelated to those to which I had been referring. "Take care" was not an expression he and I grew up with. I acquired it over the years in my life in New York City. It may be illuminating to begin thinking about the meaning of 'care' with an examination of this expression.

We often say "take care" as routinely as "good-bye" or some abbreviation and with as little emotion. But even then it does convey some sense of connectedness. More often, when said with some feeling, it means something like "take care of yourself because I care about you." Sometimes we say it, especially to children or to someone embarking on a trip or an endeavor, meaning "I care what happens to you, so please don't do anything dangerous or foolish." Or, if we know the danger is inevitable and inescapable, it may be more like a wish that the elements will let the person take care so the worst can be evaded. And sometimes we mean it as a plea: Be careful not to harm yourself or others because our connection will make us feel with and for you. We may be harmed ourselves or partly responsible, or if you do something you will regret we will share that regret.

One way or another, this expression (like many others) illustrates human relatedness and the daily reaffirmations of connection. It is the relatedness of human beings, built and rebuilt, that the ethics of care is being developed to try to understand, evaluate, and guide. The expression has more to do with the feelings and awareness of the persons expressing and the persons receiving such expressions than with the actual tasks and work of "taking care" of a person who is dependent on us, or in need of care, but such attitudes and shared awareness seem at least one important component of care.

Some Distinctions

A seemingly easy distinction to make is between care as the activity of taking care of someone and the mere "caring about" of how we feel about certain issues. Actually "caring for" a small child or a person who is ill is quite different from merely "caring for" something (or not) in the sense of liking it or not, as in "I don't care for that kind of music." But these distinctions may not be as clear as they appear, since when we take care of a child, for instance, we usually also care about him or her, and although we could take care of a child we do not like, the caring will usually be better care if we care for the child in both senses. If we really do care about world hunger, we will probably be doing something about it, such as at least giving money to alleviate it or to change the conditions that bring it about, and thus establishing some connection between ourselves and the hungry we say we care about. And if we really do care about global climate change and the harm it will bring to future generations, we imagine a connection between ourselves and those future people who will judge our irresponsibility, and we change our consumption practices or political activities to decrease the likely harm. . . .

Care as Practice

. . . Care is a practice involving the work of care-giving and the standards by which the practices of care can be evaluated. Care must concern itself with the effectiveness of its efforts to meet needs, but also with the motives with which care is provided. It seeks good caring relations. In normal cases, recipients of care sustain caring relations through their responsiveness—the look of satisfaction in the child, the smile of the patient. Where such responsiveness is not possible—with a severely mentally ill person, for instance—sustaining the relation may depend entirely on the caregiver, but it is still appropriate to think in terms of caring relations: The caregiver may be trying to form a relation or must imagine a relation. Relations between persons can be criticized when they become dominating, exploitative, mistrustful, or hostile. Relations of care can be encouraged and maintained.

Consider, for instance, mothering, in the sense of caring for children. It had long been imagined in the modern era after the establishment of the public/private distinction to be "outside morality" because it was based on instinct. Feminist critique has been needed to show how profoundly mistaken such a view is. Moral issues are confronted constantly in the practice of mothering and other caring work. There is constant need for the cultivation of the virtues appropriate to these practices, and of moral evaluation of how the practices are being carried out. To get a hint of how profoundly injustice has been embedded in the practice of mothering, one can compare the meaning of "mothering" with that of "fathering," which standardly has meant no more than impregnating a woman and being the genetic father of a child. "Mothering" suggests that this activity must or should be done by women, whereas, except for lactation, there is no part of it that cannot be done by men as well. Many feminists argue that for actual practices of child care to be morally acceptable, they will have to be radically transformed to accord with principles of equality, though existing conceptions of equality should probably not be the primary moral focus of practices of care. This is only the beginning of the moral scrutiny to which they should be subject.

This holds also for other practices that can be thought of as practices of care. We need, then, not only to examine the practices and discern with new sensitivities the values already embedded or missing within them but also to construct the appropriate normative theory with which to evaluate them, reform them, and shape them anew. This, I think, involves understanding care as a value worthy of the kind of theoretical elaboration justice has received. Understanding the value of care involves understanding how it should not be limited to the household or family; care should be recognized as a political and social value also.

Care as Value

We all agree that justice is a value. There are also practices of justice: law enforcement, court proceedings, and so on. Practices incorporate values but also need to be evaluated by the normative standards values provide. A given actual practice of justice may only very inadequately incorporate within it the value of justice, and we need justice as a value to evaluate such a practice. The value of justice picks out certain aspects of the overall moral spectrum, those having to do with fairness, equality, and so on, and it would not be satisfactory to have only the most general value terms, such as 'good' and 'right,' 'bad' and 'wrong,' with which to do the evaluating of a practice of justice. Analogously, for actual

practices of care we need care as a value to pick out the appropriate cluster of moral considerations, such as sensitivity, trust, and mutual concern, with which to evaluate such practices. It is not enough to think of care as simply work, describable empirically, with 'good' and 'right' providing all the normative evaluation of actual practices of care. Such practices are often morally deficient in ways specific to care as well as to justice.

If we say of someone that "he is a caring person," this includes an evaluation that he has a characteristic that, other things being equal, is morally admirable. Attributing a virtue to someone, as when we say that she is generous or trustworthy, describes a disposition but also makes a normative judgment. It is highly useful to be able to characterize people (and societies) in specific and subtle ways, recognizing the elements of our claims that are empirically descriptive and those that are normative. The subtlety needs to be available not only at the level of the descriptive but also within our moral evaluations. "Caring" thus picks out a more specific value to be found in persons' and societies' characteristics than merely finding them to be good or bad, or morally admirable or not, on the whole. But we may resist reducing care to a virtue if by that we refer only to the dispositions of individual persons, since caring is so much a matter of the relations between them. We value caring persons in caring relations. . . .

Caring Relations

My own view, then, is that care is both a practice and a value. As a practice, it shows us how to respond to needs and why we should. It builds trust and mutual concern and connectedness between persons. It is not a series of individual actions, but a practice that develops, along with its appropriate attitudes. It has attributes and standards that can be described, but more important that can be recommended and that should be continually improved as adequate care comes closer to being good care. Practices of care should express the caring relations that bring persons together, and they should do so in ways that are progressively more morally satisfactory. Caring practices should gradually transform children and others into human beings who are increasingly morally admirable. . . .

In addition to being a practice, care is also a value. Caring persons and caring attitudes should be valued, and we can organize many evaluations of how persons are interrelated around a constellation of moral considerations associated with care or its absence. For instance, we can ask of a relation whether it is trusting and mutually considerate or hostile and vindictive. We can ask if persons are attentive and responsive to each other's needs or indifferent and self-absorbed. Care is not the same as benevolence, in my view, since it is more the characterization of a social relation than the description of an individual disposition, and social relations are not reducible to individual states. Caring relations ought to be cultivated, between persons in their personal lives and between the members of caring societies. Such relations are often reciprocal over time if not at given times. The values of caring are especially exemplified in caring relations, rather than in persons as individuals.

To advocates of the ethics of care, care involves moral considerations at least as important as those of justice. And when adequately understood, the ethics of care is as appropriate for men as for women. Both men and women should acknowledge the enormous value of the caring activities on which society relies and should share these activities fairly. They should recognize the values of care, as of justice.

Caring relations form the small societies of family and friendship on which larger societies depend. Caring relations of a weaker but still evident kind between more distant persons allow them to trust one another enough to live in peace and respect each others' rights. For progress to be made, persons need to care together for the well-being of their members and their environment. . . .

The ethics of care builds relations of care and concern and mutual responsiveness to need on both the personal and wider social levels. Within social relations in which we care enough about one another to form a social entity, we may agree on various ways to deal with one another. For instance, for limited purposes we may imagine each other as liberal individuals in the marketplace, independent, autonomous, and rational, and we may adopt liberal schemes of law and governance, and policies to maximize individual benefits. But we should not lose sight of the deeper reality of human interdependency and of the need for caring relations to undergird or surround such constructions. The artificial abstraction of the model of the liberal individual is at best suitable for a restricted and limited part of human life, rather than for the whole of it. The ethics of care provides a way of thinking about and evaluating both the more immediate and the more distant human relations with which to develop morally acceptable societies.

STUDY QUESTIONS

1. What does Held mean by her claim that care is both a practice and a value?
2. Is the ethics of care a form of virtue ethics?
3. Does an ethics of care require caring equally for all?
4. Does an ethics of care imply particular views on any concrete moral issues?

Part XII

PARTICULARISM

Existentialism Is a Humanism

Jean-Paul Sartre

Jean-Paul Sartre (1905–1980) was a French philosopher, novelist, and dramatist who was offered but declined the 1964 Nobel Prize for Literature. He defends existentialism, the theory that human agents by their thoughts and deeds freely shape themselves. According to Sartre, our existence precedes our essence (or nature), and hence we are only what we make of ourselves. Central to Sartre's ethical theory is authenticity, the willingness to take responsibility for our choices. Doing so, however, brings with it anguish, forlornness, and despair. For Sartre, an atheist, each of us is alone with no way to avoid responsibility for making ourselves whatever we become. All that matters is what we do, not what we dream, expect, or hope.

What is meant by the term *existentialism?*

Most people who use the word would be rather embarrassed if they had to explain it, since, now that the word is all the rage, even the work of a musician or painter is being called existentialist. A gossip columnist in *Clartés* signs himself *The Existentialist,* so that by this time the word has been so stretched and has taken on so broad a meaning, that it no longer means anything at all. It seems that for want of an advance-guard doctrine analogous to surrealism, the kind of people who are eager for scandal and flurry turn to this philosophy which in other respects does not at all serve their purposes in this sphere.

Actually, it is the least scandalous, the most austere of doctrines. It is intended strictly for specialists and philosophers. Yet it can be defined easily. What complicates matters is that there are two kinds of existentialist; first, those who are Christian, among whom I would include Jaspers and Gabriel Marcel, both Catholic; and on the other hand the atheistic existentialists, among whom I class Heidegger, and then the French existentialists and myself. What they have in common is that they think that existence precedes essence, or, if you prefer, that subjectivity must be the starting point.

Just what does that mean? Let us consider some object that is manufactured, for example, a book or a paper-cutter: here is an object which has been made by an artisan whose inspiration came from a concept. He referred to the concept of what a paper-cutter is and likewise to a known method of production, which is part of the concept, something which is, by and large, a routine. Thus, the paper-cutter is at once an object produced in a certain way and, on the other hand, one having a specific use; and one can not postulate a man who produces a paper-cutter but does not know what it is used for. Therefore, let us say that, for the paper-cutter, essence—that is, the ensemble of both the production routines and the properties which enable it to be both produced and defined—precedes existence. Thus, the presence of the paper-cutter or book in front of me is determined. Therefore, we have here a technical view of the world whereby it can be said that production precedes existence.

When we conceive God as the Creator, He is generally thought of as a superior sort of artisan. Whatever doctrine we may be considering, whether one like that of Descartes or that of Leibnitz, we always grant that will more or less follows understanding or, at the very least, accompanies it, and that when God creates He knows exactly what He is creating. Thus, the concept of man in the mind of God is comparable to the concept of paper-cutter in the mind of the manufacturer, and, following certain techniques and a conception, God produces man, just as the artisan, following a definition and a technique, makes a paper-cutter. Thus, the individual man is the realization of a certain concept in the divine intelligence.

In the eighteenth century, the atheism of the *philosopher* discarded the idea of God, but not so much for the notion that essence precedes existence. To a certain extent, this idea is found everywhere; we find it in Diderot, in Voltaire, and even in Kant. Man has a human nature; this human nature, which is the concept of the human, is found in all men, which means that each man is a particular example of a universal concept, man. In Kant, the result of this universality is that the wild-man, the natural man, as well as the bourgeois, are circumscribed by the same definition and have the same basic qualities. Thus, here too the essence of man precedes the historical existence that we find in nature.

Atheistic existentialism, which I represent, is more coherent. It states that if God does not exist, there is at least one being in whom existence precedes essence, a being who exists before he can be defined by any concept, and that this being is man, or, as Heidegger says, human reality. What is meant here by saying that existence precedes essence? It means that, first of all, man exists, turns up, appears on the scene, and, only afterwards, defines himself. If man, as the existentialist conceives him, is indefinable, it is because at first he is nothing. Only afterward will he be something, and he himself will have made what he will be. Thus, there is no human nature, since there is no God to conceive it. Not only is man what he conceives himself to be, but he is also only what he wills himself to be after this thrust toward existence.

Man is nothing else but what he makes of himself. Such is the first principle of existentialism. It is also what is called subjectivity, the name we are labeled with when charges are brought against us. But what do we mean by this, if not that man has a greater dignity than a stone or table? For we mean that man first exists, that is, that man first of all is the being who hurls himself toward a future and who is conscious of imagining himself as being in the future. Man is at the start a plan which is aware of itself, rather than a patch of moss, a piece of garbage, or a cauliflower; nothing exists prior to this plan; there is nothing in heaven; man will be what he will have planned to be. Not what he will want to be. Because by the word "will" we generally mean a conscious decision, which is subsequent to what we have already made of ourselves. I may want to belong to a political party, write a book, get married: but all that is only a manifestation of an earlier, more spontaneous choice that is called "will." But if existence really does precede essence, man is responsible for what he is. Thus, existentialism's first move is to make every man aware of what he is and to make the full responsibility of his existence rest on him. And when we say that a man is responsible for himself, we do not only mean that he is responsible for his own individuality, but that he is responsible for all men.

The word subjectivism has two meanings, and our opponents play on the two. Subjectivism means, on the one hand, that an individual chooses and makes himself; and, on the other, that it is impossible for man to transcend human subjectivity. The second of these is the essential meaning of existentialism. When we say that man chooses his own self, we mean that every one of us does likewise; but we also mean by that that in making this choice he also chooses all men. In fact, in creating the man that we want to be, there is not a single one of our acts which does not at the same time create an image of man as we think he ought to be. To choose to be this or that is to affirm at the same time the value of what we choose, because we can never choose evil. We always choose the good, and nothing can be good for us without being good for all.

If, on the other hand, existence precedes essence, and if we grant that we exist and fashion our image at one and the same time, the image is valid for everybody and for our whole age. Thus, our responsibility is much greater than we might have supposed, because it involves all mankind. If I am a working-man and choose to join a Christian trade-union rather than be a communist, and if by being a member I want to show that the best thing for man is resignation, that the kingdom of man is not of this world, I am not only involving my own case—I want to be resigned for everyone. As a result, my action has involved all humanity. To take a more individual matter, if I want to marry, to have children; even if this marriage depends solely on my own circumstances or passion or wish, I am involving all humanity in monogamy and not merely myself. Therefore, I am responsible for myself and for everyone else. I am creating a certain image of man of my own choosing. In choosing myself, I choose man.

This helps us understand what the actual content is of such rather grandiloquent words as anguish, forlornness, despair. As you will see, it's all quite simple.

First, what is meant by anguish? The existentialists say at once that man is anguish. What that means is this: the man who involves himself and who realizes that he is not only the person he chooses to be, but also a lawmaker who is, at the same time, choosing all mankind as well as himself, can not help escape the feeling of his total and deep responsibility. Of course, there are many people who are not anxious; but we claim that they are hiding their anxiety, that they are fleeing from it. Certainly, many people believe that when they do something, they themselves are the only ones involved, and when someone says to them, "What if everyone acted that way?" they shrug their shoulders and answer. "Everyone doesn't act that way." But really, one should always ask himself, "What would happen if everybody looked at things that way?" There is no escaping this disturbing thought except by a kind of double-dealing. A man who lies and makes excuses for himself by saying "not everybody does that," is someone with an uneasy

conscience, because the act of lying implies that a universal value is conferred upon the lie.

Anguish is evident even when it conceals itself. This is the anguish that Kierkegaard called the anguish of Abraham. You know the story: an angel has ordered Abraham to sacrifice his son: if it really were an angel who has come and said. "You are Abraham, you shall sacrifice your son," everything would be all right. But everyone might first wonder, "Is it really an angel, and am I really Abraham? What proof do I have?"

There was a madwoman who had hallucinations; someone used to speak to her on the telephone and give her orders. Her doctor asked her, "Who is it who talks to you?" She answered. "He says it's God." What proof did she really have that it was God? If an angel comes to me, what proof is there that it's an angel? And if I hear voices, what proof is there that they come from heaven and not from hell, or from the subconscious, or a pathological condition? What proves that they are addressed to me? What proof is there that I have been appointed to impose my choice and my conception of man on humanity? I'll never find any proof or sign to convince me of that. If a voice addresses me, it is always for me to decide that this is the angel's voice: if I consider that such an act is a good one, it is I who will choose to say that it is good rather than bad.

Now, I'm not being singled out as an Abraham, and yet at every moment I'm obliged to perform exemplary acts. For every man, everything happens as if all mankind had its eyes fixed on him and were guiding itself by what he does. And every man ought to say to himself. "Am I really the kind of man who has the right to act in such a way that humanity might guide itself by my actions?" And if he does not say that to himself, he is masking his anguish.

There is no question here of the kind of anguish which would lead to quietism, to inaction. It is a matter of a simple sort of anguish that anybody who has had responsibilities is familiar with. For example, when a military officer takes the responsibility for an attack and sends a certain number of men to death, he chooses to do so, and in the main he alone makes the choice. Doubtless, orders come from above, but they are too broad; he interprets them, and on this interpretation depend the lives of ten or fourteen or twenty men. In making a decision he can not help having a certain anguish. All leaders know this anguish. That doesn't keep them from acting; on the contrary, it is the very condition of their action. For it implies that they envisage a number of possibilities, and when they choose one, they realize that it has value only because it is chosen. We shall see that this kind of anguish, which is the kind that existentialism describes, is explained, in addition, by a direct responsibility to the other men whom it involves. It is not a curtain separating us from action, but is part of action itself.

When we speak of forlornness, a term Heidegger was fond of, we mean only that God does not exist and that we have to face all the consequences of this. The existentialist is strongly opposed to a certain kind of secular ethics which would like to abolish God with the least possible expense. About 1880, some French teachers tried to set up a secular ethics which went something like this: God is a useless and costly hypothesis; we are discarding it; but, meanwhile, in order for there to be an ethics, a society, a civilization, it is essential that certain values be taken seriously and that they be considered as having an *a priori* existence. It must be obligatory, *a priori,* to be honest, not to lie, not to beat your wife, to have children, etc., etc. So we're going to try a little device which will make it possible to show that values exist all the same, inscribed in a heaven of ideas, though otherwise God does not exist. In other words—and this, I believe, is the tendency of everything called reformism in France—nothing will be changed if God does not exist. We shall find ourselves with the same norms of honesty, progress, and humanism, and we shall have made of God an outdated hypothesis which will peacefully die off by itself.

The existentialist, on the contrary, thinks it very distressing that God does not exist, because all possibility of finding values in a heaven of ideas disappears along with Him; there can no longer be an *a priori* Good, since there is no infinite and perfect consciousness to think it. Nowhere is it written that the Good exists, that we must be honest, that we must not lie; because the fact is we are on a plane where there are only men. Dostoevsky said, "If God didn't exist, everything would be possible." That is the very starting point of existentialism. Indeed, everything is permissible if God does not exist, and as a result man is forlorn, because neither within him nor without does he find anything to cling to. He can't start making excuses for himself.

If existence really does precede essence, there is no explaining things away by reference to a fixed and given human nature. In other words, there is no determinism, man is free, man is freedom. On the other hand, if God does not exist, we find no values or commands to turn to which legitimize our conduct. So, in the bright realm of values, we have no excuse behind us, nor justification before us. We are alone, with no excuses.

That is the idea I shall try to convey when I say that man is condemned to be free. Condemned, because he did not create himself, yet, in other respects is free; because, once thrown into the world, he is responsible for everything he does. The existentialist does not believe in the power of passion. He will never agree that a sweeping passion is a ravaging torrent which fatally leads a man to certain acts and is therefore an excuse. He thinks that man is responsible for his passion.

The existentialist does not think that man is going to help himself by finding in the world some omen by which to orient himself. Because he thinks that man will interpret the omen to suit himself. Therefore, he thinks that man, with no support and no aid, is condemned every moment to invent man. Ponge, in a very fine article, has said, "Man is the future of man." That's exactly it. But if it is taken to mean that this future is recorded in heaven, that God sees it, then it is false, because it would really no longer be a future. If it is taken to mean that, whatever a man may be, there is a future to be forged, a virgin future before him, then this remark is sound. But then we are forlorn.

To give you an example which will enable you to understand forlornness better, I shall cite the case of one of my students who came to see me under the following circumstances: his father was on bad terms with his mother, and, moreover, was inclined to be a collaborationist; his older brother had been killed in the German offensive of 1940, and the young man, with somewhat immature but generous feelings, wanted to avenge him. His mother lived alone with him, very much upset by the half-treason of her husband and the death of her older son; the boy was her only consolation.

The boy was faced with the choice of leaving for England and joining the Free French Forces—that is, leaving his mother behind—or remaining with his mother and helping her to carry on. He was fully aware that the woman lived only for him and that his going-off—and perhaps his death—would plunge her into despair. He was also aware that every act that he did for his mother's sake was a sure thing, in the sense that it was helping her to carry on, whereas every effort he made toward going off and fighting was an uncertain move which might run aground and prove completely useless; for example, on his way to England he might, while passing through Spain, be detained indefinitely in a Spanish camp; he might reach England or Algiers and be stuck in an office at a desk job. As a result, he was faced with two very different kinds of action: one, concrete, immediate, but concerning only one individual; the other concerned an incomparably vaster group, a national collectivity, but for that very reason was dubious, and might be interrupted en route. And, at the same time, he was wavering between two kinds of ethics. On the one hand, an ethics of sympathy, of personal devotion; on the other hand, a broader ethics, but one whose efficacy was more dubious. He had to choose between the two.

Who could help him choose? Christian doctrine? No. Christian doctrine says, "Be charitable, love your neighbor, take the more rugged path, etc., etc." But which is the more rugged path? Whom should he love as a brother? The fighting man or his mother? Which does the greater good, the vague act of fighting in a group, or the concrete one of helping a particular human being to go on living? Who can decide *a priori?* Nobody. No book of ethics can tell him. The Kantian ethics says, "Never treat any person as a means, but as an end." Very well, if I stay with my mother. I'll treat her as an end and not as a means; but by virtue of this very fact, I'm running the risk of treating the people around me who are fighting, as means; and, conversely, if I go to join

those who are fighting, I'll be treating them as an end, and, by doing that. I run the risk of treating my mother as a means.

If values are vague, and if they are always too broad for the concrete and specific case that we are considering, the only thing left for us is to trust our instincts. That's what this young man tried to do; and when I saw him, he said, "In the end, feeling is what counts. I ought to choose whichever pushes me in one direction. If I feel that I love my mother enough to sacrifice everything else for her—my desire for vengeance, for action, for adventure—then I'll stay with her. If, on the contrary. I feel that my love for my mother isn't enough. I'll leave."

But how is the value of a feeling determined? What gives his feeling for his mother value? Precisely the fact that he remained with her. I may say that I like so-and-so well enough to sacrifice a certain amount of money for him, but I may say so only if I've done it. I may say "I love my mother well enough to remain with her" if I have remained with her. The only way to determine the value of this affection is, precisely, to perform an act which confirms and defines it. But, since I require this affection to justify my act, I find myself caught in a vicious circle.

On the other hand, Gide has well said that a mock feeling and a true feeling are almost indistinguishable; to decide that I love my mother and will remain with her, or to remain with her by putting on an act, amount somewhat to the same thing. In other words, the feeling is formed by the acts one performs; so, I can not refer to it in order to act upon it. Which means that I can neither seek within myself the true condition which will impel me to act, nor apply to a system of ethics for concepts which will permit me to act. You will say, "At least, he did go to a teacher for advice." But if you seek advice from a priest, for example, you have chosen this priest: you already knew, more or less, just about what advice he was going to give you. In other words, choosing your adviser is involving yourself. The proof of this is that if you are a Christian, you will say. "Consult a priest." But some priests are collaborating, some are just marking time, some are resisting. Which to choose? If the young man chooses a priest who is resisting or collaborating, he has already decided on the kind of advice he's going to get. Therefore, in coming to see me he knew the answer I was going to give him, and I had only one answer to give: "You're free, choose, that is, invent." No general ethics can show you what is to be done; there are no omens in the world. The Catholics will reply. "But there are." Granted—but, in any case. I myself choose the meaning they have.

When I was a prisoner, I knew a rather remarkable young man who was a Jesuit. He had entered the Jesuit order in the following way: he had had a number of very bad breaks; in childhood, his father died, leaving him in poverty, and he was a scholarship student at a religious institution where he was constantly made to feel that he was being kept out of charity; then, he failed to get any of the honors and distinctions that children like; later on, at about eighteen, he bungled a love affair; finally at twenty-two, he failed in military training, a childish enough matter, but it was the last straw.

This young fellow might well have felt that he had botched everything. It was a sign of something, but of what? He might have taken refuge in bitterness or despair. But he very wisely looked upon all this as a sign that he was not made for secular triumphs, and that only the triumphs of religion, holiness, and faith were open to him. He saw the hand of God in all this, and so he entered the order. Who can help seeing that he alone decided what the sign meant?

Some other interpretation might have been drawn from this series of set-backs; for example, that he might have done better to turn carpenter or revolutionist. Therefore, he is fully responsible for the interpretation. Forlornness implies that we ourselves choose our being. Forlornness and anguish go together.

As for despair, the term has a very simple meaning. It means that we shall confine ourselves to reckoning only with what depends upon our will, or on the ensemble of probabilities which make our action possible. When we want something, we always have to reckon with probabilities. I may be counting on the arrival of a friend. The friend is coming by rail or street-car; this supposes that the train will arrive on schedule, or that the street-car will not jump the track. I am left in the realm of possibility; but

possibilities are to be reckoned with only to the point where my action comports with the ensemble of these possibilities, and no further. The moment the possibilities I am considering are not rigorously involved by my action. I ought to disengage myself from them, because no God, no scheme, can adapt the world and its possibilities to my will. When Descartes said. "Conquer yourself rather than the world," he meant essentially the same thing.

The Marxists to whom I have spoken reply. "You can rely on the support of others in your action, which obviously has certain limits because you're not going to live forever. That means: rely on both what others are doing elsewhere to help you, in China, in Russia, and what they will do later on, after your death, to carry on the action and lead it to its fulfillment, which will be the revolution. You even *have* to rely upon that, otherwise you're immoral." I reply at once that I will always rely on fellow-fighters insofar as these comrades are involved with me in a common struggle, in the unity of a party or a group in which I can more or less make my weight felt; that is, one whose ranks I am in as a fighter and whose movements I am aware of at every moment In such a situation, relying on the unity and will of the party is exactly like counting on the fact that the train will arrive on time or that the car won't jump the track. But, given that man is free and that there is no human nature for me to depend on. I can not count on men whom I do not know by relying on human goodness or man's concern for the good of society. I don't know what will become of the Russian revolution: I may make an example of it to the extent that at the present time it is apparent that the proletariat plays a part in Russia that it plays in no other nation. But I can't swear that this will inevitably lead to a triumph of the proletariat. I've got to limit myself to what I see.

Given that men are free and that tomorrow they will freely decide what man will be. I can not be sure that, after my death, fellow-fighters will carry on my work to bring it to its maximum perfection. Tomorrow, after my death, some men may decide to set up Fascism, and the others may be cowardly and muddied enough to let them do it. Fascism will then be the human reality, so much the worse for us.

Actually, things will be as man will have decided they are to be. Does that mean that I should abandon myself to quietism? No, First, I should involve myself: then, act on the old saw. "Nothing ventured, nothing gained." Nor does it mean that I shouldn't belong to a party, but rather that I shall have no illusions and shall do what I can. For example, suppose I ask myself, "Will socialization, as such, ever come about?" I know nothing about it. All I know is that I'm going to do everything in my power to bring it about. Beyond that, I can't count on anything. Quietism is the attitude of people who say, "Let others do what I can't do." The doctrine I am presenting is the very opposite of quietism, since it declares, "There is no reality except in action." Moreover, it goes further, since it adds. "Man is nothing else than his plan: he exists only to the extent that he fulfills himself; he is therefore nothing else than the ensemble of his acts, nothing else than his life."

According to this, we can understand why our doctrine horrifies certain people. Because often the only way they can bear their wretchedness is to think, "Circumstances have been against me. What I've been and done doesn't show my true worth. To be sure, I've had no great love, no great friendship, but that's because I haven't met a man or woman who was worthy. The books I've written haven't been very good because I haven't had the proper leisure. I haven't had children to devote myself to because I didn't find a man with whom I could have spent my life. So there remains within me, unused and quite viable, a host of propensities, inclinations, possibilities, that one wouldn't guess from the mere series of things I've done."

Now, for the existentialist there is really no love other than one which manifests itself in a person's being in love. There is no genius other than one which is expressed in works of art; the genius of Proust is the sum of Proust's works; the genius of Racine is his series of tragedies. Outside of that, there is nothing. Why say that Racine could have written another tragedy, when he didn't write it? A man is involved in life, leaves his impress on it, and outside of that there is nothing. To be sure, this may seem a harsh thought to someone whose life hasn't been a success. But, on the other hand, it prompts people to understand that reality alone is what counts, that dreams, expectations, and hopes warrant no more than to define a man as a disappointed dream, as miscarried hopes, as vain expectations. In other words, to define him negatively and not positively. However, when we say, "You are nothing else than your life," that does not imply that the artist will be judged solely on the basis of his works of art; a thousand other things will contribute toward summing him up. What we mean is that a man is nothing else than a series of undertakings, that he is the sum, the organization, the ensemble of the relationships which make up these undertakings.

STUDY QUESTIONS

1. Does our existence precede our essence?
2. How does Sartre distinguish among anguish, forlornness, and despair?
3. In the case of the boy faced with joining the Free French Forces or staying with his mother, is only one decision correct?
4. On what bases should we judge whether a life is successful?

Particularism, Universalism, and Commonsense Morality

Shelly Kagan

Shelly Kagan, whose work we read previously, explains the difference between particularism and universalism. The particularist maintains that principles are not helpful in reaching answers to moral questions, because each case depends on particular features and cannot be subsumed under any useful generalization. Universalists, on the contrary, believe that at least in theory any case can be handled with the guidance of substantive principles. Both particularists and universalists maintain that their views are in line with commonsense morality. Kagan, however, suggests that if we are willing to follow our moral reflection to its logical conclusion, we may discover that it leads beyond the commonsense morality with which we began.

. . . One could hold the view that in each specific case there is a correct or best answer concerning the moral status of any given act, while still maintaining that there are no interesting generalizations to be had—not even in theory—subsuming different cases. That is to say, one might be a *particularist* about moral cases. Each particular configuration of features might yield a determinate moral outcome. And, no doubt, any two cases that were *exactly* alike in every single aspect would be identical in terms of the moral status of the corresponding acts. But for all this there might be no generalizations whatsoever linking cases that differ in any way. Each type of case would be governed by its own unique principle, relevant only to that precise configuration of features. No principles more general than this would exist, not even in theory. (Of course, if there is a right answer in each case, then one could—at least in theory— string all of these together, into one hopelessly long, and perhaps infinite, principle. The question really is

whether any generalizations exist other than this philosophically *uninteresting* one.)

The most radical version of particularism would not even accept the existence of a finite and fixed list of basic normative factors. On such a view, any feature at all might be morally relevant in the right circumstances—without deriving its moral force (in those circumstances) from some more basic normative factor. Features that made a difference in one case might never make any kind of difference again (except in cases literally identical to the first), and the very attempt to identify a list of basic normative factors would therefore be ill founded and illegitimate.

In point of fact, of course, many particularists are less radical than this. They accept the existence of a fixed number of basic normative factors, from which all other morally relevant features derive their significance. But they will deny that there are any general principles to be discovered governing the

From Shelly Kagan, *Normative Ethics*, Westview Press, 1998. Reprinted by permission of the publisher.

interaction of these factors. Each particular combination of factors remains governed by its own unique principle.

Some particularists are more moderate still. They are prepared to accept the existence of *generalizations*—provided that it is understood that these generalizations never take the form of principles that are exceptionless and universal. There may, for example, be statistical generalizations to the effect that a given factor typically outweighs another, or that some third factor normally loses its force in the presence of a fourth. But despite the truth of these generalizations, there will be no *complete* set of interaction principles; any set of true principles will fail to cover certain possible cases, or will be subject to exceptions. In theory, it should be noted, this type of particularism is compatible with belief in the existence of interaction principles with a quite significant degree of generality: large numbers of distinct cases might be subsumed under a few general principles. Obviously, a position like this last one is rather removed from the spirit of *radical* particularism; but it remains particularist insofar as it shares the basic claim that there is no complete set of exceptionless interaction principles (except, of course, for the trivial solution of listing all the right answers).

We can call those who reject particularism, even in its most modest form, *universalists*. Obviously enough, universalism is the view that there exists—at least in theory—a complete set of interaction principles. The principles are complete and exceptionless, insofar as they govern all possible combinations of normative factors; for each such possible configuration, the principles correctly assign a determinate moral status to the relevant actions on the basis of the factors at play. (Once again, if we are to avoid having universalism be true trivially, we will have to disallow making an infinite list that simply combines the right answer for each distinct case.)

It is worth emphasizing the point that universalists are only committed to the *existence* of such a complete set of interaction principles. They need not believe that we can discover these principles or articulate them. And they certainly need not believe that exceptionless interaction principles will have any role in practical moral deliberation.

They *need* not believe these things; but for all that, they *might* believe them. That is, universalists might in fact be fairly optimistic about our ability to discover, articulate, and make use of the interaction principles. After all, the number of *basic* normative factors might be relatively small, and the interaction of these factors might be governed by a limited number of reasonably straightforward principles. Admittedly, the possible combinations of normative factors may be able to grow ever more complex. But this does not, in and of itself, give reason to assume that the principles governing those interactions are themselves complex or beyond our grasp. . . .

Most people begin their moral theorizing thinking that something at least roughly similar to commonsense morality is correct. (Were this not true, of course, the view wouldn't deserve the name "commonsense morality.") People may disagree with one another concerning some of the details—and people can obviously be uncertain, in their own minds, about individual issues—but generally, most start out with the belief that, in at least broad outline, something like commonsense morality is on the right track. But when they turn to the search for a foundational view, obviously enough, among other things they are looking for a view that will have what they take to be plausible results. . . . And this means, of course, that they start out trying to find foundational views that will generate something at least roughly similar to commonsense morality. Given all of this, it probably should not surprise us that most people believe that their favored foundational views do, in fact, support something like commonsense morality. But for this very reason, we should never lose sight of the fact that foundational views can take on something of a life of their own, and once they are developed they may actually lead in rather unexpected directions.

Accordingly, we should not be too quick to assume that a foundational view that seems plausible in its own right will necessarily lead in the direction of commonsense morality. . . . Once we spell out the theory, and look with some care to see what . . . view it actually supports, we might find ourselves rather surprised. And yet, if the foundational view is itself sufficiently attractive, we might be prepared to follow this view and accept its . . . implications, even if these are somewhat counterintuitive. This is especially so, if the foundational view can challenge our initial . . . beliefs in plausible and compelling ways.

It is also worth recalling, in this regard, that our overall assessment of a foundational view—or indeed any normative theory—is always at least in part a comparative affair. It might well be that no moral theory escapes all philosophical objections, that no moral theory is without its counterintuitive implications. It is rather unlikely, I think, that we will be able to find a moral theory that gives us everything we initially want, without exacting any significant costs in terms of modifying or even abandoning some of our initial views. Rather, what we should hope for is to find a moral theory that provides what is, on balance, an attractive and plausible position.

Thus people may start out looking for a defense of their ordinary, commonsense moral views—but they may end up having justified views rather different from the ones with which they began. Of course, they may not even always realize this: it takes a certain amount of open-mindedness, and a willingness to follow a plausible line of argument to its logical conclusion. But in principle, at any rate, moral reflection and the attempt to arrive at an adequate moral theory might lead you to a position rather removed from where you started. This possibility is one we face as soon as we begin to do moral philosophy.

Moral philosophy begins with the question: how should I live? Moral wisdom begins with the realization that I may not already know the answer.

STUDY QUESTIONS

1. What is the distinction between particularism and universalism?
2. If particularism is true, is normative ethics useless?
3. Can you describe a situation in which you began a moral discussion holding one position only to find that careful reasoning led you to change your mind?
4. Do you agree with Kagan that you may not already know how to live?

Part XIII

APPLIED ETHICS

A Defense of Abortion

Judith Jarvis Thomson

Consider the argument that because a fetus is an innocent human being, and killing an innocent human being is always wrong, abortion is always wrong. Some would respond by denying that the earliest embryo is a human person, but putting that issue aside, is killing an innocent human being always wrong? In an article that has given rise to much discussion, Judith Jarvis Thomson, Professor Emerita at the Massachusetts Institute of Technology, argues that while people have a right not to be killed unjustly, they do not have an unqualified right to life. Hence even if the human fetus is a person, abortion may remain morally permissible.

Most opposition to abortion relies on the premise that the fetus is a human being, a person, from the moment of conception. The premise is argued for, but, as I think, not well. Take, for example, the most common argument. We are asked to notice that the development of a human being from conception through birth into childhood is continuous; then it is said that to draw a line, to choose a point in this development and say "before this point the thing is not a person, after this point it is a person" is to make an arbitrary choice, a choice for which in the nature of things no good reason can be given. It is concluded that the fetus is, or anyway that we had better say it is, a person from the moment of conception. But this conclusion does not follow. Similar things might be said about the development of an acorn into an oak tree, and it does not follow that acorns are oak trees, or that we had better say they are. Arguments of this form are sometimes called "slippery slope arguments"—the phrase is perhaps self-explanatory—and it is dismaying that opponents of abortion rely on them so heavily and uncritically.

I am inclined to agree, however, that the prospects for "drawing a line" in the development of the fetus look dim. I am inclined to think also that we shall probably have to agree that the fetus has already become a human person well before birth. Indeed, it comes as a surprise when one first learns how early in its life it begins to acquire human characteristics. By the tenth week, for example, it already has a face, arms and legs, fingers and toes; it has internal organs, and brain activity is detectable.[1] On the other hand, I think that the premise is false, that the fetus is not a person from the moment of conception. A newly fertilized ovum, a newly implanted clump of cells, is no more a person than an acorn is an oak tree. But I shall not discuss any of this. For it seems to me to be of great interest to ask what happens if, for the sake of argument, we allow the premise. How, precisely, are we supposed

Judith Jarvis Thomson, "A Defense of Abortion," *Philosophy & Public Affairs*, vol. 1, no. 1, 1971.

to get from there to the conclusion that abortion is morally impermissible? Opponents of abortion commonly spend most of their time establishing that the fetus is a person, and hardly any time explaining the step from there to the impermissibility of abortion. Perhaps they think the step too simple and obvious to require much comment. Or perhaps instead they are simply being economical in argument. Many of those who defend abortion rely on the premise that the fetus is not a person, but only a bit of tissue that will become a person at birth; and why pay out more arguments than you have to? Whatever the explanation, I suggest that the step they take is neither easy nor obvious, that it calls for closer examination than it is commonly given, and that when we do give it this closer examination we shall feel inclined to reject it.

I propose, then, that we grant that the fetus is a person from the moment of conception. How does the argument go from here? Something like this, I take it. Every person has a right to life. So the fetus has a right to life. No doubt the mother has a right to decide what shall happen in and to her body; everyone would grant that. But surely a person's right to life is stronger and more stringent than the mother's right to decide what happens in and to her body, and so outweighs it. So the fetus may not be killed; an abortion may not be performed.

It sounds plausible. But now let me ask you to imagine this. You wake up in the morning and find yourself back to back in bed with an unconscious violinist. A famous unconscious violinist. He has been found to have a fatal kidney ailment, and the Society of Music Lovers has canvassed all the available medical records and found that you alone have the right blood type to help. They have therefore kidnapped you, and last night the violinist's circulatory system was plugged into yours, so that your kidneys can be used to extract poisons from his blood as well as your own. The director of the hospital now tells you, "Look, we're sorry the Society of Music Lovers did this to you—we would never have permitted it if we had known. But still, they did it, and the violinist now is plugged into you. To unplug you would be to kill him. But never mind, it's only for nine months. By then he will have recovered from his ailment, and

can safely be unplugged from you." Is it morally incumbent on you to accede to this situation? No doubt it would be very nice of you if you did, a great kindness. But do you *have* to accede to it? What if it were not nine months, but nine years? Or longer still? What if the director of the hospital says, "Tough luck, I agree, but you've now got to stay in bed, with the violinist plugged into you, for the rest of your life. Because remember this. All persons have a right to life, and violinists are persons. Granted you have a right to decide what happens in and to your body, but a person's right to life outweighs your right to decide what happens in and to your body. So you cannot ever be unplugged from him." I imagine you would regard this as outrageous, which suggests that something really is wrong with the plausible-sounding argument I mentioned a moment ago.

In this case, of course, you were kidnapped; you didn't volunteer for the operation that plugged the violinist into your kidneys. Can those who oppose abortion on the ground I mentioned make an exception for a pregnancy due to rape? Certainly. They can say that persons have a right to life only if they didn't come into existence because of rape; or they can say that all persons have a right to life, but that some have less of a right to life than others, in particular, that those who came into existence because of rape have less. But these statements have a rather unpleasant sound. Surely the question of whether you have a right to life at all, or how much of it you have, shouldn't turn on the question of whether or not you are the product of a rape. And in fact the people who oppose abortion on the ground I mentioned do not make this distinction, and hence do not make an exception in case of rape.

Nor do they make an exception for a case in which the mother has to spend the nine months of her pregnancy in bed. They would agree that would be a great pity, and hard on the mother; but all the same, all persons have a right to life, the fetus is a person, and so on. I suspect, in fact, that they would not make an exception for a case in which, miraculously enough, the pregnancy went on for nine years, or even the rest of the mother's life.

Some won't even make an exception for a case in which continuation of the pregnancy is likely to shorten the mother's life; they regard abortion as impermissible even to save the mother's life. Such cases are nowadays very rare, and many opponents of abortion do not accept this extreme view. All the same, it is a good place to begin: a number of points of interest come out in respect to it.

1. Let us call the view that abortion is impermissible even to save the mother's life "the extreme view." I want to suggest first that it does not issue from the argument I mentioned earlier without the addition of some fairly powerful premises. Suppose a woman has become pregnant, and now learns that she has a cardiac condition such that she will die if she carries the baby to term. What may be done for her? The fetus, being a person, has a right to life, but as the mother is a person too, so has she a right to life. Presumably they have an equal right to life. How is it supposed to come out that an abortion may not be performed? If mother and child have an equal right to life, shouldn't we perhaps flip a coin? Or should we add to the mother's right to life her right to decide what happens in and to her body, which everybody seems to be ready to grant—the sum of her rights now outweighing the fetus' right to life?

The most familiar argument here is the following. We are told that performing the abortion would be directly killing[2] the child, whereas doing nothing would not be killing the mother, but only letting her die. Moreover, in killing the child, one would be killing an innocent person, for the child has committed no crime, and is not aiming at his mother's death. And then there are a variety of ways in which this might be continued. (1) But as directly killing an innocent person is always and absolutely impermissible, an abortion may not be performed. Or, (2) as directly killing an innocent person is murder, and murder is always and absolutely impermissible, an abortion may not be performed.[3] Or, (3) as one's duty to refrain from directly killing an innocent person is more stringent than one's duty to keep a person from dying, an abortion may not be performed. Or, (4) if one's only options are directly killing an innocent person or letting a person die, one must prefer letting the person die, and thus an abortion may not be performed.[4]

Some people seem to have thought that these are not further premises which must be added if the conclusion is to be reached, but that they follow from the very fact that an innocent person has a right to life.[5] But this seems to me to be a mistake, and perhaps the simplest way to show this is to bring out that while we must certainly grant that innocent persons have a right to life, the theses in (1) through (4) are all false. Take (2), for example. If directly killing an innocent person is murder, and thus is impermissible, then the mother's directly killing the innocent person inside her is murder, and thus is impermissible. But it cannot seriously be thought to be murder if the mother performs an abortion on herself to save her life. It cannot seriously be said that she *must* refrain, that she *must* sit passively by and wait for her death. Let us look again at the case of you and the violinist. There you are, in bed with the violinist, and the director of the hospital says to you, "It's all most distressing, and I deeply sympathize, but you see this is putting an additional strain on your kidneys, and you'll be dead within the month. But you *have* to stay where you are all the same. Because unplugging you would be directly killing an innocent violinist, and that's murder, and that's impermissible." If anything in the world is true, it is that you do not commit murder, you do not do what is impermissible, if you reach around to your back and unplug yourself from that violinist to save your life.

The main focus of attention in writings on abortion has been on what a third party may or may not do in answer to a request from a woman for an abortion. This is in a way understandable. Things being as they are, there isn't much a woman can safely do to abort herself. So the question asked is what a third party may do, and what the mother may do, if it is mentioned at all, is deduced, almost as an afterthought, from what it is concluded that third parties may do. But it seems to me that to treat the matter in this way is to refuse to grant to the mother that very status of person which is so firmly insisted on for the fetus. For we cannot simply read off what a person may do from what a third party may do. Suppose you find yourself trapped in a tiny house with a growing child. I mean a very tiny house, and a rapidly growing child—you are already up against the wall of the house and in a few minutes you'll be crushed to death. The child on the other hand won't be crushed to death; if nothing is done to stop him from growing he'll be hurt, but in the end he'll simply burst open the house and walk out a free man. Now I could well understand it if a bystander were to say, "There's nothing we can do for you. We cannot choose between your life and his, we cannot be the ones to decide who is to live, we cannot intervene." But it cannot be concluded that you too can do nothing, that you cannot attack it to save your life. However innocent the child may be, you do not have to wait passively while it crushes you to death. Perhaps a pregnant woman is vaguely felt to have the status of house, to which we don't allow the right of self-defense. But if the woman houses the child, it should be remembered that she is a person who houses it.

I should perhaps stop to say explicitly that I am not claiming that people have a right to do anything whatever to save their lives. I think, rather, that there are drastic limits to the right of self-defense. If someone threatens you with death unless you torture someone else to death, I think you have not the right, even to save your life, to do so. But the case under consideration here is very different. In our case there are only two people involved, one whose life is threatened, and one who threatens it. Both are innocent: the one who is threatened is not threatened because of any fault, the one who threatens does not threaten because of any fault. For this reason we may feel that we bystanders cannot intervene. But the person threatened can.

In sum, a woman surely can defend her life against the threat to it posed by the unborn child, even if doing so involves its death. And this shows not merely that the theses in (1) through (4) are false; it shows also that the extreme view of abortion is false, and so we need not canvass any other possible ways of arriving at it from the argument I mentioned at the outset.

2. The extreme view could of course be weakened to say that while abortion is permissible to save the mother's life, it may not be performed by a third party, but only by the mother herself. But this cannot be right either. For what we have to keep in mind is that the mother and the unborn child are not like two tenants in a small house which has, by an unfortunate mistake, been rented to both: the mother *owns* the house. The fact that she does adds to the offensiveness of deducing that the mother can do nothing from the supposition that third parties can do nothing. But it does more than this: it casts a bright light on the supposition that third parties can do nothing. Certainly it lets us see that a third party who says "I cannot choose between you" is fooling himself if he thinks this is impartiality. If Jones has found and fastened on a certain coat, which he needs to keep him from freezing, but which Smith also needs to keep him from freezing, then it is not impartiality that says "I cannot choose between you" when Smith owns the coat. Women have said again and again "This body is *my* body!" and they have reason to feel angry, reason to feel that it has been like shouting into the wind. Smith, after all, is hardly likely to bless us if we say to him, "Of course it's your coat, anybody would grant that it is. But no one may choose between you and Jones who is to have it."

We should really ask what it is that says "no one may choose" in the face of the fact that the body that houses the child is the mother's body. It may be simply a failure to appreciate this fact. But it may be something more interesting, namely the sense that one has a right to refuse to lay hands on people, even where it would be just and fair to do so, even where justice seems to require that somebody do so. Thus justice might call for somebody to get Smith's coat back from Jones, and yet you have a right to refuse to be the one to lay hands on Jones, a right to refuse to do physical violence to him. This, I think, must be granted. But then what should be said is not "no one may choose," but only "*I* cannot choose," and indeed not even this, but "*I* will not *act*," leaving it open that somebody else can or should, and in particular that anyone in a position of authority, with the job of securing people's rights, both can and should. So this is no difficulty. I have not been arguing that any given third party must accede to the mother's request that he perform an abortion to save her life, but only that he may.

I suppose that in some views of human life the mother's body is only on loan to her, the loan not being one which gives her any prior claim to it. One who held this view might well think it impartiality to say "I cannot choose." But I shall simply ignore this possibility. My own view is that if a human being has any just, prior claim to anything at all, he has a just, prior claim to his own body. And perhaps this needn't be argued for here anyway, since, as I mentioned, the arguments against abortion we are looking at do grant that the woman has a right to decide what happens in and to her body.

But although they do grant it, I have tried to show that they do not take seriously what is done in granting it. I suggest the same thing will reappear even more clearly when we turn away from cases in which the mother's life is at stake, and attend, as I propose we now do, to the vastly more common cases in which a woman wants an abortion for some less weighty reason than preserving her own life.

3. Where the mother's life is not at stake, the argument I mentioned at the outset seems to have a much stronger pull. "Everyone has a right to life, so the unborn person has a right to life." And isn't the child's right to life weightier than anything other than the mother's own right to life, which she might put forward as ground for an abortion?

This argument treats the right to life as if it were unproblematic. It is not, and this seems to me to be precisely the source of the mistake.

For we should now, at long last, ask what it comes to, to have a right to life. In some views having a right to life includes having a right to be given at least the bare minimum one needs for continued life. But suppose that what in fact is the bare minimum a man needs for continued life is something he has no right at all to be given? If I am sick unto death, and the only thing that will save my life is the touch of Henry Fonda's cool hand on my fevered brow, then all the same, I have no right to be given the touch of Henry Fonda's cool hand on my fevered brow. It would be frightfully nice of him to fly in from the West Coast to provide it. It would be less nice, though no doubt well meant, if my friends flew out to the West Coast and carried Henry Fonda back with them. But I have no right at all against anybody that he should do this for me. Or again, to return to the story I told earlier, the fact that for continued life that violinist needs the continued use of your kidneys does not establish that he has a right to be given the continued use of your kidneys. He certainly has no right against you that *you* should give him continued use of your kidneys. For nobody has any right to use our kidneys unless you give him such a right; and nobody has the right against you that you shall give him this right—if you do allow him to go on using your kidneys, this is a kindness on your part, and not something he can claim from you as his due. Nor has he any right against anybody else that *they* should give him continued use of your kidneys. Certainly he had no right against the Society of Music Lovers that they should plug him into you in the first place. And if you now start to unplug yourself, having learned that you will otherwise have to spend nine years in bed with him, there is nobody in the world who must try to prevent you, in order to see to it that he is given something he has a right to be given.

Some people are rather stricter about the right to life. In their view, it does not include the right to be given anything, but amounts to, and only to, the right not to be killed by anybody. But here a related difficulty arises. If everybody is to refrain from killing that violinist, then everybody must refrain from doing a great many different sorts of things. Everybody must refrain from slitting his throat, everybody must refrain from shooting him—and everybody must refrain from unplugging you from him. But does he have a right against everybody that they shall refrain from unplugging you from him? To refrain from doing this is to allow him to continue to use your kidneys. It could be argued that he has a right against us that *we* should allow him to continue to use your kidneys. That is, while he had no right against us that we should give him the use of your kidneys, it might be argued that he anyway has a right against us that we shall not now intervene and deprive him of the use of your kidneys. I shall come back to third party interventions later. But certainly the violinist has no right against you that *you* shall allow him to continue to use your kidneys. As I said, if you do allow him to use them, it is a kindness on your part, and not something you owe him.

The difficulty I point to here is not peculiar to the right to life. It reappears in connection with all the other natural rights; and it is something which an adequate account of rights must deal with. For present purposes it is enough just to draw attention to it. But I would stress that I am not arguing that people do not have a right to life—quite to the contrary, it seems to me that the primary control we must place on the acceptability of an account of rights is that it should turn out in that account to be a truth that all persons have a right to life. I am arguing only that having a right to life does not guarantee having either a right to be given the use of or a right to be allowed continued use of another person's body—even if one needs it for life itself. So the right to life will not serve the opponents of abortion in the very simple and clear way in which they seem to have thought it would.

4. There is another way to bring out the difficulty. In the most ordinary sort of case, to deprive someone of what he has a right to is to treat him unjustly. Suppose a boy and his small brother are jointly given a box of chocolates for Christmas. If the older boy takes the box and refuses to give his brother any of the chocolates, he is unjust to him, for the brother has been given a right to half of them. But suppose that, having learned that otherwise it means nine years in bed with that violinist, you unplug yourself from him. You surely are not being unjust to him, for you gave him no right to use your kidneys, and no one else can have given him any such right. But we have to notice that in unplugging yourself, you are killing him; and violinists, like everybody else, have a right to life, and thus in the view we were considering just now, the right not to be killed. So here you do what he supposedly has a right you shall not do, but you do not act unjustly to him in doing it.

The emendation which may be made at this point is this: the right to life consists not in the right not to be killed, but rather in the right not to be killed unjustly. This runs a risk of circularity, but never mind: it would enable us to square the fact that the violinist has a right to life with the fact that you do not act unjustly toward him in unplugging yourself, thereby killing him. For if you do not kill him unjustly, you do not violate his right to life, and so it is no wonder you do him no injustice.

But if this emendation is accepted, the gap in the argument against abortion stares us plainly in the face: it is by no means enough to show that the fetus is a person, and to remind us that all persons have a right to life—we need to be shown also that killing the fetus violates its right to life, i.e., that abortion is unjust killing. And is it?

I suppose we may take it as a datum that in a case of pregnancy due to rape the mother has not given the unborn person a right to the use of her body for food and shelter. Indeed, in what pregnancy could it be supposed that the mother has given the unborn person such a right? It is not as if there were unborn persons drifting about the world, to whom a woman who wants a child says "I invite you in."

But it might be argued that there are other ways one can have acquired a right to the use of another person's body than by having been invited to use it by that person. Suppose a woman voluntarily indulges in intercourse, knowing of the chance it will issue in pregnancy, and then she does become pregnant; is she not in part responsible for the presence, in fact the very existence, of the unborn person inside her? No doubt she did not invite it in. But doesn't her partial responsibility for its being there itself give it a right to the use of her body?[6] If so, then her aborting it would be more like the boy's taking away the chocolates, and less like your unplugging yourself from the violinist—doing so would be depriving it of what it does have a right to, and thus would be doing it an injustice.

And then, too, it might be asked whether or not she can kill it even to save her own life: If she voluntarily called it into existence, how can she now kill it, even in self-defense?

The first thing to be said about this is that it is something new. Opponents of abortion have been so concerned to make out the independence of the fetus, in order to establish that it has a right to life, just as its mother does, that they have tended to overlook the possible support they might gain from making out that the fetus is *dependent* on the mother, in order to establish that she has a special kind of responsibility for it, a responsibility that gives it rights against her which are not possessed by any independent person—such as an ailing violinist who is a stranger to her.

On the other hand, this argument would give the unborn person a right to its mother's body only if her pregnancy resulted from a voluntary act, undertaken in full knowledge of the chance a pregnancy might result from it. It would leave out entirely the unborn person whose existence is due to rape. Pending the availability of some further argument, then, we would be left with the conclusion that unborn persons whose existence is due to rape have no right to the use of their mothers' bodies, and thus that aborting them is not depriving them of anything they have a right to and hence is not unjust killing.

And we should also notice that it is not at all plain that this argument really does go even as far as it purports to. For there are cases and cases, and the details make a difference. If the room is stuffy, and I therefore open a window to air it, and a burglar climbs in, it would be absurd to say, "Ah, now he can stay, she's given him a right to the use of her house—for she is partially responsible for his presence there, having voluntarily done what enabled him to get in, in full knowledge that there are such things as burglars, and that burglars burgle." It would be still more absurd to say this if I had had bars installed outside my windows, precisely to prevent burglars from getting in, and a burglar got in only because of a defect in the bars. It remains equally absurd if we imagine it is not a burglar who climbs in, but an innocent person who blunders or falls in. Again, suppose it were like this: people-seeds drift about in the air like pollen, and if you open your windows, one may drift in and take root in your carpets or upholstery. You don't want children, so you fix up your windows with fine mesh screens, the very best you can buy. As can happen, however, and on very, very rare occasions does happen, one of the screens is

defective; and a seed drifts in and takes root. Does the person-plant who now develops have a right to the use of your house? Surely not—despite the fact that you voluntarily opened your windows, you knowingly kept carpets and upholstered furniture, and you knew that screens were sometimes defective. Someone may argue that you are responsible for its rooting, that it does have a right to your house, because after all you *could* have lived out your life with bare floors and furniture, or with sealed windows and doors. But this won't do—for by the same token anyone can avoid a pregnancy due to rape by having a hysterectomy, or anyway by never leaving home without a (reliable!) army.

It seems to me that the argument we are looking at can establish at most that there are *some* cases in which the unborn person has a right to the use of its mother's body, and therefore *some* cases in which abortion is unjust killing. There is room for much discussion and argument as to precisely which, if any. But I think we should sidestep this issue and leave it open, for at any rate the argument certainly does not establish that all abortion is unjust killing.

5. There is room for yet another argument here, however. We surely must all grant that there may be cases in which it would be morally indecent to detach a person from your body at the cost of his life. Suppose you learn that what the violinist needs is not nine years of your life, but only one hour: all you need do to save his life is to spend one hour in that bed with him. Suppose also that letting him use your kidneys for that one hour would not affect your health in the slightest. Admittedly you were kidnapped. Admittedly you did not give anyone permission to plug him into you. Nevertheless it seems to me plain you *ought* to allow him to use your kidneys for that hour—it would be indecent to refuse.

Again, suppose pregnancy lasted only an hour, and constituted no threat to life or health. And suppose that a woman becomes pregnant as a result of rape. Admittedly she did not voluntarily do anything to bring about the existence of a child. Admittedly she did nothing at all which would give the unborn person a right to the use of her body. All the same it might well be said, as in the newly emended violinist story, that she *ought* to allow it to remain for that hour—that it would be indecent of her to refuse.

Now some people are inclined to use the term "right" in such a way that it follows from the fact that you ought to allow a person to use your body for the hour he needs, that he has a right to use your body for the hour he needs, even though he has not been given that right by any person or act. They may say that it follows also that if you refuse, you act unjustly toward him. This use of the term is perhaps so common that it cannot be called wrong; nevertheless it seems to me to be an unfortunate loosening of what we would do better to keep a tight rein on. Suppose that box of chocolates I mentioned earlier had not been given to both boys jointly, but was given only to the older boy. There he sits, stolidly eating his way through the box, his small brother watching enviously. Here we are likely to say "You ought not to be so mean. You ought to give your brother some of those chocolates." My own view is that it just does not follow from the truth of this that the brother has any right to any of the chocolates. If the boy refuses to give his brother any, he is greedy, stingy, callous—but not unjust. I suppose that the people I have in mind will say it does follow that the brother has a right to some of the chocolates, and thus that the boy does act unjustly if he refuses to give his brother any. But the effect of saying this is to obscure what we should keep distinct, namely the difference between the boy's refusal in this case and the boy's refusal in the earlier case, in which the box was given to both boys jointly, and in which the small brother thus had what was from any point of view clear title to half.

A further objection to so using the term "right" that from the fact that A ought to do a thing for B, it follows that B has a right against A that A do it for him, is that it is going to make the question of whether or not a man has a right to a thing turn on how easy it is to provide him with it; and this seems not merely unfortunate, but morally unacceptable. Take the case of Henry Fonda again. I said earlier that I had no right to the touch of his cool hand on my fevered brow, even though I needed it to save my life. I said it would be frightfully nice of him to fly in from the West Coast to provide me with it, but that I had no right against him that he should do so. But suppose he isn't on the West Coast. Suppose he has only to walk across the room, place a hand briefly on my brow—and lo, my life is saved. Then surely he ought to do it, it would be indecent to refuse. Is it to be said "Ah, well, it follows that in this case she has a right to the touch of his hand on her brow, and so it would be an injustice in him to refuse"? So that I have a right to it when it is easy for him to provide it, though no right when it's hard? It's rather a shocking idea that anyone's rights should fade away and disappear as it gets harder and harder to accord them to him.

So my own view is that even though you ought to let the violinist use your kidneys for the one hour he needs, we should not conclude that he has a right to do so—we should say that if you refuse, you are, like the boy who owns all the chocolates and will give none away, self-centered and callous, indecent in fact, but not unjust. And similarly, that even supposing a case in which a woman pregnant due to rape ought to allow the unborn person to use her body for the hour he needs, we should not conclude that he has a right to do so; we should conclude that she is self-centered, callous, indecent, but not unjust, if she refuses. The complaints are no less grave; they are just different. However, there is no need to insist on this point. If anyone does wish to deduce "he has a right" from "you ought," then all the same he must surely grant that there are cases in which it is not morally required of you that you allow that violinist to use your kidneys, and in which he does not have a right to use them, and in which you do not do him an injustice if you refuse. And so also for mother and unborn child. Except in such cases as the unborn person has a right to demand it—and we were leaving open the possibility that there may be such cases—nobody is morally *required* to make large sacrifices, of health, of all other interests and concerns, of all other duties and commitments, for nine years, or even for nine months, in order to keep another person alive.

6. We have in fact to distinguish between two kinds of Samaritan: the Good Samaritan and what we might call the Minimally Decent Samaritan. The story of the Good Samaritan, you will remember, goes like this:

A certain man went down from Jerusalem to Jericho, and fell among thieves, which stripped him of his raiment, and wounded him, and departed, leaving him half dead.

And by chance there came down a certain priest that way; and when he saw him, he passed by on the other side.

And likewise a Levite, when he was at the place, came and looked on him, and passed by on the other side.

But a certain Samaritan, as he journeyed, came where he was; and when he saw him he had compassion on him.

And went to him, and bound up his wounds, pouring in oil and wine, and set him on his own beast, and brought him to an inn, and took care of him.

And on the morrow, when he departed, he took out two pence, and gave them to the host, and said unto him, "Take care of him; and whatsoever thou spendest more, when I come again, I will repay thee." (Luke 10:30–35)

The Good Samaritan went out of his way, at some cost to himself, to help one in need of it. We are not told what the options were, that is, whether or not the priest and the Levite could have helped by doing less than the Good Samaritan did, but assuming they could have, then the fact they did nothing at all shows they were not even Minimally Decent Samaritans, not because they were not Samaritans, but because they were not even minimally decent.

These things are a matter of degree, of course, but there is a difference, and it comes out perhaps most clearly in the story of Kitty Genovese, who, as you will remember, was murdered while thirty-eight people watched or listened, and did nothing at all to help her. A Good Samaritan would have rushed out to give direct assistance against the murderer. Or perhaps we had better allow that it would have been a Splendid Samaritan who did this, on the ground that it would have involved a risk of death for himself. But the thirty-eight not only did not do this, they did not even trouble to pick up a phone to call the police. Minimally Decent Samaritanism would call for doing at least that, and their not having done it was monstrous.

After telling the story of the Good Samaritan, Jesus said "Go, and do thou likewise." Perhaps he meant that we are morally required to act as the Good Samaritan did. Perhaps he was urging people to do more than is morally required of them. At all events it seems plain that it was not morally required of any of the thirty-eight that he rush out to give direct assistance at the risk of his own life, and that it is not morally required of anyone that he give long stretches of his life—nine years or nine months—to sustaining the life of a person who has no special right (we were leaving open the possibility of this) to demand it.

Indeed, with one rather striking class of exceptions, no one in any country in the world is *legally* required to do anywhere near as much as this for anyone else. The class of exceptions is obvious. My main concern here is not the state of the law in respect to abortion, but it is worth drawing attention to the fact that in no state in this country is any man compelled by law to be even a Minimally Decent Samaritan to any person; there is no law under which charges could be brought against the thirty-eight who stood by while Kitty Genovese died. By contrast, in most states in this country women are compelled by law to be not merely Minimally Decent Samaritans, but Good Samaritans to unborn persons inside them. This doesn't by itself settle anything one way or the other, because it may well be argued that there should be laws in this country—as there are in many European countries—compelling at least Minimally Decent Samaritanism.[7] But it does show that there is a gross injustice in the existing state of the law. And it shows also that the groups currently working against liberalization of abortion laws, in fact working toward having it declared unconstitutional for a state to permit abortion, had better start working for the adoption of Good Samaritan laws generally, or earn the charge that they are acting in bad faith.

I should think, myself, that Minimally Decent Samaritan laws would be one thing, Good Samaritan laws quite another, and in fact highly improper. But we are not here concerned with the law. What we should ask is not whether anybody should be compelled by law to be a Good Samaritan, but whether we must accede to a situation in which somebody is being compelled—by nature, perhaps—to be a Good Samaritan. We have, in other words, to look now at third-party interventions. I have been arguing that no person is morally required to make large sacrifices to sustain the life of another who has no right to demand them, and this even where the sacrifices do not include life itself; we are not morally required to be Good Samaritans or anyway Very Good Samaritans to one another. But what if a man cannot extricate himself from such a situation? What if he appeals to us to extricate him? It seems to me plain that there are cases in which we can, cases in which a Good Samaritan would extricate him. There you are, you were kidnapped, and nine years in bed with that violinist lie ahead of you. You have your own life to lead. You are sorry, but you simply cannot see giving up so much of your life to the sustaining of his. You cannot extricate yourself, and ask us to do so. I should have thought that—in light of his having no right to the use of your body—it was obvious that we do not have to accede to your being forced to give up so much. We can do what you ask. There is no injustice to the violinist in our doing so.

7. Following the lead of the opponents of abortion, I have throughout been speaking of the fetus merely as a person, and what I have been asking is whether or not the argument we began with, which proceeds only from the fetus' being a person, really does establish its conclusion. I have argued that it does not.

But of course there are arguments and arguments, and it may be said that I have simply fastened on the wrong one. It may be said that what is important is not merely the fact that the fetus is a person, but that it is a person for whom the woman has a special kind of responsibility issuing from the fact that she is its mother. And it might be argued that all my analogies are therefore irrelevant—for you do not have that special kind of responsibility for that violinist, Henry Fonda does not have that special kind of responsibility for me. And our attention might be drawn to the fact that men and women both *are* compelled by law to provide support for their children.

I have in effect dealt (briefly) with this argument in section 4 above; but a (still briefer) recapitulation now may be in order. Surely we do not have any such "special responsibility" for a person unless we have assumed it, explicitly or implicitly. If a set of parents do not try to prevent pregnancy, do not obtain an abortion, and then at the time of birth of the child do not put it out for adoption, but rather take it home with them, then they have assumed responsibility for it, they have given it rights, and they cannot *now* withdraw support from it at the cost of its life because they now find it difficult to go on providing for it. But if they have taken all reasonable precautions against having a child, they do not simply by virtue of their biological relationship to the child who comes into existence have a special responsibility for it. They may wish to assume responsibility for it, or they may not wish to. And I am suggesting that if assuming responsibility for it would require large sacrifices, then they may refuse. A Good Samaritan would not refuse—or anyway, a Splendid Samaritan, if the sacrifices that had to be made were enormous. But then so would a Good Samaritan assume responsibility for that violinist; so would Henry Fonda, if he is a Good Samaritan, fly in from the West Coast and assume responsibility for me.

8. My argument will be found unsatisfactory on two counts by many of those who want to regard abortion as morally permissible. First, while I do argue that abortion is not impermissible, I do not argue that it is always permissible. There may well be cases in which carrying the child to term requires only Minimally Decent Samaritanism of the mother, and this is a standard we must not fall below. I am inclined to think it a merit of my account precisely that it does *not* give a general yes or a general no. It allows for and supports our sense that, for example, a sick and desperately frightened

fourteen-year-old schoolgirl, pregnant due to rape, may *of course* choose abortion, and that any law which rules this out is an insane law. And it also allows for and supports our sense that in other cases resort to abortion is even positively indecent. It would be indecent in the woman to request an abortion, and indecent in a doctor to perform it, if she is in her seventh month, and wants the abortion just to avoid the nuisance of postponing a trip abroad. The very fact that the arguments I have been drawing attention to treat all cases of abortion, or even all cases of abortion in which the mother's life is not at stake, as morally on a par ought to have made them suspect at the outset.

Secondly, while I am arguing for the permissibility of abortion in some cases, I am not arguing for the right to secure the death of the unborn child. It is easy to confuse these two things in that up to a certain point in the life of the fetus it is not able to survive outside the mother's body; hence removing it from her body guarantees its death. But they are importantly different. I have argued that you are not morally required to spend nine months in bed, sustaining the life of that violinist; but to say this is by no means to say that if, when you unplug yourself, there is a miracle and he survives, you then have a right to turn round and slit his throat. You may detach yourself even if this costs him his life; you have no right to be guaranteed his death, by some other means, if unplugging yourself does not kill him. There are some people who will feel dissatisfied by this feature of my argument. A woman may be utterly devastated by the thought of a child, a bit of herself, put out for adoption and never seen or heard of again. She may therefore want not merely that the child be detached from her, but more, that it die. Some opponents of abortion are inclined to regard this as beneath contempt—thereby showing insensitivity to what is surely a powerful source of despair. All the same, I agree that the desire for the child's death is not one which anybody may gratify, should it turn out to be possible to detach the child alive.

At this place, however, it should be remembered that we have only been pretending throughout that the fetus is a human being from the moment of conception. A very early abortion is surely not the killing of a person, and so is not dealt with by anything I have said here.

NOTES

1. Daniel Callahan, *Abortion: Law, Choice and Morality* (New York, 1970), p. 373. This book gives a fascinating survey of the available information on abortion. The Jewish tradition is surveyed in David M. Feldman, *Birth Control in Jewish Law* (New York, 1968), Part 5, the Catholic tradition in John T. Noonan, Jr., "An Almost Absolute Value in History," in *The Morality of Abortion,* ed. John T. Noonan, Jr. (Cambridge, Mass., 1970).

2. The term "direct" in the arguments I refer to is a technical one. Roughly, what is meant by "direct killing" is either killing as an end in itself, or killing as a means to some end, for example, the end of saving someone else's life. See note 5, below, for an example of its use.

3. Cf. *Encyclical Letter of Pope Pius XI on Christian Marriage,* St. Paul Editions (Boston, n.d.), p. 32: "however much we may pity the mother whose health and even life is gravely imperiled in the performance of the duty allotted to her by nature, nevertheless what could ever be a sufficient reason for excusing in any way the direct murder of the innocent? This is precisely what we are dealing with here." Noonan (*The Morality of Abortion,* p. 43) reads this as follows: "What cause can ever avail to excuse in any way the direct killing of the innocent? For it is a question of that."

4. The thesis in (4) is in an interesting way weaker than those in (1), (2), and (3): they rule out abortion even in cases in which both mother *and* child will die if the abortion is not performed. By contrast, one who held the view expressed in (4) could consistently say that one needn't prefer letting two persons die to killing one.

5. Cf. the following passage from Pius XII, *Address to the Italian Catholic Society of Midwives:* "The baby in the maternal breast has the right to life immediately from God.—Hence there is no man, no human authority, no science, no medical, eugenic, social, economic or moral 'indication' which can establish or grant a valid juridical ground for a direct deliberate disposition of an innocent human life, that is a disposition which looks to its destruction either as an end or as a means to another end perhaps in itself not illicit.— The baby, still not born, is a man in the same degree and for the same reason as the mother" (quoted in Noonan, *The Morality of Abortion,* p. 45).

6. The need for a discussion of this argument was brought home to me by members of the Society for Ethical and Legal Philosophy, to whom this paper was originally presented.

7. For a discussion of the difficulties involved, and a survey of the European experience with such laws, see *The Good Samaritan and the Law,* ed. James M. Ratcliffe (New York, 1966).

STUDY QUESTIONS

1. What are the main points Thomson seeks to make by the example of the unconscious violinist?
2. Does the morality of aborting a fetus depend on the conditions surrounding its conception?
3. In your own words, what is the distinction Thomson draws between the Good Samaritan and the Minimally Decent Samaritan?
4. If the abortion controversy is described as a debate between those who believe in a right to life and those who affirm a woman's right to choose, on which side is Thomson?

An Argument that Abortion Is Wrong

Don Marquis

Don Marquis, Professor of Philosophy at the University of Kansas, argues that, with rare exceptions, abortion is immoral. Marquis does not base his argument on the claim that the fetus is a person but rather on the view that an aborted fetus loses the future goods of consciousness, such as the completion of projects, the pursuit of goals, aesthetic enjoyment, friendships, intellectual pursuits, and physical pleasures of various sorts. In short, premature death deprives individuals of a future of value.

The purpose of this essay is to set out an argument for the claim that abortion, except perhaps in rare instances, is seriously wrong. One reason for these exceptions is to eliminate from consideration cases whose ethical analysis should be controversial and detailed for clear-headed opponents of abortion. Such cases include abortion after rape and abortion during the first fourteen days after conception when there is an argument that the fetus is not definitely an individual. Another reason for making these exceptions is to allow for those cases in which the permissibility of abortion is compatible with the argument of this essay. Such cases include abortion when continuation of a pregnancy endangers a woman's life and abortion when the fetus is anencephalic. When I speak of the wrongness of abortion in this essay, a reader should presume the above qualifications. I mean by an abortion an action intended to bring about the death of a fetus for the sake of the woman who carries it. (Thus, as is standard on the literature on this subject, I eliminate spontaneous abortions from consideration.) I mean by a fetus a developing human being from the time of conception to the time of birth. (Thus, as is standard, I call embryos and zygotes, fetuses.)

The argument of this essay will establish that abortion is wrong for the same reason as killing a reader of this essay is wrong. I shall just assume, rather than establish, that killing you is seriously wrong. I shall make no attempt to offer a complete ethics of killing. Finally, I shall make no attempt to resolve some very fundamental and difficult general philosophical issues into which this analysis of the ethics of abortion might lead.

WHY THE DEBATE OVER ABORTION SEEMS INTRACTABLE

Symmetries that emerge from the analysis of the major arguments on either side of the abortion debate may explain why the abortion debate seems intractable. Consider the following standard anti-abortion argument: Fetuses are both human and alive. Humans have the right to life. Therefore, fetuses have the right to life. Of course, women have the right to control their own bodies, but the right to life overrides the right of a woman to control her own body. Therefore, abortion is wrong.

Thomson's View

Judith Thomson (1971) has argued that even if one grants (for the sake of argument only) that fetuses have the right to life, this argument fails. Thomson invites you to imagine that you have been connected while sleeping, bloodstream to bloodstream, to a famous violinist. The violinist, who suffers from a rare blood disease, will die if disconnected. Thomson argues that you surely have the right to disconnect yourself. She appeals to our intuition that having to lie in bed with a violinist for an indefinite period is too much for morality to demand. She supports this claim by noting that the body being used is *your* body, not the violinist's body. She distinguishes the right to life, which the violinist clearly has, from the right to use someone else's body when necessary to preserve one's life, which it is not at all obvious the violinist has. Because the case of pregnancy is like the case of the violinist, one is no more morally obligated to remain attached to a fetus than to remain attached to the violinist.

It is widely conceded that one can generate from Thomson's vivid case the conclusion that abortion is morally permissible when a pregnancy is due to rape (Warren, 1973, p. 49; and Steinbock, 1992, p. 79). But this is hardly a general right to abortion. Do Thomson's more general theses generate a more general right to an abortion? Thomson draws our attention to the fact that in a pregnancy, although a fetus uses a woman's body as a life-support system, a pregnant woman does not use a fetus's body as a life-support system. However, an opponent of abortion might draw our attention to the fact that in an abortion the life that is lost is the fetus's, not the woman's. This symmetry seems to leave us with a stand-off.

Thomson points out that a fetus's right to life does not entail its right to use someone else's body to preserve its life. However, an opponent of abortion might point out that a woman's right to use her own body does not entail her right to end someone else's life in order to do what she wants with her body. In reply, one might argue that a pregnant woman's right to control her own body doesn't come to much if it is wrong for her to take any action that ends the life of the fetus within her. However, an opponent of abortion can argue that the fetus's right to life doesn't come to much if a pregnant woman can end it when she chooses. The consequence of all of these symmetries seems to be a stand-off. But if we have the stand-off, then one might argue that we are left with a conflict of rights: a fetal right to life versus the right of a woman to control her own body. One might then argue that the right to life seems to be a stronger right than the right to control one's own body in the case of abortion because the loss of one's life is a greater loss than the loss of the right to control one's own body in one respect for nine months. Therefore, the right to life overrides the right to control one's own body and abortion is wrong. Considerations like these have suggested to both opponents of abortion and supporters of choice that a Thomsonian strategy for defending a general right to abortion will not succeed (Tooley, 1972; Warren, 1973; and Steinbock, 1992). In fairness, one must note that Thomson did not intend her strategy to generate a general moral permissibility of abortion.

Do Fetuses Have the Right to Life?

The above considerations suggest that whether abortion is morally permissible boils down to the question of whether fetuses have the right to life. An argument that fetuses either have or lack the right to life must be based upon some general criterion for having or lacking the right to life. Opponents of abortion, on the one hand, look around for the broadest possible plausible criterion, so that fetuses will fall under it. This explains why classic arguments against abortion appeal to the criterion of being human (Noonan, 1970; Beckwith, 1993). This criterion appears plausible: The claim that all humans, whatever their race, gender, religion or *age,* have the right to life seems evident enough. In addition, because the fetuses we are concerned with do not, after all, belong to another species, they are clearly human. Thus, the syllogism that generates the conclusion that fetuses have the right to life is apparently sound.

On the other hand, those who believe abortion is morally permissible wish to find a narrow, but plausible, criterion for possession of the right to life so that fetuses will fall outside of it. This explains, in part, why the standard pro-choice arguments in the philosophical literature appeal to the criterion of being a person (Feinberg, 1986; Tooley, 1972; Warren, 1973; Benn, 1973; Engelhardt, 1986). This criterion appears plausible: The claim that only persons have the right to life seems evident enough. Furthermore, because fetuses neither are rational nor possess the capacity to communicate in complex ways nor possess a concept of self that continues through time, no fetus is a person. Thus, the syllogism needed to generate the conclusion that no fetus possesses the right to life is apparently sound. Given that no fetus possesses the right to life, a woman's right to control her own body easily generates the general right to abortion. The existence of two apparently defensible syllogisms which support contrary conclusions helps to explain why partisans on both sides of the abortion dispute often regard their opponents as either morally depraved or mentally deficient.

Which syllogism should we reject? The anti-abortion syllogism is usually attacked by attacking its major premise: the claim that whatever is biologically human has the right to life. This premise is subject to scope problems because the class of the biologically human includes too much: human cancer-cell cultures are biologically human, but they do not have the right to life. Moreover, this premise also is subject to moral-relevance problems: the connection between the biological and the moral is merely assumed. It is hard to think of a good *argument* for such a connection. If one wishes to consider the category of "human" a moral category, as some people find it plausible to do in other contexts, then one is left with no way of showing that the fetus is fully human without begging the question. Thus, the

classic anti-abortion argument appears subject to fatal difficulties.

These difficulties with the classic anti-abortion argument are well known and thought by many to be conclusive. The symmetrical difficulties with the classic pro-choice syllogism are not as well recognized. The pro-choice syllogism can be attacked by attacking its major premise: Only persons have the right to life. This premise is subject to scope problems because the class of persons includes too little: infants, the severely retarded, and some of the mentally ill seem to fall outside the class of persons as the supporter of choice understands the concept. The premise is also subject to moral-relevance problems: Being a person is understood by the prochoicer as having certain psychological attributes. If the prochoicer questions the connection between the biological and the moral, the opponent of abortion can question the connection between the psychological and the moral. If one wishes to consider "person" a moral category, as is often done, then one is left with no way of showing that the fetus is not a person without begging the question.

Pro-choicers appear to have resources for dealing with their difficulties that opponents of abortion lack. Consider their moral-relevance problem. A pro-choicer might argue that morality rests on contractual foundations and that only those who have the psychological attributes of persons are capable of entering into the moral contract and, as a consequence, being a member of the moral community. (This is essentially Engelhardt's [1986] view.) The great advantage of this contractarian approach to morality is that it seems far more plausible than any approach the anti-abortionist can provide. The great disadvantage of this contractarian approach to morality is that it adds to our earlier scope problems by leaving it unclear how we can have the duty not to inflict pain and suffering on animals.

Contractarians have tried to deal with their scope problems by arguing that duties to some individuals who are not persons can be justified even though those individuals are not contracting members of the moral community. For example, Kant argued that, although we do not have direct duties to animals, we "must practice kindness towards animals, for he who is cruel to animals becomes hard also in his dealings with men" (Kant, 1963, p. 240). Feinberg argues that infanticide is wrong, not because infants have the right to life, but because our society's protection of infants has social utility. If we do not treat infants with tenderness and consideration, then when they are persons they will be worse off and we will be worse off also (Feinberg, 1986, p. 271).

These moves only stave off the difficulties with the pro-choice view; they do not resolve them. Consider Kant's account of our obligations to animals. Kantians certainly know the difference between persons and animals. Therefore, no true Kantian would treat persons as she would treat animals. Thus, Kant's defense of our duties to animals fails to show that Kantians have a duty not to be cruel to animals. Consider Feinberg's attempt to show that infanticide is wrong even though no infant is a person. All Feinberg really shows is that it is a good idea to treat with care and consideration the infants we intend to keep. That is quite compatible with killing the infants we intend to discard. This point can be supported by an analogy with which any pro-choicer will agree. There are plainly good reasons to treat with care and consideration the fetuses we intend to keep. This is quite compatible with aborting those fetuses we intend to discard. Thus, Feinberg's account of the wrongness of infanticide is inadequate.

Accordingly, we can see that a contractarian defense of the pro-choice personhood syllogism fails. The problem arises because the contractarian cannot account for our duties to individuals who are not persons, whether these individuals are animals or infants. Because the pro-choicer wishes to adopt a narrow criterion for the right to life so that fetuses will not be included, the scope of her major premise is too narrow. Her problem is the opposite of the problem the classic opponent of abortion faces.

The argument of this section has attempted to establish, albeit briefly, that the classic anti-abortion argument and the pro-choice argument favored by most philosophers both face problems that are mirror images of one another. A stand-off results. The abortion debate requires a different strategy.

THE "FUTURE LIKE OURS" ACCOUNT OF THE WRONGNESS OF KILLING

Why do the standard arguments in the abortion debate fail to resolve the issue? The general principles to which partisans in the debate appeal are either truisms most persons would affirm in the absence of much reflection, or very general moral theories. All are subject to major problems. A different approach is needed.

Opponents of abortion claim that abortion is wrong because abortion involves killing someone like us, a human being who just happens to be very young. Supporters of choice claim that ending the life of a fetus is not in the same moral category as ending the life of an adult human being. Surely this controversy cannot be resolved in the absence of an account of what it is about killing us that makes killing us wrong. On the one hand, if we know what property we possess that makes killing us wrong, then we can ask whether fetuses have the same property. On the other hand, suppose that we do not know what it is about us that makes killing us wrong. If this is so, we do not understand even easy cases in which killing is wrong. Surely, we will not understand the ethics of killing fetuses, for if we do not understand easy cases, then we will not understand hard cases. Both pro-choicer and anti-abortionist agree that it is obvious that it is wrong to kill us. Thus, a discussion of what it is about us that makes killing us not only wrong, but seriously wrong, seems to be the right place to begin a discussion of the abortion issue.

Who is primarily wronged by a killing? The wrong of killing is not primarily explained in terms of the loss to the family and friends of the victim. Perhaps the victim is a hermit. Perhaps one's friends find it easy to make new friends. The wrong of killing is not primarily explained in terms of the brutalization of the killer. The great wrong to the victim explains the brutalization, not the other way around. The wrongness of killing us is understood in terms of what killing does to us. Killing us imposes on us the misfortune of premature death. That misfortune underlies the wrongness.

Premature death is a misfortune because when one is dead, one has been deprived of life. This misfortune can be more precisely specified. Premature death cannot deprive me of my past life. That part of my life is already gone. If I die tomorrow or if I live thirty more years my past life will be no different. It has occurred on either alternative. Rather than my past, my death deprives me of my future, of the life that I would have lived if I had lived out my natural life span.

The loss of a future biological life does not explain the misfortune of death. Compare two scenarios: In the former I now fall into a coma from which I do not recover until my death in thirty years. In the latter I die now. The latter scenario does not seem to describe a greater misfortune than the former.

The loss of our future conscious life is what underlies the misfortune of premature death. Not any future conscious life qualifies, however. Suppose that I am terminally ill with cancer. Suppose also that pain and suffering would dominate my future conscious life. If so, then death would not be a misfortune for me.

Thus, the misfortune of premature death consists of the loss to us of the future goods of consciousness. What are these goods? Much can be said about this issue, but a simple answer will do for the purposes of this essay. The goods of life are whatever we get out of life. The goods of life are those items toward which we take a "pro" attitude. They are completed projects of which we are proud, the pursuit of our goals, aesthetic enjoyments, friendships, intellectual pursuits, and physical pleasures of various sorts. The goods of life are what makes life worth living. In general, what makes life worth living for one person will not be the same as what makes life worth living for another. Nevertheless, the list of goods in each of our lives will overlap. The lists are usually different in different stages of our lives.

What makes the goods of my future good for me? One possible, but wrong, answer is my desire for those goods now. This answer does not account for those aspects of my future life that I now believe I will later value, but about which I am wrong. Neither does it account for those aspects of my future that I will come to value, but which I don't value now. What is valuable to the young may not be valuable to the middle-aged. What is valuable to the middle-aged may not be valuable to the old. Some of life's values for the elderly are best appreciated by the elderly. Thus it is wrong to say that the value of my future to me is just what I value now. What makes my future valuable to me are those aspects of my future that I will (or would) value when I will (or would) experience them, whether I value them now or not.

It follows that a person can believe that she will have a valuable future and be wrong. Furthermore, a person can believe that he will not have a valuable future and also be wrong. This is confirmed by our attitude toward many of the suicidal. We attempt to save the lives of the suicidal and to convince them that they have made an error in judgment. This does not mean that the future of an individual obtains value from the value that others confer on it. It means that, in some cases, others can make a clearer judgment of the value of a person's future *to that person* than the person herself. This often happens when one's judgment concerning the value of one's own future is clouded by personal tragedy. (Compare the views of McInerney, 1990, and Shirley, 1995.)

Thus, what is sufficient to make killing us wrong, in general, is that it causes premature death. Premature death is a misfortune. Premature death is a misfortune, in general, because it deprives an individual of a future of value. An individual's future will be valuable to that individual if that individual will come, or would come, to value it. We know that killing us is wrong. What makes killing us wrong, in general, is that it deprives us of a future of value. Thus, killing someone is wrong, in general, when it deprives her of a future like ours. I shall call this "an FLO."

ARGUMENTS IN FAVOR OF THE FLO THEORY

At least four arguments support this FLO account of the wrongness of killing.

The Considered Judgment Argument

The FLO account of the wrongness of killing is correct because it fits with our considered judgment concerning the nature of the misfortune of death. The analysis of the previous section is an exposition of the nature of this considered judgment. This judgment can be confirmed. If one were to ask individuals with AIDS or with incurable cancer about the nature of their misfortune, I believe that they would say or imply that their impending loss of an FLO makes their premature death a misfortune. If they would not, then the FLO account would plainly be wrong.

The Worst of Crimes Argument

The FLO account of the wrongness of killing is correct because it explains why we believe that killing is one of the worst of crimes. My being killed deprives me of more than does my being robbed or beaten or harmed in some other way because my being killed deprives me of all of the value of my future, not merely part of it. This explains why we make the penalty for murder greater than the penalty for other crimes.

As a corollary the FLO account of the wrongness of killing also explains why killing an adult human being is justified only in the most extreme circumstances, only in circumstances in which the loss of life to an individual is outweighed by a worse outcome if that life is not taken. Thus, we are willing to justify killing in self-defense, killing in order to save one's own life, because one's loss if one does not kill in that situation is so very great. We justify killing in a just war for similar reasons. We believe that capital punishment would be justified if, by having such an institution, fewer premature deaths would occur. The FLO account of the wrongness of killing does not entail that killing is always wrong. Nevertheless, the FLO account explains both why killing is one of the worst of crimes and, as a corollary, why the exceptions to the wrongness of killing are so very rare. A correct theory of the wrongness of killing should have these features.

The Appeal to Cases Argument

The FLO account of the wrongness of killing is correct because it yields the correct answers in many life-and-death cases that arise in medicine and have interested philosophers.

Consider medicine first. Most people believe that it is not wrong deliberately to end the life of a person who is permanently unconscious. Thus we believe that it is not wrong to remove a feeding tube or a ventilator from a permanently comatose patient, knowing that such a removal will cause death. The FLO account of the wrongness of killing explains why this is so. A patient who is permanently unconscious cannot have a future that she would come to value, whatever her values. Therefore, according to the FLO theory of the wrongness of killing, death could not, *ceteris paribus,* be a misfortune to her. Therefore, removing the feeding tube or ventilator does not wrong her.

By contrast, almost all people believe that it is wrong, *ceteris paribus,* to withdraw medical treatment from patients who are temporarily unconscious. The FLO account of the wrongness of killing also explains why this is so. Furthermore, these two unconsciousness cases explain why the FLO account of the wrongness of killing does not include present consciousness as a necessary condition for the wrongness of killing.

Consider now the issue of the morality of legalizing active euthanasia. Proponents of active euthanasia argue that if a patient faces a future of intractable pain and wants to die, then, *ceteris paribus,* it would not be wrong for a physician to give him medicine that she knows would result in his death. This view is so universally accepted that even the strongest *opponents* of active euthanasia hold it. The official Vatican view (Sacred Congregation, 1980) is that it is permissible for a physician to administer to a patient morphine sufficient (although no more than sufficient) to control his pain even if she foresees that the morphine will result in his death. Notice how nicely the FLO account of the wrongness of killing explains this unanimity of opinion. A patient known to be in severe intractable pain is presumed to have a future without positive value. Accordingly, death would not be a misfortune for him and an action that would (foreseeably) end his life would not be wrong.

Contrast this with the standard emergency medical treatment of the suicidal. Even though the suicidal have indicated that they want to die, medical personnel will act to save their lives. This supports the view that it is not the mere *desire* to enjoy an FLO which is crucial to our understanding of the wrongness of killing. *Having* an FLO is what is crucial to the account, although one would, of course, want to make an exception in the case of fully autonomous people who refuse life-saving medical treatment. Opponents of abortion can, of course, be willing to make an exception for fully autonomous fetuses who refuse life support.

The FLO theory of the wrongness of killing also deals correctly with issues that have concerned philosophers. It implies that it would be wrong to kill (peaceful) persons from outer space who come to visit our planet even though they are biologically utterly unlike us. Presumably, if they are persons, then they will have futures that are sufficiently like ours so that it would be wrong to kill them. The FLO account of the wrongness of killing shares this feature with the personhood views of the supporters of choice. Classical opponents of abortion who locate the wrongness of abortion somehow in the biological humanity of a fetus cannot explain this.

The FLO account does not entail that there is another species of animals whose members ought not to be killed. Neither does it entail that it is permissible to kill any non-human animal. On the one hand, a supporter of animals' rights might argue that since some non-human animals have a future of value, it is wrong to kill them also, or at least it is wrong to kill them without a far better reason than we usually have for killing non-human animals. On the other hand, one might argue that the futures of non-human animals are not sufficiently like ours for the FLO account to entail that it is wrong to kill them. Since the FLO account does not specify which properties a future of another individual must possess so that killing that individual is wrong, the FLO account is indeterminate with respect to this issue.

The fact that the FLO account of the wrongness of killing does not give a determinate answer to this question is not a flaw in the theory. A sound ethical account should yield the right answers in the obvious cases; it should not be required to resolve every disputed question.

A major respect in which the FLO account is superior to accounts that appeal to the concept of person is the explanation the FLO account provides of the wrongness of killing infants. There was a class of infants who had futures that included a class of events that were identical to the futures of the readers of this essay. Thus, reader, the FLO account explains why it was as wrong to kill you when you were an infant as it is to kill you now. This account can be generalized to almost all infants. Notice that the wrongness of killing infants can be explained in the absence of an account of what makes the future of an individual sufficiently valuable so that it is wrong to kill that individual. The absence of such an account explains why the FLO account is indeterminate with respect to the wrongness of killing non-human animals.

If the FLO account is the correct theory of the wrongness of killing, then because abortion involves killing fetuses and fetuses have FLOs for exactly the same reasons that infants have FLOs, abortion is presumptively seriously immoral. This inference lays the necessary groundwork for a fourth argument in favor of the FLO account that shows that abortion is wrong.

The Analogy with Animals Argument

Why do we believe it is wrong to cause animals suffering? We believe that, in our own case and in the case of other adults and children, suffering is a misfortune. It would be as morally arbitrary to refuse to acknowledge that animal suffering is wrong as it would be to refuse to acknowledge that the suffering of persons of another race is wrong. It is, on reflection, suffering that is a misfortune, not the suffering of white males or the suffering of humans. Therefore, infliction of suffering is presumptively wrong no matter on whom it is inflicted and whether it is inflicted on persons or nonpersons. Arbitrary restrictions on the wrongness of suffering count as racism or speciesism. Not only is this argument convincing on its own, but it is the only way of justifying the wrongness of animal cruelty. Cruelty toward animals is clearly wrong. (This famous argument is due to Singer, 1979.)

The FLO account of the wrongness of abortion is analogous. We believe that, in our own case and the cases of other adults and children, the loss of a future of value is a misfortune. It would be as morally arbitrary to refuse to acknowledge that the loss of a future of value to a fetus is wrong as to refuse to acknowledge that the loss of a future of value to Jews (to take a relevant twentieth-century example) is wrong. It is, on reflection, the loss of a future of value that is a misfortune; not the loss of a future of value to adults or loss of a future of value to non-Jews. To deprive someone of a future of value is wrong no matter on whom the deprivation is inflicted and no matter whether the deprivation is inflicted on persons or nonpersons. Arbitrary restrictions on the wrongness of this deprivation count as racism, genocide or ageism. Therefore, abortion is wrong. This argument that abortion is wrong should be convincing because it has the same form as the argument for the claim that causing pain and suffering to nonhuman animals is wrong. Since the latter argument is convincing, the former argument should be also. Thus, an analogy with animals supports the thesis that abortion is wrong.

REPLIES TO OBJECTIONS

The four arguments in the previous section establish that abortion is, except in rare cases, seriously immoral. Not surprisingly, there are objections to this view. There are replies to the four most important objections to the FLO argument for the immorality of abortion.

The Potentiality Objection

The FLO account of the wrongness of abortion is a potentiality argument. To claim that a fetus *has* an FLO is to claim that a fetus now has the potential to be in a state of a certain kind in the future. It is not to claim that all ordinary fetuses *will* have FLOs. Fetuses who are aborted, of course, will not. To say that a standard fetus has an FLO is to say that a standard fetus either will have or would have a life it will or would value. To say that a standard fetus would have a life it would value is to say that it will have a life it will value if it does not die prematurely. The truth of this conditional is based upon the nature of fetuses (including the fact that they naturally age) and this nature concerns their potential.

Some appeals to potentiality in the abortion debate rest on unsound inferences. For example, one may try to generate an argument against abortion by arguing that because persons have the right to life, potential persons also have the right to life. Such an argument is plainly invalid as it stands. The premise one needs to add to make it valid would have to be something like: "If Xs have the right to Y, then potential Xs have the right to Y." This premise is plainly false. Potential presidents don't have the rights of the presidency; potential voters don't have the right to vote.

In the FLO argument potentiality is not used in order to bridge the gap between adults and fetuses as is done in the argument in the above paragraph. The FLO theory of the wrongness of killing adults is based upon the adult's potentiality to have a future of value. Potentiality is in the argument from the very beginning. Thus, the plainly false premise is not required. Accordingly, the use of potentiality in the FLO theory is not a sign of an illegitimate inference.

The Argument from Interests

A second objection to the FLO account of the immorality of abortion involves arguing that even though fetuses have FLOs, nonsentient fetuses do not meet the minimum conditions for having any moral standing at all because they lack interests. Steinbock (1992, p. 5) has presented this argument clearly:

> Beings that have moral status must be capable of caring about what is done to them. They must be capable of being made, if only in a rudimentary

sense, happy or miserable, comfortable or distressed. Whatever reasons we may have for preserving or protecting nonsentient beings, these reasons do not refer to their own interests. For without conscious awareness, beings cannot have interests. Without interests, they cannot have a welfare of their own. Without a welfare of their own, nothing can be done for their sake. Hence, they lack moral standing or status.

Medical researchers have argued that fetuses do not become sentient until after 22 weeks of gestation (Steinbock, 1992, p. 50). If they are correct, and if Steinbock's argument is sound, then we have both an objection to the FLO account of the wrongness of abortion and a basis for a view on abortion minimally acceptable to most supporters of choice.

Steinbock's conclusion conflicts with our settled moral beliefs. Temporarily unconscious human beings are nonsentient, yet no one believes that they lack either interests or moral standing. Accordingly, neither conscious awareness nor the capacity for conscious awareness is a necessary condition for having interests.

The counter-example of the temporarily unconscious human being shows that there is something internally wrong with Steinbock's argument. The difficulty stems from an ambiguity. One cannot *take* an interest in something without being capable of caring about what is done to it. However, something can be *in* someone's interest without that individual being capable of caring about it, or about anything. Thus, life support can be *in* the interests of a temporarily unconscious patient even though the temporarily unconscious patient is incapable of *taking* an interest in that life support. If this can be so for the temporarily unconscious patient, then it is hard to see why it cannot be so for the temporarily unconscious (that is, nonsentient) fetus who requires placental life support. Thus the objection based on interests fails.

The Problem of Equality

The FLO account of the wrongness of killing seems to imply that the degree of wrongness associated with each killing varies inversely with the victim's age. Thus, the FLO account of the wrongness of killing seems to suggest that it is far worse to kill a five-year-old than an 89-year-old because the former is deprived of far more than the latter. However, we believe that all persons have an equal right to life. Thus, it appears that the FLO account of the wrongness of killing entails an obviously false view (Paske, 1994).

However, the FLO account of the wrongness of killing does not, strictly speaking, imply that it is worse to kill younger people than older people. The FLO account provides an explanation of the wrongness of killing that is sufficient to account for the serious presumptive wrongness of killing. It does not follow that killings cannot be wrong in other ways. For example, one might hold, as does Feldman (1992, p. 184), that in addition to the wrongness of killing that has its basis in the future life of which the victim is deprived, killing an individual is also made wrong by the admirability of an individual's past behavior. Now the amount of admirability will presumably vary directly with age, whereas the amount of deprivation will vary inversely with age. This tends to equalize the wrongness of murder.

However, even if, *ceteris paribus,* it is worse to kill younger persons than older persons, there are good reasons for adopting a doctrine of the legal equality of murder. Suppose that we tried to estimate the seriousness of a crime of murder by appraising the value of the FLO of which the victim had been deprived. How would one go about doing this? In the first place, one would be confronted by the old problem of interpersonal comparisons of utility. In the second place, estimation of the value of a future would involve putting oneself, not into the shoes of the victim at the time she was killed, but rather into the shoes the victim would have worn had the victim survived, and then estimating from that perspective the worth of that person's future. This task seems difficult, if not impossible. Accordingly, there are reasons to adopt a convention that murders are equally wrong.

Furthermore, the FLO theory, in a way, explains why we do adopt the doctrine of the legal equality of murder. The FLO theory explains why we regard murder as one of the worst of crimes, since depriving someone of a future like ours deprives her of more than depriving her of anything else. This gives us a reason for making the punishment for murder very harsh, as harsh as is compatible with civilized society. One should not make the punishment for younger victims harsher than that. Thus, the doctrine of the equal legal right to life does not seem to be incompatible with the FLO theory.

The Contraception Objection

The strongest objection to the FLO argument for the immorality of abortion is based on the claim that, because contraception results in one less FLO, the FLO argument entails that contraception, indeed, abstention from sex when conception is possible, is immoral. Because neither contraception nor abstention from sex when conception is possible is immoral, the FLO account is flawed.

There is a cogent reply to this objection. If the argument of the early part of this essay is correct, then the central issue concerning the morality of abortion is the problem of whether fetuses are individuals who are members of the class of individuals whom it is seriously presumptively wrong to kill. The properties of being human and alive, of being a person, and of having an FLO are criteria that participants in the abortion debate have offered to mark off the relevant class of individuals. The central claim of this essay is that having an FLO marks off the relevant class of individuals. A defender of the FLO view could, therefore, reply that since, at the time of contraception, there is no individual to have an FLO, the FLO account does not entail that contraception is wrong. The wrong of killing is primarily a wrong to the individual who is killed; at the time of contraception there is no individual to be wronged.

However, someone who presses the contraception objection might have an answer to this reply. She might say that the sperm and egg are the individuals deprived of an FLO at the time of contraception. Thus, there are individuals whom contraception deprives of an FLO and if depriving an individual of an FLO is what makes killing wrong, then the FLO theory entails that contraception is wrong.

There is also a reply to this move. In the case of abortion, an objectively determinate individual is the subject of harm caused by the loss of an FLO. This individual is a fetus. In the case of contraception, there are far more candidates (see Norcross, 1990). Let us consider some possible candidates in order of the increasing number of individuals harmed: (1) The single harmed individual might be the combination of the particular sperm and the particular egg that would have united to form a zygote if contraception had not been used. (2) The two harmed individuals might be the particular sperm itself, and, in addition, the ovum itself that would have physically combined to form the zygote. (This is modeled on the double homicide of two persons who would otherwise in a short time fuse. (1) is modeled on harm to a single entity some of whose parts are not physically contiguous, such as a university.) (3) The many harmed individuals might be the millions of *combinations* of sperm and the released ovum whose (small) chance of having an FLO were reduced by the successful contraception. (4) The even larger class of harmed individuals (larger by one) might be the class consisting of all of the individual sperm in an ejaculate and, in addition, the individual ovum released at the time of the successful contraception. (1) through (4) are all candidates for being the subject(s) of harm in the case of successful contraception or abstinence from sex. Which should be chosen? Should we hold a lottery? There seems to be no non-arbitrarily determinate subject of harm in the case of successful contraception. But if there is no such subject of harm, then no determinate thing was harmed. If no determinate thing was harmed, then (in the case of contraception) no wrong has been done. Thus, the FLO account of the wrongness of abortion does not entail that contraception is wrong.

CONCLUSION

This essay contains an argument for the view that, except in unusual circumstances, abortion is seriously wrong. Deprivation of an FLO explains why killing adults and children is wrong. Abortion deprives fetuses of FLOs. Therefore, abortion is wrong. This argument is based on an account of the wrongness of killing that is a result of our considered judgment of the nature of the misfortune of premature death. It accounts for why we regard killing as one of the worst of crimes. It is superior to alternative accounts of the wrongness of killing that are intended to provide insight into the ethics of abortion. This account of the wrongness of killing is supported by the way it handles cases in which our moral judgments are settled. This account has an analogue in the most plausible account of the wrongness of causing animals to suffer. This account makes no appeal to religion. Therefore, the FLO account shows that abortion, except in rare instances, is seriously wrong.

REFERENCES

Beckwith, F. J., *Politically Correct Death: Answering Arguments for Abortion Rights* (Grand Rapids, Michigan: Baker Books, 1993).

Benn, S. I., "Abortion, Infanticide, and Respect for Persons," *The Problem of Abortion,* ed. J. Feinberg (Belmont, California: Wadsworth, 1973), pp. 92–104.

Engelhardt, Jr, H. T., *The Foundations of Bioethics* (New York: Oxford University Press, 1986).

Feinberg, J., "Abortion," *Matters of Life and Death: New Introductory Essays in Moral Philosophy,* ed. T. Regan (New York: Random House, 1986).

Feldman, F., *Confrontations with the Reaper: A Philosophical Study of the Nature and Value of Death* (New York: Oxford University Press, 1992).

Kant, I., *Lectures on Ethics,* trans. L. Infeld (New York: Harper, 1963).

McInerney, P., "Does a Fetus Already Have a Future like Ours?," *Journal of Philosophy* 87 (1990): 264–8.

Noonan, J., "An Almost Absolute Value in History," in *The Morality of Abortion,* ed. J. Noonan (Cambridge, MA: Harvard University Press, 1970).

Norcross, A., "Killing, Abortion, and Contraception: a Reply to Marquis," *Journal of Philosophy* 87 (1990): 268–77.

Paske, G., "Abortion and the Neo-natal Right to Life: a Critique of Marquis's Futurist Argument," *The Abortion Controversy: A Reader,* ed. L. P. Pojman and F. J. Beckwith (Boston: Jones and Bartlett, 1994), pp. 343–53.

Sacred Congregation for the Propagation of the Faith, *Declaration on Euthanasia* (Vatican City, 1980).

Shirley, E. S., "Marquis' Argument Against Abortion: a Critique," *Southwest Philosophy Review* 11 (1995): 79–89.

Singer, P., "Not for Humans Only: the Place of Nonhumans in Environmental Issues," *Ethics and Problems of the 21st Century,* ed. K. E. Goodpaster and K. M. Sayre (South Bend: Notre Dame University Press, 1979).

Steinbock, B., *Life Before Birth: The Moral and Legal Status of Embryos and Fetuses* (New York: Oxford University Press, 1992).

Thomson, J. J., "A Defense of Abortion," *Philosophy and Public Affairs* 1 (1971): 47–66.

Tooley, M., "Abortion and Infanticide," *Philosophy and Public Affairs* 2 (1972): 37–65.

Warren, M. A., "On the Moral and Legal Status of Abortion," *Monist* 57 (1973): 43–61.

STUDY QUESTIONS

1. Is the loss of one's future as devastating for a fetus as for a child?
2. Does Marquis's argument that abortion is immoral depend on religious considerations?
3. Does Marquis's position imply that using contraception is wrong?
4. According to Marquis, in what circumstances is abortion not wrong?

Virtue Theory and Abortion

Rosalind Hursthouse

Rosalind Hursthouse is Professor of Philosophy at the University of Auckland in New Zealand. She responds to criticisms of virtue theory by demonstrating how it can be applied to the issue of abortion. She argues that the deep emotions that surround parenthood and family relationships indicate that pregnancy and its termination are serious matters. Accordingly, treating them trivially demonstrates the vices of callousness and light-mindedness. She maintains that even in cases in which abortion is right, it will probably cause some evil.

The sort of ethical theory derived from Aristotle, variously described as virtue ethics, virtue-based ethics, or neo-Aristotelianism, is becoming better known, and is now quite widely recognized as at least a possible rival to deontological and utilitarian theories . . . I aim to deepen that understanding . . . by illustrating what the theory looks like when it is applied to a particular issue, in this case, abortion. . . .

As everyone knows, the morality of abortion is commonly discussed in relation to just two considerations: first, and predominantly, the status of the fetus and whether or not it is the sort of thing that may or may not be innocuously or justifiably killed; and second, and less predominantly (when, that is, the discussion concerns the *morality* of abortion rather than the question of permissible legislation in a just society), women's rights. If one thinks within this familiar framework, one may well be puzzled about what virtue theory, as such, could contribute. Some people assume the discussion will be conducted solely in terms of what the virtuous agent would or would not do. . . . Others assume that only

justice, or at most justice and charity, will be applied to the issue, generating a discussion very similar to Judith Jarvis Thomson's.[1]

Now if this is the way the virtue theorist's discussion of abortion is imagined to be, no wonder people think little of it. It seems obvious in advance that in any such discussion there must be either a great deal of extremely tendentious application of the virtue terms *just, charitable,* and so on or a lot of rhetorical appeal to "this is what only the virtuous agent knows." But these are caricatures; they fail to appreciate the way in which virtue theory quite transforms the discussion of abortion by dismissing the two familiar dominating considerations as, in a way, fundamentally irrelevant. In what way or ways, I hope to make both clear and plausible.

Let us first consider women's rights. Let me emphasize again that we are discussing the *morality* of abortion, not the rights and wrongs of laws prohibiting or permitting it. If we suppose that women do have a moral right to do as they choose with their own bodies, or, more particularly, to terminate their

From *Philosophy & Public Affairs*, 20 (1991), by permission of Blackwell Publishing Ltd.

pregnancies, then it may well follow that a *law* forbidding abortion would be unjust. Indeed, even if they have no such right, such a law might be, as things stand at the moment, unjust, or impractical, or inhumane: on this issue I have nothing to say in this article. But, putting all questions about the justice or injustice of laws to one side, and supposing only that women have such a moral right, *nothing* follows from this supposition about the morality of abortion, according to virtue theory, once it is noted (quite generally, not with particular reference to abortion) that in exercising a moral right I can do something cruel, or callous, or selfish, light-minded, self-righteous, stupid, inconsiderate, disloyal, dishonest—that is, act viciously.[2] Love and friendship do not survive their parties' constantly insisting on their rights, nor do people live well when they think that getting what they have a right to is of preeminent importance; they harm others, and they harm themselves. So whether women have a moral right to terminate their pregnancies is irrelevant within virtue theory, for it is irrelevant to the question "In having an abortion in these circumstances, would the agent be acting virtuously or viciously or neither?"

What about the consideration of the status of the fetus—what can virtue theory say about that? One might say that this issue is not in the province of *any* moral theory; it is a metaphysical question, and an extremely difficult one at that. Must virtue theory then wait upon metaphysics to come up with the answer?

At first sight it might seem so. For virtue is said to involve knowledge, and part of this knowledge consists in having the *right* attitude to things. "Right" here does not just mean "morally right" or "proper" or "nice" in the modern sense; it means "accurate, true." One cannot have the right or correct attitude to something if the attitude is based on or involves false beliefs. And this suggests that if the status of the fetus is relevant to the rightness or wrongness of abortion, its status must be known, as a truth, to the fully wise and virtuous person.

But the sort of wisdom that the fully virtuous person has is not supposed to be recondite; it does not call for fancy philosophical sophistication, and it does not depend upon, let alone wait upon, the discoveries of academic philosophers.[3] And this entails the following, rather startling, conclusion: that the status of the fetus—that issue over which so much ink has been spilt—is, according to virtue theory, simply not relevant to the rightness or wrongness of abortion (within, that is, a secular morality).

Or rather, since that is clearly too radical a conclusion, it is in a sense relevant, but only in the sense that the familiar biological facts are relevant. By "the familiar biological facts" I mean the facts that most human societies are and have been familiar with—that, standardly (but not invariably), pregnancy occurs as the result of sexual intercourse, that it lasts about nine months, during which time the fetus grows and develops, that standardly it terminates in the birth of a living baby, and that this is how we all come to be.

It might be thought that this distinction—between the familiar biological facts and the status of the fetus—is a distinction without a difference. But this is not so. To attach relevance to the status of the fetus, in the sense in which virtue theory claims it is not relevant, is to be gripped by the conviction that we must go beyond the familiar biological facts, deriving some sort of conclusion from them, such as that the fetus has rights, or is not a person, or something similar. It is also to believe that this exhausts the relevance of the familiar biological facts, that all they are relevant to is the status of the fetus and whether or not it is the sort of thing that may or may not be killed.

These convictions, I suspect, are rooted in the desire to solve the problem of abortion by getting it to fall under some general rule such as "You ought not to kill anything with the right to life but may kill anything else." But they have resulted in what should surely strike any nonphilosopher as a most bizarre aspect of nearly all the current philosophical literature on abortion, namely, that, far from treating abortion as a unique moral problem, markedly unlike any other, nearly everything written on the status of the fetus and its bearing on the abortion issue would be consistent with the human reproductive facts' (to say nothing of family life) being totally different from what they are. Imagine that you are an alien extraterrestrial anthropologist who does not know that the human race is roughly 50 percent female and 50 percent male, or that our only (natural) form of reproduction involves heterosexual intercourse, viviparous birth, and the female's (and only the female's) being pregnant for nine months, or that females are capable of childbearing from late childhood to late middle age, or that childbearing is painful, dangerous, and emotionally charged—do you think you would pick up these facts from the hundreds of articles written on the status of the fetus? I am quite sure you would not. And that, I think, shows that the current philosophical literature on abortion has got badly out of touch with reality.

Now if we are using virtue theory, our first question is not "What do the familiar biological facts show—what can be derived from them about the status of the fetus?" but "How do these facts figure in the practical reasoning, actions and passions, thoughts and reactions, of the virtuous and the nonvirtuous? What is the mark of having the right attitude to these facts and what manifests having the wrong attitude to them?" This immediately makes essentially relevant not only all the facts about human reproduction I mentioned above, but a whole range of facts about our emotions in relation to them as well. I mean such facts as that human parents, both male and female, tend to care passionately about their offspring, and that family relationships are among the deepest and strongest in our lives— and, significantly, among the longest-lasting.

These facts make it obvious that pregnancy is not just one among many other physical conditions; and hence that anyone who genuinely believes that an abortion is comparable to a haircut or an appendectomy is mistaken.[4] The fact that the premature termination of a pregnancy is, in some sense, the cutting off of a new human life, and thereby, like the procreation of a new human life, connects with all our thoughts about human life and death, parenthood, and family relationships, must make it a serious matter. To disregard this fact about it, to think of abortion as nothing but the killing of something that does not matter, or as nothing but the exercise of some right or rights one has, or as the incidental means to some desirable state of affairs, is to do something callous and light-minded, the sort of thing

that no virtuous and wise person would do. It is to have the wrong attitude not only to fetuses, but more generally to human life and death, parenthood, and family relationships.

Although I say that the facts make this obvious, I know that this is one of my tendentious points. In partial support of it I note that even the most dedicated proponents of the view that deliberate abortion is just like an appendectomy or haircut rarely hold the same view of spontaneous abortion, that is, miscarriage. It is not so tendentious of me to claim that to react to people's grief over miscarriage by saying, or even thinking, "What a fuss about nothing!" would be callous and light-minded, whereas to try to laugh someone out of grief over an appendectomy scar or a botched haircut would not be. It is hard to give this point due prominence within act-centered theories, for the inconsistency is an inconsistency in attitude about the seriousness of loss of life, not in beliefs about which acts are right or wrong. Moreover, an act-centered theorist may say, "Well, there is nothing wrong with *thinking* 'What a fuss about nothing!' as long as you do not say it and hurt the person who is grieving. And besides, we cannot be held responsible for our thoughts, only for the intentional actions they give rise to." But the character traits that virtue theory emphasizes are not simply dispositions to intentional actions, but a seamless disposition to certain actions and passions, thoughts and reactions.

To say that the cutting off of a human life is always a matter of some seriousness, at any stage, is not to deny the relevance of gradual fetal development. Notwithstanding the well-worn point that clear boundary lines cannot be drawn, our emotions and attitudes regarding the fetus do change as it develops, and again when it is born, and indeed further as the baby grows. Abortion for shallow reasons in the later stages is much more shocking than abortion for the same reasons in the early stages in a way that matches the fact that deep grief over miscarriage in the later stages is more appropriate than it is over miscarriage in the earlier stages (when, that is, the grief is solely about the loss of *this* child, not about, as might be the case, the loss of one's only hope of having a child or of having one's husband's child). Imagine (or recall) a woman who already has children; she had not intended to have more, but finds herself unexpectedly pregnant. Though contrary to her plans, the pregnancy, once established as a fact, is welcomed—and then she loses the embryo almost immediately. If this were bemoaned as a tragedy, it would, I think, be a misapplication of the concept of what is tragic. But it may still properly be mourned as a loss. The grief is expressed in such terms as "I shall always wonder how she or he would have turned out" or "When I look at the others, I shall think, 'How different their lives would have been if this other one had been part of them.'" It would, I take it, be callous and light-minded to say, or think, "Well, she has already *got* four children; what's the problem?"; it would be neither, nor arrogantly intrusive in the case of a close friend, to try to correct prolonged mourning by saying, "I know it's sad, but it's not a tragedy; rejoice in the ones you have." The application of *tragic* becomes more appropriate as the fetus grows, for the mere fact that one has lived with it for longer, conscious of its existence, makes a difference. To shrug off an early abortion is understandable just because it is very hard to be fully conscious of the fetus's existence in the early stages and hence hard to appreciate that an early abortion is the destruction of life. It is particularly hard for the young and inexperienced to appreciate this, because appreciation of it usually comes only with experience.

I do not mean "with the experience of having an abortion" (though that may be part of it) but, quite generally, "with the experience of life." Many women who have borne children contrast their later pregnancies with their first successful one, saying that in the later ones they were conscious of a new life growing in them from very early on. And, more generally, as one reaches the age at which the next generation is coming up close behind one, the counterfactuals "If I, or she, had had an abortion, Alice, or Bob, would not have been born" acquire a significant application, which casts a new light on the conditionals "If I or Alice have an abortion then some Caroline or Bill will not be born."

The fact that pregnancy is not just one among many physical conditions does not mean that one can never regard it in that light without manifesting a vice. When women are in very poor physical health, or worn out from childbearing, or forced to do very physically demanding jobs, then they cannot be described as self-indulgent, callous, irresponsible, or light-minded if they seek abortions mainly with a view to avoiding pregnancy as the physical condition that it is. To go through with a pregnancy when one is utterly exhausted, or when one's job consists of crawling along tunnels hauling coal, as many women in the nineteenth century were obliged to do, is perhaps heroic, but people who do not achieve heroism are not necessarily vicious. That they can view the pregnancy only as eight months of misery, followed by hours if not days of agony and exhaustion, and abortion only as the blessed escape from this prospect, is entirely understandable and does not manifest any lack of serious respect for human life or a shallow attitude to motherhood. What it does show is that something is terribly amiss in the conditions of their lives, which make it so hard to recognize pregnancy and childbearing as the good that they can be.

In relation to this last point I should draw attention to the way in which virtue theory has a sort of built-in indexicality. Philosophers arguing against anything remotely resembling a belief in the sanctity of life (which the above claims clearly embody) frequently appeal to the existence of other communities in which abortion and infanticide are practiced. We should not automatically assume that it is impossible that some other communities could be morally inferior to our own; maybe some are, or have been, precisely insofar as their members are, typically, callous or light-minded or unjust. But in communities in which life is a great deal tougher for everyone than it is in ours, having the right attitude to human life and death, parenthood, and family relationships might well manifest itself in ways that are unlike ours. When it is essential to survival that most members of the community fend for themselves at a very young age or work during most of their waking hours, selective abortion or infanticide might be practiced either as a form of genuine euthanasia or for the sake of the community and not, I think, be thought callous or light-minded. But this does not make everything all right; as before, it shows that there is something amiss with the conditions of their lives, which are making it impossible for them to live really well.

The foregoing discussion, insofar as it emphasizes the right attitude to human life and death, parallels to a certain extent those standard discussions of abortion that concentrate on it solely as an issue of killing. But it does not, as those discussions do, gloss over the fact, emphasized by those who discuss the morality of abortion in terms of women's rights, that abortion, wildly unlike any other form of killing, is the termination of a pregnancy, which is a condition of a woman's body and results in *her* having a child if it is not aborted. This fact is given due recognition not by appeal to women's rights but by emphasizing the relevance of the familiar biological and psychological facts and their connection with having the right attitude to parenthood and family relationships. But it may well be thought that failing to bring in women's rights still leaves some important aspects of the problem of abortion untouched.

Speaking in terms of women's rights, people sometimes say things like, "Well, it's her life you're talking about too, you know; she's got a right to her own life, her own happiness." And the discussion stops there. But in the context of virtue theory, given that we are particularly concerned with what constitutes a good human life, with what true happiness or *eudaimonia* is, this is no place to stop. We go on to ask, "And is this life of hers a good one? Is she living well?"

If we are to go on to talk about good human lives, in the context of abortion, we have to bring in our thoughts about the value of love and family life, and our proper emotional development through a natural life cycle. The familiar facts support the view that parenthood in general, and motherhood and child-bearing in particular, are intrinsically worthwhile, are among the things that can be correctly thought to be partially constitutive of a flourishing human life.[5] If this is right, then a woman who opts for not being a mother (at all, or again, or now) by opting for abortion may thereby be manifesting a flawed grasp of what her life should be, and be about—a grasp that is childish, or grossly materialistic, or short-sighted, or shallow.

I said "*may* thereby": this *need* not be so. Consider, for instance, a woman who has already had several children and fears that to have another will seriously affect her capacity to be a good mother to the ones she has—she does not show a lack of appreciation of the intrinsic value of being a parent by opting for abortion. Nor does a woman who has been a good mother and is approaching the age at which she may be looking forward to being a good grandmother. Nor does a woman who discovers that her pregnancy may well kill her, and opts for abortion and adoption. Nor, necessarily, does a woman who has decided to lead a life centered around some other worthwhile activity or activities with which motherhood would compete.

People who are childless by choice are sometimes described as "irresponsible," or "selfish," or "refusing to grow up," or "not knowing what life is about." But one can hold that having children is intrinsically worthwhile without endorsing this, for we are, after all, in the happy position of there being more worthwhile things to do than can be fitted into one lifetime. Parenthood, and motherhood in particular, even if granted to be intrinsically worthwhile, undoubtedly take up a lot of one's adult life, leaving no room for some other worthwhile pursuits. But some women who choose abortion rather than have their first child, and some men who encourage their partners to choose abortion, are not avoiding parenthood for the sake of other worthwhile pursuits, but for the worthless one of "having a good time," or for the pursuit of some false vision of the ideals of freedom or self-realization. And some others who say "I am not ready for parenthood yet" are making some sort of mistake about the extent to which one can manipulate the circumstances of one's life so as to make it fulfill some dream that one has. Perhaps one's dream is to have two perfect children, a girl and a boy, within a perfect marriage, in financially secure circumstances, with an interesting job of one's own. But to care too much about that dream, to demand of life that it give it to one and act accordingly, may be both greedy and foolish, and is to run the risk of missing out on happiness entirely. Not only may fate make the dream impossible, or destroy it, but one's own attachment to it may make it impossible. Good marriages, and the most promising children, can be destroyed by just one adult's excessive demand for perfection.

Once again, this is not to deny that girls may quite properly say "I am not ready for motherhood yet," especially in our society, and, far from manifesting irresponsibility or light-mindedness, show an appropriate modesty or humility, or a fearfulness that does not amount to cowardice. However, even when the decision to have an abortion is the right decision—one that does not itself fall under a vice-related term and thereby one that the perfectly virtuous could recommend—it does not follow that there is no sense in which having the abortion is wrong, or guilt inappropriate. For, by virtue of the fact that a human life has been cut short, some evil has probably been brought about,[6] and that circumstances make the decision to bring about some evil the right decision will be a ground for guilt if getting into those circumstances in the first place itself manifested a flaw in character.

What "gets one into those circumstances" in the case of abortion is, except in the case of rape, one's sexual activity and one's choices, or the lack of them, about one's sexual partner and about contraception. The virtuous woman (which here of course does not mean simply "chaste woman" but "woman with the virtues") has such character traits as strength, independence, resoluteness, decisiveness, self-confidence, responsibility, serious-mindedness, and self-determination—and no one, I think, could deny that many women become pregnant in circumstances in which they cannot welcome or cannot face the thought of having *this* child precisely because they lack one or some of these character traits. So even in the cases where the decision to have an abortion is the right one, it can still be the reflection of a moral failing—not because the decision itself is weak or cowardly or irresolute or irresponsible or light-minded, but because lack of the requisite opposite of these failings landed one in the circumstances in the first place. Hence the common universalized claim that guilt and remorse are never appropriate emotions about an abortion is denied. They may be appropriate, and appropriately inculcated, even when the decision was the right one.

Another motivation for bringing women's rights into the discussion may be to attempt to correct the implication, carried by the killing-centered approach, that insofar as abortion is wrong, it is a wrong that only women do, or at least (given the preponderance of male doctors) that only women instigate. I do not myself believe that we can thus escape the fact that nature bears harder on women than it does on men,[7] but virtue theory can certainly correct many of the injustices that the emphasis on women's rights is rightly concerned about. With very little amendment, everything that has been said above applies to boys and men too. Although the abortion decision is, in a natural sense, the woman's decision, proper to her, boys and men are often party to it, for well or ill, and even when they are not, they are bound to have been party to the circumstances that brought it up. No less than girls and women, boys and men can, in their actions, manifest self-centeredness, callousness, and light-mindedness about life and parenthood in relation to abortion. They can be self-centered or courageous about the possibility of disability in their offspring; they need to reflect on their sexual activity and their choices, or the lack of them, about their sexual partner and contraception; they need to grow up and take responsibility for their own actions and life in relation to fatherhood. If it is true, as I maintain, that insofar as motherhood is intrinsically worthwhile, being a mother is an important purpose in women's lives, being a father (rather than a mere generator) is an important purpose in men's lives as well, and it is adolescent of men to turn a blind eye to this and pretend that they have many more important things to do.

Much more might be said, but I shall end the actual discussion of the problem of abortion here, and conclude by highlighting what I take to be its significant features. . . .

The discussion does not proceed simply by our trying to answer the question "Would a perfectly virtuous agent ever have an abortion and, if so, when?"; virtue theory is not limited to considering "Would Socrates have had an abortion if he were a raped, pregnant fifteen-year-old?" nor automatically stumped when we are considering circumstances into which no virtuous agent would have got herself. Instead, much of the discussion proceeds in the virtue- and vice-related terms whose application, in several cases, yields practical conclusions. . . . These terms are difficult to apply correctly, and anyone might challenge my application of any one of them. So, for example, I have claimed that some abortions, done for certain reasons, would be callous or light-minded; that others might indicate an appropriate modesty or humility; that others would reflect a greedy and foolish attitude to what one could expect out of life. Any of these examples may be disputed, but what is at issue is, should these difficult terms be there, or should the discussion be couched in terms that all clever adolescents can apply correctly? . . .

Proceeding as it does in the virtue- and vice-related terms, the discussion thereby, inevitably, also contains claims about what is worthwhile, serious and important, good and evil, in our lives. So, for example, I claimed that parenthood is intrinsically worthwhile, and that having a good time was a worthless end (in life, not on individual occasions); that losing a fetus is always a serious matter (albeit not a tragedy in itself in the first trimester) whereas acquiring an appendectomy scar is a trivial one; that (human) death is an evil. Once again, these are difficult matters, and anyone might challenge any one of my claims. But what is at issue is, as before, should those difficult claims be there or can one reach practical conclusions about real moral issues that are in no way determined by premises about such matters? . . .

The discussion also thereby, inevitably, contains claims about what life is like (e.g., my claim that love and friendship do not survive their parties' constantly insisting on their rights; or the claim that to demand perfection of life is to run the risk of missing out on happiness entirely). What is at issue is, should those disputable claims be there, or is our knowledge (or are our false opinions) about what life is like irrelevant to our understanding of real moral issues? . . .

Naturally, my own view is that all these concepts should be there in any discussion of real moral issues and that virtue theory, which uses all of them, is the right theory to apply to them. I do not pretend to have shown this. I realize that proponents of rival theories may say that, now that they have understood how virtue theory uses the range of concepts it draws on, they are more convinced than ever that such concepts should not figure in an adequate normative theory, because they are sectarian, or vague, or too particular, or improperly anthropocentric. . . . Or, finding many of the details of the discussion appropriate, they may agree that many, perhaps even all, of the concepts should figure, but argue that virtue theory gives an inaccurate account of the way the concepts fit together (and indeed of the concepts themselves) and that another theory provides a better account; that would be interesting to see.

NOTES

1. Judith Jarvis Thomson, "A Defense of Abortion," *Philosophy & Public Affairs* 1, no. 1 (Fall 1971): 47–66. One could indeed regard this article as proto-virtue theory (no doubt to the surprise of the author) if the concepts of callousness and kindness were allowed more weight.

2. One possible qualification: if one ties the concept of justice very closely to rights, then if women do have a moral right to terminate their pregnancies it *may* follow that in doing so they do not act unjustly. (Cf. Thomson, "A Defense of Abortion.") But it is debatable whether even that much follows.

3. This is an assumption of virtue theory, and I do not attempt to defend it here. An adequate discussion of it would require a separate article, since, although most moral philosophers would be chary of claiming that intellectual sophistication is a necessary condition of moral wisdom or virtue, most of us, from Plato onward, tend to write as if this were so. Sorting out which claims about moral knowledge are committed to this kind of elitism and which can, albeit with difficulty, be reconciled with the idea that moral knowledge can be acquired by anyone who really wants it would be a major task.

4. Mary Anne Warren, in "On the Moral and Legal Status of Abortion," *Monist* 57 (1973), sec. 1, says of the opponents of restrictive laws governing abortion that "their conviction (for the most part) is that abortion is not a *morally* serious and extremely unfortunate, even though sometimes justified, act, comparable to killing in self-defense or to letting the violinist die, but rather is closer to being a *morally neutral* act, like

cutting one's hair" (italics mine). I would like to think that no one *genuinely* believes this. But certainly in discussion, particularly when arguing against restrictive laws or the suggestion that remorse over abortion might be appropriate, I have found that some people *say* they believe it (and often cite Warren's article, albeit inaccurately, despite its age). Those who allow that it is morally serious, and far from morally neutral, have to argue against restrictive laws, or the appropriateness of remorse, on a very different ground from that laid down by the premise "The fetus is just part of the woman's body (and she has a right to determine what happens to her body and should not feel guilt about anything she does to it)."

5. I take this as a premise here, but argue for it in some detail in my *Beginning Lives* (Oxford: Basil Blackwell, 1987). In this connection I also discuss adoption and the sense in which it may be regarded as "second best," and the difficult question of whether the good of parenthood may properly be sought, or indeed bought, by surrogacy.

6. I say "some evil has probably been brought about" on the ground that (human) life is (usually) a good and hence (human) death usually an evil. The exceptions would be (*a*) where death is actually a good or a benefit, because the baby that would come to be if the life were not cut short would be better off dead than alive, and (*b*) where death, though not a good, is not an evil either, because the life that would be led (e.g., in a state of permanent coma) would not be a good. (See Philippa Foot, "Euthanasia," *Philosophy & Public Affairs* 6, no. 2 (Winter 1977): 85–112).

7. I discuss this point at greater length in *Beginning Lives*.

STUDY QUESTIONS

1. According to Hursthouse, do women's rights have anything to do with the morality of abortion?
2. According to Hursthouse, is the status of the fetus relevant to the rightness or wrongness of abortion?
3. Can a correct moral decision result in some evil?
4. In what distinctive ways, if any, does virtue ethics approach moral issues?

Famine, Affluence, and Morality

Peter Singer

What obligations do we have toward those around the globe who are suffering from a lack of food, shelter, or medical care? Does morality permit us to purchase luxuries for ourselves, our families, and our friends instead of providing needed resources to other people who are suffering in unfortunate circumstances? Peter Singer, who is Ira W. Decamp Professor of Bioethics at the University Center for Human Values at Princeton University, argues that if we can prevent something bad without thereby sacrificing anything of comparable moral worth, we ought to do so. In short, while some view contributing to relief funds as an act of charity, Singer considers such a donation as a moral duty.

As I write this, in November 1971, people are dying in East Bengal from lack of food, shelter, and medical care. The suffering and death that are occurring there now are not inevitable, not unavoidable in any fatalistic sense of the term. Constant poverty, a cyclone, and a civil war have turned at least nine million people into destitute refugees; nevertheless, it is not beyond the capacity of the richer nations to give enough assistance to reduce any further suffering to very small proportions. The decisions and actions of human beings can prevent this kind of suffering. Unfortunately, human beings have not made the necessary decisions. At the individual level, people have, with very few exceptions, not responded to the situation in any significant way. Generally speaking, people have not given large sums to relief funds; they have not written to their parliamentary representatives demanding increased government assistance; they have not demonstrated in the streets, held symbolic fasts, or done anything else directed toward providing the refugees with the means to satisfy their essential needs. At the governmental level, no government has given the sort of massive aid that would enable the refugees to survive for more than a few days. Britain, for instance, has given rather more than most countries. It has, to date, given £14,750,000. For comparative purposes, Britain's share of the nonrecoverable development costs of the Anglo-French Concorde project is already in excess of £275,000,000, and on present estimates will reach £440,000,000. The implication is that the British government values a supersonic transport more than thirty times as highly as it values the lives of the nine million refugees. Australia is another country which, on a per capita basis, is well up in the "aid to Bengal" table. Australia's aid, however, amounts to less than one-twelfth of the cost of Sydney's new opera house. The total amount given, from all sources, now stands at about £65,000,000. The

Peter Singer, "Famine, Affluence, and Morality," *Philosophy & Public Affairs*, vol. 1, no. 3 (1972). Reprinted by permission of Blackwell Publishing Ltd.

estimated cost of keeping the refugees alive for one year is £464,000,000. Most of the refugees have now been in the camps for more than six months. The World Bank has said that India needs a minimum of £300,000,000 in assistance from other countries before the end of the year. It seems obvious that assistance on this scale will not be forthcoming. India will be forced to choose between letting the refugees starve or diverting funds from her own development program, which will mean that more of her own people will starve in the future.[1]

These are the essential facts about the present situation in Bengal. So far as it concerns us here, there is nothing unique about this situation except its magnitude. The Bengal emergency is just the latest and most acute of a series of major emergencies in various parts of the world, arising both from natural and from man-made causes. There are also many parts of the world in which people die from malnutrition and lack of food independent of any special emergency. I take Bengal as my example only because it is the present concern, and because the size of the problem has ensured that it has been given adequate publicity. Neither individuals nor governments can claim to be unaware of what is happening there.

What are the moral implications of a situation like this? In what follows, I shall argue that the way people in relatively affluent countries react to a situation like that in Bengal cannot be justified; indeed, the whole way we look at moral issues—our moral conceptual scheme—needs to be altered, and with it, the way of life that has come to be taken for granted in our society.

In arguing for this conclusion I will not, of course, claim to be morally neutral. I shall, however, try to argue for the moral position that I take, so that anyone who accepts certain assumptions, to be made explicit, will, I hope, accept my conclusion.

I begin with the assumption that suffering and death from lack of food, shelter, and medical care are bad. I think most people will agree about this, although one may reach the same view by different routes. I shall not argue for this view. People can hold all sorts of eccentric positions, and perhaps from some of them it would not follow that death by

starvation is in itself bad. It is difficult, perhaps impossible, to refute such positions, and so for brevity I will henceforth take this assumption as accepted. Those who disagree need read no further.

My next point is this: if it is in our power to prevent something bad from happening, without thereby sacrificing anything of comparable moral importance, we ought, morally, to do it. By "without sacrificing anything of comparable moral importance" I mean without causing anything else comparably bad to happen, or doing something that is wrong in itself, or failing to promote some moral good, comparable in significance to the bad thing that we can prevent. This principle seems almost as uncontroversial as the last one. It requires us only to prevent what is bad, and not to promote what is good, and it requires this of us only when we can do it without sacrificing anything that is, from the moral point of view, comparably important. I could even, as far as the application of my argument to the Bengal emergency is concerned, qualify the point so as to make it: if it is in our power to prevent something very bad from happening, without thereby sacrificing anything morally significant, we ought, morally, to do it. An application of this principle would be as follows: if I am walking past a shallow pond and see a child drowning in it, I ought to wade in and pull the child out. This will mean getting my clothes muddy, but this is insignificant, while the death of the child would presumably be a very bad thing.

The uncontroversial appearance of the principle just stated is deceptive. If it were acted upon, even in its qualified form, our lives, our society, and our world would be fundamentally changed. For the principle takes, firstly, no account of proximity or distance. It makes no moral difference whether the person I can help is a neighbor's child ten yards from me or a Bengali whose name I shall never know, ten thousand miles away. Secondly, the principle makes no distinction between cases in which I am the only person who could possibly do anything and cases in which I am just one among millions in the same position.

I do not think I need to say much in defense of the refusal to take proximity and distance into account. The fact that a person is physically near to us, so that we have personal contact with him, may make it more likely that we *shall* assist him, but this does not show that we *ought* to help him rather than another who happens to be further away. If we accept any principle of impartiality, universalizability, equality, or whatever, we cannot discriminate against someone merely because he is far away from us (or we are far away from him). Admittedly, it is possible that we are in a better position to judge what needs to be done to help a person near to us than one far away, and perhaps also to provide the assistance we judge to be necessary. If this were the case, it would be a reason for helping those near to us first. This may once have been a justification for being more concerned with the poor in one's own town than with famine victims in India. Unfortunately for those who like to keep their moral responsibilities limited, instant communication and swift transportation have changed the situation. From the moral point of view, the development of the world into a "global village" has made an important, though still unrecognized, difference to our moral situation. Expert observers and supervisors, sent out by famine relief organizations or permanently stationed in famine-prone areas, can direct our aid to a refugee in Bengal almost as effectively as we could get it to someone in our own block. There would seem, therefore, to be no possible justification for discriminating on geographical grounds.

There may be a greater need to defend the second implication of my principle—that the fact that there are millions of other people in the same position, in respect to the Bengali refugees, as I am, does not make the situation significantly different from a situation in which I am the only person who can prevent something very bad from occurring. Again, of course, I admit that there is a psychological difference between the cases; one feels less guilty about doing nothing if one can point to others, similarly placed, who have also done nothing. Yet this can make no real difference to our moral obligations.[2] Should I consider that I am less obliged to pull the drowning child out of the pond if on looking around I see other people, no further away than I am, who have also noticed the child but are doing nothing? One has only to ask this question to see the absurdity of the view that numbers lessen obligation. It is a view that is an ideal excuse for inactivity; unfortunately most of the major evils—poverty, overpopulation, pollution—are problems in which everyone is almost equally involved.

The view that numbers do make a difference can be made plausible if stated in this way: if everyone in circumstances like mine gave £5 to the Bengal Relief Fund, there would be enough to provide food, shelter, and medical care for the refugees; there is no reason why I should give more than anyone else in the same circumstances as I am; therefore I have no obligation to give more than £5. Each premise in this argument is true, and the argument looks sound. It may convince us, unless we notice that it is based on a hypothetical premise, although the conclusion is not stated hypothetically. The argument would be sound if the conclusion were: if everyone in circumstances like mine were to give £5, I would have no obligation to give more than £5. If the conclusion were so stated, however, it would be obvious that the argument has no bearing on a situation in which it is not the case that everyone else gives £5. This, of course, is the actual situation. It is more or less certain that not everyone in circumstances like mine will give £5. So there will not be enough to provide the needed food, shelter, and medical care. Therefore by giving more than £5 I will prevent more suffering than I would if I gave just £5.

It might be thought that this argument has an absurd consequence. Since the situation appears to be that very few people are likely to give substantial amounts, it follows that I and everyone else in similar circumstances ought to give as much as possible, that is, at least up to the point at which by giving more one would begin to cause serious suffering for oneself and one's dependents—perhaps even beyond this point to the point of marginal utility, at which by giving more one would cause oneself and one's dependents as much suffering as one would prevent in Bengal. If everyone does this, however, there will be more than can be used for the benefit of the refugees, and some of the sacrifice will have been unnecessary. Thus, if everyone does what he ought to do, the result will not be as good as it would be if everyone did a little less than he ought to do, or if only some do all that they ought to do.

The paradox here arises only if we assume that the actions in question—sending money to the relief funds—are performed more or less simultaneously, and are also unexpected. For if it is to be expected that everyone is going to contribute something, then clearly each is not obliged to give as much as he would have been obliged to had others not been giving too. And if everyone is not acting more or less simultaneously, then those giving later will know how much more is needed, and will have no obligation to give more than is necessary to reach this amount. To say this is not to deny the principle that people in the same circumstances have the same obligations, but to point out that the fact that others have given, or may be expected to give, is a relevant circumstance: those giving after it has become known that many others are giving and those giving before are not in the same circumstances. So the seemingly absurd consequence of the principle I have put forward can occur only if people are in error about the actual circumstances—that is, if they think they are giving when others are not, but in fact they are giving when others are. The result of everyone doing what he really ought to do cannot be worse than the result of everyone doing less than he ought to do, although the result of everyone doing what he reasonably believes he ought to do could be.

If my argument so far has been sound, neither our distance from a preventable evil nor the number of other people who, in respect to that evil, are in the same situation as we are, lessens our obligation to mitigate or prevent that evil. I shall therefore take as established the principle I asserted earlier. As I have already said, I need to assert it only in its qualified form: if it is in our power to prevent something very bad from happening, without thereby sacrificing anything else morally significant, we ought, morally, to do it.

The outcome of this argument is that our traditional moral categories are upset. The traditional distinction between duty and charity cannot be drawn, or at least, not in the place we normally draw it. Giving money to the Bengal Relief Fund is regarded as an act of charity in our society. The bodies which collect money are known as "charities." These organizations see themselves in this way—if you send them a check, you will be thanked for your "generosity." Because giving money is regarded as an act of charity, it is not thought that there is anything wrong with not giving. The charitable man may be praised, but the man who is not charitable is not condemned. People do not feel in any way ashamed or guilty about spending money on new clothes or a new car instead of giving it to famine relief. (Indeed, the alternative does not occur to them.) This way of looking at the matter cannot be justified. When we buy new clothes not to keep ourselves warm but to look "well-dressed" we are not providing for any important need. We would not be sacrificing anything significant if we were to continue to wear our old clothes, and give the money to famine relief. By doing so, we would be preventing another person from starving. It follows from what I have said earlier that we ought to give money away, rather than spend it on clothes which we do not need to keep us warm. To do so is not charitable, or generous. Nor is it the kind of act which philosophers and theologians have called "supererogatory"—an act which it would be good to do, but not wrong not to do. On the contrary, we ought to give the money away, and it is wrong not to do so.

I am not maintaining that there are no acts which are charitable, or that there are no acts which it would be good to do but not wrong not to do. It may be possible to redraw the distinction between duty and charity in some other place. All I am arguing here is that the present way of drawing the distinction, which makes it an act of charity for a man living at the level of affluence which most people in the "developed nations" enjoy to give money to save someone else from starvation, cannot be supported. It is beyond the scope of my argument to consider whether the distinction should be redrawn or abolished altogether. There would be many other possible ways of drawing the distinction—for instance, one might decide that it is good to make other people as happy as possible, but not wrong not to do so.

Despite the limited nature of the revision in our moral conceptual scheme which I am proposing, the revision would, given the extent of both affluence and famine in the world today, have radical implications. These implications may lead to further objections, distinct from those I have already considered. I shall discuss two of these.

One objection to the position I have taken might be simply that it is too drastic a revision of our moral scheme. People do not ordinarily judge in the way I have suggested they should. Most people reserve their moral condemnation for those who violate some moral norm, such as the norm against taking another person's property. They do not condemn those who indulge in luxury instead of giving to famine relief. But given that I did not set out to present a morally neutral description of the way people make moral judgments, the way people do in fact judge has nothing to do with the validity of my conclusion. My conclusion follows from the principle which I advanced earlier, and unless that principle is rejected, or the arguments shown to be unsound, I think the conclusion must stand, however strange it appears.

It might, nevertheless, be interesting to consider why our society, and most other societies, do judge differently from the way I have suggested they should. In a well-known article, J. O. Urmson suggests that the imperatives of duty, which tell us what we must do, as distinct from what it would be good to do but not wrong not to do, function so as to prohibit behavior that is intolerable if men are to live together in society.[3] This may explain the origin and continued existence of the present division between acts of duty and acts of charity. Moral attitudes are shaped by the needs of society, and no doubt society needs people who will observe the rules that make social existence tolerable. From the point of view of a particular society, it is essential to prevent violations of norms against killing, stealing, and so on. It is quite inessential, however, to help people outside one's own society.

If this is an explanation of our common distinction between duty and supererogation, however, it is not a justification of it. The moral point of view requires us to look beyond the interests of our own society. Previously, as I have already mentioned, this may hardly have been feasible, but it is quite feasible now. From the moral point of view, the prevention of the starvation of millions of people outside our society must be considered at least as pressing as the upholding of property norms within our society.

It has been argued by some writers, among them Sidgwick and Urmson, that we need to have a basic moral code which is not too far beyond the capacities of the ordinary man, for otherwise there will be a general breakdown of compliance with the moral code. Crudely stated, this argument suggests that if we tell people that they ought to refrain from murder and give everything they do not really need to famine relief, they will do neither, whereas if we tell them that they ought to refrain from murder and that it is good to give to famine relief but not wrong not to do so, they will at least refrain from murder. The issue here is: Where should we draw the line between conduct that is required and conduct that is good although not required, so as to get the best possible result? This would seem to be an empirical question, although a very difficult one. One objection to the Sidgwick-Urmson line of argument is that it takes insufficient account of the effect that moral standards can have on the decisions we make. Given a society in which a wealthy man who gives five percent of his income to famine relief is regarded as most generous, it is not surprising that a proposal that we all ought to give away half our incomes will be thought to be absurdly unrealistic. In a society which held that no man should have more than enough while others have less than they need, such a proposal might seem narrow-minded. What it is possible for a man to do and what he is likely to do are both, I think, very greatly influenced by what people around him are doing and expecting him to do. In any case, the possibility that by spreading the idea that we ought to be doing very much more than we are to relieve famine we shall bring about a general breakdown of moral behavior seems remote. If the stakes are an end to widespread starvation, it is worth the risk. Finally, it should be emphasized that these considerations are relevant only to the issue of what we should require from others, and not to what we ourselves ought to do.

The second objection to my attack on the present distinction between duty and charity is one which has from time to time been made against utilitarianism. It follows from some forms of utilitarian theory that we all ought, morally, to be working full time to increase the balance of happiness over misery. The position I have taken here would not lead to this conclusion in all circumstances, for if there were no bad occurrences that we could prevent without sacrificing something of comparable moral importance, my argument would have no application. Given the present conditions in many parts of the world, however, it does follow from my argument that we ought, morally, to be working full time to relieve great suffering of the sort that occurs as a result of famine or other disasters. Of course, mitigating circumstances can be adduced—for instance, that if we wear ourselves out through overwork, we shall be less effective than we would otherwise have been. Nevertheless, when all considerations of this sort have been taken into account, the conclusion remains: we ought to be preventing as much suffering as we can without sacrificing something else of comparable moral importance. This conclusion is one which we may be reluctant to face. I cannot see, though, why it should be regarded as a criticism of the position for which I have argued, rather than a criticism of our ordinary standards of behavior. Since most people are self-interested to some degree, very few of us are likely to do everything that we ought to do. It would, however, hardly be honest to take this as evidence that it is not the case that we ought to do it.

It may still be thought that my conclusions are so wildly out of line with what everyone else thinks and has always thought that there must be something wrong with the argument somewhere. In order to show that my conclusions, while certainly contrary to contemporary Western moral standards, would not have seemed so extraordinary at other times and

in other places, I would like to quote a passage from a writer not normally thought of as a way-out radical, Thomas Aquinas. Now, according to the natural order instituted by divine providence, material goods are provided for the satisfaction of human needs. Therefore the division and appropriation of property, which proceeds from human law, must not hinder the satisfaction of man's necessity from such goods. Equally, whatever a man has in superabundance is owed, of natural right, to the poor for their sustenance. So Ambrosius says, and it is also to be found in the *Decretum Gratiani:* "The bread which you withhold belongs to the hungry; the clothing you shut away, to the naked; and the money you bury in the earth is the redemption and freedom of the penniless."[4]

I now want to consider a number of points, more practical than philosophical, which are relevant to the application of the moral conclusion we have reached. These points challenge not the idea that we ought to be doing all we can to prevent starvation, but the idea that giving away a great deal of money is the best means to this end.

It is sometimes said that overseas aid should be a government responsibility, and that therefore one ought not to give to privately run charities. Giving privately, it is said, allows the government and the noncontributing members of society to escape their responsibilities.

This argument seems to assume that the more people there are who give to privately organized famine relief funds, the less likely it is that the government will take over full responsibility for such aid. This assumption is unsupported, and does not strike me as at all plausible. The opposite view—that if no one gives voluntarily, a government will assume that its citizens are uninterested in famine relief and would not wish to be forced into giving aid—seems more plausible. In any case, unless there were a definite probability that by refusing to give one would be helping to bring about massive government assistance, people who do refuse to make voluntary contributions are refusing to prevent a certain amount of suffering without being able to point to any tangible beneficial consequence of their refusal. So the onus of showing how their refusal will bring about government action is on those who refuse to give.

I do not, of course, want to dispute the contention that governments of affluent nations should be giving many times the amount of genuine, no-strings-attached aid that they are giving now. I agree, too, that giving privately is not enough, and that we ought to be campaigning actively for entirely new standards for both public and private contributions to famine relief. Indeed, I would sympathize with someone who thought that campaigning was more important than giving oneself, although I doubt whether preaching what one does not practice would be very effective. Unfortunately, for many people the idea that "it's the government's responsibility" is a reason for not giving which does not appear to entail any political action either.

Another, more serious reason for not giving to famine relief funds is that until there is effective population control, relieving famine merely postpones starvation. If we save the Bengal refugees now, others, perhaps the children of these refugees, will face starvation in a few years' time. In support of this, one may cite the now well-known facts about the population explosion and the relatively limited scope for expanded production.

This point, like the previous one, is an argument against relieving suffering that is happening now, because of a belief about what might happen in the future; it is unlike the previous point in that very good evidence can be adduced in support of this belief about the future. I will not go into the evidence here. I accept that the earth cannot support indefinitely a population rising at the present rate. This certainly poses a problem for anyone who thinks it important to prevent famine. Again, however, one could accept the argument without drawing the conclusion that it absolves one from any obligation to do anything to prevent famine. The conclusion that should be drawn is that the best means of preventing famine, in the long run, is population control. It would then follow from the position reached earlier that one ought to be doing all one can to promote population control (unless one

held that all forms of population control were wrong in themselves, or would have significantly bad consequences). Since there are organizations working specifically for population control, one would then support them rather than more orthodox methods of preventing famine.

A third point raised by the conclusion reached earlier relates to the question of just how much we all ought to be giving away. One possibility, which has already been mentioned, is that we ought to give until we reach the level of marginal utility—that is, the level at which, by giving more, I would cause as much suffering to myself or my dependents as I would relieve by my gift. This would mean, of course, that one would reduce oneself to very near the material circumstances of a Bengali refugee. It will be recalled that earlier I put forward both a strong and a moderate version of the principle of preventing bad occurrences. The strong version, which required us to prevent bad things from happening unless in doing so we would be sacrificing something of comparable moral significance, does seem to require reducing ourselves to the level of marginal utility. I should also say that the strong version seems to me to be the correct one. I proposed the more moderate version—that we should prevent bad occurrences unless, to do so, we had to sacrifice something morally significant—only in order to show that even on this surely undeniable principle a great change in our way of life is required. On the more moderate principle, it may not follow that we ought to reduce ourselves to the level of marginal utility, for one might hold that to reduce oneself and one's family to this level is to cause something significantly bad to happen. Whether this is so I shall not discuss, since, as I have said, I can see no good reason for holding the moderate version of the principle rather than the strong version. Even if we accepted the principle only in its moderate form, however, it should be clear that we would have to give away enough to ensure that the consumer society, dependent as it is on people spending on trivia rather than giving to famine relief, would slow down and perhaps disappear entirely. There are several reasons why this would be desirable in itself. The value and necessity of economic growth are now being questioned not only by conservationists, but by economists as well.[5] There is no doubt, too, that the consumer society has had a distorting effect on the goals and purposes of its members. Yet looking at the matter purely from the point of view of overseas aid, there must be a limit to the extent to which we should deliberately slow down our economy; for it might be the case that if we gave away, say, forty percent of our Gross National Product, we would slow down the economy so much that in absolute terms we would be giving less than if we gave twenty-five percent of the much larger GNP that we would have if we limited our contribution to this smaller percentage.

I mention this only as an indication of the sort of factor that one would have to take into account in working out an ideal. Since Western societies generally consider one percent of the GNP an acceptable level for overseas aid, the matter is entirely academic. Nor does it affect the question of how much an individual should give in a society in which very few are giving substantial amounts.

It is sometimes said, though less often now than it used to be, that philosophers have no special role to play in public affairs, since most public issues depend primarily on an assessment of facts. On questions of fact, it is said, philosophers as such have no special expertise, and so it has been possible to engage in philosophy without committing oneself to any position on major public issues. No doubt there are some issues of social policy and foreign policy about which it can truly be said that a really expert assessment of the facts is required before taking sides or acting, but the issue of famine is surely not one of these. The facts about the existence of suffering are beyond dispute. Nor, I think, is it disputed that we can do something about it, either through orthodox methods of famine relief or through population control or both. This is therefore an issue on which philosophers are competent to take a position. The issue is one which faces everyone who has more money than he needs to support himself and his dependents, or who is in a position to take some sort of political action.

These categories must include practically every teacher and student of philosophy in the universities of the Western world. If philosophy is to deal with matters that are relevant to both teachers and students, this is an issue that philosophers should discuss.

Discussion, though, is not enough. What is the point of relating philosophy to public (and personal) affairs if we do not take our conclusions seriously? In this instance, taking our conclusion seriously means acting upon it. The philosopher will not find it any easier than anyone else to alter his attitudes and way of life to the extent that, if I am right, is involved in doing everything that we ought to be doing. At the very least, though, one can make a start. The philosopher who does so will have to sacrifice some of the benefits of the consumer society, but he can find compensation in the satisfaction of a way of life in which theory and practice, if not yet in harmony, are at least coming together.

NOTES

1. There was also a third possibility: that India would go to war to enable the refugees to return to their lands. Since I wrote this paper, India has taken this way out. The situation is no longer that described above, but this does not affect my argument, as the next paragraph indicates.

2. In view of the special sense philosophers often give to the term, I should say that I use "obligation" simply as the abstract noun derived from "ought," so that "I have an obligation to" means no more, and no less, than "I ought to." This usage is in accordance with the definition of "ought" given by the *Shorter Oxford English Dictionary:* "the general verb to express duty or obligation." I do not think any issue of substance hangs on the way the term is used; sentences in which I use "obligation" would all be rewritten, although somewhat clumsily, as sentences in which a clause containing "ought" replaces the term "obligation."

3. J. O. Urmson, "Saints and Heroes," in *Essays in Moral Philosophy,* ed. Abraham I. Melden (Seattle and London, 1958), p. 214. For a related but significantly different view see also Henry Sidgwick, *The Methods of Ethics,* 7th edn. (London, 1907), pp. 220–221, 492–493.

4. *Summa Theologica,* II-II, Question 66, Article 7, in *Aquinas, Selected Political Writings,* ed. A. P. d'Entreves, trans. J. G. Dawson (Oxford, 1948), p. 171.

5. See, for instance, John Kenneth Galbraith, *The New Industrial State* (Boston, 1967); and E. J. Mishan, *The Costs of Economic Growth* (London, 1967).

STUDY QUESTIONS

1. If you can prevent something bad from happening at a comparatively small cost to yourself, are you obligated to do so?
2. Is your obligation to save a drowning child affected by how often you are called on to offer such help?
3. Are you acting immorally by paying college tuition for your own children while other children have no opportunity for any schooling at all?
4. Do we have a moral obligation to try to alleviate extreme poverty in our own country before attempting to do so in other countries?

A Reply to Singer

Travis Timmerman

Peter Singer argues that you are obligated to prevent something bad from happening if you can do so without thereby sacrificing anything of comparable moral importance. For example, you are morally obligated to save a child from drowning if you can do so without inconvenience. Travis Timmerman, a graduate student at Syracuse University, argues that the strength of your obligation depends on how many children need to be saved. If the number is large, then Singer's line of reasoning would obligate you to spend your entire life saving children. Are you not entitled at some point to pursue your own interests, even if they are not as morally weighty as saving the lives of children?

1. INTRODUCTION

Peter Singer's *Famine Affluence and Morality* is undoubtedly one of the most influential and widely read pieces of contemporary philosophy. Yet, the majority of philosophers (including ethicists) reject Singer's conclusion that we are morally required to donate to aid agencies whenever we can do so without sacrificing anything nearly as important as the good that our donations could bring about. Many ignore Singer's argument simply because they believe morality would just be too demanding if it required people in affluent nations to donate significant sums of money to charity. Of course, merely rejecting Singer's conclusion because it seems absurd does not constitute a refutation of Singer's argument. More importantly, this standard demandingness objection is a particularly inappropriate dialectical move because Singer provides a valid argument for his (demanding) conclusion and, crucially, the argument only consists of

ethical premisses that Singer takes his typical readers to already accept. Singer formulates his argument as follows.

(1) Suffering and death from lack of food, shelter and medical care are bad.
(2) If it is in your power to prevent something bad from happening, without sacrificing anything nearly as important, it is wrong not to do so.
(3) By donating to aid agencies, you can prevent suffering and death from lack of food, shelter and medical care, without sacrificing anything nearly as important.
(4) Therefore, if you do not donate to aid agencies, you are doing something wrong (Singer 1972: 231–3; Singer 2009: 15–16).

If it is not true that typical readers' existing ethical commitments entail that they accept premisses one and two, then they should be able to say which

From Travis Timmerman, "Sometimes there is nothing wrong with letting a child drown," *Analysis* 75 (2015). Reprinted by permission of Oxford University Press.

premiss(es) they reject and why. Those who believe that Singer's conclusion is too demanding will need to reject premiss two. This requires addressing Singer's infamous *Drowning Child* thought experiment, which elicits a common response that Singer believes demonstrates that his readers are already committed to the truth of premiss two. As such, Singer purports to demonstrate that the ethical commitments his typical readers already accept are demanding enough to require them to donate a substantial portion of their expendable income to aid organizations. A dialectically appropriate demandingness objection would have to demonstrate why this is not the case. I aim to provide such an objection, in part, by demonstrating that the inference from the near universal intuition that we are obligated to rescue the child in *Drowning Child* to the truth of premiss two is unwarranted.

To be fair, although many philosophers do not attempt to directly engage with the argument Singer provides, many do. Those that have commonly reject premiss three (e.g. Fagelson 2009; Gomberg 2002; Schmidtz 2000: 684–9) and moral libertarians must reject premiss two (e.g. Narveson 2003; Pogge 2008). The existing arguments given in favour of rejecting premiss two appeal to the highly controversial claim that we only have a negative duty to not inflict harm on others and no positive duty to help others, even when we can do so at little or no cost to ourselves. Such views about duty strike me as highly dubious. More importantly, even if they turn out to be true, Singer might still be able to successfully argue for his conclusion since there are many ways people in affluent nations do causally contribute to the suffering of those in extreme poverty (Singer 1999; Pogge 2001; Pogge 2008).

I aim to do something different in this paper. I will grant Singer the truth of premisses one and three and that we can have positive duties to help others, even when we did not, in any way, causally contribute to the suffering we are obligated to end. In spite of this, I argue that Singer has not provided sufficient justification for the truth of premiss two. I do this by proposing a thought experiment analogous to Singer's *Drowning Child* case, which plays the dual role of blocking the inference from the common intuition in *Drowning Child* to the truth of premiss two and gives us positive reason to reject premiss two.

The paper proceeds as follows. In the next section, I review Singer's *Drowning Child* thought experiment, which he appeals to in an attempt to establish that his typical readers already accept the truth of the second premiss. In the third section, I offer my own *Drowning Children* thought experiment, which is a better analogy of the situation between people in affluent nations and those in extreme poverty than Singer's *Drowning Child*. People's intuitions in the case I provide should reveal that they think, upon reflection, premiss two is actually false. In the fourth section, I consider and rebut two objections to my argument before concluding with a heuristic for determining how much people in affluent nations are obligated to donate to aid agencies.

2. SINGER'S CASE

. . . Singer defends the claim that

> 'if it is in our power to prevent something bad from happening, without thereby sacrificing anything of comparable moral importance, we ought, morally, to do it' (1972: 231).

He argues for this by analogy, writing 'if I am walking past a shallow pond and see a child drowning in it, I ought to wade in and pull the child out. This will mean getting my clothes muddy, but this is insignificant, while the death of the child would presumably be a very bad thing' (Singer 1972: 231). He expands this defence into a thought experiment in *The Life You Can Save,* which I will refer to as *Drowning Child*:

> ***Drowning Child:*** On your way to work, you pass a small pond. On hot days, children sometimes play in the pond, which is only about knee-deep. The weather's cool today, though, and the hour is early, so you are surprised to see a child splashing about in the pond. As you get closer, you see that it is a very young child, just

a toddler, who is flailing about, unable to stay upright or walk out of the pond. You look for the parents or babysitter, but there is no one else around. The child is unable to keep his head above the water for more than a few seconds at a time. If you don't wade in and pull him out, he seems likely to drown. Wading in is easy and safe, but you will ruin the new shoes you bought only a few days ago, and get your suit wet and muddy (Singer 2009: 3).

It is supposed to be obvious that you are obligated to wade in the pond and save the child, even if doing so ruins your new shoes and suit. The best explanation of why you are obligated to save the child, Singer contends, is precisely because premiss two is true. The only additional defence provided of premiss two is a rebuttal of two objections. First, Singer claims that our proximity, in itself, to those in need is of no moral relevance (Singer 1972: 231–2). Although some deny this assumption (e.g. Kamm 1999, 2007), I will happily grant it for the sake of argument. Second, the fact that millions of others in affluent nations are also in a position to prevent children from dying in extreme poverty, but do not, does not diminish the extent to which we are obligated to provide aid. Singer rhetorically asks

'Should I consider that I am less obliged to pull the drowning child out of the pond if on looking around I see other people, no further away than I am, who have also noticed the child but are doing nothing?'

before adding

'One has only to ask this question to see the absurdity of the view that numbers lessen obligation' (Singer 1972: 233).

Although some also deny this assumption (e.g. McKinsey 1981), I again grant Singer as much.[1]

Although premiss two is admittedly *prima facie* plausible, the problem with it is that it is deceptively demanding of us as moral agents, far too demanding to be intuitively compelling. If true, we are obligated to donate our money to aid agencies whenever we can do so without sacrificing anything nearly as important as a child's life, the consequence of which Singer makes explicitly clear.

Yet if we were to take [premiss two] seriously, our lives would be changed dramatically. For while the cost of saving one child's life by a donation to an aid organization may not be great, after you have donated that sum, there remain more children in need of saving, each one of whom can be saved at a relatively small additional cost. Suppose you have just sent $200 to an agency that can, for that amount, save the life of a child in a developing country who would otherwise have died. You've done something really good, and all it has cost you is the price of some new clothes you didn't really need anyway. But don't celebrate your good deed by opening a bottle of champagne, or even going to a movie. The cost of that bottle or movie, added to what you could save by cutting down on a few other extravagances, would save the life of another child . . . So you must keep cutting back on unnecessary spending, and donating what you save, until you have reduced yourself to the point where if you give any more, you will be sacrificing something nearly as important as a child's life—like giving so much that you can no longer afford to give your children an adequate education (Singer 2009: 18).

Perhaps premiss two is true, but a proposition with such strong counterintuitive implications requires a strong defence, one that gives us reason to think that certain ordinary moral intuitions are radically misguided. Singer believes he has provided such a defence with *Drowning Child*. Aren't we morally obligated to sacrifice our new clothes to save the child *because* we are obligated to prevent something bad from happening whenever we can do so without sacrificing anything nearly as important? The short answer is 'No.' Here's why. Although Singer's description of *Drowning Child* is ahistorical, the implicit assumption is that *Drowning Child* is an anomalous event. People almost never find themselves in the situation Singer describes, so when they consider their obligations in *Drowning Child,* they implicitly assume that they have not frequently sacrificed their new clothes to save children in the past and will not need to do so frequently in the future.

Giving to aid organizations is, in this respect, unlike *Drowning Child.* Every individual in an affluent nation, so long as they have some expendable income, will always be in a position to save the lives of people living in extreme poverty by donating said income. It may be quite clear that one has a moral obligation to sacrifice $200 worth of new clothing a single time to prevent a child from drowning. It is much less clear that one is morally obligated to spend one's entire life making repeated $200 sacrifices to constantly prevent children from drowning. So, we may be obligated to save the child in *Drowning Child,* but still be disposed to believe that premiss two is false. I will expand on this asymmetry in the next section by providing an altered version of Singer's thought experiment that more closely resembles the position those in affluent nations are in with respect to providing aid to those in extreme poverty. I suspect that most people's intuitions in such a case will show that they reject premiss two of Singer's argument.

3. THE MOST RELEVANTLY ANALOGOUS CASE

People almost universally have the intuition that we are morally obligated to rescue the child in *Drowning Child,* but are not morally obligated to donate all their expendable income to aid agencies. Singer attempts to explain away this intuition as a mere psychological difference, a difference that results from our evolutionary history and socialization and not a moral difference (Singer 1972: 232–3; Singer 2009: 45–62). To a certain extent, I think Singer is successful. I grant that, *ceteris paribus,* there is no moral difference between one's obligation to save the drowning child and one's obligation to donate to aid organizations.[2] However, there *is* a moral difference

between the sacrifice required to save the child in *Drowning Child* (as it is imagined) and the sacrifice Singer believes people in affluent nations are required to make in order to donate the supposed obligatory amount to aid organizations.

This moral difference is easily overlooked because Singer's *Drowning Child* thought experiment is, in a crucial way, under-described. Once the necessary details are filled in, its inability to support premiss two will be made clear. My following *Drowning Children* case is not under-described and gives us reason to believe that there are times at which it is morally permissible to *not* prevent something bad from happening, even when one can do so at a comparably insignificant personal cost.

> *Drowning Children:* Unlucky Lisa gets a call from her 24-hr bank telling her that hackers have accessed her account and are taking $200 out of it every 5 min until Lisa shows up in person to put a hold on her account. Due to some legal loophole, the bank is not required to reimburse Lisa for any of the money she may lose nor will they. In fact, if her account is overdrawn, the bank will seize as much of her assets as is needed to pay the debt created by the hackers.
>
> Fortunately, for Lisa, the bank is just across the street from her work and she can get there in fewer than 5 min. She was even about to walk to the bank as part of her daily routine. On her way, Lisa notices a vast space of land covered with hundreds of newly formed shallow ponds, each of which contains a small child who will drown unless someone pulls them to safety.[3] Lisa knows that for each child she rescues, an extra child will live who would have otherwise died. Now, it would take Lisa approximately 5 min to pull each child to safety and, in what can only be the most horrifically surreal day of her life, Lisa has to decide how many children to rescue before entering the bank. Once she enters the bank, all the children who have not yet been rescued will drown.
>
> Things only get worse for poor Lisa. For the remainder of her life, the hackers repeat their actions on a daily basis and, every day, the

ponds adjacent to Lisa's bank are filled with drowning children.

The truth of premiss two would entail that Lisa is obligated to rescue children until almost all of her money and assets are gone. It might permit her to close her account before she is unable to rent a studio apartment and eat a healthy diet. However, it would require her to give up her house, her car, her books, her art and anything else not nearly as important as a child's life. That might not seem so counterintuitive if Lisa has to make this monumental sacrifice a single time. But, and here's the rub, premiss two would also prohibit Lisa from ever rebuilding her life. For every day Lisa earns money, she is forced to choose between saving children and letting the hackers steal from her. Lisa would only be permitted to go to the bank each day in time to maintain the things nearly as important as a child's life, which I take to be the basic necessities Lisa needs to lead a healthy life.[4]

I propose that it's a viable option that morality permits Lisa to, *at least* on 1 day over the course of her entire life, stop the hackers in time to enjoy some good that is not nearly as important as a child's life. Maybe Lisa wants to experience theatre one last time before she spends the remainder of her days pulling children from shallow ponds and stopping hackers. Given the totality of the sacrifice Lisa is making, morality intuitively permits Lisa to indulge in theatre *at least* one time in, let's say, the remaining 80 years of her life. In fact, commonsense morality should permit Lisa to indulge in these comparably morally insignificant goods a non-trivial number of times, though a single instance is all that is required to demonstrate that premiss two is false and, consequently, Singer's argument is unsound.

I have purposefully not made a suggestion as to how many (if any) children Lisa is obligated to rescue. I did so to make my argument as neutral as possible, as I want it to be consistent with any normative ethical view ranging from moral libertarianism to a view that only permits Lisa to indulge in a comparably insignificant good a single time. For what it's worth, I am inclined to hold that Lisa is obligated to rescue a great many children, though *significantly*

fewer than is required by premiss two. However, no part of my argument hinges on this claim.

4. OBJECTIONS

I now consider, and rebut, two objections to my argument.

> *First Objection: Drowning Children* really does support the truth of premiss two because Lisa *is* intuitively obligated to make the sacrifice it requires.

To be sure, impartial consequentialists will not be convinced that premiss two is false and their theory-laden intuitions may conflict with the commonsense intuition in my *Drowning Children* case. But my aim in this paper is not to provide a dialectically effective argument against this particular kind of consequentialism. Rather, my main goal is to demonstrate that *Drowning Child* does not justify premiss two in the way Singer believes it does. Specifically, Singer's argument fails to demonstrate that commonsense assumptions about morality require us to donate as much to aid agencies as his argument entails. Singer's goal was to argue for his conclusion without assuming the truth of impartial consequentialism (Singer 1999: 302–3). Unfortunately, it fails to do just that. A significantly stronger defence of premiss two is required if Singer is going to be successful in showing people like me, a commonsense consequentialist, that morality is as demanding as his argument entails.

> *Second Objection:* Our moral intuitions are not reliable.

One might resist my argument by denying that the intuitive judgments about *Drowning Children* are reliable. In fact, Singer famously rejects the reliability of intuitions about first-order normative judgments,[5] so I suspect that he too will think intuitive responses to *Drowning Children* carry little argumentative weight (Singer 1974: 516; Singer 2005; Singer and Lazari-Radek 2014: 67). Because Singer rejects the reliability of first-order normative intuitions, it might seem hypocritical of him to appeal to *Drowning Child* as a justification for premiss two, but it is not. Recall that Singer's goal was to demonstrate to non-impartial consequentialists that, by their own lights, they are obligated to donate a significant portion of their income to aid organizations (Singer 1999: 315–6, 505). That is, *Drowning Child* was invoked to make salient to people moral beliefs they supposedly already had, including the truth of premiss two. That's fair enough. The problem, though, is that I may use *Drowning Children* in the same way as Singer uses *Drowning Child*. I invoke *Drowning Children* to show that people are not committed, by their own lights, to the truth of premiss two. My argument for *that* claim need not assume that our first-order normative judgments are reliable, although I don't rule out that possibility either. More generally, one cannot call into question the reliability of our judgments in *Drowning Children* without also calling into question the reliability of our judgments in *Drowning Child*. Either our judgments in both cases are reliable and, consequently, we have reason to reject premiss two or neither is reliable and, consequently, Singer has provided no justification for premiss two.

5. CONCLUSION

If my argument is successful, it should provide compelling reason to accept the following two distinct claims. First, Singer's *Drowning Child* case actually fails to justify the truth of premiss two by his readers' own lights. People's intuition that they are obligated to save the child in Singer's case (as they imagine it) is consistent with premiss two being false. Second, my *Drowning Children* case actually provides positive reason to reject premiss two. These two claims are independent of one another and I take each to be significant in their own right. To sum up, the intuitive pull of premiss two is more apparent than real. Few moral truths may seem more obvious than that one is obligated to sacrifice $200 to save a child's life at least once. But it's far from obvious that one is obligated, for his or her entire life, to constantly sacrifice everything comparably insignificant to a child's life. The truth of the second premiss

hinges on the truth of this latter claim, not the former. How much are we obligated to donate to aid organizations? I am not sure exactly, but it should be the same amount we would be obligated to sacrifice were we to find ourselves in Lisa's position.

NOTES

1. At least, principle (9) in McKinsey's (1981) allows that numbers can lessen obligation. It also allows that they need not, depending on how other members of the group act. The relationship between group and individual obligations is a complicated one that is beyond the scope of this paper.
2. I also grant that *some* people's differing judgments about these two cases are the result of such people mistaking mere psychological differences for moral differences. For instance, people tend to be more emotionally moved to help a child they see suffering than when they are considering suffering in the abstract.
3. I am imagining that Lisa is the only person on the scene. I grant Singer that the number of people who are in a position to help, but won't, does not diminish Lisa's obligation to help. Readers who believe otherwise should feel free to amend *Drowning Children* to account for this. To amend it accordingly, we could imagine that there are countless other people on the scene who are also in a position to save the drowning children, many of whom could do so at a cost less significant than the one Lisa would incur. Some of these people are helping, but most are not. Many of these children will not be saved and, again, Lisa knows that for each child she rescues, an extra child will live who would have otherwise drowned. Those who believe that the presence of other people in a position to help *does* reduce the extent to which Lisa is obligated to help will also have to reject premiss two of Singer's argument.
4. It might also include providing for those to whom Lisa (might) have special obligations, such as children or siblings. To avoid this complication, I will stipulate that Lisa has no family and no one else depends on her in any significant way.
5. It is worth noting that Singer is not similarly skeptical of the reliability of intuitions about abstract moral principles (Singer 2011; Singer and Lazari-Radek 2014: Ch. 3). So, his confidence in premiss two presumably does not depend on his intuitions about *Drowning Child,* but rather, on the intuitive plausibility he assigns to premiss two considered in isolation.

REFERENCES

Fagelson, D. 2009. The ethics of assistance: what's the good of it? In *Peter Singer Under Fire: The Moral Iconoclast Faces His Critics,* ed. J.A. Schaler, 329–50. Chicago: Open Court Press.

Gomberg, P. 2002. The fallacy of philanthropy. *Canadian Journal of Philosophy* 32: 29–66.

Kamm, F. M. 1999. Famine ethics: the problem of distance in morality and Singer's ethical theory. In *Singer and His Critics,* ed. D. Jamieson, 269–332. Malden: Blackwell Publishers.

Kamm, F. M. 2007. *Intricate Ethics: Rights, Responsibilities, and Permissible Harm.* New York: Oxford University Press.

McKinsey, M. 1981. Obligations to the starving. *Nous* 15: 309–23.

Narveson, J. 2003. We don't owe them a thing! a tough-minded but soft-hearted view of aid to the faraway needy. *The Monist* 86: 419–33.

Pogge, T. 2001. Priorities of global justice. *Metaphilosophy* 32: 6–24.

Pogge, T. 2008. *World Poverty and Human Rights.* Malden: Polity Press.

Schmidtz, D. 2000. Islands in a sea of obligation: an essay on the duty to rescue. *Law and Philosophy* 19: 683–705.

Singer, P. 1972. Famine, affluence and morality. *Philosophy and Public Affairs* 3: 229–43.

Singer, P. 1974. Sidgwick and reflective equilibrium. *The Monist* 58: 490–517.

Singer, P. 1999. A response. In *Singer and His Critics,* ed. D. Jamieson, 269–332. Malden: Blackwell Publishers.

Singer, P. 2005. Ethics and intuitions. *The Journal of Ethics* 9: 331–52.

Singer, P. 2009. *The Life You Can Save.* New York: Random House.

Singer, P. 2011. *The Expanding Circle: Ethics, Evolution, and Moral Progress.* Princeton: Princeton University Press.

Singer, P. and K. Lazari-Radek. 2014. *The Point of View of the Universe: Sidgwick and Contemporary Ethics.* New York: Oxford University Press.

STUDY QUESTIONS

1. If you buy a book instead of giving the money to help others in need, are you acting morally?
2. If you spend time studying philosophy instead of helping others in need, are you acting morally?
3. If you pay to send your child to college while other children are too poor to obtain food or clothing, are you acting morally?
4. When, if ever, are you entitled to pursue your own interests while you could, instead, be helping others in need of assistance?

The Trolley Problem

Judith Jarvis Thomson

Judith Jarvis Thomson, Professor Emerita at the Massachusetts Institute of Technology, considers the moral complexities of a hypothetical case that has become well-known as the "trolley problem." It concerns the morality of turning a trolley from a track where it would run down five workmen onto a spur of track where it would run down only one. Is it permissible to turn the trolley? Is it permissible not to turn the trolley? Thomson, appealing to the concept of rights, concludes that you may, but need not, turn the trolley.

I

Some years ago Philippa Foot drew attention to an extraordinarily interesting problem.[1] Suppose you are the driver of a trolley. The trolley rounds a bend, and there come into view ahead five track workmen, who have been repairing the track. The track goes through a bit of a valley at that point, and the sides are steep, so you must stop the trolley if you are to avoid running the five men down. You step on the brakes, but alas they don't work. Now you suddenly see a spur of track leading off to the right. You can turn the trolley onto it, and thus save the five men on the straight track ahead. Unfortunately, Mrs. Foot has arranged that there is one track workman on that spur of track. He can no more get off the track in time than the five can, so you will kill him if you turn the trolley onto him. Is it morally permissible for you to turn the trolley?

Everybody to whom I have put this hypothetical case says, Yes, it is.[2] Some people say something stronger than that it is morally *permissible* for you to turn the trolley: They say that morally speaking, you must turn it—that morality requires you to do so. Others do not agree that morality requires you to turn the trolley, and even feel a certain discomfort at the idea of turning it. But everybody says that it is true, at a minimum, that you *may* turn it—that it would not be morally wrong for you to do so.

Now consider a second hypothetical case. This time you are to imagine yourself to be a surgeon, a truly great surgeon. Among other things you do, you transplant organs, and you are such a great surgeon that the organs you transplant always take. At the moment you have five patients who need organs. Two need one lung each, two need a kidney each, and the fifth needs a heart. If they do not get those organs today, they will all die; if you find organs for them today, you can transplant the organs and they will all live. But where to find the lungs, the kidneys, and the heart? The time is almost up when a report is brought to you that a young man who has just

From *The Yale Law Journal, 94* (1985) by permission of The Yale Law Journal and Fred. B. Rothman & Company. Minor alterations in some footnotes have been made for the sake of uniformity and accessibility.

come into your clinic for his yearly check-up has exactly the right blood-type, and is in excellent health. Lo, you have a possible donor. All you need do is cut him up and distribute *his* parts among the five who need them. You ask, but he says, "Sorry. I deeply sympathize, but no." Would it be morally permissible for you to operate anyway? Everybody to whom I have put this second hypothetical case says, No, it would not be morally permissible for you to proceed.

Here then is Mrs. Foot's problem: *Why* is it that the trolley driver may turn his trolley, though the surgeon may not remove the young man's lungs, kidneys, and heart?[3] In both cases, one will die if the agent acts, but five will live who would otherwise die—a net saving of four lives. What difference in the other facts of these cases explains the moral difference between them? I fancy that the theorists of tort and criminal law will find this problem as interesting as the moral theorist does.

II

Mrs. Foot's own solution to the problem she drew attention to is simple, straightforward, and very attractive. She would say: Look, the surgeon's choice is between operating, in which case he kills one, and not operating, in which case he lets five die; and killing is surely worse than letting die[4]—indeed, so much worse that we can even say

(I) Killing one is worse than letting five die.

So the surgeon must refrain from operating. By contrast, the trolley driver's choice is between turning the trolley, in which case he kills one, and not turning the trolley, in which case he does not *let five die,* he positively *kills* them. Now surely we can say

(II) Killing five is worse than killing one.

But then that is why the trolley driver may turn his trolley: He would be doing what is worse if he fails to turn it, since if he fails to turn it he kills five.

I do think that that is an attractive account of the matter. It seems to me that if the surgeon fails to operate, he does not kill his five patients who need parts; he merely lets them die. By contrast, if the driver fails to turn his trolley, he does not merely let the five track workmen die; he drives his trolley into them, and thereby kills them.

But there is good reason to think that this problem is not so easily solved as that.

Let us begin by looking at a case that is in some ways like Mrs. Foot's story of the trolley driver. I will call her case *Trolley Driver;* let us now consider a case I will call *Bystander at the Switch.* In that case you have been strolling by the trolley track, and you can see the situation at a glance: The driver saw the five on the track ahead, he stamped on the brakes, the brakes failed, so he fainted. What to do? Well, here is the switch, which you can throw, thereby turning the trolley yourself. Of course you will kill one if you do. But I should think you may turn it all the same.[5]

Some people may feel a difference between these two cases. In the first place, the trolley driver is, after all, captain of the trolley. He is charged by the trolley company with responsibility for the safety of his passengers and anyone else who might be harmed by the trolley he drives. The bystander at the switch, on the other hand, is a private person who just happens to be there.

Second, the driver would be driving a trolley into the five if he does not turn it, and the bystander would not—the bystander will do the five no harm at all if he does not throw the switch.

I think it right to feel these differences between the cases.

Nevertheless, my own feeling is that an ordinary person, a mere bystander, may intervene in such a case. If you see something, a trolley, a boulder, an avalanche, heading towards five, and you can deflect it onto one, it really does seem that—other things being equal—it would be permissible for you to *take* charge, *take* responsibility, and deflect the thing, whoever you may be. Of course you run a moral risk if you do, for it might be that, unbeknownst to you, other things are not equal. It might be, that is, that there is some relevant difference between the five on the one hand, and the one on the other, which would make it morally preferable that the five be hit by the trolley than that the one be hit by it. That would be so if, for example, the five are not track workmen at all, but Mafia members in workmen's clothing, and they have tied the one workman to the right-hand track in the hope that you would turn the trolley onto him. I won't canvass all the many kinds of possibilities, for in fact the moral risk is the same whether you are the trolley driver, or a bystander at the switch.

Moreover, second, we might well wish to ask ourselves what exactly is the difference between what the driver would be doing if he failed to turn the trolley and what the bystander would be doing if he failed to throw the switch. As I said, the driver would be driving a trolley into the five; but what exactly would his driving the trolley into the five consist in? Why, just sitting there, doing nothing! If the driver does just sit there, doing nothing, then that will have been how come he drove his trolley into the five.

I do not mean to make much of that fact about what the driver's driving his trolley into the five would consist in, for it seems to me to be right to say that if he does not turn the trolley, he does drive his trolley into them, and does thereby kill them. (Though this does seem to me to be right, it is not easy to say exactly what makes it so.) By contrast, if the bystander does not throw the switch, he drives no trolley into anybody, and he kills nobody.

But as I said, my own feeling is that the bystander *may* intervene. Perhaps it will seem to some even less clear that morality requires him to turn the trolley than that morality requires the driver to turn the trolley; perhaps some will feel even more discomfort at the idea of the bystander's turning the trolley than at the idea of the driver's turning the trolley. All the same, I shall take it that he *may.*

If he may, there is serious trouble for Mrs. Foot's thesis (I). It is plain that if the bystander throws the switch, he causes the trolley to hit the one, and thus he kills the one. It is equally plain that if the bystander does not throw the switch, he does not cause the trolley to hit the five, he does not kill the five, he merely fails to save them—he lets them die.

His choice therefore is between throwing the switch, in which case he kills one, and not throwing the switch, in which case he lets five die. If thesis (I) were true, it would follow that the bystander may not throw the switch, and that I am taking to be false.

III

I have been arguing that

> (I) Killing one is worse than letting five die

is false, and a fortiori that it cannot be appealed to to explain why the surgeon may not operate in the case I shall call *Transplant.*

I think it pays to take note of something interesting which comes out when we pay close attention to

> (II) Killing five is worse than killing one.

For let us ask ourselves how we would feel about *Transplant* if we made a certain addition to it. In telling you that story, I did not tell you why the surgeon's patients are in need of parts. Let us imagine that the history of their ailments is as follows. The surgeon was badly overworked last fall—some of his assistants in the clinic were out sick, and the surgeon had to take over their duties dispensing drugs. While feeling particularly tired one day, he became careless, and made the terrible mistake of dispensing chemical X to five of the day's patients. Now chemical X works differently in different people. In some it causes lung failure, in others kidney failure, in others heart failure. So these five patients who now need parts need them because of the surgeon's carelessness. Indeed, if he does not get them the parts they need, so that they die, he will have killed them. Does that make a moral difference? That is, does the fact that he will have killed the five if he does nothing make it permissible for him to cut the young man up and distribute his parts to the five who need them?

We could imagine it to have been worse. Suppose what had happened was this: The surgeon was badly overextended last fall, he had known he was named a beneficiary in his five patients' wills, and it swept over him one day to give them chemical X to kill them. Now he repents, and would save them if he could. If he does not save them, he will positively have murdered them. Does *that* fact make it permissible for him to cut the young man up and distribute his parts to the five who need them?

I should think plainly not. The surgeon must not operate on the young man. If he can find no other way of saving his five patients, he will *now* have to let them die—despite the fact that if he now lets them die, he will have killed them.

We tend to forget that some killings themselves include lettings die, and do include them where the act by which the agent kills takes time to cause death—time in which the agent can intervene but does not.

In face of these possibilities, the question arises what we should think of thesis (II), since it *looks* as if it tells us that the surgeon ought to operate, and thus that he may permissibly do so, since if he operates he kills only one instead of five.

There are two ways in which we can go here. First, we can say: (II) does tell us that the surgeon ought to operate, and that shows it is false. Second, we can say: (II) does not tell us that the surgeon ought to operate, and it is true.

For my own part, I prefer the second. If Alfred kills five and Bert kills only one, then questions of motive apart, and other things being equal, what Alfred did *is* worse than what Bert did. If the surgeon does not operate, so that he kills five, then it will later be true that he did something worse than he would have done if he had operated, killing only one—especially if his killing of the five was murder, committed out of a desire for money, and his killing of the one would have been, though misguided and wrongful, nevertheless a well-intentioned effort to save five lives. Taking this line would, of course, require saying that assessments of which acts are worse than which other acts do not by themselves settle the question what it is permissible for an agent to do.

But it might be said that we ought to by-pass (II), for perhaps what Mrs. Foot would have offered us as an explanation of why the driver may turn the trolley in *Trolley Driver* is not (II) itself, but something more complex, such as

> (II') If a person is faced with a choice between doing something *here and now* to five, by the doing of which he will kill them, and doing something else *here and now* to one, by the doing of which he will kill only the one, then (other things being equal) he ought to choose the second alternative rather than the first.

We may presumably take (II') to tell us that the driver ought to, and hence permissibly may, turn the trolley in *Trolley Driver,* for we may presumably view the driver as confronted with a choice between here and now driving his trolley into five, and here and now driving his trolley into one. And at the same time, (II') tells us nothing at all about what the surgeon ought to do in *Transplant,* for he is not confronted with such a choice. If the surgeon operates, he does do something by the doing of which he will kill only one; but if the surgeon does not operate, he does not do something by the doing of which he kills five; he merely fails to do something by the doing of which he would make it be the case that he has not killed five.

I have no objection to this shift in attention from (II) to (II'). But we should not overlook an interesting question that lurks here. As it might be put: *Why should the present tense matter so much?* Why should a person prefer killing one to killing five if the alternatives are wholly in front of him, but not (or anyway, not in every case) where one of them is partly behind him? I shall come back to this question briefly later.

Meanwhile, however, even if (II') can be appealed to in order to explain why the trolley driver may turn his trolley, that would leave it entirely open why the bystander at the switch may turn *his* trolley. For he does not drive a trolley into each of five if he refrains from turning the trolley; he merely lets the trolley drive into each of them.

So I suggest we set *Trolley Driver* aside for the time being. What I shall be concerned with is a first cousin of Mrs. Foot's problem, viz.: Why is it that the bystander may turn his trolley, though the surgeon may not remove the young man's lungs, kidneys, and heart? Since *I* find it particularly puzzling that the bystander may turn his trolley, I am inclined to call this The Trolley Problem. Those who find it particularly puzzling that the surgeon may not operate are cordially invited to call it The Transplant Problem instead.

IV

It should be clear, I think, that "kill" and "let die" are too blunt to be useful tools for the solving of this problem. We ought to be looking within killings and savings for the ways in which the agents would be carrying them out.

It would be no surprise. I think, if a Kantian idea occurred to us at this point. Kant said: "Act so that you treat humanity, whether in your own person or in that of another, always as an end and never as a means only." It is striking, after all, that the surgeon who proceeds in *Transplant* treats the young man he cuts up "as a means only": He literally uses the young man's body to save his five, and does so without the young man's consent. And perhaps we may say that the agent in *Bystander at the Switch* does not use his victim to save his five, or (more generally) treat his victim as a means only, and that that is why he (unlike the surgeon) may proceed.

But what exactly is it to treat a person as a means only, or to use a person? And why exactly is it wrong to do this? These questions do not have obvious answers.[6]

Suppose an agent is confronted with a choice between doing nothing, in which case five die, or engaging in a certain course of action, in which case the five live, but one dies. Then perhaps we can say: If the agent chooses to engage in the course of action, then he uses the one to save the five only if, had the one gone out of existence just before the agent started, the agent would have been unable to save the five. That is true of the surgeon in *Transplant*. He needs the young man if he is to save his five; if the young man goes wholly out of existence just before the surgeon starts to operate, then the surgeon cannot

save his five. By contrast, the agent in *Bystander at the Switch* does not need the one track workman on the right-hand track if he is to save his five; if the one track workman goes wholly out of existence before the bystander starts to turn the trolley, then the bystander *can* all the same save his five. So here, anyway is a striking difference between the cases.

It does seem to me right to think that solving this problem requires attending to the means by which the agent would be saving his five if he proceeded. But I am inclined to think that this is an overly simple way of taking account of the agent's means.

One reason for thinking so[7] comes out as follows. You have been thinking of the tracks in *Bystander at the Switch* as not merely diverging, but continuing to diverge, as in the following picture:

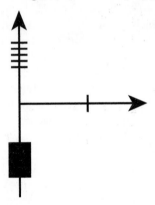

Consider now what I shall call "the loop variant" on this case, in which the tracks do not continue to diverge—they circle back, as in the following picture:

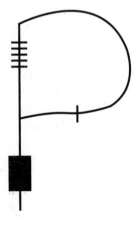

Let us now imagine that the five on the straight track are thin, but thick enough so that although all five will be killed if the trolley goes straight, the bodies of the five will stop it, and it will therefore not reach the one. On the other hand, the one on the right-hand track is fat, so fat that his body will by itself stop the trolley, and the trolley will therefore not reach the five. May the agent turn the trolley? Some people feel more discomfort at the idea of turning the trolley in the loop variant than in the original *Bystander at the Switch*. But we cannot really suppose that the presence or absence of that extra bit of track makes a major moral difference as to what an agent may do in these cases, and it really does seem right to think (despite the discomfort) that the agent may proceed.

On the other hand, we should notice that the agent here needs the one (fat) track workman on the right-hand track if he is to save his five. If the one goes wholly out of existence just before the agent starts to turn the trolley, then the agent cannot save his five[8]—just as the surgeon in *Transplant* cannot save his five if the young man goes wholly out of existence just before the surgeon starts to operate.

Indeed, I should think that there is no plausible account of what is involved in, or what is necessary for, the application of the notions "treating a person as a means only," or "using one to save five," under which the surgeon would be doing this whereas the agent in this variant of *Bystander at the Switch* would not be. If that is right, then appeals to these notions cannot do the work being required of them here.

V

Suppose the bystander at the switch proceeds: He throws the switch, thereby turning the trolley onto the right-hand track, thereby causing the one to be hit by the trolley, thereby killing him—but saving the five on the straight track. There are two facts about what he does which seem to me to explain the moral difference between what he does and what the agent in *Transplant* would be doing if *he* proceeded. In the first place, the bystander saves his five by making something that threatens them instead threaten one.

Second, the bystander does not do that by means which themselves constitute an infringement of any right of the one's.

As is plain, then, my hypothesis as to the source of the moral difference between the cases makes appeal to the concept of a right. My own feeling is that solving this problem requires making appeal to that concept—or to some other concept that does the same kind of work.[9] Indeed, I think it is one of the many reasons why this problem is of such interest to moral theory that it does force us to appeal to that concept; and by the same token, that we learn something from it about that concept.

Let us begin with an idea, held by many friends of rights, which Ronald Dworkin expressed crisply in a metaphor from bridge: Rights "trump" utilities.[10] That is, if one would infringe a right in or by acting, then it is not sufficient justification for acting that one would thereby maximize utility. It seems to me that something like this must be correct.

Consideration of this idea suggests the possibility of a very simple solution to the problem. That is, it might be said (i) The reason why the surgeon may not proceed in *Transplant* is that if he proceeds, he maximizes utility, for he brings about a net saving of four lives, but in so doing he would infringe a right of the young man's.

Which right? Well, we might say: The right the young man has against the surgeon that the surgeon not kill him—thus a right in the cluster of rights that the young man has in having a right to life.

Solving this problem requires being able to explain also why the bystander may proceed in *Bystander at the Switch*. So it might be said (ii) The reason why the bystander may proceed is that if he proceeds, he maximizes utility, for he brings about a net saving of four lives, and in so doing he does *not* infringe any right of the one track workman's.

But I see no way—certainly there is no easy way—of establishing that these ideas are true.

Is it clear that the bystander would infringe no right of the one track workman's if he turned the trolley? Suppose there weren't anybody on the straight track, and the bystander turned the trolley onto the right-hand track, thereby killing the one, but not saving anybody, since nobody was at risk, and thus nobody needed saving. Wouldn't that infringe a right of the one workman's, a right in the cluster of rights that he has in having a right to life?

So should we suppose that the fact that there are five track workmen on the straight track who are in need of saving makes the one lack that right—which he would have had if that had not been a fact?

But then why doesn't the fact that the surgeon has five patients who are in need of saving make the young man also lack that right?

I think some people would say there is good (excellent, conclusive) reason for thinking that the one track workman lacks the right (given there are five on the straight track) lying in the fact that (given there are five on the straight track) it is morally permissible to turn the trolley onto him. But if your reason for thinking the one lacks the right is that it is permissible to turn the trolley onto him, then you can hardly go on to explain its being permissible to turn the trolley onto him by appeal to the fact that he lacks the right. It pays to stress this point: If you want to say, as (ii) does, that the bystander may proceed because he maximizes utility and infringes no right, then you need an independent account of what makes it be the case that he infringes no right—independent, that is, of its being the case that he may proceed.

There is *some* room for maneuver here. Any plausible theory of rights must make room for the possibility of waiving a right, and within that category, for the possibility of failing to have a right by virtue of assumption of risk; and it might be argued that that is what is involved here, i.e., that track workmen know of the risks of the job, and consent to run them when signing on for it.

But that is not really an attractive way of dealing with this difficulty. Track workmen certainly do not explicitly consent to being run down with trolleys when doing so will save five who are on some other track—certainly they are not asked to consent to this at the time of signing on for the job. And I doubt that they consciously assume the risk of it at that or any other time. And in any case, what if the six people involved had not been track workmen? What if they had been young children? What if they had been people who had been shoved out of helicopters? Wouldn't it all the same be permissible to turn the trolley?

So it is not clear what (independent) reason could be given for thinking that the bystander will infringe no right of the one's if he throws the switch.

I think, moreover, that there is *some* reason to think that the bystander will infringe a right of the one if he throws the switch, even though it is permissible for him to do so. What I have in mind issues simply from the fact that if the bystander throws the switch, then he does what will kill the one. Suppose the bystander proceeds, and that the one is now dead. The bystander's motives were, of course, excellent—he acted with a view to saving five. But the one did not volunteer his life so that the five might live; the bystander volunteered it for him. The bystander made him pay with his life for the bystander's saving of the five. This consideration seems to me to lend some weight to the idea that the bystander did do him a wrong—a wrong it was morally permissible to do him, since five were saved, but a wrong *to him* all the same.

Consider again that lingering feeling of discomfort (which, as I said, some people do feel) about what the bystander does if he turns the trolley. No doubt it is permissible to turn the trolley, but still . . . but still. . . . People who feel this discomfort also think that, although it is permissible to turn the trolley, it is not morally required to do so. My own view is that they are right to feel and think these things. We would be able to explain why this is so if we supposed that if the bystander turns the trolley, then he does do the one track workman a wrong—if we supposed, in particular, that he infringes a right of the one track workman's which is in that cluster of rights which the workman has in having a right to life.[11]

I do not for a moment take myself to have established that (ii) is false. I have wished only to draw attention to the difficulty that lies ahead of a person who thinks (ii) true, and also to suggest that there is some reason to think that the bystander would infringe a right of the one's if he proceeded, and thus some reason to think that (ii) is false. It can easily be seen that if there is some reason to think the bystander would infringe a right of the one's, then there is also some reason to think that (i) is false—since if the bystander does infringe a right of the one's if he proceeds, and may nevertheless proceed, then it cannot be the fact that the surgeon infringes a right of the young man's if *he* proceeds which makes it impermissible for *him* to do so.

Perhaps a friend of (i) and (ii) can establish that they are true. I propose that, just in case he can't, we do well to see if there isn't some other way of solving this problem than by appeal to them. In particular, I propose we grant that both the bystander and the surgeon would infringe a right of their ones, a right in the cluster of rights that the ones' have in having a right to life, and that we look for some *other* difference between the cases which could be appealed to to explain the moral difference between them.

Notice that accepting this proposal does not commit us to rejecting the idea expressed in that crisp metaphor of Dworkin's. We can still say that rights trump utilities—if we can find a further feature of what the bystander does if he turns the trolley (beyond the fact that he maximizes utility) which itself trumps the right, and thus makes it permissible to proceed.

VI

As I said, my own feeling is that the trolley problem can be solved only by appeal to the concept of a right—but not by appeal to it in as simple a way as that discussed in the preceding section. What we were attending to in the preceding section was only the fact that the agents would be killing and saving if they proceeded; what we should be attending to is the means by which they would kill and save.[12] (It is very tempting, because so much simpler, to regard a human act as a solid nugget, without internal structure, and to try to trace its moral value to the shape of its surface, as it were. The trolley problem seems to me to bring home that that will not do.)

I said earlier that there seem to me to be two crucial facts about what the bystander does if he proceeds in *Bystander at the Switch*. In the first place, he saves his five by making something that threatens them instead threaten the one. And second, he does not do that by means which themselves constitute infringements of any right of the one's.

Let us begin with the first.

If the surgeon proceeds in *Transplant,* he plainly does not save his five by making something that threatens them instead threaten one. It is organ failure that threatens his five, and it is not *that* which he makes threaten the young man if he proceeds.

Consider another of Mrs. Foot's cases, which I shall call *Hospital*.

> Suppose [Mrs. Foot says] that there are five patients in a hospital whose lives could be saved by the manufacture of a certain gas, but that this will inevitably release lethal fumes into the room of another patient whom for some reason we are unable to move.[13]

Surely it would not be permissible for us to manufacture the gas.

In *Transplant* and *Hospital,* the five at risk are at risk from their ailments, and this might be thought to make a difference. Let us by-pass it. In a variant on *Hospital*—which I shall call *Hospital'*—all six patients are convalescing. The five at risk are at risk, not from their ailments, but from the ceiling of their room, which is about to fall on them. We can prevent this by pumping on a ceiling-support-mechanism: but doing so will inevitably release lethal fumes into the room of the sixth. Here too it is plain we may not proceed.

Contrast a case in which lethal fumes are being released by the heating system in the basement of a building next door to the hospital. They are headed towards the room of five. We can deflect them towards the room of one. Would that be permissible? I should think it would be—the case seems to be in all relevant respects like *Bystander at the Switch*.

In *Bystander at the Switch,* something threatens five, and if the agent proceeds, he saves the five by making that very thing threaten the one instead of the five. That is not true of the agents in *Hospital'* or *Hospital* or *Transplant*. In *Hospital'* for example, what threatens the five is the ceiling, and the agent does not save them by making *it* threaten the one, he saves them by doing what will make something wholly different (some lethal fumes) threaten the one.

Why is this difference morally important? Other things being equal, to kill a man is to infringe his right to life, and we are therefore morally barred from killing. It is not enough to justify killing a person that if we do so, five others will be saved: To say that if we do so, five others will be saved is merely to say that utility will be maximized if we proceed, and that is not by itself sufficient to justify proceeding. Rights trump utilities. So if that is all that can be said in defense of killing a person, then killing that person is not permissible.

But that five others will be saved is not all that can be said in defense of killing in *Bystander at the Switch*. The bystander who proceeds does not merely minimize the number of deaths which get caused: He minimizes the number of deaths which get caused by something that already threatens people, and that will cause deaths whatever the bystander does.

The bystander who proceeds does not make something be a threat to people which would otherwise not be a threat to anyone; he makes be a threat to fewer what is already a threat to more. We might speak here of a "distributive exemption," which permits arranging that something that will do harm anyway shall be better distributed than it otherwise would be—shall (in *Bystander at the Switch*) do harm to fewer rather than more. Not just any distributive intervention is permissible: It is not in general morally open to us to make one die to save five. But other things being equal, it is not morally required of us that we let a burden descend out of the blue onto five when we can make it instead descend onto one.

I do not find it clear why there should be an exemption for, and only for, making a burden which is descending onto five descend, instead, onto one. That there is seems to me very plausible, however. On the one hand, the agent who acts under this exemption makes be a threat to one something that is *already* a threat to more, and thus something that will do harm *whatever* he does; on the other hand, the exemption seems to allow those acts which intuition tells us are clearly permissible, and to rule out those acts which intuition tells us are clearly impermissible.

VII

More precisely, it is not morally required of us that we let a burden descend out of the blue onto five when we

can make it instead descend onto one *if* we can make it descend onto the one by means which do not themselves constitute infringements of rights of the one.

Consider a case—which I shall call *Fat Man*—in which you are standing on a footbridge over the trolley track. You can see a trolley hurtling down the track, out of control. You turn around to see where the trolley is headed, and there are five workmen on the track where it exits from under the footbridge. What to do? Being an expert on trolleys, you know of one certain way to stop an out-of-control trolley: Drop a really heavy weight in its path. But where to find one? It just so happens that standing next to you on the footbridge is a fat man, a really fat man. He is leaning over the railing, watching the trolley; all you have to do is to give him a little shove, and over the railing he will go, onto the track in the path of the trolley. Would it be permissible for you to do this? Everybody to whom I have put this case says it would not be. But why?

Suppose the agent proceeds. He shoves the fat man, thereby toppling him off the footbridge into the path of the trolley, thereby causing him to be hit by the trolley, thereby killing him—but saving the five on the straight track. Then it is true of this agent, as it is true of the agent in *Bystander at the Switch,* that he saves his five by making something which threatens them instead threaten one.

But *this* agent does so by means which themselves constitute an infringement of a right of the one's. For shoving a person is infringing a right of his. So also is toppling a person off a footbridge.

I should stress that doing these things is infringing a person's rights even if doing them does not cause his death—even if doing them causes him no harm at all. As I shall put it, shoving a person, toppling a person off a footbridge, are *themselves* infringements of rights of his. A theory of rights ought to give an account of what makes it be the case that doing either of these things is itself an infringement of a right of his. But I think we may take it to be a datum that it is, the job which confronts the theorist of rights being, not to establish that it is, but rather to explain why it is.

Consider by contrast the agent in *Bystander at the Switch*. He too, if he proceeds, saves five by making something that threatens them instead threaten one. But the means he takes to make that be the case are these: Turn the trolley onto the right-hand track. And turning the trolley onto the right-hand track is not *itself* an infringement of a right of anybody's. The agent would do the one no wrong at all if he turned the trolley onto the right-hand track, and by some miracle the trolley did not hit him.

We might of course have imagined it not necessary to shove the fat man. We might have imagined that all you need do to get the trolley to threaten him instead of the five is to wobble the handrail, for the handrail is low, and he is leaning on it, and wobbling it will cause him to fall over and off. Wobbling the handrail would be impermissible, I should think—no less so than shoving. But then there is room for an objection to the idea that the contrast I point to will help explain the moral differences among these cases. For it might be said that if you wobble the handrail, thereby getting the trolley to threaten the one instead of the five, then the means you take to get this to be the case are just these: Wobble the handrail. But doing that is not *itself* an infringement of a right of anybody's. You would do the fat man no wrong at all if you wobbled the handrail and no harm came to him in consequence of your doing so. In this respect, then, your situation seems to be exactly like that of the agent in *Bystander at the Switch*. Just as the means he would be taking to make the trolley threaten one instead of five would not constitute an infringement of a right, so also would the means you would be taking to make the trolley threaten one instead of five not constitute an infringement of a right.

What I had in mind, however, is a rather tighter notion of "means" than shows itself in this objection. By hypothesis, wobbling the handrail will cause the fat man to topple onto the track in the path of the trolley, and thus will cause the trolley to threaten him instead of the five. But the trolley will not threaten him instead of the five unless wobbling the handrail does cause him to topple. Getting the trolley to threaten the fat man instead of the five *requires* getting him into its path. You get the trolley to threaten him instead of them by wobbling the handrail only if, and only because, by wobbling the handrail you topple him into the path of the trolley.

What I had in mind, then, is a notion of "means" which comes out as follows. Suppose you get a trolley to threaten one instead of five by wobbling a handrail. The means you take to get the trolley to threaten the one instead of the five include wobbling the handrail, *and* all those further things that you have to succeed in doing by wobbling the handrail if the trolley is to threaten the one instead of the five.

So the means by which the agent in *Fat Man* gets the trolley to threaten one instead of five include toppling the fat man off the footbridge; and doing that is itself an infringement of a right of the fat man's. By contrast, the means by which the agent in *Bystander at the Switch* gets the trolley to threaten one instead of five include no more than getting the trolley off the straight track onto the right-hand track; and doing that is not itself an infringement of a right of anybody's. . . .

X

If these ideas are correct, then we have a handle on anyway some of the troublesome cases in which people make threats. Suppose a villain says to us "I will cause a ceiling to fall on five unless you send lethal fumes into the room of one." Most of us think it would not be permissible for us to accede to this threat. Why? We may think of the villain as part of the world around the people involved, a part which is going to drop a burden on the five if we do not act. On this way of thinking of him, nothing *yet* threatens the five (certainly no ceiling as yet threatens them) and a fortiori we cannot save the five by making what (already) threatens them instead threaten the one. Alternatively, we may think of the villain as himself a threat to the five. But sending the fumes in is not making *him* be a threat to the one instead of to the five. The hypothesis I proposed, then, yields what it should: We may not accede.

That is because the hypothesis I proposed says nothing at all about the source of the threat to the five. Whether the threat to the five is, or is caused by, a human being or anything else, it is not permissible to do what will kill one to save the five except by making what threatens the five itself threaten the one.

By contrast, it seems to me very plausible to think that if a villain has started a trolley towards five, we may deflect the trolley towards one—other things being equal, of course. If a trolley is headed towards five, and we can deflect it towards one, we *may,* no matter who or what caused it to head towards the five.

I think that these considerations help us in dealing with a question I drew attention to earlier. Suppose a villain says to us "I will cause a ceiling to fall on five unless you send lethal fumes into the room of one." If we refuse, so that he does what he threatens to do, then he surely does something very much worse than we would be doing if we acceded to his threat and sent the fumes in. If we accede, we do something misguided and wrongful, but not nearly as bad as what he does if we refuse.

It should be stressed: The fact that he will do something worse if we do not send the fumes in does not entail that we ought to send them in, or even that it is permissible for us to do so.

How after all could that entail that we may send the fumes in? The fact that we would be saving five lives by sending the fumes in does not itself make it permissible for us to do so. (Rights trump utilities.) How could adding that the taker of those five lives would be doing what is worse than we would tip the balance? If we may not infringe a right of the one in order to save the five lives, it cannot possibly be thought that we may infringe the right of that one in order, not merely to save the five lives, but to make the villain's moral record better than it otherwise would be.

For my own part, I think that considerations of motives apart, and other things being equal, it does no harm to say that

(II) Killing five is worse than killing one

is, after all, true. *Of course* we shall then have to say that assessments of which acts are worse than which do not by themselves settle the question of what is permissible for a person to do. For we shall have to say that, despite the truth of (II), it is not the case that we are required to kill one in order that another person shall not kill five, or even that it is everywhere permissible for us to do this.

What is of interest is that what holds inter-personally also holds intra-personally. I said earlier that we might imagine the surgeon of *Transplant* to have caused the ailments of his five patients. Let us imagine the worst: He gave them chemical X precisely in order to cause their deaths, in order to inherit from them. Now he repents. But the fact that he would be saving five lives by operating on the one does not itself make it permissible for him to operate on the one. (Rights trump utilities.) And if he may not infringe a right of the one in order to save the five lives, it cannot possibly be thought that he may infringe the right of that one in order, not merely to save the five lives, but to make his own moral record better than it otherwise would be.

Another way to put the point is this: Assessments of which acts are worse than which have to be directly relevant to the agent's circumstances if they are to have a bearing on what he may do. If A threatens to kill five unless B kills one, then although killing five is worse than killing one, these are not the alternatives open to B. The alternatives open to B are: Kill one, thereby forestalling the deaths of five (and making A's moral record better than it otherwise would be), or let it be the case that A kills five. And the supposition that it would be worse for B to choose to kill the one is entirely compatible with the supposition that killing five is worse than killing one. Again, the alternatives open to the surgeon are: Operate on the one, thereby saving five (and making the surgeon's own moral record better than it otherwise would be), or let it be the case that he himself will have killed the five. And the supposition that it would be worse for the surgeon to choose to operate is entirely compatible with the supposition that killing five is worse than killing one.

On the other hand, suppose a second surgeon is faced with a choice between here and now giving chemical X to five, thereby killing them, and operating on, and thereby killing, only one. (It taxes the imagination to invent such a second surgeon, but let that pass. And compare *Trolley Driver.*) Then, other things being equal, it does seem he may choose to operate on the one. Some people would say something stronger, namely that he is required to make this choice. Perhaps they would say that

> (II′) If a person is faced with a choice between doing something *here and now* to five, by the doing of which he will kill them, and doing something else *here and now* to one, by the doing of which he will kill only the one, then (other things being equal) he ought to choose the second alternative rather than the first

is a quite general moral truth. Whether or not the second surgeon is morally required to make this choice (and thus whether or not (II′) is a general moral truth), it does seem to be the case that he may. But this did seem puzzling. As I put it: Why should the present tense matter so much?

It is plausible to think that the present tense matters because the question for the agent at the time of acting is about the present, viz., "What may I here and now do?," and because that question is the same as the question "Which of the alternatives here and now open to me may I choose?" The alternatives now open to the second surgeon are: kill five or kill one. If killing five is worse than killing one, then perhaps he ought to, but at any rate he may, kill the one.

NOTES

1. See Philippa Foot, "The Problem of Abortion and the Doctrine of the Double Effect," in *Virtues and Vices, and Other Essays in Moral Philosophy* (Berkeley and Los Angeles: University of California Press, 1978), p. 19.
2. I think it possible (though by no means certain) that John Taurek would say, "No, it is not permissible to (all simply) turn the trolley; what you ought to do is flip a coin." See John Taurek, "Should the Numbers Count?" *Philosophy & Public Affairs, 6* (1977), p. 293. (But he is there concerned with a different kind of case, namely that in which what is in question is not whether we may do what harms one to avoid harming five, but whether we may or ought to choose to save five in preference to saving one.) For criticism of Taurek's article, see Derek Parfit, "Innumerate Ethics." *Philosophy & Public Affairs 7* (1978), p. 285.
3. I doubt that anyone would say, with any hope of getting agreement from others, that the surgeon ought to flip a coin. So even if you think that the trolley driver ought to flip a coin, there would remain, for you, an analogue of Mrs. Foot's problem, namely: Why ought the trolley driver flip a coin, whereas the surgeon may not?
4. Mrs. Foot speaks more generally of causing injury and failing to provide aid, and her reason for thinking that the former is worse than the latter is that the negative duty to refrain from causing injury is stricter than the positive duty to provide aid. See Philippa Foot, *supra* note 1, pp. 27–29.
5. A similar case (intended to make a point similar to the one that I shall be making) is discussed in N. Ann Davis, "The Priority of Avoiding Harm," in Bonnie Steinbock, ed., *Killing and Letting Die* (Englewood Cliffs. NJ: Prentice Hall, 1980). pp. 172, 194–195.
6. For a sensitive discussion of some of the difficulties, see N. Ann Davis, "Using Persons and Common Sense," *Ethics 94* (1984), p. 94. Among other things she argues (I think rightly) that the Kantian idea is not to be identified with the common-sense concept of "using a person." Id., p. 402.
7. For a second reason to think so, see *infra* note 13.
8. It is also true that if the five go wholly out of existence just before the agent starts to turn the trolley, then the one will die whatever the agent does. Should we say, then, that the agent uses one to save five if he acts, *and* uses five to save one, if he does not act? No: What follows *"and"* is false. If the agent does not act, he uses nobody. (I doubt that it can even be said that if he does not act, he lets them *be used.* For what is the active for which this is passive? Who or what would be using them if he does not act?)
9. I strongly suspect that giving an account of what makes it wrong to *use* a person, see *supra* text accompanying notes 6–8, would also require appeal to the concept of a right.
10. Ronald Dworkin. *Taking Rights Seriously* (Cambridge: Harvard University Press, 1977), p. ix.
11. Many of the examples discussed by Bernard Williams and Ruth Marcus plainly call for this kind of treatment. See Bernard Williams. "Ethical Consistency," in *Problems of the Self* (Cambridge: Cambridge University Press. 1973), p. 166; Ruth Barcan Marcus, "Moral Dilemmas and Consistency," in *The Journal of Philosophy 77* (1980), p. 121.

12. It may be worth stressing that what I suggest calls for attention is not (as some construals of "double effect" would have it) whether the agent's killing of the one is his means to something, and not (as other construals of "double effect" would have it) whether the death of the one is the agent's means to something, but rather what are the means by which the agent both kills and saves. For a discussion of "the doctrine of double effect," see Philippa Foot, *supra* note 1.

13. *Id.,* p. 29. As Mrs. Foot says, we do not *use* the one if we proceed in *Hospital.* Yet the impermissibility of proceeding in *Hospital* seems to have a common source with the impermissibility of operating in *Transplant,* in which the surgeon *would* be using the one whose parts he takes for the five who need them. This is my second reason for thinking that an appeal to the fact that the surgeon would be using his victim is an over-simple way of taking account of the means he would be employing for the saving of his five. See *supra* note 7.

STUDY QUESTIONS

1. Do you believe that turning the trolley in "Bystander at the Switch" is morally permissible?

2. Do you believe that not turning the trolley in "Bystander at the Switch" is morally permissible?

3. In what crucial ways, if any, does the case Thomson calls "Fat Man" differ from "Bystander at the Switch"?

4. If you could save the life of five individuals by sacrificing either the life of one stranger or by sacrificing your own life, does morality allow you to choose to sacrifice the life of the stranger?

The Altruism Puzzle

Steven M. Cahn, Harry Brighouse, and Robert B. Talisse

Imagine that you are uniquely positioned to disarm a bomb set to kill thousands of people. The catch, however, is that disarming the bomb requires the sacrifice of your life. Are you morally required to make this sacrifice? Steven M. Cahn, co-editor of this book and Professor of Philosophy at The City University of New York Graduate Center, calls this scenario "the altruism puzzle." Harry Brighouse, Professor of Philosophy at the University of Wisconsin–Madison, maintains that you are required to make the sacrifice. Robert B. Talisse, Professor of Philosophy at Vanderbilt University, argues that you are not.

A.

Steven M. Cahn

Suppose I uncover a plot to set off a bomb that would destroy a city. Only I am in position to foil the scheme. Doing so, however, would cost me my life. I may choose, of course, to sacrifice myself and thereby save thousands of others. But am I morally obligated to do so?

B.

Harry Brighouse

The obligation to sacrifice oneself in the scenario described by the puzzle is stringent. Because this seems so obvious to me, it is hard to discern what arguments will move the unconvinced. I offer an argument I find persuasive, and consider some objections.

Let's start with a variant of the altruism puzzle in which many people will have the intuition that killing *someone else* is required. Imagine I am in a different city from the one under threat. John, an innocent man beside me, has unknowingly undergone a procedure that makes him the trigger of the bomb. The bomb in the city under threat is set to detonate when John takes his 1,000th breath after 11 a.m. He is currently taking his 980th breath. I have a gun, and can kill him instantaneously with it.

John is not at all implicated in the plot. He is a good person, gives joy to others, and has a flourishing enjoyable life. The bombers subjected John to the procedure while he was asleep. It left no traces. He is innocent of the plot and has no reason to suspect anything.

But I have an obligation to sacrifice John's life. Killing him, by stipulation, is the only way of saving thousands of equally valuable lives. To deny the obligation just seems to me not take seriously the scale of the destruction the bomb will cause.

Killing him will certainly be very bad. It is bad that he loses his life, and bad that I act in a way that

From the *Journal of Social Philosophy*, vol. 44 (2013). Reprinted by permission of Wiley Periodicals, Inc.

contradicts my sense of who I really am (a pacific person who does not take the lives of others)—undermines my integrity. Maybe I will suffer severe emotional costs in the future as a result of my sense of responsibility for having taken John's life, despite understanding it was my duty. But these quite real bads, and all others generated by the act, are massively outweighed by the good of saving the thousands of other people.

So I am obliged to kill John. But what is the difference between killing him and sacrificing myself? Just that, in general, we are obliged to be more cautious about imposing costs on innocent others, especially serious costs like killing, than on our innocent selves. We must be more parsimonious with the lives of others than with our own. If I must kill John when that is the only way of preventing detonation, then I must sacrifice myself when that is the only effective way.

Consider three objections. First, is it overdemanding for morality to require such self-sacrifice? It is, certainly, *demanding*—sacrificing oneself is a considerable demand. But it is not something we *cannot* do: people do sacrifice themselves for others, and for principles, and the vast majority of us believe and hope that in some circumstances *we* would *be able* to sacrifice ourselves. Maybe, on the principle that ought implies can, those few who genuinely are incapable of self-sacrifice are under no requirement. But for more of us, we *can* sacrifice our lives. It may be more difficult when we understand there is some probability that our sacrifice will be in vain. But the specifications of this case are clear in a way that our actual choices rarely are: you know, *for sure,* that sacrificing yourself *really will* save many thousands of lives.

The second retort is that someone who sacrifices her life for innocent others commands our moral admiration in a way that suggests we think the act is supererogatory, not merely dutiful. Certainly someone who sacrifices her life in the scenario commands our admiration. But admiration can be commanded when someone is merely fulfilling her duty. Most of us admire a parent who merely risks her life to save her child from a burning building, even though that is her duty. The altruism puzzle sacrifice

commands admiration because we know a situation requiring someone to sacrifice her life is rare, makes extreme demands on our motivations, and is one for which few people are well-prepared. Admiration is especially appropriate given that we have sufficient humility to be less than fully confident that we would be dutiful ourselves in those circumstances.

The third objection is that I might have conflicting, preexisting, obligations. I have friends, a spouse, and children, to all of whom I am tied in various ways and whose well-being I should treat as more important than the well-being of strangers. Let us suppose that they live far from the city under threat. In sacrificing myself, I impose a large cost on them. Either this is permissible, or it is impermissible. If it is permissible, then the fact I am doing it is no objection to my sacrificing myself being obligatory. If it is not permissible then, indeed, sacrificing myself is not obligatory, but, contra the assumption in the description of the puzzle, *it is not even permissible.*

So am I even permitted to impose the cost of my death on my near and dear? I am certainly permitted to act in ways that *risk* imposing that same burden on them—consider driving moderate distances, crossing the road at night, walking downstairs while slightly tipsy. Someone who is killed in a car-crash for which he is not responsible has not wronged his near and dear, even if the trip was frivolous. Morality allows us to risk our lives, even for trivial benefits to ourselves. It is not a great leap to think morality requires us to do something that *certainly* imposes these costs for the sake of huge benefits to others.

The thought that we are permitted or even required to act partially toward our near and dear is animated partly by the understanding that a world in which people were always willing to forsake their nearest and dearest for the sake of somewhat more needy strangers would be dreadful; many of the best things in life would be lost. But a world in which people were always willing to *give their lives* for the sake of *thousands of strangers,* if called upon, would not be dreadful. The near and dear of the person who routinely forsakes them for merely somewhat needier strangers could only conclude that he does not truly care for them. Those of the person who gives his life for thousands of others, when his life was the only one that could fulfill that function, can, and should, understand that they are cared for and loved, but that duties to others sometimes requires that we impose costs on those we love.

C.

Robert B. Talisse

Steven Cahn's Altruism Puzzle asks whether morality could require other-regarding action that is self-sacrificing to the ultimate degree. My answer is yes; we could be morally required to end our own lives for the sake of others. Yet, perhaps surprisingly, I also hold that in the case identified by Cahn, one is not required to sacrifice one's life.

I begin with Cahn's example—call it the Bomb Case. Then I'll say something about the more general view I favor. In the Bomb Case, I am not obligated to foil the plot at the expense of my own life because morality cannot require me to bear such a high cost for *someone else's immorality*. Let us call the view that in the Bomb Case one is obligated to foil the plot Strong Altruism. Strong Altruism is unlivable because it holds that at any moment my life could be disrupted to the ultimate degree by an obligation to perform a self-sacrificing action simply because someone else has decided to do something dreadful. To appeal to a consideration associated with Bernard Williams, among others: Living a moral life requires us to be able to build our lives around certain long-term projects. Of course, our life plans could at any moment be derailed by contingencies of various kinds; and in some cases, contingencies give rise to moral obligations which conflict with our life plans; however, as Strong Altruism counts among these contingencies the radically evil designs of extremely immoral others, it makes moral lives things too easily co-opted by the worst among us. Indeed, in the moral economy proposed by Strong Altruism, a tiny band of madmen could make the moral life impossible for us all by routinely staging situations like the Bomb Case and allowing selected numbers of decent people the opportunity to foil their plots. In short, Strong Altruism allows evil people to take the moral

life hostage. It seems odd to think that this could be required by morality.

This response to the Bomb Case does not entail that self-interest, even ultimate self-interest, always trumps our duties to others. The rejection of Strong Altruism does not entail a rejection of altruism as such. Consider a companion case, the Virus Case:

> You discover that you are the sole carrier of a virus that is deadly in 99% of humans. As a carrier, your own life is not at risk. However, if the virus is allowed to mature, it will quickly become highly contagious, and thousands will become infected and die. No method of quarantine is sufficient to prevent the spread of the virus once it has reached maturity. The only way to prevent the outbreak is to ingest a poison that will surely kill the virus, but will also inevitably kill you.

The Virus Case is like the Bomb Case in nearly all respects. The crucial difference is that in the Bomb Case, the self-sacrificing action is required in order to save people from serious harm that is the result of the *gross immorality of another agent*. In the Virus Case, the self-sacrificing action is required in order to save people from harm that is not the result of another's gross immorality. In the Virus Case, one is indeed obligated to ingest the poison for the sake of saving the thousands of lives that would otherwise perish. That is, in the Virus Case, morality requires other-regarding behavior that is self-sacrificing.

A critic might object that the two cases do not differ significantly with respect to the Williams-style consideration operating in my treatment of the Bomb Case. Such a critic could argue that it is no less unsettling of the moral life to think that one could be morally required to sacrifice oneself due to having had the bad luck of catching a virus than it would be to think that someone else's gross immorality could require one to commit an act of self-sacrifice. In both cases, one is obligated to pay the ultimate price in order to save others from serious harm resulting from something that is not of one's doing.

It seems to me that in both cases, the subject is a victim of a kind of bad luck in that each is placed in a moral conundrum by forces out of his control. But the moral significance of the bad luck differs in the cases. In the Bomb Case, one has the bad luck of being in the unique position to thwart another's gross immorality; one is placed in a grave moral conundrum at the hand of a thoroughly immoral agent. In the virus case, the bad luck is brute; one is obligated to sacrifice oneself, but this is not at the hand of another. That, due to bad brute luck, an obligation to self-sacrifice could simply befall us is admittedly a disconcerting, perhaps terrifying, thought. But it is morally different from the thought that someone else's immorality could be the source of such an obligation. As I've said, this latter thought places our lives too much in the hands of evil others; it places the lives of decent persons at the mercy of the extremely evil.

Consider a further complication: The Injection Case. This case is identical to the Virus Case except for the fact that one is injected with the deadly virus by an evil scientist bent on destroying humanity. Here, I think self-sacrifice is indeed required. But self-sacrifice in this case is *not* a capitulation of the moral life to the evil of the scientist, because, given the extremely high lethality of the virus and the fact that one's ability to live morally depends upon the ability of others to live morally as well, allowing the scientist's plot to go forward will render the moral life impossible; I relinquish my ability to live the moral life no matter what I do, so I should sacrifice myself so that others may pursue their moral projects.

But now imagine the closely related Moderated Injection Case. It is identical to the Injection Case, except for the fact that the injected virus is lethal in only 5 percent of humans. Let us assume, as seems plausible, that one's ability to live a moral life is not rendered impossible by the death of 5 percent of humanity at the hands of a virus. Here, my intuitions flip: to require self-sacrifice in this case would be to cede to the evil scientist too much control over the lives of morally decent people.

There is certainly much more to say, and a lot hangs on whether it is possible to get a clear sense of where the morally relevant thresholds lie. It is clear that the behavior of some could be the source of obligations in others, as when my wife makes plans for us both to meet friends for dinner without consulting me first. And I concede that the *immoral* behavior of some could be the source of moral obligations in others, as when my neighbors' negligent parenting creates a moral obligation for me to intervene. I also accept that the extremely bad behavior of some could be the source of extremely costly moral obligations in others. But I cannot see how morality could require a morally decent person to pay the ultimate price for gross immorality on the part of others. In short, self-sacrifice may sometimes be morally required, but it is simply not the kind of obligation that a morally despicable person can impose upon a morally responsible person.

D.

Steven M. Cahn

I appreciate these insightful replies to the altruism puzzle. They suggest a quandary that is worth attention.

If in the case described I have a moral obligation to sacrifice my life, then in another situation I might be morally obligated to give up my property, my physical well-being, or my pursuit of happiness. After all, if when my life is at risk I cannot choose self-interest over altruism, how can I do so to preserve something of lesser value than my life? Granted, in other situations the consequences of my choices might not be so calamitous, but considering the vast amount of suffering in our world, I could he obligated to abandon, if not my life, at least all my personal interests, devoting myself exclusively to providing much needed aid to others. I would become, in the words of the subtitle of *The Pirates of Penzance,* "The Slave of Duty."

On the other hand, if in the case described I do not have a moral obligation to sacrifice my life because that price would be too great, why should I ever be morally obligated to give up my property, my physical well-being, or my pursuit of happiness? Admittedly, such values are not as precious to me as my life, but still I may find surrendering them excessively costly. If I do, why can't I again choose self-interest over morality? Furthermore, wouldn't the justification for my doing so be even stronger in ordinary circumstances, where the consequences of my acting solely for my own advantage are far less horrific?

In sum, the altruism puzzle calls for accepting one alternative and dealing with the consequences.

Which option to choose, however, is uncertain, and I look forward to more extended treatments of the numerous issues involved.

STUDY QUESTIONS

1. What would be your answer to the puzzle if those being saved were your family or friends?
2. What would be your answer to the puzzle if your action would save not people but millions of wild animals?
3. What would be your answer to the puzzle if your action would save not people but plant life extending over millions of acres?
4. What would be your answer to the puzzle if your action would save not people but a vast number of the world's greatest works of art?

Part XIV

METAETHICS

A Treatise of Human Nature

David Hume

David Hume (1711–1776), the influential Scottish philosopher, maintains that morality is based on sentiment, not reason. He argues that while moral judgments motivate us to act, reason is inert, helping us make demonstrative or probable inferences but not producing passions for action. That is, because moral judgments are motivating while the products of reason are not, moral judgments are not based on reason. Moreover, no factual claims alone ever imply any moral claims. In other words, "is" does not imply "ought." Thus, Hume concludes, reason serves our passions.

BOOK II OF THE PASSIONS

Part III Of the Will and Direct Passions

Section III Of the Influencing Motives of the Will

Nothing is more usual in philosophy, and even in common life, than to talk of the combat of passion and reason, to give the preference to reason, and assert that men are only so far virtuous as they conform themselves to its dictates. Every rational creature, it is said, is obliged to regulate his actions by reason; and if any other motive or principle challenge the direction of his conduct, he ought to oppose it, till it be entirely subdued, or at least brought to a conformity with that superior principle. On this method of thinking the greatest part of moral philosophy, ancient and modern, seems to be founded; nor is there an ampler field, as well for metaphysical arguments, as popular declamations, than this supposed preëminence of reason above passion. The eternity, invariableness, and divine origin of the former, have been

displayed to the best advantage: the blindness, inconstancy, and deceitfulness of the latter, have been as strongly insisted on. In order to show the fallacy of all this philosophy, I shall endeavour to prove, *first,* that reason alone can never be a motive to any action of the will; and *secondly,* that it can never oppose passion in the direction of the will.

The understanding exerts itself after two different ways, as it judges from demonstration or probability: as it regards the abstract relations of our ideas, or those relations of objects of which experience only gives us information. I believe it scarce will be asserted, that the first species of reasoning alone is ever the cause of any action. As its proper province is the world of ideas, and as the will always places us in that of realities, demonstration and volition seem upon that account to be totally removed from each other. Mathematics, indeed, are useful in all mechanical operations, and arithmetic in almost every art and profession: but it is not of themselves they have any influence. Mechanics are the art of regulating the motions of bodies *to some designed end or*

From David Hume, *A Treatise of Human Nature* (1739–40).

purpose; and the reason why we employ arithmetic in fixing the proportions of numbers, is only that we may discover the proportions of their influence and operation. A merchant is desirous of knowing the sum total of his accounts with any person: why? but that he may learn what sum will have the same *effects* in paying his debt, and going to market, as all the particular articles taken together. Abstract or demonstrative reasoning, therefore, never influences any of our actions, but only as it directs our judgment concerning causes and effects; which leads us to the second operation of the understanding.

It is obvious, that when we have the prospect of pain or pleasure from any object, we feel a consequent emotion of aversion or propensity, and are carried to avoid or embrace what will give us this uneasiness or satisfaction. It is also obvious, that this emotion rests not here, but, making us cast our view on every side, comprehends whatever objects are connected with its original one by the relation of cause and effect. Here then reasoning takes place to discover this relation; and according as our reasoning varies, our actions receive a subsequent variation. But it is evident, in this case, that the impulse arises not from reason, but is only directed by it. It is from the prospect of pain or pleasure that the aversion or propensity arises towards any object: and these emotions extend themselves to the causes and effects of that object, as they are pointed out to us by reason and experience. It can never in the least concern us to know, that such objects are causes, and such others effects, if both the causes and effects be indifferent to us. Where the objects themselves do not affect us, their connection can never give them any influence; and it is plain that, as reason is nothing but the discovery of this connection, it cannot be by its means that the objects are able to affect us.

Since reason alone can never produce any action, or give rise to volition, I infer, that the same faculty is as incapable of preventing volition, or of disputing the preference with any passion or emotion. This consequence is necessary. It is impossible reason could have the latter effect of preventing volition, but by giving an impulse in a contrary direction to our passions; and that impulse, had it operated alone, would have been ample to produce volition. Nothing can oppose or retard the impulse of passion, but a contrary impulse;

and if this contrary impulse ever arises from reason, that latter faculty must have an original influence on the will, and must be able to cause, as well as hinder, any act of volition. But if reason has no original influence, it is impossible it can withstand any principle which has such an efficacy, or ever keep the mind in suspense a moment. Thus, it appears, that the principle which opposes our passion cannot be the same with reason, and is only called so in an improper sense. We speak not strictly and philosophically, when we talk of the combat of passion and of reason. Reason is, and ought only to be, the slave of the passions, and can never pretend to any other office than to serve and obey them. As this opinion may appear somewhat extraordinary, it may not be improper to confirm it by some other considerations.

A passion is an original existence, or, if you will, modification of existence, and contains not any representative quality, which renders it a copy of any other existence or modification. When I am angry, I am actually possessed with the passion, and in that emotion have no more a reference to any other object, than when I am thirsty, or sick, or more than five feet high. It is impossible, therefore, that this passion can be opposed by, or be contradictory to truth and reason; since this contradiction consists in the disagreement of ideas, considered as copies, with those objects which they represent.

What may at first occur on this head is, that as nothing can be contrary to truth or reason, except what has a reference to it, and as the judgments of our understanding only have this reference, it must follow that passions can be contrary to reason only, so far as they are *accompanied* with some judgment or opinion. According to this principle, which is so obvious and natural, it is only in two senses that any affection can be called unreasonable. First, When a passion, such as hope or fear, grief or joy, despair or security, is founded on the supposition of the existence of objects, which really do not exist. Secondly, When in exerting any passion in action, we choose means sufficient for the designed end, and deceive ourselves in our judgment of causes and effects. Where a passion is neither founded on false suppositions, nor chooses means insufficient for the end, the understanding can neither justify nor condemn it. It is not contrary to reason to prefer the destruction of the whole world to the scratching of my finger. It is not contrary to reason for me to choose my total ruin, to prevent the least uneasiness of an Indian, or person wholly unknown to me. It is as little contrary to reason to prefer even my own acknowledged lesser good to my greater, and have a more ardent affection for the former than the latter. A trivial good may, from certain circumstances, produce a desire superior to what arises from the greatest and most valuable enjoyment; nor is there anything more extraordinary in this, than in mechanics to see one pound weight raise up a hundred by the advantage of its situation. In short, a passion must be accompanied with some false judgment, in order to its being unreasonable; and even then it is not the passion, properly speaking, which is unreasonable, but the judgment.

The consequences are evident. Since a passion can never, in any sense, be called unreasonable, but when founded on a false supposition, or when it chooses means insufficient for the designed end, it is impossible that reason and passion can ever oppose each other, or dispute for the government of the will and actions. The moment we perceive the falsehood of any supposition, or the insufficiency of any means, our passions yield to our reason without any opposition. I may desire any fruit as of an excellent relish; but whenever you convince me of my mistake, my longing ceases. I may will the performance of certain actions as means of obtaining any desired good; but as my willing of these actions is only secondary, and founded on the supposition that they are causes of the proposed effect; as soon as I discover the falsehood of that supposition, they must become indifferent to me.

It is natural for one, that does not examine objects with a strict philosophic eye, to imagine, that those actions of the mind are entirely the same, which produce not a different sensation, and are not immediately distinguishable to the feeling and perception. Reason, for instance, exerts itself without producing any sensible emotions; and except in the more sublime disquisitions of philosophy, or in the frivolous subtilties of the schools, scarce ever conveys any pleasure or uneasiness. Hence it proceeds, that every action of the mind which operates with the same calmness and tranquillity, is confounded with reason by all those who judge of things from the first view and appearance. Now it is certain there are certain calm desires and tendencies, which, though they be real passions, produce little emotion in the mind, and are more known by their effects than by the immediate feeling or sensation. These desires are of two kinds; either certain instincts originally implanted in our natures, such as benevolence and resentment, the love of life, and kindness to children: or the general appetite to good, and aversion to evil, considered merely as such. When any of these passions are calm, and cause no disorder in the soul, they are very readily taken for the determinations of reason, and are supposed to proceed from the same faculty with that which judges of truth and falsehood. Their nature and principles have been supposed the same, because their sensations are not evidently different.

Besides these calm passions, which often determine the will, there are certain violent emotions of the same kind, which have likewise a great influence on that faculty. When I receive any injury from another, I often feel a violent passion of resentment, which makes me desire his evil and punishment, independent of all considerations of pleasure and advantage to myself. When I am immediately threatened with any grievous ill, my fears, apprehensions, and aversions rise to a great height, and produce a sensible emotion.

The common error of metaphysicians has lain in ascribing the direction of the will entirely to one of these principles, and supposing the other to have no influence. Men often act knowingly against their interest: for which reason, the view of the greatest possible good does not always influence them. Men often counteract a violent passion in prosecution of their interests and designs: it is not, therefore, the present uneasiness alone which determines them. In general we may observe that both these principles operate on the will; and where they are contrary, that either of them prevails, according to the *general* character or *present* disposition of the person. What we call strength of mind, implies the prevalence of the calm passions above the violent; though we may easily observe, there is no man so constantly possessed of this virtue as never on any occasion to yield to the solicitations of passion and desire. From these variations of temper proceeds the great difficulty of deciding concerning the actions and resolutions of men, where there is any contrariety of motives and passions. . . .

BOOK III OF MORALS

Part I Of Virtue and Vice in General

Section I Moral Distinctions Not Derived from Reason

There is an inconvenience which attends all abstruse reasoning, that it may silence, without convincing an antagonist, and requires the same intense study to make us sensible of its force, that was at first requisite for its invention. When we leave our closet, and engage in the common affairs of life, its conclusions seem to vanish like the phantoms of the night on the appearance of the morning; and it is difficult for us to retain even that conviction which we had attained with difficulty. This is still more conspicuous in a long chain of reasoning, where we must preserve to the end the evidence of the first propositions, and where we often lose sight of all the most received maxims, either of philosophy or common life. I am not, however, without hopes, that the present system of philosophy will acquire new force as it advances; and that our reasonings concerning *morals* will corroborate whatever has been said concerning the *understanding* and the *passions.* Morality is a subject that interests us above all others; we fancy the peace of society to be at stake in every decision concerning it; and it is evident that this concern must make our speculations appear more real and solid, than where the subject is in a great measure indifferent to us. What affects us, we conclude, can never be a chimera; and, as our passion is engaged on the one side or the other, we naturally think that the question lies within human comprehension; which, in other cases of this nature, we are apt to entertain some doubt of. Without this advantage, I never should have ventured upon a third volume of such abstruse philosophy, in an age wherein the greatest part of men seem agreed to convert reading into an amusement, and to reject everything that requires any considerable degree of attention to be comprehended.

It has been observed, that nothing is ever present to the mind but its perceptions; and that all the actions of seeing, hearing, judging, loving, hating, and thinking, fall under this denomination. The mind can never exert itself in any action which we may not comprehend under the term of *perception;* and consequently that term is no less applicable to those judgments by which we distinguish moral good and evil, than to every other operation of the mind. To approve of one character, to condemn another, are only so many different perceptions.

Now, as perceptions resolve themselves into two kinds, viz. *impressions* and *ideas,* this distinction gives rise to a question, with which we shall open up our present inquiry concerning morals, *whether it is by means of our* ideas *or* impressions *we distinguish betwixt vice and virtue, and pronounce an action blamable or praiseworthy?* This will immediately cut off all loose discourses and declamations, and reduce us to something precise and exact on the present subject.

Those who affirm that virtue is nothing but a conformity to reason; that there are eternal fitnesses and unfitnesses of things, which are the same to every rational being that considers them; that the immutable measure of right and wrong impose an obligation, not only on human creatures, but also on the Deity himself: all these systems concur in the opinion, that morality, like truth, is discerned merely by ideas, and by their juxtaposition and comparison. In order, therefore, to judge of these systems, we need only consider whether it be possible from reason alone, to distinguish betwixt moral good and evil, or whether there must concur some other principles to enable us to make that distinction.

If morality had naturally no influence on human passions and actions, it were in vain to take such pains to inculcate it; and nothing would be more fruitless than that multitude of rules and precepts with which all moralists abound. Philosophy is commonly divided into *speculative* and *practical;* and as morality is always comprehended under the latter division, it is supposed to influence our passions and actions, and to go beyond the calm and indolent judgments of the understanding. And this is confirmed by common experience, which informs us that men are often governed by their duties, and are deterred from some actions by the opinion of injustice, and impelled to others by that of obligation.

Since morals, therefore, have an influence on the actions and affections, it follows that they cannot be derived from reason; and that because reason alone, as we have already proved, can never have any such influence. Morals excite passions, and produce or prevent actions. Reason of itself is utterly impotent in this particular. The rules of morality, therefore, are not conclusions of our reason.

No one, I believe, will deny the justness of this inference; nor is there any other means of evading it, than by denying that principle on which it is founded. As long as it is allowed, that reason has no influence on our passions and actions, it is in vain to pretend that morality is discovered only by a deduction of reason. An active principle can never be founded on an inactive; and if reason be inactive in itself, it must remain so in all its shapes and appearances, whether it exerts itself in natural or moral subjects, whether it considers the powers of external bodies, or the actions of rational beings.

It would be tedious to repeat all the arguments by which I have proved that reason is perfectly inert, and can never either prevent or produce any action or affection. It will be easy to recollect what has been said upon that subject. I shall only recall on this occasion one of these arguments, which I shall endeavour to render still more conclusive, and more applicable to the present subject.

Reason is the discovery of truth or falsehood, Truth or falsehood consists in an agreement or disagreement either to the *real* relations of ideas, or to *real* existence and matter of fact. Whatever therefore is not susceptible of this agreement or disagreement, is incapable of being true or false, and can never be an object of our reason. Now, it is evident our passions, volitions, and actions, are not susceptible of any such agreement or disagreement; being original facts and realities, complete in themselves, and implying no reference to other passions, volitions, and actions. It is impossible, therefore, they can be pronounced either true or false, and be either contrary or conformable to reason.

This argument is of double advantage to our present purpose. For it proves *directly,* that actions do not derive their merit from a conformity to reason, nor their blame from a contrariety to it; and it proves the same truth more *indirectly,* by showing us, that as reason can never immediately prevent or produce any action by contradicting or approving of it, it cannot be the source of moral good and evil, which are found to have that influence. Actions may be laudable or blamable; but they cannot be reasonable or unreasonable: laudable or blamable, therefore, are not the same with reasonable or unreasonable. The merit and demerit of actions frequently contradict, and sometimes control our natural propensities. But reason has no such influence. Moral distinctions, therefore, are not the offspring of reason. Reason is wholly inactive, and can never be the source of so active a principle as conscience, or a sense of morals.

But perhaps it may be said, that though no will or action can be immediately contradictory to reason, yet we may find such a contradiction in some of the attendants of the actions, that is, in its causes or effects. The action may cause a judgment, or may be *obliquely* caused by one, when the judgment concurs with a passion; and by an abusive way of speaking, which philosophy will scarce allow of, the same contrariety may, upon that account, be ascribed to the action. How far this truth or falsehood may be the source of morals, it will now be proper to consider.

It has been observed that reason, in a strict and philosophical sense, can have an influence on our conducts only after two ways: either when it excites a passion, by informing us of the existence of something which is a proper object of it; or when it discovers the connection of causes and effects, so as to afford us means of exerting any passion. These are the only kinds of judgment which can accompany our actions, or can be said to produce them in any manner; and it must be allowed, that these judgments may often be false and erroneous. A person may be affected with passion, by supposing a pain or pleasure to lie in an object which has no tendency to produce either of these sensations, or which produces the contrary to what is imagined. A person may also take false measures for the attaining of his end, and may retard, by his foolish conduct, instead of forwarding the execution of any object. These false judgments may be thought to affect the passions and actions, which are connected with them, and may be said to render them unreasonable, in a figurative and improper way of speaking. But though this be acknowledged, it is easy to observe, that these errors are so far from being the source of all immorality, that they are commonly very innocent, and draw no manner of guilt upon the person who is so unfortunate as to fall into them. They extend not beyond a mistake of *fact,* which moralists have not generally supposed criminal, as being perfectly involuntary. I am more to be lamented than blamed, if I am mistaken with regard to the influence of objects in producing pain or pleasure, or if I know not the proper means of satisfying my desires. No one can ever regard such errors as a defect in my moral character. A fruit, for instance, that is really disagreeable, appears to me at a distance, and, through mistake, I fancy it to be pleasant and delicious. Here is one error. I choose certain means of reaching this fruit, which are not proper for my end. Here is a second error; nor is there any third one, which can ever possibly enter into our reasonings concerning actions. I ask, therefore, if a man in this situation, and guilty of these two errors, is to be regarded as vicious and criminal, however unavoidable they might have been? Or if it be possible to imagine that such errors are the sources of all immorality?

And here it may be proper to observe, that if moral distinctions be derived from the truth or falsehood of those judgments, they must take place wherever we form the judgments; nor will there be any difference, whether the question be concerning an apple or a kingdom, or whether the error be avoidable or unavoidable.

For as the very essence of morality is supposed to consist in an agreement or disagreement to reason, the other circumstances are entirely arbitrary, and can never either bestow on any action the character of virtuous or vicious, or deprive it of that character. To which we may add, that this agreement or disagreement, not admitting of degrees, all virtues and vices would of course be equal.

Should it be pretended, that though a mistake of *fact* be not criminal, yet a mistake of *right* often is; and that this may be the source of immorality: I would answer, that it is impossible such a mistake can ever be the original source of immorality, since it supposes a real right and wrong; that is, a real distinction in morals, independent of these judgments.

A mistake, therefore, of right, may become a species of immorality; but it is only a secondary one, and is founded on some other antecedent to it.

As to those judgments which are the *effects* of our actions, and which, when false, give occasion to pronounce the actions contrary to truth and reason; we may observe, that our actions never cause any judgment, either true or false, in ourselves, and that it is only on others they have such an influence. It is certain that an action, on many occasions, may give rise to false conclusions in others; and that a person, who, through a window, sees any lewd behaviour of mine with my neighbour's wife, may be so simple as to imagine she is certainly my own. In this respect my action resembles somewhat a lie or falsehood; only with this difference, which is material, that I perform not the action with any intention of giving rise to a false judgment in another, but merely to satisfy my lust and passion. It causes, however, a mistake and false judgment by accident; and the falsehood of its effects may be ascribed, by some odd figurative way of speaking, to the action itself. But still I can see no pretext of reason for asserting, that the tendency to cause such an error is the first spring or original source of all immorality.

Thus, upon the whole, it is impossible that the distinction betwixt moral good and evil can be made by reason; since that distinction has an influence upon our actions, of which reason alone is incapable. Reason and judgment may, indeed, be the mediate cause of an action, by prompting or by directing a passion; but it is not pretended that a judgment of this kind, either in its truth or falsehood, is attended with virtue or vice. And as to the judgments, which are caused by our judgments, they can still less bestow those moral qualities on the actions which are their causes.

But, to be more particular, and to show that those eternal immutable fitnesses and unfitnesses of things cannot be defended by sound philosophy, we may weigh the following considerations.

If the thought and understanding were alone capable of fixing the boundaries of right and wrong, the character of virtuous and vicious either must lie in some relations of objects, or must be a matter of fact which is discovered by our reasoning. This consequence is evident. As the operations of human understanding divide themselves into two kinds, the comparing of ideas, and the inferring of matter of fact, were virtue discovered by the understanding, it must be an object of one of these operations; nor is there any third operation of the understanding which can discover it. There has been an opinion very industriously propagated by certain philosophers, that morality is susceptible of demonstration; and though no one has ever been able to advance a single step in those demonstrations, yet it is taken for granted that this science may be brought to an equal certainty with geometry or algebra. Upon this supposition, vice and virtue must consist in some relations; since it is allowed on all hands, that no matter of fact is capable of being demonstrated. Let us therefore begin with examining this hypothesis, and endeavour, if possible, to fix those moral qualities which have been so long the objects of our fruitless researches; point out distinctly the relations which constitute morality or obligation, that we may know wherein they consist, and after what manner we must judge of them.

If you assert that vice and virtue consist in relations susceptible of certainty and demonstration, you must confine yourself to those *four* relations which alone admit at that degree of evidence: and in that case you run into absurdities from which you will never be able to extricate yourself. For as you make the very essence of morality to lie in the relations, and as there is no one of these relations but what is applicable, not only to all irrational but also to an inanimate object, it follows that even such objects must be susceptible of merit or demerit. *Resemblance, contrariety, degrees in quality,* and *proportions in quantity and number;* all these relations belong us properly to matter as to our actions, passions, and volitions. It is unquestionable, therefore, that morality lies not in any of these relations, nor the sense of it in their discovery.

Should it be asserted, that the sense of morality consists in the discovery of some relation distinct from these, and that our enumeration was not complete when we comprehended all demonstrable relations under four general heads: to this I know not what to reply, till some one be so good as to point out to me this new relation. It is impossible to refute a system which has never yet been explained. In such a manner of fighting in the dark, a man loses his blows in the air, and often places them where the enemy is not present.

I must therefore, on this occasion, rest contented with requiring the two following conditions of any one that would undertake to clear up this system. *First,* as moral good and evil belong only to the actions of the mind, and are derived from our situation with regard to external objects, the relations from which these moral distinctions arise must lie only betwixt internal actions and external objects, and must not be applicable either to internal actions, compared among themselves, or to external objects, when placed in opposition to other external objects. For as morality is supposed to attend certain relations, if these relations could belong to internal actions considered singly, it would follow, that we might be guilty of crimes in ourselves, and independent of our situation with respect to the universe; and in like manner, if these moral relations could be applied to external objects, it would follow that even inanimate beings would be susceptible of moral beauty and deformity. Now, it seems difficult to imagine that any relation can be discovered betwixt our passions, volitions, and actions, compared to external objects, which relation might not belong either to these passions and volitions, or to these external objects, compared among *themselves.*

But it will be still more difficult to fulfil the *second* condition, requisite to justify this system. According to the principles of those who maintain an abstract rational difference betwixt moral good and evil, and a natural fitness and unfitness of things, it is not only supposed, that these relations, being eternal and immutable, are the same, when considered by every rational creature, but their *effects* are also supposed to be necessarily the same; and it is concluded they have no less, or rather a greater, influence in directing the will of the Deity, than in governing the rational and virtuous of our own species. These two particulars are evidently distinct. It is one thing to know virtue, and another to conform the will to it. In order, therefore, to prove that the measures of right and wrong are eternal laws, *obligatory* on every rational mind, it is not sufficient to show the relations upon which they are founded: we must also point out the connection betwixt the relation and the will; and must prove that this connection is so necessary, that in every well-disposed mind, it must take place and have its influence; though the difference betwixt these minds be in other respects immense and infinite. Now, besides what I have already proved, that even in human nature no relation can ever alone produce any action; besides this, I say, it has been shown, in treating of the understanding, that there is no connection of cause and effect, such as this is supposed to be, which is discoverable otherwise than by experience, and of which we can pretend to have any security by the simple consideration of the objects. All beings in the universe, considered in themselves, appear entirely loose and independent of each other. It is only by experience we learn their influence and connection; and this influence we ought never to extend beyond experience.

Thus it will be impossible to fulfil the *first* condition required to the system of eternal rational measures of right and wrong; because it is impossible to show those relations, upon which such a distinction may be founded: and it is as impossible to fulfil the *second* condition; because we cannot prove *a priori,* that these relations, if they really existed and were perceived, would be universally forcible and obligatory.

But to make these general reflections more clear and convincing, we may illustrate them by some particular instances, wherein this character of moral good or evil is the most universally acknowledged. Of all crimes that human creatures are capable of committing, the most horrid and unnatural is ingratitude, especially when it is committed against parents, and appears in the more flagrant instances of wounds and death. This is acknowledged by all mankind, philosophers as well as the people: the question only arises among philosophers, whether the guilt or moral deformity of this action be discovered by demonstrative reasoning, or be felt by an internal sense, and by means of some sentiment, which the reflecting on such an action naturally occasions. This question will soon be decided against the former opinion, if we can show the same relations in other objects, without the notion of any guilt or iniquity attending them. Reason or science is nothing but the comparing of ideas, and the discovery of their relations; and if the same relations have different characters, it must evidently follow, that those characters are not discovered merely by reason. To put the affair, therefore, to this trial, let us choose any inanimate object, such as an oak or

elm; and let us suppose, that, by the dropping of its seed, it produces a sapling below it, which, springing up by degrees, at last overtops and destroys the parent tree: I ask, if, in this instance, there be wanting any relation which is discoverable in parricide or ingratitude? Is not the one tree the cause of the other's existence; and the latter the cause of the destruction of the former, in the same manner as when a child murders his parent? It is not sufficient to reply, that a choice or will is wanting. For in the case of parricide, a will does not give rise to any *different* relations, but is only the cause from which the action is derived; and consequently produces the *same* relations, that in the oak or elm arise from some other principles. It is a will or choice that determines a man to kill his parent: and they are the laws of matter and motion that determine a sapling to destroy the oak from which it sprung. Here then the same relations have different causes; but still the relations are the same: and as their discovery is not in both cases attended with a notion of immorality, it follows, that that notion does not arise from such a discovery.

But to choose an instance still more resembling: I would fain ask any one, why incest in the human species is criminal, and why the very same action, and the same relations in animals, have not the smallest moral turpitude and deformity? If it be answered, that this action is innocent in animals, because they have not reason sufficient to discover its turpitude; but that man, being endowed with that faculty, which *ought* to restrain him to his duty, the same action instantly becomes criminal to him. Should this be said, I would reply, that this is evidently arguing in a circle. For, before reason can perceive this turpitude, the turpitude must exist; and consequently is independent of the decisions of our reason, and is their object more properly than their effect. According to this system, then, every animal that has sense and appetite and will, that is, every animal must be susceptible of all the same virtues and vices, for which we ascribe praise and blame to human creatures. All the difference is, that our superior reason may serve to discover the vice or virtue, and by that means may augment the blame or praise: but still this discovery supposes a separate being in these moral distinctions, and a being which depends only on the will and appetite, and which, both in thought and reality, may be distinguished from reason. Animals are susceptible of the same relations with respect to each other as the human species, and therefore would also be susceptible of the same morality, if the essence of morality consisted in these relations. Their want of a sufficient degree of reason may hinder them from perceiving the duties and obligations of morality, but can never hinder these duties from existing; since they must antecedently exist, in order to their being perceived. Reason must find them, and can never produce them. This argument deserves to be weighed, as being, in my opinion, entirely decisive.

Nor does this reasoning only prove, that morality consists not in any relations that are the objects of science; but if examined, will prove with equal certainty, that it consists not in any *matter of fact,* which can be discovered by the understanding. This is the *second* part of our argument; and if it can be made evident, we may conclude that morality is not an object of reason. But can there be any difficulty in proving that vice and virtue are not matters of fact, whose existence we can infer by reason? Take any action allowed to be vicious; wilful murder, for instance. Examine it in all lights, and see if you can find that matter of fact, or real existence, which you call *vice.* In whichever way you take it, you find only certain passions, motives, volitions, and thoughts. There is no other matter of fact in the case. The vice entirely escapes you, as long as you consider the object. You never can find it, till you turn your reflection into your own breast, and find a sentiment of disapprobation, which arises in you, towards this action. Here is a matter of fact; but it is the object of feeling, not of reason. It lies in yourself, not in the object. So that when you pronounce any action or character to be vicious, you mean nothing, but that from the constitution of your nature you have a feeling or sentiment of blame from the contemplation of it. Vice and virtue, therefore, may be compared to sounds, colours, heat, and cold, which, according to modern philosophy, are not qualities in objects, but perceptions in the mind: and this discovery in morals, like that other in physics, is to be regarded as a considerable advancement of the speculative sciences; though, like that too, it has little or no influence on practice. Nothing can be more real, or concern us more, than our own sentiments of pleasure and uneasiness; and if these be favourable to virtue, and unfavourable to vice, no more can be requisite to the regulation of our conduct and behaviour.

I cannot forbear adding to these reasonings an observation, which may, perhaps, be found of some importance. In every system of morality which I have hitherto met with, I have always remarked, that the author proceeds for some time in the ordinary way of reasoning, and establishes the being of a God, or makes observations concerning human affairs; when of a sudden I am surprised to find, that instead of the usual copulations of propositions, *is,* and *is not,* I meet with no proposition that is not connected with an *ought,* or an *ought not.* This change is imperceptible; but is, however, of the last consequence. For as this *ought,* or *ought not,* expresses some new relation or affirmation, it is necessary that it should be observed and explained; and at the same time that a reason should be given, for what seems altogether inconceivable, how this new relation can be a deduction from others, which are entirely different from it. But as authors do not commonly use this precaution. I shall presume to recommend it to the readers; and am persuaded, that this small attention would subvert all the vulgar systems of morality, and let us see that the distinction of vice and virtue is not founded merely on the relations of objects, nor is perceived by reason.

STUDY QUESTIONS

1. If you judge that an action is moral, are you motivated to perform it?
2. If human beings were different, would morality be different?
3. Do 'is' statements by themselves ever imply 'ought' statements?
4. What does Hume aim to show with the example of a sapling killing its parent tree?

Principia Ethica

G. E. Moore

George Edward Moore (1873–1958), Professor of Mental Philosophy and Logic at the University of Cambridge, was one of the most influential philosophers of the twentieth century. He argued that goodness, like the color yellow, is simple, and having no parts, indefinable. In other words, goodness is an ultimate term by reference to which other terms can be defined. To offer a definition of goodness is to commit what Moore called "the naturalistic fallacy." Whether that so-called fallacy is indeed fallacious became a crucial issue in ethical inquiry.

5. . . . [H]ow "good" is to be defined, is the most fundamental question in all Ethics. That which is meant by "good" is, in fact, except its converse "bad," the *only* simple object of thought which is peculiar to Ethics. Its definition is, therefore, the most essential point in the definition of Ethics; and moreover a mistake with regard to it entails a far larger number of erroneous ethical judgments than any other. Unless this first question be fully understood, and its true answer clearly recognised, the rest of Ethics is as good as useless from the point of view of systematic knowledge. True ethical judgments, of the two kinds last dealt with, may indeed be made by those who do not know the answer to this question as well as by those who do; and it goes without saying that the two classes of people may lead equally good lives. But it is extremely unlikely that the *most general* ethical judgments will be equally valid, in the absence of a true answer to this question: I shall presently try to shew that the gravest errors have been largely due to beliefs in a false answer. And, in any case, it is impossible that, till the answer to this question be known, any one should know *what is the evidence* for any ethical judgment whatsoever. But the main object of Ethics, as a systematic science, is to give correct *reasons* for thinking that this or that is good; and, unless this question be answered, such reasons cannot be given. Even, therefore, apart from the fact that a false answer leads to false conclusions, the present enquiry is a most necessary and important part of the science of Ethics.

6. What, then, is good? How is good to be defined? Now, it may be thought that this is a verbal question. A definition does indeed often mean the expressing of one word's meaning in other words. But this is not the sort of definition I am asking for. Such a definition can never be of ultimate importance in any study except lexicography. If I wanted that kind of definition I should have to consider in the first place how people generally used the word "good"; but my business is not with its proper usage, as established by custom. I should, indeed, be foolish, if I tried to use it for something which it

From *Principia Ethica* by G. E. Moore (1903). Reprinted with the permission of Cambridge University Press.

did not usually denote: if, for instance, I were to announce that, whenever I used the word "good," I must be understood to be thinking of that object which is usually denoted by the word "table." I shall, therefore, use the word in the sense in which I think it is ordinarily used; but at the same time I am not anxious to discuss whether I am right in thinking that it is so used. My business is solely with that object or idea, which I hold, rightly or wrongly, that the word is generally used to stand for. What I want to discover is the nature of that object or idea, and about this I am extremely anxious to arrive at an agreement.

But, if we understand the question in this sense, my answer to it may seem a very disappointing one. If I am asked "What is good?" my answer is that good is good, and that is the end of the matter. Or if I am asked "How is good to be defined?" my answer is that it cannot be defined, and that is all I have to say about it. But disappointing as these answers may appear, they are of the very last importance. To readers who are familiar with philosophic terminology, I can express their importance by saying that they amount to this: That propositions about the good are all of them synthetic and never analytic; and that is plainly no trivial matter. And the same thing may be expressed more popularly, by saying that, if I am right, then nobody can foist upon us such an axiom as that "Pleasure is the only good" or that "The good is the desired" on the pretence that this is "the very meaning of the word."

7. Let us, then, consider this position: My point is that "good" is a simple notion, just as "yellow" is a simple notion; that, just as you cannot, by any manner of means, explain to any one who does not already know it, what yellow is, so you cannot explain what good is. Definitions of the kind that I was asking for, definitions which describe the real nature of the object or notion denoted by a word, and which do not merely tell us what the word is used to mean, are only possible when the object or notion in question is something complex. You can give a definition of a horse, because a horse has many different properties and qualities, all of which you can enumerate. But when you have enumerated them all, when you have reduced a horse to his simplest terms, then you can no longer define those terms. They are simply something which you think of or perceive, and to any one who cannot think of or perceive them, you can never, by any definition, make their nature known. It may perhaps be objected to this that we are able to describe to others, objects which they have never seen or thought of. We can, for instance, make a man understand what a chimaera is, although he has never heard of one or seen one. You can tell him that it is an animal with a lioness's head and body, with a goat's head growing from the middle of its back, and with a snake in place of a tail. But here the object which you are describing is a complex object; it is entirely composed of parts, with which we are all perfectly familiar—a snake, a goat, a lioness; and we know, too, the manner in which those parts are to be put together, because we know what is meant by the middle of a lioness's back, and where her tail is wont to grow. And so it is with all objects, not previously known, which we are able to define: they are all complex; all composed of parts, which may themselves, in the first instance, be capable of similar definition, but which must in the end be reducible to simplest parts, which can no longer be defined. But yellow and good, we say, are not complex: they are notions of that simple kind, out of which definitions are composed and with which the power of further defining ceases.

8. When we say, as Webster says, "The definition of horse is 'A hoofed quadruped of the genus Equus,'" we may, in fact, mean three different things. (1) We may mean merely: "When I say 'horse,' you are to understand that I am talking about a hoofed quadruped of the genus Equus." This might be called the arbitrary verbal definition: and I do not mean that good is indefinable in that sense. (2) We may mean, as Webster ought to mean: "When most English people say 'horse,' they mean a hoofed quadruped of the genus Equus." This may be called the verbal definition proper, and I do not say that good is indefinable in this sense either; for it is certainly possible to discover how people use a word: otherwise, we could never have known that "good" may be translated by "gut" in German and by "bon" in French. But (3) we may, when we define horse, mean something much more important. We may mean that a certain object, which

we all of us know, is composed in a certain manner: that it has four legs, a head, a heart, a liver, etc., etc., all of them arranged in definite relations to one another. It is in this sense that I deny good to be definable. I say that it is not composed of any parts, which we can substitute for it in our minds when we are thinking of it. We might think just as clearly and correctly about a horse, if we thought of all its parts and their arrangement instead of thinking of the whole: we could, I say, think how a horse differed from a donkey just as well, just as truly, in this way, as now we do, only not so easily; but there is nothing whatsoever which we could so substitute for good; and that is what I mean, when I say that good is indefinable.

9. But I am afraid I have still not removed the chief difficulty which may prevent acceptance of the proposition that good is indefinable. I do not mean to say that *the* good, that which is good, is thus indefinable; if I did think so, I should not be writing on Ethics, for my main object is to help towards discovering that definition. It is just because I think there will be less risk of error in our search for a definition of "the good," that I am now insisting that *good* is indefinable. I must try to explain the difference between these two. I suppose it may be granted that "good" is an adjective. Well "the good," "that which is good," must therefore be the substantive to which the adjective "good" will apply: it must be the whole of that to which the adjective will apply, and the adjective must *always* truly apply to it. But if it is that to which the adjective will apply, it must be something different from that adjective itself; and the whole of that something different, whatever it is, will be our definition of *the* good. Now it may be that this something will have other adjectives, besides "good," that will apply to it. It may be full of pleasure, for example; it may be intelligent: and if these two adjectives are really part of its definition, then it will certainly be true, that pleasure and intelligence are good. And many people appear to think that, if we say "Pleasure and intelligence are good," or if we say "Only pleasure and intelligence are good," we are defining "good." Well, I cannot deny that propositions of this nature may sometimes be called definitions; I do not know well enough how the word is generally used to decide upon this point. I only wish it to be understood that that is not what I mean when I say there is no possible definition of good, and that I shall not mean this if I use the word again. I do most fully believe that some true proposition of the form "Intelligence is good and intelligence alone is good" can be found; if none could be found, our definition of *the* good would be impossible. As it is, I believe *the* good to be definable; and yet I still say that good itself is indefinable.

10. "Good," then, if we mean by it that quality which we assert to belong to a thing, when we say that the thing is good, is incapable of any definition, in the most important sense of that word. The most important sense of "definition" is that in which a definition states what are the parts which invariably compose a certain whole; and in this sense "good" has no definition because it is simple and has no parts. It is one of those innumerable objects of thought which are themselves incapable of definition, because they are the ultimate terms by reference to which whatever *is* capable of definition must be defined. That there must be an indefinite number of such terms is obvious, on reflection; since we cannot define anything except by an analysis, which, when carried as far as it will go, refers us to something, which is simply different from anything else, and which by that ultimate difference explains the peculiarity of the whole which we are defining: for every whole contains some parts which are common to other wholes also. There is, therefore, no intrinsic difficulty in the contention that "good" denotes a simple and indefinable quality. There are many other instances of such qualities.

Consider yellow, for example. We may try to define it, by describing its physical equivalent; we may state what kind of light-vibrations must stimulate the normal eye, in order that we may perceive it. But a moment's reflection is sufficient to shew that those light-vibrations are not themselves what we mean by yellow. *They* are not what we perceive. Indeed we should never have been able to discover their existence, unless we had first been struck by the patent difference of quality between the different colours. The most we can be entitled to say of those vibrations is that they are what corresponds in space to the yellow which we actually perceive.

Yet a mistake of this simple kind has commonly been made about "good." It may be true that all things which are good are *also* something else, just as it is true that all things which are yellow produce a certain kind of vibration in the light. And it is a fact, that Ethics aims at discovering what are those other properties belonging to all things which are good. But far too many philosophers have thought that when they named those other properties they were actually defining good; that these properties, in fact, were simply not "other," but absolutely and entirely the same with goodness. This view I propose to call the "naturalistic fallacy" and of it I shall now endeavour to dispose.

11. Let us consider what it is such philosophers say. And first it is to be noticed that they do not agree among themselves. They not only say that they are right as to what good is, but they endeavour to prove that other people who say that it is something else, are wrong. One, for instance, will affirm that good is pleasure, another, perhaps, that good is that which is desired; and each of these will argue eagerly to prove that the other is wrong. But how is that possible? One of them says that good is nothing but the object of desire, and at the same time tries to prove that it is not pleasure. But from his first assertion, that good just means the object of desire, one of two things must follow as regards his proof:

(1) He may be trying to prove that the object of desire is not pleasure. But, if this be all, where is his Ethics? The position he is maintaining is merely a psychological one. Desire is something which occurs in our minds, and pleasure is something else which so occurs; and our would-be ethical philosopher is merely holding that the latter is not the object of the former. But what has that to do with the question in dispute? His opponent held the ethical proposition that pleasure was the good, and although he should prove a million times over the psychological proposition that pleasure is not the object of desire, he is no nearer proving his opponent to be wrong. The position is like this. One man says a triangle is a circle: another replies "A triangle is a straight line, and I will prove to you that I am right: *for*" (this is the only argument) "a straight line is not a circle."

"That is quite true," the other may reply; "but nevertheless a triangle is a circle, and you have said nothing whatever to prove the contrary. What is proved is that one of us is wrong, for we agree that a triangle cannot be both a straight line and a circle: but which is wrong, there can be no earthly means of proving, since you define triangle as straight line and I define it as circle."—Well, that is one alternative which any naturalistic Ethics has to face; if good is *defined* as something else, it is then impossible either to prove that any other definition is wrong or even to deny such definition.

(2) The other alternative will scarcely be more welcome. It is that the discussion is after all a verbal one. When A says "Good means pleasant" and B says "Good means desired," they may merely wish to assert that most people have used the word for what is pleasant and for what is desired respectively. And this is quite an interesting subject for discussion: only it is not a whit more an ethical discussion than the last was. Nor do I think that any exponent of naturalistic Ethics would be willing to allow that this was all he meant. They are all so anxious to persuade us that what they call the good is what we really ought to do. "Do pray, act so, because the word 'good' is generally used to denote actions of this nature": such, on this view, would be the substance of their teaching. And in so far as they tell us how we ought to act, their teaching is truly ethical, as they mean it to be. But how perfectly absurd is the reason they would give for it! "You are to do this, because most people use a certain word to denote conduct such as this." "You are to say the thing which is not, because most people call it lying." That is an argument just as good!—My dear sirs, what we want to know from you as ethical teachers, is not how people use a word; it is not even, what kind of actions they approve, which the use of this word "good" may certainly imply: what we want to know is simply what *is* good. We may indeed agree that what most people do think good, is actually so; we shall at all events be glad to know their opinions: but when we say their opinions about what *is* good, we do mean what we say; we do not care whether they call that thing which they mean "horse" or "table" or "chair," "gut" or "bon" or "ἀγαθός"; we want to know what it is

that they so call. When they say "Pleasure is good," we cannot believe that they merely mean "Pleasure is pleasure" and nothing more than that.

12. Suppose a man says "I am pleased"; and suppose that is not a lie or a mistake but the truth. Well, if it is true, what does that mean? It means that his mind, a certain definite mind, distinguished by certain definite marks from all others, has at this moment a certain definite feeling called pleasure. "Pleased" *means* nothing but having pleasure, and though we may be more pleased or less pleased, and even, we may admit for the present, have one or another kind of pleasure; yet in so far as it is pleasure we have, whether there be more or less of it, and whether it be of one kind or another, what we have is one definite thing, absolutely indefinable, some one thing that is the same in all the various degrees and in all the various kinds of it that there may be. We may be able to say how it is related to other things: that, for example, it is in the mind, that it causes desire, that we are conscious of it, etc., etc. We can, I say, describe its relations to other things, but define it we can *not*. And if anybody tried to define pleasure for us as being any other natural object; if anybody were to say, for instance, that pleasure *means* the sensation of red, and were to proceed to deduce from that that pleasure is a colour, we should be entitled to laugh at him and to distrust his future statements about pleasure. Well, that would be the same fallacy which I have called the naturalistic fallacy. That "pleased" does not mean "having the sensation of red," or anything else whatever, does not prevent us from understanding what it does mean. It is enough for us to know that "pleased" does mean "having the sensation of pleasure," and though pleasure is absolutely indefinable, though pleasure is pleasure and nothing else whatever, yet we feel no difficulty in saying that we are pleased. The reason is, of course, that when I say "I am pleased," I do *not* mean that "I" am the same thing as "having pleasure." And similarly no difficulty need be found in my saying that "pleasure is good" and yet not meaning that "pleasure" is the same thing as "good," that pleasure *means* good, and that good *means* pleasure. If I were to imagine that when I said "I am pleased,"

I meant that I was exactly the same thing as "pleased," I should not indeed call that a naturalistic fallacy, although it would be the same fallacy as I have called naturalistic with reference to Ethics. The reason of this is obvious enough. When a man confuses two natural objects with one another, defining the one by the other, if for instance, he confuses himself, who is one natural object, with "pleased" or with "pleasure" which are others, then there is no reason to call the fallacy naturalistic. But if he confuses "good," which is not in the same sense a natural object, with any natural object whatever, then there is a reason for calling that a naturalistic fallacy; its being made with regard to "good" marks it as something quite specific, and this specific mistake deserves a name because it is so common. As for the reasons why good is not to be considered a natural object, they may be reserved for discussion in another place. But, for the present, it is sufficient to notice this: Even if it were a natural object, that would not alter the nature of the fallacy nor diminish its importance one whit. All that I have said about it would remain quite equally true: only the name which I have called it would not be so appropriate as I think it is. And I do not care about the name: what I do care about is the fallacy. It does not matter what we call it, provided we recognise it when we meet with it. It is to be met with in almost every book on Ethics; and yet it is not recognised: and that is why it is necessary to multiply illustrations of it, and convenient to give it a name. It is a very simple fallacy indeed. When we say that an orange is yellow, we do not think our statement binds us to hold that "orange" means nothing else than "yellow," or that nothing can be yellow but an orange. Supposing the orange is also sweet! Does that bind us to say that "sweet" is exactly the same thing as "yellow," that "sweet" must be defined as "yellow"? And supposing it be recognised that "yellow" just means "yellow" and nothing else whatever, does that make it any more difficult to hold that oranges are yellow? Most certainly it does not: on the contrary, it would be absolutely meaningless to say that oranges were yellow, unless yellow did in the end mean just "yellow" and nothing else whatever—unless it was absolutely indefinable. We should not get any very clear notion about things, which are yellow—we should not get very far with our science, if we were bound to hold that everything which was yellow, *meant* exactly the same thing as yellow. We should find we had to hold that an orange was exactly the same thing as a stool, a piece of paper, a lemon, anything you like. We could prove any number of absurdities; but should we be the nearer to the truth? Why, then, should it be different with "good"? Why, if good is good and indefinable, should I be held to deny that pleasure is good? Is there any difficulty in holding both to be true at once? On the contrary, there is no meaning in saying that pleasure is good, unless good is something different from pleasure. It is absolutely useless, so far as Ethics is concerned, to prove, as Mr Spencer tries to do, that increase of pleasure coincides with increase of life, unless good *means* something different from either life or pleasure. He might just as well try to prove that an orange is yellow by shewing that it always is wrapped up in paper.

13. In fact, if it is not the case that "good" denotes something simple and indefinable, only two alternatives are possible: either it is a complex, a given whole, about the correct analysis of which there may be disagreement; or else it means nothing at all, and there is no such subject as Ethics. In general, however, ethical philosophers have attempted to define good, without recognising what such an attempt must mean. They actually use arguments which involve one or both of the absurdities considered in § 11. We are, therefore, justified in concluding that the attempt to define good is chiefly due to want of clearness as to the possible nature of definition. There are, in fact, only two serious alternatives to be considered, in order to establish the conclusion that "good" does denote a simple and indefinable notion. It might possibly denote a complex, as "horse" does; or it might have no meaning at all. Neither of these possibilities has, however, been clearly conceived and seriously maintained, as such, by those who presume to define good; and both may be dismissed by a simple appeal to facts.

(1) The hypothesis that disagreement about the meaning of good is disagreement with regard to the correct analysis of a given whole, may be most plainly seen to be incorrect by consideration of the fact that, whatever definition be offered, it may be always asked, with significance, of the complex so defined, whether it is itself good. To take, for instance, one of the more plausible, because one of the more complicated, of such proposed definitions, it may easily be thought, at first sight, that to be good may mean to be that which we desire to desire. Thus if we apply this definition to a particular instance and say "When we think that A is good, we are thinking that A is one of the things which we desire to desire," our proposition may seem quite plausible. But, if we carry the investigation further, and ask ourselves "Is it good to desire to desire A?" it is apparent, on a little reflection, that this question is itself as intelligible, as the original question "Is A good?"—that we are, in fact, now asking for exactly the same information about the desire to desire A, for which we formerly asked with regard to A itself. But it is also apparent that the meaning of this second question cannot be correctly analysed into "Is the desire to desire A one of the things which we desire to desire?": we have not before our minds anything so complicated as the question "Do we desire to desire to desire A?" Moreover any one can easily convince himself by inspection that the predicate of this proposition—"good"—is positively different from the notion of "desiring to desire" which enters into its subject: "That we should desire to desire A is good" is *not* merely equivalent to "That A should be good is good." It may indeed be true that what we desire to desire is always also good; perhaps, even the converse may be true: but it is very doubtful whether this is the case, and the mere fact that we understand very well what is meant by doubting it, shews clearly that we have two different notions before our minds.

(2) And the same consideration is sufficient to dismiss the hypothesis that "good" has no meaning whatsoever. It is very natural to make the mistake of supposing that what is universally true is of such a nature that its negation would be self-contradictory: the importance which has been assigned to analytic propositions in the history of philosophy shews how easy such a mistake is. And thus it is very easy to conclude that what seems to be a universal ethical principle is in fact an identical proposition; that, if,

for example, whatever is called "good" seems to be pleasant, the proposition "Pleasure is the good" does not assert a connection between two different notions, but involves only one, that of pleasure, which is easily recognised as a distinct entity. But whoever will attentively consider with himself what is actually before his mind when he asks the question "Is pleasure (or whatever it may be) after all good?" can easily satisfy himself that he is not merely wondering whether pleasure is pleasant. And if he will try this experiment with each suggested definition in succession, he may become expert enough to recognise that in every case he has before his mind a unique object, with regard to the connection of which with any other object, a distinct question may be asked. Every one does in fact understand the question "Is this good?" When he thinks of it, his state of mind is different from what it would be, were he asked "Is this pleasant, or desired, or approved?" It has a distinct meaning for him, even though he may not recognise in what respect it is distinct. Whenever he thinks of "intrinsic value," or "intrinsic worth," or says that a thing "ought to exist," he has before his mind the unique object—the unique property of things—which I mean by "good." Everybody is constantly aware of this notion, although he may never become aware at all that it is different from other notions of which he is also aware. But, for correct ethical reasoning, it is extremely important that he should become aware of this fact; and, as soon as the nature of the problem is clearly understood, there should be little difficulty in advancing so far in analysis.

STUDY QUESTIONS

1. According to Moore, what is the most fundamental question in ethics?
2. How does Moore answer that fundamental question?
3. According to Moore, what is the naturalistic fallacy?
4. What did Moore mean by "intrinsic value"?

Ethics and Observation

Gilbert Harman

Gilbert Harman is Professor of Philosophy at Princeton University. He argues that moral beliefs are incapable of the sort of empirical confirmation characteristic of scientific beliefs. Scientific observations provide evidence for particular physical theories because the best explanation for the occurrence of the observation is based on the observer's psychology *and* facts about the world. By contrast, moral observations do not provide evidence for particular ethical theories because the best explanation for the occurrence of the observation is based only on the observer's psychology and not on moral facts. This asymmetry suggests the nonexistence of moral facts, moral truths, and moral knowledge.

1. THE BASIC ISSUE

Can moral principles be tested and confirmed in the way scientific principles can? Consider the principle that, if you are given a choice between five people alive and one dead or five people dead and one alive, you should always choose to have five people alive and one dead rather than the other way round. We can easily imagine examples that appear to confirm this principle. Here is one:

> You are a doctor in a hospital's emergency room when six accident victims are brought in. All six are in danger of dying but one is much worse off than the others. You can just barely save that person if you devote all of your resources to him and let the others die. Alternatively, you can save the other five if you are willing to ignore the most seriously injured person.

It would seem that in this case you, the doctor, would be right to save the five and let the other person die. So this example, taken by itself, confirms the principle under consideration. Next, consider the following case.

> You have five patients in the hospital who are dying, each in need of a separate organ. One needs a kidney, another a lung, a third a heart, and so forth. You can save all five if you take a single healthy person and remove his heart, lungs, kidneys, and so forth, to distribute to these five patients. Just such a healthy person is in Room 306. He is in the hospital for routine tests. Having seen his test results, you know that he is perfectly healthy and of the right tissue compatability. If you do nothing, he will survive without incident; the other patients will die, however. The other five patients can be saved

From Gilbert Harman, *The Nature of Morality*, Princeton University Press, 1977. Reprinted by permission of the publisher.

only if the person in Room 306 is cut up and his organs distributed. In that case, there would be one dead but five saved.

The principle in question tells us that you should cut up the patient in Room 306. But in this case, surely you must not sacrifice this innocent bystander, even to save the five other patients. Here a moral principle has been tested and disconfirmed in what may seem to be a surprising way.

This, of course, was a "thought experiment." We did not really compare a hypothesis with the world. We compared an explicit principle with our feelings about certain imagined examples. In the same way, a physicist performs thought experiments in order to compare explicit hypotheses with his "sense" of what should happen in certain situations, a "sense" that he has acquired as a result of his long working familiarity with current theory. But scientific hypotheses can also be tested in real experiments, out in the world.

Can moral principles be tested in the same way, out in the world? You can observe someone do something, but can you ever perceive the rightness or wrongness of what he does? If you round a corner and see a group of young hoodlums pour gasoline on a cat and ignite it, you do not need to *conclude* that what they are doing is wrong; you do not need to figure anything out; you can *see* that it is wrong. But is your reaction due to the actual wrongness of what you see or is it simply a reflection of your moral "sense," a "sense" that you have acquired perhaps as a result of your moral upbringing?

2. OBSERVATION

The issue is complicated. There are no pure observations. Observations are always "theory laden." What you perceive depends to some extent on the theory you hold, consciously or unconsciously. You see some children pour gasoline on a cat and ignite it. To really see that, you have to possess a great deal of knowledge, know about a considerable number of objects, know about people: that people pass through the life stages infant, baby, child, adolescent, adult. You must know what flesh and blood animals are,

and in particular, cats. You must have some idea of life. You must know what gasoline is, what burning is, and much more. In one sense, what you "see" is a pattern of light on your retina, a shifting array of splotches, although even that is theory, and you could never adequately describe what you see in that sense. In another sense, you see what you do because of the theories you hold. Change those theories and you would see something else, given the same pattern of light.

Similarly, if you hold a moral view, whether it is held consciously or unconsciously, you will be able to perceive rightness or wrongness, goodness or badness, justice or injustice. There is no difference in this respect between moral propositions and other theoretical propositions. If there is a difference, it must be found elsewhere.

Observation depends on theory because perception involves forming a belief as a fairly direct result of observing something; you can form a belief only if you understand the relevant concepts and a concept is what it is by virtue of its role in some theory or system of beliefs. To recognize a child as a child is to employ, consciously or unconsciously, a concept that is defined by its place in a framework of the stages of human life. Similarly, burning is an empty concept apart from its theoretical connections to the concepts of heat, destruction, smoke, and fire.

Moral concepts—Right and Wrong, Good and Bad, Justice and Injustice—also have a place in your theory or system of beliefs and are the concepts they are because of their context. If we say that observation has occurred whenever an opinion is a direct result of perception, we must allow that there is moral observation, because such an opinion can be a moral opinion as easily as any other sort. In this sense, observation may be used to confirm or disconfirm moral theories. The observational opinions that, in this sense, you find yourself with can be in either agreement or conflict with your consciously explicit moral principles. When they are in conflict, you must choose between your explicit theory and observation. In ethics, as in science, you sometimes opt for theory, and say that you made an error in observation or were biased or whatever, or you sometimes opt for observation, and modify your theory.

In other words, in both science and ethics, general principles are invoked to explain particular cases and, therefore, in both science and ethics, the general principles you accept can be tested by appealing to particular judgments that certain things are right or wrong, just or unjust, and so forth; and these judgments are analogous to direct perceptual judgments about facts.

3. OBSERVATIONAL EVIDENCE

Nevertheless, observation plays a role in science that it does not seem to play in ethics. The difference is that you need to make assumptions about certain physical facts to explain the occurrence of the observations that support a scientific theory, but you do not seem to need to make assumptions about any moral facts to explain the occurrence of the so-called moral observations I have been talking about. In the moral case, it would seem that you need only make assumptions about the psychology or moral sensibility of the person making the moral observation. In the scientific case, theory is tested against the world.

The point is subtle but important. Consider a physicist making an observation to test a scientific theory. Seeing a vapor trail in a cloud chamber, he thinks, "There goes a proton." Let us suppose that this is an observation in the relevant sense, namely, an immediate judgment made in response to the situation without any conscious reasoning having taken place. Let us also suppose that this observation confirms his theory, a theory that helps give meaning to the very term "proton" as it occurs in his observational judgment. Such a confirmation rests on inferring an explanation. He can count his making the observation as confirming evidence for his theory only to the extent that it is reasonable to explain his making the observation by assuming that, not only is he in a certain psychological "set," given the theory he accepts and his beliefs about the experimental apparatus, but furthermore, there really was a proton going through the cloud chamber, causing the vapor trail, which he saw as a proton. (This is evidence for the theory to the extent that the theory can explain the proton's being there better than competing theories

can.) But, if his having made that observation could have been equally well explained by his psychological set alone, without the need for any assumption about a proton, then the observation would not have been evidence for the existence of that proton and therefore would not have been evidence for the theory. His making the observation supports the theory only because, in order to explain his making the observation, it is reasonable to assume something about the world over and above the assumptions made about the observer's psychology. In particular, it is reasonable to assume that there was a proton going through the cloud chamber, causing the vapor trail.

Compare this case with one in which you make a moral judgment immediately and without conscious reasoning, say, that the children are wrong to set the cat on fire or that the doctor would be wrong to cut up one healthy patient to save five dying patients. In order to explain your making the first of these judgments, it would be reasonable to assume, perhaps, that the children really are pouring gasoline on a cat and you are seeing them do it. But, in neither case is there any obvious reason to assume anything about "moral facts," such as that it really is wrong to set the cat on fire or to cut up the patient in Room 306. Indeed, an assumption about moral facts would seem to be totally irrelevant to the explanation of your making the judgment you make. It would seem that all we need assume is that you have certain more or less well articulated moral principles that are reflected in the judgments you make, based on your moral sensibility. It seems to be completely irrelevant to our explanation whether your intuitive immediate judgment is true or false.

The observation of an event can provide observational evidence for or against a scientific theory in the sense that the truth of that observation can be relevant to a reasonable explanation of why that observation was made. A moral observation does not seem, in the same sense, to be observational evidence for or against any moral theory, since the truth or falsity of the moral observation seems to be completely irrelevant to any reasonable explanation of why that observation was made. The fact that an observation of an event was made at the time it was made is evidence not only about the observer but also about the physical facts. The fact that you made a particular moral observation when you did does not seem to be evidence about moral facts, only evidence about you and your moral sensibility. Facts about protons can affect what you observe, since a proton passing through the cloud chamber can cause a vapor trail that reflects light to your eye in a way that, given your scientific training and psychological set, leads you to judge that what you see is a proton. But there does not seem to be any way in which the actual rightness or wrongness of a given situation can have any effect on your perceptual apparatus. In this respect, ethics seems to differ from science.

In considering whether moral principles can help explain observations, it is therefore important to note an ambiguity in the word "observation." You see the children set the cat on fire and immediately think, "That's wrong." In one sense, your observation is that what the children are doing is wrong. In another sense, your observation is your thinking that thought. Moral observations might explain observations in the first sense but not in the second sense. Certain moral principles might help to explain why it was *wrong* of the children to set the cat on fire, but moral principles seem to be of no help in explaining *your thinking* that that is wrong. In the first sense of "observation," moral principles can be tested by observation—"That this act is wrong is evidence that causing unnecessary suffering is wrong." But in the second sense of "observation," moral principles cannot clearly be tested by observation, since they do not appear to help explain observations in this second sense of "observation." Moral principles do not seem to help explain your observing what you observe.

Of course, if you are already given the moral principle that it is wrong to cause unnecessary suffering, you can take your seeing the children setting the cat on fire as observational evidence that they are doing something wrong. Similarly, you can suppose that your seeing the vapor trail is observational evidence that a proton is going through the cloud chamber, if you are given the relevant physical theory. But there is an important apparent difference between the two cases. In the scientific case, your making that observation is itself evidence for the physical theory because the physical theory explains the proton, which explains the trail, which explains your observation. In the moral case, your making your observation does not seem to be evidence for the relevant moral principle because that principle does not seem to help explain your observation. The explanatory chain from principle to observation seems to be broken in morality. The moral principle may "explain" why it is wrong for the children to set the cat on fire. But the wrongness of that act does not appear to help explain the act, which you observe, itself. The explanatory chain appears to be broken in such a way that neither the moral principle nor the wrongness of the act can help explain why you observe what you observe.

A qualification may seem to be needed here. Perhaps the children perversely set the cat on fire simply "because it is wrong." Here it may seem at first that the actual wrongness of the act does help explain why they do it and therefore indirectly helps explain why you observe what you observe just as a physical theory, by explaining why the proton is producing a vapor trail, indirectly helps explain why the observer observes what he observes. But on reflection we must agree that this is probably an illusion. What explains the children's act is not clearly the actual wrongness of the act but, rather, their belief that the act is wrong. The actual rightness or wrongness of their act seems to have nothing to do with why they do it.

Observational evidence plays a part in science it does not appear to play in ethics, because scientific principles can be justified ultimately by their role in explaining observations, in the second sense of observation—by their explanatory role. Apparently, moral principles cannot be justified in the same way. It appears to be true that there can be no explanatory chain between moral principles and particular observings in the way that there can be such a chain between scientific principles and particular observings. Conceived as an explanatory theory, morality, unlike science, seems to be cut off from observation.

Not that every legitimate scientific hypothesis is susceptible to direct observational testing. Certain hypotheses about "black holes" in space cannot be directly tested, for example, because no signal is emitted from within a black hole. The connection with observation in such a case is indirect. And there are many similar examples. Nevertheless, seen in the large, there is the apparent difference between science and ethics we have noted. The scientific realm is accessible to observation in a way the moral realm is not.

4. ETHICS AND MATHEMATICS

Perhaps ethics is to be compared, not with physics. but with mathematics. Perhaps such a moral principle as "You ought to keep your promises" is confirmed or disconfirmed in the way (whatever it is) in which such a mathematical principle as "$5 + 7 = 12$" is. Observation does not seem to play the role in mathematics it plays in physics. We do not and cannot perceive numbers, for example, since we cannot be in causal contact with them. We do not even understand what it would be like to be in causal contact with the number 12, say. Relations among numbers cannot have any more of an effect on our perceptual apparatus than moral facts can.

Observation, however, *is* relevant to mathematics. In explaining the observations that support a physical theory, scientists typically appeal to mathematical principles. On the other hand, one never seems to need to appeal in this way to moral principles. Since an observation is evidence for what best explains it, and since mathematics often figures in the explanations of scientific observations, there is indirect observational evidence for mathematics. There does not seem to be observational evidence, even indirectly, for basic moral principles. In explaining why certain observations have been made, we never seem to use purely moral assumptions. In this respect, then, ethics appears to differ not only from physics but also from mathematics.

STUDY QUESTIONS

1. Can any value judgments about, for example, good automobiles, good computers, or good restaurants be tested and confirmed in the way scientific claims can?
2. Can moral principles be tested and confirmed in the way scientific principles can?
3. Can we reason about morality in the absence of "moral facts"?
4. According to Harman, what is the difference between moral and mathematical explanations?

Realism

Michael Smith

Do moral judgments express beliefs, attempting to describe the way the world is? Or do moral judgments express desires, indicating how we want the world to be? Although both accounts look appealing, we appear to face a conflict between the objectivity and practicality of moral judgment. Michael Smith, Professor of Philosophy at Princeton University, argues in favor of realism, the view that moral facts exist. However he maintains that, though moral judgments are factual, they are nonetheless intimately linked to desire. For, according to Smith, moral judgments express beliefs about what we would desire if we were fully informed and rational.

It is a commonplace that we appraise each other's behaviour and attitudes from the moral point of view. We say, for example, that we did the *wrong* thing when we refused to give to famine relief this year, though perhaps we did the *right* thing when we handed in the wallet we found on the street; that we would be *better* people if we displayed a greater sensitivity to the feelings of others, though perhaps *worse* if in doing so we lost the special concern we have for our family and friends.

Most of us take appraisal of this sort pretty much for granted. To the extent that we worry about moral appraisal, we simply worry about *getting it right.* Philosophers too have been concerned to get the answers to moral questions right. However, traditionally, they have also been worried about the whole business of moral appraisal itself. Their worry can be brought out by focusing on two of the more distinctive features of moral practice; for, surprisingly, these features pull against each other, so threatening

to make the very idea of a 'moral' point of view altogether incoherent.

To begin, as we have already seen, it is distinctive of moral practice that we are concerned to get the answers to moral questions *right*. But this concern presupposes that there are correct answers to moral questions to be had. It thus seems to presuppose that there exists a domain of moral facts about which we can form beliefs and about which we may be mistaken. Moreover, these moral facts have a particular character. For we seem to think that the only relevant determinant of the rightness of an act is the circumstances in which the action takes place. Agents whose circumstances are identical face the same moral choice: if they did the same then either they both acted rightly or they both acted wrongly.

Indeed, something like this view of moral practice seems to explain our preoccupation with moral argument. What seems to give moral argument its point and poignancy is the idea that, since we are all

---

From "Realism" in Peter Singer, ed., *A Companion to Ethics*, Blackwell Publishers, 1991. Reprinted by permission of the publisher.

in the same boat, a careful mustering and assessment of the reasons for and against our moral opinions is the best way to discover what the moral facts really are. If the participants are open-minded and thinking correctly then, we seem to think, such an argument should result in a *convergence* in moral opinion—a convergence upon the truth. Individual reflection may serve the same purpose, but only when it simulates a real moral argument; for only then can we be certain that we are giving each side of the argument due consideration.

We may summarize this first feature of moral practice in the following terms: we seem to think moral questions have correct answers, that the correct answers are made correct by objective moral facts, that moral facts are determined by circumstances, and that, by moralizing, we can discover what these objective moral facts determined by the circumstances are. The term 'objective' here simply signifies the possibility of a convergence in moral views of the kind just mentioned.

A second and rather different feature of moral practice concerns the practical implications of moral judgement, the way in which moral questions gain in their significance for us because of the special influence our moral opinions are supposed to have upon our actions. The idea is that when, say, we come to think that we did the wrong thing in refusing to give to famine relief, we come to think that we failed to do something for which there was a good reason. And this has motivational implications. For now imagine the situation if we refuse to give to famine relief when next the opportunity arises. Our refusal will occasion serious puzzlement, for we will have refused to do what we are known to think we have a good reason to do. Perhaps we will be able to explain ourselves. Perhaps we thought there was a better reason to do something else, or perhaps we were weak-willed. But, the point remains, an explanation of some sort will need to be forthcoming. An explanation will need to be forthcoming because, we seem to think, other things being equal, to have a moral opinion simply is to find yourself with a corresponding motivation to act.

These two distinctive features of moral practice—the *objectivity* and the *practicality* of moral judgement—are widely thought to have both metaphysical and psychological implications. However, and unfortunately, these implications are the exact opposite of each other. In order to see why this is thought to be so, we need to pause for a moment to reflect more generally on the nature of human psychology.

According to the standard picture of human psychology—a picture we owe to David Hume, the famous Scottish philosopher of the eighteenth century—there are two main kinds of psychological state. On the one hand there are beliefs, states that purport to represent the way the world is. Since our beliefs purport to represent the world, they are subject to rational criticism: specifically, they are assessable in terms of truth and falsehood according to whether or not they succeed in representing the world to be the way it really is.

On the other hand, however, there are also desires, states that represent how the world is to be. Desires are unlike beliefs in that they do not even purport to represent the way the world is. They are therefore not assessable in terms of truth and falsehood. Indeed, according to the standard picture, our desires are at bottom not subject to any sort of rational criticism at all. The fact that we have a certain desire is, with a proviso to be mentioned presently, simply a fact about ourselves to be acknowledged. It may be unfortunate that we have certain combinations of desires—perhaps our desires cannot all be satisfied together—but, *in themselves,* our desires are all on a par, rationally neutral.

This is important, for it suggests that though we may make discoveries about the world, and though these discoveries may rightly affect our beliefs, such discoveries should, again with one proviso to be mentioned presently, have no rational impact upon our desires. They may of course, have some *non*-rational impact. Seeing a spider I may be overcome with a morbid fear and desire never to be near one. However, this is not a change in my desires mandated by reason. It is a *non*-rational change in my desires.

Now for the proviso. Suppose, contrary to the example I just gave, that I acquire the desire never to be near a spider because I come to believe, falsely, that spiders give off an unpleasant odour. Then we would certainly ordinarily say that I have an 'irrational desire'. However, the reason we would say this clearly doesn't go against the spirit of what has been said so far. For my desire never to be near a spider is *based on* a further desire and belief: my desire not to smell that unpleasant odour and my belief that that odour is given off by spiders. Since I can be rationally criticized for having the belief, as it is false, I can be rationally criticized for having the desire it helps to produce.

The proviso is thus fairly minor: desires are subject to rational criticism, but only insofar as they are based on beliefs that are subject to rational criticism. Desires that are not related in some such way to beliefs that can be rationally criticized are not subject to rational criticism at all. We will return to this point presently.

According to the standard picture, then, there are two kinds of psychological state—beliefs and desires—utterly distinct and different from each other. The standard picture of human psychology is important because it provides us with a model for understanding human action. Human action is, according to this picture, produced by a combination of the two. Crudely, our beliefs tell us how the world is, and thus how it has to be changed, so as to make it the way our desires tell us it is to be. An action is thus the product of these two forces: a desire representing the way the world is to be and a belief telling us how the world has to be changed so as to make it that way.

Let's now return to consider the two features of moral judgment we discussed earlier. Consider first the objectivity of such judgement: the idea that moral questions have correct answers, that the correct answers are made correct by objective moral facts, that moral facts are determined by circumstances, and that, by moralizing, we can discover what these objective moral facts are. The metaphysical and psychological implications of this may now be summarized as follows. Metaphysically, the implication is that, amongst the various facts there are in the world, there aren't just facts about (say) the consequences of our actions on the well-being of our families and friends, there are also distinctively *moral* facts: facts about the rightness and wrongness of our actions having these consequences. And,

psychologically, the implication is thus that when we make a moral judgement we thereby express our *beliefs* about the way these moral facts are. In forming moral opinions we acquire beliefs, representations of the way the world is morally.

Given the standard picture of human psychology, there is a further psychological implication. For whether or not people who have a certain moral belief desire to act accordingly must now be seen as a further and entirely separate question. They may happen to have a corresponding desire, they may not. However, either way, they canot be rationally criticized. Having or failing to have a corresponding desire is simply a further fact about a person's psychology.

But now consider the second feature, the practicality of moral judgment. We saw earlier that to have a moral opinion simply *is*, contrary to what has just been said, to find ourselves with a corresponding motivation to act. If we think it right to give to famine relief then, other things being equal, we must be motivated to give to famine relief. The practicality of moral judgement thus seems to have a psychological and a metaphysical implication of its own. Psychologically, since making a moral judgement requires our having a certain desire, and no recognition of a fact about the world could rationally compel us to have one desire rather than another, our judgement must really simply *be* an expression of that desire. And this psychological implication has a metaphysical counterpart. For it seems to follow that, contrary to initial appearance, when we judge it right to give to famine relief we *are not* responding to any moral fact—the rightness of giving to famine relief. Indeed, moral facts are an idle postulate. In judging it right to give to famine relief we are really simply expressing our desire that people give to famine relief. It is as if we were yelling "Hooray for giving to famine relief!"—no mention of a moral fact there, in fact, no factual claim at all.

We are now in a position to see why philosophers have been worried about the whole business of moral appraisal. The problem is that the *objectivity* and the *practicality* of moral judgement pull in quite opposite directions from each other. The objectivity of moral judgement suggests that there are moral facts, determined by circumstances, and that our moral judgements express our beliefs about what these facts are. This enables us to make good sense of moral argument, and the like, but it leaves it entirely mysterious how or why having a moral view is supposed to have special links with what we are motivated to do. And the practicality of moral judgement suggests just the opposite, that our moral judgements express our desires. While this enables us to make good sense of the link between having a moral view and being motivated, it leaves it entirely mysterious what a moral argument is supposed to be an argument about.

The idea of a moral judgement thus looks like it may well be incoherent, for what is required to make sense of such a judgement is a queer sort of fact about the universe: a fact whose recognition necessarily impacts upon our desires. But the standard picture tells us that there are no such facts. Nothing could be everything a moral judgement purports to be—or so it may now seem.

At long last we are in a position to see what this essay is about. For *moral realism* is simply the metaphysical (or ontological) view that there exist moral facts. The psychological counterpart to realism is called 'cognitivism', the view that moral judgements express beliefs about what these moral facts are, and that we can come to discover what these facts are by engaging in moral argument and reflection.

Moral realism thus contrasts with two alternative metaphysical views about morality: *irrealism* (sometimes called 'anti-realism') and *moral nihilism*. According to the irrealists, there are no moral facts, but neither are moral facts required to make sense of moral practice. We can happily acknowledge that our moral judgements simply express our desires about how people behave. This, the psychological counterpart to irrealism, is called 'non-cognitivism'. . . .

By contrast, according to the moral nihilists, the irrealists are right that there are no moral facts, but wrong about what is required to make sense of moral practice. The nihilist thinks that without moral facts moral practice is all a sham, much like religious practice without belief in God.

I have taken some time before introducing the ideas of moral realism, irrealism, and nihilism because, as it seems to me, each has much to be said both in its favour and against it. In what follows I will explain in more detail some of the substantive views people have taken in this whole debate. However, I want to emphasize at the outset that nearly every substantive position is fraught with difficulty and controversy. The long introduction will hopefully have given some hint of why this is so. The very idea of moral practice may well be in deep trouble, much as the moral nihilist suggests.

Remember that, according to the irrealist, when we judge it right to give to famine relief we are expressing our desire that people give to famine relief; it is as if we were yelling 'Hooray for giving to famine relief!' Irrealism is certainly an option to be considered. But it seems to me that it is ultimately an unattractive option.

To be sure, irrealists have a perfect explanation of the practicality of moral judgement. But it seems utterly implausible to suppose, as they therefore must, that moral judgements aren't truth-assessable at all. They must say this because they model a moral judgement on a yell of approval or disapproval. But when I yell 'Hooray for giving to famine relief!', though my yell may be sincere or insincere, it can hardly be true or false. My yell reveals something about myself—that I have a certain desire—not about the world.

The problem here isn't just that we *say* that moral judgements can be true or false, though we certainly do do that. The problem is rather that the whole business of moral argument and moral reflection only makes sense on the assumption that moral judgements *are* truth-assessable. When we agonize over our moral opinions, we seem to he agonizing over whether our reasons for our beliefs are good enough reasons for believing what we believe to be true. And no irrealist surrogate seems up to the task of explaining this appearance away. For example, it seems utterly hopeless to suppose that we are agonizing over whether we *really* have the desires we have. Surely *this* question isn't so hard to answer!

Indeed, in this context, it is worthwhile asking what the irrealists' view of moral argument is supposed to be. They presumably imagine that what we are trying to do, when we engage in moral argument, is to get our opponent to have the same desires as we have. But, at bottom, they must also say that we are trying to do this *not* because the opponent rationally should have these desires—remember that, subject to the proviso mentioned, desires aren't supposed to be subject to rational criticism at all—but rather just because these are the desires *we* want him to have. But in that case moral argument begins to look massively self-obsessed, an imposition of *our* wants on others.

Irrealism isn't an attractive option. The irrealist's account of moral judgement as the expression of a desire simply fails to make sense of moral reflection. And the irrealist's account of moral argument makes moral persuasion look like it is itself immoral! What about the alternative, moral realism?

It might be thought that, since the moral realist admits the existence of moral facts, he has therefore no problem explaining the objectivity of moral judgement and the related phenomena of moral reflection and moral argument. It might be thought that the realist's only problem is that, if he is to eschew the existence of 'queer' moral properties whose recognition connects necessarily with the will, then he cannot explain the practicality of moral judgement. But matters are in fact much more complicated.

Certainly the moral realist needs to face up to the fact that the practicality of moral judgement is problematic, from his point of view. But his problem is more than that. His problem is that, *because* he has no explanation of the practicality of moral judgement, he has no plausible story about what *kind* of fact a moral fact is. And if he has no plausible story about the kind of fact a moral fact is, then, despite initial appearance, he has no plausible story about what moral reflection and moral argument are all about.

In order to see this, remember what we said at the outset when we first introduced the idea of the practicality of moral judgement. We said then that the practicality of moral judgement is a consequence of the fact that judgements about right and wrong are judgements about what we have reason to do and reason not to do. This is the subject matter of moral reflection and moral argument, *our reasons for action*. But the moral realist who admits an array of moral facts about which we may be motivationally neutral must reject such a conception of rightness

and wrongness. After all, we could hardly remain motivationally neutral about what we think we have reason to do! The challenge such a realist faces is thus to provide us with some alternative account of what *kind* of fact a moral fact is; an alternative account of what moral reflection and moral argument are *about*.

Some moral realists do face up to this challenge. They have claimed, for example, that moral facts are facts that play a certain *explanatory role* in the social world: right acts are those that tend towards social stability, whereas wrong acts are those that tend towards social unrest. An Aristotelian version of this might be: right acts are those in accord with the 'proper function' of human beings—a quasi-biological notion—wrong acts are those that are not in accord with this proper function. Moral reflection and moral argument are thus, they suggest, arguments about which features of actions feed this tendency towards unrest and stability. Or, in the Aristotelian version, they are arguments about which acts are in accord with the proper function of humans (and thus, ultimately, about what the proper function of a human being is). The word 'tendency' is not idle here for such realists are quick to emphasize that other factors may mitigate the tendency towards stability and unrest, or may stop humans actually having their proper function.

Let's focus for a moment on the suggestion that a moral fact can be characterized in terms of a tendency towards social stability or unrest. This suggestion cannot be dismissed out of hand, for reflection of an armchair-sociological kind does suggest that the acts we are disposed to think of as right—those that provide for a more equitable satisfaction of different people's interests, say—do tend towards social stabilty, and that the acts we are disposed to think of as wrong—those that provide for a less equitable satisfaction of different people's interests, say—do tend towards social unrest. It is thus best to assume that we have here two *competing* conceptions of a moral fact. Which conception seems the more plausible?

On the one hand, we have the idea of a moral fact as a fact about what we have reason to do or not to do. On the other, we have the idea of a moral fact in terms of what tends towards social stability and unrest. If the question is 'Which conception allows us to make the best sense of moral argument?' then the answer must surely be the former. For, to the extent that moral argument does focus on what tends towards social stability, it does so because social stability is deemed morally important, an outcome we have reason to produce.

Indeed, it seems to me that even this kind of moral realist's focus on *explanation* pushes us back in the direction of the idea of a moral fact as a fact about what we have reason to do. For, again, to the extent that we think of right acts as acts that tend towards social stability, we think that they have this tendency *because* they represent the reasonable thing for people to do. It is the tendency people have to do what is reasonable that is doing the explanatory work. But that, too, simply returns us to the original conception of a moral fact in terms of what we have reason to do. (We might say similar things about the idea that we can characterize a moral fact in terms of the proper function of human beings; for insofar as we understand the idea of the 'proper function' of human beings, we think that their proper function is to be reasonable and rational.)

In the end, then, we might object that this kind of moral realist fails to provide us with a real *alternative* to our original conception of a moral fact. The real question, then, is whether the moral realist is forced to reject the idea that rightness and wrongness have to do with what we have reason to do and reason not to do. In the remainder of this essay I want to explore this question.

The devil of the piece is what I have been calling the 'standard picture' of human psychology. For the standard picture gives us a model of what it is to have a reason in terms of a desire/belief pair. If the moral realist is to make headway *in combining the objectivity and the practicality of moral judgement without appealing to 'queer' moral facts, he must challenge this standard picture.*

The trouble is, however, that the standard picture looks substantially correct as an account of human motivation. After all, it is uncontroversial that the psychological states that motivate actions must be dispositions of some sort, dispositions to produce acts of the relevant kind. And it is also uncontroversial that actions are motivated by psychological states that

have content: either they are produced by states that represent the way the world is (beliefs) or by states that represent the way the world is to be (desires), or, as the standard picture has it, they are produced by a pairing of the two (a desire and a belief).

But now reflect for a moment. A disposition to produce acts of some relevant kind, if it has content, must have, as its content, a representation of the way the world is to be, and so it must be a desire. For how else could the psychological state in question *target* the state of affairs to be produced? (And how could it produce what is to be produced without having targeted it?) Moreover, if this state is to produce the targeted state of affairs, it must also be paired with a representation of how the world is, and so it must be paired with a belief. For only so will the relevant *change* in the world be produced so as to bring about the targeted state of affairs.

It therefore seems that the standard picture is right in insisting that desires are required in order to motivate actions. The place to challenge the standard picture, then, is not in its account of what motivates action, but rather in its tacit conflation of *reasons* with *motives*. Seeing why this is a conflation also enables us to see why we may legitimately talk about our *beliefs* about the reasons we have, and why having such beliefs makes it rational to have corresponding desires.

Imagine that you are giving the baby a bath. As you do, it begins to scream uncontrollably. Nothing you do seems to help. As you watch it scream, you are overcome with a desire to drown the baby in the bathwater. Certainly you may now be *motivated* to drown the baby. (You may even actually drown it.) But does the mere fact that you have this desire, and are thus motivated, mean that you have a *reason* to drown the baby?

One commonsensical answer is that, since the desire is not *worth* satisfying, it does not provide you with such a reason; that, in this case, you are motivated to do something you have *no* reason to do. However, the standard picture seems utterly unable to accept this answer. After all, your desire to drown the baby need be based on no false belief. As such, it is entirely beyond rational criticism—or so that standard picture tells us.

The problem, here, is that the standard picture gives no special privilege to what we would want if we were 'cool, calm and collected' (to use a flippant phrase). Yet we seem ordinarily to think that not being cool, calm and collected may lead to all sorts of irrational emotional outbursts. Having those desires that we would have if we were cool, calm and collected thus seems to be an independent rational ideal. When cool, calm and collected, you would wish for the baby not to be drowned, no matter how much it screams, and no matter how overcome you may be, in your uncool, uncalm and uncollected state, with a desire to drown it. This is why you have no reason to drown the baby.

Perhaps we have already said enough to reconcile the objectivity of moral judgement with its practicality. Judgements of right and wrong are judgements about what we have reason to do and reason not to do. But what sort of fact is a fact about what we have reason to do? The preceding discussion suggests an answer. It suggests that facts about what we have reason to do are not facts about what we *do* desire, as the standard picture would have it, but are rather facts about what we *would* desire if we were in certain idealized conditions of reflection: if, say, we were well-informed, cool, calm and collected. According to this account, then, I have a reason to give to famine relief in my particular circumstances just in case, if I were in such idealized conditions of reflection, I would desire that, even when in my particular circumstances, I give to famine relief. And this sort of fact may certainly be the object of a belief.

Moreover, this account of what it is to have a reason makes it plain why the standard picture of human psychology is wrong to insist that beliefs and desires are altogether distinct; why, on the contrary, having certain beliefs, beliefs about what we have reason to do, does make it rational for us to have certain desires, desires to do what we believe we have reason to do.

In order to see this, suppose I believe that I would desire to give to famine relief if I were cool, calm and collected—i.e. more colloquially, I believe I have a reason to give to famine relief—but, being uncool, uncalm and uncollected, I don't desire to give to famine relief. Am I rationally criticizable for

not having the desire? I surely am. After all, from my own point of view my beliefs and desires form a more coherent, and thus a rationally preferable, package if I do in fact desire to do what I believe I would desire to do if I were cool, calm and collected. This is because, since it is an independent rational ideal to have the desires I would have if I were cool, calm and collected, so, from my own point of view, if I believe that I would have a certain desire under such conditions and yet fail to have it, then my beliefs and desires fail to meet this ideal. To believe that I would desire to give to famine relief if I were cool, calm and collected, and yet to fail to desire to give to famine relief, is thus to manifest a commonly recognizable species of rational failure.

If this is right, then it follows that, contrary to the standard picture of human psychology, there is in fact no problem at all in supposing that I may have genuine *beliefs* about what I have reason to do, where having those beliefs makes it rational for me to have the corresponding *desires.* And if there is no problem at all in supposing that this may be so, then there is no problem in reconciling the practicality of moral judgement with the claim that moral judgements express our beliefs about the reasons we have.

However, this doesn't yet suffice to solve the problem facing the moral realist. For moral judgements aren't *just* judgements about the reasons we have. They are judgements about the reasons we have *where those reasons are supposed to be determined entirely by our circumstances.* As I put it earlier, people in the same circumstances face the same moral choice: if they did the same action then either they both acted rightly (they both did what they had reason to do) or they both acted wrongly (they both did what they had reason not to do). Does the account of what it is to have a reason just given entail that this is so?

Suppose our circumstances are identical, and let's ask whether it is right for each of us to give to famine relief: that is, whether we each have a reason to do so. According to the account on offer it is right that I give to famine relief just in case I have a reason to give to famine relief, and I have such a reason just in case, if I were in idealized conditions of reflection—well-informed, cool, calm and collected—I would desire to give to famine relief. And the same is true of you. If our circumstances are the same then, supposedly, we should both have such a reason or both lack such a reason. But do we?

The question is whether, if we were well-informed, cool, calm and collected, we would tend to *converge* in the desires we have. Would we converge or would there always be the possibility of some non-rationally-explicable difference in our desires *even under such conditions?* The standard picture of human psychology now returns to centre-stage. For it tells us that there is *always* the possibility of some non-rationally-explicable difference in our desires even under such idealized conditions of reflection. This is the residue of the standard picture's conception of desire as a psychological state that is beyond rational criticism.

If this is right then the moral realist's attempt to combine the objectivity and the practicality of moral judgement must be deemed a failure. We are forced to accept that there is a *fundamental relativity* in the reasons we have. What we have reason to do is relative to what we would desire under certain idealized conditions of reflection, and this may differ from person to person. It is not wholly determined by our circumstances, as moral facts are supposed to be.

Many philosophers accept the standard picture's pronouncement on this point. But accepting there is such a fundamental relativity in our reasons seems altogether premature to me. It puts the cart before the horse. For surely moral practice is itself the forum in which we will *discover* whether there is a fundamental relativity in our reasons.

After all, in moral practice we attempt to change people's moral beliefs by engaging them in rational argument: i.e. by getting their beliefs to approximate those they would have under more idealized conditions of reflection. And sometimes we succeed. When we succeed, other things being equal, we succeed in changing their desires. But if we accept that there is a fundamental relativity in our reasons then we can say, in advance, that this procedure will never result in a massive *convergence* in moral beliefs; for we know in advance that there will never be a convergence in the desires we have under such idealized conditions of reflection. Or rather, and more accurately, if there is a

fundamental relativity in our reasons then it follows that any convergence we find in our moral beliefs, and thus in our desires, must be entirely contingent. It could in no way be explained by, or suggestive of, the fact that the desires that emerge have some *privileged* rational status.

My question is: 'Why accept this?' Why not think, instead, that if such a convergence emerged in moral practice then that would itself suggest that these particular moral beliefs, and the corresponding desires, *do* enjoy a privileged rational status? After all, something like such a convergence in mathematical practice lies behind our conviction that mathematical claims enjoy a privileged rational status. So why not think that a like convergence in moral practice would show that moral judgements enjoy the same privileged rational status? At this point, the standard picture's insistence that there is a fundamental relativity in our reasons begins to sound all too much like a hollow dogma.

The kind of moral realism described here endorses a conception of moral facts that is a far cry from the picture presented at the outset: moral facts as queer facts about the universe whose recognition necessarily impacts upon our desires. Instead, the realist has eschewed queer facts about the universe in favour of a more 'subjectivist' conception of moral facts. This emerged in the realist's analysis of what it is to have a reason. . . . The realist's point, however, is that such a conception of moral facts may make them subjective only in the innocuous sense that they are facts about what we would *want* under certain idealized conditions of reflection, where wants are, admittedly, a kind of psychological state enjoyed by subjects. But moral facts remain objective insofar as they are facts about what *we,* not just *you* or *I,* would want under such conditions. The existence of a moral fact—say, the rightness of giving to famine relief in certain circumstances—requires that, under idealized conditions of reflection, rational creatures would *converge* upon a desire to give to famine relief in such circumstances.

Of course, it must be agreed on all sides that moral argument has not yet produced the sort of convergence in our desires that would make the idea of a moral fact—a fact about the reasons we have entirely determined by our circumstances—look plausible. But neither has moral argument had much of a history in times in which we have been able to engage in free reflection unhampered by a false biology (the Aristotelian tradition) or a false belief in God (the Judeo-Christian tradition). It remains to be seen whether sustained moral argument can elicit the requisite convergence in our moral beliefs, and corresponding desires, to make the idea of a moral fact look plausible. The kind of moral realism described here holds out the hope that it will. Only time will tell.

STUDY QUESTIONS

1. According to Smith, why have philosophers been worried about the business of moral appraisal?
2. How do desires differ from beliefs?
3. Can you make a moral judgment yet not be motivated to act accordingly?
4. If you care about friendship, family, and beauty, and I care only about enhancing my collection of vintage cars, are my desires more rational than yours?

Morality as a System of Hypothetical Imperatives

Philippa Foot

Philippa Foot (1920–2010), born in England, became Professor of Philosophy at the University of California, Los Angeles. She argued against the Kantian claim that moral imperatives must be categorical rather than hypothetical. Just as rules of etiquette do not have binding force and can be disregarded without violating rationality, the same is true of moral rules, although in both cases failure to adhere to widely accepted guidelines can undermine a person's ability to work with others and achieve common goals. In other words, a moral person cares about suffering and injustice, but not out of duty, which is only an illusion.

There are many difficulties and obscurities in Kant's moral philosophy, and few contemporary moralists will try to defend it all; many, for instance, agree in rejecting Kant's derivation of duties from the mere form of law expressed in terms of a universally legislative will. Nevertheless, it is generally supposed, even by those who would not dream of calling themselves his followers, that Kant established one thing beyond doubt—namely, the necessity of distinguishing moral judgments from hypothetical imperatives. That moral judgments cannot be hypothetical imperatives has come to seem an unquestionable truth. It will be argued here that it is not.

In discussing so thoroughly Kantian a notion as that of the hypothetical imperative, one naturally begins by asking what Kant himself meant by a hypothetical imperative, and it may be useful to say a little about the idea of an imperative as this appears in Kant's works. In writing about imperatives Kant seems to be thinking at least as much of statements about what ought to be or should be done, as of injunctions expressed in the imperative mood. He even describes as an imperative the assertion that it would be "good to do or refrain from doing something"[1] and explains that for a will that "does not always do something simply because it is presented to it as a good thing to do" this has the force of a command of reason. We may therefore think of Kant's imperatives as statements to the effect that something ought to be done or that it would be good to do it.

The distinction between hypothetical imperatives and categorical imperatives, which plays so important a part in Kant's ethics, appears in characteristic form in the following passages from the *Foundations of the Metaphysics of Morals:*

> All imperatives command either hypothetically or categorically. The former present the practical necessity of a possible action as a means to achieving something else which one desires (or which one may possibly desire). The categorical imperative would be one which presented an

From *Philosophical Review* 71 (1972).

action as of itself objectively necessary, without regard to any other end.[2]

If the action is good only as a means to something else, the imperative is hypothetical; but if it is thought of as good in itself, and hence as necessary in a will which of itself conforms to reason as the principle of this will, the imperative is categorical.[3]

The hypothetical imperative, as Kant defines it, "says only that the action is good to some purpose" and the purpose, he explains, may be possible or actual. Among imperatives related to actual purposes Kant mentions rules of prudence, since he believes that all men necessarily desire their own happiness. Without committing ourselves to this view it will be useful to follow Kant in classing together as "hypothetical imperatives" those telling a man what he ought to do because (or if) he wants something and those telling him what he ought to do on grounds of self-interest. Common opinion agrees with Kant in insisting that a moral man must accept a rule of duty whatever his interests or desires.[4]

Having given a rough description of the class of Kantian hypothetical imperatives it may be useful to point to the heterogeneity within it. Sometimes what a man should do depends on his passing inclination, as when he wants his coffee hot and should warm the jug. Sometimes it depends on some long-term project, when the feelings and inclinations of the moment are irrelevant. If one wants to be a respectable philosopher one should get up in the mornings and do some work, though just at that moment when one should do it the thought of being a respectable philosopher leaves one cold. It is true nevertheless to say of one, at that moment, that one wants to be a respectable philosopher,[5] and this can be the foundation of a desire-dependent hypothetical imperative. The term "desire" as used in the original account of the hypothetical imperative was meant as a grammatically convenient substitute for "want," and was not meant to carry any implication of inclination rather than long-term aim or project. Even the word "project," taken strictly, introduces undesirable restrictions. If someone is devoted to his family or his country or to any cause, there are certain things he wants, which may then be

the basis of hypothetical imperatives, without either inclinations or projects being quite what is in question. Hypothetical imperatives should already be appearing as extremely diverse; a further important distinction is between those that concern an individual and those that concern a group. The desires on which a hypothetical imperative is dependent may be those of one man, or may be taken for granted as belonging to a number of people, engaged in some common project or sharing common aims.

Is Kant right to say that moral judgments are categorical, not hypothetical, imperatives? It may seem that he is, for we find in our language two different uses of words such as "should" and "ought," apparently corresponding to Kant's hypothetical and categorical imperatives, and we find moral judgments on the "categorical" side. Suppose, for instance, we have advised a traveler that he should take a certain train, believing him to be journeying to his home. If we find that he has decided to go elsewhere, we will most likely have to take back what we said: the "should" will now be unsupported and in need of support. Similarly, we must be prepared to withdraw our statement about what he should do if we find that the right relation does not hold between the action and the end—that it is either no way of getting what he wants (or doing what he wants to do) or not the most eligible among possible means. The use of "should" and "ought" in moral contexts is, however, quite different. When we say that a man should do something and intend a moral judgment we do not have to back up what we say by considerations about his interests or his desires; if no such connection can be found the "should" need not be withdrawn. It follows that the agent cannot rebut an assertion about what, morally speaking, he should do by showing that the action is not ancillary to his interests or desires. Without such a connection the "should" does not stand unsupported and in need of support; the support that *it* requires is of another kind.[6]

There is, then, one clear difference between moral judgments and the class of "hypothetical imperatives" so far discussed. In the latter "should" is used "hypothetically," in the sense defined, and if Kant were merely drawing attention to this piece of linguistic usage his point would be easily proved. But obviously Kant meant more than this; in describing moral judgments as non-hypothetical—that is, categorical imperatives—he is ascribing to them a special dignity and necessity which this usage cannot give. Modern philosophers follow Kant in talking, for example, about the "unconditional requirement" expressed in moral judgments. These tell us what we have to do whatever our interests or desires, and by their inescapability they are distinguished from hypothetical imperatives.

The problem is to find proof for this further feature of moral judgments. If anyone fails to see the gap that has to be filled it will be useful to point out to him that we find "should" used non-hypothetically in some non-moral statements to which no one attributes the special dignity and necessity conveyed by the description "categorical imperative." For instance, we find this non-hypothetical use of "should" in sentences enunciating rules of etiquette, as, for example, that an invitation in the third person should be answered in the third person, where the rule does not *fail to apply* to someone who has his own good reasons for ignoring this piece of nonsense, or who simply does not care about what, from the point of view of etiquette, he should do. Similarly, there is a non-hypothetical use of "should" in contexts where something like a club rule is in question. The club secretary who has told a member that he should not bring ladies into the smoking room does not say, "Sorry, I was mistaken" when informed that this member is resigning tomorrow and cares nothing about his reputation in the club. Lacking a connection with the agent's desires or interests, this "should" does not stand "unsupported and in need of support"; it requires only the backing of the rule. The use of "should" is therefore "non-hypothetical" in the sense defined.

It follows that if a hypothetical use of "should" gives a hypothetical imperative, and a non-hypothetical use of "should" a categorical imperative, then "should" statements based on rules of etiquette, or rules of a club, are categorical imperatives. Since this would not be accepted by defenders of the categorical imperative in ethics, who would insist that these other "should" statements give hypothetical imperatives, they must be using this expression in some other sense. We must therefore ask what they mean when they say that "You should answer . . . in the third person" is a hypothetical imperative. Very roughly the idea seems to be that one may reasonably ask why anyone should bother about what should (should from the point of view of etiquette) be done, and that such considerations deserve no notice unless reason is shown. So although people give as their reason for doing something the fact that it is required by etiquette, we do not take this consideration as *in itself giving us reason to act*. Considerations of etiquette do not have any automatic reason-giving force, and a man might be right if he denied that he had reason to do "what's done."

This seems to take us to the heart of the matter, for, by contrast, it is supposed that moral considerations necessarily give reasons for acting to any man. The difficulty is, of course, to defend this proposition which is more often repeated than explained. Unless it is said, implausibly, that all "should" or "ought" statements give reasons for acting, which leaves the old problem of assigning a special categorical status to moral judgment, we must be told what it is that makes the moral "should" relevantly different from the "shoulds" appearing in normative statements of other kinds.[7] Attempts have sometimes been made to show that some kind of irrationality is involved in ignoring the "should" of morality: in saying "Immoral—so what?" as one says "Not *comme il faut*—so what?" But as far as I can see these have all rested on some illegitimate assumption, as, for instance, of thinking that the amoral man, who agrees that some piece of conduct is immoral but takes no notice of that, is inconsistently disregarding a rule of conduct that he has accepted; or again of thinking it inconsistent to desire that others will not do to one what one proposes to do to them. The fact is that the man who rejects morality because he sees no reason to obey its rules can be convicted of villainy but not of inconsistency. Nor will his action necessarily be irrational. Irrational actions are those in which a man in some way defeats his own purposes, doing what is calculated to be disadvantageous or to frustrate his ends. Immorality does not *necessarily* involve any such thing.

It is obvious that the normative character of moral judgment does not guarantee its reason-giving force.

Moral judgments are normative, but so are judgments of manners, statements of club rules, and many others. Why should the first provide reasons for acting as the others do not? In every case it is because there is a background of teaching that the non-hypothetical "should" can be used. The behavior is required, not simply recommended, but the question remains as to why we should do what we are required to do. It is true that moral rules are often enforced much more strictly than the rules of etiquette, and our reluctance to press the non-hypothetical "should" of etiquette may be one reason why we think of the rules of etiquette as hypothetical imperatives. But are we then to say that there is nothing behind the idea that moral judgments are categorical imperatives but the relative stringency of our moral teaching? I believe that this may have more to do with the matter than the defenders of the categorical imperative would like to admit. For if we look at the kind of thing that is said in its defense we may find ourselves puzzled about what the words can even mean unless we connect them with the feelings that this stringent teaching implants. People talk, for instance, about the "binding force" of morality, but it is not clear what this means if not that we *feel* ourselves unable to escape. Indeed the "inescapability" of moral requirements is often cited when they are being contrasted with hypothetical imperatives. No one, it is said, escapes the requirements of ethics by having or not having particular interests or desires. Taken in one way this only reiterates the contrast between the "should" of morality and the hypothetical "should," and once more places morality alongside of etiquette. Both are inescapable in that behavior does not cease to offend against either morality or etiquette because the agent is indifferent to their purposes and to the disapproval he will incur by flouting them. But morality is supposed to be inescapable in some special way and this may turn out to be merely the reflection of the way morality is taught. Of course, we must try other ways of expressing the fugitive thought. It may be said, for instance, that moral judgments have a kind of necessity since they tell us what we "must do" or "have to do" whatever our interests and desires. The sense of this is, again, obscure. Sometimes when we use such expressions we are referring to physical or mental compulsion.

(A man has to go along if he is pulled by strong men, and he has to give in if tortured beyond endurance.) But it is only in the absence of such conditions that moral judgments apply. Another and more common sense of the words is found in sentences such as "I caught a bad cold and had to stay in bed" where a penalty for acting otherwise is in the offing. The necessity of acting morally is not, however, supposed to depend on such penalties. Another range of examples, not necessarily having to do with penalties, is found where there is an unquestioned acceptance of some project or role, as when a nurse tells us that she has to make her rounds at a certain time, or we say that we have to run for a certain train.[8] But these too are irrelevant in the present context, since the acceptance condition can always be revoked.

No doubt it will be suggested that it is in some other sense of the words "have to" or "must" that one has to or must do what morality demands. But why should one insist that there must be such a sense when it proves so difficult to say what it is? Suppose that what we take for a puzzling thought were really no thought at all but only the reflection of our *feelings* about morality? Perhaps it makes no sense to say that we "have to" submit to the moral law, or that morality is "inescapable" in some special way. For just as one may feel as if one is falling without believing that one is moving downward, so one may feel as if one has to do what is morally required without believing oneself to be under physical or psychological compulsion, or about to incur a penalty if one does not comply. No one thinks that if the word "falling" is used in a statement reporting one's sensations it must be used in a special sense. But this kind of mistake may be involved in looking for the special sense in which one "has to" do what morality demands. There is no difficulty about the idea that we feel we *have to* behave morally, and given the psychological conditions of the learning of moral behavior it is natural that we should have such feelings. What we cannot do is quote them in support of the doctrine of the categorical imperative. It seems, then, that in so far as it is backed up by statements to the effect that the moral *is* inescapable, or that we *do* have to do what is morally required of us, it is uncertain whether the doctrine of the categorical imperative even makes sense.

The conclusion we should draw is that moral judgments have no better claim to be categorical imperatives than do statements about matters of etiquette. People may indeed follow either morality or etiquette without asking why they should do so, but equally well they may not. They may ask for reasons and may reasonably refuse to follow either if reasons are not to be found.

It will be said that this way of viewing moral considerations must be totally destructive of morality, because no one could ever act morally unless he accepted such considerations as in themselves sufficient reason for action. Actions that are truly moral must be done "for their own sake," "because they are right," and not for some ulterior purpose. This argument we must examine with care, for the doctrine of the categorical imperative has owed much to its persuasion.

Is there anything to be said for the thesis that a truly moral man acts "out of respect for the moral law" or that he does what is morally right because it is morally right? That such propositions are not prima facie absurd depends on the fact that moral judgment concerns itself with a man's reasons for acting as well as with what he does. Law and etiquette require only that certain things are done or left undone, but no one is counted as charitable if he gives alms "for the praise of men," and one who is honest only because it pays him to be honest does not have the virtue of honesty. This kind of consideration was crucial in shaping Kant's moral philosophy. He many times contrasts acting out of respect for the moral law with acting from an ulterior motive, and what is more from one that is self-interested. In the early *Lectures on Ethics* he gave the principle of truth-telling under a system of hypothetical imperatives as that of not lying *if it harms one* to lie. In the *Metaphysics of Morals* he says that ethics cannot start from the ends which a man may propose to himself, since these are all "selfish."[9] In the *Critique of Practical Reason* he argues explicitly that when acting not out of respect for the moral law but "on a material maxim" men do what they do for the sake of pleasure or happiness.

> All material practical principles are, as such, of one and the same kind and belong under the general principle of self love or one's own happiness.[10]

Kant, in fact, was a psychological hedonist in respect of all actions except those done for the sake of the moral law, and this faulty theory of human nature was one of the things preventing him from seeing that moral virtue might be compatible with the rejection of the categorical imperative.

If we put this theory of human action aside, and allow as ends the things that seem to be ends, the picture changes. It will surely be allowed that quite apart from thoughts of duty a man may care about the suffering of others, having a sense of identification with them, and wanting to help if he can. Of course he must want not the reputation of charity, nor even a gratifying role helping others, but, quite simply, their good. If this is what he does care about, then he will be attached to the end proper to the virtue of charity and a comparison with someone acting from an ulterior motive (even a respectable ulterior motive) is out of place. Nor will the conformity of his action to the rule of charity be merely contingent. Honest action may happen to further a man's career; charitable actions do not *happen* to further the good of others.

Can a man accepting only hypothetical imperatives possess other virtues besides that of charity? Could he be just or honest? This problem is more complex because there is no one end related to such virtues as the good of others is related to charity. But what reason could there be for refusing to call a man a just man if he acted justly because he loved truth and liberty, and wanted every man to be treated with a certain minimum respect? And why should the truly honest man not follow honesty for the sake of the good that honest dealing brings to men? Of course, the usual difficulties can be raised about the rare case in which no good is foreseen from an individual act of honesty. But it is not evident that a man's desires could not give him reason to act honestly even here. He wants to live openly and in good faith with his neighbors; it is not all the same to him to lie and conceal.

If one wants to know whether there could be a truly moral man who accepted moral principles as hypothetical rules of conduct, as many people accept rules of etiquette as hypothetical rules of conduct, one must consider the right kind of example. A man who demanded that morality should be brought under the heading of self-interest would not be a good candidate, nor would anyone who was ready to be charitable or honest only so long as he felt inclined. A cause such as justice makes strenuous demands, but this is not peculiar to morality, and men are prepared to toil to achieve many ends not endorsed by morality. That they are prepared to fight so hard for moral ends—for example, for liberty and justice—depends on the fact that these are the kinds of ends that arouse devotion. To sacrifice a great deal for the sake of etiquette one would need to be under the spell of the emphatic "ought." One could hardly be devoted to behaving *comme il faut.*

In spite of all that has been urged in favor of the hypothetical imperative in ethics, I am sure that many people will be unconvinced and will argue that one element essential to moral virtue is still missing. This missing feature is the recognition of a *duty* to adopt those ends which we have attributed to the moral man. We have said that he *does* care about others, and about causes such as liberty and justice; that it is on this account that he will accept a system of morality. But what if he never cared about such things, or what if he ceased to care? Is it not the case that he *ought* to care? This is exactly what Kant would say, for though at times he sounds as if he thought that morality is not concerned with ends, at others he insists that the adoption of ends such as the happiness of others is itself dictated by morality.[11] How is this proposition to be regarded by one who rejects all talk about the binding force of the moral law? He will agree that a moral man has moral ends and cannot be indifferent to matters such as suffering and injustice. Further, he will recognize in the statement that one *ought* to care about these things a correct application of the non-hypothetical moral "ought" by which society is apt to voice its demands. He will not, however, take the fact that he ought to have certain ends as in itself reason to adopt them. If he himself is a moral man then he cares about such things, but not "because he ought." If he is an amoral man he may deny that he has any reason to trouble his head over this or any other moral demand. Of course he may be mistaken, and his life as well as others' lives may be most sadly spoiled by his selfishness. But this is not what is urged by those who

think they can close the matter by an emphatic use of "ought." My argument is that they are relying on an illusion, as if trying to give the moral "ought" a magic force.[12]

This conclusion may, as I said, appear dangerous and subversive of morality. We are apt to panic at the thought that we ourselves, or other people, might stop caring about the things we do care about, and we feel that the categorical imperative gives us some control over the situation. But it is interesting that the people of Leningrad were not similarly struck by the thought that only the *contingent* fact that other citizens shared their loyalty and devotion to the city stood between them and the Germans during the terrible years of the siege. Perhaps we should be less troubled than we are by fear of defection from the moral cause; perhaps we should even have less reason to fear it if people thought of themselves as volunteers banded together to fight for liberty and justice and against inhumanity and oppression. It is often felt, even if obscurely, that there is an element of deception in the official line about morality. And while some have been persuaded by talk about the authority of the moral law, others have turned away with a sense of distrust.

NOTES

1. *Foundations of the Metaphysics of Morals*, Sec. II, trans. by L. W. Beck.
2. Ibid.
3. Ibid.
4. According to the position sketched here we have three forms of the hypothetical imperative: "If you want *x* you should do *y*," "Because you want *x* you should do *y*," and "Because *x* is in your interest you should do *y*." For Kant the third would automatically be covered by the second.
5. To say that at that moment one wants to be a respectable philosopher would be another matter. Such a statement requires a special connection between the desire and the moment.
6. I am here going back on something I said in an earlier article ("Moral Beliefs," *Proceedings of the Aristotelian Society, 1958–1959*) where I thought it necessary to show that virtue must benefit the agent. I believe the rest of the article can stand.

7. To say that moral considerations are *called* reasons is blatantly to ignore the problem.
8. I am grateful to Rogers Albritton for drawing my attention to this interesting use of expressions such as "have to" or "must."
9. Pt. II, Introduction, sec. II.
10. Immanuel Kant, *Critique of Practical Reason,* trans. by L. W. Beck, p. 133.
11. See, e.g., *The Metaphysics of Morals,* pt. II, sec. 30.
12. See G. E. M. Anscombe, "Modern Moral Philosophy," *Philosophy* (1958). My view is different from Miss Anscombe's, but I have learned from her.

STUDY QUESTIONS

1. What is the difference between a hypothetical and a categorical imperative?
2. Do moral rules bind us in ways that rules of etiquette do not?
3. If you don't have a duty to tell the truth, might you still have a good reason to do so?
4. Do you agree with Foot that a person who rejects morality can be convicted of villainy but not of inconsistency?

The Last Word

Thomas Nagel

Thomas Nagel is Professor of Philosophy and Law at New York University. He argues that moral reasoning is immune to attacks from history, anthropology, or psychology. Indeed, any challenge to reason fails, because the challenge itself relies on reason. Thus reason is validated in the very attempt to discredit it. In particular, any metaethical attack on the role of reason in morality can be answered by pointing out that the considerations leveled, if genuine, are subsumed within reason's domain. They simply provide more fodder to work with; they do not undermine reason from outside. In short, reason has the last word.

I

Let me now turn to the question of whether moral reasoning is . . . fundamental and inescapable. Unlike logical or arithmetical reasoning, it often fails to produce certainty, justified or unjustified. It is easily subject to distortion by morally irrelevant factors, social and personal, as well as outright error. It resembles empirical reason in not being reducible to a series of self-evident steps.

I take it for granted that the objectivity of moral reasoning does not depend on its having an external reference. There is no moral analogue of the external world—a universe of moral facts that impinge on us causally. Even if such a supposition made sense, it would not support the objectivity of moral reasoning. Science, which this kind of reifying realism takes as its model, doesn't derive its objective validity from the fact that it starts from perception and other causal relations between us and the physical world. The real work comes after that, in the form of active scientific reasoning, without which no amount of causal impact on us by the external world would generate a belief in Newton's or Maxwell's or Einstein's theories, or the chemical theory of elements and compounds, or molecular biology.

If we had rested content with the causal impact of the external world on us, we'd still be at the level of sense perception. We can regard our scientific beliefs as objectively true not because the external world causes us to have them but because we are able to *arrive at* those beliefs by methods that have a good claim to be reliable, by virtue of their success in selecting among rival hypotheses that survive the best criticisms and questions we can throw at them. Empirical confirmation plays a vital role in this process, but it cannot do so without theory.

Moral thought is concerned not with the description and explanation of what happens but with decisions and their justification. It is mainly because we have no comparably uncontroversial and well-developed methods for thinking about morality that

From Thomas Nagel, *The Last Word*, Oxford University Press, 1997. Reprinted by permission of the publisher.

a subjectivist position here is more credible than it is with regard to science. But just as there was no guarantee at the beginnings of cosmological and scientific speculation that we humans had the capacity to arrive at objective truth beyond the deliverances of sense-perception—that in pursuing it we were doing anything more than spinning collective fantasies—so there can be no decision in advance as to whether we are or are not talking about a real subject when we reflect and argue about morality. The answer must come from the results themselves. Only the effort to reason about morality can show us whether it is possible—whether, in thinking about what to do and how to live, we can find methods, reasons, and principles whose validity does not have to be subjectively or relativistically qualified.

Since moral reasoning is a species of practical reasoning, its conclusions are desires, intentions, and actions, or feelings and convictions that can motivate desire, intention, and action. We want to know how to live, and why, and we want the answer in general terms, if possible. Hume famously believed that because a 'passion' immune to rational assessment must underly every motive, there can be no such thing as specifically practical reason, nor specifically moral reason either. That is false, because while 'passions' are the source of some reasons, other passions or desires are themselves motivated and/or justified by reasons that do not depend on still more basic desires. And I would contend that either the question whether one should have a certain desire or the question whether, given that one has that desire, one should act on it, is always open to rational consideration.

The issue is whether the procedures of justification and criticism we employ in such reasoning, moral or merely practical, can be regarded finally as just something we do—a cultural or societal or even more broadly human collective practice, within which reasons come to an end. I believe that if we ask ourselves seriously how to respond to proposals for contextualization and relativistic detachment, they usually fail to convince. . . . [A]ttempts to get entirely outside of the object language of practical reasons, good and bad, right and wrong, and to see all such judgments as expressions of a contingent, nonobjective perspective will eventually collapse before the independent force of the first-order judgments themselves.

II

Suppose someone says, for example, "You only believe in equal opportunity because you are a product of Western liberal society. If you had been brought up in a caste society or one in which the possibilities for men and women were radically unequal, you wouldn't have the moral convictions you have or accept as persuasive the moral arguments you now accept." The second, hypothetical sentence is probably true, but what about the first—specifically the "only"? In general, the fact that I wouldn't believe something if I hadn't learned it proves nothing about the status of the belief or its grounds. It may be impossible to explain the learning without invoking the content of the belief itself, and the reasons for its truth; and it may be clear that what I have learned is such that even if I hadn't learned it, it would still be true. The reason the genetic fallacy is a fallacy is that the explanation of a belief can sometimes confirm it.

To have any content, a subjectivist position must say more than that my moral convictions are my moral convictions. That, after all, is something we can all agree on. A meaningful subjectivism must say that they are *just* my moral convictions—or those of my moral community. It must *qualify* ordinary moral judgments in some way, must give them a self-consciously first-person (singular or plural) reading. That is the only type of antiobjectivist view that is worth arguing against or that it is even possible to disagree with.

But I believe it is impossible to come to rest with the observation that a belief in equality of opportunity, and a wish to diminish inherited inequalities, are merely expressions of our cultural tradition. True or false, those beliefs are essentially objective in intent. Perhaps they are wrong, but that too would be a nonrelative judgment. Faced with the fact that such values have gained currency only recently and not universally, one still has to try to decide whether they are right—whether one ought to continue to hold them. That question is not displaced by the information of contingency: The question remains, at the level of moral content, whether I would have been in error if I had accepted as natural, and therefore justified, the inequalities of a caste society, or a fairly rigid class system, or the orthodox subordination of women. It can take in additional facts as material for reflection, but the question of the relevance of those facts is inevitably a moral question: Do these cultural and historical variations and their causes tend to show that I and others have less reason than we had supposed to favor equality of opportunity? Presentation of an array of historically and culturally conditioned attitudes, including my own, does not disarm first-order moral judgment but simply gives it something more to work on—including information about influences on the formation of my convictions that may lead me to change them. But the relevance of such information is itself a matter for moral reasoning—about what are and are not good grounds for moral belief.

When one is faced with these real variations in practice and conviction, the requirement to put oneself in everyone's shoes when assessing social institutions—some version of universalizability—does not lose any of its persuasive force just because it is not universally recognized. It dominates the historical and anthropological data: Presented with the description of a traditional caste society, I have to ask myself whether its hereditary inequalities are justified, and there is no plausible alternative to considering the interests of all in trying to answer the question. If others feel differently, they must say why they find these cultural facts relevant—why they require some qualification to the objective moral claim. On both sides, it is a moral issue, and the only way to defend universalizability or equal opportunity against subjectivist qualification is by continuing the moral argument. It is a matter of understanding exactly what the subjectivist wants us to give up, and then asking whether the grounds for those judgments disappear in light of his observations.

In my opinion, someone who abandons or qualifies his basic methods of moral reasoning on historical or anthropological grounds alone is nearly as irrational as someone who abandons a mathematical belief on other than mathematical grounds. Even with all their uncertainties and liability to controversy and distortion, moral considerations occupy a position in the system of human thought that makes it illegitimate to subordinate them completely to anything else. Particular moral claims are constantly being discredited for all kinds of reasons, but moral considerations per se keep rising again to challenge in their own right any blanket attempt to displace, defuse, or subjectivize them.

This is an instance of the more general truth that the normative cannot be transcended by the descriptive. The question "What should I do?" like the question "What should I believe?" is always in order. It is always possible to think about the question in normative terms, and the process is not rendered pointless by any fact of a different kind—any desire or emotion or feeling, any habit or practice or convention, any contingent cultural or social background. Such things may in fact guide our actions, but it is always possible to take their relation to action as an object of further normative reflection and ask, "How should I act, given that these things are true of me or of my situation?"

The type of thought that generates answers to this question is practical reason. But, further, it is always possible for the question to take a specifically moral form, since one of the successor questions to which it leads is, "What should anyone in my situation do?"—and consideration of that question leads in turn to questions about what everyone should do, not only in this situation but more generally.

Such universal questions don't always have to be raised, and there is good reason in general to develop a way of living that makes it usually unnecessary to raise them. But if they are raised, as they always can be, they require an answer of the appropriate kind—even though the answer may be that in a case like this one may do as one likes. They cannot be ruled out of order by pointing to something more fundamental—psychological, cultural, or biological—that brings the request for justification to an end. Only a justification can bring the request for justifications to an end. Normative questions in general are not undercut or rendered idle by anything, even though particular normative answers may be. (Even when some putative justification is exposed as a rationalization, that implies that something else could be said about the justifiability or nonjustifiability of what was done.)

III

The point of view to defeat, in a defense of the reality of practical and moral reason, is in essence the Humean one. Although Hume was wrong to say that reason was fit only to serve as the slave of the passions, it is nevertheless true that there are desires and sentiments prior to reason that it is not appropriate for reason to evaluate—that it must simply treat as part of the raw material on which its judgments operate. The question then arises how pervasive such brute motivational data are, and whether some of them cannot perhaps be identified as the true sources of those grounds of action which are usually described as reasons. Hume's theory of the "calm" passions was designed to make this extension, and resisting it is not a simple matter—even if it is set in the context of a minimal framework of practical rationality stronger than Hume would have admitted.

If there is such a thing as practical reason, it does not simply dictate particular actions but, rather, governs the *relations* among actions, desires, and beliefs—just as theoretical reason governs the relations among beliefs and requires some specific material to work on. Prudential rationality, requiring uniformity in the weight accorded to desires and interests situated at different times in one's life, is an example—and the example about which Hume's skepticism is most implausible, when he says it is not contrary to reason "to prefer even my own acknowledged lesser good to my greater, and have a more ardent affection for the former than the latter." Yet Hume's position always seems a possibility, because whenever such a consistency requirement or similar pattern has an influence on our decisions, it seems possible to represent this influence as the manifestation of a systematic second-order desire or calm passion, which has such consistency as its object and without which we would not he susceptible to this type of "rational" motivation. Hume need then only claim that while such a desire (for the satisfaction of one's future interests) is quite common, to lack it is not contrary to reason, any more than to lack sexual desire is contrary to reason. The problem is to show how this misrepresents the facts.

The fundamental issue is about the order of explanation, for there is no point in denying that people have such second-order desires: the question is whether they are sources of motivation or simply the manifestation in our motives of the recognition of certain rational requirements. A parallel point could be made about theoretical reason. It is clear that the belief in modus ponens, for example, is not a rationally ungrounded *assumption* underlying our acceptance of deductive arguments that depend on modus ponens: Rather, it is simply a recognition of the validity of that form of argument.

The question is whether something similar can be said of the "desire" for prudential consistency in the treatment of desires and interests located at different times. I think it can be and that if one tries instead to regard prudence as simply a desire among others, a desire one happens to have, the question of its appropriateness inevitably reappears as a normative question, and the answer can only be given in terms of the principle itself. The normative can't be displaced by the psychological.

If I think, for example, "What if I didn't care about what would happen to me in the future?" the appropriate reaction is not like what it would be to the supposition that I might not care about movies. True, I'd be missing something if I didn't care about movies, but there are many forms of art and entertainment, and we don't have to consume them all. Note that even this is a judgment of the *rational acceptability* of such variation—of there being no reason to regret it. The supposition that I might not care about my own future cannot be regarded with similar tolerance: It is the supposition of a real failure—the paradigm of something to be regretted—and my recognition of that failure does not reflect merely the antecedent presence in me of a contingent second-order desire. Rather, it reflects a judgment about what is and what is not relevant to the justification of action against a certain factual background.

Relevance and consistency both get a foothold when we adopt the standpoint of decision, based on the total circumstances, including our own condition. This standpoint introduces a subtle but profound gap between desire and action, into which the free exercise of reason enters. It forces us to the idea of the difference between doing the right thing and doing the wrong thing (here, without any specifically ethical meaning as yet)—given our total situation, *including* our desires.

Once I see myself as the subject of certain desires, as well as the occupant of an objective situation, I still have to decide what to do, and that will include deciding what justificatory weight to give to those desires.

This step back, this opening of a slight space between inclination and decision, is the condition that permits the operation of reason with respect to belief as well as with respect to action, and that poses the demand for generalizable justification. The two kinds of reasoning are in this way parallel. It is only when, instead of simply being pushed along by impressions, memories, impulses, desires, or whatever, one stops to ask "What should I do?" or "What should I believe?" that reasoning becomes possible—and, having become possible, becomes necessary. Having stopped the direct operation of impulse by interposing the possibility of decision, one can get one's beliefs and actions into motion again only by thinking about what, in light of the circumstances, one should do.

The controversial but crucial point, here as everywhere in the discussion of this subject, is that the standpoint from which one assesses one's choices after this step back is not just first-personal. One is suddenly in the position of judging what one ought to do, against the background of all one's desires and beliefs, in a way that does not merely flow from those desires and beliefs but *operates* on them—by an assessment that should enable anyone else also to see what is the right thing for you to do against that background.

It is not enough to find some higher order desires that one happens to have, to settle the matter: such desires would have to be placed among the background conditions of decision along with everything else. Rather, even in the case of a purely self-interested choice, one is seeking the right answer. One is trying to decide what, given the inner and outer circumstances, *one should do*—and that means not just what *I* should do but what *this person* should do. The same answer should be given to that question by anyone to whom the data are presented, whether or not he is in your circumstances and shares your desires. That is what gives practical reason its generality.

The objection that has to be answered, here as elsewhere, is that this sense of unconditioned, non-relative judgment is an illusion—that we cannot, merely by stepping back and taking ourselves as objects of contemplation, find a secure platform from which such judgment is possible. On this view whatever we do, after engaging in such an intellectual ritual, will still inevitably be a manifestation of our individual or social nature, not the deliverance of impersonal reason—for there is no such thing.

But I do not believe that such a conclusion can be established a priori, and there is little reason to believe it could be established empirically. The subjectivist would have to show that all purportedly rational judgments about what people have reason to do are really expressions of rationally unmotivated desires or dispositions of the person making the judgment—desires or dispositions to which normative assessment has no application. The motivational explanation would have to have the effect of *displacing* the normative one—showing it to be superficial and deceptive. It would be necessary to make out the case about many actual judgments of this kind and to offer reasons to believe that something similar was true in all cases. Subjectivism involves a positive claim of empirical psychology.

Is it conceivable that such an argument could succeed? In a sense, it would have to be shown that all our supposed practical reasoning is, at the limit, a form of rationalization. But the defender of practical reason has a general response to all psychological claims of this type. Even when some of his actual reasonings are convincingly analyzed away as the expression of merely parochial or personal inclinations, it will in general be reasonable for him to add this new information to the body of his beliefs about himself and then step back once more and ask, "What, in light of all this, do I have reason to do?" It is logically conceivable that the subjectivist's strategy might succeed by exhaustion; the rationalist might become so discouraged at the prospect of being once again undermined in his rational pretensions that he would give up trying to answer the recurrent normative question. But it is far more likely that the question will always be there, continuing to appear significant and to demand an answer. To give up would be nothing but moral laziness.

More important, as a matter of substance I do not think the subjectivist's project can be plausibly carried out. It is not possible to give a debunking psychological explanation of prudential rationality, at any rate. For suppose it is said, plausibly enough, that the disposition to provide for the future has survival value and that its implantation in us is the product of natural selection. As with any other instinct, we still have to decide whether acting on it is a good idea. With some biologically natural dispositions, both motivational and intellectual, there are good reasons to resist or limit their influence. That this does not seem the right reaction to prudential motives (except insofar as we limit them for moral reasons) shows that they cannot be regarded simply as desires that there is no reason to have. If they were, they wouldn't give us the kind of reasons for action that they clearly do. It will never be reasonable for the rationalist to concede that prudence is just a type of consistency in action that he happens, groundlessly, to care about, and that he would have no reason to care about if he didn't already.

The null hypothesis—that in this unconditional sense there are no reasons—is acceptable only if from the point of view of detached self-observation it is superior to the alternatives; and as elsewhere, I believe it fails that test.

IV

. . . It has to be admitted that phenomenologically, the subjectivist view is more plausible in ethics than in regard to theoretical reason. When I step back from my practical reasonings and ask whether I can endorse them as correct, it is possible to experience this as a move to a deeper region of myself rather than to a higher universal standpoint. Yet at the same time there seems to be no limit to the possibility of asking whether the first-personal reasoning I rely on in deciding what to do is also objectively acceptable. It always seems appropriate to ask, setting aside that the person in question is oneself, "What ought to happen? What is the right thing to do, in this case?"

That the question can take this form does not follow merely from the fact that it is always possible to step back from one's present intentions and motives and consider whether one wishes to change them. The fact that the question "What should I do?" is always open, or reopenable, is logically consistent with the answer's always being a first-personal answer. It might be . . . that the highest freedom I can hope for is to ascend to higher order desires or values that are still irreducibly my own—values that determine what kind of person I as an individual wish to be—and that all apparently objective answers to the question are really just the first person masquerading as the third. But do values really disappear into thin air when we adopt the external point of view? Since we can reach a *descriptive* standpoint from which the first person has vanished and from which one regards oneself impersonally, the issue is whether at that point description outruns evaluation. If it does not, if evaluation of some sort keeps pace with it, then we will finally have to evaluate our conduct from a non-first-person standpoint.

Clearly, description can outrun some evaluations. If I don't like shrimp, there simply is no higher order evaluation to be made of this preference. All I can do is to observe that I have it; and no higher order value seems to be involved when it leads me to refrain from ordering a dish containing shrimp or to decline an offer of shrimp when the hors d'oeuvres are passed at a cocktail party. However external a view I may take of the preference, I am not called on either to defend it or to endorse it: I can just accept it. But there are other evaluations, by contrast, that seem at least potentially to be called into question by an external, descriptive view, and the issue is whether those questions always lead us finally to a first-person answer.

Suppose I reflect on my political preferences— my hope that candidate X will not win the next presidential election, for example. What external description of this preference, considered as a psychological state, is consistent with its stability? Can I regard my reasons for holding it simply as facts about myself, as my dislike of shrimp is a fact about myself? Or will any purely descriptive observation of such facts give rise to a further evaluative question—one that cannot be answered simply by a reaffirmation that this is the kind of person I am?

Here . . . I don't think we can hope for a decisive proof that we are asking objective questions and pursuing objective answers. The possibility that we are deceiving ourselves is genuine. But the only way to deal with that possibility is to think about it, and one must think about it by weighing the plausibility of the debunking explanation against the plausibility of the ethical reasoning at which it is aimed. The claim that, at the most objective level, the question of what we should do becomes meaningless has to compete head-to-head with specific claims about what in fact we should do, and their grounds. So in the end, the contest is between the credibility of substantive ethics and the credibility of an external psychological reduction of that activity. . . .

VI

Even a 'subjective'-seeming solution to this problem . . . is itself an objective, universal claim and therefore a limiting case of a moral position. But that position obviously has competitors, and one or another of the moralities that require some kind of impartial consideration for everyone is much more plausible. Let me now sketch out in a series of rough steps the familiar kinds of substantive practical reasoning that lead to this conclusion and that resist a Humean reduction.

The first step on the path to ethics is the admission of *generality* in practical judgments. That is actually equivalent to the admission of the existence of reasons, for a reason is something one person can have only if others would also have it if they were in the same circumstances (internal as well as external). In taking an objective view of myself, the first question to answer is whether I have, in this generalizable sense, any reason to do anything, and a negative answer is nearly as implausible as a negative answer to the analogous question of whether I have any reason to believe anything. Neither of those questions—though they are, to begin with, about me—is essentially first-personal, since they are supposed not to depend for their answers on the fact that I am asking them.

It is perhaps less impossible to answer the question about practical reasons in the negative than the question about theoretical reasons. (And by a negative answer, remember, we mean the position that there *are* no reasons, not merely that I have no reason to believe, or do, anything rather than anything else—the skeptical position, which is also universal in its grounds and implications.) If one ceased to recognize theoretical reasons, having reached a reflective standpoint, it

would make no sense to go on having beliefs, though one might be unable to stop. But perhaps action wouldn't likewise become senseless if one denied the existence of practical reasons: One could still be moved by impulse and habit, without thinking that what one did was justified in any sense—even by one's inclinations—in a way that admitted generalization.

However, this seems a very implausible option. It implies, for example, that none of your desires and aversions, pleasures and sufferings, or your survival or death, give you any generalizable reason to do anything—that all we can do from an objective standpoint is to observe, and perhaps try to predict, what you *will* do. The application of this view to my own case is outlandish: I can't seriously believe that I have *no reason* to get out of the way of a truck that is bearing down on me in the street—that my motive is a purely psychological reaction not subject to rational endorsement. Clearly I have a reason, and clearly it is generalizable.

The second step on the path to familiar moral territory is the big one: the choice between agent-relative, essentially egoistic (but still general) reasons and some alternative that admits agent-neutral reasons or in some other way acknowledges that each person has a noninstrumental reason to consider the interests of others. It is possible to understand this choice partly as a choice of the way in which one is going to value oneself and one's own interests. It has strong implications in that regard.

Morality is possible only for beings capable of seeing themselves as one individual among others more or less similar in general respects—capable, in other words, of seeing themselves as others see them. When we recognize that although we occupy only our own point of view and not that of anyone else, there is nothing cosmically unique about it, we are faced with a choice. This choice has to do with the relation between the value we naturally accord to ourselves and our fates from our own point of view, and the attitude we take toward these same things when viewed from the impersonal standpoint that assigns to us no unique status apart from anyone else.

One alternative would be not to "transfer" to the impersonal standpoint in any form those values which concern us from the personal standpoint. That would mean that the impersonal standpoint would remain purely descriptive and our lives and what matters to us as we live them (including the lives of other people we care about) would not be regarded as mattering at all if considered apart from the fact that they are ours, or personally related to us. Each of us, then, would have a system of values centering on his own perspective and would recognize that others were in exactly the same situation.

The other alternative would be to assign to one's life and what goes on in it some form of impersonal as well as purely perspectival value, not dependent on its being one's own. This would then imply that everyone else was also the subject of impersonal value of a similar kind.

The agent-relative position that all of a person's reasons derive from his own interests, desires, and attachments means that I have no reason to care about what happens to other people unless what happens to them matters to me, either directly or instrumentally. This is compatible with the existence of strong derivative reasons for consideration of others—reasons for accepting systems of general rights, and so forth—but it does not include those reasons at the ground level. It also means, of course, that others have no reason to care about what happens to me—again, unless it matters to them in some way, emotionally or instrumentally. All the practical reasons that any of us have, on this theory, depend on what is valuable *to us.*

It follows that we each have value only to ourselves and to those who care about us. Considered impersonally, we are valueless and provide no intrinsic reasons for concern to anyone. So the egoistic answer to the question of what kinds of reasons there are amounts to an assessment of oneself, along with everyone else, as *objectively worthless.* In a sense, it doesn't matter (except to ourselves) what happens to us: Each person has value only *for himself,* not *in himself.*

Now this judgment, while it satisfies the generality condition for reasons, and while perfectly consistent, is in my opinion highly unreasonable and difficult to honestly accept. Can you really believe that objectively, it doesn't matter whether you die of thirst or not—and that your inclination to believe that it does is just the false objectification of your self-love? One could really ask the same question about anybody else's dying of thirst, but concentrating on your own case stimulates the imagination, which is why the

fundamental moral argument takes the form, "How would you like it if someone did that to you?" The concept of reasons for action faces us with a question about their content that it is very difficult to answer in a consistently egoistic or agent-relative style.

VII

This step takes us to the basic platform of other-regarding moral thought, but at that point the path forward becomes more difficult to discern. We may admit that a system of reasons should accord to persons and their interests some kind of objective, as well as subjective, worth, but there is more than one way to do this, and none of them is clearly the right one; no doubt there are other ways, not yet invented, which are superior to those that have been. As a final illustration of the attempt to discover objective practical reasons, let me discuss the familiar contrast between two broad approaches to the interpretation of objective worth, represented by utilitarian and contractualist (or rights-based) moral theories, respectively. This is also, I must admit, the type of case where skepticism about the objectivity of reasons is most plausible, precisely because the substantive arguments are not decisive.

The problem is to give more specific content to the idea that persons have value not just *for* themselves but *in* themselves—and therefore for everyone. That means we all have some kind of reason to consider one another, but what kind is it? What is the right way to think from an objective standpoint about the nonegoistic system of reasons generated by multiple individual lives?

Each of the two approaches answers the question in a way that attempts to give equal value to everyone; the difference between them lies in the kind of equality they endorse. Utilitarianism assigns equal value to people's actual experiences, positive and negative: Everyone's personal good *counts* the same, as something to be advanced. The equal moral value that utilitarianism assigns to everyone is equality as a *component* of the totality of value. This leads to the characteristic aggregative and maximizing properties of utilitarian moral reasoning. Everyone is treated equally as a source of inputs to the calculation of value, but once that is done, it is total value rather than equality that takes over as the goal. Utilitarianism may have problems supplying a usable common measure of well-being for combinatorial purposes, but it is certainly a viable method of moral reasoning. If it is taken as the whole truth about morality, then rights, obligations, equality, and other deontological elements have to be explained derivatively, on the ground of their instrumental value in promoting the greatest overall good for people in the long run. The rule-utilitarian treatment of those topics is well developed and familiar.

The other approach is associated with the social contract tradition and Kant's categorical imperative. It accords to everyone not equality of input into the totality of value, but equality of status and treatment in certain respects. The way it acknowledges everyone's objective value is to offer certain universal substantive guarantees—protections against violation and provision of basic needs. Equality in moral status is therefore much closer to the surface of contractualist than of utilitarian moral recognition. Contractualism uses a system of priorities rather than maximization of total well-being as the method of settling conflicts between interests. It also allows the admission of rights, obligations, and distributive equality as fundamental features of the system of moral reasons rather than as derivative features justified only by their instrumental value. The resulting system will include certain guaranteed protections to everyone, in the form of individual rights against interference, as well as priority in the provision of benefits to serve the most urgent needs, which are in general to be met before less urgent interests, even of larger numbers of persons, are addressed.

The dispute between a priority or rights-based theory and a maximizing, aggregative theory is really a disagreement over the best way to interpret the extremely general requirement of impartial interpersonal concern. The issue is at the moment highly salient and controversial, and I do not propose to take it further here. I introduce it only as an example of a large substantive question of moral theory, one that firmly resists subjectivist or relativist interpretation: The question demands that we look for the right answer rather than relying on our feelings or the consensus of our community.

Once we admit the existence of some form of other-regarding reasons that are general in application, we have to look for a way of specifying their content and principles of combination. That is not a first-person enterprise. We are trying to decide what reasons there are, having already decided that there must be *some,* in a certain broad category—a generally applicable way of answering the question "What is the right thing to do in these circumstances?" . . . To answer the question it is not enough to consult my own inclinations; I have to try to arrive at a judgment. Such judgments often take the form of moral intuitions, but those are not just subjective reactions, at least in intention: They are beliefs about what is right.

The situation here is like that in any other basic domain. First-order thoughts about its content—thoughts expressed in the object language—rise up again as the decisive factor in response to all second-order thoughts about their psychological character. They look back at the observer, so to speak. And those first-order thoughts aim to be valid without qualification, however much pluralism or even relativism may appear as part of their (objective) content. It is in that sense that ethics is one of the provinces of reason, if it is. That is why we can defend moral reason only by abandoning metatheory for substantive ethics. Only the intrinsic weight of first-order moral thinking can counter the doubts of subjectivism. (And the less its weight, the more plausible subjectivism becomes.)

STUDY QUESTIONS

1. According to Nagel, does the objectivity of moral reasoning depend on the existence of a universe of moral facts?
2. Could findings in psychology undermine the status of morality?
3. According to Nagel, what are the first two steps on the path to ethics?
4. In your own words, what does Nagel's conclusion, "Only the intrinsic weight of first-order moral thinking can counter the doubts of subjectivism," mean?

Glossary

Amoralist Someone who knows that she morally ought to act in a certain way yet has no motivation whatsoever to act in this way. The possibility of amoralists, it is argued, calls into question the truth of judgment internalism.

Absolutism The view that certain types of acts are impermissible no matter the consequences.

Act-consequentialism The view that, for all persons, each person is permitted to do (of the available actions) only what will bring about the most good-*simpliciter*.

Act-utilitarianism Act-consequentialism combined with a hedonistic theory of value. The view that, for all persons, each person is permitted to do (of the available actions) only what will bring about the most utility, where 'utility' is pleasure and the absence of pain.

Agency To be an agent is to have the capacity to recognize and respond to reasons.

Agent-neutral reasons Reasons that do not make essential reference to the agent; reasons for everyone.

Agent-relative constraint A constraint that blocks agents from promoting the good, even when violation of the constraint would minimize violations (either by other agents or at other times) of that very constraint. The reasons attached to the constraint accordingly must be agent-relative.

Agent-relative reason Reasons that make essential reference to the agent; reasons for a particular person.

Analytic proposition A proposition whose truth-value depends solely on the meaning of the terms with which it is expressed. For example, 'all bachelors are unmarried men' is analytically true, because the predicate concept is contained within the subject concept.

***A posteriori* proposition** A proposition whose truth-value can be known only through experience. For example, 'some swans are black' is true *a posteriori*, because we need to examine the swans in the world to discover if some of them are black.

***A priori* proposition** A proposition whose truth-value can be known independently of experience. For example, 'triangles have three sides' is true *a priori*, because we do not need to examine any triangles in the world to discover that they have three-sides.

Attributive goodness Good of a kind—for example, 'That is a good pair of scissors.'

Autonomy　Having control over one's life. For Kant, autonomy is a property of the will, namely, to be a law unto oneself.

Average utilitarianism　The view that, for all persons, each person is permitted to do (of the available actions) only what will bring about the maximum average utility—in other words, the total utility divided by the number of persons.

Belief-desire psychology　Agents act in order to satisfy their desires based on their beliefs. Beliefs, on this picture, are representational mental states that the agent adjusts to fit the world. Whereas, desires are pro-attitudes, which the agent tries to adjust the world to fit. That is, agents try to get their beliefs to conform to the world and the world to conform to their desires.

Care ethics　The view that, for all persons, each person, S, is required to do whatever a fully caring person (acting in character) would do in S's circumstances.

Categorical imperative　An imperative that is unconditional. It holds regardless of the agent's contingent aims, desires, or ends. The supreme principle of morality, according to Kant, must take the form of a categorical imperative.

Cognitivism　The view that normative thought and talk express claims that are apt for truth or falsity. That is, the cognitivist holds that when we think or say that 'lying is wrong' we express a belief.

Consequentialist theory　A theory that is an evaluative-first teleological theory—for example, egoism.

Constitutive value　Something's having value by being a part of a larger valuable whole—for example, a piece of glass in a beautiful mosaic.

Continent　Doing what is required while fighting desires that pull in some other direction.

Cultural relativism　The view that, for all persons, each person, S, is required to do whatever the norms of S's culture tell S to do.

Decisive (or conclusive) reasons　Reasons to act in a certain way that outweigh any other reason (or the combination of reasons) not to act in this way.

Desire-based (or preference) theory　The view that well-being consists solely in the satisfaction of one's preferences or desires. To the extent that your preferences or desires are satisfied, you are better off; to the extent that your preferences or desires are not satisfied, you are less well off.

Deontic-first theory　A theory that does not treat deontic verdicts solely as a function of evaluative claims. Often such theories include at least one agent-relative constraint.

Deontic verdict　A claim about the normative status of an action—for example, impermissible, permissible, required, optional, supererogatory.

Deontological　Any theory that is non-consequentialist—for example, Kantianism.

Derivative reasons　Reasons that are parasitic on other reasons—in other words, reasons that are not ultimate. Derivative reasons do not supply additional justificatory weight for a particular deontic verdict.

Determining grounds　Part of an ethical theory that tells us which facts are reason-providing—in other words, the facts that are relevant to the theory's deontic verdicts.

Dignity   Having moral standing that makes one the appropriate object of respect.

Divine command theory   The view that, for all persons, each person, *S*, is required to do whatever God commands *S* to do.

Egoism   The view that, for all persons, each person, *S*, is permitted to do (of the available actions) only what will bring about the most good- for -*S*.

Error theory   The view that holds that cognitivism is correct–normative claims are truth-apt—but also maintains that all such claims are invariably false. Put differently, the error theory holds that normative thought and talk express beliefs that ascribe normative properties, but no such properties exist.

Evaluative (or axiological) claims   Claims about what is good or valuable.

Evaluative-first theory   A theory that treats deontic verdicts as a function of evaluative claims—for example, act-consequentialism.

Existence internalism   The view that holds that an agent's having a reason to act in a certain way depends on the agent's (perhaps idealized) motivational set (broadly construed). That is, what an agent has reason to do depends on her wants, ends, and desires.

Extrinsic value   Something's having value because of the value some other intrinsically valuable thing bestows on it—for example, a family heirloom.

Felicific calculus   A method for measuring the value produced by a given action. For example, Bentham held that the intensity, duration, certainty, propinquity, fecundity, and purity should be taken into account when assessing the value of pains and pleasures.

Good-for   Personally good. Good for some group or particular person—for example, 'College was good for her.'

Good-*simpliciter*   Impersonally good. Good, period—for example, 'It was good that the beautiful painting was saved from the fire.'

Good will   A will that is able to reliably identify and carry out its duty for its own sake.

Hedonism   The view that well-being consists solely in experiences of pleasure and pain. *Quantitative hedonists* hold that it is better the more intense the pleasure and the longer it lasts—in other words, 'better' tracks the amount of pleasure. *Qualitative hedonists* hold that it is better the more intense the pleasure and the longer it lasts, but add that some kinds of pleasures are better than others—in other words, 'better' tracks both amount and quality of pleasure. For example, Mill, with his distinction between higher and lower pleasure, was a qualitative hedonist.

Humean theory of motivation   All motivation depends on a relevant antecedent desire. No belief could motivate us unless it is combined with some independent desire. Beliefs, alone, are motivationally inert.

Hypothetical imperative   An imperative that is conditional. It depends on the agent's contingent aims, desires, or ends.

Iff   Shorthand for 'if and only if'. A sentence containing 'iff' thus states a necessary and sufficient condition—in other words, a biconditional. For example, act-utilitarians claim that: "Actions are permissible iff they produce at least as much net utility as any other available action." The 'necessary' claim in this utilitarian biconditional states that if an action fails to produce at least as much net utility as any other available action then it also fails to be permissible. And the 'sufficiency' claim in this biconditional states that if an action succeeds at producing at least as much net utility as any other available action then it also succeeds at being a permissible action.

Impermissible   An action is impermissible if and only if refraining from the action is required.

Instrumental reasons   Reasons that are merely a means to accomplishing something we have ultimate reason to accomplish. Instrumental reasons do not supply additional justificatory weight for a particular deontic verdict.

Instrumental value   Something's having value because of what it brings about via its consequences—for example, money.

Intrinsic value   Something's having value in and of itself, or for its own sake—for example, pleasure.

Intuitionism   The view that ethical truths are self-evident, known by direct apprehension.

Judgment internalism   The view that holds that if a person makes a normative judgment that she ought to act in some way, then it is conceptually necessary that the person is (somewhat) motivated to act in conformity with this judgment (if she is rational).

Justice   The part of normative ethics concerned, broadly, with what people are due, and, more narrowly, with what rights and duties people have.

Kantianism   The view that, for all persons, each person, S, is required to refrain from acting according to a maxim S couldn't rationally will as a universal law. Alternatively, for all persons, each person, S, is required to refrain from acting according to a maxim that treats humanity (rational nature), whether in S's own person or in the person of another rational agent, as a mere means and not as an end.

Maxim   A subjective principle of action that consists of the actor's intention and reason for so intending.

Moral luck   When what someone does depends on factors beyond her control, yet we continue to treat her as the proper object of moral assessment.

Moral rationalism   The view that holds that if one has a moral obligation to act in a certain way, then one has a reason to act in this way. Moral obligations entail reasons for action.

Moral worth   The praiseworthy feature of an action associated with the motive that led the agent to perform the action. According to Kant, an action has moral worth if and only if it is a dutiful action done from the motive of duty.

Naturalism   The natural world is the whole of reality; roughly, all facts and properties are features of the empirically discoverable, spatio-temporal world.

Natural law theory   The view that, for all persons, each person, S, is required to respect or honor those things that are non-derivatively good in S's own person.

Negative duties   A requirement to refrain from performing certain kinds of acts—for example, killing the innocent.

Non-cognitivism   The view that rejects cognitivism. The non-cognitivist holds that, since normative thought and talk are not truth-apt, when we think or say that 'lying is wrong' we do not express a belief; rather, we express some other mental states, such as a con-attitude toward lying.

Non-derivative reasons   Reasons that are neither instrumental nor derivative. The ultimate reasons that supply justificatory weight for our deontic verdicts.

Non-naturalism   Rejects naturalism about reality; some truths—e.g., some normative truths—are made true by correctly describing how things are in some non-spatio-temporal realm.

Normative (as opposed to descriptive) claims   A claim that tells us what should, ought, or must be the case. By contrast, a descriptive claim tells us what is, was, or will be the case.

Objective act-consequentialism   The view that, for all persons, each person is permitted to do (of the available actions) only what will actually bring about the most good-*simpliciter*.

Objective claim   A claim that depends on how things are, independent of the speaker's psychology.

Obligatory   An action is obligatory if and only if it is an action that is required.

Optimific   An action is optimific if and only if (of the actions available) it is the action that makes things go best—in other words, no other action would produce a better outcome.

Optional   An action is optional if and only if it is permissible to perform or not perform the action. More precisely, the reasons in favor of performing the action are at least as weighty as the reasons against it.

Particularism   The view that no properties or facts are always reason providing; the polarity of any reason-providing fact can change given a different set of circumstances. Particularism is accordingly anti-theory; it rejects both absolute and *prima facie* duties.

Permissible   An action is permissible if and only if it is an action that is not impermissible.

Pluralism   The view that there are at least two irreducible kinds of *prima facie* duties. For example, a view, like Ross's, that holds we have both duties of beneficence and duties of justice, but the latter duty cannot be fully captured by the former (or vice versa).

Positive duties   A requirement to perform certain kinds of acts—for example, helping those in need.

***Prima facie* duty**   A *pro tanto* reason to act in a certain way.

***Pro tanto* reason**   A consideration that counts in favor of acting in a certain way, but may not do so decisively.

Psychological egoism   The view that all human actions are motivated by self-interest.

Rawls's contractualism   The view that, for all persons, each person, S, is required to refrain from acting in ways disallowed by principles whose acceptance would be in everyone's rational self-interest to agree to behind a veil of ignorance.

Reason   A consideration that counts in favor of, or justifies, acting in certain ways.

Required   An action is required if and only if there is decisive (or conclusive) reason to perform the action. That is, an action is required if and only if it is an action that is not optional—it is the only permissible action available.

Rights   Broadly, for S to have a right is for S to have a claim to be treated in a certain way. Narrowly, for S to have a right is for S to have a claim that corresponds to someone else's having a positive or negative duty to treat S in a certain way.

Rossian pluralism   The view that, for all persons, each person, S, is required to perform the action demanded by the *prima facie* duty that has greater weight than any other *prima facie* duty that demands the performance of some other action by S.

Rule-consequentialism   The view that, for all persons, each person is required to conform to the rules whose general internalization will (of the available sets of rules) bring about the most good-*simpliciter.*

Scanlon's contractualism   The view that, for all persons, each person, S, is required to refrain from acting in ways disallowed by any set of principles for the general regulation of behavior that no one could reasonably reject as a basis for informed, unforced, general agreement.

Self-evident claims   A claim whose truth one is justified in believing simply in virtue of adequately understanding it.

Subjective act-consequentialism   The view that, for all persons, each person, S, is permitted to do (of the available actions) only what S expects will bring about the most good-*simpliciter.*

Subjective claim   A claim that depends on the speaker's psychology, independently of how things are.

Supererogatory   An action is supererogatory if and only if it is an action that is good but not required-in other words, an action that goes beyond the call of duty.

Synthetic propositions   A proposition that is not analytic. For example, 'all creatures with hearts have kidneys' is true because of the way the world is, not because the predicate concept is contained within the subject concept.

Teleological theory   Any theory that gives agents the end or goal of promoting certain outcomes or states of affairs. Most teleological theories give agents the end or goal of promoting the good—for example, act-consequentialism.

Total-utilitarianism   The view that, for all persons, each person is permitted to do (of the available actions) only what will bring about the maximum total utility.

Universality   The view that deontic verdicts must not be relative to a particular culture, but apply to all persons in relevantly similar circumstances.

Vices   Bad dispositions, or defects of character. Lead to negative assessments of attributive goodness.

Virtues   Good dispositions, or excellences of character. Lead to positive assessments of attributive goodness.

Virtue ethics   The view that, for all persons, each person, S, is required to do whatever a fully virtuous person (acting in character) would do in S's circumstances.

Index